OXFORD IB DIPLOMA PROGRAMME

# PHILOSOPHY: BEING HUMAN

COURSE COMPANION

Nancy Le Nezet
Guy Williams
Chris White
Daniel Lee

OXFORD

OXFORD
UNIVERSITY PRESS

Great Clarendon Street, Oxford, OX2 6DP, United Kingdom

Oxford University Press is a department of the University of Oxford. It furthers the University's objective of excellence in research, scholarship, and education by publishing worldwide. Oxford is a registered trade mark of Oxford University Press in the UK and in certain other countries



First published in 2014



British Library Cataloguing in Publication Data
Data available

978-0-19-839283-5

10 9 8 7 6 5 4 3

Paper used in the production of this book is a natural, recyclable product made from wood grown in sustainable forests.
The manufacturing process conforms to the environmental regulations of the country of origin.

Printed in Great Britain by CPI Group (UK) Ltd., Croydon CR0 4YY

**Acknowledgements**

The authors and the publisher are grateful for permission to reprint extracts from the following copyright material:

*The Holy Bible, New International Version®*, NIV®, copyright © 1973, 1978, 1984, 2011 by Biblica, Inc.®, reprinted by permission of Biblica, Inc. All rights reserved worldwide.

Saheeh International Version *The Qur'an: English meanings and Notes*, verses 22: 5-7 translated by Umm Muhammad, Aminah Assami (Dar Abul-Qasim 1997–2001, Al Muntada Al-Islami Trust 2011–2012), reprinted by permission.

**David Leech Anderson**: 'What is a Person?, The Mind Project, Illinois State University, copyright © David L Anderson 2014, reprinted by permission of the author.

**Jorge Luis Borges** translated by Andrew Hurley: 'Borges and I', first published in *The Maker* (1960), from *Collected Fictions* (Viking Penguin, 1998), copyright © Maria Kodama 2012, translation copyright © 1998 by Penguin Putnam Inc, reprinted by permission of the publishers, Penguin Books Ltd, Viking Penguin, a division of Penguin Group (USA) LLC, and Penguin Canada, and of The Wylie Agency.

**Ken Browne**: 'Social Inequality' in *An Introduction to Sociology* (4e, Polity, 2011), p 398, reprinted by permission of Polity Press.

**Jonathan Cainer**: horoscope for 8 Feb 2014, reprinted by permission of Jonathan Cainer

**Andrew J Elliott & Daniela Niesta**: 'Romantic Red: Red enhances men's attraction to women', *Journal of Personality & Social Psychology*, Vol 95:5 (20008), pp 1150–1164, reprinted by permission of American Psychological Association (APA).

**Harry G Frankfurt**: 'Freedom of the Will and the Concept of a Person', *Journal of Philosophy*, Vol LXVIII, No 1 (January, 1971) pp 5–20, reprinted by permission of the Journal of Philosophy, Columbia University.

**Jonardon Ganeri**: *The Concealed Art of the Soul* (Clarendon P, 2007/OUP 2012), reprinted by permission of Oxford University Press.

**Richelle E Goodrich**: *Eena, The Dawn and the Rescue* (2012), copyright © Richelle E Goodrich 2012, reprinted by permission of the author.

**R M Hare**: 'The simple Believer' Appendix, Theology and Falsification in *Essays on Religion and Education* (Clarendon Press, 1992), reprinted by permission of Oxford University Press.

**Georg Wilhelm Friedrich Hegel**: *The Encyclopedia of Philosophy* translated by Gustav E Mueller (Philosophical Library, 1959), reprinted by permission of the Philosophical Library, Inc.

**Judith Hooper** and **Dick Teresi**: *The Three-Pound Universe* (G P Putnams Sons, 1986), copyright © Judith Hooper and Dick Teresi 1986, reprinted by permission of Lowenstein Associates, Inc.

**Charlie Kaufman**: *Being John Malkovich* screenplay (Propaganda Films, 1999), copyright © 1999 Universal City Studios, Inc, reprinted by permission of Universal Studios and the author.

**KyÇu Shooku zÇ**: 'KyÇu's Moral Discourse Continued' in *Self as Person in Asian Theory and Practice* edited by Roger T Ames, Wimal Dissanayake and Thomas P Kasuli (SUNY Press, 1994), copyright © 1994, reprinted by permission of the publishers, State University of New York Press.

**Robert Langbaum**: *Mysteries of Identity: A Theme in Modern Literature* (OUP, 1977), reprinted by permission of Oxford University Press, USA.

**Tessa Livingstone**: 'The New Gender Divide' in *Times Educational Supplement (TES)* 4. Aug 2008, reprinted by permission of the author.

**Raymond Martin**: *The Rise and Fall of the Soul and Self: An Intellectual History of Personal Identity* (Columbia University Press, 2006), reprinted by permission of the publishers.

**Kate Millett**: *Sexual Politics* (Univ of Illinois Press, 2000), copyright © 1969, 1970, 1990, 2000 by Kate Millett, reprinted by permission of Georges Borchardt, Inc, on behalf of the author.

**Willard A Mullins**: 'Truth and Ideology: Reflections on Mannheim's Paradox', *History and Theory*, Vol 18, No 2 (May, 1979) p 141, reprinted by permission of Blackwell Publishing Inc.

**Thomas Nagel**: *The View from Nowhere* (OUP, 1986), reprinted by permission of Oxford University Press, USA; 'What is it like to be a bat?', *The Philosophical Review*, LXXXIII, 4 (October 1974), reprinted by permission of the author.

**Raymond S Nickerson**: 'Confirmation Bias: A Ubiquitous Phenomenon in Many Guises, *Review of General Psychology*, Vol 2: 2 (1998) p 175, reprinted by permission of American Psychologic
Association (APA).

**Eric Olson**: 'Is there a Bodily Criterion of Personal Ide
in *Identity and Modality* edited by Fraser McBride (OU , reprinted
p 242–259, copyright © Eric Olson 2006, reprinte
the author.

11e, Cengage,
**Plato**: *Phaedo* translated by David Gallop ngage Learning.
by permission of Oxford University Pr
*A Text with Readings* translated by M a lecture given in April
2011), reprinted by permission thor.

**Adrian Raine**: 'Neuroscie elf-awareness as they unfold early
2009, reprinted by perm n Vol 12, Issue 4, December 2003, pp
printed by permission of Elsevier Ltd.
**Philippe Rochat**:
in life', *Consciou*
725-6, copyri

*Continued on back page.*

## Course Companion definition

The IB Diploma Programme course books are resource materials designed to support students throughout their two-year Diploma Programme course of study in a particular subject. They will help students gain an understanding of what is expected from the study of an IB Diploma Programme subject while presenting content in a way that illustrates the purpose and aims of the IB. They reflect the philosophy and approach of the IB and encourage a deep understanding of each subject by making connections to wider issues and providing opportunities for critical thinking.

The books mirror the IB philosophy of viewing the curriculum in terms of a whole-course approach; the use of a wide range of resources, international mindedness, the IB learner profile and the IB Diploma Programme core requirements, theory of knowledge, the extended essay, and creativity, action, service (CAS).

Each book can be used in conjunction with other materials and indeed, students of the IB are required and encouraged to draw conclusions from a variety of resources. Suggestions for additional and further reading are given in each book and suggestions for how to extend research are provided.

In addition, the course books provide advice and guidance on the specific course assessment requirements and on academic honesty protocol. They are distinctive and authoritative without being prescriptive.

## IB mission statement

The International Baccalaureate aims to develop inquiring, knowledgable and caring young people who help to create a better and more peaceful world through intercultural understanding and respect.

To this end the IB works with schools, governments and international organizations to develop challenging programmes of international education and rigorous assessment.

These programmes encourage students across the world to become active, compassionate, and lifelong learners who understand that other people, with their differences, can also be right.

## The IB Learner Profile

The aim of all IB programmes is to develop internationally minded people who, recognizing their common humanity and shared guardianship of the planet, help to create a better and more peaceful world. IB learners strive to be:

**Inquirers** They develop their natural curiosity. They acquire the skills necessary to conduct inquiry and research and show independence in learning. They actively enjoy learning and this love of learning will be sustained throughout their lives.

**Knowledgable** They explore concepts, ideas, and issues that have local and global significance. In so doing, they acquire in-depth knowledge and develop understanding across a broad and balanced range of disciplines.

**Thinkers** They exercise initiative in applying thinking skills critically and creatively to recognize and approach complex problems, and make reasoned, ethical decisions.

**Communicators** They understand and express ideas and information confidently and creatively in more than one language and in a variety of modes of communication. They work effectively and willingly in collaboration with others.

**Principled** They act with integrity and honesty, with a strong sense of fairness, justice, and respect for the dignity of the individual, groups, and communities. They take responsibility for their own actions and the consequences that accompany them.

**Open-minded** They understand and appreciate their own cultures and personal histories, and are open to the perspectives, values, and traditions of other individuals and communities. They are accustomed to seeking and evaluating a range of points of view, and are willing to grow from the experience.

**Caring** They show empathy, compassion, and respect towards the needs and feelings of others. They have a personal commitment to service, and act to make a positive difference to the lives of others and to the environment.

**Risk-takers** They approach unfamiliar situations and uncertainty with courage and forethought, and have the independence of spirit to explore new roles, ideas, and strategies. They are brave and articulate in defending their beliefs.

**Balanced** They understand the importance of intellectual, physical, and emotional balance to achieve personal well-being for themselves and others.

**Reflective** They give thoughtful consideration to their own learning and experience. They are able to assess and understand their strengths and limitations in order to support their learning and personal development.

## A note of academic honesty

It is of vital importance to acknowledge and appropriately credit the owners of information when that information is used in your work. After all, owners of ideas (intellectual property) have property rights. To have an authentic piece of work, it must be based on your individual and original ideas with the work of others fully acknowledged. Therefore, all assignments, written or oral, completed for assessment must use your own language and expression. Where sources are used or referred to, whether in the form of direct quotation or paraphrase, such sources must be appropriately acknowledged.

### How do I acknowledge the work of others?

The way that you acknowledge that you have used the ideas of other people is through the use of footnotes and bibliographies.

**Footnotes** (placed at the bottom of a page) or endnotes (placed at the end of a document) are to be provided when you quote or paraphrase from another document, or closely summarize the information provided

in another document. You do not need to provide a footnote for information that is part of a 'body of knowledge'. That is, definitions do not need to be footnoted as they are part of the assumed knowledge.

**Bibliographies** should include a formal list of the resources that you used in your work. 'Formal' means that you should use one of the several accepted forms of presentation. This usually involves separating the resources that you use into different categories (e.g. books, magazines, newspaper articles, Internet-based resources, CDs and works of art) and providing full information as to how a reader or viewer of your work can find the same information. A bibliography is compulsory in the extended essay.

## What constitutes malpractice?

**Malpractice** is behaviour that results in, or may result in, you or any student gaining an unfair advantage in one or more assessment component. Malpractice includes plagiarism and collusion.

**Plagiarism** is defined as the representation of the ideas or work of another person as your own. The following are some of the ways to avoid plagiarism:

- Words and ideas of another person used to support one's arguments must be acknowledged.
- Passages that are quoted verbatim must be enclosed within quotation marks and acknowledged.
- CD-ROMs, email messages, web sites on the Internet, and any other electronic media must be treated in the same way as books and journals.
- The sources of all photographs, maps, illustrations, computer programs, data, graphs, audio-visual, and similar material must be acknowledged if they are not your own work.
- Works of art, whether music, film, dance, theatre arts, or visual arts, and where the creative use of a part of a work takes place, must be acknowledged.

**Collusion** is defined as supporting malpractice by another student. This includes:

- allowing your work to be copied or submitted for assessment by another student
- duplicating work for different assessment components and/or diploma requirements.

**Other forms of malpractice** include any action that gives you an unfair advantage or affects the results of another student. Examples include, taking unauthorized material into an examination room, misconduct during an examination, and falsifying a CAS record.

## About the authors

**Daniel Lee** taught IB philosophy, psychology and sociology for over six years. He has worked and lived in both Bridgewater and Oxford in the UK.

**Nancy Le Nezet** has been teaching IB courses - including Philosophy, Psychology and Theory of Knowledge - for over ten years, in London and Bangkok. She holds a PhD in Philosophy and specialized in political theory and gender studies.

**Dr Guy Williams** is Head of the Philosophy and Religion Department at Wellington College in Berkshire, England. He is a graduate of the universities of Cambridge, Oxford, and Cardiff. He has taught for many years, specialising in the philosophy and history of religion, as well as the core issues of the IB Philosophy course. Guy has worked with IB teachers and schools around the world.

**Chris White** is an experienced IB Diploma teacher of History, Philosophy, and TOK. He has taught in Australia, Singapore, and the UK. He holds a PhD in Philosophy where he specialised in the work of Hannah Arendt, the concept of love, and the phenomenological self.

# Contents

1. Introduction 1

2. Human Nature 17

→ *Man is a rational being*

→ *Man is an irrational animal*

→ *Man is a blank slate*

3. Personhood 71

→ *Self-consciousness*

→ *Agency*

→ *Morality and moral responsibility*

→ *Responsibility and authenticity*

4. Mind and Body 125

→ *Concepts of mind and body*

→ *The mind–body problem*

→ *The problem of other minds*

→ *Consciousness*

5. The Self and The Other 179

→ *Self/non-self*

→ *Solipsism and inter-subjectivity*

→ *Authenticity*

6. Freedom 263

→ *Freedom and determinism*

→ *Social conditioning*

→ *Existential angst*

7. Identity 321

→ *Personal identity*

→ *Identity over time*

→ *Social and cultural identity*

8. IB Philosophy Assessment 365

Index 402

# BEING HUMAN

# 1 Introduction

Welcome to philosophy. The IB Diploma's philosophy course is an exciting option as part of the Diploma Programme. It is a subject that seeks to challenge you in ways that are at the heart of the educational ambitions of the IB Diploma - as critical inquirers, global citizens with international mindedness, and compassionate action-takers. Philosophy has these ambitions as part of its practice. This book focuses on the core theme of **being human** that all students undertaking the subject must complete at part of the prescribed course. The core theme explores the fundamental question of what it is to be human and does so by looking at the six **key concepts** that are at the heart of exploring the question.

The key concepts encourage us to seek answers to the following questions:

- What does it mean to be human?
- Is there such a thing as the self?
- Can we really ever know the other?
- Is how we interact with others what makes us human?
- Has what it means to be human been changed/shaped by technologies such as the internet?
- What can discoveries in neuroscience tell us about what it is to be human?[1]

However, before this systematic investigation is undertaken, it is worth reflecting on philosophy as both a discipline and as an activity. This allows you to engage with the ambitions of the course while preparing yourself for the final assessments from your first experience of philosophy.

## What is philosophy?

### Philosophers as plumbers

"We cannot learn philosophy; for where is it, who is in possession of it, and how shall we recognise it? We can only learn to philosophize"

—Immanuel Kant - Critique of Pure Reason

Immanuel Kant, one of the greatest philosophers of all time, provides a clear insight into the ambitions of the IB Diploma philosophy course. However, Kant makes it sound as if philosophy is something that just happens and that everyone can do it. In a sense this is true but it does

[1] International Baccalaureate, *Philosophy Guide* (Diploma Programme) (Geneva: International Baccalaureate Organization, 2014), p. 15.

not mean that everyone can do it well. There is a focus which defines philosophy. As Woodhouse has put it,

> ... what catches the philosopher's eye concerning the statement "Ralph told the truth" is not the potential issue of whether Ralph actually told the truth. Instead, the philosopher's curiosity is aroused by the challenge of determining the standards that any sentence in principle must meet in order to merit the label 'truth' - that is, of inquiring into the meaning of the concept of truth.[2]

Woodhouse's point is simple; philosophers are interested in what lies behind the words, ideas and concepts that we tend to use without thinking about their deeper meaning. Mary Midgley once made a rather controversial claim that philosophers were like plumbers:

> Plumbing and philosophy are both activities that arise because elaborate cultures like ours have, beneath their surface, a fairly complex system which is usually unnoticed, but which sometimes goes wrong. In both cases, this can have serious consequences. Each is hard to repair when it goes wrong, because neither of them was ever consciously planned as a whole.[3]

### Philosophy and international-mindedness

When Midgley referred to 'cultures like ours' she is addressing a western audience but there is no doubt she would now extend her point to all cultures. Every culture or tradition of thought has a set of concepts that underpin their understanding of the world around them. Sometimes they are unique to that culture or tradition though often comparable concepts are found in other cultures as they too seek to respond to satisfy a desire to understand the world and issues that emerge out of these attempts. Philosophy as a tool is used across cultures and is an excellent way of increasing your international-mindedness.

While some commentators were concerned that philosophers were being compared to 'intellectual sanitation workers', the point she is making is very insightful. The philosophical plumbing refers to the network of concepts that underpin our understanding of the world and therefore the way we live, how we make decisions and interact with others. Perhaps, the analogy would be more contemporary if it was replaced with electricity and the electrician. We are usually only concerned with our electrical supply when the power goes off and our lights, computers and televisions become obsolete.

## 'Doing' philosophy

Perhaps Professor Simon Blackburn is right when he says "[t]he word "philosophy" carries unfortunate connotations: impractical, unworldly,

[2] Quoted from http://philosophy.louisiana.edu/what.html (accessed 20 October 2014).

[3] Mary Midgley, *Utopias, Dolphins and Computers: Problems of Philosophical Plumbing* (Oxford: Psychology Press, 2000), p. 1.

weird."[4] To a certain extent this is still true. Have you ever had anyone ask you why you are studying philosophy as part of your Diploma, or comment that philosophy is impractical? It can be an interesting conversation.

Still, the word philosophy is a translation of the ancient greek word, '*philosophia*' and is usually translated as 'the love of wisdom'. As a practice philosophy found its foundation in Socrates and his dialectic method of inquiry. However, while the actions of Socrates, and the writings of his student, Plato, are commonly perceived as the foundation of the western tradition of thought, each culture has pursued wisdom using different methodologies and with different areas of interest. Consequently, not all pathways to wisdom require the centrality of rationality and argumentation to be called philosophy. Instead, wisdom can be expressed through poetry, storytelling, even in song, while using analytical strategies that are not based on dispute or refutation to develop an understanding. There are numerous occasions where the purpose of thinking and the conceptual frameworks used are so far apart there is limited commonality to enable valid contrast between different traditions. Despite these differences, there are significant areas where direct comparison can occur, enabling a student to look at issues from different perceptives, bringing insight into these traditions and their cultures and being able to assess the viability or sustainability of their own prevailing understandings. These different perspectives occur in a number of the key concepts covered in this book.

The focus of philosophy is questions that continue to intrigue people; perennial and perplexing questions (that often confound us with their simplicity). They tend to be big questions with equally big answers. Often understanding the question is an equal challenge to understanding the answer.

Philosophy asks you to think about the questions, how to answer them, how to present the answers, and to do so as a philosopher. Consequently, the emphasis of the Diploma Programme philosophy course is on "doing philosophy", that is, on actively engaging in 'philosophical activity' and in the process allowing your own philosophical voice to emerge and 'to grow into independent thinkers'.

This not a straight 'history of ideas' course. It seeks to equip you with the understanding that will help you to appreciate your own thinking and the thinking of others. The course will enable you to engage with the debates that will shape the future of humankind, the ecosystem, and therefore the planet. Some of the debates are yet to emerge, as societies face new challenges on a number of fronts. Advances in technology and science impact upon the way we live, and what we can achieve in our lives. The changing nature of the world through globalisation brings the need to reflect on our morality, our laws, our expectations, and our relationship with those we are connected with in an increasingly contracting world. To do so requires sensitivity to different ways of thinking, appreciating the assumptions that are then used to reflect upon and offer a particular solution to an issue.

---

[4] Simon Blackburn, *Think: A Compelling Introduction to Philosophy* (Oxford: Oxford University Press, 1999), p. 1.

## What do philosophers do?

### Philosophers as conceptual engineers

Perhaps Midgley's association with plumbing is not how we want to leave our picture of doing philosophy. Blackburn, when asked what he does, replies that he prefers "to introduce myself as doing **conceptual engineering**. For just as the engineer studies the structure of material things, so the philosopher studies the structure of thought."[5] The ambition is therefore to understand these structures or frameworks and

> [u]nderstanding the structure involves seeing how parts function and how they interconnect. It means knowing what would happen for better or worse if changes were made. This is what we aim at when we investigate the structures that shape our view of the world. Our concepts or ideas form the mental housing in which we live. We may end up proud of the structures we have built. Or we may believe that they need dismantling and starting afresh.[6]

This is an important endeavor and not one to be taken lightly. It is part of a dialogue that has been going on for many millennia. Occasionally, these structures have been dismantled dramatically and rebuilt although not all believe these rebuilds have been successful. These bring about disputes, creating even more dialogue as each participant pursues greater understanding and clarity of the issues and the positions being taken.

With this mind, is it fair to suggest that philosophy is all about ideas? Peter Hacker expresses this idea of doing philosophy, while comparing the knowledge pursued and obtained in science with that in philosophy, and this leads him to claim that

> [p]hilosophy does not contribute to our knowledge of the world we live in after the manner of any of the natural sciences. You can ask any scientist to show you the achievements of science over the past millennium, and they have much to show: libraries full of well-established facts and well-confirmed theories. *If you ask a philosopher to produce a handbook of well-established and unchallengeable philosophical truths, there's nothing to show.* I think that is because philosophy is not a quest for knowledge about the world, but rather a quest for understanding the **conceptual scheme** in terms of which we conceive of the knowledge we achieve about the world. One of the rewards of doing philosophy is a clearer understanding of the way we think about ourselves and about the world we live in, not fresh facts about reality.[7]

It is hard to believe that after at least 3 millennia of debate, philosophy has nothing to show for itself. However, Hacker's point is that the

---

[5] Blackburn, *Think*, p. 1–2.

[6] Ibid., p. 2.

[7] Quoted in "Peter Hacker tells James Garvey that neuroscientists are talking nonsense". Originally published in *The Philosophers' Magazine* but now available at http://jamesgarveyactually.files.wordpress.com/2011/03/hackers-challenge.pdf (accessed 20 October 2014).

nature of knowledge in philosophy is different to the empirical sciences. Philosophy can change the world, hopefully for the better. Philosophy should, and often does, lead to action. Ideas change the world and good ideas change the world for the better.[8]

### The relationship between TOK and philosophy

As you might realise there are some aspects of TOK evident in this discussion. The *Philosophy Guide* explores the relationship of TOK and philosophy. It is worth reflecting on the differences to ensure you are aware of their similarities, the differences and their shared features. The following is an extract from the *Guide*:

Philosophy allows us to explore and reflect on the nature and meaning of being human. By presenting an opportunity to engage in these activities, the DP philosophy course shares many common concerns with TOK. Like TOK, philosophy places a premium on the development of critical thinking skills, on encouraging students to reflect on their own perspectives, and engaging with a diverse range of perspectives and interpretations. However, TOK is not intended to be a course in philosophy, and care should be taken not to turn the TOK course into an overly technical philosophical investigation into the nature of knowledge. While there might be a degree of overlap in the terms used, the questions asked, or the tools applied to answer these questions, the approach is quite different.[9]

## Why philosophize?

In *A Preface to Philosophy*, Mark B Woodhouse provides an indication of the potential benefits of studying philosophy when he asks, "what's in philosophy besides the pursuit of knowledge for its own sake?" He provides a practical response:

> A critical involvement with philosophy can change our fundamental beliefs, including both our general view of the world and our system of values. The change of these can change our personal happiness and our goal within a chosen profession or simply our general lifestyle. However, such benefits are generally by-products, and not the specific goal of philosophical investigation.[10]

Philosophy can be empowering, exposing an individual to insights about the way the world works, generating an understanding into important matters that affect an individual, their community and global events. This provides a greater sense of awareness and security. However, what is particular about philosophy is that it engages with the ideas, and therefore concepts, that underlie these matters; key concepts such as

[8] It is tempting to say that philosophers are not plumbers or engineers but conceptual architects, seeking to build a better world that also takes into consideration our 'lived world' not just our structural world.

[9] IB, *Philosophy Guide*, p. 8.

[10] Mark B. Woodhouse, *A Preface to Philosophy* (Wadsworth: Cengage Learning, 2003), p. 31.

truth, causality, justice and beauty. This is why philosophy is regarded as the first subject; the subject all others have emerged from, particularly in the west. These are the specific goals of philosophical investigation that make up the purpose of this textbook.

### Philosophy and international-mindedness

A philosophy course is well-placed to support your development of a global perspective and increase inter-cultural understanding. The Philosophy guide provides the following insight into this potential:

> The DP philosophy course develops international-mindedness in students by encouraging them to engage with multiple perspectives and to carefully consider alternative points of view. The course encourages dialogue and debate, nurturing students' capacity to interpret competing and contestable claims. In addition to encouraging students to explore and draw upon a wide range of traditions and perspectives, the course also provides an opportunity to engage in an examination of concepts and debates of global significance.[11]

## Philosophizing with attitude

In *Philosophers*, contemporary philosopher Geoffrey Warnock asks a simple but far-reaching question 'What is the aim of philosophy?' He answers not with an exact destination but with an expectation,

> [t]o be clear-headed rather than confused; lucid rather than obscure; rational rather than otherwise; and to be neither more, nor less, sure of things than is justifiable by argument or evidence.[12]

But what do you philosophize about? Any philosopher, including a young philosopher such as yourself, is required to engage with a number of different traditions of thought as they explore themes, issues and questions that are becoming more and more pertinent to society in the 21st century. Issues such as advances in medical research, including transplants and genome technologies, new claims in science such as the multiverse and neuroscience, and the issues of consciousness and artificial intelligence. Many of these are central to the key question of the core theme of the IB Diploma Course; the question of what it means to be human. In a similar expectation of any philosopher, you are expected to take a position on these themes and issues as you increase your understanding, develop your own philosophical voice and sustain an argument on any number of questions.

It is therefore important to understand the context of philosophical debates and the way they draw upon the dialogue that has been established over thousands of years, responding to contributions in the form of clarifications and new perspectives. In order to philosophize

### What is philosophy? (http://vimeo.com/14348757)

This video makes two important points:

- Philosophy is an activity defined by the use of specific skills which focuses on a variety of important themes, issues and questions.
- Philosophy focuses on the importance of formulating questions rather than just answering them.

[11] IB, *Philosophy Guide*, p. 6.

[12] Quoted in Steve Pyke, Philosophers (London: Zelda Cheatle Press, 1995).

though, knowing how to enter into these debates in equally important. This can be quite a daunting task at the beginning of the course. The nature of philosophy is in some ways similar to the Internet – there is no clear starting point as each concept or idea is interconnected with many others. Consequently, this philosophy textbook aims to equip you with not just knowledge of philosophical ideas and concepts involved in these debates but also with the skills and understanding required to *do* philosophy and enter into these debates with confidence.

With this in mind, the core theme presents an excellent opportunity to begin an engagement with philosophy and, through reflection, start to develop an appreciation of how to think philosophically and understand the interconnected ideas and concepts that make up philosophy. The study of philosophy is not just a matter of reading a textbook; philosophy as a reflective activity is also an attitude. For philosophy to be truly rewarding, it requires an attitude of inquiry into key themes and issues based on reflection, looking for connections as well as justifications while keeping an open mind in order to understand different perspectives and sources of ideas that could inform your own.

Then, there is philosophy as a discipline, a practice of thinking. Reflective activity involves systematic and critical exploration of concepts and issues. This exploration focuses on the positions taken by philosophers on these themes and issues – both their understanding of the themes and issues and the justification of the positions they have taken on them. In the process you become part of an ongoing dialogue that has been going on for many millennia and will continue to go on. The exploration involves an analysis and evaluation of the justifications offered to support the positions taken. This is an analysis of the assumptions or its foundations; the quality of the argument and its justifications; as well as an assessment of its implications.

## So, why do philosophy?

Finally, it is worth returning to the broad question, 'why do philosophy?'. First of all, philosophy will be an enriching experience. You will be able to not just scratch the surface but look behind events, understanding their complexities to a much better extent, evaluate other people's opinions and as well as your own and develop your understanding of the world. There is a saying that guns don't kill, people do. While this is true to a certain extent, as people do pull the trigger, it is ideas that prompt them to do so. It is ideas that are at the heart of the many crises that confront humanity at this start of this century. It is understanding those ideas - and the concepts they reflect - that is the purpose of philosophy. Similarly, it is through understanding the issues that solutions can then start to emerge and change the world for the better.

### You as philosopher

"Philosophy is simply thinking hard about life, about what we have learned, about our place in the world... Philosophy is nothing less than the attempt to understand who we are and what we think of ourselves. And that is just what the great philosophers of history, whom we study in philosophy courses, were doing: trying to understand themselves, their times, and their place in the world... But philosophy is not primarily the study of other people's ideas. Philosophy is first of all the attempt to state clearly, and as convincingly and interestingly as possible, your own views. That is doing philosophy, not just reading about how someone else has done it."

—Robert C. Solomon[13]

### Reflection Questions

How can understanding other people's views from different times help us understand who we are now?

How should we form our own views? Is it only in relation to other philosophers' views?

Can you 'do philosophy' without having studied philosophy?

[13] Quoted in Robert C. Solomon and Kathleen M. Higgins, *The Big Questions: A Short Introduction to Philosophy*, 9th edition (Wadsworth: Cengage Learning, 2013), p. xv.

### Philosophy and leadership

Peter Singer, Professor of Bioethics at Princeton University and Laureate Professor at the University of Melbourne, noted in an article published on the Project Syndicate website that

> GDI [Gottlieb Duttweiler Institute] recently released a ranked list of the top 100 Global Thought Leaders for 2013. The ranking includes economists, psychologists, authors, political scientists, physicists, anthropologists, information scientists, biologists, entrepreneurs, theologians, physicians, and people from several other disciplines. Yet three of the top five global thinkers are philosophers: Slavoj Žižek, Daniel Dennett, and me. GDI classifies a fourth, Jürgen Habermas, as a sociologist, but the report acknowledges that he, too, is arguably a philosopher.[14]

### Philosophy at work

Over the last ten years it has been consistently noted that the study of philosophy is growing and employers are increasingly appreciating the qualities that trained philosophy student bring to their professional role. Stephen Law states that the skills that are developed and appreciated by employees in exciting, innovative companies are:

- The ability to spot errors in reasoning
- The ability to make a point with clarity and precision
- The ability to analyze complex issues and arguments
- The ability to think independently and creatively (to 'think out of the box')
- The ability to build a strong, rigorous case.[16]

Philosophy can also benefit your achievements in your other Diploma subjects. As the first subject, or the subject from which all other subjects emerged, it offers insight into these other subjects. This is primarily done by providing an understanding of the foundational conceptual frameworks used in each discipline (similar to TOK, though with greater range). As such, philosophy is often referred to as a metadiscipline because it goes beyond individual disciplines. It is also a subject that focuses on the development of your skills in argument and therefore analysis and evaluation. Each of these aspects of philosophy should provide you with a firm foundation for success across your Diploma. In return, they can also provide your studies in philosophy with evidence that can be used to determine positions and make arguments as philosophy frequently draws upon the research done in science, mathematics, literary studies, and so on.

It also can be a worthy contribution to your professional career. Recently the Australasian Association of philosophy blog reflected on Singer's article where he says that

> Doing philosophy – thinking and arguing about it, not just passively reading it – develops our critical reasoning abilities, and so equips us for many of the challenges of a rapidly changing world. Perhaps that is why many employers are now keen to hire graduates who have done well in philosophy courses.[15]

These critical reasoning abilities are transferable skills, not bound to discipline specific content-based knowledge. They are skills that allow you to think outside the box (so you need to know what the box looks like, why it looks like that, how and what can be changed with the budget, even when to throw the box out). These include creative thinking, or the ability to develop new insights into established issues, ask new questions of the established issues, even identify new issues in a rapidly changing world. These transferrable skills include those skills that are central to your assessment.

---

[14] Peter Singer, 'Philosophy on Top', *Project Syndicate*, 9 April 2014, available at http://www.project-syndicate.org/commentary/peter-singer-explains-why-the-world-s-leading-thinkers-are-philosophers (accessed 20 October 2014).

[15] Ibid.

[16] Stephen Law, "Why Study Philosophy?", *Think* 33, no. 12 (Spring 2013): 5.

## How do you start philosophizing?

It is now common to hear the claim that everyone is a philosopher, mostly because they have asked the question 'Why?' While there is some truth in this broad statement, asking 'Why?' does not necessarily make you a philosopher. A philosopher adheres to certain standards of intellectual inquiry and argument.

This defines a set of skills that are very important to being a good philosopher. While knowledge is also important to good philosophy, the emphasis is on the use of this knowledge not just its acquisition and therefore on argument and the correct use of evidence.

This skill set is outlined in the marking criteria which have been designed to reward good philosophy in the IB course. (These are discussed in greater detail in the Assessment chapter.) They are the skills of philosophizing and getting into the habit of doing philosophy throughout the course is ideal preparation for your final assessments. Your assessments will ask you to explore concepts in response to questions by taking a position and assessing its validity, often in relation to positions taken by others.

As you proceed through your course it is worth remaining conscious of the demands of good philosophy. One such way of outlining good philosophy is to require the 6 Cs – (1) conceptual *clarity*, (2) *consistency*, (3) rational *coherence*, (4) *comprehensiveness*, (5) *compatibility* with well-established facts and theories, and (6) having the support of *compelling* arguments.[17]

These 6 aspects of good philosophy demonstrate the complexity of sound philosophy. While each of the 6 Cs require further unpacking, above all they require you to take a position that is sustainable and communicable and with philosophical reasoning evident in a your work.

The final one can cause concern. What is a *compelling* argument? It is an argument where philosophical reasoning is supported by the use of quality evidence.

### Argument in philosophy

Often when reading a philosopher's work it is hard to evaluate an argument being put forward. Sometimes this is due to the complexity of an argument, or sometimes the abstract nature or the depth of knowledge being offered. It is important to appreciate what a philosopher is doing other than asserting an abstract position on an issue. They are often seeking to offer a justification for this position based on numerous forms of evidence that leads them to draw a conclusion about a concept, or a system of concepts. It seems initially that philosophers only argue with other philosophers, picking over their arguments, seeking to counter them in a pedantic, overly critical manner. But philosophical argument is often explanatory as well, seeking to offer a common sense understanding of the world through the treatment of an issue, even if the complexity of this explanation can be

[17] This list comes from http://faculty.mc3.edu/barmstro/somelogic.html (accessed 20 October 2014).

quite challenging. Remember the idea that philosophy is like plumbing. Given the nature of philosophy, philosophers use a diversity of evidence from other disciplines drawing upon them to assemble an understanding and then invite you to appreciate the validity of this understanding as a solution to the issue identified. Observations or empirical evidence is also important when assessing alternative perspectives with which to contrast their own position.

A. A. Milne writes:

> It had HUNNY written on it, but, just to make sure, he took off the paper cover and looked at it, and it looked just like honey. "But you never can tell," said Pooh. "I remember my uncle saying once that he had seen cheese just this colour." So he put his tongue in, and took a large lick.[18]

Winnie-the-Pooh uses a variety of evidence to assess that it was honey in his pot but in the end his recourse is to sense perception or the experience of honey. In philosophy this is not always possible, so sometimes a philosopher has to draw a conclusion that seems to fit.

## What is evidence?

This leads to the question, 'what is sound evidence in philosophy?'. Evidence does not only have to come from the tradition itself. Evidence can come from subjects studied in the IB Diploma such as economics, anthropology, psychology, physics, biology, history, literature as well as numerous other disciplines.

Quite simply, all evidence can be valid as long as it is explained, made relevant and integrated into the argument. Good evidence supports the points being made that in turn support the argument and are ultimately judged by the reader as to whether they convince them that your position is sound. Examples can also be evidence if they are used correctly.

## Understanding the process of philosophical analysis

Philosophy as an activity seeks to identify issues with our understanding of the world and offer reasonable, well thought-out solutions. An analysis of a philosophical issue involves the analysis of the relevant arguments put forward to identify the issue, the nature of the issue, and its solution. Philosophical arguments need to be justified. Generally, arguments are justified using evidence that is shown to support a point that, in turn, supports the argument or at least an element of the argument.

This expectation, which is a key foundation to doing philosophy, also defines the process of analysis. In broad terms, philosophical analysis involves the systematic investigation of three elements of a philosophical argument. These are the **assumptions**, the **quality of the argument** and the **implications** of the argument and resulting position.

[18] A. A. Milne, *Winnie-the-Pooh* (London: Methuen & Co., 1926), pp. 61–62.

## What is analysis?

Analysis has always been key to the philosophical process. At a basic level it involves dismantling an argument or a position to reveal its constituent parts and assess them. In philosophy this involves identifying and understanding the concepts, methodology, and evidence used to justify the argument or position taken.

The first phase of an analysis is the identification of the assumptions on which the argument is founded. A philosopher, or school of philosophy, will explicitly or implicitly use these assumptions to engage with the issue.

The analysis of the assumptions involves looking at the **concepts** and resulting **conceptual framework** involved, the **methodology used** for their investigation being utilized, and the nature of the evidence used to support the argument.

The next stage of analysis is to look at the **quality of the argument** and therefore the quality of the justification of the position taken by the philosopher. This allows you to develop an understanding of the validity of the position being outlined (including the assumptions, methodologies and evidence). A key element of any argument is the quality of the evidence being used to support the point being made, how successfully it is used to support the point, and therefore the overall argument.

However, you need to measure the quality of an argument and this is the evaluative framework. For example, the following questions capture the idea of an evaluative framework. What assumptions are valid assumptions? Which methodology is a valid methodology?

The final stage of the analytical process involves the implications of an argument and therefore position on a philosophical issue. What impact does the position have on the broader philosophical worldview? This can be extended to society; such as the recognition of difference, the accountability of the actions of individuals and so on.

The best way of understanding philosophical analysis is to think about your favourite food treat. What was the best example of that food treat you have ever eaten? Ask yourself, why was it the best? Was it because of the:

- **Ingredients?**
- **Recipe?**
- **Presentation?**

In other words,

- Did you like the treat because of the quality of the ingredients?
- Did you like the treat because of the way the ingredients are brought together to produce it?
- Did you like the treat because of the way it is presented?

This is analysis – breaking something down in an ordered way to better understand it (with the intention of evaluating it).

In exactly the same way, in philosophy when we analyze a philosophical position we look at the following:

- **Assumptions** (the foundations of the position such as concepts, methodologies and evidence)
- **Argument** (the quality of the argument/how it is supported. How well were the concepts, methodologies and evidence used to support the position?)
- **Implications** (what is the impact of the argument on other arguments and even on individuals and society?)

### Evaluation

Having completed the process of analysis you can now start to argue the reasons why it was the best treat you had ever tasted. Your analysis develops into your evaluation and the establishment of a set of criteria to judge the argument or position by.

Each of these three phases of analysis produces an understanding of the argument or position being taken on an issue. This allows an evaluation of the argument. At a basic level the questions are as follows:

- Are the assumptions valid?
- Is the evidence offered sufficient to justify the argument being made?
- Are the implications of the position acceptable?

## Developing the skills of analysis

The following activity provides an opportunity to experience philosophy. It is a simple question and completing this activity provides an insight into the comments and advice given below about doing philosophy.

**Question:** Whose life is more important – your life or an insect's?

### What is your answer?

How would you justify it and demonstrate your philosophical skills at the same time!

Three sides to the argument

1. You are more important
2. The insect is more important
3. You are equal to the insect

### Understanding the question and the answer

#### Undertake analysis

What is important to answering this question from your given perspective? Or what are the key concepts, methodologies and evidence?

### Undertake evaluation

How do you decide what is important? Or the criteria to judge the answer by?

Do the three positions agree on what is important in terms of concepts (and their interpretations), the methodologies (and their worth) and relevant evidence (and its significance)?

This is now getting to the heart of good philosophical analysis; an understanding of the different perspectives and their analytical and evaluative frameworks.

The expectation in philosophy is that you will develop your own position as part of your study of the philosophers and philosophical schools you cover in your course of study. These positions, on issues in the topics you study as part of the core theme, as well as optional themes, prescribed text, and "What is philosophy?" (higher level only), will form the basis of your evaluation of these philosophers and philosophical schools.

Your position should be an outcome of your evaluation. In philosophy you should approach finding a resolution to an issue with an open mind. However, when you evaluate something – whatever it is – you have to develop a **reference point** from which you can judge it. What should the reference point be? Well, this is your own philosophically informed position on the issue being examined. This position involves a well-thought out **criterion or set of criteria** with which to assess the positions offered on the issue. These enable you to evaluate the validity of another position or argument, even suggest how to improve an aspect of it, and equally evaluate your own position with the same intention.

## Establishing your own position

It is sometimes hard to know where to start. Often we have an opinion about basic issues in society but not necessarily about metaphysical or epistemological matters. However, as your philosophical investigations proceed, you will become more aware of the context in which philosophical debate occurs.

Initially our positions on issues are influenced, sometimes significantly, by other positions. Yet, the more you do philosophy the more you are able to understand the elements that contribute to philosophical analysis and start to be able to take your own positions.

In a similar way to analysing another philosophical position you should also establish your own position using the **Assumptions – Quality of Argument – Implications** framework. This involves answering some basic questions:

- Are the assumptions valid?
- Is the evidence offered appropriate and, if so, sufficient to justify the argument being offered?
- Do I accept the implications of the position?

This is the context in which you will be undertaking analysis and evaluation. When you evaluate something you have to have a reference point with which to measure something. This enables you to measure the validity of a position or argument, even suggest how to improve it in some way. What should the reference point be? Well, this is your own philosophical position on the issue being examined.

## The core theme and this book

The core theme in the DP philosophy course is "Being human". It encourages exploration of the fundamental themes, issues, and questions associated with the question, 'what it is to be human?', both as individuals and as members of communities. It is designed to focus around six key concepts: Identity, Personhood, Freedom, Mind and Body, The Self and Others, and Human Nature. Each of these is interrelated in a number of ways and they can be studied in any order. The structure of this book is not the only way of learning about the central issue of being human. Nonetheless, as you continue through your course you will start to recognise the connectedness of the key concepts and start to appreciate how they contribute to each other and occasionally have a clear overlap.

### What do we mean by concepts?

A concept is a feature or characteristic of something. These concepts are often expressed in abstract terms but they are frequently at work in the world. Solomon provides a key insight into the nature of philosophy as well as the role of concepts.

> Concepts give form to experience; they make articulation possible. But even before we try to articulate our views, concepts make it possible for us to recognize things in the world, to see and hear particular objects and particular people instead of one big blur of a world, like looking through a movie camera that is seriously out of focus. But in addition to defining the forms of our experience, concepts also tie our experience together.[19]

Other than truth, important concepts could include time, beauty, being, identity, and cause; all evident in everyday life, they make up the pipes in Midgley's 'philosophical plumbing'. An equally important dimension to this investigation as Solomon notes is to understand their relationships with other concepts; '[c]oncepts rarely occur in isolation; they virtually always tie together into a **conceptual framework**'.[20] These conceptual frameworks provide a picture of the world or a worldview within which we make decisions. As Solomon continues,

> These all-embracing pictures and perspectives are our ultimate conceptual frameworks—that is, the most abstract concepts through which we "frame" and organize all of our more specific concepts. The term conceptual framework stresses the importance of concepts and is therefore central to the articulation of concepts that makes up most of philosophy.[21]

[19] In Solomon and Higgins, *The Big Questions*, p. 8.

[20] Ibid., p. 8.

[21] Ibid., p. 10.

## The six concepts explored in this textbook

The key concepts that form the core theme all relate to the central question of what it means to be human. This textbook is divided into six main chapters, each focusing on one of the six key concepts prescribed by the IB Programme. Although they are all important, it is not necessary, or even possible, for you to know everything about all six concepts. Your teacher may choose to focus on certain chapters, or some aspects of the chapters.

The more you study the key concepts, the more you will see that they are deeply connected to one another. Your understanding will deepen and you will get a better grasp of the complexity that underlines the question of what it means to be human. In that sense, you could probably read this textbook in any order and also re-read chapters after a few months, and get a slightly different understanding every time, as you relate the content to your previous knowledge. As outlined in this introduction, your learning to do philosophy is just as important as what philosophers have said until now.

Having said that, this textbook was not structured randomly! Despite the freedom you and your teacher have in choosing what to study and in what order, there is no doubt that Chapter 2: Human Nature and Chapter 3: Personhood are an excellent way to get you started, because they lay down some important definitions and ideas that are central to the entire core theme. Equally, the last two chapters are perhaps a little more complex and may require a bit of knowledge and experience before you dive into them.

Finally, the activities provided in this textbook are there to ensure that you practise philosophy as well as read about it. They have been chosen to help you become a philosopher in you own right and make connections between the history of ideas and their contemporary application. There is also, of course, a focus on assessment, with assessment tips peppered all along the textbook and specific assessment exercises at the end of the chapters. You will also find a full assessment chapter at the end of the textbook, with a bank of stimulus material that will allow you to practise turning non-philosophical material into good philosophical arguments.

While assessment is essential at this stage of your life and school career, the hope is that this book and IB course will also help you become a better thinker, a skill that will stay with you long after you have finished taking school examinations.

## References Cited


Blackburn, Simon. *Think: A Compelling Introduction to Philosophy*. Oxford: Oxford University Press, 1999.

International Baccalaureate. *Philosophy Guide* (Diploma Programme). Geneva: International Baccalaureate Organization, 2014.

Kant, Immanuel. *Critique of Pure Reason*. Translated from the German *Kritik der reinen Vernunft*, 1781 / 1787.

Law, Stephen. "Why Study Philosophy?". *Think* 33, no. 12 (Spring 2013): 5.

Midgley, Mary. *Utopias, Dolphins and Computers: Problems of Philosophical Plumbing*. Oxford: Psychology Press, 2000.

Milne, A. A. *Winnie-the-Pooh*. London: Methuen & Co., 1926.

Pyke, Steve. *Philosophers*. London: Zelda Cheatle Press, 1995.

Singer, Peter. 'Philosophy on Top'. *Project Syndicate*, 9 April 2014. Available at: http://www.project-syndicate.org/commentary/peter-singer-explains-why-the-world-s-leading-thinkers-are-philosophers (accessed 20 October 2014).

Solomon, Robert C., and Kathleen M. Higgins. *The Big Questions: A Short Introduction to Philosophy*, 9th edition. Wadsworth: Cengage Learning, 2013.

Woodhouse, Mark B. *A Preface to Philosophy*. Wadsworth: Cengage Learning, 2003.

# 2 Human Nature

- → Man is a rational being
- → Man is an irrational animal
- → Man is a blank slate

## Some essential questions:

- → What is at the heart of who we are?
- → Which picture of man is more suitable?

### Stimulus 1

What a piece of work is a man! How noble in reason, how infinite in faculty! In form and moving how express and admirable! In action how like an angel, in apprehension how like a god! The beauty of the world. The paragon of animals. And yet, to me, what is this quintessence of dust? Man delights not me. No, nor woman neither, though by your smiling you seem to say so.

—Shakespeare, *Hamlet*, Act II, Scene 2

In this chapter we will look at the notion of Human Nature from a number of philosophical perspectives.

The question of human nature is a philosophical problem. We will ask whether there is anything that we can meaningfully call a human nature shared by all human beings.

One way of thinking about the problem of human nature is to look for some characteristics that all people share because they are human. We also need to consider if these features are 'essential' in the sense that they define human beings. We will explore three ways in which philosophy has tried to answer these questions.

▲ Michaelangelo depicted human beings as next to the angels – pure, rational and wise.

1. **Is man a rational being?** In this section we look at the traditional Western view of man. We are creatures with a special gift – our minds. The mind is our rational self, which gives us our ability to have knowledge and to control ourselves.

   Key thinkers:
   - Plato
   - René Descartes

2. **Is man an irrational animal?** In this section we look at challenges to the traditional Western view of man. These ideas from philosophy, biology, and psychology argue that we are not in fact in control of ourselves or making choices on the basis of the reasoned evidence we have, but that we are actually driven by instincts and deep desires over which we have no control.

   Key thinkers:
   - Charles Darwin
   - Sigmund Freud
   - Friedrich Wilhelm Nietzsche

3. **Is man a blank slate?** In this section we look at challenges to the view of man as an irrational animal. These ideas from philosophy, anthropology, and psychology argue that we have no human nature. Some argue that we are free to choose any possible action and are not constrained by any built-in nature, while others argue that we are created by our culture and our experiences, and therefore we are born without any fixed nature – we can become anything.

   Key thinkers:
   - John Locke
   - John B. Watson
   - Karl Marx
   - Judith Butler

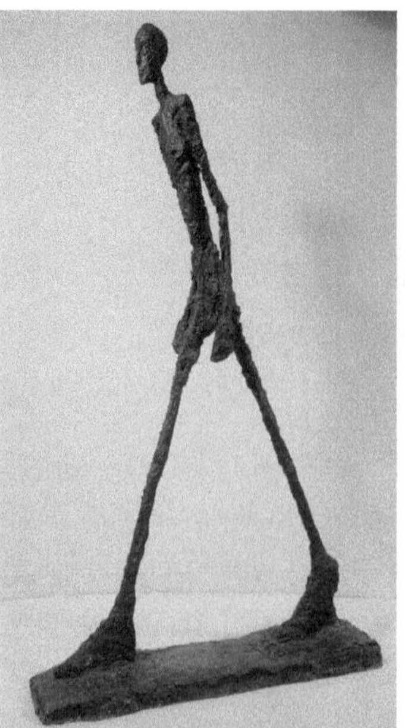

▲ In his scupltures, Giacometti depicts human beings as a bare silhouette, unfinished, and full of possibility.

▲ Francisco de Goya painted images of human beings caricatured as animals and engaged in acts of animalistic brutality.

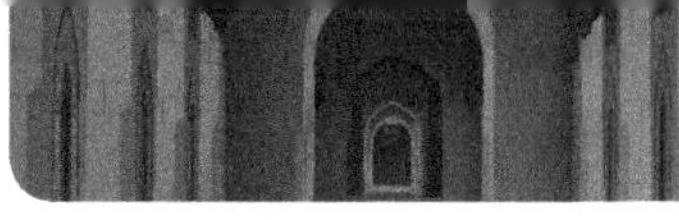

# Rationalism

## Rationality as objectivity

What does **rational** mean? This question has been answered in many different ways and is itself the subject of considerable debate. We need to make some assumptions, however, about what we mean by rationality. Historically one of the core features of rationality involves being **objective**. By "objective" we mean capable of considering the world independently of our particular perspective: without desire, impulse, or instinct.

Being objective, therefore, involves both self-control and an ability to justify our beliefs according to sound reasons rather than our own interests. This means that we must be able to separate ourselves from any interests or values, and give reasons for our beliefs that will persuade not only ourselves but also any other rational being.

> The word "rational" has as its first component "ratio", which means "proportion." So a rational inquiry is one in which the judgments reached, the conclusions drawn, are proportional to the evidence – the strength of the evidence – for them. We mean something quite serious by "rational inquiry." We mean that we are looking very, very carefully at how far we are licensed to think something on the basis of all the reasons and all the evidence that we have for sustaining it.[1]

Plato also defined rationality as involving objectivity.

He is often thought of as a precursor to philosophical rationalism and in his writings he presents a very rationalist view of human nature. In the following series of arguments Plato attempts to persuade his audience that Man is a creature who is dominated by his ability to reason and be rational. He makes the following claims:

1. All human beings have a soul ('soul' is not used in exactly the same way we use it today. It also refers to our mind and our thought).
2. The human soul has three parts, one of which is unique to human beings.
3. The uniquely human component of the soul does two key things:
    a. It controls the other parts, such as our desire.
    b. It has access to truth because it is able to think about the world objectively.

### Plato: Chariot – self-control

It is the ability to master our impulses and think objectively that Plato emphasizes in his account of man as a rational animal. Plato initially focuses on the way that we can control our impulses. He uses the example of a thirsty man controlling his desire in the face of poisoned

For more information about Plato, see Chapter 4, p. 137.

[1] A. C. Grayling, with Richard Dawkins, discussing evidence for the supernatural at Oxford ThinkWeek (2011), available at http://poddelusion.co.uk/blog/2011/02/23/richard-dawkins-ac-grayling-discuss-evidence-for-the-supernatural-at-oxford-thinkweek/ (accessed 21 October 2014).

water. When we exercise control of our impulses, we must be using a different part of ourselves to overcome desire.

Plato argues that there is a second distinction. Not only does desire compete with reason, but it also competes at times with anger. Imagine a child who refuses to eat his dinner out of anger, despite a powerful desire for food. The resentment and drive for self-assertion and power are stronger than the basic desire to eat. On the basis of a similar example, Plato concludes that there are three parts to the soul: the **appetitive** part, which consists of our basic desires; the **spirited** or passionate part, which consists of our anger, will for self-expression and recognition; and our **reason**, which consists of our ability to make correct judgments about the world and to choose a course of action on the basis of good reasons.

This seems like a sensible reason for supposing that we have a higher nature. We are controlling our desires with something else that therefore ***must be fundamentally different in nature***. If our self-control is able to withstand our desires, then it must be different from desire – it must be an objective and rational self.

However, we need to think about what really happens in the poisoned water example. The rational part prevents us from drinking the water, but for what reason? In fact, it appears that our rational self is acting on a desire itself – the desire not to die painfully from drinking poisoned water. This might suggest that in fact our rationality is not an objective and autonomous soul, but just a more powerful and refined set of impulses. Our rationality may just be a tool to get the things we want in the smartest way. After all, many animals are able to resist eating and drinking poisoned food and drink – they too have a part of them that resists their first impulse for the sake of a long-term goal. That doesn't mean that they have any special objective self – just a more refined set of desires. For more on this see the sections on Darwin and Freud, who are sceptical about rationality.

Clearly, the claim that we are all in perfect, rational, self-control seems astonishing given our experience of, for example, 17-year-old students. However, Plato includes room for irrationality and poor self-control in his model. He argues that when we are imbalanced or when our reason fails to master the two passionate parts of ourselves, then we become dysfunctional, imbalanced persons. Nevertheless, he argues that our fundamental nature, that ideal of man which we aim at, is a rational being.

## EXERCISE

Think about assumptions in philosophical argument

In this set of arguments we are arguing that human nature is to do with what kind of mind you have. Here, being human is thinking rationally. Therefore, because we have a peculiar set of mental skills or abilities that let us do unique things, such as human knowledge, we are human beings.

But this involves some big assumptions – immediately we have assumed that what it means to be a human being is to do with our conscious mind. But surely the mind is only part of our selves. Can we assume that our human nature lies in the mind and not the body. See Chapter 3: Personhood, to examine problems with the assumption that our mind is our self.

Furthermore, rationalists have assumed that we can think of our minds as separate from our bodies. While this assumption can seem natural (which is probably why it is overlooked), it is thought by many philosophers to be a very unreasonable one. See Chapter 4: Mind and Body, to examine problems with the assumption that the mind can be thought of as separate from the body.

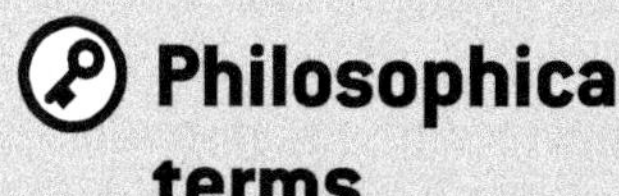

### *Three parts of the soul*

In his Socratic dialogue *Phaedrus* Plato continues to describe the soul and in doing so expands his concept of human nature. Plato's analogy of the chariot is one of his most famous. In this metaphor, expounded here by Socrates, the soul is like a chariot with three components. The two horses provide the drive that pulls the chariot and therefore represent the energetic parts of our soul. The white horse, *thumos* (often translated as passion or spirit), represents our drive for recognition and self-expression – our desire to succeed and compete, and our aggression are part of this impulse. The black horse, *epithumetikon* (often translated as appetite), represents our base worldly impulses, such as hunger, lust, and short-term gain.

These two drives battle for dominance in the pull of life. The third component is the charioteer, the natural master of the other two parts. Our reason is without drive, but it is the king of the soul. It is this that is our core nature and which must master and control our drives in order to achieve goodness.

This argument from Plato has a powerful phenomenal justification. Everyone experiences the turmoil of the soul – the different impulses within us at war with one another. We have all experienced "temptation" and been torn between two choices – often one that appeals to our impulse, while the other requires restraint for the sake of our long-term well-being. Plato's is the earliest surviving articulation of the idea of the devil and the angel in either ear. One begs for restraint, the other urges us to act on impulse. We need to master them both, and deny the basic drives, in order to be in harmony with our nature. *Logistikon*, the centre of the self, seeks one thing – truth. For Plato man is the rational truth seeker and his unique rational soul is what allows him to achieve these heights.

### *Conclusions*

Plato has presented the basic argument that man is essentially a rational being. He has justified this view by comparing our irrational drives with our capacity for self control. We see that there are different selves within and one of them is much wiser when it comes to understanding the world and making smart decisions. When presenting the argument that we are rational you could start by discussing this argument.

It is important to also note what Plato's argument does not do. His argument has demonstrated that we are capable of making decisions which sacrifice short term gain in favor of long term benefits. This is not the same as showing that rationality is 'divine' or something over and above what other creatures can do – we can respond that it is just a more complex form of self interested instinct.

In the next section we attempt to justify the view that rationality is separate from ordinary instinct. We look at reasons for thinking that when we make rational choices it involves something extra: objective knowledge.

### *Plato's epistemology – forms and perfect knowledge*

How is it possible for us to exercise self-control? If we make decisions which sacrifice short-term for long-term benefit, it seems that it must involve a better understanding of the world, and a better ability to predict the future outcomes of our actions. If I decide not to drink the poisoned water, I must have good knowledge of the nature of poison and what it will do

#### Philosophical terms

**Phenomenal:** Having to do with first hand experience. A phenomenal justification is one which asks you to consider your own subjective experiences as evidence.

**Epistemology:** The philosophical study of knowledge. epistemology concerns what we can know and how we can know it.

to me – much better knowledge than an instinct-driven creature who drinks the poison. Plato's idea of reason as the core of our nature is intimately connected to his epistemology. Plato was, like the later rationalists, very sceptical about the world we experience. He thought that because it was subject to change and decay, and because it was imprecise and uncertain, the objects we can see – the "visible" world – are not genuinely real. In fact, it was only those things that are eternal and unchanging, as well as perfect and complete, which can be said to be real. Let's see how Plato justifies the claim that the things we see aren't the real things.

Mathematics, for example, seems to be a special category of thing. Its unchanging and eternal truths are the only really true things – they are absolutely true. Plato extends this to other aspects of reason and logic and argues that abstract philosophy is the path to ultimate truth. If a thing can change, decay, and one day not be what it is, then for Plato it isn't actually "real" enough. He is tantalized by the final certainties that mathematics and logic give us – the way they describe absolute claims – and he thinks that only something that participates in the same finality, certainty, and infallibility can really deserve the name of "truth". The **forms** are the purely intellectual objects that never change and are ultimate reality. They enable us to understand and identify the changing world we experience, and our reason helps us to access knowledge that would be impossible without the forms to pin it down.

For example, consider the difference between 1+1=2 and the words "it is sunny today". The claim "it is sunny today" is relative to who is saying it, where, and when. Its truth is location relative – it's probably sunny somewhere, isn't it? Its truth is dependent on interpretation and perspective – your sunny might not be the same as my sunny. Its truth is relative to time – it might be true now but that will change. Its truth is relative to whether or not we are accurately perceiving the world – what if I am dreaming or intoxicated? Finally, the objects that we are talking about, these particular things, are only individual instances of "sunniness". What is "sunniness"? Is it this day? Or is this day just an example of it? Plato thought that the particular things that have the characteristics of "sunniness" did not amount to "sunniness" itself.

The real sunniness is "sunniness itself" and must be a different sort of thing from the objects that have the quality of sunniness. Lots of things look sunny, but each in a different way. Where is the thing that gives them all that quality and is "sunniness"? Plato argues that the world we see is just made of particular instances of "sunniness" and that none of these are the thing itself. The real "sunniness" is a complete and perfect object – what Plato calls a form. Behind this temporary and ephemeral world there must be a more perfect structure, which is hinted at in our knowledge of mathematics and reason. It is a world where all the objects of our world get their nature. A world better than this one, not limited by time and space, where the perfectly real exists without end.

If this idea is a challenge for you, don't worry – it is for most people. Plato's forms have the quality of an exotic religious system – some philosophers argue that they are the point of origin for Christian beliefs about the divine.

A classic example used to illustrate Plato's notion of the forms is the concept of "horse". We see lots of particular horses, but are any of them

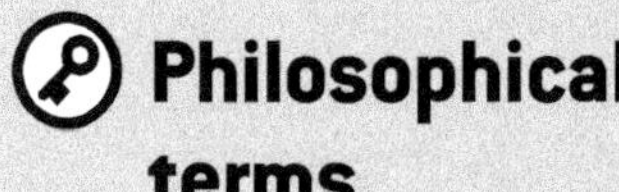

*the* horse? Do any of them encapsulate completely the meaning of the concept "horse"? No, each particular horse has horseness in a particular way and therefore it does not have everything that makes a thing a horse. Horses also die. If a horse can become no longer a horse, then it isn't the *real* "horse". Plato thinks that there must be something that is permanent, unchanging, and perfect which is the real horse.

Plato has to reconcile the unchanging nature of our concepts with the changing and contingent nature of the objects we experience.

Plato's forms are apparent only intellectually through the exercise of thought. It is for this reason that Plato argues we have access to a second world of abstract rational mental objects that are ultimate reality. The forms are the perfect, eternal, unchanging things that are temporarily mirrored in the things we observe in this world. The world we experience, says Plato, is a shadow of ultimate reality.

This access to unchanging truth, what Plato thinks is real knowledge, is what makes us uniquely human. Our ability **to reason and grasp the absolute** is the defining characteristic of man.

### Philosophical terms

**Empirical:** Coming from the senses. Here it refers to the everyday world that we experience.

**Transcendent:** Existing in, or coming from, somewhere above and beyond the ordinary realm of experience. Plato saw something divine in human reason.

### *Conclusions*

This argument presents reasons for thinking that man's rationality is special. The rationalist view holds the key assumption that our reason is something divine, or at least totally different from the mundane. Plato's argument concerning the perfection of our knowledge is really an attempt to draw a distinction between our reason and the empirical world around us. Like Hamlet, Plato wants to find in human beings a nature which is more than animal, and this argument helps to widen the gap between us and them by showing that we have a transcendent ability to have knowledge of reality.

In the next section we look at very similar arguments from Descartes, a much later rationalist, who supports the same conclusion: the character of human thought is such that we stand apart from the rest of nature in our ability to have knowledge of eternal certainties.

## Support from later rationalism: Descartes

While Plato is usually not included within the philosophical school of rationalism he is credited as laying the groundwork on which most of its ideas were built. The later rationalists' alterations to Plato's account of human nature will be discussed in Chapter 4: Mind and Body and Chapter 6: Freedom. Descartes and other Enlightenment rationalists from the late 17th century onwards increased the separation between the rational part of our "true selves" and the desires and drives. However, the essential point with respect to our basic nature – that we are autonomous, rational beings – remains the same.

Descartes is often credited to be the father of modern philosophy. (See biography on p. 100 of Chapter 3: Mind and Body.) He is also the first of the Enlightenment rationalists who thought in ways broadly similar to Plato. Descartes was the arch-rationalist and it is not incidental to his philosophical views that he was also a famous mathematician. It was his love of mathematics that grounded his belief in the power of reason.

▲ Mathematical patterns in nature

> How can it be that mathematics, being after all a product of human thought independent of experience, is so admirably adapted to the objects of reality?
>
> —Albert Einstein[2]

In this quote, Einstein summarizes what is really special about mathematics. When mathematicians do research they do so entirely in their offices. They don't need to experiment, they don't need to measure anything, or watch anything. If we had the space we could do maths completely in our head. And yet mathematicians make discoveries! They find out interesting things about the world. Using their own minds they realize that black holes exist and that objects accelerate towards the earth at equal rates. For Descartes this cut to the heart of human nature – it is our ability to do mathematics and unlock what Galileo called "the language of the universe" that makes us human. We are able to use our reason in the pursuit of real knowledge – knowledge that is absolute and certain and reveals the ultimate nature of reality.

### *Self-evidence and foundationalism*

Reason is notoriously difficult to explain. Descartes attempts to explain it in terms of **self-evidence**. Self-evident truths are the foundation of reason. From these unarguably certain foundations we can build a whole system of knowledge that we can be sure of because of its basis in these absolute principles. Descartes thought that these foundational truths were known because they were indubitable – they provided their own clear evidence and cannot be challenged.

Descartes' classic example of a self-evident truth is the claim that "I exist". The truth of this statement is demonstrated in the very act of thinking or speaking it. It only needs to be understood in order to be known as true. Consider the opposite – "I do not exist". But of course in the very act of saying or thinking it you guarantee your own existence. This paradox shows us that "I exist" is a self-evident truth – its opposite is impossible.

The following truths are some of the **basic logical principles** or laws that are thought by rationalists to be self-evident and therefore provide the foundation of philosophical reason. Here they are explained by the 19th-century German philosopher Arthur Schopenhauer, who usefully included both a complicated and a simplified version of each in his writing.

- Law of identity

  "A subject is equal to the sum of its predicates, or a = a."

  "Everything that is, exists."

  *This is the principle of self-identity. It means that a thing always is itself, as in 1=1.*

---

[2] Albert Einstein, *Sidelights on Relativity* (London/Montana, USA: Methuen & Co./Kessinger Publishing, 1922/2004), p. 12. Also available at http://www.ibiblio.org/ebooks/Einstein/Sidelights/Einstein_Sidelights.pdf (accessed 21 October 2014).

- Law of non-contradiction

  "No predicate can be simultaneously attributed and denied to a subject, or a ≠ ~a."

  "Nothing can simultaneously be and not be."

  *This principle says that nothing can be both true and false at the same time.*

- Law of excluded middle

  "Of every two contradictorily opposite predicates one must belong to every subject."

  "Each and every thing either is or is not."

  *This principle says that everything is either true or false, there's no third option. This means it can't be both true and false, and it can't be neither true nor false.*

- Principle of sufficient reason

  "Truth is the reference of a judgment to something outside it as its sufficient reason or ground."

  "Of everything that is, it can be found why it is."

  *This is the principle of causality. It states that there is a sufficient explanation for everything that exists or occurs.* This principle is not always included in the list of the laws of thought – you will see why when you read about David Hume further on. Gottfried Wilhelm von Leibniz was its most famous advocate and summed it up thus: "The principle of sufficient reason, namely, that nothing happens without a reason."

Each of these principles was considered by rationalists to be self-evident – to deny them is to state an absurd contradiction. For Descartes and the other modern rationalists, these principles underpin all of our reasoning and allow us to take that all-important, rigidly objective look at the world. Our ability to use them is evidenced by our success in mathematics, physics, and philosophy.

### *An example of a priori reasoning: the Cosmological Argument*

In order to better understand this idea of self-evident reasoning we can look at an example from the philosophy of religion. The Cosmological Argument is an attempt to prove the existence of God using the principle of sufficient reason.

The Cosmological Argument is an ancient one, but a modern version was put forward by Frederick Copleston in 1948 during a BBC radio debate with his fellow British philosopher Bertrand Russell. During the debate Copleston argued that everything that exists in the universe is a "contingent being", that it might not have existed and that the principle of sufficient reason applies to it – it "demands an explanation". Copleston argues that when we explain things causally (using the principle of sufficient reason) we can proceed in a chain of explanations going back as far as we like. For example, my parents are the sufficient reason for my existence, and their parents are the sufficient reason for both me and my parents' existence. In order to get a "full" explanation we need to go back as far as we can – ultimately we end up needing to explain the big bang in order to have any explanation for existence at all.

### Questions

Be careful to think about how each idea can be used in a discussion of human nature. What is significant about these ideas is both their certainty – Leibniz believed that no human being could deny the truth of these principles – and their place in our thinking. For Leibniz and the other rationalists these basic principles underpin all of our knowledge and are the tools with which we discover truth.

Is an implication of Leibniz' argument that **doing philosophy** is at the centre of human nature?

### EXERCISE

Try this: Ask a friend to explain some particular thing. Maybe ask her to explain her own existence or to explain how your school might have come to be. Each time your friend offers an explanation check if it is a complete explanation by asking, "And how did *that* come about?", referring to the new explanation. You will annoy your friend and discover that a total explanation for anything is very hard to come by.

Copleston makes a clever point here – in terms of fully explaining things, for example the law of gravity or the existence of insects, we end up needing an account of why anything exists at all. Otherwise these particular things are never given a really full explanation. Physics, for example, argues that the laws of nature are the most fundamental explanation for everything that happens on earth, from our behaviour, to the weather, to the history of art, but the laws of nature themselves are contingent things – they might have been different – and we need an account of how they were made the way they are. Copleston concludes that in order to explain anything at all we need to come to a being about which the question "and how did that come about?" is no longer needed. He calls this being a **Necessary Being** – one who is its own sufficient reason. God is this remarkable being – the one whose existence is self-evident and provides the ultimate explanation for why there is anything at all. If all there are, are contingent beings requiring explanation, "then there's *no explanation* of existence at *all*".

This argument is a good example of reasoning from logical principles to further conclusions. Copleston has used the principle of sufficient reason to demonstrate that there must be some being that is its own sufficient reason.

The early modern rationalist idea of human nature is as a being capable of recognizing the eternal necessity of these truths and being able to use them in the discovery of further knowledge. We are capable of objective knowledge because of our faculty to use reason. These self-evident principles and their products are evidence that reason is a transcendent truth-acquiring tool.

### *Conclusions*

Descartes and Leibniz' foundationalism is arguing the same point as Plato's epistemological arguments: reason is special because it gives us knowledge of eternal certainties. However, whereas Plato's argument depended on obscure esoteric objects called 'Forms', the later rationalists are appealing to our everyday reasonings about the world. Accepting the laws of logic is much more reasonable than accepting transcendent forms, but for the rationalists, the conclusion is the same – we have the astounding ability to have certain knowledge and we can't explain it with experience.

▲ A judge in most court proceedings represents the ideal of rationality. They try to judge the truth of two arguments objectively, without involving any of their own feelings and biases.

## Combining self-control and knowledge: objectivity as rationality

The knowledge reached through our powers of reason demonstrate another feature of rationality. We have the ability to be objective. We all understand the difference between thinking clearly and clouded judgment. In the first we assume a position from which none of our desires or feelings distorts what we believe about the world. In the second we are influenced and biased by our perspective, values, and attitudes. We have good reasons to think that human beings are capable of objectivity. Firstly we have our experience of the difference. Compare the experience of "seeing red" with thinking about a mathematical problem. In the first case your perception of the world around you is completely transformed by your emotions – your anger causes you to misinterpret the things you see. In the second case you have no particular feelings either way, and you don't allow your views, values, or attitudes to influence what you think is the right answer. Your belief is formed strictly on the basis of the evidence you have.

The success of scientific knowledge, which emphasizes the strict reliance on evidence alone when making judgments, is a typical example of this feature of rationalism. The scientific attitude involves an attempt to be as objective as possible so as to derive beliefs from evidence in the most direct and reliable way.

For Plato and the rationalist view of human nature, our ability to be objective is connected to our ability to control our emotions and desires. When the rational part of our selves is in control we are able to have true knowledge and choose a course of action instead of being compelled to it by our values. **Autonomy**, or self-control, is the third feature of rationality that we seem to have. We experience ourselves as taking charge of our impulses and mastering them. We overcome our passions and choose our actions, on the basis of our understanding of the world rather than on the basis of a compulsion. (See the discussion of free will and determinism in Chapter 6: Freedom.)

### *Conclusion*

According to the rationalist view of human nature, man is a rational animal whose essential property consists in having the capacity of reason or rationality, which itself consists in three key capacities to do with knowledge and freedom:

1. Man can discover certainty and truth through use of abstract certainties.
2. Man can separate himself from his feelings to make objective judgments.
3. Man can make choices independently of his impulses.

#### Assessment tip

In a philosophy essay you are specifically asked to discuss implications and assumptions as part of your argument. In this next section we will contextualize the rationalist perspective by exploring just a couple of assumptions and implications. When we consider the rationalist view, we may need to think about it from a cultural perspective. Why, in the history of philosophy did such an idea appear? Why was it so popular and what does that say about the ideas themselves?

When writing an essay on human nature, you can use these implications to enhance argumentation, discussion, and your personal response. When we think about whether or not we want to commit to a rationalist view of human nature, these are some of the concerns, beyond direct philosophical argument, that we use to decide.

## Why do we believe this?

Most of European philosophy has accepted this idea of man as a rational animal for the better part of 2,000 years. In various forms this idea of a human being as a creature with an autonomous, rational soul has dominated various religious and philosophical views of human beings. Why has this idea of man dominated for so long?

When we consider Plato's account of man as a being whose primary nature is his core of reason or rationality we appear to have three intertwining reasons for having believed this idea so often and for so long.

- **Autonomy:** We are able to control ourselves. This is an important piece of phenomenal evidence. Our ability to restrain actions caused by desire seems a powerful reason for supposing that we are governed by a separate faculty that is above desire.
- **Objectivity:** We seem able to think independently of our perspective, to consider things as they are without being influenced by our own interests.
- **Knowledge:** We are able to *understand* the world instead of only responding to it. Most animals respond to stimuli, whereas human beings consider possibilities and select from among them.

## The good life

The rationalist idea of human nature is strongly tied to the question of how we ought to live. In fact, both Plato and his pupil Aristotle (see biography on p. 140 of Chapter 4: Mind and Body) use arguments about the good life to support their claims about our nature.

In Plato's Socratic dialogue *Gorgias,* Plato argues that the best way to live is to control our desires, live temperately, and in accordance with reason. Socrates' adversary, Callicles, suggests that the best way to live is just to seek pleasure. He thinks that although most people won't admit it because of the pressure put on them by social norms, everyone knows that the life of pleasure is the best one.

Plato responds, through Socrates, with two key arguments:

1. He argues that the pursuit of pleasure is an impossible goal. Pleasures are never satisfied – they are like a leaky vessel and we would spend our whole lives frustrated from never achieving satisfaction.
2. Some desires are repulsive or lead to destructiveness. He uses the example of a catamite, but we might use the example of a sex offender. To pursue our desires without restraint is clearly not the same as living "the good life". And so, argues Plato, the good life means acting in accordance with rationality, justice, and virtue.

Each of these can be seen as an argument for Plato's theory of human nature. For Plato and Aristotle living well was living in accordance with our nature. This "teleological" reasoning actually underpins a surprising amount of philosophy and commonsense wisdom. The belief that both Plato and Aristotle share is that all things are made with a kind of purpose or nature. Their "telos", or ultimate object, is what they are supposed to do and amounts to being "good". A good tree is a big, strong, leafy one. In short, one that is good at treeness, or tree nature. In the same way, a "good" human is one who is good at human nature.

Because what is good always comes back to being rational for Plato and Aristotle, it becomes clear to them that our nature consists in rationality.

Aristotle's argument runs in the other direction. Whereas Plato identified the good life and used it to identify our nature, Aristotle identifies our nature, and uses it to identify the good life. He claims that we can see the nature of things by examining their tendencies and capacities. Human beings are good at using reason to think about their world so our reason must be the core of our nature. This reveals our purpose or telos. We are reasoning creatures who, by nature, ought to exercise our reason as well as possible. This means that we must be political and social creatures because it is in the debate of politics that we most use our reason.

So, for Plato goodness means living in accordance with our reason, and for Aristotle, living according to our nature is good.

The relationship between the rationalist idea of the good life and the rationalist account of human nature is an important one. It hints at a crucial explanation for the rationalists' beliefs about our nature.

It hints also at an important discussion. Is this ideal too good to be true? There seem to be a lot of reasons why we might want to believe that reason is our core self. We want to believe we are in control of our actions, that we are able to see the world as it really is, and that we can access truth. But is this a good reason to think we're rational or is it a reason to be suspicious?

## Conclusion

The rationalist view is an old and venerable account of human nature. It dignifies human beings by granting us a number of special powers, including the ability to know the world around us. It appeals to our pride in ourselves, and much of our global culture depends on some aspect of rationalism.

We have looked at a number of arguments in favour of the rationalist concept of human nature.

- Self-control
- Mathematics
- Self-evidence

## A warning

While we will see strong arguments against the rationalist view, it is important not to dismiss it too easily, if at all. For many perspectives, the doing of philosophy and the belief in its value may require some commitment to rationalism, and in giving it up we may also have to give up our belief in human knowledge. Furthermore, the rationalist perspective is the oldest and most popular account of our human nature for a reason. For many historical philosophers it was seen as essential in the preservation of human dignity and in our ability to know. We should be careful to consider the implications of holding – or of not holding – a philosophical perspective.

## Critiques of the rational view

### Reason is less powerful than we imagine: Hobbes and Hume

> ... no one man's reason, nor the reason of any one number of men, makes the certainty; no more than an account is therefore well cast up, because a great many men have unanimously approved it.
>
> —Thomas Hobbes[3]

One criticism of the rationalist perspective stems from some scepticism about reason itself. Thomas Hobbes and David Hume have both argued that "reason" is a much less powerful faculty than philosophers have so far believed.

Thomas Hobbes argued that reason was nothing more than "calculation" in which we compare potential costs and benefits of given actions when choosing what to do next. When we describe the world we give the objects in it names and meanings – we create concepts. For Hobbes, when we reason we are using these concepts to calculate a judgment about what will happen in the future.

For example, we have given the name "water" to a substance and as part of that concept we have included the claim that "water helps to clean things". Therefore I can reason that if I soak my shirt in water after spilling food on it, it will help to remove the mess. I have combined what I know of the world – my concepts about it – into a prediction of what will happen next. Rationality, for Hobbes, is just using this to pursue our interests.

All of this even a rationalist might agree with but Hobbes adds a key assumption that undermines the value and usefulness of reason. The trouble is that reasoning always involves using concepts that we have invented rather than ones that perfectly fit the world.

Nominalists such as Hobbes and Hume reject the claim that our concepts carve up the world as it is – our ideas do not necessarily "cut nature at the joints". We derive our concepts from our experience, according to Hobbes, and as a result it is based on an account that is limited by our ways of seeing the world. We see through our own interests and perspective, and through our particular sense organs – eyes, ears, and so on.

Consider that bats conceptualize their world through echolocation, and some snakes perceive through thermoception. You could also imagine aliens that see the world not in colour but according to the chemical elements that compose it. In each case it stands to reason that they might develop a radically different set of concepts by which to organize their view of the world.

The conclusion of this argument is that reason is a much weaker and more uncertain tool than the rationalists argue. Hobbes rejects the claim that reason offers certainty. This is because it is a mundane and imprecise tool for helping us to navigate life and get what we want, not a means of accessing the divine or absolute. If this is the case, what does

[3] Quoted in Noel Malcolm (ed.), *The Clarendon Edition of the Works of Thomas Hobbes, Volume 3: Leviathan* (Oxford: Oxford University Press, 2012).

it mean for Hobbes to say that man is rational? Only that he is very good at pursuing his own interests – nothing more.

## Biography: Thomas Hobbes (1588–1679)

Hobbes was an English philosopher of the 17th century: an era of intense political turmoil in his native country. He grew up in a small West Country town and later went to Oxford for his studies. Travelling through Europe as a young man, Hobbes learned about developments in continental philosophy and the Enlightenment, and his works were informed by classical learning. However, his main focus on political philosophy courted controversy in his works *The Elements of Law* and, most famously, *Leviathan*. Feeling endangered in revolutionary England, Hobbes spent much of his life in Paris and became a tutor to the exiled Prince of Wales (later, Charles II). Beyond political philosophy, Hobbes was known as a critic of Descartes and some of his objections were published, with replies, in certain editions of the French philosopher's works. Hobbes was sometimes accused of having unorthodox religious views but, on his eventual return to England, he was protected at the restored Stuart court.

## Biography: David Hume (1711–1776)

Hume was a Scottish philosopher, a leading figure of the Scottish Enlightenment, and has proved one of the most influential philosophers to write in the English language. Hume grew up in a respectable middle class family, the son of lawyer, and the recipient of a good education from an early age at Edinburgh University. Relying on his learning (he had no great inherited wealth), Hume progressed from his studies to a series of clerical jobs that saw him work in England, France and Scotland. He hoped to work as a professor, but long-term suspicion about his religious beliefs (or lack thereof) prevented him from rising to an academic post. Hume's works as a philosopher were incredibly wide ranging, covering human nature, epistemology, ethics and politics. Curiously, although he is now regarded as one of the greatest philosophers of all time, in his own life he made his reputation as an historian, and his best-selling work was the multi-volume *History of England*.

A century later Hume presented a similar view of reason that can be seen as more detailed fleshing out of Hobbes' arguments. Hume was an **empiricist**, meaning that he based his philosophy on the principle that the entire contents of our mind comes from our experiences. This means he rejects the rationalist view that we have innate rationality.

Hume's argument begins with the same basic claim as Hobbes' – we derive our concepts from experience. His argument for this is to demonstrate that all of the ideas we have can be broken down into **sense experience**, or "impressions" as he calls them. Hume takes it for granted that the majority of our ideas can be explained in terms of sense experience. Most of the things that we think about and talk about are actually things out there in the world that we have seen or heard. Therefore Hume focuses on ideas that are less obviously derived from experience.

He begins with imaginary ideas. "Nothing, at first view, may seem more unbounded than the imagination of man," he writes in *An Enquiry Concerning Human Understanding* (1748).[4] Hume notes that the freedom given to us by our imagination takes us far beyond our own limited daily experience – we can travel to worlds completely different from our own inside our heads. At least, this is how it seems. In fact, if you consider the things you can imagine, says Hume, you will find that it always has its roots in your everyday experience. Consider the last sci-fi book, film, or video game you encountered. Notice how the aliens always look like some kind of animal from earth? Maybe a blue human being, or one with big eyes, or something that looks like an insect. But ultimately the imagination of Hollywood scriptwriters seems to be limited to combining the things they've seen. They haven't come up with a *truly* imaginary idea at all.

## EXERCISE

Try to design a world or a creature that is unlike anything your classmates have ever experienced. Now share them – they may be new as a whole, but can you show how each part has come from something from your everyday experience?

So far so good, but rationalists have found other ideas that they argue cannot be derived from sense experience. Here is how Hume deals with a few of them:

- **God:** Rationalists argue that the idea of a perfect being could not possibly have come from our experience because we only have experience of limited and imperfect things. Hume responds that we simply take qualities that we value in others, such as power, compassion, and mercy, and "amalgamate them without limit". By this means we have imagined the idea of God.
- **Morality:** Yet another rationalist idea that could not possibly have come from experience is our knowledge of right and wrong. Nowhere in experience do we encounter values such as good and evil, so we must have intuitive rational access to the moral law on earth. Hume responds that morality is nothing more than a feeling of liking or disliking that is so strong that we feel that it must be a universal truth. We are so convinced of their value that we extend it to others.
- **Basic principles of reason:** Hume presents an argument that these are nothing more than complex ideas just like imaginary ideas. He picks on a key rationalist principle, the law of causation, in order to undermine the whole rationalist project. He does so mercilessly, concluding that this pillar of logical thought is in fact nothing but passionate prejudice. This argument is one of Hume's most famous and significant, so let's look at it in detail.

[4] David Hume, "Section II: Of the Origin of Ideas", in *An Enquiry Concerning Human Understanding and Concerning the Principles of Morals*, edited by L. A. Selby-Bigge, 3rd edition revised by P. H. Nidditch (Oxford: Clarendon Press, 1975), p. 18.

### Hume's critique of necessary causation

The principle that everything must have a cause is one of the most basic parts of the logical toolkit we use to make reasoned judgments about the world. The principle underpins all of scientific inquiry because it amounts to saying that everything must have an explanation – that every natural fact happens for some reason. When Hume attacks causation he attacks the foundation of every inference we can make about the world around us.

▲ When you play pool you are relying on a lawful universe to predict the result of your shots. For homework go play a game of pool, and explain Hume's account to your opponent.

## A WORLD WITHOUT CAUSATION

Imagine if we could not be certain of the law of causation. When we explain events in the natural world we look for the most plausible, but if causation is uncertain then it could just happen for no reason. If we don't assume necessary causation, we can never be sure of our explanations – maybe gravity makes us fall towards large bodies, maybe it happens for no reason.

Hume begins by asking if we can actually observe cause and effect when we look at the world. He uses the example of billiard balls to illustrate causation in its purest form. When one billiard ball hits another we see it cause the other one to move, right? Or do we? Hume asks us to think carefully about what we really do see. If we break our experience down to its barest parts we actually don't see any "cause" at all. All we see is a white circular shape move across our field of vision, then stop, then we hear a noise, then we see another contiguous circular shape, this time red, move in another direction. Nowhere in this catalogue of experience is any actual experience of the "necessary connection" between the two events – we don't actually see anything that demonstrates that the one event caused the other.

The rationalists would argue that the knowledge of cause and effect is given by our intuition – the reasoning nature within ourselves. However, Hume rejects this in favour of a naturalistic account that argues that our belief in causation is learned through a kind of training.

Initially when we encounter two events happening contemporaneously we form no belief about their relationship. After repeatedly experiencing two events together, what Hume calls "constant conjunction", we come to have a feeling of "expectation" when we encounter one of them. For example, if we repeatedly experience a loud frightening noise at the same time as seeing a rat, we will eventually come to expect the noise whenever we encounter a rat. Once we have the belief that one event entails the other, we will have formed a belief in "necessary connection", that there is a causal relationship between the two events. This clever argument suggests that our belief in causation is based on a combination of empirical experience and our feelings in response to them.

## OBJECT PERMANENCE

There is a similar debate in psychology concerning the extent to which our basic reasoning faculties are acquired through experience or are innate. Jean Piaget famously presents a similar argument for the acquisition of rational principles through experience. Object permanence is a basic developmental stage for babies. It consists of the belief that objects that they sense continue to exist even when they cannot be seen. If infants have no understanding of object permanence, then they don't understand that objects have a separate existence or that the world exists beyond themselves. Piaget argues that children in fact learn to believe in the outside world through repeated interactions with objects and coordinated experience – experiences that happen in systematic relation to one another. This argument mirrors Hume's account of reason by showing that even the most basic principles by which we understand our world are learned through repeated processes. The game of peek-a-boo is a classic example of an object permanence test. Not until four months old do babies show evidence of understanding that the person's face is hidden.

### Conclusion

What Hume has really done here is to reduce reasoning down to emotions. He is showing that our beliefs about cause and effect are not rational, but dependent on our passions – which eliminates the clarity and objectivity that rationalists think our reason has. If Hume is right, then to call us rational animals is really empty because rationality (or at least a very important part of it – the principle of causation) is based on irrationality.

Furthermore, if our beliefs about cause and effect are just based on limited experiences, they can never be considered certain – Hume famously declares that there is no reason to be sure that the sun will rise tomorrow other than it always has done. Just because it always has risen is not sufficient evidence that it must continue to rise. Russell illustrated the idea with a turkey, the traditional centrepiece of the British Christmas Day meal. The turkey wakes up every morning for a year and gets fed. Christmas Day dawns and the turkey has a year's worth of evidence to support its belief that it will be fed today – but it will be sorely disappointed... This therefore calls into question the claim that reason has the power to give us certain knowledge. We may be rational animals but that doesn't give us any claim to really know the world.

Hobbes' and Hume's arguments have cast doubt on the status of reason. It is from this position of scepticism about the history of philosophy and rationalism that our next question makes sense: if certainty was never a plausible goal, what were all those rationalist philosophers really doing? The philosophers Nietzsche and Michel Foucault provide a philosophical approach that helps us to reinterpret the rationalist project. They see the arguments of rationalist philosophers as part of a quest for power in the battle of ideas.

### Questions

It's important to think about these ideas in terms of human nature. With his attack on causation Hume is really attacking the idea that knowledge is central to human nature. Whereas Leibniz argued that our thinking had special qualities which separate us from the animal kingdom, Hume argues that **doing philosophy** is a combination of guess work and invention.

How is Hume 'pulling the rug out from under' the Rationalist view that it is human nature to **do philosophy**?

## Relativism

Scepticism about the power and value of rationality often comes in the form of **relativism**. Relativists make one essential argument: what constitutes reason and rationality depends on **cultural norms**, not on transcendent or universal truth. Therefore, reason itself, as a basic set of principles that guide thinking and a standard by which to judge the validity of arguments, is socially constructed. Furthermore, there is a plurality of different notions of reason and we have no universal standard or position from which to judge them. This perspective is a very common feature of postmodern 20th-century thought but its roots go as far back as the sceptics of ancient Greece.

One set of arguments in support of this view uses the history of ideas and science in order to provide evidence and support for relativism. Thomas Kuhn and Foucault, although working in different philosophical traditions, developed similar arguments that reason is not a permanent or fixed thing, but that in fact the idea of reason changes depending on the culture and historical period in which it exists.

### *Kuhn*

The idea of a **paradigm shift** is central to Thomas Kuhn's (1922–96) philosophy of science. He begins his argument by spelling out the traditional picture of scientific progress: for most historians and lay people, science is seen as a unified constant progression where ideas are developed and improved as we proceed linearly towards a full understanding of natural history.

This view, argues Kuhn, is founded on mistaken assumptions and is the result of an over-optimistic view of scientific reason. Kuhn rejects two assumptions of the traditional view:

- Science heads towards the truth: It is a common belief that we will eventually arrive at a complete and final account of the natural world.
- Scientific history is a linear process of improvement. It is also believed that scientific discovery builds on and improves the ideas that came before.

Kuhn challenges this picture with the notion of paradigm shifts. In this model science is not a single unified history but a series of independent, "**incommensurable**" pictures of the world that cannot be understood or meaningfully explored from the perspective of another. Each paradigm is self-contained and its principles and assumptions determine how scientific knowledge of the world is meaningful and valid. These paradigms are so completely different from one another that it is impossible to evaluate the ideas of one paradigm from the perspective of another – we cannot make claims about the truth or falsity of one paradigm without committing ourselves to it.

So how do we come to switch to a new paradigm? This happens because anomalies appear in our current way of thinking. As new scientific questions appear that are unanswerable in the current paradigm this stresses our way of looking at the world to the point where it collapses and a new conceptual framework is put in its place.

> There is no neutral algorithm for theory choice, no systematic decision procedure which, properly applied, must lead each individual in the group to the same decision.
>
> —Thomas Kuhn[5]

The upshot of all this is that describing man as a "reasoning" animal does not actually describe any essential feature of human beings because the idea of reason itself is relative and therefore a constantly changing notion. If there are different conceptions of reason, and we switch between them on the basis of social convention, then we have serious reason to doubt the rationalist claim that our reason is a tool for uncovering truth:

> In the sciences there need not be progress of another sort. We may, to be more precise, have to relinquish the notion, explicit or implicit, that changes of paradigm carry scientists and those who learn from them closer and closer to the truth.
>
> —Thomas Kuhn[6]

### *Foucault*

The French philosopher Michel Foucault (1926–84) took Kuhn's ideas to a relativistic extreme with his concept of **episteme**. An episteme is a basic unconscious way of seeing the world and of using reason. Therefore it runs even further than the scientific paradigm; it touches every thought because it is the framework for meaning and use of language.

> In any given culture and at any given moment, there is always only one episteme that defines the conditions of possibility of all knowledge, whether expressed in a theory or silently invested in a practice.
>
> —Michel Foucault[7]

Consider the shift from a teleological worldview to a **mechanistic** worldview. Before the Enlightenment age the very notion of "explanation" was radically different. From the Enlightenment onwards, to explain something generally means to give an account of the causes that bring it into being. However, from Aristotle until Francis Bacon the typical way of explaining the natural world is described

---

[5] Thomas Kuhn, *The Structure of Scientific Revolutions*, 2nd edition (Chicago: University of Chicago Press, 1970), p. 200.

[6] Ibid, p. 170.

[7] Michel Foucault, *The Order of Things: An Archaeology of the Human Sciences*, 2nd edition (London: Routledge, 1970), p. 183.

as a teleological worldview. Rather than inquiring into the physical causes that came before, Aristotle and his followers would ask what the purpose of something is. For example, while we might explain the rising of the sun in terms of gravitational forces and the spinning of the earth, a teleological explanation sees its cause in terms of its purpose, such as to enable crops to grow and to allow us to see. These differing sets of assumptions about the world determine what we mean by "explanation" and therefore fix the sorts of things that can count as an explanation.

### *An illustration*

R. M. Hare provides a useful example to illustrate this idea:

> A certain lunatic is convinced that all dons want to murder him. His friends introduce him to all the mildest and most respectable dons that they can find, and after each of them has retired, they say, "You see, he doesn't really want to murder you; he spoke to you in a most cordial manner; surely you are convinced now?" But the lunatic replies, "Yes, but that was only his diabolical cunning; he's really plotting against me the whole time, like the rest of them; I know it I tell you." However many kindly dons are produced, the reaction is still the same.[8]

While this seems obviously insane to us, from the perspective of the "lunatic" all of the evidence presented serves to support a completely different view to our own. Hare called this a "*blik*" and while he used this example to illustrate the nature of a religious perspective we can apply it to our case. In this case the assumptions that determine the explanation are not based on reasoning or evidence, but are the conditions for what counts as reasoning and evidence.

As Hare said, "without a *blik* there can be no explanation; for it is by our paranoid *bliks* that we decide what is and what is not an explanation".[9]

For Hare, everyone has a *blik*. There are no "theory-neutral" observations of the world. You and I bring with us basic assumptions about reason and evidence every time we make judgments about the world. They are beyond justification because they determine how we justify things, and they are an assumption so deep that we never notice them. Our *blik* may seem obviously right to us, but that is only when seen through our own perspective.

The paranoid man above has what might be called a "paranoid" *blik*. Others might include the "mechanistic" *blik* in which only explanations based on the physical theory of the universe are legitimate (for example, religious or metaphysical ones are silly), or a fundamentalist religious *blik* in which evidence from religious authority outweighs the evidence of science.

---

[8] R. M. Hare, "The Simple Believer, Appendix: Theology and Falsification", *Essays on Religion and Education* (Oxford: Clarendon Press, 1992), p. 37.

[9] Ibid., p. 38.

In each of these cases you can point to why you do or don't like it, and why you do or don't find the assumptions plausible, but you cannot justify your view without first making some assumptions about what a good justification is. Try it.

## EXERCISE

Consider this student's response to this challenge:

> I like the "mechanistic" *blik* whereby science informs us as to why the universe behaves the way it does. I find this legitimate because these theories have to be backed up with evidence, whereas religious explanations of the universe are based on narratives which have no grounding in what is actually happening. They are just stories based on interpretations a very long time ago.

The trouble with this answer is that it is full of assumptions. The student assumes that "backed up with evidence" improves the quality of the viewpoint and that "what is actually happening" is what our senses tell us is happening – note that these are just assumptions rather than justifiable. What other assumptions can you identify?

### Conclusion

Relativism offers three general arguments that we can use when doing philosophy on the question of human nature. In each we will be challenging the view that man's nature is as a rational being that is capable of perceiving objective truth.

1. **The pessimistic meta-induction:** This argument is a simple one (in spite of its title). It argues from the fact that there are multiple conceptions of reason and rationality depending on time and culture. Furthermore, we do not have a higher position from which to judge them so our own notion of reason has no more authority than any other conception. Therefore there is no good reason to think we have the right conception now or that we ever will.
2. **The social and ecological construction of reason:** Having argued that different times and places have different conceptions of reason, we can argue that these differences are derived from something relative to those cultures and times, and not from a transcendent or divine source. Different forms of rationality may be the result of cultural norms and values or the concerns and interests that dominated the time and place in which people lived. Therefore, because reason and rationality are the product of mundane causes, they have no claim to absolute truth or certainty.
3. **Feeling sure is not being right:** A key argument from rationalist philosophers is from self-evidence. Reasoned truths are certain because they are apparently undeniable. By stripping away any metaphysical foundation for reason and replacing it with the everyday, relativists can argue that simply because something seems self-evident to us that doesn't make it certain. Feeling sure is not enough justification to demonstrate that you are right.

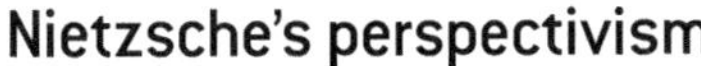

## Nietzsche's perspectivism

In the first chapter of *Beyond Good and Evil* (1886), the German philosopher Nietzsche launches a spectacular attack on philosophy in general and in particular on the rationalist assumptions that he perceives in nearly the whole history of philosophy. His critique involves a rejection of the key tenets of the rationalist perspective on human nature.

### Biography: Friedrich Wilhelm Nietzsche (1844–1900)

Nietzsche was a German philosopher who wrote on numerous subjects including philology, ancient Greek drama, religion, culture as well as philosophy. Nietzsche became the professor of classical philology at the University of Basel in Switzerland at the age of 24. However, he is most famous for his radical critique of western philosophy; in particular his radical questioning of the value and objectivity of truth through a rejection of Plato's metaphysics. In his early works, Nietzsche was a philosopher of pessimism due to the influence of Arthur Schopenhauer and Richard Wagner on his thinking. However, these influences were eventually rejected and the resulting nihilism with a philosophy of "life-affirmation". He was never tenured as a philosopher. Instead, he chose to retire early from the University and wrote his later works while living off a small pension. During this period of time he travelled throughout Europe and wrote *Beyond Good and Evil*, *On the Genealogy of Morals*, *Twilight of the Idols*, *The Antichrist*, and *Ecco Homo*. His life was plagued with ill heath that included prolonged migraines, and eventually lose of sight towards the end of his life. Nietzsche suffered a mental breakdown in1889 but lived until 1900. Nietzsche's reception was limited during his own life and his work was distorted by selective publication posthumously of his writings by his sister, an avowed anti-Semite herself, in a book called *Will to Power*. His work is hard to read due his aphoristic style of writing. Nonetheless, his influence has been profound; including the philosophy schools of phenomenology and existentialism, numerous movements in the arts, musicians, writers and poets.

Objectivity and the ability of human beings to use reason in the discovery of truth are his targets. Nietzsche points out that there are no philosophical truths yet and after at least 2500 years you'd think a discipline would have made some progress – yet philosophy seems to have made none. This suggests there is something seriously wrong with our perception of philosophy as "**the search for truth**" and of man as a creature who searches for it. Rationalists have used the myth of reason while all the while they've secretly been trying to push their own prejudices on to the rest of us.

Nietzsche begins this critique with an argument for what he calls **perspectivism**. Nietzsche argues that "**perspectivity**" is the most obvious pre-condition of any kind of knowledge. Perspectivism refers to the fact that any knowledge we may have of the world is an **interpretation** that is filtered through our values and ways of seeing. Our way of seeing the world is based on ourselves – on our particular needs, on our particular values, and on our particular bodies. We don't see reality from the perspective of an ant any more than we see it from the perspective of a god. A knower can only have a perspective, not a god's eye view, and as a result our knowledge of the world will always be incomplete. Consider the fact that anything you see must be viewed from a perspective – we must picture things from a position. The idea of seeing without perspective is absurd and Nietzsche ridicules the notion of objectivity in the same way. To be objective is to have a "view from nowhere" – an incoherent impossibility – and in fact Nietzsche goes so far as to conclude that perspectivity is "the fundamental condition – of life".

Our perspective comes from our nature as beings in the world. Everything we do is an expression of some deep desire or fear, and the way we create our beliefs and knowledge is no exception. We choose all of our beliefs not according to rational principles but according to our interests. Nietzsche's perspectives are fixed by the human values that underpin them:

> the greater part of the conscious thinking of a philosopher is secretly influenced by his instincts, and forced into definite channels.[10]

Therefore the "rational" theories that we develop are in fact vast falsifications and simplifications in which we overemphasize what appeals to us and ignore what doesn't. All knowledge always involves an interpretation and simplification – we attempt to reduce the world, or describe it in a system that is intelligible to ourselves. But in simplifying we also make false.

Nietzsche gives examples of the hidden values behind rationalism. The emphasis on the life of the mind rather than lived experience reveals that rationalists are "**despisers of the body**". Rationalism takes what is most real – daily lived experience – and turns it into an illusion. In Descartes' and Plato's philosophies sense experience is the great illusion to be scorned in favour of reason. In this, argues Nietzsche, they are simply demonstrating their own lack of vitality and life – their inability to enjoy and succeed in the passions and pleasures of daily living. He goes on to argue that rationalism is the result of the resentment felt by the physically fearful and weak. Because they are unable to succeed on the terms of life, they have used philosophy to make thinking more important and living less important.

So while different philosophers may come to opposing conclusions they are still "chasing one another around the same orbit" – they share the same values and assumptions so are nonetheless on the same track, or thinking from the same perspective. They still have the same global value set.

### Conclusion

Nietzsche rejects the rationalist theory of human nature because the principles and assumptions on which it rests are incoherent. We cannot be rational beings because:

- All philosophy is derived from the hidden desires and prejudices of the men who wrote it.
- "Philosophical Truth" is a myth. This is because objectivity is nonsense – there can be no belief that is separated from the particulars of the one who writes it.

[10] Friedrich Nietzsche, *Beyond Good and Evil*, revised edition, translated by R. J. Hollingdale (London: Penguin, 2003), p. 2.

We can therefore say that human beings are not interested in truth for its own sake; what we seek in an opinion is that it be of use to us:

> The falseness of an opinion is not for us any objection to it: it is here, perhaps, that our new language sounds most strangely. The question is, how far an opinion is life-furthering, life-preserving, species-preserving, perhaps species-rearing, and we are fundamentally inclined to maintain that the falsest opinions (to which the synthetic judgments a priori belong), are the most indispensable to us, that without a recognition of logical fictions, without a comparison of reality with the purely IMAGINED world of the absolute and immutable, without a constant counterfeiting of the world by means of numbers, man could not live—that the renunciation of false opinions would be a renunciation of life, a negation of life.[11]

In fact we are irrational to the point that in order to face life we need to lie to ourselves:

> TO RECOGNISE UNTRUTH AS A CONDITION OF LIFE; that is certainly to impugn the traditional ideas of value in a dangerous manner, and a philosophy which ventures to do so, has thereby alone placed itself beyond good and evil.[12]

## EXERCISE

Compare the lyrics of the song *Clouds*, by Joni Mitchell, with Wallace Stevens' poem *Tea at the Palaz of Hoon*.

- How do Mitchell and Stevens express some of the ideas discussed in relativism and perspectivism?
- How do their poems challenge some of the rationalist arguments we looked at earlier?

## Irrational animal

**Darwinian Man, though well behaved,**

**At best is only a monkey shaved!**

—W. S. Gilbert, *Princess Ida*, libretto (1884)

Are human beings no more than a shaved ape? The perspective that man is an animal is the precise opposite of the rationalist view. Instead of a being with one foot in heaven and a faculty that separates him from the world, the animal view sees us as much more mundane. In this perspective we lack objectivity, rational knowledge, and self-control. The good life is not one of contemplation or of reasoned moderation and there is often nothing to do but control man as you would a beast.

[11] Ibid., p. 3.

[12] Ibid., p. 3.

When we describe man as an animal it is generally not a compliment. When most philosophers do so they are saying that he is irrational, that he makes judgments not on the basis of facts and evidence but on the basis of his flawed perspective and limited understanding. We are saying that man is not objective, but **subjective**, that he is not able to see the world as it is independently of himself, but always interprets according to his own interests. We are arguing that he does not have self-control, that he is a **creature of impulse and instinct**, and it is those deepest desires that ultimately govern all we do.

This view is as old as the rationalist view. Many of the earliest philosophers such as Protagoras and Xenophanes had a less hopeful view of human nature and often emphasized the irrationality of man. While there are very early views emphasizing the irrationality of man, the argument isn't put forward in a really powerful way until biological theories emerge claiming to demonstrate that man is an animal.

▲ "'A Veritable Orang-outang: a contribution to unnatural history": Charles Darwin caricatured in *The Hornet* (1871)

## Darwin

> The difference in mind between man and the higher animals, great as it is, certainly is one of degree and not of kind.
>
> —Charles Darwin (1871)[13]

### How natural selection works

1. When creatures reproduce they generate variation – all of their offspring are different in lots of small subtle ways.
2. Some of these subtle differences help an organism to survive and reproduce.
3. The offspring who have these adaptations are the ones who survive and pass on their genes.
4. The next generation therefore has more of these adaptations.

▲ Darwin's illustrations of beak variation in the finches of the Galápagos Islands, which hold 13 closely related species that differ most markedly in the shape of their beaks. The beak of each species is suited to its preferred food, suggesting that beak shapes evolved by natural selection.

In 1858 Darwin's account of the biological world in terms of **natural selection** was published in his book *On the Origin of Species*. It provoked an enormous response because of the way that it challenged the long-established theological account of how the world was created: rather than being made instantaneously by God as the Holy Bible stated, Darwin's natural history argued that all organisms were the product of a slow incremental development over millions of years. However, what was more deeply upsetting were the briefly suggested implications for our theory of human nature. At the end of *On the Origin of Species* Darwin only dared to hint at what the theory of evolution implied about human beings: "Light will be thrown on the origin of man and his history."[14] What Darwin is implying is that with his new theory there is no escape

[13] Charles Darwin, *The Descent of Man*, revised edition (London: Penguin, 2004), p. 151.

[14] Charles Darwin, *On the Origin of Species* (John Murray, 1859), p. 488, now available at http://darwin-online.org.uk/content/frameset?itemID=F373&viewtype=text&pageseq=1 (accessed 21 October 2014).

for human beings. If evolution is true, then it obviously applies to humans as well, making us just one species among the other animals. In the light of this new theory people started to look at themselves in a very different light and our physical similarity to primates was obvious even to ordinary people. Debate about Darwin's theory was heated, but most of the controversy revolved around this issue, which was never actually discussed in his book. People saw the clear link between human beings and primates and were deeply upset by the implication that man was no more than an animal. In the words of Benjamin Disraeli, the British Conservative politician, in 1864: "The question is this – Is man an ape or an angel? My Lord, I am on the side of the angels. I repudiate with indignation and abhorrence these new fangled theories."[15]

The rationalist perspective is, at its root, strongly connected with religious perspectives on the nature of human beings. For Plato, our reason is the part that connects us to the absolute and eternal realm of forms. Our immortal soul enables us to grasp perfect reality. For Descartes, reason is a gift from God that allows us to see the world as it really is.

However, without a divine origin the power of reason becomes dubious. If our reason is from the divine, whether it be the forms of Plato or a theistic god, this provides justification for its power – it justifies the claim that reason allows us to see eternal truth and that it grants us **autonomy**.

Darwin's arguments and the whole history of evolutionary arguments after him suggest a very different origin for reason and a very different idea of human nature.

In the theory of evolution the nature of our bodies is the result of natural processes. When Darwin considered the behavioural similarities between human beings and certain animals he came to the conclusion that our brains and our minds are likely produced by the same mundane processes.

In a later book, *The Descent of Man* (1871), Darwin finally had the courage to apply evolutionary thinking to human beings. When applied to our bodies this seemed uncontroversial: we share so much of our physiology with other mammals that it is very reasonable to say that the body of *Homo sapiens* is related to them. A more threatening problem for Darwin was explaining human behaviour.

Our nervous system is just as much a result of evolutionary processes as the rest of our bodies, and any good biologist would argue that our nervous system produces our behaviour. Furthermore, behaviour is at least as important for evolution as our physical state. After all, you can give a lion an excellent body for hunting – sharp teeth, good eyesight, speed, and strength – but if it doesn't have any hunting impulses then its survival is not improved at all. The implication of evolutionary theory when we look at animal behaviour is that most of the things animals do, from pack hunting, to flocking, to burrowing, to mating, all have adaptive value – they increase the likelihood of survival. There is every reason, therefore, from an evolutionary perspective, to believe that the large part of human behaviours are also driven by evolutionary adaptations and not the product of a reasoned

## Questions

What does a difference of degree and not of kind mean?

In your view, are the following differences one of degree or of kind:

**a.** Murder and involuntary manslaughter

**b.** Adults and children

**c.** American and Chinese people

When Darwin says that man only differs from animals in degree, what does that do to the rationalist view of human nature?

[15] Benjamin Disraeli, speech given at the Oxford Diocesan Conference, 25 November 1864.

judgment. This shift, from explaining the physical components of the biological world, to explaining behaviour using evolution, is known as **evolutionary psychology**.

However even many of Darwin's supporters could not conceive of our mind being a product of evolution. Our higher faculties and moral reasoning, they argued, must remain the domain of God.

## Why the resistance?

Charles Lyell and other contemporary scientists could not accept that our behaviours could be explained through evolution. The sheer complexity of our mental faculties seemed too much to explain in evolutionary terms. Furthermore, many scientists used arguments similar to those proposed by Descartes and others for substance dualism. They argued that the nature of the mind was such that it couldn't be built through small increments – they argued that the mind was irreducible. Still others argued that the mind could not possibly be a biological sort of thing – that it must be a spiritual or mental sort of thing. We can also argue that the large part of the resistance to Darwin's theory was about the dignity given to human beings by the rationalist theory of human nature.

In spite of this resistance Darwin attempted to demonstrate that our behaviour may have an evolutionary explanation. If this is true, then we are not guided by a divine light or objectivity but by our "selfish genes", which have retained behaviours in the form of instincts. These impulses exist because they improved our fitness and therefore they do not necessarily include faculties that are the most rational, moral, or objective.

## Evolutionary psychology

> In the distant future I see open fields for far more important researches. Psychology will be based on a new foundation, that of the necessary acquirement of each mental power and capacity by gradation.
>
> —Charles Darwin[16]

Darwin spent a great deal of his text examining behavioural differences in the sexes. More recently a large body of research has grown which supports the claim that we are driven by instincts similar to animals, stretching from our basic impulses to our higher reasoning behaviours. Leda Cosmides and John Tooby identify the assumptions that evolutionary psychology makes when it applies Darwin's ideas to the human mind.

1. The brain is a physical system whose operation is governed solely by the laws of chemistry and physics. What does this mean? It means that all of your thoughts and hopes and dreams and feelings are produced by chemical reactions going on in your head (a sobering thought).
2. Our brains were designed by natural selection to solve problems that our ancestors faced during our species' evolutionary history. Our behaviour is therefore designed by natural selection for the same reason.

[16] Darwin, *Origin of Species*, p. 488.

3. Consciousness is just the tip of the iceberg; most of what goes on in your mind is hidden from you. As a result, your conscious experience can mislead you into thinking that thinking is simpler than it really is. Most problems that you experience as easy to solve are very difficult to solve – they require very complicated neural circuitry.
4. Our modern skulls house a stone age mind.[17]

## Male aggression

One example Darwin picks on is male aggression and competitiveness. He points out that this "must be our natural birth right" as men, and that it has obvious survival and reproductive benefits, but that it is not a rational or moral behaviour. Darwin therefore claimed it as an impulse built into us rather than something reasoned through and judged.

Darwin gave the following argument about sex differences in favour of the claim that man is an animal, both in his physical composition and in his behaviour. He provides a fairly crude account of the differences between male and female behaviour. Male aggressiveness and competitiveness are the result of the struggle to acquire mates and to protect them from competitors. He has also been given a stronger power of reason to enable him to fashion weapons and outthink his enemies. Female tenderness and selflessness are the result of the adaptive maternal instincts which ensure that her young are cared for.

## Mating preferences

[17] Adapted from Leda Cosmides and John Tooby, *Evolutionary Psychology: A Primer* (Santa Barbara, USA: Center for Evolutionary Psychology, University of California, 1997), available at http://www.cep.ucsb.edu/primer.html (accessed 21 October 2014).

Another idea from evolutionary psychology is the suggestion that when we choose a mate we are hard wired to seek certain things that make sense in evolutionary terms. For example, research suggests that men seek younger partners, which increases the likelihood of fertility.

For a case study about the science of attraction and its philosophical implications, turn to Chapter 6: Freedom.

Furthermore, what people find attractive in a mate is thought to indicate their useful genes. The facial and bodily features that are sexually attractive to people are signs of health, strength, and a sound immune system. By seeking these features, people ensure that they get the best genes for their offspring. A healthy mate increases the likelihood of healthy offspring, and this is what attractiveness is really about.

Another aspect of distinct mating preferences is the tendency for men to prefer short-term mating opportunities (yes, that is what it sounds like) and women to have long-term mating preferences. This is because of the different investments that men and women have to make as parents. While males can produce millions of sperm immediately, females have a limited monthly fertile window and produce a much smaller number of zygotes at greater cost. Furthermore, a male can reproduce and walk away and be reproducing again within minutes. A female, on the other hand, can conceive around once per year at best, and is encumbered with carrying the child and then nursing it thereafter. So the commitment in terms of energy and time for females is much greater. Therefore evolution has programmed males to seek the greatest **quantity** of mating opportunities, while it has given women the impulse to seek the greatest **quality** mating opportunity – evolution made women more selective about who they have sex with.

## Evaluation

Bear in mind that arguments from evolutionary psychology are far from uncontroversial. Many philosophers and psychologists argue that they are speculative inventions designed to support a misogynistic and oppressive politics of gender inequality. Look at the feminist arguments in the section on man as a blank slate at the end of this chapter.

### Morality

Perhaps the theory most objected to is that which attempts to explain virtue and vice as evolutionary adaptations. Darwin himself offered an account of "selfless" behaviour in terms of adaptation. **Altruism** is a problem for evolutionary theory because, according to the theory, our behaviour is adapted to increase the likelihood of our survival and reproduction. Altruism is any behaviour that costs the organism but does not provide any benefit. For example, giving away hard-won resources or even laying down one's life to preserve another organism is severely detrimental to our chances of reproduction, so evolution would have removed these behaviours through selection.

However, altruism is found in nature, including in our closest relatives, chimpanzees. Two evolutionary explanations have been offered for this behaviour.

### *Kin selection*

According to kin selection theory organisms that help closely related family members to survive and reproduce are helping their own genes to be passed on. By enduring the cost of resource sharing, they increase the likelihood of offspring or other close relatives surviving to reproduce. Because they share genes, altruism can lead to more effective reproduction and survival. Altruistic behaviour increases the likelihood of passing on our shared genes. This theory explains the sacrifices that mother animals and humans make for their offspring. It can also be used to explain why we tend to be more altruistic with members of our own family and with people who are similar to ourselves. We have an adaptive interest in saving their lives and helping them reproduce.

> Let us suppose that you carry a rare gene that affects your behaviour so that you jump into a flooded river and save a child, but you have one chance in ten of being drowned, while I do not possess the gene, and stand on the bank and watch the child drown. If the child's your own child or your brother or sister, there is an even chance that this child will also have this gene, so five genes will be saved in children for one lost in an adult. If you save a grandchild or a nephew, the advantage is only two and a half to one. If you only save a first cousin, the effect is very slight. If you try to save your first cousin once removed the population is more likely to lose this valuable gene than to gain it. ... It is clear that genes making for conduct of this kind would only have a chance of spreading in rather small populations when most of the children were fairly near relatives of the man who risked his life.
>
> —John B. S. Haldane[18]

The British scientist John B. S. Haldane, when asked if he would lay down his life for a drowning brother, jokingly replied, "No, but I would for two brothers or eight cousins."[19] We share half our genes with a brother and an eighth with a cousin. Therefore saving the lives of eight cousins would preserve his own genes just as well as staying alive himself does.

### *Reciprocal altruism*

In this approach, altruistic behaviours are the product of our sociality. Primates have similar kinship and social groups to human beings and this is seen as evidence for the view that our social and moral behaviours are evolved instincts. In fact, the great apes share with us lots of social behaviours:

> ... attachment and bonding, cooperation and mutual aid, sympathy and empathy, direct and indirect reciprocity, altruism and reciprocal altruism, conflict resolution and peacemaking, deception and deception detection, community concern and caring about what others think about you, and awareness of and response to the social rules of the group.[20]

[18] John B. S. Haldane, "Population Genetics", *New Biology* 18 (1955): 44.

[19] John B. S. Haldane, attributed (in a public conversation), "Accidental Career", *New Scientist* (8 August 1974): 325.

[20] Joycelyn M. Pollock, *Ethical Dilemmas and Decisions in Criminal Justice*, 8th edition (Wadsworth: Cengage Learning, 2013), p. 12.

The advantages of socializing and having bonded groups is enormous. We are better at defending ourselves, we can hunt better (consider pack hunting), we can share resources and we can better extract and find resources. Altruistic behaviours are connected to sociality in two ways. In the first, we are reciprocally altruistic. That is to say we are altruistic with others insofar as they will be altruistic back to us. For example, vampire bats often return from feeding trips having failed to find any food. Those who successfully found a food source will often take more than they need and share it with those who were unsuccessful. The next night those latter bats will, in return, share their food with those that shared it with them before. In this way a group is able to manage an unreliable resource through cooperation. Human generosity works in a similar way in most societies. In fact, much of our morality involves dealing with those who fail to return generosity – "free riders" – who are harshly punished with ostracism and exclusion from the group. Altruism, therefore, exists only because we gain from it.

According to evolutionary psychology our moral instincts are an old adaptation that helps us to survive and reproduce. In this view, altruism is something we share with the animal kingdom and its origin is neither rational nor traditionally moral. It exists as an unconscious impulse that serves the interests of our selfish genes.

## Cognitive biases

Since Darwin's original book on human evolution, some surprising research from psychology and economics has provided evidence that our higher cognitive processes, including inference, judgement, and estimation, produce systematic patterns of irrational behaviour. We are, in one author's words, "predictably irrational".

### *Confirmation bias*

> If one were to attempt to identify a single problematic aspect of human reasoning that deserves attention above all others, the confirmation bias would have to be among the candidates for consideration. Many have written about this bias, and it appears to be sufficiently strong and pervasive that one is led to wonder whether the bias, by itself, might account for a significant fraction of the disputes, altercations, and misunderstandings that occur among individuals, groups, and nations.
>
> —Raymond S. Nickerson[21]

A well-documented tendency that human beings demonstrate is the irrational way they take in information. According to rationalism, a rational being treats all evidence equally and comes to a balanced judgment based purely on the evidence to hand. However, in psychological testing we find that people tend to respond to the evidence they see in ways that we would want to describe as rational.

[21] Raymond S. Nickerson, "Confirmation Bias: A Ubiquitous Phenomenon in Many Guises", *Review of General Psychology* 2, No. 2 (1998): 175.

### *Wason Selection Task*

The most famous of the experiments into reasoning is the Wason Selection Task. In 1966, the cognitive psychologist Peter C. Wason devised a simple means of testing the inferential strategies of human beings. The testing process is simple: participants are shown four cards. In the original experiment all four cards had a letter on one side and a number on the other. Then the participants are asked: "Which cards do you have to turn over in order to determine if the following rule is true: 'If a card has a vowel on one side, then it has an odd number on the other side.'"

Here are four cards. Each of them has a letter on one side and a number on the other side. Two of these cards are shown with the letter side up, and two with the number side up.

Indicate which of these cards you have to turn over in order to determine whether the following claim is true:

**If a card has a vowel on one side, then it has an odd number on the other side.**

▲ The Wason Selection Task experiment

Incredibly, more than 90% of the people who do this test get it wrong. The correct answer is "E" and "4". Interestingly, there are patterns to the wrong answers; most people pick "E" and "5". The task has the form of a conditional: if x, then y. So in this example, we would say "if vowel, then odd". In order to know if this rule stands we need to turn over the E card – if there is an even number underneath then our rule is false. We also need to turn over 4 because, if there is a vowel underneath, then we have a vowel with an even number on the other side and our rule is again false. Note the key mistake: whether the 5 has an even or an odd number on the other side makes no difference. If it has a vowel, this is an example of our rule. If a consonant, then it doesn't matter, because we have no rules for consonants. The mistake seems to be in thinking that an odd number must have a vowel – but this is not what is stated by the rule. The rule says "If vowel, then odd", not "If odd, then vowel". These are two different rules that most of us confuse very easily.

This amazing example shows that human rationality is not universal and is a far from perfect match for reality. Our ability to make inferences is not just faulty, but systematically so – as though we are made with specific error tendencies built in.

Interestingly, if the problem is put in the form of a concrete pragmatic problem, people start getting it right. In the example below more than 75% of the participants get it right.

In its crackdown against drunk drivers, Massachusetts law enforcement officials are revoking liquor licences left and right. You are a bouncer in a Boston bar, and you'll lose your job unless you enforce the following law:

**"If a person is drinking beer, then he must be over 20 years old."**

The cards below have information about four people sitting at a table in your bar. Each card represents one person. One side of a card tells what a person is drinking and the other side of the card tells that person's age. Indicate only those card(s) you definitely need to turn over to see if any of these people are breaking the law.

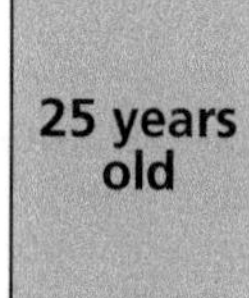


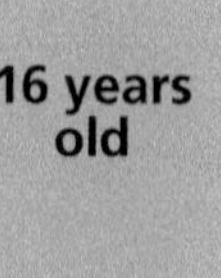


▲ The Wason Selection Task experiment

Wason concluded that this exposes a bias in our way of thinking. Rather than look for what might disprove their ideas, people seek confirming information. So in the selection task participants ignore the information that could refute the rule, instead seeking information that would confirm it!

This is a far from trivial insight. Wason used a clever method to teach his students about confirmation bias.

Confirmation bias is involved in any case where people find meaning in meaninglessness or patterns in chaos. According to this theory we are hard wired to seek for patterns even when they are not there, and this means discounting evidence against the theories we create.

Confirmation bias has been implicated in the following areas of human behaviour:

- **Finance:** Stock traders have been shown to make regular use of this bias. In searching for patterns in the economic noise they find reasons to confirm their own theories. In fact, stock traders are guilty of a great number of cognitive biases and fallacies common among the superstitious. Financial astrology is a booming business and an example of how people will always find a way to invent a pattern.
- **Paranormal and superstitious thinking:** Some of the most vivid examples of the confirmation bias in action come from paranormal beliefs. In paranormal readings the psychic exploits the natural confirmation bias by making predictions that are ambiguous and vague. In doing so the psychic leaves the work to the client; the person being read will find ways to fit the reading into their lives.

## EXERCISE

Have a look at your horoscope for the day (mine is given below), and consider how tempting it is to fit it to your life. Then look at a friend's horoscope. Notice how you find ways to relate it to your own experiences? Horoscopes are usually vague enough to exploit our confirmation bias. By letting you draw the connections to your own life, the astrologer is letting your biases do the work.

> The author's horoscope:
>
> You are putting the right thing in the right place now. The process may not seem especially glamorous or exciting but it is immensely constructive. There is now a real chance for you to banish confusion and chaos from a part of your emotional life. This in turn will allow the growth of something that you have inwardly needed to nurture for a very long time.[22]

▲ Skinner's pigeon experiment

The American behaviourist B. F. Skinner famously showed that confirmation bias was also a cause of superstitious thinking in pigeons. He placed pigeons in a box with a slot that automatically dispensed food, "at regular intervals with no reference whatsoever to the bird's behavior". The pigeons began to associate being fed with whatever behaviour they were doing at the time. They believed that their actions had caused the dispensing of food. This was apparent because they began to repeat whatever behaviours they had been doing, often developing into complex "rituals":

> One bird was conditioned to turn counter-clockwise about the cage, making two or three turns between reinforcements. Another repeatedly thrust its head into one of the upper corners of the cage. A third developed a 'tossing' response, as if placing its head beneath an invisible bar and lifting it repeatedly. Two birds developed a pendulum motion of the head and body, in which the head was extended forward and swung from right to left with a sharp movement followed by a somewhat slower return...
>
> The experiment might be said to demonstrate a sort of superstition. The bird behaves as if there were a causal relation between its behavior and the presentation of food, although such a relation is lacking. There are many analogies in human behavior. Rituals for changing one's fortune at cards are good examples. A few accidental connections between a ritual and favorable consequences suffice to set up and maintain the behavior in spite of many unreinforced instances. The bowler who has released a ball down the alley but continues to behave as if he were controlling it by twisting and turning his arm and shoulder is another case in point. These behaviors have, of course, no real effect upon one's luck or upon a ball half way down an alley, just as in the present case the food would appear as often if the pigeon did nothing—or, more strictly speaking, did something else.[23]

[22] Jonathan Cainer, 8 February 2014. Cainer's daily horoscopes are available at www.cainer.com.

[23] B. F. Skinner, "'Superstition' in the Pigeon", *Journal of Experimental Psychology* 38 (1948): 168–172.

Superstitions come from looking for relationships where there are none. We are too quick to make a causal connection between things on the basis of unreasonably limited evidence. Think about any superstitions you might have. Do they follow a similar pattern to the making of lucky charms?

### How lucky charms are made

1. The "charm" happens to be there when something good happens.
2. You instantly believe it was the "charm" that caused the good event.
3. You bring the charm with you to other events.
4. When it does not bring you luck you selectively dismiss this evidence as an anomaly: "Maybe there was something cancelling the effect of my lucky charm...?"
5. When it happens to be there the next time something good happens the charm gets the credit.
6. Even though the charm does nothing and is there when bad things happen just as often as good, you continue to select evidence to support your theory and the charm retains its lucky status in spite of the actual balance of evidence.

- **Juries:** Confirmation bias is an especially troubling problem in criminal prosecutions. If people are unable to evaluate evidence objectively, and instead selectively ignore evidence that does not fit with their expectations, then we have a very serious problem indeed. Research has found that jurors have a strong predisposition to make up their mind early on and then skew the evidence to fit with their belief. "Innocent until proven guilty" is a courtroom adage because people need constantly to be reminded to withhold judgment until they have seen all the evidence.

### *Optimism bias*

The final cognitive bias shows that people unconsciously reject facts in favour of an attractive fiction. The optimism bias concerns the way we use inductive reasoning to develop predictions about the world. People tend towards overoptimistic estimations of favourable outcomes. More interestingly, the optimism bias also shows that the way we update our beliefs in the face of new evidence has an optimistic skew.

Tali Sharot developed an ingenious experiment to examine the way that people estimate the likelihood of good things compared with bad things and the way our brains ignore what they don't want to believe. Her team asked participants to estimate the likelihood of a number of negative life events. So they were asked to guess the likelihood of them getting cancer, or dying in a car accident, or having a heart attack, etc. Afterwards, they were shown the real probabilities for each of these events. When they were asked the same set of questions later they only remembered the real probabilities if they were better than they had thought to begin with. If the real probability was worse than they had estimated participants selectively "forgot" the real probability! So if they estimated the likelihood of cancer at 5% but it was more like 30%, their brains had ignored the information and they gave the 5% estimate again! But if they thought the chance of a car accident was 10% but in fact the probability was only 2%, they had updated their beliefs and gave something closer to the real probability.

This shows that our brain defends us from unhappy truths in much the way Nietzsche and Freud describe. It shows that the way we select beliefs involves picking and choosing unconsciously according to their attractiveness at least as much as their truth.

## Conclusion

These examples attack rationalism at its very heart. The claim that we use pure cold reason in the construction of our beliefs and knowledge seems to be undermined. We do two remarkable things:

1. We deal with evidence irrationally: we seek out and incorporate evidence that confirms our existing theories, while ignoring evidence that refutes it.
2. We select beliefs irrationally: our unconscious mind selects beliefs on the basis of their attractiveness to us.

## Responses to evolutionary psychology and cognitive biases

### *Falsifiable?*

The evolutionary and psychological theories discussed so far are compelling but it can be argued that they are based on speculation rather than on solid argument or evidence. Evolutionary explanations of behaviour, for instance, cannot be tested. The claim that moral feeling, for example, is an adaptation that evolved from our need to cooperate with one another is plausible but there is no way to know if it is true or false. Evolutionary explanations for behaviour have been called "just so stories", after Rudyard Kipling's children's stories, for this reason. Kipling's stories, such as "How the Leopard Got His Spots", are made-up explanations for features of the natural world. The argument, therefore, is that evolutionary explanations share this speculative and made-up nature and cannot constitute a scientific or rigorous explanation of our behaviour.

Is this a fair criticism? Perhaps it applies more evenly to evolutionary psychology than it does to cognitive biases. The evidence that we are systematically irrational is strong and consistent. This criticism applies only when we try to explain *why* we make the irrational choices we do.

### *Universal and necessary?*

A second point applies more directly to cognitive biases. While the claim that we make "lazy" choices does appear to have support, we can ask whether we always make choices in this way and whether we must. The best explanation for cognitive biases is that we use them as a "short cut" in our thinking. When we don't have the time to reason through something fully, cognitive biases are adaptations that help us to make quick decisions which help us more often than not.

While this may be true, it doesn't mean that we are incapable of rational thought, or that we do not, when we have the time and it matters, use reason in the pursuit of truth. Most research on cognitive biases concerns everyday judgments such as economic decisions for which we may have neither the need nor the desire on which to use the full power of our intellect.

### *Self-awareness*

This brings us to a further problem. If we are aware of our cognitive biases, does that make us more likely to think rationally? By discovering more about ourselves and our own prejudices it seems reasonable to think that we would be able to overcome them. The key to our human nature and the exercise of our rationality may be our capacity to overcome our instinctive prejudices and desires. The whole history of psychology and the human sciences demonstrates that while rationality does not come easily, we do seek it, and, being the purpose and goal of human life, we can rightly describe it as our true nature.

Evolution may describe some of our natural tendencies but we can argue, in line with Plato, that we have another self – a rational one – that is able to control the desires of our evolved nature. We can master the beast within and look at the world dispassionately.

Furthermore, even if our reason is evolved, that doesn't necessarily diminish its status. We may have evolved a truth seeking, and truth knowing, faculty. Removing the divine cause of reason does leave new room for doubt, but we can respond that we do seem to be very good at knowing. The human mastery of our environment and the success of our fields of knowledge seem to suggest that we are more than irrational animals.

### Nagel's modern rationalism

In his book *The View from Nowhere* (1986) Thomas Nagel argues in favour of a near Platonic perspective on human nature. We are the subjects of two ways of approaching and thinking about experience. We have a view that is personal, subjective, and limited by our place in the world, but we also are able to transcend that viewpoint and see the world "from nowhere in particular". Our ability to know is indeed limited by our particular perspective and it may well be that we will only ever have a very narrow and simplified view of reality. Nevertheless, we do have the capacity to develop appropriate hypotheses about the world as it is, independently of our particular viewpoint, and to evaluate that hypothesis dispassionately. For Nagel, the goal is "how to combine the perspective of a particular person inside the world with an objective view of that same world, the person and his viewpoint included. It is a problem that faces every creature with the impulse and the capacity to transcend its particular point of view and to conceive of the world as a whole."[24]

The evolutionary perspective on human nature involves a dismissal of thought as anything over and above the mechanistic workings out of our instincts. But thought, Nagel argues, does involve the capacity to

[24] Thomas Nagel, *The View from Nowhere* (Oxford: Oxford University Press, 1989), p. 3.

extend beyond our local experience and concerns, to consider the world as a whole – as it is, independently of ourselves. So while we may be subject to cognitive biases and other impulses evolved over millions of years, we also have the ability to remain detached from these drives and think objectively. Nagel doesn't think we can ever be certain about the conclusions we reach – scepticism about reality will always be possible – but we are able to consider these problems, understand the limitations of our own knowledge, and make judgments about what it would be wisest to believe. For Nagel, this ability cannot be captured by an objective materialist perspective. In Chapter 4: Mind and Body, we discuss arguments against reductive materialism – the view that all we have is a brain – and Nagel presents one such argument. Human thought, he believes, cannot be captured by an evolutionary model of man as a "meat machine" whose every thought is explained as an evolutionary adaptation.

## Freud

The Austrian psychoanalyst Sigmund Freud drew on many of the scientific ideas of his day including Darwin's theory of evolution. He developed a model of the human psyche in which our actions are driven by forces hidden even from ourselves. His psychoanalytic account of the mind focuses on what he calls the "**unconscious**".

### The unconscious

The development of Freud's theory came from his experience of neurotic patients. Freud worked particularly with patients diagnosed with "hysteria". In the past people with disturbed behaviour, delusions, and irrational fears had been dismissed as having an inexplicable dysfunction. Freud instead insisted, in accord with the scientific principles of his day, that everything has an explanation, including neurosis.

### Biography: Sigmund Freud (1856–1939)

Sigmund Freud was a late-19th- and early-20th-century Austrian who was one of the founding fathers of modern psychology. In his early career he worked as a medical doctor and neurologist focusing on neurological disorder. As a result of his work and many case studies with which he experimented, he developed a non-medical form of treatment, 'Psychoanalysis' often referred to as the 'talking cure'. Freud theorised that the roots of neurological disorder led not in the brain, but in the past, usually the childhood experiences, of his patients. By talking through their experiences, his patients would learn to accept and 'get over' there neuroses. His approach is now known as 'Psychodynamic' and involves a formalised theory around the 'Unconscious' – the idea that our mind hides our deepest desires and darkest feelings from us. He enjoyed large success during his lifetime, in part due no doubt to his infamous emphasis on, and openness about, human sexuality. His work was scandalous for some, and honest science to others, but either way he got a lot of attention. His significant works include The *Psychoanalysis of Everyday Life*, which includes the idea of the 'Freudian slip' – a moment when our unconscious reveals itself in accidental mistakes of wording or behaviour. Other important books are *The Psychoanalysis of Dreams* in which he argues that our dreams are a way of revealing our unconscious feelings, and *Civilisation and its Discontents*, in which he argues that our animalistic urges put us into violent emotional conflict when suppressed by civilisation and moral codes.

His early case studies begin with himself, and continue to the famous cases "Anna O." and "Little Hans". In each case Freud began to suspect that the symptoms of irrational fear and disturbed behaviour had a hidden cause. The fantasies and fears of Anna and Hans were particular and hinted at a relationship to some part of their past. Hans' fear of horses was connected to a latent "Oedipus Complex", the horse representing his father of whom he was afraid because of his early sexual feelings towards his mother. According to Freud and his colleague Josef Breuer, Anna was cured only when the origins of each symptom had been gone through in what she called the "talking cure". Once the early childhood origins of her problems had been discovered "each symptom disappeared ... after she had described its first occurrence. In this way, too, the whole illness was brought to a close."[25]

These case studies provided Freud with evidence for his theory that the behaviour of neurotics was caused by early childhood traumas that had been buried deep in the unconscious mind and never successfully integrated or dealt with. Freud took this analysis and applied it to everyone – neurotic or not. He generalized that all people's personalities – their particular tendencies, desires, and fears – were the result of their early childhood experiences. He theorized that all people began life with fundamental drives for pleasure, sexuality, and aggression. When these drives are confronted with social norms they produce feelings of shame and guilt. These feelings need to be resolved or they will produce neurosis into adulthood.

## The tripartite theory of the unconscious

Freud explained neurosis by positing three components of the mind, two of them entirely unconscious.

- **Id:** The id is our basic instincts. It contains the energy and drive behind all of our actions. Our will and libido reside here and it is this animalistic part of the mind that contains our sexual desire and our aggression.
- **Super-ego:** This part of our mind is given to us from "civilization". Social behaviour requires that we restrain our aggressive and sexual impulses and the super-ego is a kind of suppression mechanism that controls the id. The super-ego is formed of social norms that have been internalized into an unconscious morality. This part of our mind "shames" us into self-restraint.
- **Ego:** The only part of our mind that is conscious is the ego, which has to take the contradictory impulses from the id and super-ego and resolve them into coherent behaviours that meet the demands of living in the world.

## Defence mechanisms

The key to Freud's theory for our purposes is the limited control, awareness, and honesty of the ego. While we all give reasons to ourselves and others for our behaviour, Freud thought that these were mostly self-delusions. The ego is actually a weak component of the mind that had been given an impossible task: the control and harmonizing of the unconscious parts. Because of its inability to keep control of these impulses it has to lie to itself in order to deal with the irreconcilable tensions of the unconscious and the world.

[25] Josef Breuer and Sigmund Freud, *Studies on Hysteria (1893–1895)*, translated and edited by James Strachey, with the collaboration of Anna Freud (USA: Basic Books, 2000), p. 40.

> Thus the ego, driven by the id, confined by the super-ego, repulsed by reality, struggles ... [in] bringing about harmony among the forces and influences working in and upon it ... it breaks out in anxiety – realistic anxiety regarding the external world, moral anxiety regarding the super-ego and neurotic anxiety regarding the strength of the passions in the id.
>
> One might compare the relation of the ego to the id with that between a rider and his horse. The horse provides the locomotor energy, and the rider has the prerogative of determining the goal and of guiding the movements of his powerful mount towards it. But all too often in the relations between the ego and the id we find a picture of the less ideal situation in which the rider is obliged to guide his horse in the direction in which it itself wants to go.
>
> —Sigmund Freud[26]
>
> All the defensive measures of the ego against the id are carried out silently and invisibly. The most we can ever do is to reconstruct them in retrospect: we can never really witness them in operation. This statement applies, for instance, to successful repression. The ego knows nothing of it; we are aware of it only subsequently, when it becomes apparent that something is missing.
>
> —Anna Freud[27]

For Freud, the stories we tell ourselves about who we are and why we do the things we do are nothing more than fictions that he calls "defence mechanisms". The theory of defence mechanisms was refined and developed by Freud's daughter Anna, one of the founders of child psychoanalysis. Below are just a few of the extensive catalogue of defence mechanisms thought to be routinely used by the ego.

- **Denial:** In this classic defence mechanism, the ego defends itself by rejecting a fact that is too uncomfortable to accept. For example, when an alcoholic denies being addicted to alcohol, or someone who is seriously ill insists that their illness is less serious than it really is. These are extreme examples, but denial can also happen in everyday life when we deny the truths that we don't like or that upset us.
- **Rationalization:** In this defence mechanism, the ego invents reasons for an action or feeling that has already occurred when the real cause of the action or feeling is unacceptable to the ego. That is to say, the person justifies an event or emotion in a self-deceiving way after the fact.

[26] Sigmund Freud, "Lecture XXXI: The Dissection of the Psychical Personality", in *New Introductory Lectures on Psycho-Analysis: The Standard Edition*, with a biographical introduction by Peter Gay (New York: W. W. Norton & Co., 1990), pp. 96–97.

[27] Anna Freud, *The Ego and the Mechanisms of Defence* (London: Karnac Books, 1993), p. 8.

- **Reaction formation:** In this defence mechanism, the ego deals with an uncomfortable truth by asserting an extreme version of its opposite. The often-cited example is when a homosexual behaves in an overly "macho" way to attempt to master his feelings. Other examples might include severe moralism as a way of offsetting a hidden deviant behaviour.
- **Sublimation:** This mechanism is unusual in that it can form a perfectly healthy way of dealing with socially inappropriate impulses. In sublimation, instead of expressing the basic drives for aggression and sexuality in their raw form, we transform them into socially useful energies. For example, the creation of art, science, or any other passionate vocation or activity, is thought by Freud to be the expression of sexual energy transformed.
- **Repression:** This defence mechanism is a key part of psychoanalytic philosophy because it plays a central role in most mental illnesses. In repression, the ego suppresses a difficult feeling or impulse by forcing it into the unconscious. When inappropriate desires are repressed, however, they create a tension in the unconscious that may explode in the expression of some neurosis or anxiety. The exposure of repressed sexuality in order to treat emotional problems, for example, is one of the staples of psychoanalysis.

### Conclusion

Freud's psychoanalysis is an argument that we are irrational animals. The part of ourselves that rationalists identify as our core – the reasoning, objective, part that controls us – is for Freud nothing more than a confused passenger. Our conscious mind is made up of irrational tricks and lies that are used to help us live with the animalistic drives that really control our behaviour.

## The blank slate

> Give me a dozen healthy infants, well-formed, and my own specified world to bring them up in and I'll guarantee to take any one at random and train him to become any type of specialist I might select – doctor, lawyer, artist, merchant-chief and, yes, even beggar-man and thief, regardless of his talents, penchants, tendencies, abilities, vocations, and race of his ancestors.
>
> —John B. Watson[28]

So far we have looked at two accounts of human nature. We have considered the view that we are rational beings and the view that we are irrational creatures dominated by unconscious forces. What we have yet to consider is the idea that there is *no* human nature.

The idea that we are not born with any significant behaviours, preferences, or impulses is often referred to as the **tabula rasa** or **blank slate**

[28] John B. Watson, *Behaviourism*, with a new introduction by Gregory A. Kimble (New Brunswick, NJ: Transaction Publishers, 1998), p. 82.

philosophy of human nature. In this view human beings are born with an empty mind that is filled with ideas from our experience.

## Empiricism

During the 17th and 18th centuries, European philosophy underwent a revolution known as the Enlightenment. During this period philosophers and scientists began to provide justifications for their ideas that were based on observation or reason instead of on religious sources of knowledge.

During this period two schools of philosophy emerged. The first, which we looked at in the first section, is known as rationalism and argues that our reason is the source of our knowledge and that it provides certainty in justifying our beliefs.

The second is known as empiricism and involves the rejection of everything the rationalists believed. Empiricist philosophers argue the following:

- We are born without ideas already in our mind.
- Everything we know and believe comes from our experiences of the world around us.

Because of their rejection of rationalism and their focus on experience as the source of all knowledge, empiricists tend to be sceptical about the certainty of the things we can know. Experience is a very limited and uncertain source of knowledge.

## Locke

For more information on Locke, see Chapter 5.

The blank slate view of human beings can be traced back as far as Aristotle and a number of his contemporaries. However, the first really famous account was offered by the British empiricists.

In his *An Essay Concerning Human Understanding* (1690), John Locke (1632–1704) describes the mind as a "white paper, void of all characters", and claims that experience is "from whence all the ideas we have, or can naturally have, do spring".[29]

This is the "tabula rasa" (Latin for blank slate) axiom of empiricism. At birth we are empty vessels – our mind contains nothing at all – and experience begins to inscribe on the mind with every sense experience we have.

Locke spends the rest of the *Essay* explaining what essentially child cognitive development is. He gives an account of how we acquire a whole range of ideas from general names to logical principles.

### Associationism

As we saw earlier in the discussion on Hume, when we come to apply empiricism and the tabula rasa we come up against a number of problems. How is it that our ideas can be derived only from sense experience? As in Descartes' Wax argument, it seems that we

[29] John Locke, *An Essay Concerning Human Understanding* (New York: Prometheus Books, 1995), p. 59.

understand more than what is given only in experience. For example, how do we come to the idea that the wax is the same in spite of our experience differing? Descartes would argue that we must use reason in order to effectively interpret experience, and the identity of the wax before and after is known not by the senses but by intuition.

These questions require a complex theory of learning and development. The empiricist view of the process by which we build ideas from experience is known as **associationism**. This is a philosophical and psychological approach to learning that claims our experiences are organized and related to one another by association.

According to this philosophy our ideas are experiences that have been written onto the tabula rasa of the mind. When these experiences occur together, over time they can become associated. When I see the shape of a cat, for example, it also brings to mind the other sights, sounds, and colours that I have in the past tended to experience at the same time. When I experience other objects that are similar, they recall to mind the same set of associated ideas. I can then give this set of related experiences a general name – cat. So my idea of "cat" is a set of experiences that has been bundled together (furry, purrs, sharp claws, etc.).

In fact, this account of abstract and general ideas allowed Hume to develop a critique of reason. Hume's attack on the principle of causation, which we looked at earlier, uses this same analysis to show that our understanding of cause and effect can come from experience alone.

The key to this philosophy is that the formation of complex ideas happens without the mind needing to have any ideas already. Ideas become naturally associated on the blank slate without there needing to be any innate ideas or reason that analyse experience.

### Conclusion

Locke's account of the tabula rasa and his theory of how the slate becomes furnished with ideas leads to the conclusion that there is no human nature. If we are an empty container at birth, then our beliefs and attitudes are unfixed. This means also that our behaviours are not fixed before birth but are the result of our lives and our experiences. So we are neither rational nor irrational by nature, but can become them only by nurture. This idea was developed into the next theory we will look at: **psychological behaviourism**.

## Watson: behaviourism

The American psychologist John B. Watson (1878–1958) drew on the long tradition of empiricism and associationism. If we are born without ideas, then we can be made into anything. It is this plasticity that Watson assumed was the only nature of man: given the right experiences a person can be made into anything.

The quote from *Behaviorism* (1930) at the start of this section neatly summarizes Watson's view. He thought that because a human being is born a blank slate, he is entirely the sum of his experiences. Any philosophy which claims that there are natural tendencies for human beings – a human nature – has mistaken learning for instinct:

> There are ... for us no instincts—we no longer need the term in psychology. Everything we have been in the habit of calling an "instinct" today is a result largely of training—belonging to man's learned behavior.[30]

We may share many things with other people but this is because we are raised within the same culture by people who also share that culture. Any human universals are the result of a similar environment, not a shared human nature.

▲ John B. Watson

Watson was sceptical of both the rationalist and irrationalist perspectives. He rejected the very idea of instincts, but he also rejected the notion of reason as a special or "higher" faculty. He argued that learning and behaviour are produced in the exact same way in both animals and man, saying that, "The behaviorist, in his efforts to get a unitary scheme of animal response, recognizes no dividing line between man and brute."[31]

The "dividing line" that Watson rejected is the separation between human beings and animals based on reason. For Watson, rats, pigeons, and human children all learn behaviours in the same way.

A further component of behaviourism is its rejection of our internal processes. Watson believed that because "feelings", "desires", and "beliefs" were not observable things, they could not properly be studied and therefore they would have no place in a serious science of human nature.

A human being is nothing more than an organism like any other that is organized to behave according to stimulus and response. According to Watson, we have no human nature that separates us from other creatures apart from our incidental physical features. Therefore all behaviour, no matter how complex, is nothing more than a **trained response to stimuli**.

## Classical conditioning

The process by which people were said to learn was called **conditioning**. Watson and other behaviourists took the basic principle of associationism – that we learn by associating our experiences – and developed it into a theory of behaviour. The result was the claim that any behaviour is a response to stimuli.

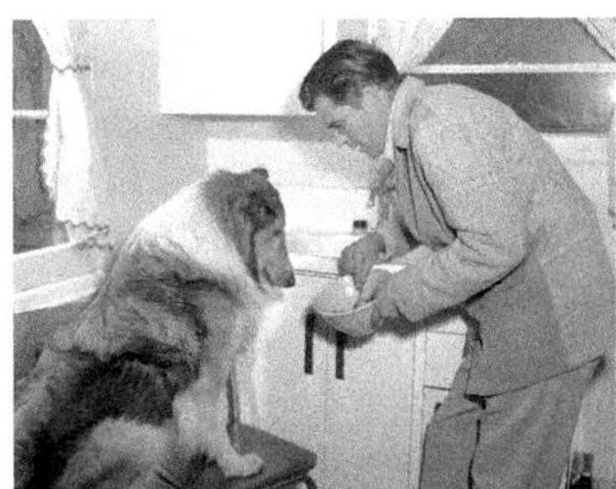

▲ Animals and human beings are essentially the same for the early behaviourists – all behaviour is a matter of training.

According to classical conditioning, learning involves taking a behaviour that we already do in response to a stimulus – for example, fear behaviour in response to loud noises – and then associating another stimulus – for example, a rat or other small fluffy animal – by repeatedly presenting the stimuli together. Eventually conditioning takes place and we respond with fear to the sight of a rat or other small fluffy animal.

[30] Watson, *Behaviourism*, p. 74.

[31] John B. Watson, "Psychology as the Behaviourist Views It", *Psychological Review* 20 (1913): 158.

Watson argued that every behaviour we do, including the use of language, or what is often described as complex reasoning, amounts to a conditioned response to stimuli. We have been trained by the subtle mass of our enormous experience into all of the things we do, and even complex philosophical writing, he argued, is a conditioned response.

## Critique

These two classic presentations of the blank slate view have been the subject of fearsome criticism and are now largely unpopular in philosophy and the behavioural sciences. Both Locke and Watson presented fascinating shifts in the way people think about human nature. The reduction of all human thoughts and behaviours to experience was an audacious goal that both thinkers pursued with brilliance. However, for many philosophers the task was always an impossible one and reducing all of our nature to our experiences just cannot be done.

### Kant

One of the earliest attacks on empiricism comes from *Critique of Pure Reason* (1781) by the German philosopher Immanuel Kant. In this book he argues that experience alone is insufficient to explain thought. This criticism ultimately applies to both Locke and Watson in their mutual attempt to eliminate any innate mental mechanisms with which we are born.

Kant's argument consists of showing that thought, as it occurs, would be impossible given nothing more than a blank slate receiving experience. Some means of processing our experience – of deriving meaningful information from it – is a precondition of having thoughts and experiences. In the empiricist model, we simply receive data and it turns into ideas, but as Kant points out, sense data on its own is meaningless. If we were nothing more than a blank slate, we would never be able to derive anything meaningful from experience. We would remain a blank slate forever because experience would always be what it is for a newborn – a "blooming buzzing confusion" in the words of William James (1890). When the confused totality of our experience hits the mind we have to do something with it – experiencing the world is an active process that requires us to be dealing with data from the senses rather than passively soaking up information. A baby must be able to start sorting out what it sees and hears, and that sorting out must happen through innate faculties already built in.

In the same way, when Locke explains our ideas as the result of "associations" made because of the relationships between sense data, he leaves an unanswered question. How, if we were a blank slate, could we identify relationships between sense data? How could we recognize anything in the raw unprocessed information? We must have some innate machinery that takes raw information and processes it.

Consider a metaphor: learning how to play football for the first time. You might think that you don't need to know anything already, but

## Biography: Immanuel Kant (1724–1804)

Kant was a German philosopher of the 18th century, who wrote during the Age of Enlightenment. He was born in Konigsberg, Prussia (now Kaliningrad, Russia) and famously never travelled more than 20 km from his birthplace even though he lived for 80 years. In fact, unlike many other prominent philosophers he led an exceptionally unremarkable life. The only aspect of his life worth noting seems to be his diligence and time keeping and the fact that he was a witty and engaging host. While he was accomplished in mathematics and science he established his reputation as a philosopher, publishing influential work on metaphysics, epistemology, ethics, political philosophy, and aesthetics. Late in his life Kant was awoken from his 'dogmatic slumber' after reading David Hume's sceptical philosophy. In response he wrote his most famous works, and in particular, *The Critique of Pure Reason*. Kant sought to resolve many of the outstanding debates, especially in epistemology focusing on the role of reason in the human experience of the world. In the process he combined rationalism and empiricism into a single system. In the process, he redefined the western philosophy's conceptual framework through his "Copernican revolution" arguing that the mind already has necessary structures for understanding the world. His arguments had a profound impact of western philosophy and he is considered the father of modern philosophy. His most important contribution was his belief that an individual should always be treated with respect - the precursor to modern human rights. Nearly all subsequent philosophy in the western tradition has either worked within the framework he established by seeking to refine it or has consciously sought to overturn it.

actually there is lots of understanding that you need already in order for it to be possible for you to learn how to play football. You need to know what a game is and what rules are: they at the very least are the absolute minimal understanding required before you can learn about football. For this reason my students often refer to this as the problem of "learning to learn". The idea that we can learn how to learn is paradoxical – in order to acquire the learning we must have those skills already.

### *The categories*

The question that remains from all this is what are the **prerequisites of experience**? What is it that must be, as a bare minimum, in the mind already for us to be able to have ideas?

Kant's answer is that we must have what he calls the "**categories**" already present in the mind. These categories are a very basic set of organizing tools for dealing with sense data. They are not knowledge or ideas, but are a mechanism that provides ways of dealing with experience. Among these categories are things like cause and effect, and substance and unity, which we already have an understanding of in order to have sense experience.

The two most basic categories or concepts that must be present in our mind in order for us to experience the world the way we do are **time and space**. We'll look at space in detail.

Space, Kant argues, is one of the most basic preconditions of experience. Without it we would be unable to identify objects or to recognize them as related to one another. Space is a concept or category by which the mind is able to interpret experience:

> Space is not an empirical concept which has been derived from outer experiences ... it is the subjective condition of sensibility, under which alone outer intuition is possible for us.[32]

Kant's argument is powerful. It does seem that because we perceive and understand objects *in terms of* space it cannot be derived from our perceptions.

> We can never represent to ourselves the absence of space, though we can quite well think it as empty of objects. It must therefore be regarded as the condition of the possibility of appearances, and not as a determination dependent upon them.[33]

Furthermore, any experience of the world is only imaginable spatially: whether in our dreams or in fantasy, events, objects, and actions require being understood in terms of space.

### Conclusion

What we can take from this argument is that we must have an innate human nature. The empiricist attempt to argue for a blank slate fails because the subject must process experience and in doing so must interpret it according to innate concepts. We have seen this view in other forms – in Nietzsche and in Freud – and here we find the foundations on which so much psychological insight is built. Kant was among the earliest philosophers to argue that every act of looking is an interpretation; that we must have a way of seeing which changes the world as it meets our mind.

### Chomsky

Recent psychological research reinforces Kant's argument. According to Noam Chomsky (1928– ) we appear to have an innate capacity for language, what he calls a "universal grammar". His argument is intended as a refutation of the behaviourist theory of language learning. For behaviourists language is a skill learned through conditioning processes of trial and error like any other.

Chomsky noticed that language learning had unique characteristics. Language involves using a finite set of words to generate an infinite number of unique possible sentences. Children master language without

[32] Kant, *Critique of Pure Reason*, p. A23 / B38.

[33] Ibid., p. A24 / B39.

formal training and with startling ease. This is an enormously complex task (natural language processing in computers has only got as far as Apple's Siri, and that isn't all that far), which underscores how amazing it is that children are able to take their understanding of language and apply it beyond what they have experienced. Behaviourism has trouble explaining this because if conditioning alone were the mechanism behind language acquisition we would be unprepared to use language in novel ways: we would have to be conditioned to respond to each situation appropriately.

Instead, Chomsky suggests that the best explanation for how quickly children are able to take their limited use of words and apply them in new situations is that they are born with some network or system in the brain that enables them to use language more easily. This makes sense in evolutionary terms and it also seems to explain the empirical evidence. Our survival very much depends on us being capable of the cooperation that language use allows. We learn language much more easily than we acquire other skills, and this suggests an innate element.

The **universal grammar** that Chomsky argues for is a very basic structure that underpins all languages. It involves the basic understanding of what is required to compose sentences – distinctions between verbs and nouns, for example. Of course we are not born *knowing* a language, we are just born able to learn one quickly.

## Ideology and human nature: Marxism, feminism, and postmodernism

In this section we will look at a final critique of the idea of human nature. So far we have explored competing perspectives on what our nature is, including some that have argued that we are naturally blank slates. Our next set of theories do not themselves offer substantial theories of human nature. Rather they argue that the very attempt to isolate and identify our essence involves an emphasis that begins with political and ideological beliefs. Debates about human nature are ideological wars in which philosophers attempt to use truth in the pursuit of power.

These philosophies have their roots in Nietzsche's scepticism and Marx's cultural canon. The concept of ideology comes from Marxist thought but has been used in many contexts to identify beliefs or knowledge systems that are systematically untruthful in order to affirm some form of power.

In this section we look at Foucault, who offers a classic account of knowledge as ideology. We then build on his ideas by exploring the agendas that may underpin our theories of human nature.

### Reason as a power discourse: Foucault

Foucault is referred to as a post-structuralist and a postmodernist in the philosophical canon. He was not a Marxist, and was in fact frequently critical of Marxist thought, but his approach to knowledge is a useful starting point in understanding the claim that theories of human nature are ideologies.

▲ Foucault

Foucault uses the concept of **discourse** to describe ideas and theories that are secretly means of granting power to sets of people. Foucault was extremely sceptical of ideas and belief systems such as rationalism because he thought that, while they argue on what seems to be reasonable grounds, their reasoning is always full of prejudice and assumptions.

For Foucault, **power** is the operating force behind the language and arguments of philosophy and the sciences of human nature. The reasoning as it appears to us is contingent – it exists in virtue of the conventions of reasoning and the structure of language that we currently accept. Foucault's point is, firstly, that these conventions are neither necessary nor universal, and secondly, that if they aren't necessary and universal they require an explanation in terms of historical forces.

Foucault uses the same analytic tools and perspective as Nietzsche does to cast doubt on the dominant views of society. He begins with the assumption that claims to truth are always linked to a cultural agenda and the pursuit of power. Foucault criticizes the rationalist perspective by arguing that it is a "discourse" that is organized not on the grounds of any objective system of argument but on the culture and systems existing in that place at that time. Foucault's central argument is that "Truth" is created by the discourse, or culture, that generates it. The rules that govern what counts as true are particular to that given discourse or culture and are not an absolute or objective criterion for truth. For Foucault a claim to truth is entirely dependent on the sets of rules which govern language in that society. The claim that man is a rational being is therefore dependent on the values and agendas pertinent to a particular culture at a particular time.

What arises from this scepticism is that what is true is not dependent on reality or on a universal standard but is actually dependent on power. Many of Foucault's books focus on exposing and analysing the origins and roots of modern disciplines. In one text he undertakes to explain the history of psychiatry as a story in which the "rational" discourse seeks to control, confine, and cure the irrational by labelling it as an illness. Foucault's point is that the truth makers always do so with an agenda – they do so for the purpose of securing and affirming their own power and they are able to do so because of their power.

This allows us to generate a criticism of rationalism that rejects its assumptions and casts doubt on its conclusions. By presenting itself as "objective" and "rational" the rationalist perspective claims a monopoly of truth and seeks to acquire power over other ways of thinking. These may be non-European views or other religious perspectives, which can then be judged negatively according to the rules of our rationalist power/discourse.

In sum Foucault argues that rationalists have invented their idea of human nature as a way of preserving a set of political and moral beliefs. The rationalists were almost all linked to Christian religion and their rationalism reflects Christian criticism of the sensual everyday world. Throughout Christian writing and thought there is an ongoing hostility towards the "sinful body", "the sensual world", and the evil passions. Our animal nature and our interest in sexuality and feeling are continually scorned as the source of sin and evil. In the same way rationalists attempt to cut away our animal natures as supplemental and unnecessary, arguing that the "real you" is the spiritual and rational being underneath. For Foucault this is the real underlying agenda behind rationalism and it is founded on the pursuit of power, not on an objective appraisal of reality. So the rationalist view is both:

- founded on shaky reasoning that is far from objective, and
- an authoritarian attempt to use a discourse as a means of power.

## Horkheimer and Mannheim

The German sociologist and philosopher, Max Horkheimer (1895–1973) is credited as the founder of the Frankfurt School of neo-Marxists, a group of thinkers who applied Marxism and other ideas in a critique of culture and the history of ideas.

Horkheimer argues that the rationalist perspective on human nature was a means of reconciling religious ideology with developments in modern science. By linking man to God, rationalists helped to maintain the Christian Church's power structures and keep in place man's duty to God.

Locke's empiricist critique also lay on ideological foundations. It was a means by which the English bourgeoisie could wrest power away from the monarchy and the Church by eliminating the divine in favour of the practical or real world.

The Hungarian sociologist Karl Mannheim (1893–1947) goes even further by collapsing the distinction between truth and ideology. He argues that there is no way in which the truth can be untangled from its political and social uses. Therefore any attempt to use truth always involves moral and political assumptions.

> The very juxtaposition of the terms "truth" and "ideology" may suggest that they are antagonistic and irreconcilable; and, indeed, when they are treated together it is usually by writers who deplore ideology, alleging that it is a misrepresentation of truth or reality. Often, moreover, this attitude is accompanied by claims that ideology is impractical, absolute, dogmatic, totalitarian, or all of these; and usually there is a plea for the end of ideology in politics, or a prediction that ideology will eventually be overcome.
>
> —Willard A. Mullins[34]

## Not in our genes

> Science is the ultimate legitimator of bourgeois ideology.
>
> —R. C. Lewontin, Steven Rose, and Leon J. Kamin[35]

[34] Willard A. Mullins, "Truth and Ideology: Reflections on Mannheim's Paradox", *History and Theory* 18, No. 2 (May 1979): 141.

[35] R. C. Lewontin, Steven Rose, and Leon J. Kamin, *Not in Our Genes: Biology, Ideology and Human Nature* (New York: Pantheon Books, 1984),

During the radical counterculture of the 1960s, biological theories of human nature were fiercely attacked as pushing a capitalist agenda. The biological theory, it is argued, contains an ideology that reinforces class divisions and justifies the class system. By arguing that differences between human beings are "natural", the biological theory implies that a hierarchy in which some people have more power and property is justified by their natural capacities. Furthermore, the biological approach suggests that people being innately self-interested, aggressive, and competitive implies that they require a system of control in order to prevent chaotic violence. The theory that man is an irrational animal is a means of selling lies to the proletariat, which will help in preserving the position of the owners of the means of production.

In a controversial book called *Not in Our Genes*, Richard Lewontin, Steven Rose, and Leon Kamin reiterated the neo-Marxist rejection of evolutionary psychology as capitalist ideology:

> If biological determinism is a weapon in the struggle between classes, then the universities are weapons factories, and their teaching and research faculties are the engineers, designers, and production workers.[36]

The book was panned by many critics who thought that the assumption that they must be working for the capitalists in an elaborate conspiracy was ridiculous.

▲ Judith Butler

## Feminism: Butler

Radical feminists are sceptical of any view that sees fundamental or innate features of human beings. For a feminist these are based on **patriarchal** assumptions, and used by those with a patriarchal agenda to oppress women and other marginalized groups (such as homosexuals and intersex people).

Thus, the biological view of Darwin and later thinkers is based not simply on fact and evidence but riddled throughout with the prejudices and assumptions of patriarchal society. Both Darwin and Freud's ideas have been subjected to powerful feminist attacks. In each case, while they seem to be deriving theories simply from the facts they encounter, feminists have argued that cultural bias is the real foundation for their ideas.

Darwin, for example, included passages in *The Descent of Man* (1871) that show both shocking prejudice and stunning ignorance. In his book he points to the fact that women have historically not achieved as much as men in the dominant fields of science, art, philosophy, etc., and uses this as evidence that women are intellectually inferior. At no point does this man with an estimated IQ of 160 consider the extent to which cultural barriers and lack of access to opportunities have prevented women from exercising their abilities.

[36] Ibid.,

Feminists often reject the idea that there is an innate gender identity. The existentialist philosopher Simone de Beauvoir, for example, rejected the idea of "femininity" as a myth, given the fundamental existential freedom that every conscious being faces.

The critique by the American philosopher and gender theorist Judith Butler, however, goes deeper. Her rejection of innate gender differences extends to the idea of biological sex. Butler argues that even the notion of a distinct "male" and "female" sex is a means of control with which the patriarchal system keeps those designated non-male in a subordinated position.

### Conclusion

In this final section we have seen arguments that reject the very act of doing philosophy about human nature. These thinkers see the philosophy of human nature as a sinister, or at the very least deceptive, attempt either to maintain or to establish power structures. Human nature, from this perspective, is a loaded question and one that should ideally be rejected. Butler concludes her argument by suggesting that the ethical solution is to **celebrate diversity** and **reject predetermined categories**. If we apply this to the whole study of human nature we would resist the impulse to pick a theory and instead take a **postmodern approach**, in which we accept that in the study of human nature there may be a variety of worthwhile interpretations.

## References Cited


Breuer, Josef, and Sigmund Freud. *Studies on Hysteria (1893–1895)*. Translated and edited by James Strachey, with the collaboration of Anna Freud. USA: Basic Books, 2000.

Cosmides, Leda, and John Tooby. *Evolutionary Psychology: A Primer*. Santa Barbara, USA: Center for Evolutionary Psychology, University of California, 1997. Available at http://www.cep.ucsb.edu/primer.html (accessed 21 October 2014).

Darwin, Charles. *On the Origin of Species*. John Murray, 1859. Now available at http://darwin-online.org.uk/content/frameset?itemID=F373&viewtype=text&pageseq=1 (accessed 21 October 2014).

Darwin, Charles. *The Descent of Man*, revised edition. London: Penguin, 2004.

Einstein, Albert. *Sidelights on Relativity*. London/Montana, USA: Methuen & Co./Kessinger Publishing, 1922/2004. Available at http://www.ibiblio.org/ebooks/Einstein/Sidelights/Einstein_Sidelights.pdf (accessed 21 October 2014).

Foucault, Michel. *The Order of Things: An Archaeology of the Human Sciences*, 2nd edition. London: Routledge, 1970.

Freud, Anna. *The Ego and the Mechanisms of Defence*. London: Karnac Books, 1993.

Freud, Sigmund. "Lecture XXXI: The Dissection of the Psychical Personality". *In New Introductory Lectures on Psycho-Analysis: The Standard Edition*, with a biographical introduction by Peter Gay. New York: W. W. Norton & Co., 1990, pp. 71–100.

Graylin, A. C., and Richard Dawkins. "Evidence for the Supernatural". Oxford ThinkWeek, 2011. Available at http://poddelusion.co.uk/blog/2011/02/23/richard-dawkins-ac-grayling-discuss-evidence-for-the-supernatural-at-oxford-thinkweek/ (accessed 21 October 2014).

Haldane, John B. S. "Population Genetics". *New Biology* 18 (1955): 34–51.

Haldane, John B. S. "Accidental Career". *New Scientist* (8 August 1974).

Hare, R. M. "The Simple Believer, Appendix: Theology and Falsification", in *Essays on Religion and Education*. Oxford: Clarendon Press, 1992.

Hume, David. "Section II: Of the Origin of Ideas". In *An Enquiry Concerning Human Understanding and Concerning the Principles of Morals*. Edited by L. A. Selby-Bigge, 3rd edition revised by P. H. Nidditch. Oxford: Clarendon Press, 1975.

Kant, Immanuel. *Critique of Pure Reason*. Translated from the German *Kritik der reinen Vernunft*, 1781/1787.

Kuhn, Thomas. *The Structure of Scientific Revolutions*, 2nd edition. Chicago: University of Chicago Press, 1970.

Lewontin, R. C., Steven Rose, and Leon J. Kamin. *Not in Our Genes: Biology, Ideology and Human Nature*. New York: Pantheon Books, 1984.

Locke, John. *An Essay Concerning Human Understanding*. New York: Prometheus Books, 1995.

Malcolm, Noel (ed.). *The Clarendon Edition of the Works of Thomas Hobbes, Volume 3: Leviathan*. Oxford: Oxford University Press, 2012.

Mullins, Willard A. "Truth and Ideology: Reflections on Mannheim's Paradox". *History and Theory* 18, No. 2 (May 1979): 141–154.

Nagel, Thomas. *The View from Nowhere*. Oxford: Oxford University Press, 1989.

Nickerson, Raymond S. "Confirmation Bias: A Ubiquitous Phenomenon in Many Guises". *Review of General Psychology* 2, No. 2 (1998): 175–220.

Nietzsche, Friedrich. *Beyond Good and Evil*, revised edition. Translated by R. J. Hollingdale. London: Penguin, 2003.

Pollock, Joycelyn M. *Ethical Dilemmas and Decisions in Criminal Justice*, 8th edition. Wadsworth: Cengage Learning, 2013.

Skinner, B. F. " 'Superstition' in the Pigeon". *Journal of Experimental Psychology* 38 (1948): 168–172.

Watson, John B. "Psychology as the Behaviourist Views It". *Psychological Review* 20 (1913): 158–177.

Watson, John B. *Behaviourism*, with a new introduction by Gregory A. Kimble. New Brunswick, NJ: Transaction Publishers, 1998.

# BEING HUMAN

## 3 Personhood

- → Self-consciousness
- → Agency
- → Morality and moral responsibility
- → Responsibility and authenticity

### Some essential questions:

- → What is it to be a person?
- → Could animals or machines be considered persons?
- → Is being morally responsible the defining feature of being human?

### Stimulus 1

If I was once a foetus – and this human organism was, once – it seems to follow that I once wasn't a person. To be a person you need to have some significant mental life, or at least that is how most people would understand the notion of person. Maybe there will come a time when this physical organism is still operating as an organism but has no conscious life. Maybe at the end of my life this will be a physical organism, after the personhood has gone. So it might seem to follow that being a person is an accidental property of mine rather than an essential property, and that may seem to be rather an uncomfortable position, to think of myself as not necessarily a person…

Could we not then identify the person with the developed functioning brain rather than the whole organism? So in other words maybe we want to say that the person only comes into existence not when the embryo is formed, not at conception, not even when there's a very early foetus, but when the brain starts developing, when consciousness emerges, that's when a person comes along, and the person is to be identified with the developed functioning brain rather than the whole organism.

—Peter Millican[1]

[1] Peter Millican, "Persons, Humans and Brains", Lecture delivered to first-year Philosophy students, Oxford University, Oxford, 2009, available at http://www.youtube.com/watch?v=9HhWqBJtPP8 (accessed 21 October 2014).

## Stimulus 2

We present this individual for your consideration: She communicates in sign language, using a vocabulary of over 1,000 words. She also understands spoken English, and often carries on "bilingual" conversations, responding in sign to questions asked in English. She is learning the letters of the alphabet, and can read some printed words, including her own name. She has achieved scores between 85 and 95 on the Stanford-Binet Intelligence Test.

She demonstrates a clear self-awareness by engaging in self-directed behaviours in front of a mirror, such as making faces or examining her teeth, and by her appropriate use of self-descriptive language. She lies to avoid the consequences of her own misbehaviour, and anticipates others' responses to her actions. She engages in imaginary play, both alone and with others. She has produced paintings and drawings which are representational. She remembers and can talk about past events in her life. She understands and has used appropriately time-related words like "before", "after", "later", and "yesterday".

She laughs at her own jokes and those of others. She cries when hurt or left alone, screams when frightened or angered. She talks about her feelings, using words like "happy", "sad", "afraid", "enjoy", "eager", "frustrate", "mad" and, quite frequently, "love". She grieves for those she has lost – a favourite cat who has died, a friend who has gone away. She can talk about what happens when one dies, but she becomes fidgety and uncomfortable when asked to discuss her own death or the death of her companions. She displays a wonderful gentleness with kittens and other small animals. She has even expressed empathy for others seen only in pictures.

Does this individual have a claim to basic moral rights? It is hard to imagine any reasonable argument that would deny her these rights based on the description above. She is self-aware, intelligent, emotional, communicative, has memories and purposes of her own, and is certainly able to suffer deeply. There is no reason to change our assessment of her moral status if I add one more piece of information: namely that she is not a member of the human species. The person I have described – and she is nothing less than a person to those who are acquainted with her – is Koko, a twenty-year-old lowland gorilla.

—Francine Patterson and Wendy Gordon[2]

[2] Francine Patterson and Wendy Gordon, "The Case for the Personhood of Gorillas", in The Great Ape Project, edited by Paola Cavalieri and Peter Singer (New York: St Martin's Griffin, 1993), p. 58; also available at http://www.animal-rights-library.com/texts-m/patterson01.htm (accessed 21 October 2014).

## Questions

1. In the stimuli above, what characteristics define what a person is? Write a comprehensive list.
2. Which one of these characteristics do you think is the most important one?
3. Can you think of characteristics of personhood that are not identified in the extracts above?

## What is a person?

In many conventional dictionaries, a person is defined as a human being. In this chapter, however, we will unpack this view and ask whether non-human entities could also be called "persons". We will also wonder whether absolutely all human beings are "persons". In order to do this, we will examine the characteristics of personhood. What is it, exactly, that makes someone or something a person? What qualities does an entity need to possess in order to be granted personhood?

### Personhood: a historical perspective

It is worth noting that equating personhood with humanity in its entirety, although it can seem obvious to most of us now, is a fairly recent phenomenon. Throughout history, many human beings have been excluded from personhood and from the rights it could have conferred on them. From women, disabled people and children to slaves and foreigners, it is fair to say that in many cultures, including the most "advanced" of their time, human beings that were considered persons were a minority.

This is well illustrated by the following extract from an 1856 Law Dictionary:

PERSON. This word is applied to men, women and children, who are called natural persons. In law, man and person are not exactly synonymous terms. Any human being is a man, whether he be a member of society or not, whatever may be the rank he holds, or whatever may be his age, sex, &c. A person is a man considered according to the rank he holds in society, with all the rights to which the place he holds entitles him, and the duties which it imposes.

2. It is also used to denote a corporation which is an artificial person.
3. But when the word "Persons" is spoken of in legislative acts, natural persons will be intended, unless something appear in the context to show that it applies to artificial persons.
4. Natural persons are divided into males, or men; and females or women. Men are capable of all kinds of engagements and functions, unless by reasons applying to particular individuals. Women cannot be appointed to any public office, nor perform any civil functions, except those which the law specially declares them capable of exercising.
5. They are also sometimes divided into free persons and slaves. Freemen are those who have preserved their natural liberty, that is to say, who have the right of doing what is not forbidden by the law. A slave is one who is in the power of a master to whom he belongs. Slaves are sometimes ranked not with persons but things. But sometimes

they are considered as persons, for example, a negro is in contemplation of law a person, so as to be capable of committing a riot in conjunction with white men.

6. Persons are also divided into citizens, (q.v.) and aliens, (q.v.) when viewed with regard to their political rights. When they are considered in relation to their civil rights, they are living or civilly dead; vide Civil Death; outlaws; and infamous persons.

7. Persons are divided into legitimates and bastards, when examined as to their rights by birth.

8. When viewed in their domestic relations, they are divided into parents and children; husbands and wives; guardians and wards; and masters and servants, as it is understood in law.[3]

**Question**

Can you think of people who, despite being human, are still not granted full personhood (in the sense of full legal rights and responsibilities) today?

## Why is personhood important?

It is very important to be able to define what makes a person, because personhood tends to imply rights. Once a being is granted personhood, it is granted a certain dignity, respect, and basic rights such as protection from harm.

Because of the rights that are given to persons, some groups campaign for the personhood of certain beings in order to change their social and legal status.

For instance, there are currently pro-life movements, such as Personhood USA, that demand that embryos be recognized as persons from conception, in order to ban abortion completely. In such a case, the personhood debate has huge moral, political, and social implications. Philosophically, it is also interesting, because it asks us to think about the limits between personhood and non-personhood: when does one become a person? Do foetuses become persons when they acquire a functioning brain, or perhaps consciousness? Or does personhood come at birth? Or even later, when reason and cognition develop? Equally, when does one cease to be a person? Are people in a coma or a vegetative state still persons? Are severely mentally disabled people or people with dementia persons?

Non-human beings have also been part of the personhood debate. For instance, groups have been fighting to have certain animals, such as apes, included in the definition of personhood, in order to protect them from torture, experimentation, and captivity. Others would like to see all non-human animals considered as persons, simply because they can suffer and feel emotions. These people are often, politically and philosophically,

[3] http://legal-dictionary.thefreedictionary.com/person

at odds with those who want embryos to be recognized as persons. Philosophically, of course, this raises the interesting questions of whether human beings are the only ones who can be granted personhood, and whether some animals deserve personhood more than others.

▲ The television series *True Blood* explores the personhood and legal rights of vampires. But does one need to be alive to be a person?

Giving non-human beings personhood and rights has been a fascinating debate for a long time, and is as popular as ever today, as illustrated by science fiction and fantasy literature, films, and TV series. Many plots revolve around the treatment of vampires, human hybrids and even aliens. Indeed, what characteristics would aliens need to possess for us to treat them like persons?

Strangely, in legal terms, entities such as corporations and organizations are described as persons in some countries:

> ***Person***
>
> In general usage, a human being; by statute, however, the term can include firms, labor organizations, partnerships, associations, corporations, legal representatives, trustees, trustees in bankruptcy, or receivers.
>
> A corporation is a "person" for purposes of the constitutional guarantees of Equal Protection of Laws and Due Process of Law.
>
> Foreign governments otherwise eligible to sue in United States courts are "persons" entitled to institute a suit for treble damages for alleged antitrust violations under the Clayton Act (15 U.S.C.A. § 12 et seq.).[4]

▲ The film *District 9* depicts human beings discriminating against aliens. What characteristics would aliens need to possess for us to treat them as persons?

[4] http://legal-dictionary.thefreedictionary.com/person

This shows the extent to which personhood is intimately connected with rights and the protection of the law. In this case, our usual logic is somewhat reversed: protection by the law grants personhood, instead of the opposite.

Of course, governments, corporations, and organizations are still composed of human beings, which can justify such an approach. However, a day may come when the personhood debate goes much beyond human beings and even animals: with the rapid progress of artificial intelligence, computers, and robots, it is worth asking ourselves if there is any way machines could ever gain personhood, and under what conditions. Again, this topic has been explored in many works of science fiction, perhaps because it threatens the idea that personhood is exclusively human and forces us to explore the limits of our humanity.

Given the implications, you can now understand why the question of what makes a person is a crucial and contemporary one. Before we explore some of the characteristics associated with personhood, here are some philosophical tools you may find particularly useful in this chapter.

## Philosophical terms

### Sufficient and necessary conditions

Sufficient means "enough" and a **sufficient condition** is a characteristic that is "enough" to make something belong to a category. For example, being a woman is a sufficient condition of being a human being. This means that being a woman is enough to make someone a human being: no other condition or characteristic is required. When you hear the word "woman", you know that it is a human being that is being mentioned. All women are human beings, therefore being a woman is a sufficient condition of being a human being.

Be careful: it only works one way! For instance, being a woman is a sufficient condition of being a human being, but being a human being is not a sufficient condition of being a woman. In other words, to be a human being it is not quite enough to be a woman because, of course, a human being could also be a man.

A **necessary condition** is a characteristic that is absolutely required for something to belong to a certain category. For instance, being male is a necessary condition of being a monk. You cannot be a monk unless you are male.

Examples can also be used to understand how necessary conditions are different from sufficient conditions: being male is a necessary condition of being a monk, but being male is not a sufficient condition of being a monk. In other words, you have to be male to be a monk, but not all male individuals are monks.

In some cases, though, a characteristic is both a necessary and sufficient condition. This means that sufficient and necessary conditions are **not mutually exclusive**. For instance, having a child is both a sufficient and necessary condition of being a parent.

These concepts are useful tools when we think about the attributes of a person.

For instance, we can ask ourselves how important *reason* is to the definition of a person. The first question we can ask ourselves is: is the ability to reason a sufficient condition of personhood? In other words, is it enough to possess reason in order to be a person? Is every rational being a person? You can see that this immediately leads to extremely interesting philosophical points, which will be tackled later in this chapter.

Similarly, we can ask if rationality is a necessary condition of personhood: does a being *need* to be rational in order to be called a person?

The concepts of sufficient and necessary conditions can help refine definitions and lead to in-depth philosophical discussions. Remember, however, that these concepts are fairly complex: use them in essays only if you can do so clearly and concisely, without losing track of your initial argument.

## Consciousness and self-consciousness

### Consciousness

One of the characteristics that is most often cited as a condition of personhood is consciousness. Consciousness has many different levels and definitions. As described in the *Oxford Companion to Philosophy,* "Consciousness exists, but it resists definition".[5] Philosophers disagree as to what constitutes consciousness, and there are countless philosophical questions raised by each definition. To keep things manageable here, let us start with a few basic characteristics that usually define consciousness.

At its most basic, consciousness is simply a state of **wakefulness**, where a being is conscious in a clinical sense, **aware** of its immediate surroundings, and able to **respond** to them, at least mentally. This basic consciousness is shared by most human beings and sentient animals. Although these characteristics are simple, they already raise some questions, as we will see.

Another popular view of consciousness was developed by Thomas Nagel, according to whom consciousness is what it is like, or what it feels like, to be oneself and to perceive the world as oneself. Nagel includes animals in his definition, since they must experience the world in a certain way that feels unique too. Such a definition emphasizes subjectivity: consciousness can never really be shared. There is a certain quality to each being's experience and consciousness, and that quality is unique.

Here is an extract from his classic philosophical text, "What Is It Like to Be a Bat?"

> Conscious experience is a widespread phenomenon. It occurs at many levels of animal life, though we cannot be sure of its presence in the simpler organisms, and it is very difficult to say in general what provides evidence of it. (Some extremists have been prepared to deny it even of mammals other than man.) No doubt it occurs in countless forms totally unimaginable to us, on other planets in other solar systems throughout the universe. But no matter how the form may vary, the fact that an organism has conscious experience at all means, basically, that there is something it is like to be that organism. There may be further implications about the form of the experience; there may even (though I doubt it) be implications about the behavior of the organism. But fundamentally an organism has conscious mental states if and only if there is something that it is to be that organism—something it is like for the organism.
>
> We may call this the subjective character of experience.[6]

[5] Ted Honderich (ed.), *The Oxford Companion to Philosophy* (Oxford: Oxford University Press, 1995), p. 152.

[6] Thomas Nagel, "What Is it Like to Be a Bat?", *The Philosophical Review* LXXXIII, No. 4 (October 1974): 435–436.

## Who and what possesses consciousness?

The first, basic characteristics of consciousness (wakefulness, awareness, responsiveness) are very inclusive. If we unpack them, we can see that many beings can qualify as conscious, because they form such an open and undemanding definition of consciousness.

- **Wakefulness**: wakefulness, in a human sense, is the opposite of being asleep. For many living beings, however, it is simply a state of awareness of the world. As we will see, this does not exclude many living beings at all. There are obvious questions regarding sleep and coma states that are raised by this characteristic, however, and we will have to address them in a moment.
- **Awareness**: like consciousness, awareness is an elusive concept and can be found in many degrees. When we talk about human beings, awareness tends to include self-awareness, which would exclude many animals whose self-awareness is either non-existent or non-evident to us. Some people take an even more elevated view of awareness with a more spiritual approach to the term, seeing it as a rare quality that is only fully accessed through meditation or similar practices. Such a definition would obviously exclude animals, as well as most human beings.

  The fact is, however, that there is such a thing as basic awareness. Some might say that responding to one's environment is already a basic form of awareness. A typical dictionary's definition of awareness, after all, is "knowledge or perception of a situation or fact".[7] How could anything respond to a stimulus without having perceived it first?
- **Responsiveness**: this characteristic is perhaps the most inclusive of all, because it doesn't even seem to require a mind. After all, if animals were unable to respond to their environment, they would quickly become extinct. The very definition of "animal" – "a living organism which feeds on organic matter, typically having specialized sense organs and nervous system and able to respond rapidly to stimuli"[8] – includes responsiveness.

Therefore, according to the most basic definitions of consciousness, many living beings can be called "conscious". One problem, of course, is to find a cut-off point. Mammals, for instance, obviously seem awake and responsive. Insects can perhaps also be seen as "awake", and are certainly able to respond to environmental stimuli. But what about very simple organisms, composed of a few cells? And what about plants? They do respond to threats and stimuli too, but can they really be called "conscious"?

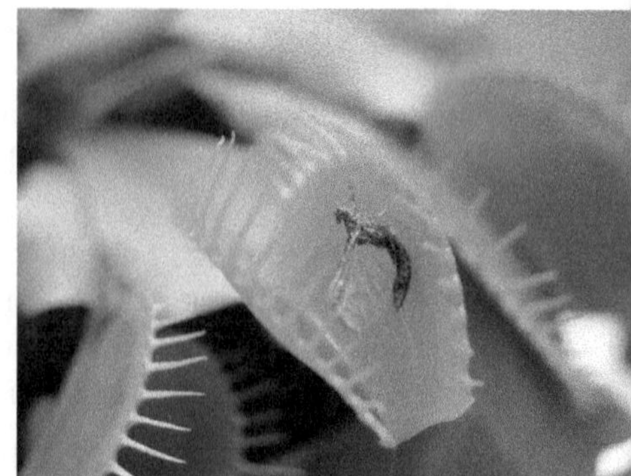

▲ This plant responds to its environment, but does that make it conscious?

Such a simple definition of consciousness seems to leave many beings in a grey area, depending on what we mean by awareness and responsiveness. Perhaps a good way to refine the definition is to ask what beings it definitely excludes. Inanimate objects, for instance, can surely never be called "aware". It is true that a piece of dead wood, for instance,

[7] http://www.oxforddictionaries.com/definition/english/awareness

[8] http://www.oxforddictionaries.com/definition/english/animal?q=animal

will react to its environment by expanding or changing shape slightly. This, to an extent, could be mistaken for "responsiveness". However, the piece of wood does not "perceive" its environment. Its reaction is just physics and involves neither wakefulness nor awareness. We must therefore distinguish between "being changed by the environment" and responding to it actively. The thing that "responds" must have some degree of awareness, and therefore some degree of subjectivity.

This is where Nagel's definition becomes useful, as it adds the subjective element to any definition of consciousness: instead of focusing on a list of necessary and sufficient conditions, Nagel centres everything on the subject. Consciousness is what is at the centre of all the experiences that are felt by a subject.

This means that, instead of wondering whether a human, an animal, or an inanimate object can qualify as "aware" or "awake", we can focus on whether it is able to experience the world in a specific, unique way. This approach is so inclusive that it is worth asking, once again, what kind of beings it actually excludes. For instance, it is very difficult to imagine that machines possess an individual way to feel the world. Although computers can be described as "awake" and can even, to an extent, respond to the world around them, as soon as we start talking about "what it feels like to be a computer", we can very well see that machines are not, in fact, conscious. Of course, it is possible to believe that some machines will, one day, acquire a form of consciousness, but it is clear that they haven't yet.

Animals are, as in the case of awareness, more problematic, because it is difficult to establish whether simpler animals such as insects or fish are really able to *feel* what it is like to be themselves. Although there is probably *something that it feels like* to be a cockroach, it is so far remote from human consciousness that it starts to make the definition look too open. This is particularly true if consciousness is to be the basis of personhood. Can a cockroach really be a person, based on the fact that it may possess the type of very basic consciousness Nagel talks about?

### Consciousness as a condition of personhood

This brings us back to the link between consciousness and personhood.

Firstly, is consciousness a necessary condition of personhood? In other words, can anyone or anything be a person if it does not possess consciousness? This would exclude inanimate objects such as computers and robots, however intelligent they are. More disturbingly, it would also seem to exclude people in a coma, especially if they have lost all awareness of the world. Coma is a very interesting state for our question, because most people would hesitate before they say that someone in a coma is no longer a person. Why is that?

In order to answer this question, let us consider two states that are somewhat similar to a coma: death and sleep. In the case of death, it is pretty clear that the corpse has ceased to be conscious, and ceased to be a person too. Although some religions instruct us to respect the body of the dead, their adherents would never argue that the body still possesses legal rights, for instance. Personhood is well and truly gone. In the case of sleep, on the other hand, it would make very little sense to say that we stop being a person every time we sleep. Yet, we are certainly unconscious, in every sense: wakefulness, responsiveness, awareness, and "what it feels to be us" are temporarily suspended (especially when we are not dreaming). So, why do we think of sleeping people as "persons" even though they possess no consciousness?

The answer is probably that we know their consciousness will return in a few hours, or instantly if we wake them up. The absence of consciousness is temporary, and sleepers are *potentially conscious*. This is probably why we refuse to exclude comatose people from personhood: they may well wake up. A coma is closer to a prolonged sleep than it is to death, as *potential consciousness* is still there. Many people resume life after a coma, and some even say that they possessed a certain degree of awareness of the world while they were in a coma.

As long as there is a chance that consciousness is present, even in a reduced form, or that it will return, we maintain the personhood of people. Once a doctor tells us someone's brain is entirely dead and there is no way they will ever come back to life, personhood seems to leave, as it does with death.

This example can help us refine our definition: consciousness, or the potential return of consciousness, is probably a necessary condition of personhood. Once we manage to include sleepers and people in a coma in our definition of consciousness, there seems to be little reason to say that anything unconscious can be a person.

There are, as always, alternative views, such as the idea that consciousness is a mere epiphenomenon or illusion and should not be given much importance. Another criticism you could develop is that, of course, it is very difficult to find definite proof of the existence of consciousness, especially in animals. "There must be a way it feels like to be this animal" is not a satisfying piece of evidence for some thinkers.

**Making connections: ethics (optional theme and TOK)**

The inclusion of "the potential return of consciousness" can be problematic too. The word *return* is key here, because it assumes that consciousness was once present in that very person, and may come back, just like it does in a sleeper.

However, many people believe that personhood should also include beings who will become conscious in the future. This would include embryos, from the time of conception. Since they have *potential consciousness* (this time, there is no idea of *returned* consciousness), some argue that they should be granted personhood.

This is a very important point, because it would also grant rights to those embryos from the very start of pregnancy, and would change the way we view abortion. Removing an embryo would essentially become a form of murder, since a person is eliminated.

There are also strong arguments against such a position. Firstly, *potential consciousness* is a can of worms. In theory, every sperm and every egg has potential consciousness, and yet we cannot possibly treat them as persons! As with many personhood debates, there is a problem with the cut-off point.

Does fertilization mean that that egg and that sperm suddenly become a person?

A second argument against personhood of embryos is that the personhood of the mother also needs to be respected. If a woman doesn't want to have a baby, and the embryo is protected by the law as a person, who is protecting the mother as a person? Some argue that the personhood of the mother – who is fully conscious and making a choice – takes precedence over that of a potential being who has not yet acquired full personhood. Philosophically, this is just as problematic as granting personhood to eggs, because it implies that the mother is, somehow, more of a person than the embryo or foetus. But can there be degrees of personhood? Is personhood something that embryos, foetuses or babies acquire gradually, or does it come overnight at some stage? If it is a sudden quality, at what stage does it appear?

Consciousness as a necessary condition of personhood can help answer this question: for many thinkers and scientists, the foetus becomes a person when it acquires consciousness. Scientists are constantly trying to determine when that is, and their efforts are made easier by developments in brain imaging technology.

As you can see, although consciousness is a good condition for personhood, there are many questions raised by the beginning of life, where consciousness is only there as a potential quality.

A second question about the link between consciousness and personhood is whether consciousness is a sufficient condition of personhood. Is every conscious being a person, or does it take more than simple consciousness in order to be granted personhood?

The answer, of course, entirely depends on the definition of consciousness that is used. If we stick with the simple criteria we have used so far, such as Nagel's "what it feels like" idea, we end up with a very open door. If every conscious being is a person, we may end up with a definition of personhood that is so inclusive it becomes meaningless. As discussed, fairly basic animals such as insects and fish most probably possess a primitive form of consciousness. Yet, their consciousness is also probably very different from that of human beings or higher order mammals. Somehow, such a rudimentary form of consciousness, reduced to a few impressions and basic awareness, does not seem enough to make a person. This is especially true if we consider that personhood is the basis for fundamental rights. Most thinkers, therefore, would not count basic consciousness as a sufficient condition of personhood.

## Self-consciousness/self-awareness

Self-consciousness is a more refined, higher level criterion than simple consciousness. It can be defined as "consciousness about consciousness", or a being's knowledge that it exists as a conscious being and an individual. For animals or young children, self-consciousness may simply mean that they are aware that they exist and that they are distinct from others and the world around them. In other words, they are aware of their own individuality and subjectivity.

A more mature and developed kind of self-consciousness involves thinking about oneself and one's consciousness in more depth. It is one thing to understand that I exist and am a separate being from others, but quite another for me to reflect on my own personality traits, way of thinking, emotions, and existence.

### ACTIVITY

Research the development of foetuses and newborn babies, and particularly of the brain and cognitive abilities. Do you think there is a specific point when personhood begins?

### FIND OUT MORE

A comprehensive web page on consciousness that reflects all the complexity of the topic:

**http://plato.stanford.edu/entries/consciousness/**

Another detailed page on consciousness that includes a section on animal and machine consciousness:

**http://www.iep.utm.edu/consciou/#H6**

The following extract from David L. Anderson's article on personhood clearly explains some of the qualities of self-awareness and self-consciousness:

> The standard idea is probably that the self, though capable of being aware of things external to it, is also capable of being aware of its own states. Some have described this as a kind of experience. I might be said to have an "inner experience" of my own mental activity, being directly aware, say, of the thoughts that I am presently thinking and the attitudes ("I hope the White Sox win") that I presently hold. But even if we grant that we have such "inner experiences," they do not, by themselves, supply everything that we intend to capture by the term, "self-awareness." When I say that I am aware of my own mental activity (my thoughts, dreams, hopes, etc.) I do not mean merely that I have some inner clue to the content of that mental activity, I also mean that the character of that awareness is such that it gives me certain abilities to critically reflect upon my mental states and to make judgments about those states. If I am aware of my own behavior and mental activity in the right way, then it may be possible for me to decide that my behavior should be changed, that an attitude is morally objectionable or that I made a mistake in my reasoning and that a belief that I hold is unjustified and should be abandoned.[9]

There are many philosophical complexities and debates surrounding self-consciousness, what it is exactly, what purpose it serves and the different qualities it possesses. These debates remain philosophical because, scientifically, we still know very little about the true nature of self-consciousness. This leads to an interesting paradox, as highlighted in this extract from the *Internet Encyclopedia of Philosophy*'s entry on self-consciousness:

> These forms of self-consciousness—consciousness of ourselves and our personal existence, of our character traits and standing features, and of the thoughts that occur to us and the feelings that we experience—are philosophically fascinating, inasmuch as they are at once quite mysterious and closest to home. Our scientific theories of astrophysical objects that are incredibly distant from us in both space and time, or of the smallest particles that make up the sub-atomic layer of reality, are mature, sophisticated, and impressive. By contrast, we barely have anything worth the name "scientific theory" for self-consciousness and its various manifestations, in spite of self-consciousness being so much more familiar a phenomenon—indeed the most familiar phenomenon of all.
>
> Here, as elsewhere, the immaturity of our scientific understanding of self-consciousness invites philosophical reflection on the topic, and is anyway partly due precisely to deep philosophical puzzles about the nature of self-consciousness. Many philosophers have thought that self-consciousness exhibits certain peculiarities not to be found in consciousness of things other than ourselves, and indeed possibly not to be found anywhere else in nature.[10]

[9] David L. Anderson, "What Is a Person?", *Consortium on Cognitive Science Instruction*, 2000, available at http://www.mind.ilstu.edu/curriculum/what_is_a_person/what_is_a_person.php (accessed 21 October 2014).
[10] http://www.iep.utm.edu/self-con/

## Who and what possesses self-consciousness?

In human babies, self-consciousness is thought to appear gradually. When babies are born, they do not possess self-consciousness as such.

The following is a summary of Philippe Rochat's article "Five Levels of Self-Awareness as They Unfold Early in Life":[11]

| Approximate age and level | Characteristics |
|---|---|
| From birth (Level 1) | Babies demonstrate "a sense of their own body as a differentiated entity" (p. 722), "an entity that is experienced differently from other entities *out there* in the environment" (p. 723). |
| From 2 months (Level 2) | Babies now "have a sense of how their own body is *situated* in relation to other entities in the environment" (p. 723). They can, for instance, imitate facial expressions and explore the consequence of their actions of their environment (pp. 723– 724). |
| Around 18 months (Level 3) | Babies start passing the classic test that involves putting a mark on their forehead to see if they touch it and/or remove it when they see it in the mirror (see extract below). They also start to separate themselves from others through language. However, they refer to their mirror image in the third person until they are 3 or 4, and may not recognize themselves in a film because of the time delay (pp. 725– 727). |
| From 3 years old (Level 4) | "It is not prior to approximately 3 years that children begin to grasp the temporal dimension of the self. That the self pertains not only to what is experienced now but also to what was experienced then, what can be seen in a mirror now or in a movie tomorrow: the same enduring self" (p. 727). |
| From 4 to 5 years old (Level 5) | Children now possess a much better understanding of others and their own self in relation to others. This is proper self-awareness, where children, for instance, can imagine what others may think of them (pp. 727– 728). |

### The mirror: a classic test for self-awareness

Despite all [the] remarkable perceptual discriminability between what pertains to the self and what pertains to others, up to the middle of the first year infants are oblivious that some rouge has surreptitiously been smeared on their face or that a yellow "Post-It" might appear on their forehead when looking at their own specular image.

It is only by 18 months that ... infants start to reach for the mark on their own body, often in order to remove it (Level 3). This behavior is considered by most developmental and comparative psychologists as the Litmus test of self-awareness (but see Loveland, 1986, for

[11] Philippe Rochat, "Five Levels of Self-Awareness as They Unfold Early in Life", *Consciousness and Cognition* 12 (2003): 717–731.

a critic of this view). It is often viewed as the evidence of a conceptual or "represented" sense of self in any organism behaving like this in front of mirrors, whether the human child, non-human primates, avian, mammals like elephants, or even cetaceans like dolphins. But why? It is mainly because by showing this behavior, individuals demonstrate the ability to refer to the specular image as standing to their own body. In other words, they refer the silhouette they see reflected in the mirror to precise regions of their own body they cannot see directly (e.g., their forehead). This would be impossible without a body schema or own body representation that is mapped onto what is seen in the mirror. Therefore, this behavior indicates that the mirror reflection is seen by the individual as standing for this representation (Level 3). It is identified as referring to the body experienced and represented from within, not anybody else's. Identity is used here in the literal, dictionary sense of "recognizing the condition of being oneself, not another"...

Identifying oneself in the mirror is a major feat, not only for the referential mapping between the mirror reflection and the own body schema, but also because what the child sees in the mirror is the way he or she always sees others: in an "en face" posture often with eye contact. In relation to this basic experience of social encounters, what the child experiences in the mirror might be "Me", but it is also what others typically look like. The child therefore has to suspend and override their overall visual experience of others, the specular image standing for "Me as an other" (pp. 725–726).[12]

Rochat's summary would suggest that babies acquire self-consciousness and self-awareness gradually, and that what they possess before 18 months, and possibly even before the age of 3, does not quite count as self-consciousness. Therefore, although self-consciousness is usually associated with human beings, it is worth remembering that it is not something we are born with, and that there are plenty of human beings who do not possess it yet.

In addition to babies, there are other human beings who may not possess self-consciousness. As discussed in the case of consciousness, comatose people may lose self-consciousness for a period of time, until they either wake up or die. The implications are similar to those discussed in the consciousness section. However, we can also add people who are severely mentally ill or disabled. While severely disabled people are still conscious, in the sense that it feels a certain way to be them, they may be unable to access self-consciousness, as it is a slightly higher cognitive ability. There is evidence that severely autistic patients, for instance, are unable to distinguish themselves from others and from their surroundings. Similarly, people with severe psychopathic disorders may be unable to think of themselves as a unique and separate entity, as a result of hallucinations or extreme multiple personality disorders.

While not all human beings possess self-consciousness, it also seems that not all self-conscious beings are human. Some animal species, such as elephants and gorillas, show consistent signs of self-consciousness and some individuals, although rare, have passed mirror tests. They may not quite reach "Level 5" of self-consciousness, but many are able to recognize themselves in films and pictures, and to wipe marks off their forehead when they see their reflection in a mirror.

[12] Ibid.

### Self-consciousness as a condition of personhood

At first sight, it seems that self-consciousness could be an excellent necessary condition of personhood. Claiming that you need to have self-consciousness in order to have personhood is not a shocking idea. Indeed, it eliminates animals that have a lower form of consciousness, such as insects and fish, and includes those that keep demonstrating higher cognitive abilities in a variety of domains, such as apes and elephants. Of course, there is always the problem of the cut-off point: as we discover more ingenious ways to understand animals, are we likely to increase the list of those that show signs of self-consciousness?

More problematic, however, is the exclusion of some human beings. We are so accustomed to equating personhood with humanity that we find it very hard to conceive of human beings who are not persons. Historically, as we saw earlier, this was not always the case: many people were excluded from personhood. Perhaps our reluctance to exclude anyone comes from the memory of those times, when racism and sexism, for instance, were normal practices, even though they tend to be deeply shocking to many of us now. Excluding human beings from personhood would seem like a step backwards.

This leads us to a difficult dilemma, however:

| Claim | Advantages | Problems |
|---|---|---|
| All human beings are persons and only human beings can be persons. | Simple definition; clear distinction between what is a person and what is not | Why would both words (human and person) even exist if they meant the same thing? What exact attributes of human beings grant them the exclusive right to be persons? |
| All human beings are persons and some other beings may be persons too. | Open definition; allows philosophical debate; slightly less anthropocentric | Cut-off point problems: if all humans can be persons, why can't all animals be persons? For instance, why is a non-self-conscious human still a person, but a non-self-conscious animal isn't? What makes human beings so special? |
| Most human beings are persons and some other beings are persons. | Consistent: some specific criteria of personhood that apply equally to humans, animals and other beings; much less anthropocentric | What is the status of human beings who do not fit the criteria for personhood? Could it be a slippery slope? |

As you can see, this is not an easy dilemma! **Ethically**, you may feel that all human beings must be considered as persons if we want to treat them fairly, while **logically**, you may find that the only consistent claim is the third one.

Such a dilemma may also call for a **personal response**. Beliefs and values will inform what answer you tend to go with. For instance, if you are a religious believer, you may think that God clearly set human beings apart from the rest of creation, and you may not have a problem with the claim that human beings are all persons while other beings cannot be persons. On the other hand, you may be an animal rights activist who believes that human beings have been on an unjustified pedestal for too long, in which case you may not see why being human would grant automatic personhood, without the need to fulfil any specific criterion. These answers are both fine and, in fact, you are encouraged to formulate a personal response when you write essays. However, you must always remember to show that you possess a solid understanding of other points of view, and you must justify yours with strong, rational arguments.

To conclude this section, we need to ask whether self-consciousness could be a sufficient condition of personhood. This is perhaps less problematic: the idea that any being found to have self-consciousness is to be treated as a person would appeal to many. It does require a fairly open mind, however, since it rules out human beings as the only possible persons. Adopting such a criterion would mean accepting the idea that some animals can be persons, that every self-conscious being we ever find in the universe is a person, and that artificially reconstructed self-consciousness (however difficult it is for us to conceive of right now) would give machines personhood too.

**FIND OUT MORE**

About the notion of self-consciousness:

**http://www.iep.utm.edu/self-con/**

About personhood, consciousness and self-awareness, with entertaining examples:

**http://www.mind.ilstu.edu/curriculum/what_is_a_person/what_is_a_person.php**

## Agency

One of the most fundamental rights granted to a person is the right to self-determination: a person should be free to make choices and decide what he or she wants to do with his or her life. This, of course, assumes that there is such a thing as freedom and that persons *can* indeed exercise it.

### What is agency?

**Agency** is a term that is intimately related to freedom. Since freedom is discussed at length in Chapter 6, we will concentrate on agency and its relationship with personhood. Agency refers to the ability people have to act and, by extension, to cause their own actions in a voluntary and intentional way. Not all philosophers believe in human agency. Hard determinists, for instance, may argue that all actions are the result of a chain of causes that cannot simply start with the will of a human being. The chain of causes may be a series of chemical reactions inside the brain and the body, for instance, that was itself caused by an external event or stimulus. Philosophers who believe in human agency, on the other hand, would argue that human beings are agents, capable of being the start of the chain that causes their own actions. It does not mean that everything we do is done intentionally, but that human beings have the power to bring about certain actions just because they want to. As the philosopher Richard Taylor writes very simply, "I am sometimes the cause of my own actions."[13] (See p. 271 in Chapter 6: Freedom for this extract.)

Of course, it can seem a little naive to think that intention alone can be the cause of action, without the intention itself being shaped by anything at all. Most philosophers, even those who believe in human agency, would agree that there are factors that influence an agent's intentions. Intention does not appear out of nowhere, for no reason at all. The key point, however, is that an agent is able to weigh a variety of possibilities and make a choice, even if that choice is influenced by internal and external factors.

[13] Richard Taylor, Action and Purpose (Englewood Cliffs, NJ: Prentice-Hall, 1966), p. 111; also available at http://www.informationphilosopher.com/solutions/philosophers/taylorr/ (accessed 21 October 2014).

For instance, if it is cloudy outside and I decide to take an umbrella to school, it makes little sense to say that my intention to take an umbrella is not influenced by anything: of course, it is influenced by the clouds. However, it would also make little sense to say that the clouds *cause* me to take an umbrella: the clouds do not automatically make my hand grab an umbrella before I leave for school. The cause of my taking an umbrella remains my intention to do so. When I see the clouds, I make a conscious decision to take an umbrella and, crucially, *I could very well have decided not to take an umbrella to school.* I had a choice, yet I went with the umbrella.

Of course, a hard determinist would see things differently and could argue the following: given that I saw clouds in the sky, given that I hate getting wet, given that I tend to be cautious, and given that the last time I forgot my umbrella I got soaked, it was entirely *predictable* that I would "choose" to take my umbrella to school today. The real causes of my taking an umbrella to school occurred before I made a "choice". My intention is simply part of the chain of causes. Any deliberation is probably an illusion, a simple delay caused by my processing all the information: much like a computer, I may take a little bit of time before I reach my conclusion, but the conclusion was always going to be what it is.

These are two profoundly different views that are further discussed in the Freedom chapter. Here, however, when we talk about human agency, we will go with the first view: believers in agency – or, as some call it more precisely, in *free* agency – defend the idea that intention is indeed a possible cause of action.

## Who and what possesses agency?

In a seminal 1971 text about human agency and what it means for the concept of personhood, Harry G. Frankfurt draws an interesting distinction between agency as it is found in animals, and human agency:

> It is my view that one essential difference between persons and other creatures is to be found in the structure of a person's will. Human beings are not alone in having desires and motives, or in making choices. They share these things with the members of certain other species, some of whom appear to engage in deliberation and to make decisions based upon prior thought. It seems to be peculiarly characteristic of humans, however, that they are able to form what I shall call "second-order desires" or "desires of the second order".
>
> Besides wanting and choosing and being moved *to do* this or that, men may also want to have (or not to have) certain desires and motives. They are capable of wanting to be different, in their preferences and purposes, from what they are. Many animals appear to have the capacity for what I shall call "first-order desires" or "desires of the first order", which are simply desires to do or not to do one thing or another. No animal other than man, however, appears to have the capacity for reflective self-evaluation that is manifested in the formation of second-order desires…
>
> The essential characteristic of a wanton is that he does not care about his will. His desires move him to do certain things, without its being true of him either that he wants to be moved by those desires or that he prefers to be moved by other desires. The class of wantons includes all nonhuman animals that have desires and all very young children. Perhaps it also includes some human beings as well. In any case, adult humans may be more or less wanton; they may act wantonly, in response to first-order desires concerning which they have no volitions of the second order, more or less frequently.[14]

[14] Harry G. Frankfurt, "Freedom of the Will and the Concept of a Person", The Journal of Philosophy LXVIII, No. 1 (14 January 1971): 6–7, 11.

Frankfurt's definition of the will means that, to him, there is no doubt that human beings are the only beings who can be persons. Frankfurt considers that what he calls "second-order desires" are a necessary condition of personhood, which seems to exclude not only animals but also young children and some mentally or morally deficient adults.

It is difficult to prove that there are animals that possess second-order desires, although it is conceivable that some, such as apes, elephants or dolphins, might. If we get back a slightly less demanding definition of agency, however, there are many signs that these species and some other evolved mammals occasionally stop to reflect and then choose one path over another. Of course, such reflection is probably not on a par with the long tortures that human beings can endure when they face a difficult dilemma. Some examples are striking, however, such as those given by Nadezhda Ladygina-Kohts, an early-20th-century primatologist, who described the behaviour of her chimpanzee, Joni. According to Kohts, Joni sometimes escaped and climbed on the roof, where it was impossible for her to retrieve him. Kohts tried to use threats and rewards such as food to encourage Joni to climb back down, to no effect. The only method Kohts found effective was to pretend she was hurt and crying, at which point Joni would come running to see what was going on.[15] These kinds of anecdotes show not only the presence of empathy in animals, but also that of deliberation. Food is a powerful draw for any animal, yet Joni could resist his urge and choose playing on the roof over eating: he was able to choose one desire over another one, and to decide when the situation had become serious enough to stop playing. These are clear signs of agency, and perhaps not so far from the second-order desires Frankfurt describes.

▲ Nadezhda Ladygina-Kohts and Joni

Self-consciousness and agency that includes some sort of deliberation seem to include the same kind of beings: human beings who are no longer babies and who are not severely mentally impaired, and a few animals with high cognitive abilities. As for machines, they are perhaps not quite as far from agency as they seem to be from self-consciousness. While being aware of one's self in relation to others may be a lot to ask from a computer or a robot, making a decision after considering a variety of options is not so different from what computers already do. Of course, the ultimate decision is still very predictable, and the deliberation process has been programmed by human beings, which prevents current machines from possessing agency in the sense of the word that we use for human beings. Weighing options, however, is very close to a computation process, and it is not too far-fetched to imagine computers that are able to weigh options in a way that is fairly similar to what we do. This, of course, would weaken the claim that human beings are unique and that agency is evidence that human beings are not determined. Every time an animal and, even more so, a machine, can do what was supposed to be uniquely human, humanity becomes less special and less unique. This is why the conversation about what it means to be a person is so important, and why it has become detached from the strict boundaries of humanity.

[15] See Frans de Waal, "The Evolution of Empathy", *Greater Good*, 1 September 2005, available at http://greatergood.berkeley.edu/article/item/the_evolution_of_empathy (accessed 21 October 2014).

### Agency as a condition of personhood

Do beings need to be agents in order to be persons? Is it conceivable that a person may be unable to deliberate and make choices? It seems reasonable to say that agency is a necessary condition of personhood. The problems such a statement raises are very similar to those raised by self-consciousness as a necessary condition of personhood, because the beings that are excluded are pretty much the same ones. We notice once again, then, that it is emotionally and ethically difficult to accept that human beings such as babies and mentally impaired people are not persons, even though it makes good logical sense. Agency also raises the same questions about the status of animals and human beings: can some animals be accepted as persons while some human beings are not? Are criteria of personhood such as self-consciousness and agency more important than humanity? Do human beings have an exclusive claim to personhood that animals and other beings do not possess? If so, why?

At this point, it is also worth noting that agency does not necessarily involve freedom of action. The most important aspect of agency is freedom of will: if a being is able to consider a variety of options and choose one, most philosophers would consider it an agent. Being able to put the choice into action is also important, of course, and forms part of agency. But if external circumstances prevent an agent from acting upon its choices, what makes that being an agent has not suddenly disappeared. In other words, agency is at its best when it can be translated into action, but its most important attribute is freedom of will. To say that a person must be an agent, therefore, is to say that a person must have free will, but not necessarily political or physical freedom. This is particularly important when considering animals, since many of them have no rights and live in captivity.

Finally, agency could also be considered a sufficient quality of personhood, meaning that if a being possesses agency, it does not need to possess any other quality in order to be defined as a person. Implications would include those that have been discussed above, and that you may want to develop:

- Machines may well develop something akin to agency soon. What would make it "real" agency? Would they then become persons, even without self-consciousness or even consciousness? Is agency even possible without consciousness?
- Could it be that agency is a sufficient condition of personhood, but not a necessary one? This would allow people who are not agents (such as babies, the mentally impaired, etc.) to have access to personhood, while agency in highly sentient animals would grant them personhood. The same questions we asked when studying self-consciousness would be raised again: why would animals need to fulfil a criterion that human beings do not need to fulfil in order to be considered persons?

## Morality and moral responsibility

Another set of criteria that are often cited as conditions of personhood are morality and moral responsibility. These two notions are intimately linked with those of agency and free will.

### FIND OUT MORE

For a comprehensive account of action and agency:

**http://plato.stanford.edu/entries/action/**

For an efficient summary of the link between personhood and free will:

**http://en.wikibooks.org/wiki/Introduction_to_Philosophy/What_is_a_Person**

## What are morality and moral responsibility?

**Morality** refers to beliefs about what is right and wrong. A moral being will possess moral judgment and values, and will be able to apply them to real-life situations in order to determine what behaviour is the morally right one. **Moral responsibility**, on the other hand, is the quality of a being who is able to decide what is right or wrong, and act accordingly. A morally responsible agent makes conscious choices to act one way or another, while understanding their moral implication, and can therefore be blamed or praised for those actions. As you can see, moral responsibility assumes that all the qualities we have studied so far are present: consciousness, self-consciousness, and agency.

The relationship between moral responsibility and agency is a very important one to understand. Without free will and agency, there is no moral responsibility. This is a common criticism of hard determinism: if human actions are completely determined, it makes little sense to claim that those who perform them are responsible. The bigger the emphasis on freedom, the "heavier" moral responsibility becomes: those who claim that human beings are free agents also tend to have a rather unforgiving perspective on responsibility. Blaming external factors for our behaviour only works to an extent, but if we believe that we are free agents who make the ultimate call on whether to act one way or another, we must accept blame and punishment for the "bad" choices we make. The relationship between freedom and responsibility is discussed further in Chapter 6: Freedom.

### Who and what possesses morality and moral responsibility?

Moral responsibility goes further than agency, because it assumes an understanding of morality. Also, while agency was centred on free will, freedom of action is also required for moral responsibility: you cannot be deemed fully morally responsible if someone makes you commit a crime while holding a gun to your head, for instance.

So, what beings possess agency, freedom of action, and morality? It seems that the combination of those criteria is much more demanding than the characteristics we have explored so far. While young children only take two or three years to acquire self-consciousness or agency, they need many more years to become full moral agents. Legally, children are not fully morally responsible for their actions, although the age at which this changes varies widely across the world, as illustrated in this extract:

> A child under the age of criminal responsibility lacks the capacity to commit a crime. This means they are immune from criminal prosecution – they cannot be formally charged by authorities with an offence nor be subjected to any criminal law procedures or measures.
>
> The significance of the minimum age of criminal responsibility is that it recognises that a child has attained the emotional, mental and intellectual maturity to be held responsible for their actions. The minimum age of criminal responsibility set by different countries ranges hugely from as low as six up to 18 years of age. The median age of criminal responsibility worldwide is 12.[16]

[16] Penal Reform International, "The Minimum Age of Criminal Responsibility", Justice for Children Briefing No. 4, 2013, available at http://www.penalreform.org/wp-content/uploads/2013/05/justice-for-children-briefing-4-v6-web_0.pdf (accessed 21 October 2014).

The criterion of moral responsibility is, therefore, a demanding one. Given how intellectually able the average 12-year-old is, it seems very difficult to see how the mentally impaired, let alone animals, could come close to being considered morally responsible. If personhood is based on full moral responsibility, "persons" could become quite an exclusive club indeed!

Of course, moral responsibility does not develop overnight. Although, legally, children may not be fully responsible, we still expect them to understand morality to a fairly large extent. Young children who hurt others are blamed and punished by their parents from the time they are no longer babies. A one-year-old who pulls someone's hair may not be told off very sternly, but a three-year-old will be likely to get a firmer reprimand, which clearly shows that we do expect children to understand basic moral rules after just a few years.

Another question is whether moral responsibility completely excludes animals, as it may be too demanding a criterion. To answer this question, it is important to determine where morality comes from and explore some common theories:

| Theory of the origins of morality | Implications for non-human animals |
|---|---|
| Morality comes from God | If God has set human beings apart from animals and given them moral rules as an exclusive feature, animals cannot be considered moral agents (they are **amoral**). They may make choices and even deliberate, but those choices are never moral. |
| Morality is a human invention | Animals have no reason to understand and follow the rules of human society, just as human beings do not generally attempt to follow the rules of other species. Animals that live in close contact with human beings (pets, apes living with a primatologist, etc.) may come to follow some rules and even understand them. This will make them seem like moral creatures. |
| Morality is the result of evolution | Animals that are similar to human beings (apes) or that have highly evolved cognitive abilities (elephants, dolphins, monkeys, etc.) possess a basic form of morality. They display signs of empathy as well as guilt, emotions that are intricately related to morality. Some species, like young children, can therefore possess a degree of morality and even moral responsibility. It is unlikely human beings are the only ones who have evolved to become moral agents. |
| Morality comes from nature | If morality comes from following implicit natural laws, there is no reason to think that human beings are the only ones who can "read" such laws. In fact, human beings have become so alienated from nature that it is possible to argue that some animals may be in closer touch with natural moral laws. |

## TOK link: the ways of knowing ethics

The examples above show that different ways of knowing are connected to ethics and can give us a very different understanding of what morality means. If morality comes from God, for instance, faith will be an important way of knowing ethical values. If morality comes from human beings, it may be better understood through reason, language, and perhaps emotions. The evolutionary perspective would encourage us to use intuition as well as reason and emotions, while a natural origin of the laws would mean that we may need to rely on a mixture of sense perception, reason, and emotion to understand what the best course of action is.

### Questions

1. What do you think are the best ways of knowing what is right and wrong?
2. Is this consistent with what you believe about the origins of morality?
3. What theory of the origins of morality do you think is the best one, and why? What evidence is there to back it up?

The implications for machines are quite similar: if morality is exclusively human, there is no way machines could ever be considered morally responsible, however much they evolve. If morality is not exclusively human, then machines could, in principle, become moral. Of course, the form of morality they develop would be very different from animals' morality: while animals may understand some aspects of morality through instincts, emotions, and basic social rules, machines' strength would most probably lie in computation of logical arguments and statistical predictions. Utilitarian decisions, for instance, could conceivably be made by elaborate machines that project possible outcomes and opt for the most favourable one. In fact, computers are already used to help make decisions such as whether to release prisoners, based on the probability that they will reoffend.[17] Of course, we are a long way away from machines that can actually *understand* moral values, make moral judgments, and, most of all, be morally responsible. In fact, such machines are practically inconceivable for the time being.

In summary, although morality itself is present in children and even possibly in some animals, there is quite a jump between morality and the full moral responsibility we attribute to adult, mentally able human beings. To say that personhood requires morality excludes quite a few beings, human and non-human, but to say that it requires full moral responsibility excludes many others and is one of the most demanding criteria we have faced yet.

[17] See Joseph Walker, "State Parole Boards Use Software to Decide Which Inmates to Release", *The Wall Street Journal*, 11 October 2013, available at http://online.wsj.com/news/articles/SB10001424052702304626104579121251595240852

**Questions: your turn!**

Use the work we have done on other characteristics to answer the following questions and explore their full philosophical implications:

1. Could moral responsibility be a necessary condition of personhood? What would be the implications of such a condition? (i.e. Who would be excluded? Would such exclusions be problematic?)
2. Could moral responsibility be a sufficient condition of personhood? What would be the implications?
3. Would it be better to lower expectations and use morality as a condition of personhood, rather than full moral responsibility?
4. Is it unfair on groups such as teenagers to claim that only fully morally responsible people can be persons?

## Responsibility and authenticity

### What are responsibility and authenticity for existentialists?

In philosophy, responsibility is a concept that does not just refer to the strict moral responsibility individuals possess in the legal sense of the word. Existentialist philosophers, for instance, use the term responsibility to mean the duty people have to exercise their freedom, give meaning to their own life, and live with **authenticity**.

Existentialists believe that human beings are essentially free, to the extent that they are able to determine the meaning of their life and decide who they want to be and what kind of existence they want to lead. Those who accept this absolute freedom and the huge responsibility that accompanies it live with authenticity, whereas those who try to deny or hide from their own freedom live in **bad faith** or with **facticity**.

Most people, according to existentialists, live without wanting to think about their responsibility to give meaning to their life. They just conform and stay in a comfortable routine without thinking about the importance of their choices and actions (even though such things are very important because they constitute their identity and essence). People also face a great deal of pressure from society, which is pushing them to conform and be "normal".

According to Søren Kierkegaard (1813–1855), one of the first existentialist philosophers, it is frightening to follow our own individual choices, as they might be unpopular. Being an authentic individual is therefore filled with "fear and trembling" (the title of Kierkegaard's most famous book, published in 1843). However, conforming with the masses is not a comfortable position either, as it causes the loss of our true self, resulting in a deep despair.

Martin Heidegger, one of the founders of existentialism, talks about the "average everydayness"[18] of our lives and of the fact that the roles we fulfil every day could simply be fulfilled by someone else. We are like actors and someone else could replace us easily. We just do what is done, what "one does". Even when we decide to reject the majority and to rebel, we do so in a way that is acceptable to certain groups of individuals (punks, emos, etc.).

Although they do not systematically criticize social life, existentialists believe that we need to free ourselves from conformity and become what we really want to become, out of choice and freedom. This can be done once the despair of not being ourselves becomes too deep and pushes us to react. The move towards freedom is also a move towards responsibility and authenticity.

The notion of **project** is another very important one in existentialism. People need to focus on something they want, a main concern or a project for their life, and they need to do what needs to be done to achieve it, throwing themselves into the life they have chosen, with feeling, passion, and intensity. The *way* we live our life is more important than *what* we do with it. For instance, two great concert pianists will be seen differently by existentialists if one is following her life dream and the other was forced to play piano by her parents and secretly hates it. The only authentic being is the first one.

We need to give our life and our character some "style". According to Nietzsche, "It is crucial to 'give style to one's character', to survey all the strengths and weaknesses of one's nature and then fit them into an artistic plan ... In the end, when the work is finished, it becomes evident how the constraint of a single taste governed and formed everything large and small. Whether this taste was good or bad is less important than one might suppose, if only it was a single taste."[19] We therefore need focus, coherence, integrity, and style. In other words (although Nietzsche himself never uses the word), we need authenticity.

### Who and what possesses responsibility and authenticity in the existentialist sense?

The criteria of responsibility and authenticity in the existentialist sense could be our most demanding yet. It is very difficult to imagine an animal – and, even more so, a machine – as being able to view its life as a whole, thinking about the most authentic ways to use its freedom, and giving "style", meaning, and direction to its life. Similarly, children probably lack the maturity to reflect in such a way until they are well into their teens. There is an assumption that people need to feel the anxiety caused by facticity and conformity before they can take responsibility for their own freedom: the gap that exists between what people are and what they want to be is what causes the angst that will

[18] See Introduction (p. xxxiii) and section on Martin Heidegger in Charles Guignon and Derk Pereboom (eds), *Existentialism: Basic Writings*, 2nd edition (Indianapolis: Hackett Publishing Company, 2001).

[19] Ibid, pp. xxxiv–xxxv.

motivate them to live authentically. Can children possibly feel such a gap? Can they really have a life project they will stick to? While there might be rare exceptions, what existentialism asks from people is probably only possible for adults to achieve.

In fact, as some existentialist writers point out, most adults are unable to face the responsibilities that come with freedom and are unable to live in a truly authentic way. Although people are all, technically, free and able to shape their life in a meaningful way, many choose not to and hide away from their freedom.

One of the most potent criticisms of existentialism claims that it is an elitist philosophy. If people are busy trying to survive, eat, work hard, and protect their family, they will have neither the time nor the inclination to spend hours pondering about the meaning of their life, worrying about existential anxiety, and trying to construct a life project that makes them authentic individuals. According to Jean-Paul Sartre, every human being can feel the anxiety caused by not living authentically; it is part of our human condition. Critics point out, however, that it may be more typical of moneyed intellectuals who have no other "real" problem: existential anxiety comes from a life of luxury and possibly boredom.

While these criticisms are rather harsh, they do have a point: to say that all human beings must be concerned with freedom, authenticity, and responsibility could be described as elitist, because it assumes that they have nothing more urgent – such as survival – to worry about. While it caricatures what philosophers such as Sartre really wrote, it highlights the fact that responsibility and authenticity are incredibly demanding criteria, especially if they are required to be granted personhood.

## Responsibility and authenticity as conditions of personhood

For the reasons highlighted above, using responsibility and authenticity as necessary conditions of personhood may well prevent too many human beings, and perhaps too many non-human beings as well, from being regarded as persons. This might satisfy those who never want to see non-human beings access personhood, but what about all the infants, children, teenagers, and, according to existentialists, slightly shallow adults who do not fit the criteria either? Is personhood meant to be an exclusive club of authentic beings? Given that personhood is the basis for respect and for many rights, it seems difficult to justify the exclusion of so many people.

Of course, responsibility and authenticity would work well as sufficient conditions of personhood, because they are so hard to attain that anyone who does face up to their responsibilities and lives authentically surely deserves to be called a person. These demanding criteria illustrate the importance of the difference between necessary and sufficient conditions: saying that all authentic beings are persons is very different from saying that only authentic beings are persons!

Although we might reject existentialist ideals as too demanding to be used as necessary conditions of personhood, the message that existentialists convey is still a valuable and relevant one. It surely is worth encouraging people to think about what they want to do with their life without going through it blindly, and to reflect upon the kind of person they want to be. It seems that, instead of describing what a person is, existentialists focused on what a *good* person *should be like*. This is another subtle distinction that may be very interesting for you to think about: what is a *good* person? What are the characteristics of a *good* human being? Can animals and machines ever fit into those characteristics too?

## FIND OUT MORE

In this section we have explored some possible criteria of personhood: consciousness, self-consciousness, agency, morality and moral responsibility, and responsibility and authenticity.

There are many more possible criteria, however, including the following:

- Rationality
- Complex emotions
- Empathy
- Artistic creativity
- Spirituality or religious faith
- Language

In this section, you have been given the tools to think about one or several of those possible characteristics. You can apply the same process to any of them, following the steps you have been guided through:

- What does this characteristic mean? What does it involve?
- Who or what possesses this characteristic?
- Could this characteristic be a necessary condition of personhood?
- What would be the philosophical implications?

## What is a person? Some concluding thoughts

- Thinking about the characteristics that make a person has become an increasingly "threatening" exercise for humanity: a body of evidence seems to point out that human beings are not unique and that many of the qualities they thought they were the only ones to possess are found in very evolved animals, and are close to being replicated in machines. For this reason, we will focus on animals and machines in the rest of this chapter.
- According to some thinkers, it is futile to try to cling to the specialness and sacredness of humanity, at this moment in history. Instead, it is worth thinking seriously about implications for the beings that are similar to us. Do evolved animals need more rights? Should we be allowed to keep dolphins, elephants and apes in captivity, for example? When will machines need rights? Will that ever happen?
- Another interesting consequence of discussing the ways in which other beings are similar to us is that it allows us to understand

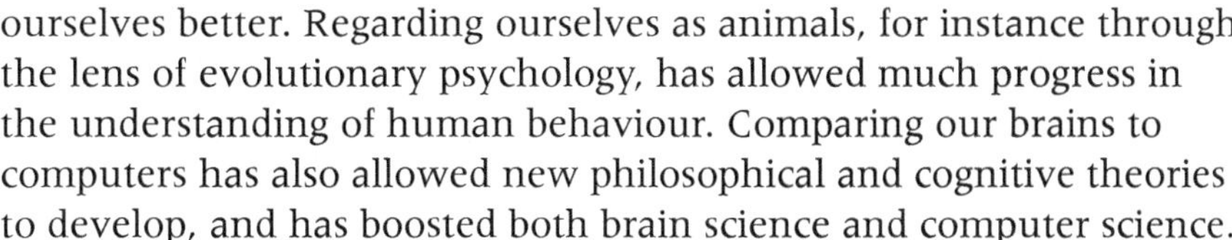

ourselves better. Regarding ourselves as animals, for instance through the lens of evolutionary psychology, has allowed much progress in the understanding of human behaviour. Comparing our brains to computers has also allowed new philosophical and cognitive theories to develop, and has boosted both brain science and computer science.

- Philosophically, we can still become immobilized by our desire to keep humanity special. This can result in logical inconsistencies. If characteristics such as self-consciousness, agency or rationality are what make a person, then some animals *are* persons, and some people just *aren't*. This is the most logical conclusion, yet we seem to find it very difficult to accept.
- As we saw in this section, this leaves us with a difficult dilemma: either we accept that there are conditions of personhood and that some human beings do not fulfil them while some animals do, or we claim that human beings are all persons, regardless of the characteristics they possess. This second option may or may not include animals and other beings as persons, but the same criteria clearly do not apply to human and non-human beings, hence the logical inconsistency. While this may be sustainable if this is backed up by religious arguments (i.e. the sanctity of human life above all other life), there is clearly a philosophical problem that needs resolving: maintaining the special status of human beings has become more and more difficult, and a new paradigm might well be emerging.

## Personhood and non-human animals

There is an obvious sense in which non-human animals are not human, by definition, because they do not belong to the species *Homo sapiens*. So, asking whether other animals are "human" is either an imprecise or a not very interesting question. However, it is still instructive to think about non-human animals in relation to human beings, as the comparison raises a number of interesting philosophical questions. The concept of personhood is a particularly helpful way of approaching the problem of how we should understand other animals and how they in turn help us understand ourselves as human beings. Could non-human animals be persons? How would we define their personhood? Why would this matter? We can begin this discussion simply by looking at the concepts already encountered.

| Are animals persons? Are they ... | If so, how do they compare with humans? |
|---|---|
| self-conscious? | Do they have "higher" or "lower" consciousness? |
| free agents? | Do they deserve similar freedoms? |
| authentic, individual? | Do they have the rights of human individuals? |
| morally responsible? | Do they have equal moral value, dignity? |
| creative, expressive, emotional? | Do they have significant feelings? |
| rational? | Do they think like humans? |

## EXERCISE

1. Write down the names of three very different types of non-human animal. Which of these is the most similar and which most different from human beings? In what sense? What animal characteristics do you regard fundamentally as: Important? Controversial? Morally significant? Ambiguous? Distinctive? Common? (Written answer/discussion.)
2. Identify media reports concerning a recent animal rights/status controversy (e.g. testing, hunting, etc.). Analyse these reports for philosophical concepts or assumptions. Is the concept of personhood used implicitly or explicitly in the articles?
3. Look at the quotes below. Write a brief explanation and response to two of them.

| | |
|---|---|
| "Man is the only animal for whom his own existence is a problem which he has to solve." —Eric Fromm | "The animal is ignorant of the fact that he knows. The man is aware of the fact that he is ignorant." —Victor Hugo |
| "Human language appears to be a unique phenomenon, without significant analogue in the animal world." —Noam Chomsky | "Man is an animal that makes bargains: no other animal does this – no dog exchanges bones with another." —Adam Smith |
| "People speak sometimes about the 'bestial' cruelty of man, but that is terribly unjust and offensive to beasts, no animal could ever be so cruel as a man, so artfully, so artistically cruel." —Fyodor Dostoevsky | "Answer me, you who believe that animals are only machines. Has nature arranged for this animal to have all the machinery of feelings only in order for it not to have any at all?" —Voltaire |
| "Animals are my friends ... and I don't eat my friends." —George Bernard Shaw | "The greatness of a nation and its moral progress can be judged by the way its animals are treated." —Mahatma Gandhi |

## Anthropocentrism: the human monopoly on personhood

Before entering in depth into the problem of whether animals could possess the qualities of personhood, and of what this would mean for humans if they did, we should first consider the "standard" view that has dominated philosophy for centuries. That is, the presumed centrality of the human species as the most important, advanced, and powerful species has kept animals out of the picture philosophically speaking. The theory that humans are of central importance to the universe as we know it is called **anthropocentrism**, and it reflects the tendency to think in human terms and from a human perspective. Remember all the books you read as a young child. Were they about animals? Were they *really* about animals? In the way that authors anthropomorphize animal characters and make their problems into human problems, they show the seemingly universal tendency to see things from a human perspective. Are animals not just another feature of the human world? What is a dog, if not man's best friend?

There are a number of sources of and arguments for anthropocentrism, and all roughly assume that significant personhood is a unique characteristic of the human species. Ancient Greek philosophy elevated the rational and linguistic capabilities of humans as a way of setting them apart from other living creatures. Aristotle, for example, sets humanity apart on the grounds that humans are politically sociable and intelligent. The classic statement of this in the *Nicomachean Ethics* (I.13) attempts to make a clear division between different forms of life, with humans having the "highest" ability of reason, beyond animal instincts and plant-like nutrition. This forms a hierarchy of life, thus:

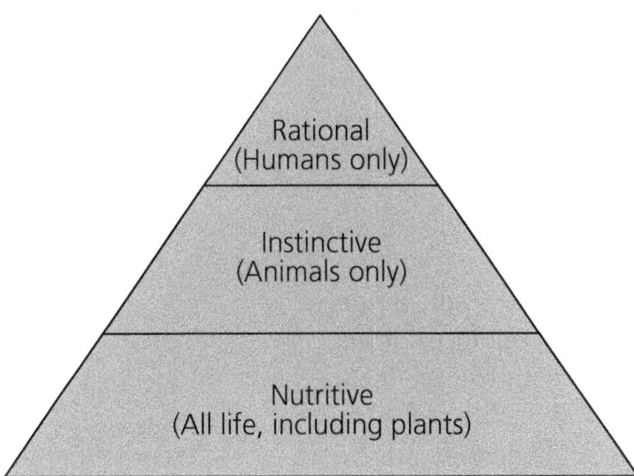


What is the evidence for this? Humans can plan and execute projects. They can think "teleologically", in terms of end results, and see intelligibility in nature. Humans build huge social institutions and advanced technologies. If you regard such observations as putting humans at the top of the pyramid, then you would tend to agree with Aristotle. There are of course some obvious objections to this and we will develop these in detail later on: certain non-human animals may be more intelligent and sociable than Aristotle realized, and some might object to rationality being used as a criterion of value in the first place (what about people with mental disabilities?). Nevertheless, we can for now observe that Aristotle's arguments have been influential and part of a dominant paradigm for how we see animals in relation to humans.

Just as influential has been religious anthropocentrism, which has advanced some different arguments from those of Aristotle. For example, in the Judeo-Christian tradition, the doctrine of Creation takes central place, arguing from the concept of God as the benevolent Creator of heaven and earth to the theory that humans are the pinnacle of that Creation: "Let us make mankind in our image, in our likeness, so that they may rule over the fish in the sea and the birds in the sky, over the livestock and all the wild animals, and over all the creatures that move along the ground" (Genesis 1:26). The idea of God is in itself somewhat anthropic, in the sense that God uses human language and professes to have a unique bond with humans as their "Father". Religious anthropocentrism also puts forward the argument that humans belong to a moral community in a way that is distinct from animals. For example, biblical commandments bind humans in a relationship, a covenant, with God, and, although right treatment of animals is mandatory (for example, "do not muzzle an ox while it is treading out the grain" (Deuteronomy 25:4), it is clear that only humans bear personal moral responsibility, as in the commandments to Israel (for example, Exodus 20). There are also objections to these arguments for their theological foundations and moral assumptions. Still, we can note for the time being that these ideas have been highly influential.

## FIND OUT MORE

Investigate the status of animals in non-Western religions, including the concepts of rebirth and reincarnation in Buddhism and Hinduism. What connections can be made with the concept of personhood?

## Questions

1. Considering the concepts of personhood discussed earlier in this chapter, how convincing are the arguments in favour of anthropocentrism? Do concepts of personhood support or undermine anthropocentrism?
2. How popular are the arguments from Aristotle and religion today? If these arguments endure, why is this?
3. Is it even possible for a human being to think in a way that does not place central importance on human beings?

## Descartes: the mental distinction between humans and animals

Anthropocentrism implicitly denies animals the quality of personhood, but the traditional arguments and assumptions have generally not offered a sustained theory supporting the inferiority of non-human life. The supposition that humans have superiority on many levels is often held at the level of assumption, seemingly being a self-evident part of the "natural order". However, the status of personhood in non-human animals rose to the level of a significant philosophical problem in the work of Descartes, who sought to identify the rational human soul as a unique entity within the world. As seen in the discussion of mind and body in Chapter 4, Descartes attempted to prove the distinct, non-physical and immortal nature of the human mind. In thus elevating the human mind, he raised the question of whether this was a singular entity within nature and set himself the task of proving that other animals could not in any way compare with human intelligence. Some of his arguments are familiar from those of Aristotle, but the extended argument he makes linking intelligence to language shows how Descartes wished to offer something much more detailed and persuasive.

Read the following extract from Part V of Descartes' *Discourse on the Method*:

### Biography: René Descartes (1596–1650)

Descartes was a French philosopher and mathematician, widely regarded as the founder of modern, Western philosophy. Initially, he trained as a lawyer, but his interests became more intellectual and philosophical, and his life became dominated by reading and travel. Descartes signed up for military service with the Dutch Republic and spent most of his life in the Netherlands, though he was not a distinguished soldier. Life in the Netherlands suited Descartes well, as it was at this time the academic centre of Europe and allowed its citizens intellectual freedom. Descartes worked intensively on mathematical and philosophical problems, his main aim being the discovery of a foundation for knowledge and a sure basis for physics and other natural sciences. His main contribution to the philosophy of mind comes in his work of 1641, *Meditations on First Philosophy*, which has become a classic text for philosophy students. His initial scepticism about sense perception and focus on self-conscious thinking leads Descartes to the conclusion that man is fundamentally a mind, *res cogitans*, a "**thinking thing**".

> Again, by means of these two tests we may likewise know the difference between men and brutes [animals]. For it is highly deserving of remark, that there are no men so dull and stupid, not even idiots, as to be incapable of joining together different words, and thereby constructing a declaration by which to make their thoughts understood; and that on the other hand, there is no other animal, however perfect or happily circumstanced, which can do the like. Nor does this inability arise from want of organs: for we observe that magpies and parrots can utter words like ourselves, and are yet unable to speak as we do, that is, so as to show that they understand what they say; in place of which men born deaf and dumb, and thus not less, but rather more than the brutes, destitute of the organs which others use in speaking, are in the habit of spontaneously inventing certain signs by which they discover their thoughts to those who, being usually in their company, have leisure to learn their language.
>
> It is also very worthy of remark, that, though there are many animals which manifest more industry than we in certain of their actions, the same animals are yet observed to show none at all in many others: so that the circumstance that they do better than we does not prove that they are endowed with mind, for it would thence follow that they possessed greater reason than any of us, and could surpass us in all things; on the contrary, it rather proves that they are destitute of reason, and that it is nature which acts in them according to the disposition of their organs: thus it is seen, that a clock composed only of wheels and weights can number the hours and measure time more exactly than we with all our skin.[20]

Studying this passage, it is clear that Descartes denies personhood to non-human animals through a range of related factors – you can identify these in the text. Firstly, there is reason and intelligence, following in the tradition of Aristotle. If we value reason above other qualities, it seemingly follows that we will use this feature to judge other forms of life; what possesses less reason would by definition be less valuable. Descartes claims that animals have some seemingly intelligent abilities, but that the overall evidence of their behaviour separates them markedly from humans. Clocks are better at calculating time than humans, but that one narrow ability does not make them intelligent. What matters is the flexible and adaptable nature of the human mind, and its readiness to solve new problems. This also then opens the door to discussion of agency and free will. Humans can have very great physical limitations – they can be deaf and dumb – and yet still possess the spontaneity, creativity, and power to choose some other solution, be it sign language, writing, or any other ingenious medium of the human mind. The parrot provides a perfect contrast for Descartes, because it has an apparent ability to use language but in fact can only mechanically repeat sounds. Think about art, poetry, and the richness of human creative output; even if non-human animals could match the physical capabilities of humans, they would not even begin to compare in terms of the qualities of their actions. Then, finally, all of this links to his wider argument about human self-consciousness. As seen in the Mind and Body chapter, humans are identified for their ability to think and also to *recognize* their own thoughts. Language and intelligence are necessary foundations for self-consciousness; I cannot acknowledge my own existence unless I have the words to do so. For Descartes, therefore, the animal that

[20] René Descartes, *Discourse on the Method of Rightly Conducting One's Reason and Seeking Truth in the Sciences* (Leiden, 1637); English translation available at http://www.gutenberg.org/files/59/59-h/59-h.htm#part5 (accessed 21 October 2014).

lacks vocabulary, grammar, syntax, etc. has no recognition of its own existence; no non-human could conceivably be a "person".

From the moment he put forward these arguments, however, Descartes caused controversy, particularly among those who wish to give moral consideration to animals. It seems challenging to suppose that animals do not experience the world in the way that we do or have qualities that we value. Would this not lead to maltreatment of animals? Contrary to Descartes, is there not some way that personhood could be found among animals, even if just in part? One popular response has been the argument that animals do possess conscious awareness in a way that is similar to human beings, even if they cannot express their own self-consciousness as acutely as humans do. The argument goes that animals are aware and have experiences, and that there is such a thing as what it is like to be a dog or a cat, just as there is an experience of being human. We reason to this conclusion by analogy. Animals have body parts like humans have body parts (legs, brains, etc.). They behave like humans behave (eat food, avoid pain, etc.). They respond to sensory stimuli like humans do (react to noise, sight, etc.). Therefore, it seems to be not a great leap of imagination to suppose that animals are aware of having real experiences, that they are conscious.

| **Cartesian argument:**<br>**Animals lack personhood** | **Objection to Descartes:**<br>**By analogy, animals are conscious** |
|---|---|
| Non-human animals lack the qualities: | Non-human animals, like humans, have: |
| • Language | • Distinct body structure/parts |
| • Reason | • Behaviour (individual, social) |
| • Agency | • Responses to stimuli |
| • Consciousness | • Therefore, they probably are conscious |

Does the analogy argument show conclusively that animals are conscious? Should they further be considered in light of concepts such as personhood? Not necessarily, although this is a popular conclusion. Consider pain, for example. Is responding to pain actually the same thing as experiencing pain? On first inspection it seems obvious: whatever responds to pain must be experiencing pain. However, it could be argued that externally observable behaviour does not prove that there is an internal state of *feeling* the pain stimulus. Taking arguments put forward by Peter Harrison (1991), we could build robots that respond to pain without them having the subjective feeling of what pain is like. The simplest organisms (amoebas) respond to pain, even though we are fairly certain that they do not experience it. So, how do we know that an animal has experiences like human experiences? Are we really justified in supposing that animal consciousness is even broadly the same as human? Such questions remain controversial. They have an obvious ethical dimension, though they are also simply part of the wider issue of how we understand non-human animals.

## Evolutionary perspective: humans as animals

The origins of human beings were something of a mystery even in early modern times, in the time of Descartes, in the sense that there seemed to be no academic way to look beyond established philosophical arguments and the biblical text. The dominant role of human beings in the natural order seemed to be a given thing (it still is to many), with humans enjoying power over domesticated animals and observing a tradition of interpreting themselves as possessing the divine image. Descartes built upon this with rationalism, trying to refine distinctions between human and non-human through mental faculties. However, part of his argument was doomed to failure in the long run, in that natural science would come to undermine the categorical distinctions between human and other animals. That is, the theory of evolution clearly links the emergence of the human species to more primitive ancestor species, and to the "cousins" of *Homo sapiens* – other primates.

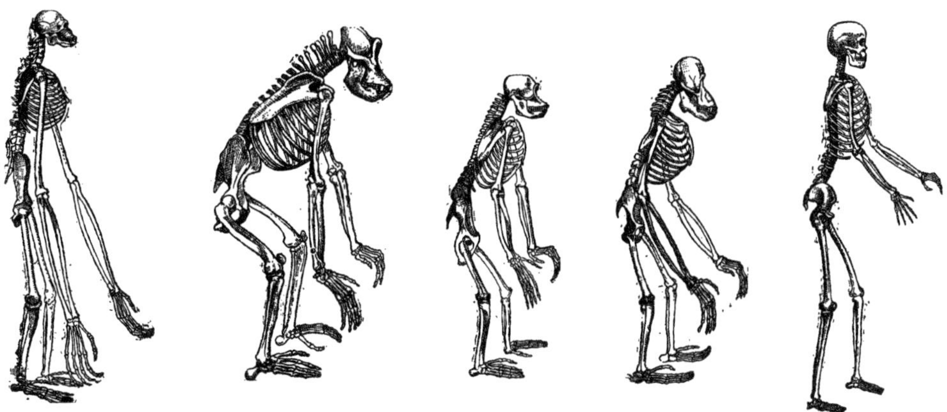

▲ Hominidae skeletons

### FIND OUT MORE

Research the details of Darwin's theory of evolution and the way it was first received by the public. Find out the reasons for the controversy that surrounded Darwin's theory.

You could start by reading the sections on Darwin in Chapters 2 and 6.

▲ A cartoon from *Punch* magazine illustrating Darwin's theory of evolution

The central argument presented by Darwin in his key work *On the Origin of Species* (1859) was that organisms develop over time (they "evolve") through their adaptation to their surroundings. Those organisms that are best suited to their environment are more likely to survive and reproduce, and thus by means of this natural selection the most advantageous characteristics are passed down. In the case of humans, previous generations of primates became biologically successful particularly through the development of language, problem solving, and social skills, and thus the very advanced primates – *Homo sapiens* (humans) – emerged.

How does this affect the concept of personhood? It could be argued that humans, since Darwin, can no longer identify themselves exclusively as persons, at the expense of other animals. The argument would go something like this:

- Human characteristics are related to and derived from animal characteristics.
- Humans cannot literally support creation myths about their own special status.
- The characteristics of all animals have developed and will develop over time.

Personhood thus becomes an evolved aspect of human beings and would be derived from a spectrum of features and abilities, rather than anything absolute. But does this entail that personhood no longer sets humans apart?

## Bentham and Singer: sentience and suffering

Another distinctive development of the modern world, alongside the natural scientific view of humans exemplified by Darwin, was the concept of social progress. Politicians, philosophers, and writers hailed the emergence of an enlightened era from the "primitive" customs of previous generations. Many of the ethical norms that are widely taken for granted today emerged from the rapid changes of the 18th and 19th centuries: the abolition of slavery, child labour, and corporal punishment, the extension of the popular vote, of legal protections, and so forth. This put moral emphasis upon the welfare of human beings, seeing their long-term happiness as a central consideration of society. Putting the interests of a wider group of humans into consideration (slaves, women, children), there seemed to be an expanded view of personhood that went beyond the intellectualism of an elite minority. Politically and ethically, modern society has become "inclusive", meaning that it has recognized the distinct value of a diverse range of persons in different ethnic groups, classes, sexual orientations, abilities, disabilities, and so on. With a wider view of the persons who have an interest in our society, the status of animals could come under renewed scrutiny. Should we not also include animals among those who receive our care and consideration?

A key theorist who brought a fresh perspective on the status of animals was the English legal reformer and philosopher Jeremy Bentham. He is famed for his development of **utilitarianism**, an ethical theory that equates goodness with the maximization of pleasure for the greatest number of people. Bentham argued accordingly that social and legal decisions should be taken in light of utilitarian principles, leading to policies that would bring the greatest benefit for the majority of all. Human values therefore are traced back to hedonism, in that all humans act in a way that will bring about pleasure and avoid what is painful. Dispensing with previous historical, mythological, and philosophical views of the human condition, Bentham put new emphasis on this seemingly simple and scientific principle. His central consideration was neither the mental prowess nor the divine origins of human beings, but instead their ability to feel, have experiences, and suffer. Bentham set aside traditional notions of personhood and instead evaluated humans in light of sentience.

### Questions

1. Does human evolution undermine the mental distinctions made by Descartes?
2. Could humans have evolved to become something very different from animals?
3. Is humanity the pinnacle of evolution, or is that an arrogant perspective?
4. Does evolution morally equalize humans and other animals?

But how does this affect animals? Bentham deals with other animals and their share in sentience in a famous passage from his key utilitarian text, *An Introduction to the Principles of Morals and Legislation* (1789):

> But is there any reason why we should be suffered to torment them [animals]? Not any that I can see. Are there any why we should *not* be suffered to torment them? Yes, several. The day has been, I grieve to say in many places it is not yet past, in which the greater part of the species, under the denomination of slaves, have been treated by the law exactly upon the same footing as, in England for example, the inferior races of animals are still. The day *may* come, when the rest of the animal creation may acquire those rights which never could have been withholden from them but by the hand of tyranny. The French have already discovered that the blackness of the skin is no reason why a human being should be abandoned without redress to the caprice of a tormentor. It may come one day to be recognized, that the number of the legs, the villosity of the skin, or the termination of the *os sacrum*, are reasons equally insufficient for abandoning a sensitive being to the same fate. What else is it that should trace the insuperable line? Is it the faculty of reason, or, perhaps, the faculty of discourse? But a full-grown horse or dog is beyond comparison a more rational, as well as a more conversable animal, than an infant of a day, or a week, or even a month, old. But suppose the case were otherwise, what would it avail? the question is not, Can they *reason*? nor, Can they *talk*? but, Can they *suffer*?[21]

## Biography: Jeremy Bentham (1748–1832)

Bentham grew up the child of a wealthy London family, gaining a reputation for academic brilliance at a young age, and entered Oxford University at the age of 12! He studied but did not practise the law, investing his energies into reforming and radical causes, and the publication of various political, legal, and ethical proposals. One such idea was the construction of a "Panopticon": a new form of prison designed to give guards constant supervision of all prisoners, cutting costs and the danger of disturbance. Such radical and practical plans give a flavour of Bentham's thinking; he advocated for the organization of society along utilitarian lines, maximizing the happiness of the majority. Throughout his career, Bentham considered himself forward thinking and a man of science, and nothing typified this better than the arrangements he made to dispose of his corpse after death. Having left his body to science, his remains were preserved in a glass box (the "auto-icon"), including his mummified head, and put on display in University College London. The icon can still be visited today, though the head is stored separately.

▲ The "auto-icon" of Jeremy Bentham, with his mummified head before it was removed for separate storage.

[21] Jeremy Bentham, "Chapter XVII: The Boundary around Penal Jurisprudence", in *An Introduction to the Principles of Morals and Legislation* (Privately printed, 1789/Oxford: Oxford University Press, 1907); now available at http://www.earlymoderntexts.com/pdfs/bentham1780.pdf (accessed 21 October 2014).

## EXERCISE

1. Rank the following organisms in terms of the consideration we should give to their suffering. Explain your approach. Or, is it impossible to rank them? (Explain.)
   - Earthworm
   - Chimpanzee
   - Cockroach
   - Rabbit
   - Shark
   - Rat
2. Examine the arguments in favour of vegetarianism put forward by a campaign group. (Research.) How important is sentience in such discussions? Is a focus on sentience rational/justified?
3. Research the current legal status of non-human animals in your country and produce a briefing document or chart. Do they have legal protections, etc.? Does the rationale for such laws connect with Bentham? (Reflections.)

In recent years, the arguments of Bentham have flourished and been reframed by utilitarian philosophers taking subtly different approaches. One such figure is the Australian ethicist Peter Singer, who advocates **preference utilitarianism**. That is, while Bentham had advocated hedonism for the majority, Singer emphasizes the satisfaction of preferences; goodness is not simple pleasure, but is the possibility of choosing things and having one's interests fulfilled. These interests are not narrowly defined, however, and one of the key components for the state of having interests is sentience, the capacity to feel, which played such a strong role in Bentham's assessment of animals. Other factors also contribute to one's possession of significant interests that are worthy of being valued, such as reason or planning for the future, but sentience is at the core. The limitation of moral thinking to humans alone would be an example of mistaken prejudice that Singer terms "speciesism". Previous discussions of personhood in philosophy thus by implication have taken wrong approaches (for example, Descartes) in drawing hard distinctions between humans and animals that, on closer inspection, seem arbitrary.

We can look at the ideas of personhood as sitting on a spectrum, as opposed to being absolute qualities that only humans have. For example, humans exercise rational thought, so do chimpanzees to a lesser extent, and dogs to a lesser extent still, and so on, but at no point is there a hard boundary between the rational and the non-rational, as Aristotle and Descartes had suggested. As Singer points out in his classic work *Animal Liberation* (1975), some adult non-human animals make a better fit with concepts of personhood than infant humans. An adult orang-utan would be a better problem-solver and more socially aware than an infant human, and thus surely would be closer to being a "person".[22]

[22] See Peter Singer, *Animal Liberation*, new edition (New York: HarperCollins, 2002).

Meanwhile, the religious absolute that is known as the Sanctity of Life doctrine (namely, God made man in his image, human dignity is inviolable) is dismissed by Singer and others as mythological, as there is no evidence for this special creation of humans. So, with its foundations seemingly demolished, how could human exceptionalism be justified?

**FIND OUT MORE**

What are the ethical implications of Singer's arguments? Research his ideas for putting preference utilitarianism into practice, in respect of animals.

Read Singer's article in the *New York Review of Books* on "Animal Liberation at 30". How does he contend with his critics?

**http://www.nybooks.com/articles/archives/2003/may/15/animal-liberation-at-30/**

## Does a difference remain?

At first sight, the various concepts of personhood seem to offer some fairly strict borderlines between human and non-human animals: humans are thinkers, planners, agents, moralists, self-aware, individual, and expressive. What other animal could produce the Sistine Chapel or travel into space? However, on closer inspection the strict and precise distinctions break down, and the distinctions between humans and animals seem quite loose and general. We could choose to shift our focus to sentience, which seems to apply strongly to non-human animals. We could also look at personhood characteristics on a spectrum, matching different animals at different developmental stages to varying degrees. Does it follow, therefore, that philosophers should abandon the practice of making distinctions along these lines?

It could be counter-argued that significant differences remain in terms of identifying humans as distinct in respect of personhood, even though these may not be "absolute" or rule out the moral consideration of animals. For example, contemporary American philosopher Christine Korsgaard supports a Kantian approach by putting aside the utilitarian concerns of pleasure and welfare, and instead focuses on the unique human concern for normativity. Only humans reflectively consider the general rightness or wrongness of their actions, or consider whether their impulses fit with the behaviour they would like to exhibit. It is not just a matter of thinking, but of humans developing a strong self-identity or practical identity that is concerned with morality. Only humans can act in a certain way because they are trying to do what is good; other animals may do something that is intelligent or even compassionate, but not *because* they have first considered the morality of their choices.

However, Korsgaard emphatically is not arguing for an absolute distinction in terms of mental characteristics (think of the brain-damaged, for example) and nor is she arguing against the moral consideration of animals. On the contrary, the similarities are as important as differences, and humans often give great value to basic needs such as avoiding pain: needs shared in common with other animals. The interests of non-persons will need to be considered. Humans could still be the only persons, even if they do not make absolute distinctions in the way they treat other life forms.

## Questions

1. How accurate is the term "speciesism" as a characterization of human (mis-) understanding of other animals?
2. If you killed an adult dog to save a human baby, would you be speciesist? Is that the moral equivalent of racism?
3. To what extent does sentience unite humans with other animals?
4. What evidence is there that humans have moral identities and think normatively?

## FIND OUT MORE

Read the essay on "Fellow Creatures" by Christine Korsgaard here: **http://www.people.fas.harvard.edu/~korsgaar/CMK.FellowCreatures.pdf**

Another type of counter-argument, re-establishing some of the distinctions between humans and animals, comes from the English philosopher Roger Scruton. In his work *Animal Rights and Wrongs* he addresses what he sees as the fundamental imbalance in some "liberal" views of the status of animals. That is, there has developed a strong focus on rights and the claims animals have, for example, to live pain-free lives. However, the idea of rights for animals takes the moral concepts out of the setting in which they normally apply. Thus, a "right" would usually apply to someone who could have a respective obligation. You have a right to have your property protected because you have an obligation to refrain from stealing from others. Meanwhile, if we said that an animal had a "right" to be protected from harm, it would be a nonsense to say that animals had obligations of non-harm. The idea of moral status comes from dialogue and interpersonal relations; it comes from the possibility of having a meaningful discussion with the interested parties. In this respect, the lack of linguistic and intellectual ability among animals seems to prevent them from entering a moral community. Animals may have something like personal qualities in some respects, but in this important area of moral equality they are not personal enough. Scruton does not deny the possibility of there being non-human persons, but claims that the current evidence weighs against it.[23]

Equally problematic for Scruton is the "sentimentality" of our thinking about animals, which emphasizes the protection of domesticated animals and those that feature in children's literature (cats, badgers). Animal rights groups may focus on certain species to capture public attention, even though such animals often cause great destruction to other species. This can "infect" our thinking about the status of animals, thinking in an emotive, empathetic, but perhaps also anthropomorphic way about the animals involved. Scruton argues that this confuses our understanding

[23] See Roger Scruton, *Animal Rights and Wrongs*, 3rd edition (New York: Continuum, 2007).

of the status of animals, as notions of personhood become blurred by our emotional attachment to bunny rabbits, for example. But should we not think with equal favour of rabbits and of rats? Or of all animals? Or, should we not rather abandon the simplistic equalizing of the value and nature of animal and human life?

We worry about the status of animals. Animals do not worry about the status of animals. Could there be a substantive distinction from humans after all?

## FIND OUT MORE

Read the interview and extract from Roger Scruton's book in the journal *Antennae*:

**http://www.antennae.org.uk/ANTENNAE%20ISSUE%2019.docx.pdf**

**Assessment tip**

If discussing the status of animals and the problem of personhood, be sure to keep a focus on the core theme issue: being human. This is different from an ethics essay concerned specifically with the treatment of animals.

## Personhood and machines

Personhood is controversial in how it is defined, in terms of what characteristics are necessary or sufficient for the acknowledgement of something/someone as a person. It is also controversial in its application, in terms of how far the status may be extended. Could it include non-human animals? Could there be any such thing as a non-human person? We could think of extra-terrestrial life forms, which would correspond to the concepts of personhood. There is a long tradition of this in philosophy; Kant speculated that there would be intelligent life on other planets. In the realm of science fiction and imagination, the Vulcans and Klingons of *Star Trek* obviously seem to be persons. However, it will not escape any careful viewer of such films that these creatures are also strongly anthropomorphic. They are basically humans with peculiar features. It seems therefore that we are good at imagining a universe full of persons, but not so good at seeing them as non-human persons. Another interesting development along these lines in fiction is the imagined emergence of machine intelligences that resemble persons: intelligent, language-using, autonomous machines. The difference here, however, is that our real-world technology seems to be bringing us increasingly sophisticated machines that resemble more closely those of *Star Trek* (for example, Commander Data), while we are as yet no closer to our first encounter with intelligent alien life forms.

So, are we on the threshold of making and encountering genuine personal machines?

Not exactly, though the speed of development in computing technology is encouraging serious philosophical reflection about what such machines *could be* in principle. Such conversations are driven by imagination, by the technological revolution of recent years,

▲ *Star Trek*'s Commander Data. Machine? Human? Human machine? Person? Non-human person? Non-person?

and by the way in which technology is saturating society and being integrated into every conceivable product. Perhaps the starting point for the idea of a machine person as a philosophical possibility is the emergence specifically of machine intelligence. We are accustomed today to referring to any number of machines as "smart" or "intelligent". We impute personal motives to computers. Does your mobile phone "recommend" things to you? Does the opponent in your video game "think" about what it is doing? Our common use of language is accepting of the idea of intelligent machines, but philosophers naturally will want to pick these ideas apart.

## CASE STUDY

### The Kasparov versus Deep Blue Chess Match

In 1997, IBM's Deep Blue became the first computer to defeat a world champion at chess, beating Garry Kasparov by a score of 3.5 to 2.5. This extraordinary feat became world news. While many celebrated this landmark in the development of artificial intelligence (AI), Kasparov was furious, accusing IBM of cheating and demanding a re-match. IBM refused and dismantled its computer. Deep Blue was capable of evaluating 200 different chess positions per second, and was progressively improved (reprogrammed) during junctures in the match, to enable it to avoid the traps that Kasparov had set for the weaker versions of its AI. Deep Blue represents a major technical achievement, but it is questionable whether this takes us nearer to the production of an artificial mind.

- Is it significant that machines can outperform humans in some mental tasks?
- Was Deep Blue "intelligent"?
- Did Deep Blue "understand" the game?
- Was Deep Blue in any sense "aware"?
- Does Deep Blue show us anything about where technology will lead in the future?

▲ Garry Kasparov contemplating his next move against Deep Blue

## Intelligence and imitation: Descartes and Turing

Let us suppose that our interest in machine persons is centred on intelligence: could machines be intelligent in the *way* that humans are intelligent? At first glance this seems like a fairly simple question. We could just see whether we can get machines to do the intelligent things that humans do, such as play chess. However, on further reflection the problem is much murkier than it initially appears. What is this quality? How do we know that humans are intelligent in the first place? One approach is to think of ways of "modelling" human intelligence, making machines that copy intelligent behaviours and processes. That is in a sense what artificial intelligence is: a model. It is an attempt to replicate something that is found organically in humans, though, intriguingly, the possibility is open according to some that such models could surpass the original form. But what kind of model is AI? Philosophers have drawn a distinction between "strong" and "weak" theories of AI, with some advocating that a machine could actually *be* a mind in matching the human form of intelligence exactly (strong AI), and others countering that a machine could achieve no such thing in its partial replications and representations of the human (weak AI). But to make any progress in this debate, some steps must first be taken to unpack the idea of how this elusive intelligence could be fairly identified and understood.

This problem has an older origin than one might expect. Going back to Descartes, we already find a hypothetical discussion of attempts to make intelligent machines, which according to Descartes were doomed to failure. In his *Discourse on the Method* he claims that there are two tests that show that machines, even if seemingly human, obviously would remain distinguishable in their lack of intelligence:

- They could not use words or signs arranged in a way that declared thoughts to others; they could make speech sounds, but not reply coherently in conversation.
- They could perform very well in certain specific tasks, but would be found lacking in others; they would lack the reason to have human mental agility.

Descartes acknowledges that these are the same objections he has to regarding non-human animals as being intelligent in the full human sense of the word. The standard he sets, therefore, is the sophisticated manipulation of symbols that is language and the adaptability of performing multiple (and new) tasks. By implication, if machines *appeared* to do such things, Descartes would have to admit that they had intelligence in the form he suggests. Looking at his wider theory of mind (see Chapter 4: Mind and Body), this fits with his contention that the mind is a non-reducible entity, separate from the body. The intelligence in the mind cannot be explained or replicated, he claims, because it is an invisible and completely basic aspect of human beings. So, it would only be possible for machines weakly to ape human actions, without there being a genuine parallel. Naturally, there are objections to his position. We could reject his theory of mind and see this as part of the biological "machine" of the brain. We could claim that computing technology will enable machines to perform sophisticated actions that Descartes could not have anticipated. Nevertheless, he has still set a high benchmark. Could any machine meet the two tests? Are these not fairly reasonable identifiers of uniquely human intelligence?

In the modern era, this Cartesian approach has been developed and challenged through the work of the English mathematician Alan Turing, who also took an interest in the external appearance of machine capabilities. Without a simple way of defining the process of human thought, Turing instead pointed to a test of the phenomenon of intelligence in what has become known as the "imitation game".

## Biography: Alan Turing (1912–1954)

Turing was a mathematician and pioneer of computer science. Born in London, he rapidly progressed in his academic career as a mathematician at Cambridge and then Princeton, and was then recruited by the UK government as part of preparations for war against Germany. With the outbreak of war in 1939, Turing was committed to the intensive work of cracking the German codes. To achieve this goal, Turing and his colleagues produced an electromechanical decryption machine known as the "bombe", which analysed intercepted German messages and tested hypotheses for how the codes could be deciphered. Such efforts met with considerable success. After the war, his expertise in analytical machinery naturally led Turing towards research in the emerging field of computing, running the Manchester University laboratory. However, Turing's life had a tragic end. In the 1950s homosexuality was still illegal in the UK, and Turing was convicted for gross indecency. He was punished in 1952 with chemical castration and died from apparent suicide in 1954. In 2009 the British Prime Minister Gordon Brown issued an apology on behalf of the government for the way Turing was treated, recognizing his contributions to the nation and to the world.

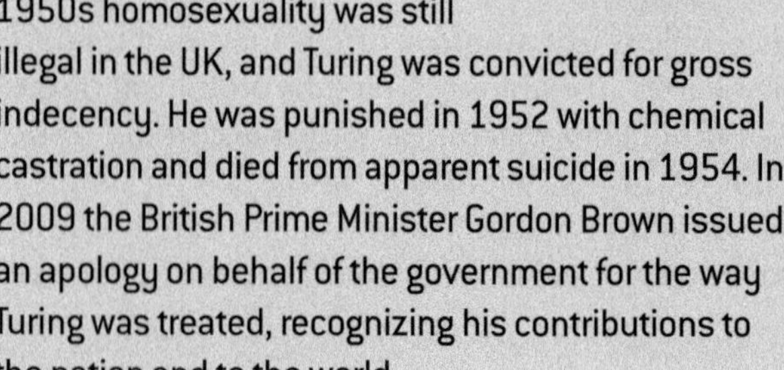

I propose to consider the question, "Can machines think?" This should begin with definitions of the meaning of the terms "machine" and "think". The definitions might be framed so as to reflect so far as possible the normal use of the words, but this attitude is dangerous. If the meaning of the words "machine" and "think" are to be found by examining how they are commonly used it is difficult to escape the conclusion that the meaning and the answer to the question, "Can machines think?" is to be sought in a statistical survey such as a Gallup poll. But this is absurd. Instead of attempting such a definition I shall replace the question by another, which is closely related to it and is expressed in relatively unambiguous words.

The new form of the problem can be described in terms of a game which we call the "imitation game". It is played with three people, a man (A), a woman (B), and an interrogator (C) who may be of either sex. The interrogator stays in a room apart from the other two. The object of the game for the interrogator is to determine which of the other two is the man and which is the woman. He knows them by labels X and Y, and at the end of the game he says either "X is A and Y is B" or "X is B and Y is A". The interrogator is allowed to put questions to A and B thus:

C: Will X please tell me the length of his or her hair?

Now suppose X is actually A, then A must answer. It is A's object in the game to try and cause C to make the wrong identification. His answer might therefore be:

"My hair is shingled, and the longest strands are about nine inches long."

In order that tones of voice may not help the interrogator the answers should be written, or better still, typewritten. The ideal arrangement is to have a teleprinter communicating between the two rooms. Alternatively the question and answers can be repeated by an intermediary. The object of the game for the third player (B) is to help the interrogator. The best strategy for her is probably to give truthful answers. She can add such things as "I am the woman, don't listen to him!" to her answers, but it will avail nothing as the man can make similar remarks.

We now ask the question, "What will happen when a machine takes the part of A in this game?" Will the interrogator decide wrongly as often when the game is played like this as he does when the game is played between a man and a woman? These questions replace our original, "Can machines think?"

—Alan Turing[24]

[24] Alan Turing, "Computing Machinery and Intelligence", *Mind* 49 (1950): 433.

With the idea of "thinking" being unclear, it is difficult to say what we would be looking for if we were to investigate the possibility of thinking machines. Can we define thinking at all? Turing suggests that a more fruitful investigation lies in the comparison of machine and human dialogue, for it is only through our conversations with others that we seem to recognize the act of thinking among our fellow human beings. In a sense, Turing is referring us back to the experience of being human, our observation of plausible language use, and then asks us to consider the question of whether a machine could attain such a level. Certainly, in Turing's own lifetime no machine was developed that could hold any kind of conversation with a human being. To this day, the most advanced computers have failed to meet the standard. However, some would argue that a successful attempt at the imitation game may not be so far away. That would raise the further and interesting question of whether machines would to some degree take on the character of being persons.

## EXERCISE

1. Investigate the Loebner Prize, which is an annual competition for computer scientists attempting to crack Turing's imitation game. Read transcripts of previous conversations and consider the challenges faced in reproducing human language (http://www.loebner.net/Prizef/loebner-prize.html).
2. The 2013 winner Mitsuku is available for conversations online. See whether you can catch her out. Or should that be "it"? (http://www.mitsuku.com/.)
3. Interview Mitsuku and other chatbots about machine intelligence. What do they have to say?

## What is understanding? The big problem for AI

We are concerned with the question of whether machines could be personal and, for that purpose, are focused on the question of whether they are intelligent. But what do we mean by that? We are looking for rational processes, but surely also something more than that. When we think about human intelligence, it is not simply a matter of some number crunching ability. We think of rational abilities as bound up with a number of faculties: language, memory, emotion, creativity, self-awareness. Can we look for something narrowly defined, or is that not misrepresenting the whole nature of the problem? Here arise some basic criticisms of Turing and the imitation game. On the one hand, the simple nature of this approach and the strong focus on our external *experiences* of intelligence make Turing's proposal attractive at first. On the other hand, is passing an intelligence test really the same thing as *being* intelligent? Having a statistical reason to say the right thing (which is how chat computers work) seems not to match with the deliberative self-conscious nature of human thinking. There seems to be a distinction between accurate output and genuine understanding.

At least, that is what John Searle, a contemporary philosopher, argues in the following extract:

Suppose that I'm locked in a room and given a large batch of Chinese writing. Suppose furthermore that I know no Chinese, either written or spoken, and that I'm not even confident that I could recognize Chinese writing. To me, Chinese writing is just so many meaningless squiggles.

Now suppose that after this first batch of Chinese writing I am given a second batch together with a set of rules for correlating the second batch with the first. The rules are in English, and I understand these rules. They enable me to correlate one set of symbols with another; I can identify the symbols entirely by their shapes. Now suppose also that I am given a third batch of Chinese symbols together with instructions in English that enable me to correlate elements of this third batch with the first two, and these rules instruct me how to give back certain Chinese symbols with certain sorts of shapes in response to certain sorts of shapes given me in the third batch. Unknown to me, the people who are giving me all of these symbols call the first batch "a script", the second batch a "story" and the third batch "questions". Furthermore, they call the symbols I give them back in response to the third batch "answers to the questions" and the set of rules in English they call "the program".

Now to complicate the story, imagine that these people also give me stories in English, which I understand, and they then ask me questions in English about these stories, and I give them answers in English. Suppose also that after a while I get so good at following the instructions that, from the external point of view, my answers to the questions are absolutely indistinguishable from those of native Chinese speakers. Nobody just looking at my answers can tell that I don't speak Chinese.

Let us also suppose that my answers to the English questions are indistinguishable from those of other native English speakers, for the simple reason that I am a native speaker. From the external point of view – from the point of view of someone reading my "answers" – the answers to the Chinese and English questions are equally good. But in the Chinese case, unlike the English case, I produce answers by manipulating uninterpreted symbols. As far as the Chinese is concerned, I simply behave like a computer; I perform operations on formally specified elements. For the purposes of the Chinese, I am simply an instantiation of the computer program.

Now the claims made by strong AI are that the programmed computer understands the stories and that the program in some sense explains human understanding. But we are now in a position to examine these claims in light of our thought experiment.

1. As regards the first claim, it seems to me obvious in the example that I do not understand a word of the Chinese stories. I have inputs and outputs that are indistinguishable from those of the native Chinese speaker, and I can have any formal program you like, but I still understand nothing. In the Chinese case the computer is me and in cases where the computer is not me, the computer has nothing more than I have in the case where I understand nothing.
2. As regards the second claim, that the program explains human understanding, we can see that the computer and its program do not provide sufficient conditions of understanding since the computer and the program are functioning, and there is no understanding.

—John Searle[25]

▲ "The Turing Test" by Darren Goossens

[25] John Searle, "Minds, Brains, and Programs", *Behavioural and Brain Sciences* 3, No. 3 (1980): 418–419.

## Questions

1. Does Turing's test lack ambition? Should computer scientists try to replicate *how* the mind works? (Strong AI.)
2. How strong is the analogy between computers and human minds? Why do we make these analogies?
3. Does Searle's thought experiment fairly characterize what is going on inside "intelligent" machines?
4. Should we accept the distinction between apparent and real understanding? What makes understanding "real"?

Seemingly, Searle knocks down the idea that genuine intelligence and understanding can simply be reproduced by computational processes. In the story of the Chinese room, the answers given to the questions could be flawless, and yet the automatic nature of the process seems to lack the qualities that we associate with understanding: no context, no memory, no imagination, no self-conscious awareness of what is happening. The statistical methods used in computing are worlds away from what it is like for us to think.

Nevertheless, there have been attempts to counter-argue against Searle's dismissal of thinking machines. One of the strongest objections is the claim that Searle takes a narrow view of agency, focusing on whether the man working in the Chinese room understands the language. However, could not the room itself be an intelligent system? Could the combination of the room, the books, the man, add up to a system that acts intelligently and understands Chinese? Searle counters by claiming that this argument produces an absurdity, that "mind is everywhere", because it could be found in any system producing intelligible results. But the whole point of investigating the mind is to look for something discrete and identifiable. A second objection is that we could hypothetically build a robot that did not learn language through written instructions only, but which gathered data about the world through sensory equipment, like a camera. The robot could then work out how language works on the basis of experiences. This argument has the advantage of matching more closely the process of human language acquisition. However, Searle remains unconvinced; merely adding the performance of operations (movement, speech) does not get around the central problem that the robot only does the right actions or sayings on the basis of formal instructions (for how else could it "understand" what it encountered?). It would still be a Chinese room on wheels.

Summary

| **Alan Turing:** **Machines can "think" in imitation** | **John Searle:** **Answering is not understanding** |
| --- | --- |
| Proposal: A form of weak AI can stand as "thinking" if it replicates the appearance of thinking through a blind language test. Any other account of thinking lacks a clear definition. | Proposal: Correct output cannot be equated with understanding, as it is possible to envisage a system that gives correct outputs without appreciating the meaning. |
| Criticisms:<br>• Surely real thinking should be linked to strong AI, thinking in the *way* humans think.<br>• In practice, machines have fared very poorly in attempting to pass the imitation game. | Criticisms:<br>• The "systems objection": the man in the Chinese room does not understand, but the system of the room does.<br>• We could build a robot that had experiences and then learned language from those experiences. |

## Minds, machines, and the problem of consciousness

As we have seen, the question of whether machines could count as rational or intelligent is a contentious one. A lot depends on our starting definitions and assumptions, and then there is the wider issue of how "reason" connects with other human attributes. Would a rational machine approximate in any way to being human? Are humans not intelligent persons in rather a broad sense, encompassing an array of emotions, dispositions, and creative capabilities that do not correspond very well to a computer program? Perhaps, although it also seems unwise to place limitations on what computers could come to be in the future.

Another way of approaching the problem of machines as persons is to reverse the question. Instead of examining the ways in which machines can be constructed to model human personalities, we could instead ask whether computing helps us to analyse the workings of the human mind. In this way, the philosophy of artificial intelligence becomes linked with the philosophy of mind. Specifically, the theory of functionalism (see Chapter 4: Mind and Body) asserts that the human mind can be fully explained by what it does (i.e. its functions), rather than what it is, so that it could in theory be replicated by other means. The mind performs a huge variety of functions and calculations at great speed, to the extent that we might best understand it as a form of biological, evolved supercomputer. After all, we have learned that computation can be used in a very basic way to control movement, give responses, and so forth, in the case of robots. This is *not* to say that we are on the threshold of building computers that really are as capable as human brains (far from it), but the example of the computer is seen as a useful way of explaining the mind. Thinking in terms of personhood, we might say that the personal human mind is defined by very high levels of functioning, and the less personal computer minds are (currently) defined by more basic levels of functioning.

In offering a reductive view of consciousness, functionalism also implicitly offers a reductive view of personhood. That is, in claiming that the human mind can be thoroughly and completely explained in terms of what it does, all of the "higher" functions of personhood would also in principle be parts of that explanation. If we are functionalists, we say that we could (one day) work out the systems that give rise to self-consciousness, reason, agency, morality, and so forth. In principle, however far off that may be, we should be able to get there in the end. That at least is the starting premise of a number of great works of science fiction, which take the future "mapping" of the personality in machine form to be an important stimulus for storytelling. Consider the opening scene from the classic film *AI: Artificial Intelligence*.

*Hobby* (a leading robotics scientist): Tell me, what is love?

*Sheila* (a robot): Love is first widening my eyes a little bit and quickening my breathing a little and warming my skin and touching with my...

*Hobby*: And so on. Exactly so. Thank you, Sheila. But I wasn't referring to sensuality simulators. The word that I used was love. Love like the love of a child for its parents. I propose that we build a robot child, who can love. A robot child who will genuinely love the parent or parents it imprints on, with a love that will never end.

*Team Member No.3*: A child substitute mecha?

*Hobby*: But a mecha with a mind, with neuronal feedback. You see what I'm suggesting is that love will be the key by which they acquire a kind of subconscious never before achieved. An inner world of metaphor, of intuition, of self-motivated reasoning. Of dreams.

*Team Member No.4*: A robot that dreams?

*Hobby*: Yes.

*Team Member No.4*: And how exactly do we pull this off?

*Female Team Member*: You know, it occurs to me ... um ... with all this animus existing against mechas today, it isn't simply a question of creating a robot who can love, but isn't the real conundrum – can you get a human to love them back?

*Hobby*: Ours will be a perfect child caught in a freeze-frame – always loving, never ill, never changing. With all the childless couples yearning in vain for a license, our little mecha would not only open an entirely new market, it will fill a great human need.

*Female Team Member*: But you haven't answered my question. If a robot could genuinely love a person, what responsibility does that person hold toward that mecha in return? It's a moral question, isn't it?

*Hobby*: The oldest one of all. But in the beginning, didn't God create Adam to love him?[26]

[26] *AI: Artificial Intelligence*, 2001, directed by Steven Spielberg, distributed by DreamWorks.

As *AI: Artificial Intelligence* so beautifully illustrates, the functionalist view of personhood is at once beguiling and also frightening, as it points towards a world in which humans can pick apart their most treasured characteristics and recreate them, synthetically. Can we create love? If we did, what then? Are humans ready for synthetic personhood, ready for the God-like power of creating life in our own image? As the film points out, this problem takes us back to a moral question.

However, the fantasy of film leans rather heavily on the assumed strength of functionalism as a way of understanding the potential of machines. If functionalists are wrong about the mind, they will also be wrong about the possibility of machine minds. The obvious criticism is that replicating human behaviour cannot be equated with the state of being a human or having the experiences of what that is like. It could be said that creating a mind artificially is self-defeating because it is by its nature only a simulation: the mind is specifically brought about by the biology of the brain. For example, it could also be said that an entirely accurate computer model of a plumbing system is distinct from something that carries real water. Similarly, it could be further argued that consciousness is subjective in its nature and the feel of what it is like to be human cannot be recreated, even if all human actions and language are successfully simulated (see the argument of David Chalmers in Chapter 4: Mind and Body). Finally, there is the claim that some questions are simply closed off from humans and there are mysteries that we are not mentally equipped to answer. The problem of human consciousness, the experience of being human, could be one such mystery. Thus, the practical problem of making the smartest possible machines rubs up against a fundamental metaphysical problem: what is the real essence of human existence?

## Questions

1. If functionalism is true, how can we know that it is true?
2. If machines could be persons, does it follow that other animals could be too?
3. Is personhood a set of functions? If it isn't, what is it?
4. Is it ethically justifiable for humans to create synthetic persons?

## FIND OUT MORE

Investigate the concept of "transhumanism". How does this link to machines? What are the implications of this for personhood?

## Assessment tip

Think about the different stimuli that could be used to connect with core theme topics. Thinking of your own ideas for a stimulus will help you develop the skill of identifying issues in the material. Look out for texts and images that will help you to do this. For example, in this topic think about: machines, technology, computers, intelligence, the internet, etc.

## FINAL REFLECTION

Looking at the concept of personhood, the problem remains of whether we can define human beings and the experience of being human through certain qualities and criteria. Are humans *defined* through self-consciousness, agency, morality, authenticity, and so forth? Can this concept of personhood be seen as the exclusive property of humans? Do humans define and shape the world around them, in light of these concepts? Philosophers have had much to say about these problems and our rapidly changing world will continue to provoke new issues and debates.

### Link with the Core Theme - Personhood and Being Human

By traditional and established ways of thinking, being a person *is* being human. We recognise the exceptional nature of human life and experience through ideas and symbols, be they religious (God created man "in his image"), philosophical (Aristotle's man, the "rational animal"), or poetic, artistic, and creative. Thus, the concepts of personhood this chapter has explored (self-consciousness, agency, morality, authenticity) have all been used to define the human condition and identify humans in an exclusive way. Anthropocentrism has been a dominant paradigm for interpreting human experience because *only* humans have been seen as self-conscious, *only* humans have been attributed with agency, morality and authenticity. Personhood seems to have been a conceptual way of bolstering human status, reinforcing the moral order, and giving meaning to the human condition. A person has a purpose.

Nevertheless, the established ways of thinking have been questioned and the simple equation of being human with personhood could be challenged on a number of levels. The concepts and criteria themselves are open for debate. What *is* self-consciousness, agency, morality, authenticity? Are these 'real' human properties or are they more dubious concepts, legacies of our language and culture? And can they be exclusively attributed to humans anyway? The differentiation between humans and non-human animals is subject to a strong and developing debate. The growth of 'smart' technology also threatens to throw the status of being human into further controversy. Perhaps the idea of personhood now challenges the idea of the 'human', rather than clarifying it.

### Personhood: assessment tips

Below are two stimuli taken from past papers, that can be related to the key concept of personhood:

## Stimulus 3:

(November 2002)

## Stimulus 4:

Human beings are animals with a peculiar character and role. They are ... alert to the values of personhood, life, order, and existence as such, to his or her community, to his or her environment, to the cosmos. As a member of the community of nature, the human being may be regarded as guardian of respect for it, to exercise reverence towards it and, if it has a maker, towards its maker.

Source: Extract from David Braine, *The Human Person: Animal and Spirit* (Notre Dame: University of Notre Dame Press) (November 2010)

## ACTIVITIES:

1. Match each stimulus with one of the topics covered in this chapter:
   - Consciousness and self-consciousness
   - Agency
   - Morality and moral responsibility
   - Responsibility and authenticity
   - Personhood and non-human animals
   - Personhood and machines
2. Why do you think the match you chose is a good one? How would you justify your choice of topic in your introduction?

Your main task in the introduction is to identify the philosophical issue you will be discussing and establish its link with three key elements: your own knowledge (the theories and philosophers you will be discussing), the stimulus and the general core theme of being human. None of these important elements must be lost along the essay, and establishing them firmly in the introduction will help you remember them as you develop your arguments.

The core of you essay is the **philosophical issue**, because it will direct you argumentation and discussion. The philosophical issue must be identified clearly. Its scope must be appropriate to the length of an essay you will write under one hour. "Personhood" in general is probably too broad. Equally, you need to know enough about an issue before you choose it as your focus for an entire essay.

Another thing to keep in mind is that the philosophical issue needs to be *discussed*. Presenting your philosophical issue as a source of debate and showing that it can be viewed from different perspectives will help you make sure you go beyond mere description in your essay. A good way to present your philosophical issue, for instance, is to use an open question that can clearly be answered in different ways.

Here is an example for the following stimulus:

**Assessment tip**

The Core Theme assessment asks you to do the following:

*With explicit reference to the stimulus and your own knowledge, discuss a philosophical issue related to the question of what it means to be human.*

Introduction written by a student:

The stimulus is an image of a man and a monkey touching each other's fingers. A philosophical theme depicted in this image is that of personhood. The monkey's action has a certain quality to it that many would describe as human. By pointing and sharing a moment with the human, the question begged is: can a non-human animal be a person? And furthermore, what constitutes a person? There are numerous approaches to the issue of personhood dating as far back as Aristotle (and also arguably Plato). This issue as an ever-growing importance as in recent years the question of how humans should treat animals has become central to numerous debates.

**Comments:** This is a good introduction, that clearly identifies a **key concept** (personhood) and narrows it down to a specific **philosophical issue** (can a non-human animal be a person?) The **stimulus** is clearly used as a basis for the philosophical issue, and the core theme **Being Human** is also present through the broader question: "what constitutes a person?"

It is a good idea to explain why the issue is important and it is done here in the last sentence. However, the writer would need to be careful not to be too side-tracked by this last point, as it could turn the essay into an ethics essay instead of focusing in personhood.

Finally, the writer could improve this introduction by making her **own knowledge** a little clearer. Although she writes that there are "numerous approaches" to this issue, it would be a good idea to explicitly state what approaches she is going to analyse in the essay. A **thesis** could also be added, although this is not always necessary if the central issue and question have been stated clearly.

## ACTIVITIES:

3. Practise turning some of the topics listed in activity 1 (page 120) into good philosophical issues. You can combine topics and make reference to broader ideas such as the key concept of personhood and being human.
4. Practise writing an introduction for stimulus 3 and 4, making sure the philosophical issue you identify is clearly linked to the stimulus, Being Human, and to the knowledge you will bring to the essay (theories and scholars).

## References Cited


Anderson, David L. "What Is a Person?". *Consortium on Cognitive Science Instruction*, 2000. Available at http://www.mind.ilstu.edu/curriculum/what_is_a_person/what_is_a_person.php (accessed 21 October 2014).

Bentham, Jeremy. "Chapter XVII: The Boundary around Penal Jurisprudence". In *An Introduction to the Principles of Morals and Legislation*. Privately printed, 1789/Oxford: Oxford University Press, 1907. Now available at http://www.earlymoderntexts.com/pdfs/bentham1780.pdf (accessed 21 October 2014).

de Waal, Frans. "The Evolution of Empathy". *Greater Good*, 1 September 2005. Available at http://greatergood.berkeley.edu/article/item/the_evolution_of_empathy (accessed 21 October 2014).

Descartes, René. *Discourse on the Method of Rightly Conducting One's Reason and Seeking Truth in the Sciences*. Leiden, 1637. English translation available at http://www.gutenberg.org/ebooks/59?msg=welcome_stranger#part5 (accessed 21 October 2014).

Frankfurt, Harry G. "Freedom of the Will and the Concept of a Person". *The Journal of Philosophy* LXVIII, No. 1 (14 January 1971): 5–20.

Guignon, Charles, and Derk Pereboom (eds). *Existentialism: Basic Writings*, 2nd edition. Indianapolis: Hackett Publishing Company, 2001.

Honderich, Ted (ed.). *The Oxford Companion to Philosophy*. Oxford: Oxford University Press, 1995.

Millican, Peter. "Persons, Humans and Brains". Lecture delivered to first-year Philosophy students. Oxford: Oxford University, 2009. Available at http://www.youtube.com/watch?v=9HhWqBJtPP8 (accessed 21 October 2014).

Nagel, Thomas. "What Is It Like to Be a Bat?". *The Philosophical Review* LXXXIII, No. 4 (October 1974): 435–450.

Patterson, Francine, and Wendy Gordon. "The Case for the Personhood of Gorillas". In *The Great Ape Project*. Edited by Paola Cavalieri and Peter Singer. New York: St Martin's Griffin, 1993, pp. 58–77. Also available at http://www.animal-rights-library.com/texts-m/patterson01.htm (accessed 21 October 2014).

Penal Reform International. "The Minimum Age of Criminal Responsibility". Justice for Children Briefing No. 4, 2013. Available at http://www.penalreform.org/wp-content/uploads/2013/05/justice-for-children-briefing-4-v6-web_0.pdf (accessed 21 October 2014).

Rochat, Philippe. "Five Levels of Self-Awareness as They Unfold Early in Life". *Consciousness and Cognition* 12 (2003): 717–731.

Scruton, Roger. *Animal Rights and Wrongs*, 3rd edition. New York: Continuum, 2007.

Searle, John. "Minds, Brains, and Programs". *Behavioural and Brain Sciences* 3, No. 3 (1980): 417–457.

Singer, Peter. *Animal Liberation*, new edition. New York: HarperCollins, 2002.

Taylor, Richard. *Action and Purpose*. Englewood Cliffs, NJ: Prentice-Hall, 1966. Also available at http://www.informationphilosopher.com/solutions/philosophers/taylorr/ (accessed 21 October 2014).

Turing, Alan. "Computing Machinery and Intelligence". *Mind 49* (1950): 433–460.

Walker, Joseph. "State Parole Boards Use Software to Decide Which Inmates to Release". *The Wall Street Journal*, 11 October 2013. Available at http://online.wsj.com/news/articles/SB10001424052702304626104579121251595240852 (accessed 21 October 2014).

# BEING HUMAN

## 4 Mind and Body

- Concepts of mind and body
- The mind–body problem
- The problem of other minds
- Consciousness

### Some essential questions:

- What does philosophy tell us about the nature of mind and body?
- What, if any, are the relationships between mind and body?
- Why do we believe that other people have minds like ours?
- What do recent advances in neuroscience tell us about how the mind works?

### Stimulus 1

*Craig*: There's a tiny door in that empty office. It's a portal, Maxine. It takes you inside John Malkovich. You see the world through John Malkovich's eyes, then, after about fifteen minutes, you're spit out into a ditch on the side of the New Jersey Turnpike.

*Maxine*: Sounds delightful. . . .

*Craig*: He's an actor. One of the great American actors of the 20th century.

*Maxine*: What's he been in?

*Craig*: Lots of things. He's very well respected. That jewel thief movie, for example. The point is that this is a very odd thing, supernatural, for lack of a better word. It raises all sorts of philosophical questions about the nature of self, about the existence of the soul. Am I me? Is Malkovich Malkovich? Was the Buddha right, is duality an illusion? Do you realize what a metaphysical can of worms this portal is? I don't think I can go on living my life as I have lived it.

—*Being John Malkovich*, screenplay by Charlie Kaufman (Propaganda Films, 1999)

## Stimulus 2

▲ *I, Robot* (2004, directed by Alex Proyas, distributed by 20th Century Fox)

One of the greatest and most recurrent themes of literature is that of a mystical journey. Imagine that you are transported far from your own land, or time, or culture, or even from your own body. You could imagine that you left your physical self far behind, while your conscious awareness floated above. Perhaps you could journey into somebody else's body and see the world through their eyes, as in the cult film *Being John Malkovich*. If you did, would you still be you? Would Malkovich be Malkovich? Would a human still be human? This scenario may seem to be a fantasy, but such stories are an important part of philosophy; they provide alternate worlds in which we can try out our ideas.

Would you enter the portal into John Malkovich's head? Would you keep your identity if you did? Do you have a soul? Would it be corrupted, by stealing somebody else's body? And, is there any such thing as "you" to begin with? Craig, the hapless protagonist and victim of the film, stumbles across these philosophical questions, much to his distress.

Now imagine a different kind of fantasy: a science fiction world. It is a world full of machines, autonomous machines, those that can do things for themselves. The machines here move around unaided, pick and complete tasks, and even use language to interact with humans. We could imagine that such machines, for the sake of convenience and understanding, have a strong resemblance to human beings: our bodily shape, our way of moving, our facial gestures. The question is posed starkly in the film *I, Robot* (adapted from an Isaac Asimov novel): how should we treat and interact with such beings? We should engage with them on the right level, but what *are* these machines? They have bodies copied from our bodies. They can do what we do. They have systems replicating the work of our brains. They have the same *functions* as our minds. Are they not, then, simply human beings?

### Questions

1. Is it possible to think of "you" without also thinking of your body?
2. What could account for the common idea of out-of-body experiences?
3. Is the human brain what makes a human being?
4. If you could replicate what the mind does with a machine, would it be a mind?

## Philosophical terms

**Body** – the physical component and extent of an organism or object

**Brain** – the most complex organ of a human being, located in the head, and the central part of the nervous system; the brain controls the sensory organs and has a decisive role in behaviour

**Consciousness** – the state of being awake or aware, or of having experiences

**Dualism** – a theory of the mind–body relationship, which sees mind and body as distinct, perhaps even as two separate entities

**Mind** – the faculty of thought, awareness and consciousness

**Mind–body problem** – the philosophical problem of defining the relationship between the mind and the body

**Monism** – a theory of the mind–body relationship, which sees them as a unity

**Problem of other minds** – the problem of knowing whether or proving that other human beings also have minds, like yours

**Soul** – the enduring essence or non-physical part of a human being, often associated with traditional or religious belief systems

**Spirit** – *either* a non-physical, invisible being or force, often associated with traditional or religious belief systems; *or* the inherent drive or character of a human being

## EXERCISE

1. Find images, videos, art, and poetry representing our concepts of body and mind. How does our imagination affect what we think of our minds and bodies?
2. Write down some initial reflections on an ancient problem: is it possible to know what happens to you when you die? Is the death of your body the end of "you"? Try to focus on reasons and counter-points.
3. Think about modern virtual communication. If you chat to somebody online who is not bodily present, is that any less "real" than face-to-face interaction? Find examples to illuminate this question.

What is the core part of a human being? There is an obvious sense in which we are more than mere physical bodies. We understand humans as being different from other objects – it is considered immoral to treat humans as "objects" – and so it seems to be a common assumption that there is something of special value "inside" humans. Humans use language to express complex emotions, they establish bonds with one another, and they can conceive of their past, present, and future. Such concepts link to another chapter of this book: personhood. However, here we are concerned with the composition of humans: the parts, features, and faculties defining them. So, the question arises, what *is* that part of us which expresses our unique awareness of ourselves?

We tend to think of the answer to that question in fairly mental terms: our thinking and awareness contain the real "us". Seeing the body as secondary is quite a common habit. For example, imagine that you lost a leg in an accident. You would have lost something in your body, but would you be any less of a human being? Indeed, we sometimes think of people with very damaged or limited bodies as having strong character or identity. The almost completely physically paralysed physicist Stephen Hawking (who has motor neurone disease) is a good example of this: his greatness lies in his thoughts and perseverance. What we value is not just the body itself, but the mind.

That may be a common way of thinking and one that is quite unphilosophical in its own right. However, such habits and uses of language give birth to enduring philosophical problems. One of the greatest and oldest is the **mind–body problem**. Are we able to define the difference between and the relationship between these two things? Is it fair to say that they are separate, or united? Do they exist distinctly? The apparent distinction between our physical bodies and our thinking minds can seem very convincing and it affects the way we see ourselves. However, philosophers are concerned to tackle this problem precisely and rigorously. They want to find out whether we can show that there is a distinction or, on the contrary, that there is not one. They want to find out whether some combination of reason, evidence, and contemplation could uncover the actual relationship.

Perhaps the simplest way to see this problem is in the distinction between two basic positions. **Dualism** proposes that the mind and the body are distinct things; perhaps they even *exist* distinctly. **Monism**, meanwhile, proposes that the mind and the body are a unity; they are aspects of the same thing. As this chapter progresses, however, you will see that there are many and varied possibilities that stretch beyond the two basic options.

| Dualism | Monism |
|---|---|
| We are two things – a mind and a body. | We are one thing – united mind/body. |
| Makes distinctions between the physical and the mental aspects of humans. | Makes links between the physical and the mental aspects of humans. |
| Traditional support from rationalist philosophers, who emphasize the primacy of thinking or mental experience. | Traditional support from empiricist philosophers, who emphasize the primacy of physical evidence. |

### Questions

1. Are most non-philosophers dualists or monists? What reasons do they have?
2. What makes the mind–body problem a *philosophy* problem?

There probably is no civilization or culture in history that has not given at least some thought to the question of what human beings are and, more specifically, whether they are "just" physical bodies. Prehistoric cultures show evidence of humans having been buried with grave goods, suggesting that some non-physical part (**soul**) would progress to a form of afterlife and enjoy those objects. It's not exactly a formal philosophy of mind, but it implies a theory about humans as something other than physical and assumes some kind of reasoning process. It's not difficult to think of arguments for this simple form of dualism. When humans die, their physical bodies remain, but something important about them goes away. When humans dream, they see and hear, and do things, but apparently without the use of their bodies. On this level, humans have been philosophers, considering the mind, for millennia. Anybody who reflects upon such matters is doing philosophy, participating in a tradition as old as the human race itself.

▲ In ancient times, people were often buried with 'grave goods', to take with them to the afterlife

Our questions about minds and bodies may be ancient, but they are also completely cutting-edge in terms of today's philosophy. These questions are socially and morally important right now. Let us say, for example, that we need to decide the fate of a patient who has suffered "brain death": her vital organs continue to function and her body lives, but all of her higher brain functions are no longer present. Minimal activity can be detected in scans. The patient cannot and will never speak again, or look someone in the eye, and so forth. Is this still a human being? In some respects obviously she is: her body clearly belongs to the human species and her outward appearance may not have changed dramatically. But is the real "her" trapped inside there? There could be a soul within, the divine spark of a human being. There could be the mind – thoughts and awareness – hampered by a damaged brain. On the contrary, though, it could well be argued that the "real" person was only ever a product of the brain and, with the physical brain severely damaged, there is no mind left to consider. Thus, we are dealing with questions that unite the neurosurgeons of today with the gravediggers of the Bronze Age: **what are our minds and our bodies?**

However, the modern problem of how we understand the mind and the body also calls into question the relationship between philosophy and science. Philosophy is interested in what humans are: it is a deep problem, concerned with the fundamental nature of things. Yet, looking at the traditional philosophical concept of the mind, we must be aware of how developments in other fields could impinge on our conversations. A hundred years ago, it would be fair to say that scientists knew almost nothing about the working of the brain. Now, with an increasingly complex array of equipment and methods, scientists are seeing progress that touches upon concepts with a traditional connection to the philosophy of mind: decision-making, aesthetic judgment, dreaming, and so forth. If scientists increasingly think they can explain these matters, it challenges the role of philosophy. It also challenges ancient philosophy, developed centuries before the modern scientific revolutions. Has it anything relevant to tell us today? Can philosophy become outdated? Or, will enduring questions about the mind always arise and remain relevant, no matter how sophisticated scientific methods become?

## FIND OUT MORE

Investigate the field of **neuroaesthetics**. What are some recent discoveries? Could this kind of brain science replace the need for philosophy in some respects? What does this tell us about the relationship between scientific and artistic knowledge?

▲ Neuro imaging at UCLA and Martinos Center for Biomedical Imaging at Massachusetts General Hospital

Regardless of how we conceive of the mind and the body, whether we view them philosophically, scientifically, or by some other method, the questions we have identified here are likely to have a continuing impact upon the popular imagination. Science fiction gives us the idea of a synthetic mind, as already mentioned, be it in a supercomputer, a robot, or in some form of organic-machine hybrid. Various spiritual revivals, meanwhile, emphasize the value of higher states of **consciousness** and mindfulness, evoking the possibility of connecting to universal truth. These approaches draw deeply from traditions of ancient wisdom and religion, but they also make connections with current science and philosophy. Finally, there are also the numerous fantasies of film, music, and wider pop culture, witnessed in the mind–body displacement of *Being John Malkovich* and in the mind-reading skills of Dr Xavier in *X-Men*. Our interest in the mind and the body seems unquenchable, but will philosophy ultimately help us in illuminating what they mean for being human?

**Questions**

1. The mind–body problem is an ancient problem. Does that make it more or less likely to be an important problem?
2. How confident are you that philosophers can solve the mind–body problem?
3. Why do so many popular films present fantasies of the mind (mind control, telepathy, switching minds, dream travel, etc.)?

## Ancient views of mind and body

- Ancient India: body and mind as friends and foes
- Ancient Greece: the nature of soul
- Abrahamic religions: raising a spiritual body

## EXERCISE

1. Look at the following quotations concerning mind and body, from ancient and traditional sources, from various cultures. Identify views that you agree or disagree with, and consider the reasons for your judgment.

| | |
|---|---|
| "Mind is everything. What we think, we become." —Buddha | "When the mind is thinking it is talking to itself." —Plato |
| "The energy of the mind is the essence of life." —Aristotle | "Difficulties strengthen the mind as labour does the body." —Seneca |
| "Oh my mind, the treasure is deep within you. Do not search for it outside." —Guru Nanak | "The body is mortal, but the person dwelling in the body is immortal." —Bhagavad Gita |
| "What we love is not the body, but what makes the body live." —Confucius | "You are dust, and to dust you shall return." —Holy Bible: Genesis |
| "The mind commands the body and it obeys. The mind orders itself and meets resistance." —Saint Augustine | "The flesh endures the storms of the present alone, the mind those of the past and future as well." —Epicurus |

NB – in some cases these are abridged or simplified quotations.

2. Try to find two sources from ancient and/or traditional cultures that seem to present contrasting views of the mind and the body. Can you explain the differences in perspective?

## Ancient India: body and mind as friends and foes

As mentioned above, there is an obvious way in which traditional cultures have considered the nature of human beings through the categories of body, mind, consciousness, and soul. There is the question of what becomes of humans at death, raising the prospect of an afterlife in some form, in the body or out of it. There are also the memories we have of dreaming: non-physical and vivid experiences that are universal features of human experience. Even more strikingly, all humans seem to be aware of their bodies, through feeling sensory inputs and being able to control what the body does. For example, you could have a conscious intention to read a book, say you will do it, and then go and do it. At first sight at least, it seems to be that "we" (in the inner self) are in charge of our bodies. The executive part of us is the *mind* and the obedient part is the *body*.

This type of reasoning seems fair enough on first inspection because it is built upon experiences we can all relate to. However, thinking in this way is more strongly philosophical than people realize, as it brings in a whole series of ideas about the fundamental nature of humans and of reality. There is a tendency to see the body as a kind of object: a tool or vehicle for carrying the mind along. Implicitly, this values the mind above the body and suggests that they have a relationship with one another, rather than being something identical or united. But is this justified?

Some of the earliest philosophical discussion of mind and body can be traced back to ancient India, a culture in which the perpetual cycle of life and death was subject to continuous scrutiny. India has given birth to some of the world's oldest and most distinguished belief systems: Hinduism, Buddhism, and Jainism, as well as more "modern" faiths such as Sikhism (15th century). One of the unifying elements of Indian religions has been the concern to address the seemingly endless process of life, suffering, and death, without humanity managing to comprehend, let alone overcome, the mental turmoil this produces. The Sanskrit word *Samsara* refers to such a cycle in the constant flow of life from the body, to death, and to new life again in the form of reincarnation or rebirth. Naturally enough, the traditional way to depict this in art has been in a great "Wheel of Life", showing the journey through the different realms of the universe.

▲ The Wheel of Life

But what keeps the Wheel of Life turning? According to Hinduism, it is the focus upon the body as the centre of awareness, being driven by sensations and the desire for things that please and preserve our physical state. This is a state of ignorance (*Avidya*), as a life focused on the body fails to perceive the wider truth that *Samsara* is happening and that the illusions of life need to be overcome. Essentially, therefore, the Hindu tradition presents the argument that the body needs to be subject to the discipline of the mind; the constant cravings of the body are evidence of this. The categories of mind and body, therefore, belong to an inner spiritual conflict in which a human is striving for an enlightened state or "liberation" (*Moksha*).

The Hindu concept of the body is ethical and spiritual in its formulation, but it also draws simply on common experience. All humans experience cravings and desires very sharply, can become conscious of these, and may struggle with what the body suggests. It could be counter-argued from a scientific perspective that such desires simply reflect physiological needs that can be understood, for example, through the science of nutrition. There could be no such thing as a conflict of mind and body, just a need for sensible diet and exercise. Nevertheless, Hinduism still offers a powerful narrative that attempts to make sense of the human condition: not just what we need, but how it feels to need things.

One answer to the problem of how we are to live with our bodies is **asceticism**. This is the practice of subduing the body by denying the things it desires: food, drink, sleep, sex, and so on. Obviously, it's not possible to remove these things completely (we would die), but there are traditions, particularly in India and Europe, of strictly limiting and managing such gratifications. One can see this in the chastity of Christian monks or in the emaciated appearance of some Hindu holy men. But why practise asceticism in the first place? One answer is that our bodily desires pollute our thoughts: they can be distracting, arise involuntarily, and are difficult to shake off. They can lead to vices, such as gluttony and lust, and in giving in to our desires we weaken our will or character. It could be argued that the body acts as a barrier to a concentrated mind and so the practice of asceticism enables one to experience discipline and clarity. Yet, on the contrary, some might say that satisfying bodily needs helps rather than hinders our thinking. This moderate view of the body was advanced by the Buddha, Siddhartha Gautama.

## Questions

1. What evidence is there that life is dominated by *Samsara*?
2. In what ways have you tried to discipline your body?
3. Could indulging the body also be seen as "good"?
4. Does science replace the need for a concept of spiritual struggle?

## Biography: Buddha (Siddhartha Gautama)

Siddhartha Gautama probably lived in the 6th and 5th centuries BCE, though the precise years of his life are disputed. He was a prince in the Shakya clan from north-eastern India, the son of the king Suddhodana, and yet renounced his royal lineage for a lifetime of meditation. His ultimate achievement according to Buddhism is reaching the status of one who is awakened (*Buddha* in Sanskrit), which led him away from the royal court. This included his perception of the nature and causes of suffering (*Dukkha*), and the possibility of overcoming it through the Four Noble Truths: there is suffering, there are causes of suffering, there is an end to suffering, and there is a way to end suffering. Deeper spiritual awareness opens up the possibility of *Nirvana*: the complete peace of mind that comes through knowledge and liberation. After his enlightenment, Gautama Buddha spent the remainder of his years teaching his insights and spreading what has become known as Buddhism. In doing so, he had an enduring impact upon how the relationship between body and mind is understood.

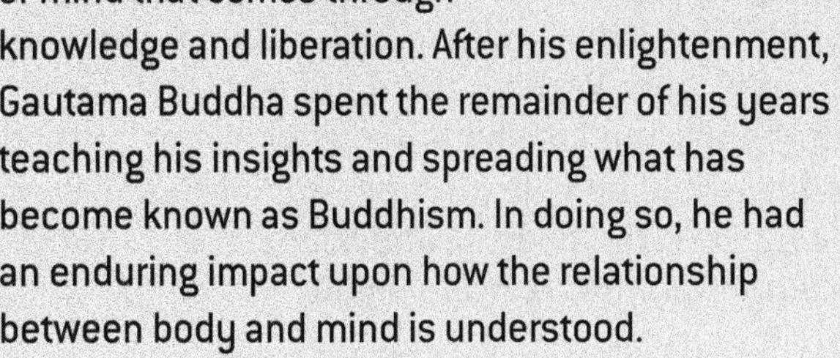

The narratives of the life of the Buddha frame the major ideas of his teaching, including concepts of being human, the nature of mind, and an ethic of compassion. The problems and limitations of our physical existence as humans are undeniable facts about our nature and condition: we know that we were children, have grown, experience sickness and suffering, will age, and must confront our own deaths. These "existential" facts are some of the key stimuli of philosophical thinking. However, for the young prince Siddhartha they were strangely unknown. Fearful that his son would abandon his royal ambitions, the king Suddhodana attempted to make his life into a gilded cage of pleasure and luxury. Siddhartha was confined to the palace, from which all sick and elderly people were banished, and in which the phenomenon of death was disguised. Not knowing the weakness of the body, it was hoped that Siddhartha could grow to be a king, rather than following his destiny to be enlightened. However, as the story goes, in journeying out from the palace he eventually caught sight of an old man and, in further journeys, he also found a diseased man, a corpse, and an ascetic (the Four Sights). The harsh reality of physical weakness hit home and Siddhartha faced the philosophical problem we all face: how to live with this knowledge. These Four Sights provide a symbol for the way in which our minds must confront our limited and mortal bodies.

Deciding to flee from his royal palace and prison, Siddhartha journeyed out into the country and joined a group of five wandering ascetics. He is said to have practised severe asceticism and punished his body, though without experiencing the spiritual realization that he was hoping for. Half starved, Siddhartha came to the conclusion that he would have to nourish his body to gain the strength for meditation; the body would need to be at peace with itself for the necessary mental equilibrium. Therefore, he turned his back on asceticism and, according to the legend, accepted rice pudding from a young woman (Sujata) before journeying on to more fruitful and decisive meditation beneath the Bodhi tree.

The importance of this story for our purposes is the way it calls into question the ascetic view of the mind–body relationship. One could think in terms of the metaphor of the master (mind) trying to gain authority over a disobedient servant (body), requiring a strict regime of punishment to bend the will. Asceticism thinks in terms of striving against wayward influences, which has the strengths of demanding self-discipline and creating genuine scope for reflection. However, working with that same metaphor, one could question whether this kind of dominance and harsh discipline is conducive to sustained and deep reflection. Perhaps the mind and the body should have a more harmonious and collaborative relationship; perhaps a well-treated servant would be of greater use and productivity in supporting the master. Or, is the body so important to our thoughts that it should not be considered the "servant" at all?

This leads to an important Buddhist concept, the Middle Way, which the Buddha proceeded to teach to the ascetics he had once travelled with. On the one hand, personal gratification obviously does not lead to enlightenment because, as the ascetics supposed, it focuses the mind on the changing world of appearances and illusions, physical sensations and desires that cloud our thinking. However, on the other hand, are extreme denial and asceticism counter-productive in the quest for truth because they cause further suffering – what meditation is supposed to overcome – and so are themselves a form of distraction? Instead of teaching the struggle of the mind against the body, the Buddha taught the Noble Eightfold Path:

- Right view
- Right thought
- Right speech
- Right action

- Right livelihood
- Right effort
- Right mindfulness
- Right concentration

This encompasses the practices of knowledge, ethics, and meditation. The path set out by the Buddha implies that it is possible to control our desires through mental effort without denying them altogether. By this view, a good life supports the body without giving in to its every craving. The problems of *Samsara* and *Dukkha* are not denied; on the contrary, the Buddha claims that the body needs to be treated gently if the painful cycle of rebirth is to be overcome.

## FIND OUT MORE

Research Buddha's meditation beneath the Bodhi tree and his confrontation with *Mara*. What does this story tell us about the Buddhist view of mind and meditation? How could you evaluate, support, or critique this perspective?

Finally, it's important to observe that Buddha not only challenged the ascetic view of the mind and the body, but also contributed further to the philosophical discussion of mind with the concept of *Anatta* ("no-self"). In accordance with Hindu culture, the Buddha affirmed that life and consciousness continue into another body after death. However, by contrast with Hindu reincarnation, the Buddha suggested that there is no fixed self or eternal element to be reborn into another body. Instead, what we regard as "us" is a constantly changing stream of consciousness. The mind is not equivalent to an immortal soul; it is not a permanent and essential self. The mind is a fluctuating series of impressions and, indeed, the idea of a fixed notion of self could be another form of attachment: a mental chain that ties us to the world. To think, therefore, that the mind drives the body like a machine would be an oversimplification for Buddhism, because the mind is just as changeable and impermanent as the body it is supposed to direct.

There are a number of arguments in favour of *Anatta*:

- If everything else is impermanent, then so is the self impermanent.
- Manifestly, our thoughts and characters change over time.
- We can become attached to or egoistic about our own spiritual quests.

It can also be said to be a form of **nondualism** because the sharp distinctions made between mind/body, internal/external, self/other, and so forth are based on the illusion of one's own enduring identity. Buddhism, for example, would deny that the mind–body problem is a real problem, because the terms themselves ("mind", "body") are uncertain and impermanent features of our experience. An important part of philosophical wisdom according to Buddhism, therefore, is learning to appreciate how pervasive illusion can be, even within one's own mind.

### TOK link

In what ways does the ego or self hamper our ways of knowing? What is the importance of personal knowledge in Buddhism?

## EXERCISE

1. Write an imaginary dialogue between the Buddha and the five ascetics, in which the Buddha argues for the Middle Way, while the ascetics argue for asceticism. Incorporate arguments for and against their views on the mind–body relationship.
2. Research the Wheel of Life and produce your own diagram of it. Analyse: what are the implications of *Samsara* for the way we view the physical body?
3. Analyse and explain: how could the Noble Eightfold Path be used to discipline the body, without hurting it?
4. Investigate ways in which modern theories or knowledge could be used in a critique of Buddhism. Is there lasting value in this philosophy?

**Assessment tip** 

If you are writing about the Buddha in an essay, avoid simply telling the stories: this shows you have knowledge, but little else. Make sure you discuss and analyse the concepts, think about criticisms of Buddhist teachings, and think how you could compare this perspective with other views. Be sure to give your comments and evaluation.

## Ancient Greece: the nature of soul

Western philosophy first flourished in ancient Greece and within that flourishing was the first philosophical discussion of mind and body. Greek civilization was dominated by rival city-states with their own subtly different dialects, cultures, and ideas. There was at times conflict and tension, as was felt particularly strongly in the 5th century BCE in the great war between Sparta and Athens. That same century saw the emergence of two founders of Western philosophy in the city of Athens: Socrates and his student Plato. Not by accident, philosophy and critical questioning emerged against a background of political rivalries, suspicion, and intrigue, and both Socrates and Plato became controversial figures within the city. Ultimately, the constant challenging, questioning, and doubting received wisdom put Socrates in great trouble. He was accused of corrupting the youth of Athens, was found guilty by the court, and was forced to commit suicide by poisoning.

This was an unfortunate end for so distinguished a figure, but Socrates is said to have faced death with courage and equanimity. Ideally, according to the Greeks, a philosopher is supposed to be virtuous and wise, and Socrates was no exception. He was said to be bold and light-hearted at his trial, refused to beg for mercy, accepted the sentence without grief, and behaved well with his friends in his final hours. Famously, his last words are said to have been "We owe a cock to Asclepius", presumably meaning that the Greek god of healing should be thanked for this end to the hardship of life. There is no sentimental attachment to life, to the body, and this could be said to be a classic case of the supposed virtue of emotional detachment. A true philosopher remains calm. At least, that is the impression given by the author recording this scene, Plato. As a pupil of Socrates, he records these events as a witness and friend of the deceased, but also very much as a philosopher in his own right. Plato constructed a dialogue around this moment, named the *Phaedo*, which takes the final conversations of Socrates as a springboard for philosophy. This is precisely what a dialogue is: a record of a real or imagined conversation between two or more parties, which advances discussion and ideas. In this case, Plato explores life and death, and the possibility of the soul living on after the body dies.

## Biography: Socrates (c. 469–399 BCE) and Plato (c. 427–347 BCE)

Socrates was an Athenian philosopher and social commentator who created a lineage of thinkers, including Plato and Aristotle. Socrates himself left no writings behind, but is a well-known figure from the works of Xenophon, Aristophanes, and (most importantly) Plato. He was the son of a sculptor father and midwife mother, perhaps working for a while as a stonecutter but then devoting his life to philosophy. Because our records are second-hand, we cannot be completely sure what are the genuine ideas of Socrates or what the later authors have imposed upon him. However, with some confidence we may say that he was known for a method of asking persistent difficult questions, particularly concerning ethical and political matters, and he gathered a strong following as a teacher. He seems to have denied his own authority, rather emphasizing his ignorance and his desire to gain wisdom from others. His popularity and the politically awkward nature of his questions may have led to his downfall in the courts and subsequent death.

Plato followed his teacher Socrates in the path of philosophy and responded to his death energetically. He was descended from an aristocratic family in Athens and grew up during the war with Sparta. A young man when Socrates died, Plato went on to a productive literary career (nearly 50 works by traditional reckoning) and founded an enduring philosophical school: the Academy. The impact of Socrates upon Plato is striking, in that Socrates is always the central character of the dialogues and always appears in a positive light. The trial and death of Socrates feature in a number of works: the *Euthyphro*, *Apology*, *Crito*, and *Phaedo*. These combine the agenda of defending the virtue of Socrates with clear advancement of Plato's ideas. Plato's philosophical concerns include the definition of justice, of virtue, and a theory that knowledge may be understood in terms of eternal truths. The death of Socrates brings a number of these themes together, including the all-important claim that the soul survives death and that human life continues beyond the body.

In the *Phaedo* we hear of the final conversations of Socrates in prison. He asserts to his visitor Simmias that a philosopher should not kill himself except when it is completely necessary (as in his own case), but still a philosopher certainly should not fear death. Indeed, philosophers have a unique appreciation of death and should take comfort as it approaches. His argument is striking and even shocking.

> Other people may well be unaware that all who actually engage in philosophy aright are practising nothing other than dying and being dead. Now if this is true, it would be odd indeed for them to be eager in their whole life for nothing but that, and yet to be resentful when it comes, the very thing they'd long been eager for and practised ... they aren't aware in what sense genuine philosophers are longing for death and deserving of it, and what kind of death they deserve. Anyway, let's discuss it amongst ourselves, disregarding them: do we suppose that death is a reality? ... And that it is nothing but the separation of the soul from the body? And that being dead is this: the body's having come to be apart, separate from the soul, alone by itself, and the soul's being apart, alone by itself, separated from the body? Death can't be anything else but that, can it?
>
> [Simmias agrees]

> Now look, my friend, and see if maybe you agree with me on these points; because through them I think we'll improve our knowledge of what we're examining. Do you think it befits a philosophical man to be keen about the so-called pleasures of, for example, food and drink?
>
> [Simmias says not]
>
> Do you think in general, then, that such a person's [a philosopher's] concern is not for the body, but so far as he can stand aside from it, is directed towards the soul? ... In such matters as these the philosopher differs from other people in releasing his soul, as far as possible, from its communion with the body ... And now, what about the actual gaining of wisdom? Is the body a hindrance or not if one enlists it as a partner in the quest? This is the sort of thing I mean: do sight and hearing afford mankind any truth, or aren't even the poets always harping on such themes, telling us that we neither see nor hear anything accurately? ... [the soul] reasons best, presumably, whenever none of these things bothers it, neither hearing nor sight nor pain, nor any pleasure either, but whenever it comes to be alone by itself as far as possible, disregarding the body, and whenever, having the least possible communion and contact with it, it strives for reality.
>
> —Plato[1]

The word that is used over and over again in this dialogue is the Greek term *psyche*, which may be translated as "life", "breath", or "soul". The translation "soul" is chosen in English because it conveys what Socrates is talking about: some immortal and immaterial essence in the human being that will even survive death. Clearly, Socrates regards it as being distinct from the body, to the extent that he speaks of separating the two: dualism. The soul is the awareness and consciousness of a human, but it is more than that; it also contains the rational element and thoughts, like the mind. It reasons best when it is alone.

As the dialogue proceeds, Plato gives a number of other arguments (via Socrates) to prove the immortality of the soul and its distinction from the body. For our purposes, they also show that the Platonic view of the mind is the same thing: it is the rational soul, continuing after death. The arguments can be summarized as follows:

- Argument from opposites and cycles: life and death are opposites, like many opposites in nature (large and small, hot and cold, awake and asleep). One state emerges from the other in a cycle. Life comes from death, death comes from life, and the process goes on. Since the living are born from the dead, the souls of the dead must still exist after death. The soul is immortal.
- The recollection argument: knowledge is derived from what we already have known in a previous life – it is to be recollected. The knowledge thus gained is evidence that the soul has lived before and is immortal (see a fuller explanation of this theory, below).
- The affinity argument: the soul has closest resemblance to things invisible, unchanging, uniform, intelligible, and things that do not die. The body by contrast has closest resemblance to things visible, changing, varied, non-intelligible, and mortal. Therefore, the body will die but the soul will not.

## Questions

1. Why does Socrates claim that philosophers practise dying and being dead?
2. What could Socrates mean by "separating" the mind and the body?
3. What is Socrates' argument that the body hinders the gaining of wisdom?

[1] Plato, *Phaedo*, translated with an introduction and notes by David Gallop (Oxford: Oxford University Press, 1999), pp. 9–11.

The middle of these, the argument from recollection, needs more explanation, being based on Plato's theory of knowledge. Philosophers have long been concerned with the question of what should be considered the most real or true. Plato's answer to this problem is that *ideas* are most real, they *exist*, and everything else is just a shadow of their reality. This is often called the **theory of the forms**, as this is another possible translation of the Greek word for ideas. Since the ideas are eternal and abstract, they can be grasped in the mind eternally also, without input from the senses and the world around us. The soul always knows that the ideas are true but forgets them on the journey from one life to the next, and so the task of gaining knowledge is the task of the soul remembering what it really eternally knows. This may seem like a strange theory but, if correct, it would support the notion that the soul is immortal and non-physical. In the *Phaedo* Plato puts Socrates to work in explaining and proving the theory.

**TOK link** 

Is it really possible for the mind to know things by reason alone? What does Plato teach about the ways of knowing?

The argument for the eternal ideas, known by the soul, goes like this. We recognize common qualities in objects in ways that are clear and intelligible. For example, we know what "equality" is (things being of the very same value or proportion) and we can see this in stones of equal weight or sticks of equal length. But how do we know "equality"? We will not have learned it from objects that are truly equal, because they never are; no two stones will ever be *exactly* the same. Indeed, without seeing true equality in the physical world, we recognize things that are nearly equal because we *already know the idea*. Pure equality in fact is completely abstract and can never be found in the world, but it is understood by the mind. The rational soul, the mind, is in possession of ideas such as equality, justice, beauty, and so forth, even though it never sees perfect examples. It would only be possible to recognize abstract qualities in objects if the knowledge were there all along, if the soul had always known these things even from before birth. Therefore, the soul must be immortal.

## FIND OUT MORE

Research the theory of ideas or forms in Plato's wider philosophical works. Look at the simile of the Cave from the *Republic* and the paradox of learning from the *Meno*. Putting the various arguments together, how convincing is Plato's theory?

In these brief arguments, Plato puts forward some of the most influential ideas from the history of philosophy. But should we be persuaded? On the one hand, there is a clear logic to the arguments, and they relate to each other and hang together as a collective proof for the immaterial, immortal soul. Our thoughts really do seem to direct our bodies and seem to cause the various activities of our lives. I thought about typing this sentence before I got my fingers to do it. So, in that sense, the mind or soul really appears to be energizing and animating the body. The mind also deals with the abstract and timeless truths, such as mathematics, and it is able to see through illusions and ever-changing nature. It is non-physical. It apprehends truths that are not lost with death.

However, as appealing as Plato's arguments may seem, they have not convinced everybody. Indeed, few philosophers today would identify themselves as Platonists or accept his proofs for the immortal, rational soul. Opposition to Plato's arguments probably arose within his own lifetime, and certainly in the next generation he was firmly criticized by his own pupil (another one of the founders of Western philosophy),

Aristotle. The key criticisms from the younger philosopher can roughly be divided into two points, directed against the theory of ideas:

1. The problem of object and idea connection: Plato said that the ideas explain universal qualities in objects, so that there is such a thing as "equality" and objects *strive* to be equal or *participate* in the idea of equality. For Aristotle, the problem arises when you try to explain how this actually works. How does an object attempt to be like an idea? This seems obscure and unexplained.
2. The problem of the third man: Plato claims that the existence of the ideal quality explains the objects possessing the quality (for example, the idea of a man explains why we can identify numerous beings as "men"). However, we now have two things with something in common (a man and the idea of a man), so we need to explain what these two things have in common. For that, we would need a third man to explain that link, but that would itself raise the question of what the three things had in common. Thus, there would be no end to these explanations, and they would not get us anywhere.

There are a number of other general criticisms we could make of the arguments for the immortality of the soul.

- Firstly, the claim that life and death are opposites, locked in a cyclical process, is questionable. In what sense are they really "opposite"? What proof is there that this forms an unbroken cycle?
- Secondly, even if we accept the theory of ideas, does "recollection" really show that the soul is immortal and has experienced a previous life? These ideas could be implanted into the mind at birth by a god, genetic coding, or some other mysterious process, and would then disappear with the deaths of our bodies.
- Thirdly, although the soul can contemplate abstract and immaterial ideas, it can also contemplate worldly and physical matters, the body, death, etc. So, does it really have an affinity with immortality?

## Biography: Aristotle (384–322 BCE)

Aristotle was one of the greatest all-round intellectuals of all time: a philosopher, scientist, legalist, and educator. He grew up in the semi-Greek kingdom of Macedonia, the son of the court physician Nicomachus. He was wealthy and well connected, and even served as tutor to the most famous Macedonian king, Alexander the Great. Aristotle studied at Plato's Academy in Athens, though eventually came to disagree with many Platonic teachings. He founded his own school in Athens, the Lyceum, where he taught for some years. Ultimately, the Athenians turned against Macedonia after the death of Alexander and Aristotle was banished from the city. He chose to live in exile rather than face execution. A distinct feature of Aristotle's works is his great interest in recording and cataloguing nature, with a kind of reverence towards the natural world. This led Aristotle towards a *natural* view of the soul as part of the physical human being, by contrast with the *metaphysical* Platonic idea of an immortal presence.

Aristotle sets out his own theories, which contrast strongly with those of Plato, in his obviously titled work *On the Soul* (widely referred to by its Latin title, *De Anima*). Aristotle's approach to writing is much less artistic than that of Plato; he does not use the method of dramatic dialogue and instead we have technical, dense, and analytical texts. This also gives a flavour of his work on the soul, which proceeds by making careful and precise distinctions in the properties and functions of the soul, its appearance in different organisms, and the varying levels of its complexity and completeness. The most important point to understand is that, while Aristotle also uses the Greek word *psyche* ("life", "soul") to refer to an important aspect of being human, his concept of what this is differs significantly from Plato's and from the meaning of "soul" in modern English. Chiefly, it is *not* an independent, distinct, non-physical substance or entity within a human. On the contrary, Aristotle's soul is a part of and a way of understanding a physical organism; it is the form, scheme, or principle that shapes a living being.

A couple of simple arguments or methods support what Aristotle is saying. Firstly, he suggests that the best way to determine the nature of the soul is to study what it does or how it functions. The soul is the thing that is commonly held to give the body life, and so the task is to look for the most characteristic form of life for a creature. The simplest life forms have souls that are merely concerned with nutrition and reproduction. More complex life forms experience sensations. Finally, the most advanced (human) life has a rational component to the soul. The "soul" is simply the ability of the organism to do these things and so is not a thing in its own right. Aristotle's other argument for his approach is that the soul must be a "form" of life rather than "matter" (a thing itself) because the soul is needed to explain what the body is putting into effect; the body obviously is material substance, brought about by some principle that is the soul. Simply, "the body is the subject, the soul what is attributed to it".[2]

By contrast with the dualism of Plato, Aristotle could be said to be the first philosopher offering a monistic theory of mind and body. He does

| Plato | Aristotle |
|---|---|
| Key work on mind/body: *Phaedo* | Key work on mind/body: *On the Soul* |
| Literary approach: dialogue | Literary approach: treatise |
| Philosophical approach: rational/abstract | Philosophical approach: rational/empirical |
| Key argument: dualism – soul deals with abstract matters, including eternal ideas, which suggests it is immortal/non-physical | Key argument: monism – soul is not a thing in its own right, because it is the form that makes the physical body alive, a unity |
| Criticism: Plato cannot explain how the theory of ideas works; proof for the cycle of life and death is debatable | Criticism: in saying that the soul is just the "form" of the body, Aristotle doesn't explain where this form comes from |

[2] Aristotle, *On the Soul* (written c. 350 BCE as treatise *De Anima*), Book II, Chapter 1; English translation by J. A. Smith available at http://classics.mit.edu/Aristotle/soul.html (accessed 22 October 2014).

not distinguish the conscious or rational component of a human being from the physical, but instead suggests that reason and awareness are natural capabilities of physical beings. There is one, unified human organism. Aristotle could also be said to take an empirical view of being human, which means that he used the observations of the senses to decide what the soul is, as opposed to purely abstract reasoning. However, although his criticisms of Plato may seem satisfying at first sight, Aristotle's own explanation runs into difficulties: if form is not matter, nor an eternal idea, then what is it? Who or what produced it?

## EXERCISE

1. Compare ancient Greek and Indian philosophy. How might Plato and Aristotle criticize the ideas of the Buddha? How might the Buddha criticize the ideas of the Greeks? Turn these points into lists, or write a dialogue between these thinkers.
2. Research concepts of mind and boy from other ancient Greek schools of philosophy: Stoicism and Epicureanism. Redraw the table above with four columns, comparing the four approaches to mind/body.
3. Look up the texts of the *Phaedo* and *On the Soul*. Compare the literary methods – what are the relative advantages or disadvantages of writing a dialogue or a treatise?

## Abrahamic religions: raising a spiritual body

While Greece was the birthplace of Western philosophy, the dominant religions of Western and Middle Eastern civilizations arose in the Near East, in ancient Israel/Palestine and Arabia. Judaism, Christianity, and Islam are commonly referred to as the Abrahamic faiths because they all claim lineage from the figure attributed with discovering monotheism (belief in one God) in the Bronze Age: Abraham. Although it might be argued that these religions are examples of "belief systems" rather than "philosophies", their impact upon concepts of body and mind in culture and popular imagination has been huge. Consider heaven and hell, or sin and redemption, in addition to the well-known rituals and rites of passage of birth, life, and death. Take, for example, the ubiquitous Western phrase on tombstones: "rest in peace". Think about it. In what sense is death a form of "rest"? What does this tell us about human life? This is just one of innumerable ways in which religion influences our thinking about mind and body. Indeed, a lot of philosophy takes place within belief systems, taking a concept of being human from a tradition, text or ritual, and then subjecting it to systematic scrutiny.

Some of the foundational ideas concerning mind and body in Judeo-Christian culture can be traced back to the story of Creation in the book of Genesis from the Hebrew Bible (what Christians call the Old Testament). This narrative describes the process by which God creates the heavens and the earth, and all of the creatures inhabiting them. It is worth taking the time to read through the first three chapters, to get a sense for how humans are understood as a part of God's handiwork.

Their relation to their divine Creator, to each other, and to their environment is explored. Picking out key points for our purposes here, note that:

- Everything God makes is "very good", including human beings.
- God shapes the man from the earth; man is and will return to "dust".
- God breathes life into the first humans to make them live.
- God names the man and the woman; they are his possessions.
- Humans are superior to other animals but must care for them.
- Humans are like God in having knowledge of good and evil.

## EXERCISE

1. Look at Michelangelo's painting of the Creation of Adam. What is the artist trying to convey about the human body and human beings?
2. Work through the first three chapters of *Genesis* and make a list of quotations that have direct relevance to the nature of humans/body/mind. Compare these with the Indian and Greek concepts discussed earlier.

In accordance with the Genesis story, Judaism traditionally teaches a monistic view of humans as essentially physical beings created by God. The Hebrew word *nefesh* ("life", "breath") has sometimes been translated as "soul", but most Jews through history have not distinguished a non-physical essence from the body (contrast Plato) and so this could be said to be misleading as a translation. The physical Creation of the world has such a dominant role within Judeo-Christian and Islamic thinking that the idea of an abstract or mental world has not held the kind of appeal that it did for some Greek philosophers. Instead, when Judaism came to consider the possibility of life after death and an ideal form of life, it focused upon the renewal of the *body* and the re-creation of the *physical* world in a perfected form. This can be summed up in the concept of **resurrection** (from Latin, "stand up again"), which is the idea of the Creation coming to new life through God's will. In Judaism today the ideal of renewal is found in prayer and liturgy in the concept of *Ha Olam Ha Ba* ("the world that is coming"), which stands in place of individualistic afterlife for the soul.

But how have Jews justified the idea that new life will come to the body and to the whole of Creation? Primarily, they have argued from the concept of God as the Creator of the Earth, using theology to illuminate the state of being human. Perhaps the first reference to resurrection in the Holy Bible is found in the book of Ezekiel, in which the prophet Ezekiel is given a vision of a valley full of dry bones. Read the following extract:

> The hand of the LORD was on me, and he brought me out by the Spirit of the LORD and set me in the middle of a valley; it was full of bones. He led me back and forth among them, and I saw a great many bones on the floor of the valley, bones that were very dry. He asked me, "Son of man, can these bones live?"
>
> I said, "Sovereign LORD, you alone know."
>
> Then he said to me, "Prophesy to these bones and say to them, 'Dry bones, hear the word of the LORD! This is what the Sovereign LORD says to these bones: I will make breath enter you, and you will come to life. I will attach tendons to you and make flesh come upon you and cover you with skin; I will put breath in you, and you will come to life. Then you will know that I am the LORD.'"
>
> So I prophesied as I was commanded. And as I was prophesying, there was a noise, a rattling sound, and the bones came together, bone to bone. I looked, and tendons and flesh appeared on them and skin covered them, but there was no breath in them.
>
> Then he said to me, "Prophesy to the breath; prophesy, son of man, and say to it, 'This is what the Sovereign LORD says: Come, breath, from the four winds and breathe into these slain, that they may live.'" So I prophesied as he commanded me, and breath entered them; they came to life and stood up on their feet—a vast army.
>
> Then he said to me: "Son of man, these bones are the people of Israel. They say, 'Our bones are dried up and our hope is gone; we are cut off.' Therefore prophesy and say to them: 'This is what the Sovereign LORD says: My people, I am going to open your graves and bring you up from them; I will bring you back to the land of Israel. Then you, my people, will know that I am the LORD, when I open your graves and bring you up from them. I will put my Spirit in you and you will live, and I will settle you in your own land. Then you will know that I the LORD have spoken, and I have done it, declares the LORD.'"
>
> Ezekiel 37:1–14 (NIV)

An important premise of the text is that life must inhabit a body, a form that is purified and dedicated to God. The logic supporting this can be unpicked from the text:

- God knows everything, including everything about life and Creation.
- God possesses the "breath of life": the ability to make things live or die.
- God has control over all of nature ("the four winds").
- God cares for the people of Israel and wants Israel to settle the land.

In other words, Judaism argues from a **monistic** view of nature – that it is a unity, is good, is God's one unique Creation – to the idea that the ideal form of human life is monistic also, inhabiting a pure body in accordance with God's will.

Developing out of Judaism, Christianity has partially kept and partially modified Jewish beliefs and arguments about the body, soul, and mind. Perhaps the most important development is the Christian opinion that the resurrection of the dead, though still a future event, is represented in and proven by the resurrection of Jesus. The spiritual founder of Christianity, Jesus of Nazareth, was a Jewish teacher and leader of the first century who was executed (crucified) by the Romans. Shortly after his death, however, a number of his followers claimed to have witnessed the "risen" Lord, i.e. the resurrected form of Jesus. The Gospels (the narratives of the life of Jesus) contain a number of accounts of post-resurrection appearances, and give the impression that the resurrection of Jesus was widely attested by the first Christians. This builds on the theological reasoning of Judaism found in Ezekiel (God is the Creator, has power over life, can purify the body) by adding physical "proofs" that the body of Jesus was raised: he appeared to many disciples, his wounds were inspected, he ate and drank, and he ascended to heaven in bodily form (so there ultimately was no corpse of Jesus).

**TOK link** 

How does the Christian belief in resurrection draw on the ways of knowing (faith, sense perception, emotion)? How would this belief be treated in different areas of knowledge (history, religion, natural science)?

Despite their strong emphasis on the bodily resurrection of Jesus, however, the first Christians also took an interest in the concepts of soul, spirit, and mind. Saint Paul warns against the weaknesses of the "flesh", the negative aspect of life in the body, and specifically criticizes adultery and sexual sin, uncleanness, drunkenness, greed, etc. In this sense, there is a parallel with the Indian ascetic tradition (see above) and the concern that bodily indulgence could pollute or distract the mind. For Paul, bodily gratifications could prevent someone from receiving the Spirit of God, for "the flesh desires what is contrary to the Spirit, and the Spirit what is contrary to the flesh" (Galatians 5:17). Paul also urges mental renewal on his followers and emphasizes the importance of thinking in accordance with God's will: "Do not conform to the pattern of this world, but be transformed by the renewing of your mind. Then you

But someone will ask, "How are the dead raised? With what kind of body will they come?" How foolish! What you sow does not come to life unless it dies. When you sow, you do not plant the body that will be, but just a seed, perhaps of wheat or of something else. But God gives it a body as he has determined, and to each kind of seed he gives its own body. Not all flesh is the same: People have one kind of flesh, animals have another, birds another and fish another. There are also heavenly bodies and there are earthly bodies; but the splendour of the heavenly bodies is one kind, and the splendour of the earthly bodies is another. The sun has one kind of splendour, the moon another and the stars another; and star differs from star in splendour.

So will it be with the resurrection of the dead. The body that is sown is perishable, it is raised imperishable; it is sown in dishonour, it is raised in glory; it is sown in weakness, it is raised in power; it is sown a natural body, it is raised a spiritual body.

1 Corinthians 15:35–44

will be able to test and approve what God's will is—his good, pleasing and perfect will" (Romans 12:2). Nevertheless, Paul still maintains the fundamentally Jewish opinion that the body must be raised and the true self is found in physical form. He gets around the problem of bodily distractions and impurity by arguing for a transformed, spiritual body.

## Questions

1. In what ways does Paul put forward Jewish monistic arguments for the unity of Creation and of the body?
2. In what ways does Paul agree or disagree with ancient Greek philosophers?
3. What could Paul mean by "spiritual body"?
4. What is the role of God in Paul's argument?

## Biography: Saint Paul (c. 5–67 CE)

Paul of Tarsus (also known as Saint Paul, Paul the Apostle) was a Jew from Asia Minor (modern-day Turkey) and originally was called Saul; he changed his name after conversion to Christianity. His early life was dominated by study of Judaism and he lived in Jerusalem as a young man at the time of the death of Jesus. Although he probably never met Jesus himself, the young Saul quickly became a persecutor of the Church and attempted to stifle the new religious movement in its early years. However, a vision of the risen Jesus changed his mind, and he became Paul: a great teacher and organizer of the Church. He founded many Churches around the Roman Empire and is perhaps best known for the letters he wrote (which form part of the New Testament), which give an important basis to Christian teaching. Ultimately, he was arrested for undermining Judaism and stirring up trouble among the Jewish populace in Jerusalem; he was sent for trial to Rome and there was executed, according to legend, by beheading.

| Jewish arguments for resurrection | Christian developments |
| --- | --- |
| God is the all-powerful Creator | God's power is shown through Jesus |
| God gives life | God restored life to Jesus |
| God made humans | God saves humans through Jesus |
| Nature is good, under God's will | All nature is subject to God/Jesus |
| God can renew life in the body | God renewed the body of Jesus |
| God's people will inhabit the earth | God will raise up "spiritual bodies" |

Jews and Christians, therefore, have argued for a form of transformational monism: on the one hand, they acknowledge the weakness and impurity of the body and accept the need for self-discipline, yet on the other hand, they see the solution to those problems in the transformation of the body by the creative power of God, as

opposed to the idea of "separating" the soul from the body. Christians have developed and differ from Jewish opinions in the sense that they make Jesus the centre of this concept and put strong emphasis on the "spiritual" nature of the resurrection of the body.

What is striking about this approach is the way in which it argues from theology, from a particular concept of God. This has a direct impact upon how the mind and the body are understood, because these things are seen as part of Creation and therefore are understood very strongly as having divine origins. The idea that everything God made was "very good" contrasts strongly with the Hindu/Buddhist concept of *Samsara*, for example, and also is quite different from the abstract conversations of Plato. It might be argued that the traditional Judeo-Christian concept of God is opposed to philosophical dualism, therefore, because God is the complete source of and explanation of everything, and so it would be problematic to say that the soul is better or purer than the body. There is real strength in this view of reality and of being human, in that it is able to embrace the goodness of nature, value life, and identifies an ultimate purpose for life. Nevertheless, such a theological approach is open to criticism:

- It depends wholly on theism, which can be denied; if there is no God then the body is not his Creation.
- The goodness of Creation can be challenged through evidence of suffering.
- There is reason behind the Hindu, Buddhist, and Platonic claim that life is characterized by illusion; the Creation could be an illusion.
- The mind still *seems* distinct from the body; our thoughts may have no relation to physical actions.

**Assessment tip** 

An important part of analysis in essays is discussing counter-arguments. Try to go beyond simply listing "points against" and think about how you can develop the criticisms: comment on them, draw connections, and weigh up the points that are most convincing. It is good practice to give a whole paragraph over to discussion of counter-arguments against a particular theory.

In terms of Christian views of the body, mind, and soul, the story does not quite end here, however, as these became extremely complicated in the course of time. One of the first major Christian philosophers was Saint Augustine, who was a student of Greek philosophy and biblical teaching. He attempted to synthesize (join together) these two seemingly very different schools of thought, arguing *both* that the rational soul is distinct from and superior to the body, *and* that the soul must be united with the body in resurrection. Augustine felt that Plato had shown convincingly that the soul is superior to the body and could be free from it. He also supposed that the Holy Bible must be explored philosophically, as it does not fully explain how God makes bodies live and how humans are constituted. Thus, Augustine claimed that God created both the body and the soul, implanting the soul within humans to give them the powers of reasoning and free will. This enabled Christians to reconcile the idea that humans are created in the body by God with mind–body dualism: thoughts come from the soul. Therefore, at this particular moment in history, there were three mind–body theories:

- A human being is primarily a *mind*, constrained by a body (Platonic view).
- A human being is primarily a *body*, created by God (biblical view).
- A human being is a *mind–body composite*, ensouled body (Augustinian view).

But is Augustine's view intellectually coherent? On the one hand, it has the obvious appeal of incorporating the arguments in favour of a distinct mind (it seems distinct, it works in abstract, etc.) with the theological hypothesis that the natural world is a good Creation and the body is part of it. However, there is a degree of tension, if not contradiction, in what Augustine is trying to put forward. He supports the Platonic view that the mind is the superior part of a human being, but has to combine that with the biblical theory that the body is created and will be perfected. Surely the body cannot be both a burden to and essential to a human being? If the non-physical soul is superior, then why should God bother with a physical resurrection?

## Biography: Saint Augustine (354–430 CE)

Augustine was a Christian philosopher and writer, and Bishop of Hippo: a town in what is now Algeria. He was the child of a pagan father and a Christian mother, and grew up in a mixed religious culture at a time when Christianity was gradually taking over from older forms of religion in Europe and North Africa. Augustine travelled to Italy to study, fell into a life of loose living (he is the patron saint of brewers), but then joined a sect called the Manicheans, who taught a severe spiritual doctrine that the physical world and body are evil, needing harsh discipline to purify the soul. However, through study of the Holy Bible he eventually abandoned the strict dualism of the Manicheans and converted to Christianity. He spent much of the rest of his life defending Christian doctrines, attacking the Manicheans and other sects, and attempting to harmonize Christian beliefs with Greek philosophy.

Finally among the Abrahamic religions is Islam, which arose in Saudi Arabia in the 7th century CE. Islam teaches that the new faith was wholly revealed to the prophet Muhammad, the final true prophet of God (Allah) by dictation from the angel Jibrail. Muhammad wrote the revelations down and this is the basis of the holy book of Islam, the Koran. The religion thus revealed, Islam, quickly spread throughout the Arabian Peninsula and, within just a couple of centuries, it also spread across the rest of the Middle East region and North Africa. Muslims do not regard the Holy Koran as the teachings of Muhammad, but rather as the direct and literal word of God. However, it is also fair to say that the conception of human beings found in the Holy Koran has affinity with Jewish and Christian ideas. Muslims hold that Islam is in continuity with and supersedes Jewish and Christian revelations: Moses and Jesus, for example, are held to be genuine prophets, though not accurately described in the Jewish and Christian scriptures. At the heart of Islam is the claim that there is one God, Allah, and his greatest, final prophet is Muhammad.

A common theme in the Holy Koran is the Day of Judgment: the time when God will resurrect the dead by judgment according to their deeds, with some expecting rewards and new life, and others expecting punishments and death. In continuity with Judeo-Christian concepts, Islam teaches that God will draw on his creative power in bringing the *body* back to life. Consider the following extract:

O you people: If you are in doubt concerning the resurrection, know that We created you from dust, then from a sperm-drop, then from a blood-clot, then from an embryo partly formed and partly unformed, in order to make clear to you. We establish in the wombs whatever We wish for an appointed time, then We bring you out as an infant, then [sustain you] until you reach maturity … You saw the earth lifeless, and then We poured down upon it water and it quivers and grows and sprouts forth all kinds of beautiful pairs. That is because God is the ultimately real. He is Who gives life to what is dead; He it is Who has power over all things. Truly the Hour is coming—there is no doubt of it—when God will resurrect those who lie in their graves (S 22:5–7).[3]

The logic is similar to that used by Ezekiel and Paul:

- God has complete power to create and did create everything.
- God gives life and has made life on earth beautiful.
- He is easily capable, therefore, of bringing the dead to life.
- He will resurrect the dead from their graves.

However, from that fundamental concept Islamic views have become diverse and complex, as has been the case for Judaism and Christianity. It is not possible to trace all the different ideas here, but a sense of the richness and variety of Islamic thought can be gained through examining the works of the Persian poet and mystic Jalal ad-Din Muhammad Rumi. His case opens up the mystical tradition of Islam, Sufism, which emphasizes personal contemplation as a means of achieving purification and unity with God. In that sense, it is possible to encounter God through mental effort and ethical life: a position also emphasized by some Jewish and Christian scholars. Rumi suggests that the ego is a barrier to unification with God and so one must 'die' in ending a life of selfishness, to be reborn in devotion to God. When the mind settles upon love and selfless living, then it receives "life": a life that is connected to the world through love cannot be cut off from it through death.

Rumi, like a number of mystical authors, claims that the mind is able to transcend the body, to reach out beyond its physical limitations, because it can become aware of its profound connection to the world and to God. This theme is explored in his poetry:

Die now! Die now! In this Love, die; when you have died in this Love, you will all receive new life.

Die now, die now, and do not fear this death, for you will come forth from this earth and seize the heavens.

Die now, die now, and break away from this carnal soul, for this carnal soul is as a chain and you are as prisoners.

Take an axe to dig through the prison; when you have broken the prison you will all be kings and princes.

Die now, die now before the beauteous King; when you have died before the King, you will all be kings and renowned.

Die now, die now and come forth from this cloud; when you come forth from this cloud, you will all be radiant full moons.

Be silent, be silent; silence is the sign of death; it is because of life that you are fleeing from the silent one.

—Rumi[4]

[3] Quoted in Jane Idleman Smith and Yvonne Yazbeck Haddad, *The Islamic Understanding of Death and Resurrection* (Oxford: Oxford University Press, 2002), p. 1.

[4] A. J. Arberry (trans.), *Mystical Poems of Rumi*, edited by Ehsan Yarshater, with a new foreword by Franklin D. Lewis (Chicago: University of Chicago Press, 2009), p. 80.

## Biography: Jalal ad-Din Muhammad Rumi (1207–1273 CE)

Rumi was a Persian poet, theologian, and Sufi mystic who has had an enormous impact upon Iranian and Islamic culture, but whose works have an enduring appeal. Improbably, in the early 2000s he became America's best-selling poet through modern translations of his works. Rumi's father was also a scholar and theologian, and so he received an intensive education at a young age. After an early career of teaching, Rumi turned to a more ascetic life and a focus upon composing poetry, his great work the *Masnavi* running to six major volumes.

## Ancient philosophy of body and mind in perspective

It would not be much of an exaggeration to say that there are as many concepts of body and mind as there are cultures around the world. Each perspective and each way of seeing the world yields a different way of seeing human beings. One of the most important points to draw from this section is that a concept of the mind or of the body is a reflection of a concept of reality as a whole. So, that concept of the body and the mind is only as convincing as the particular view of reality it relies upon. Here is a simple comparison to make the point:

| **Buddha** | **Plato** | **Saint Paul** |
|---|---|---|
| Nondualism | Dualism | Monism |
| The world is characterized by *Samsara*, the persistent cycle of life and death, and the illusions of the physical world and the self. | The world may be divided into the realms of the senses and of ideas; truth lies among the ideas, which are unchanging. | The world is the Creation of God and is "good" at origin, though it suffers from corruption; God is intent on restoration of his Creation. |
| Neither the mind nor the body contain "who we really are", as they constantly change and there is no essential self. | The core of a human being is found in the soul, which is the seat of reason and ideas; mind is distinct from the body. | The core of a human being inhabits the body, though this suffers from physical weakness; God will resurrect a spiritual body. |

If you have a Buddhist view of the world, then you will see the mind and the body in a Buddhist way. If you accept Platonic **epistemology** (concept of knowledge), then you will see the mind and the body in a Platonic way. However, any ancient or traditional concept may be criticized for the way in which it relies on an ancient worldview: an understanding of reality that could be seen as out-of-date. A common criticism of all the opinions considered in this section might be that they do not derive from a modern scientific understanding of the world, which has been shown to have more validity through its experimental method. The argument would go something like this:

- The world can be studied most accurately in scientific terms, through the laws of physics, biology, chemistry, cosmology, etc.

- There is no experimental proof for Platonic ideas, *Samsara*, God, etc., and so these are not helpful categories for analysing mind and body.
- It is best to take an analytical approach to humans, like science, by breaking down how all the different systems work; a concept of the "essence" of a human being in metaphysics or religion is therefore idle speculation.

The core of these criticisms goes beyond the remit of this chapter, as it proposes a fundamental question for all of us: is experimental science the only legitimate way to ascertain truth about our world? Nevertheless, without grappling with that greater question here, there are ways to respond to the specific critique of non-scientific concepts of mind and body. Firstly, even if a person supposedly has a "less valid" view of the world than modern scientists, this does not prevent that person from advancing some good arguments. For example, you might not believe in God, but you could still appreciate the Jewish claim that the world is a unity and that humans are physically a part of it ("you are dust, and to dust you shall return"). Secondly, although there is value in scientific analysis of humans, it could be argued that humans still need to make sense of what they are as a whole: narratives, traditions, and theologies have value in placing the human being (body, mind, soul, spirit) within a symbolic system that gives meaning. This human process of "making sense" is inevitable and could be seen as a form of truth.

## EXERCISE

1. "Ancient views of body and mind seem quaint and out-of-date in comparison with today's science." Write one paragraph in support of this statement and one paragraph counter-arguing against it.
2. Research the concepts of mind and body in a traditional culture that endures today, not discussed here (for example, Native American, African, Chinese). Consider how the worldview and assumptions of the culture inform views on mind and body. Try to uncover the reasons and logic used to support these views.
3. Discuss the extent to which common/popular views of mind and body in our culture are derived from ancient sources.

## Mind and body in rationalism and idealism

- Rationalism: humans as minds (Ficino and Descartes)
- Idealism: mind as absolute (Hegel)

### Rationalism: humans as minds (Ficino and Descartes)

How do we know what the mind or body is? Throughout much of Western history, one of the most important ways of knowing has been faith in revealed truth, from the Church. From the fall of the Roman Empire until the modern era, a rough consensus emerged on the issues we are discussing here, asserting that the nature of a human can be known through a harmony of revelation and natural reason. The scriptures would be studied, their concept of humanity would be identified, and philosophy would be used in a supporting role to clarify the ideas thus discovered. Philosophy was referred to as the "handmaiden of theology" (*ancilla theologiae*). Medieval philosophy largely followed Aristotle (mostly thanks to the preservation of his works by Muslim scholars), sparking an intellectual movement known as **scholasticism**: the programme of rationally defending and expounding theology through analytical methods. The scholastics also drew on Augustine, however, so they had a mixed legacy including Platonic ideas as a part of their system. Their general outlook on body and mind can be summarized as follows:

- Human knowledge is derived primarily from the senses (Aristotle).
- Scripture is an infallible source of knowledge, given by God.
- The mind interprets evidence from the senses and scripture.
- Therefore, humans are created in the body, as described in scripture.
- Therefore, the physical form of humans is created by God, and can be understood through the senses.
- However, the soul is held to be immortal (Plato), because the intellect is immaterial/non-physical.
- Therefore, a human is created as a composite of body and soul/intellect, the soul will survive death, and the soul will receive a renewed body at the resurrection (Augustine).

The important point to understand about this theory is that it was seen as utterly convincing for a long time. It is part of a medieval worldview in which there are two revelations: the direct revelation of scripture (the Holy Bible) and the natural revelation of a world to be studied and understood. The mind–body problem was dormant in this era (it was not considered a genuine difficulty) because the reality of nature as it appears was taken as a given thing. There would be no reason to doubt the senses, the intellect, or nature, because they were God-given. We seem to be body–soul composites and so that must be true, for God would not wish to deceive us. This type of reasoning is different from, for example, Platonic dialogue, which takes no knowledge as "given" or "revealed" and instead puts everything under question. Perhaps fittingly, therefore, the rediscovery of Plato ultimately undermined the scholastic consensus on mind and body.

## FIND OUT MORE

Investigate the concept of the soul in the writings of Thomas Aquinas. How do his ideas compare with ancient Greek philosophy?

Plato's philosophy was largely unknown in medieval Europe: with the exception of a few dialogues, it was thought that his works had not survived the collapse of Rome, in which so many writings were lost. However, the dialogues of Plato in fact *had* survived, just not in Western Europe. They were preserved in the Byzantine Empire, the successor

of the Roman Empire in the eastern half of the Mediterranean. This was a Christian, Greek-speaking power that upheld ancient culture and literature. However, the Byzantines ultimately were defeated and their empire dismantled by the Muslim Turks in the 15th century, leading to an exodus of Greek Christian scholars fleeing to Western Europe. They brought with them treasures of Greek literature, including the works of Plato. In 1464, the Italian philosopher Marsilio Ficino completed the first major translation of Plato's works from Greek into Latin, so that they would then be widely read in Europe. Ten years later, Ficino published a major work in favour of a Platonic view of the immortality of the soul, arguing for a substantial distinction between the body and the mind.

## Biography: Marsilio Ficino (1433–1499)

Ficino was one of the great scholars and philosophers of the Italian Renaissance, the era of intellectual rebirth in the arts and humanistic studies. He grew up in the city-state of Florence, ruled by the famous Medici family and to whom his father acted as a physician. Ficino studied and taught in the city for the rest of his life and was generously patronized by the Medicis. He studied Greek language and Plato under the direction of Byzantine scholars, eventually setting up a new version of Plato's Academy in Florence and acting as its tutor. His masterworks were his translation of Plato and the *Platonic Theology*, but he also took a keen interest in astrology and was investigated by the Church on suspicion of practising magic. He was acquitted by the court and spent the rest of his life in scholarship, in peace.

Ficino develops his arguments in *Platonic Theology* (1474), which has the subtitle *On the Immortality of the Soul*. These arguments are familiar from and extensions of Plato; however, Ficino has a strong agenda of uniting Platonic thought with unshakeable belief in an all-powerful Creator. He reinforces the distinction between ideas and the appearance of physical objects; ideas are the most real things and it is the goal of the mind to uncover them. He accepts, therefore, Plato's idea that the mind has an affinity to non-physical and abstract things. At this point, Ficino goes further and introduces his own arguments. The soul is not simply distinct in its immaterial nature, but it also has a *desire* towards immortality. All humans, Ficino claims, have a hope to live and wish for a kind of spiritual union after death. This desire is either true (i.e. grounded in reality), or it is a false hope. However, it cannot be a false hope, because nature is characterized by the goodness of God, and God would not give humans a universal illusion. The human desire for immortality is thus realistic and the rational soul is immortal. Ficino's other argument is that reason and the soul become more effective when isolated from the body, showing their non-physical nature. When we experience a lot of physical sensations, it is difficult to think as we are surrounded by stimulation and distraction. Clearing the mind means clearing away what is physical: "Then the soul despises corporeals and when the senses have been allayed and the clouds of phantasmata dissipated … then the intellect discerns truly and is at its brightest".[5]

[5] Marsilio Ficino, *Platonic Theology: On the Immortality of the Soul*, edited and translated by Michael J. B. Allen and James Hankins (Cambridge: Harvard University Press, 2003), vol. 3, book IX, chapter 2.2.

| Plato *(Phaedo)* | Marsilio Ficino *(Platonic Theology)* |
|---|---|
| Argument from cycles | Accepts Platonic arguments, *adds*: |
| Argument from ideas | Argument from desire, benevolent God |
| Argument from affinity | Argument from isolation |

## EXERCISE

1. Imagine that Plato were to meet a medieval Christian philosopher. How would they respond to one another on the issues of mind and body? Write an imaginary dialogue.
2. Draw a diagram representing the Platonic view of humans and of the world, and of the medieval Christian view of humans and of the world. How do the representations compare?
3. How would you criticize Ficino's arguments? Write a paragraph exploring their weaknesses.

Our knowledge of mind and body, therefore, can be derived from different sources, and after Ficino the discussion became more varied and interesting. If it is not sufficient to say that human beings are simple mind–body composites, as the Church taught, as they appear, then what are they? With the rediscovery of Plato, critical questions were being asked: How do we know what the mind is? How do we know what the body is? How do we know our senses are accurate? How do we know anything at all? That process of doubting things is known as **scepticism** and it has a powerful effect on concepts of mind and body. A natural way of arguing about being human is to start with simple statements of how life seems to be. I seem to be in this body. I seem to be thinking thoughts. I seem to be reading this sentence. If we accept all of these appearances at face value, we could use them for an idea of what being human involves in terms of mind, body, etc. However, what if we do not accept how things seem at face value? A philosopher might ask, is there any *justification* for accepting how things seem to be?

Dealing with just these questions, Descartes had a huge impact on the discussion of mind and body, stating the classic dualist argument. On the one hand, Descartes is a Platonist, because he argues from the primacy of reason towards an understanding of human beings in mental terms, as thinkers. However, on the other hand, Descartes' arguments are distinct from Plato's, because he takes the process of doubt to a new level, to the extent that mind becomes a very individual thing. His focus on the internal workings of the mind is so strong that one could even go on to question whether there is an external world, or other minds, at all. Descartes works through a series of contemplative discussions (the title of his work is *Meditations on First Philosophy,* 1641), starting by questioning all the knowledge he had simply assumed to be true. He reasons that, in his experience, he has found that many things he held to be true turned out to be falsehoods and he hopes to discern in a systematic way what is true. Therefore, he questions all his assumptions

until he arrives at what can certainly be regarded as truth. He is attempting to rebuild knowledge from the bottom up, from fundamental principles, a process known as **foundationalism**.[6]

We tend to form our knowledge and opinions on the basis of sense perception, but Descartes objects to this through his procedure of "**radical doubt**": he wishes to question *everything*. Is it possible that all of his sense perceptions are mistaken? It is possible, he argues, because humans commonly experience unreal sense perceptions in dreams. A famous passage of his argument runs as follows:

> I must nevertheless here consider that I am a man, and that, consequently, I am in the habit of sleeping, and representing to myself in dreams those same things, or even sometimes others less probable, which the insane think are presented to them in their waking moments. How often have I dreamt that I was in these familiar circumstances, that I was dressed, and occupied this place by the fire, when I was lying undressed in bed? At the present moment, however, I certainly look upon this paper with eyes wide awake; the head which I now move is not asleep; I extend this hand consciously and with express purpose, and I perceive it; the occurrences in sleep are not so distinct as all this. But I cannot forget that, at other times, I have been deceived in sleep by similar illusions; and, attentively considering those cases, I perceive so clearly that there exist no certain marks by which the state of waking can ever be distinguished from sleep, that I feel greatly astonished; and in amazement I almost persuade myself that I am now dreaming.
>
> —René Descartes[7]

Further, Descartes gives his famous thought experiment of the "**evil demon**". Imagine that there was a creature of great power that sought to deceive and confuse at every turn. This demon could create the impression of the external world wholly through illusion; it could create the impression of a physical body when in fact there are no hands and eyes. The only logical thing to do, Descartes concludes, would be to suspend judgment on all matters until sufficient reason has been found that is so clear that even a powerful demon could not deceive us on the matter. Descartes is not actually recommending to his readers that they believe in this demon; he is using it as a way of showing just how sceptical one could be. We could doubt that the world exists, that other people exist, and even that our own bodies exist.

How do we go beyond the radical scepticism given from the idea of the evil demon? For Descartes, the only way is to turn inwards, into contemplation. As he explains:

### Questions

1. What is the value of "radical doubt"? Is it possible to be "too sceptical"?
2. Does the dreaming example really show we should doubt our experiences?
3. Is it truly possible to doubt even that our bodies exist? Why/why not?
4. How does Descartes' concept of illusion compare with the Buddhist concept?

---

[6] René Descartes, *Meditations on First Philosophy: In Which the Existence of God and the Distinction of the Soul from the Body Are Demonstrated*, 3rd edition, translated from the Latin by Donald A. Cress (Indianapolis, IN: Hackett Publishing Company, 1993).

[7] In John Veitch and Frank Sewall, *The Method, Meditations and Philosophy of Descartes* (Washington and London: M. Walter Dunne, 1901), Meditation I.5.

> Thinking is another attribute of the soul; and here I discover what properly belongs to myself. This alone is inseparable from me. I am—I exist: this is certain; but how often? As often as I think; for perhaps it would even happen, if I should wholly cease to think, that I should at the same time altogether cease to be. I now admit nothing that is not necessarily true. I am therefore, precisely speaking, only a thinking thing, that is, a mind, understanding, or reason, terms whose signification was before unknown to me. I am, however, a real thing, and really existent; but what thing? The answer was, a thinking thing.
>
> —René Descartes[8]

Elsewhere, in his *Discourse on the Method*, this idea receives the famous formulation "I think, therefore I am". This is a radical view of being human, stretching the Platonic emphasis on contemplation to the limit: human beings *are* minds, thinking things. Whatever the body is, it can be distinguished from the essential core. In developing this argument, Descartes is also shifting the emphasis for philosophy of mind onto conscious awareness. It is his awareness of his own thoughts, he thinks, that enables him to prove the reality of his existence as mental substance, a mind, to the extent that even the evil demon could not mislead him. For, even if the demon were intent on twisting his thoughts, it would not be possible for Descartes not to exist in the act of thinking, because the act "is inseparable from me". Thinking requires a thinker – a logical certainty – and so the basic existence of the mind cannot be denied. Consciousness seems to be the primary characteristic of the mind – indeed, of the whole human being.

**TOK link** 

What is to be made of Descartes' claim that knowledge from sense perception is not of itself reliable? Can knowledge be founded upon "pure reason"? How could Descartes' approach be applied to the areas of knowledge?

What, then, is the relationship between mind and body? Descartes is certain that it is possible to move from knowledge of the mind – that I exist – to knowledge of the body also, but he is also adamant that these are two different types of substance. Firstly, there is the distinction. Descartes feels certain that mind and body are distinct because he has immediate logical certainty in apprehending the existence of the mind, but not so with the body. There is a further distinction in the fact that the body is characterized by "extension" (it has dimensions, size, etc.) but the mind is not characterized by extension. Then secondly, there is the possibility of reasoning from the mind, the "thinking thing", towards the physical body also. It is apparent that there is an external world and a physical body: this seems to be the case from the senses, though they can be doubted. However, because Descartes thinks that the existence of God is logically certain (as reasoned in another part of *Meditations*), the faculty of sight thus comes from God. He is perfect, does not deceive, and so the mind can put its trust in the existence of the body. So, albeit separately, both the mind and the body can be said to exist.

[8] Ibid., Meditation II.6.

They are separate, but Descartes also holds that the mind and the body *interact*, and so his version of dualism is referred to as **interactionism**. After all, how is it that our thoughts seemingly proceed to move the body? I think to touch a particular key on my computer keyboard while writing this book and I then move my finger accordingly. What else could this be other than the mind interacting with the body, "telling" it what to do? Yet, that causes a problem, perhaps the most fundamental problem of **Cartesian** dualism, of explaining *how* this interaction is supposed to work. Descartes reasoned that there must be some part of the brain housing this interaction and identified this with the **pineal gland**, producing a famous diagram thus:

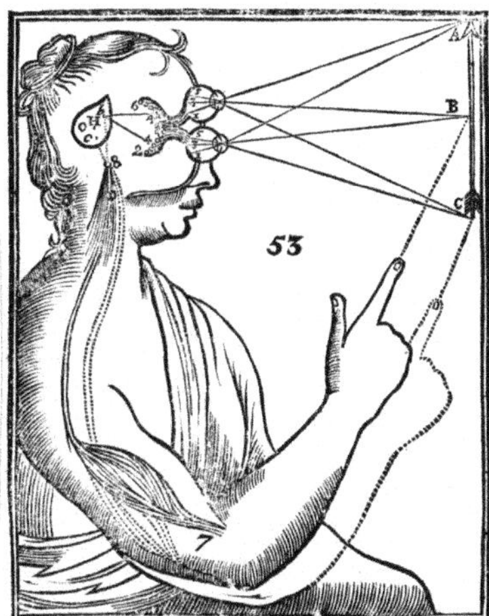


▲ Cartesian interactionism

## EXERCISE

1. Examine Descartes' diagram of interactionism. What processes is it trying to represent? What is the challenge of attempting to represent dualism visually in relation to a human body?
2. Discuss: do we *need* to be able to explain how interactionism works in order to accept the theory of mind–body dualism?

Yet, Descartes' choice of the pineal gland is difficult to understand, and his theory has proved obscure and unpopular among philosophers. The most stinging criticism of Descartes is that his interactionism involves a kind of double standard; it both separates the mind from the body and links it to the body. The contemporary philosopher Daniel C. Dennett (whom we will encounter in a later section) summarizes the problem by citing a children's cartoon, Casper the Friendly Ghost.

As Dennett asks in *Consciousness Explained* (1991), "How can Casper *both* glide through walls and grab a falling towel? How can mind stuff *both* elude all physical measurement and control the body?"[9] The objection is that dualists cannot explain this kind of interaction so they resort to the idea that it is a mystery, or beyond human understanding. However, in trying to understand the mind physically, in relation to the brain, the quest for understanding how thinking works goes on. Materialists would claim that they are going further and trying harder to explain how the mind and the body work. The classic statement of this kind of criticism of Descartes was made by the modern English philosopher Gilbert Ryle in his book *The Concept of Mind* (1949), in which Ryle refers to the Cartesian mind as the "**ghost in the machine**". That phrase has stuck in the minds of philosophers and summarizes very neatly why Descartes' theory is not popular today: how could the ghost of the mind move around the machine-like architecture of the body?

[9] Daniel C. Dennett, *Consciousness Explained* (Boston, MA: Little, Brown & Company, 1991), p. 35.

Ryle further talks about Descartes making a "**category mistake**". That is, he accuses Descartes of fundamentally misunderstanding what category of thing the mind belongs to, for it is not really a distinct object in its own right at all. He gives the example of a visitor to the English city of Oxford (where Ryle taught philosophy), who walks around the various buildings, colleges, and faculties, and then asks somebody "Where is the university?" It is a mistake, because the visitor has placed the university within the category of physical spaces and buildings, supposing that it must be somewhere in particular. However, the university belongs in another category; it is a collective term for the amalgamated departments, buildings, people, and projects that comprise it. So too with the mind: to ask "where is the mind?" or "what substance is mind?" is to make a category mistake. According to Ryle, the mind is an amalgamation of abilities and actions directed through the brain and central nervous system; it is a collective term for some of the more complex things humans can do. Therefore, Descartes is wrong in supposing that the "thinking thing" has to be some form of substance.[10]

## FIND OUT MORE

Investigate Ryle's proposal of "philosophical behaviourism" and contrast it with Descartes' theory. What is the full extent of Ryle's criticism of Descartes, and what is the alternative he suggests? What criticisms have been made of Ryle's theory?

## Philosophical terms

### Descartes

**Cartesian** – of or pertaining to the philosophy of Descartes: Cartesian doubt, Cartesian dualism, Cartesianism, etc.

**Category mistake** – the phrase coined by Ryle to criticize Descartes' opinion that mind is a type of substance

**Descartes' demon** – the thought experiment of the evil demon that distorts and misleads, supporting the idea of radical doubt that any belief could be false

**Foundationalism** – the philosophical project of building up knowledge from truly basic and certain knowledge

**Ghost in the machine** – the phrase coined by Ryle to criticize interactionism

**Interactionism** – the proposal that the mind and the body are distinct but must interact in some way (for example, the mind directing the body)

**Pineal gland** – the part of the brain where, Descartes claimed, the mind interacted with the body

**Radical doubt** – the process of doubting all beliefs, radical scepticism, to clear away all uncertain opinions

**Thinking thing** (*res cogitans*) – Descartes' definition of the mind and of a human being, primarily as a thinking substance

[10] See Gilbert Ryle, *The Concept of Mind*, new edition with an introduction by Daniel C. Dennett (Chicago: University of Chicago Press, 2002).

However, it is notable that the criticisms of Descartes tend to focus upon his speculations about non-physical mind substance, what it is, and how it interacts with the body. Dealing with the radical doubt he first proposes is another matter and it is an interesting question whether there is another route out of constant doubting, other than the one he suggests. If the individual does indeed doubt everything that seems obvious, even the existence of the external world and of the body, then a number of challenging philosophical questions arise. Can I know whether anything outside my consciousness is real? Are other humans really like me, and do they have conscious awareness like me? The first type of problem here refers to a way of thinking known as **solipsism**, the opinion that only one's own mind exists. The second type of problem is known as the **problem of other minds**, which is the difficulty of proving that people who behave in a similar way to me also have conscious minds like me. Descartes himself thought that we *can* know of the external world and of other minds, but only because he thought he had first logically proven the existence of his own mind and of God. But can his solution still convince us at any level, or are we now just left with the problems his doubting raised, without his failed dualist theory?

On the one hand, the arguments against Descartes seem compelling and his interactionism seems mystifying. Nevertheless, Descartes may have rejected the assumptions that his critics have made in arguing against him. After all, he starts from radical doubt and points out that one can even doubt the evidence of the senses. Yet it is precisely empiricism – the use of sense data – that has been used against Descartes, with the idea that concepts of mind can be reduced to an explanation of the biological brain. This criticism seems powerful and can draw on the prestige of science, but is it really logically proven that Descartes is wrong? It is interesting on this point how popular culture can illuminate a philosophical problem: think about well-known movies that present the hypothesis that the external world as it appears is some sort of illusion or simulation (for example, *The Matrix*, *Inception*, etc.). What these films show rather neatly is that there is some plausibility in questioning whether reality is exactly what we think it is. You may think it is paranoid to consider whether your life is just part of a big computer simulation, but the idea is *coherent*. Can you really know better? And so back to Descartes: we can choose to doubt pretty much anything, but is it reasonable to consider *everything* as more doubtful than the existence of our own thoughts?

## EXERCISE

1. Watch the film *The Matrix*. Does the film support or oppose mind–body dualism?
2. Imagine that Descartes watched *The Matrix*. Taking on the role of Descartes, write a review of the film from his perspective.

## Idealism: mind as absolute (Hegel)

After Descartes and the beginning of modern philosophy, the question of what mind is became an explicit and well-known philosophical problem. While humans had been understood primarily in religious terms, the composition of a human being had not seemed too problematic. They were creations of God, body, and soul. However, the logical method Descartes had used presumed that the nature of mind was first and foremost a topic for rational enquiry, which could be understood by thought alone. So, anybody willing to think independently could in principle develop an independent answer to the question "what is mind?"

**FIND OUT MORE**

Investigate the philosophy of mind of the German philosopher Gottfried Leibniz, including his criticisms of Descartes.

Descartes had given mind complete priority and independence, to the extent that he was willing to say that it was completely **irreducible** (could not be explained in terms of something else) and in no way relied upon the physical world. However, this has by no means proved to be the only way to solve the problem and Descartes had his critics from the outset. Some maintained the previous status quo: being human meant being a divinely created body–soul composite. Others argued for a position now popular in modern philosophy, that only material substances exist and that this includes the mind: **materialism**. One of the most famous materialists, writing a century after Descartes, was Paul-Henri Thiry, Baron d'Holbach (1723–1789). He adopted a thoroughgoing naturalist view of reality, including as "real" everything that could be explained "naturally" (including mind) and excluding as "false" anything metaphysical (thus excluding God). His essential position is summarized in his *System of Nature* (1770) as follows: "The universe, that vast assemblage of every thing that exists, presents only matter and motion: the whole offers to our contemplation nothing but an immense, an uninterrupted succession of causes and effects" (I.I).[11]

**Questions**

1. If the universe consists only of "matter and motion", what does that mean for our understanding of mind and body?
2. How do the ideas of Descartes and d'Holbach conflict?
3. In what ways is materialism appealing or unappealing as a worldview?
4. (Find out) how did philosophical materialism fit with the scientific advancements of d'Holbach's era?

Should we explain the state of being human in terms of mind or of matter? It is tempting to see this problem in terms of a straight choice between the mentalist dualism of Descartes and the materialism of d'Holbach: the mind is either distinct from the physical world, or it isn't. However, the problem in hand may be a little more complicated than this straight choice suggests, particularly when we come to consider the scope

[11] Paul-Henri Thiry, *The System of Nature, Or the Laws of the Moral and Physical World*, vol. 1, edited by Robert R. Richardson (Mirbaud, 1770); now available at http://www.gutenberg.org/files/8909/8909-h/8909-h.htm#link2H_4_0022 (accessed 22 October 2014).

and the power of the mind for making sense of our world. Perhaps the relationship between mind and body, between thinking and the world, could be characterized through a dynamic relationship between the two. Instead of thinking that the mind is fundamental or instead that the physical world is, these categories could be understood as contributing to each other. Perhaps the mental and the physical are in **dialogue**.

Strange as this theory may seem at first glance, it forms the basis of one of the most influential theories in the history of philosophy. The German philosopher Georg Wilhelm Friedrich Hegel attempted to bring together a number of elements of philosophy, to create a synthesis, arguing that the mind becomes "realized" *through* the physical world. Thinking and ideas form the ultimate reality for Hegel – the **absolute** – but they can only come about through their development in biological human beings. There may be no mind without body, but the body without the mind means nothing.

## Biography: Georg Wilhelm Friedrich Hegel (1770–1831)

Hegel was a German philosopher, a career academic, whose legacy has played a vital role in the development of modern philosophy. He was born in Stuttgart and received an intensive academic education, culminating in theological studies in Tübingen. Unlike many philosophers, however, Hegel had no private wealth and undertook a number of tutoring jobs to support his career. He eventually achieved fame and a well-paid professorship through his key work, *The Phenomenology of Mind* (1807), which was completed as Napoleon Bonaparte was marching across Europe to launch his Russian campaign. Hegel's life can seem fairly uneventful, though his ideas rocked the world. He used his philosophy and his reputation to align himself ultimately with the Prussian state, receiving honours and prestige in his lifetime and a later reputation for political conservatism.

To understand this argument, we have to begin with Hegel's dialectical method for understanding the world. He quite often uses a "triad" of ideas to explain how things work: a first position, a second position, and a third position that goes beyond or unites the previous two. This is sometimes called **dialectical logic**, because the first position and the second position must influence one another to produce the final idea. There is an initial *thesis*, then the contradicting idea of *antithesis*, and finally the unifying theory: *synthesis*. Essentially, Hegel argues that philosophy and even all of history advance by differing and competing ideas coming into conflict, thus creating new ways of understanding. The classic parable he tells to explain this process is known as the **master–slave dialectic**, which illuminates how philosophical ideas emerge through increasing awareness. A simple summary runs as follows:

- There are two men who both think themselves free, though at first they are not aware of each other.
- They meet and come into conflict, fighting for dominance. One is victorious and becomes the master; the defeated man is the slave.

- However, the master makes use of his slave and gradually becomes aware that he is dependent on the slave.
- Conversely, the slave becomes aware that the master needs him, and so he is the one (paradoxically) with freedom, having learned to be self-sufficient.
- So, for the sake of his own freedom, the master releases the slave.

In dialectical terms, this can be translated as follows:

- Thesis: the initial position is the desire to be the master (potential freedom).
- Antithesis: the second position is the state of being the slave (actual bondage).
- Synthesis: the new position is that of true freedom, granted by understanding (actual freedom).

This is not a strange argument in favour of slavery and Hegel is not claiming that all slaves in practice gain freedom. It is a story, a way of bringing philosophy to life. But what has it got to do with the mind and the body? In short, Hegel thinks that the mind is involved in the biggest dialectic of all, in its striving towards self-consciousness. The central idea of his philosophy is "mind", though the German word is also translated as "spirit". It is the most distinctive feature of human beings that they can grasp what is intelligible and universal, that they have minds that can think. However, in isolation the mind has nothing to comprehend and amounts to nothing. By contrast with Plato, Hegel does not think that there is some non-physical world of ideas in which the mind could flourish without the body: no body, no mind. It is only through nature that the mental development of humanity becomes possible; through the world and through history humans interact and grow in understanding. It is the interplay of the world and the human mind that enables the "absolute" to emerge, because mind becomes unified in awareness of its own limitless nature.

In Hegel's understanding of the world, reality has a mental and a physical aspect. Everything has this dual aspect and so, for Hegel, mind–body dualism in the style of Descartes would not be possible: mind goes hand-in-hand with the physical aspect (the body) of human beings. However, mind can take an ultimate form in humans, claims Hegel, because they are capable of a form of higher awareness. That is to say, human thinking can achieve a form of **self-realization**:

- Humans think.
- Humans become aware that they think.
- Humans become aware that they are among thinking humans.
- Humans become aware that they can collectively think of universal things.
- Human thinking as a whole can thus become self-aware.
- This totality or "absolute" thinking ("idealism") is infinite.
- "Absolute Mind" (or "Absolute Spirit", or "God") is realized in human thinking.

Therefore, Hegel is arguing that the mind is dependent upon the body (monism) but, in its ultimate form, becomes greater than the sum of its parts. Through my ideas, I can become united with "mind" as a whole, and so my own mind goes "beyond" my own body. For Hegel, it is essential to the appreciation of being human that we perceive this extraordinary ability to grasp the universal: the common capacity for thinking that links us all together.

Having said that, criticisms of Hegel and his idealist theory of the mind abound. It could be argued that this theory is a wilfully complicated way of saying something simple or is a grandiose way of stating the obvious: humans think, they can think a lot, and there is seemingly no limit to what they can think about. But is it really fair to say that this can prove the capacity of mind to become "absolute"? Hegel has also been accused of mystifying and misleading by referring to Absolute Mind as "God", giving the impression that thinking has some non-physical or transcendent quality, which is exactly what his theory denies. His consistent emphasis upon the great power of human ideas also puts Hegel in danger of creating an arrogant way of being human; as Robert C. Tucker argues in *Philosophy and Myth in Karl Marx* (1961), he presents the image of "a self-glorifying humanity striving compulsively ... to rise to divinity".[12] Does Hegel's view of the mind *replace* God?

## FIND OUT MORE

Investigate the "young Hegelians" and the way they interpreted philosophy. How does Marx's view of being human compare with that of Hegel?

## EXERCISE

1. "Neither Descartes nor Hegel can explain the mind, so they just write about their thoughts instead." Do you agree? (Discussion or written answer)
2. Hegel's concept of freedom cannot "keep you out of a concentration camp" (Russell). What do you think this criticism means? (Explain)
3. Identify examples from history that support and contradict Hegel's claim that history is the story of the mind developing. Write a timeline of Hegelian history.
4. Think how Hegel's philosophy could be applied to the problem of other minds. Write a paragraph explaining this application.

## Consciousness, brain, mind, and body

- Naturalism and brain science
- Functionalism: Daniel C. Dennett
- The hard problem of consciousness: David J. Chalmers
- Can the problems be solved?

[12] See Robert C. Tucker, *Philosophy and Myth in Karl Marx*, 3rd edition, with a new introduction by the author (New Brunswick, NJ: Transaction Publishers), p. 66.

## Naturalism and brain science

A lot has changed in the last hundred years or so. It seems impossible today to talk about the mind or body without talking about science. In the more distant past, perhaps, few reckoned that science could one day unlock all the mysteries of a human being: the strangeness of human behaviour, the complexity of language, or the inner workings of the mind. However, there have been many great mysteries that science has proceeded to unlock, and many modern "miracles" that would have been thought impossible by previous generations. If science can take us to the moon, then why should it not also take us into the mind itself? We take it for granted that the body can be studied scientifically: that process, in anatomy and human biology, has developed over centuries. While it might be tempting to separate the mind from this field, the obvious connections between the brain and mental events lead us to wonder whether the mind too could one day be explained with equal completeness as the beating of the heart or the inflation of the lungs. Is it only a matter of time until brain science resolves the problems of the philosophy of mind?

### Philosophical terms

#### Brain and mind

**Behaviourism** – the theory that humans should be understood by means of their external actions, not internal thoughts

**Cognition** – mental activity and processes: thinking, remembering, etc.

**Functionalism** – the theory that mind can be explained fully through its functions

**Materialism** – the theory that everything is formed of matter and nothing else exists

**Phenomena** – appearances or experiences, objects as they seem to the observer; the philosophical study of these is **phenomenology**

**Physicalism** – (equivalent to materialism) everything is physical; there is nothing else

**Naturalism** – the view that reality can and should be fully explained through natural processes and scientific laws, as opposed to the "supernatural"

**Neuroscience** – the scientific study of the brain

**Reductionism** – the process of fully explaining a theory or idea in terms of other ideas or phenomena; reducing the mind to explainable factors

One important consideration here is the question of whether the philosophy of mind can be incorporated into an understanding of nature. Can we *explain* the mind in the same way that we explain natural phenomena, through scientific laws? The philosophical tendency to see all problems as in principle solvable through the study of our world and its laws is called **naturalism**. It excludes the possibility of there being some other realities or existent things that influence our universe, but which couldn't be discovered rationally or scientifically; it excludes the idea of the "supernatural" as a genuine philosophical consideration. In that sense, naturalism tends to exclude religious and traditional belief systems as ways of acquiring knowledge. Instead, naturalism reasons from the progress of science to the principle that progress *should* be scientific. Science provides its own credentials in its myriad of success stories and seemingly

undogmatic methodology, and so it seems reasonable to incorporate everything we could hope to know into this method of natural science. Naturalism involves peeling back the mysteries and finding the reasonable explanations, and naturalists would expect that there is a reasonable explanation for the mind, even if we don't yet have it.

But why favour naturalism, as an approach to the mind or any other problem? Its supporters point out how it has seemingly superseded previous worldviews:

| Arguments for supernaturalism | Counter-arguments from naturalism |
|---|---|
| Many phenomena in the world and human experience are seemingly unexplainable or mysterious – they may have a cause beyond our natural understanding. | The phenomena that still cannot be explained are rapidly diminishing before the progress of science; it follows that we should be optimistic about naturalism. |
| Psychic evidence, miracles, and religious experiences all imply that there are "dimensions" to reality which are not readily discernible through natural senses. | The evidence for supernaturalism has at least partially been discredited, and naturalists suggest explanations for this evidence in scientific terms. |
| Supernaturalism is in continuity with the past and has been nearly universally accepted by human cultures – it is a body of received knowledge. | Continuity with the past cannot provide support to a theory in the face of evidence to the contrary; good science tends to overthrow previous understandings. |

As an approach to the mind, therefore, philosophical naturalism has some fairly straightforward consequences:

- It leads to mind–body monism, as humans are understood as organisms that can be studied holistically through natural science; there are no mysterious bits.
- Our understanding of the mind will develop gradually and improve through the application of scientific method; we know little now, but that should change.
- Arguments that are abstracted from real world experience (for example, Descartes) will have little value, as the individual is assumed to be *part* of the physical world.
- Philosophy needs to support and clarify **neuroscience**, as the brain is the organ that obviously supports the "high functionality" of humans in thinking and doing.

## TOK link

How should philosophers treat natural science as an area of knowledge? Is the success of sense perception and reason in natural science proof that these are the pre-eminent ways of knowing?

## Questions

1. Can supernaturalism respond to the criticisms from naturalism?
2. Is explaining the mind a puzzle like any other scientific puzzle?
3. Can naturalism be criticized from earlier philosophy (for example, Plato)?
4. How could naturalism affect other areas of philosophy (ethics, religion, etc.)?

One way of bringing naturalism to the philosophy of mind and body is to emphasize psychology, the way in which humans behave, and to advocate the view that the mind itself is nothing more than a way of talking about behaviour. It seems obvious that behaviour is a key observable feature about human beings: I am writing a textbook, you are reading it, and so on. We keep doing things. This behaviour can be studied and made sense of (in principle, at least) through science and the presupposition of naturalism. So, perhaps it follows that behaviour *only* follows from external stimulation and biological systems, not from thoughts or mental events. This theory is referred to as **philosophical behaviourism** or **logical behaviourism** (see the previous discussion, connected with Descartes). It is a form of mind–body monism, in the sense that it conceives of the body *only* as an object or entity and the mind has no reality of its own. The mind is just a conventional way of talking about some of the things that the body singly does in the most complex functioning of the brain and nervous system. So, when it is observed that I am typing the text for this book, the philosophical behaviourist says that there is *nothing more* going on. The typing is real; the impression that I am thinking about it is, at most, a by-product of my behaviour.

As mentioned before, this particular school of philosophy is associated with Ryle (refer back to "Find out more" task). It was popular in philosophy for a time, still has supporters, and has some obvious advantages. There is plenty of evidence to suggest that external stimulation affects or even determines the behaviour of an organism, which might imply that "thinking" does not really feature (consider how snacks can be used to manipulate dogs, and then apply that to humans). Behaviourism also coheres with naturalism and the general objective of trying to provide reasonable explanations for the world.

Nevertheless, there is a problem. I can stop writing this textbook for a minute and it certainly *seems* that I can think. I have thought of something to write in the next sentence. Now I stop and change my mind. The initial idea of what I would write next *never* featured in my behaviour, but does that mean that it was not *real*? It seems that the behaviourist is committed to saying that it was not. It certainly seems possible to have mental events that do not affect behaviour, and so the behaviourist is faced with the difficult challenge of explaining this supposedly mistaken impression. How can I be wrong in thinking that I think?

## EXERCISE

1. Write out a list of mental events that seemingly do not feature in our external behaviour. Then reflect, is there a way to explain even these in behaviourist terms?
2. Draw two diagrams representing different worldviews in relation to human beings as minds and bodies: from naturalist and supernaturalist perspectives.
3. Define the word "thinking". Is it possible? Can you do this without assuming a particular theory of the mind and the body?
4. Investigate the science of brain imaging/scanning. Does this lend any support to behaviourism, or any other theory of what constitutes a human being?

### History of brain science

The history of brain science and the attempt to perform surgical operations on the brain stretches back thousands of years, though genuine advances in understanding have been few and far between until the last hundred years or so. Traditional cultures have recognized the importance of the brain to the performance of recognizably "human" behaviour, performing trepanation (drilling or scraping into the skull) to relieve mental disorders and headaches. Some ancient sources recognized ways in which damage to the brain could affect personality or ability, and so some sort of mind–brain connection has long been assumed. These observations, combined with the eventual development of staining brain sections and sophisticated microscopes (around the turn of the 19th/20th centuries), ultimately enabled neuroscientists to begin "mapping" functions within the brain. For example, the question could be asked, which parts (loosely speaking) of the brain could correspond to language functions, social behaviour, memory, etc.? Understandably, modern neuroscience is now a diverse and highly complex field of study, encompassing studies of a psychological, mathematical, biochemical, and anthropological (etc.) nature. There is both rapid advancement in knowledge and a clear understanding that much of the brain still remains a mystery. As the great science fiction writer Isaac Asimov suggested in his Foreword for *The 3-Pound Universe*, the brain "is the most complicated organization of matter that we know of".[13]

### FIND OUT MORE

Read Barry Smith's article on neuroscience and philosophy in the *Guardian* newspaper.

**http://www.theguardian.com/commentisfree/2012/mar/04/consciousness-neuroscience-self-philosophy**

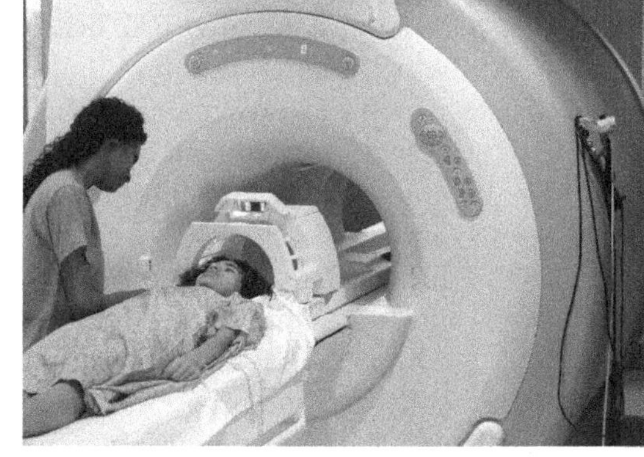

But could neuroscience ever advance so far as to render the philosophy of mind unnecessary? How would this happen? It depends upon the way in which we clarify and comprehend what we are looking at in terms of "mind". There certainly are some features at least of the mind that, one by one, are being targeted for successful scientific explanations. Your emotions could be explained through biochemical processes in the brain. Your memories are of great interest to researchers trying to combat dementia. Your appreciation of art can produce some fascinating results in fMRI scans. These are all important areas of life that have traditionally been associated with the mind, and they are now subject to scientific investigation. It seems that in some respects science is taking over from philosophical speculations. Nevertheless, that is not necessarily a problem for philosophy; some philosophers would argue that it is their job to help clarify the scope and approach of science, and so they should celebrate when science is able to be successful. Other philosophers would question whether the deeper problems of the mind have really been touched upon by the scientific discussion of mental abilities. Has the essence of mind really been explained? Has its role in relation to the body really been clarified?

## Functionalism: Daniel C. Dennett

If behaviourism fails to account for how the mind can be understood naturalistically, because it fails when we confront it with our private experiences, then could there be some other way for philosophy to

[13] Quoted in Isaac Asimov, "Foreword", in Judith Hooper and Dicki Teresi, *The 3-Pound Universe* (New York: Macmillan, 1986).

smooth the path of neuroscientific progress? One approach would be to acknowledge the greater complexity of the mind–brain relationship as part of a system that is greater and more sophisticated than the classic behaviourist arguments allowed. Instead of focusing on the overt behaviour of the human being (i.e. what we can see her or him doing), it could be possible instead to start from all the different jobs the mind could do, both in leading to external action but also to the so-called internal experiences of thinking. The mind could be defined through its capabilities; perhaps it is nothing more than a collection of processes and functions. The attempt to understand these coherently, together, to provide a satisfying explanation in the philosophy of mind is known as **functionalism**.

Functionalism differs from behaviourism in looking at mental states as being distinct from physical states: you can have private thoughts, make up sentences in your head, or daydream about eating ice-cream. All these things can be "real" to the functionalist, who would say that we will have understood the mind once we understand how all of these various functions work. Ultimately, in the case of human beings, we should be able to ascribe most or all of these functions to the brain, because that is the main piece of infrastructure we have for mental activities. Nevertheless, functionalism does *not* propose that the brain and mind are identical, because the core of this theory is the *way* in which mental functions happen, not the specific physical matter in which they are manifested. The mind is not a particular type of physical object (i.e. a brain), but is a way of talking about some pretty important and special capabilities that *happen* to be manifested in human brains but could conceivably be manifested in other ways. In this sense, functionalism differs from what is called the **identity theory** of mind (i.e. which identifies the mind with the brain exactly). To make a comparison with a computer, functionalists see the mind in terms of software: the programs and applications that the computer runs. The mind is distinct from the physical computer itself, the hardware (by analogy, the brain), because the same tasks could conceivably be run on different systems.

This leads on to another distinctive part of the functionalist theory, that the mind could receive multiple and varying forms of realization. We happen to know these functions best from our own brains, but our brains really are just a bit like organic computers. It seems reasonable to suppose that the functions could be transferred between different types of system, and so the mind as a whole in principle is transferable between different realizations. This is *not* to say that scientists should be able to build a robot mind of equal stature to humans any time soon; it is no practical possibility. Rather, this is a logical and hypothetical possibility resulting from this way of understanding the mind. This point about multiple realization shows a distinctive feature and strength of functionalism; it avoids the problem of saying narrowly that the mind is a simple part of our anatomy (clearly, having a mind feels a bit different from having a foot), yet it also avoids the problem of saying that the mind is some kind of special or mysterious entity. If the older, dualistic arguments are rejected, then functionalism seems a likely alternative.

The most important advocate of functionalism today is the American philosopher and cognitive scientist Daniel C. Dennett. In *Consciousness Explained*, he has sought to address the challenges faced in the philosophy of mind – most importantly the problems of consciousness, how and why we have experiences, and how things seem – by developing new perspectives and language for handling the problems. One of the most important of these is the assertion that consciousness should be treated as something that in principle could be studied and analysed, and, although it obviously is not possible to "get inside" somebody else's mind, it is possible to record their descriptions carefully, check them against other data, and not simply assume that the reporting of what one experiences is always accurate. Therefore, Dennett argues that we should not treat the study of experiences (**phenomenology**) as dealing with the unique and mysterious, in a completely private world of the mind. On the contrary, he claims, we should suppose that it is possible to study what somebody else's experiences are like (**heterophenomenology**), and thus consider that we could know something about experiences and consciousness in general. The "first person" experiences of the individual (what they are like for me) need to be acknowledged by philosophy, against behaviourism, but Dennett claims they need to be studied with the scientific scruples of the "third person" (i.e. the outsider, the investigator) perspective. Simply, functionalism considers what the mind *does* by discussing *scientifically* what experiences are like.

## Biography: Daniel C. Dennett (1942– )

Dennett is an American philosopher and specialist in cognitive science who has been seeking throughout his career to provide a thoroughgoing scientific approach to consciousness, with solid philosophical foundations. Naturalism is an important presupposition to Dennett: without the belief that the natural world is causally closed (that is, has no external interference from the supernatural or mysterious), he claims that it would not be possible for science, and thereby knowledge, to progress. Unsurprisingly, therefore, Dennett's career has also been characterized by polemic against religion, which he sees as one of the most significant barriers to human understanding and progress. In his work *Breaking the Spell* (2006) Dennett argues that religion itself is a purely natural phenomenon that in principle can receive a thorough explanation (making particular use of evolution as a model for understanding). Therefore, Dennett's project of explaining the mind and the body needs to be understood against this wider background; his chief aim as a philosopher is to clarify the ways in which science can explain everything we encounter in life, even the seemingly deep mysteries of the human mind. Today, Dennett is Professor of Philosophy at Tufts University in Boston, USA, and heads up the Center for Cognitive Studies.

To understand Dennett's particular view of the mind, it is helpful to start with his rejection of what he sees as the most popular alternative paradigm, that of Descartes. To understand the mind–body connection properly, claims Dennett, it is first necessary for philosophers to get the

Cartesian view of the problem completely out of our systems, because it is a long-enduring and rather subtle view of human beings. Even if we do not think of ourselves as followers of Descartes, he argues, we may still be tempted to take on some of the older philosophical assumptions. That is, it is easy to accept that the physical system of the eye and optic nerve, for example, translates light into an image that is then passed on to the brain. But how do we talk about what happens next? A common trap would be to suppose there must be something in the brain that "sees" this image, like a projection in a movie theatre. The mind "sees" the images of sight. Dennett claims that any such thinking along these lines is assuming a Cartesian way of looking at the problem, creating the need for an extra entity to view the sense data coming in. Descartes thought this was the soul (i.e. a non-physical entity) but some materialists may still take the assumption that there is something in the brain looking at the sense data, which Dennett parodies as belief in a homunculus (a tiny man) watching tiny movies in a **Cartesian Theatre**. The logical problem with this extra viewer of sense data is that it simply defers the problem one step: if there is something "inside" that absorbs external experiences, then surely there needs to be something inside this inside thing to absorb the experiences thus absorbed, and so on, infinitely. The starting point for functionalism is to get rid of the Cartesian question: what extra thing exists in order to explain what it is like to have a mind? Functionalism asserts that there is nothing *to* the mind beyond the use of various systems, including sight.

Dennett illustrates the problem of the homunculus and the Cartesian Theatre in the following image:

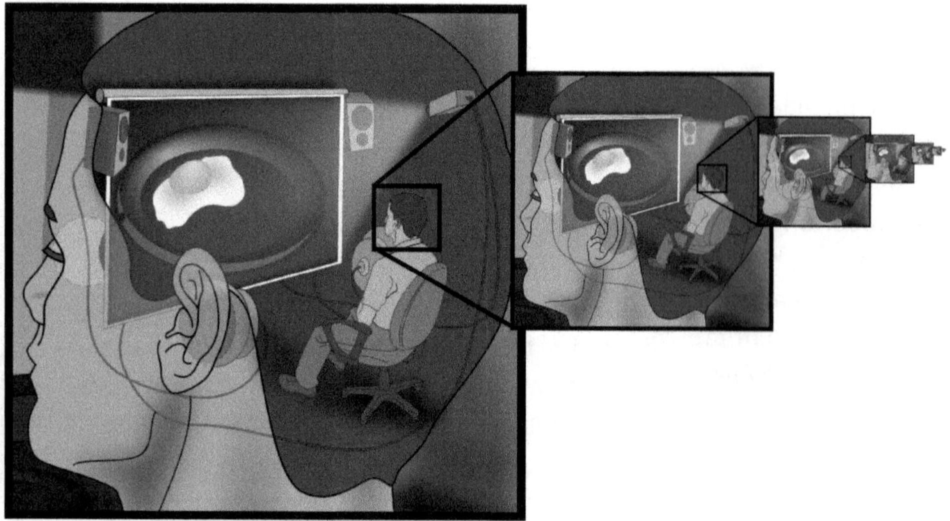

▲ The Cartesian Theatre

Dennett thinks that consciousness is no mystery (against Descartes) and thinks that he has a method for studying it (heterophenomenology). But what *is* it? It is difficult to explain something so fundamental without giving up or separating it from the natural world, so Dennett challenges us to change our perspective on the issue. Instead of thinking of consciousness in terms of "pure" experience of phenomena,

as something completely distinct in its own right, Dennett encourages his readers to think in terms of "**multiple drafts**": "there is no reality of conscious experience independent of the effects of various vehicles of content on subsequent action".[14] In other words, over a series of moments, there are many impressions of "input" (sight, sound, touch, etc.) and a number of corresponding actions in terms of behaviour, and our consciousness is just the collective accumulation of these impressions and actions. It is the "centre of gravity" for multiple functions and features of a system. Fundamental, of course, is memory, which is the ability and process of recording the multiple drafts of the sensations and actions. What we think of as "thinking" in the privacy of our minds is just the chatter of the system: comparing humans with computers in this respect is a helpful way of understanding functionalism. The idea of having a "mind" is simply the product of such a sophisticated system acknowledging its own processes.

### Questions

1. Is heterophenomenology possible?
2. How successfully does functionalism avoid the problems faced by behaviourism?
3. How does functionalism define the mind–body relationship?

### EXERCISE

1. Investigate science fiction depictions of machines *functioning* like humans with minds. How do these popular depictions compare with Dennett's theory of mind?
2. "Dennett has stripped the human mind of its grandeur and dignity." Do you agree? Write a critical response to this statement.
3. Write an imaginary dialogue between Dennett and the Buddha, discussing the concept of mind and its relation to the body.
4. Compile a glossary of the key jargon used to explain functionalism.

## The hard problem of consciousness: David J. Chalmers (1966– )

Functionalism clearly is a serious attempt to make sense of the mind and the body within the scope of science and naturalism as they are commonly understood. It is a **physicalist theory**, considering nothing beyond the tangible physical stuff that we all encounter and study. Functionalism says that studying the mind is hard, but we can do it. Explaining the mind is not a task of a qualitatively different order from studying a bicycle: once we work out what all the bits do, it makes sense as a whole. Functionalism also tells us that it is possible to know the mind of another human being, even if we cannot

[14] Dennett, *Consciousness Explained*, p. 132.

re-experience their exact experiences ourselves. I can surmise that the experience of what it is like to be *you* is pretty much the same as the experience of what it is like to be *me* insofar as your conscious experience should not be radically different from mine. After all, your feet work the same way my feet do, as do your hands, etc. Can we not say the same of the mind?

If we can, that makes a claim about the problem of other minds. As previously mentioned in the case of Descartes, it seems obvious to oneself that one's own mind exists (you can hardly doubt it), but is there a way to *prove* that other people have minds also? By the very nature of the problem, it is not possible to check in a conventional sense, because you cannot climb inside somebody else's head (unless you are in the film *Being John Malkovich*). So, the positive claim to know that other people have minds like yours seems to require a more sophisticated level of thinking. There have been a number of proposed solutions to the problem, a common one being the argument from analogy:

- Other humans seem to be quite a lot like me.
- The presence of many similarities implies fundamental similarity.
- I have a mind.
- Therefore, other humans have minds.

Superficially, it seems a reasonable argument, but on closer inspection it falls apart. How much similarity is enough? Cannot objects be almost the same but different in one or two fundamental aspects?

Functionalism, of course, attempts to get around the problem of other minds in the case of Dennett by positing the ability to study consciousness as an outsider: if you are careful, you really can know what other people's experiences are like. Talk to other people, see what they say, compare those reports with those of others and what we know about the brain. It may not be perfect, but it is still real, hard-won knowledge. Yet, is this really correct?

The Australian philosopher David J. Chalmers (1966– ) makes a very different proposal, being sceptical about the ability of functionalism to identify the existence of and to give knowledge about the minds of others. He begins with a definition of consciousness not as mere awareness or a collection of sensory inputs; it is the *subjective* quality of experience. As he puts it, "a mental state is conscious if there is something it is like to be in that mental state".[15] Consciousness is surprising, he claims, because even if we knew all the facts about the physics and dynamics of a system, there would still be no reason to suppose that the system would be conscious. Chalmers then distinguishes between the "phenomenal" and the "psychological" concepts of the mind: the phenomenal mind refers to the state of experiencing things, whereas the psychological mind refers to behaviour. Looking at functionalism, Chalmers argues that it confuses

**TOK link** 

Are there some fields of study that are simply closed off to the acquisition of knowledge? Is it impossible *in principle* to learn whether other people have minds like yours? Are there any other similar problems of knowledge you can think of?

[15] David J. Chalmers, *The Conscious Mind: In Search of a Fundamental Theory* (Oxford: Oxford University Press, 1996), p. 4.

the phenomenal and the psychological: it tries to analyse all mental states in terms of what they do. The question of whether someone *processes* vision of a colour in a certain way is different from the question of whether that person *experiences* that vision of a colour in a certain way. Against Dennett and others, he argues that the first-person experience of what something is *like for me* is conceptually different from the study of mental processes.

So, the problem with many other attempts to solve the mind–body problem, claims Chalmers, is that they have become fixated on the "easy problems" of explaining behaviour. That is the psychological mind–body problem, the question of why we do what we do. The answers lie in straightforward studies of humans as organisms and, over time, will become more refined through the advance of psychology and brain science. The success of such analyses might tempt us to suppose that they offer a complete explanation of mind and body, therefore. However, as Chalmers points out, it thus seems very strange that we were ever worried about the mind in the first place. Why was there ever a need to go beyond the question of how humans work? That need arose from conscious experience and raises the "hard problems" of addressing phenomenal consciousness. The link with the body is not so much of a problem according to Chalmers. It is more a question of why the mind gives rise to consciousness: why does the mind produce *what it is like* to experience?

At this point, it is important to note that Chalmers is making a logical distinction, rather than a practical proposal of what we should believe about the world. He is not saying that it is a good idea to stop believing that other people have consciousness; it is just that we are not logically compelled to this conclusion. The example he gives to support this point is the idea of "**philosophical zombies**": a thought experiment that has been used in philosophy for some time but has been popularized by Chalmers' persistent and well-known argument against **physicalism** and functionalism. The philosophical idea of a zombie is different from that of horror films: it is not a walking corpse, disgusting to look at. On the contrary, a philosophical zombie is exactly identical to a "normal" human in every way, except in respect of consciousness. A philosophical zombie looks like a human, acts like a human, and is able to talk about experiences in the same way that humans do. However, this zombie never *has* experiences; it behaves perfectly as though it does, but it does not.

We may not think that philosophical zombies actually exist but it is logically possible that they do. So, Chalmers claims that a complete understanding of the mind as a functioning system does nothing to "explain" consciousness, because consciousness is in no way necessary to the functioning of the system. There *could* be zombies with all the functions described by functionalism, but with nothing in the way of what it is like to be such a zombie. Similarly, if there were a hypothetical computer that was capable of simulating all the functions of the mind, there is no reason to suppose that there would be such a thing as what it is like to be that computer.

## EXERCISE

1. Get hold of red and green objects and experience the colours red and green. Now imagine that these colours were flipped (green became red, red became green: see images at http://plato.stanford.edu/entries/qualia-inverted/#LocInvSpeSce). Would it affect you physically in any way? How is this question similar to the zombie problem? (Discussion, written answers)
2. Do you think that your friends are philosophical zombies? Ask them to help you write a list of reasons for supposing that they also have consciousness.
3. Compare and contrast the arguments of Chalmers with those of Descartes.

The contribution to the philosophy of mind that Chalmers has made is striking because it seemingly reverses a strong trend towards mind–body monism and materialism in modern Western philosophy. Unsurprisingly, it has thus received a controversial reception among philosophers and the current debate in the early 21st century is lively. Could it be that dualism is correct after all (albeit in a very different way from that first proposed by Plato)? At this point, it is important to point out that Chalmers takes pains to distance himself from earlier strands of dualism. He argues that it is possible to say that materialism is false but still to adhere to naturalism. Although consciousness could not be explained physically, Chalmers suggests that it may still be possible to develop some other form of theoretical framework and that this need have nothing to do with a mysterious entity (i.e. the soul). On the contrary, he implies that consciousness is a fundamental property of the universe, like mass or time, that cannot be reduced to other, simpler explanations.

## FIND OUT MORE

Research the history of the inverted spectrum hypothesis, starting from the philosopher John Locke.

Read the article by Steven Pinker on the "mystery" of consciousness:

**http://content.time.com/time/magazine/article/0,9171,1580394,00.html**

| Daniel C. Dennett | David J. Chalmers |
|---|---|
| Monism | Naturalistic dualism |
| External observers acquire knowledge of the minds or consciousness of others (heterophenomenology) | External observers could possibly (logically) be talking to philosophical zombies, without consciousness |
| Mind reducible to its functions | Mind irreducible |

## Questions

1. Is Chalmers right to distinguish between "hard" and "easy" problems in the philosophy of mind?
2. Does the example of philosophical zombies refute functionalism?
3. How convincing is Chalmers' claim that dualism can be naturalistic?
4. What are the implications for science in supporting either Dennett or Chalmers?

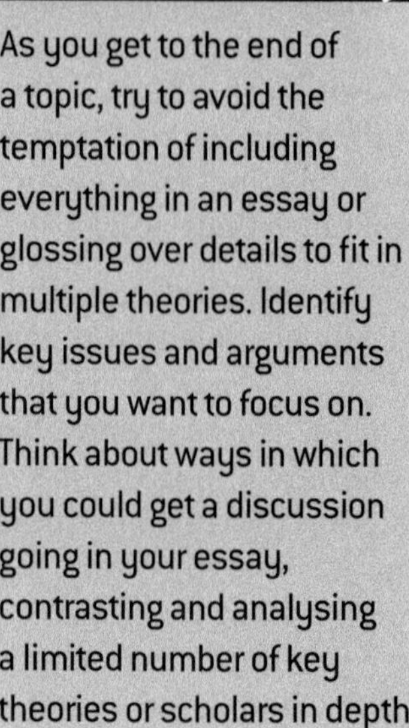

## Assessment tip

As you get to the end of a topic, try to avoid the temptation of including everything in an essay or glossing over details to fit in multiple theories. Identify key issues and arguments that you want to focus on. Think about ways in which you could get a discussion going in your essay, contrasting and analysing a limited number of key theories or scholars in depth.

## Can the problems be solved?

It is tempting to suppose that the recent disagreement in the philosophy of mind puts us right back where we started: searching for something that is mysterious, controversial, and deeply personal. Perhaps humans have too much invested, emotionally and historically, in the idea of the human mind. There will always be arguments and debate over what it means to be human. Nevertheless, the continuing dispute is perhaps a good sign that progress is being made and no one can deny that the progress of neuroscience is reframing our understanding of the mind in various ways. The dialogue goes on today and a number of responses have been made to the recent relaunch of dualism by Chalmers. For example, one response would be to attack the point that the logical possibility of zombies shows that materialism is false. That is, if we can *conceive* of zombies, does that really show that there *could be* such creatures? Does this logical thought experiment really show the non-physical nature of phenomenal consciousness? Another criticism is the "wait-and-see" approach, emphasizing the development of brain science. We know much more than we used to about the brain and will know much more in the future. Could it be that the "hard problem" of consciousness will eventually just vanish beneath the steady roll of scientific explanation? Perhaps so, though there is obviously a speculative element in that argument. Chalmers would counter that hard logic is on his side and claim that no amount of science *on principle* could unpack the subjective aspect of consciousness.

So, over time, philosophy has progressively changed our understanding of the mind and the body. Many centuries of debate have sharpened the concepts and language we use, and with each episode of new reflections or disagreements finer distinctions and more accurate tools for discussion have been created. The Buddha showed us that illusion can be both external and internal, and can touch on the mind itself. Plato and Aristotle identified the power of reason as the universal feature of the human soul, but parted company in the causes they identified for it. Jewish, Christian, and Islamic scholars identified concepts of mind and body with the Creation. Descartes then introduced a new wave of scepticism, approaching the definition of the mind only with what he saw as logical certainties. Hegel called attention to the "absolute" nature of infinite human consciousness. In more recent years, behaviourists and functionalists have sought to bring the mind within the scope of materialism. These are all important stages in the human journey of self-understanding.

But is there a destination?

Some philosophers would suggest that the problems are not as great or as serious as they first seem, as they are linguistic misunderstandings more than actual difficulties for our knowledge. In the tradition of Wittgenstein (who is famous for a wider critique of the language of philosophy), it could be argued that different types of language are being taken out of context in philosophy. There are subjective ways of speaking and objective ways of speaking, and it could be a simple mistake to ask what is "real" or "true" in our assorted vocabulary of mind and body. Moreover, other philosophers, including the British philosopher Colin McGinn (1950– ), have questioned the capability of humans to deal with such questions. Consciousness is a closed-off area of investigation, because there simply is no way "in" for humans to get to the cause of their own consciousness. By either of these approaches, the debate over mind and body could be limitless, and ultimately futile. Nevertheless, history shows that many philosophers have thought that they *have* solved the problems of mind and body. In the future, many more may reach the same conclusion about their own theories. Ultimately, the answers produced may depend on wider questions about the nature of philosophy itself: how it should work, what its scope should be, its relationship with science, and so forth. In that sense, the most exciting theories concerning mind and body may still lie ahead of us.

## FINAL REFLECTION

Looking at the debate over mind and body, how we define them, and what we make of their relationship, how are we then to develop our understanding of being human? Can we answer this problem through a particular theory of mind, through philosophical, scientific, or religious arguments?

## LINK WITH THE CORE THEME

## MIND AND BODY, AND BEING HUMAN

The various philosophical problems of the mind and body give us challenging ways to reflect upon the Core Theme problem of what it means to be human. One key issue is the mind-body problem itself, since various philosophers have attempted to define humans through a specific answer to this: humans are 'souls' or 'thinking things' or perhaps simply very complicated organisms driven by biological brains. Do the solutions to the mind-body problem 'answer' the challenge of the Core Theme? There is also the issue of how being human relates to a particular attitude towards the mind and body. Should humans see one as better or higher than the other? Should the mind act upon the body? What are the implications of us seeing the mind and body in a certain way?

Ultimately, this topic shows us that theories about being human greatly depend upon wider theories about the nature of reality. Are humans naturalistic beings in a naturalistic world? Or, could a religious, spiritual perspective be maintained? Perhaps, on the contrary, we should not seek to define humans, minds and bodies through such sharp distinctions. Looking to the future, we can anticipate an on-going debate about the nature of consciousness and advancing brain science, challenging us to keep reappraising our understanding of philosophy and of being human.

## Mind and Body: Assessment Tips

Below are some stimuli taken from past papers, which can be related to the problems of mind and body:

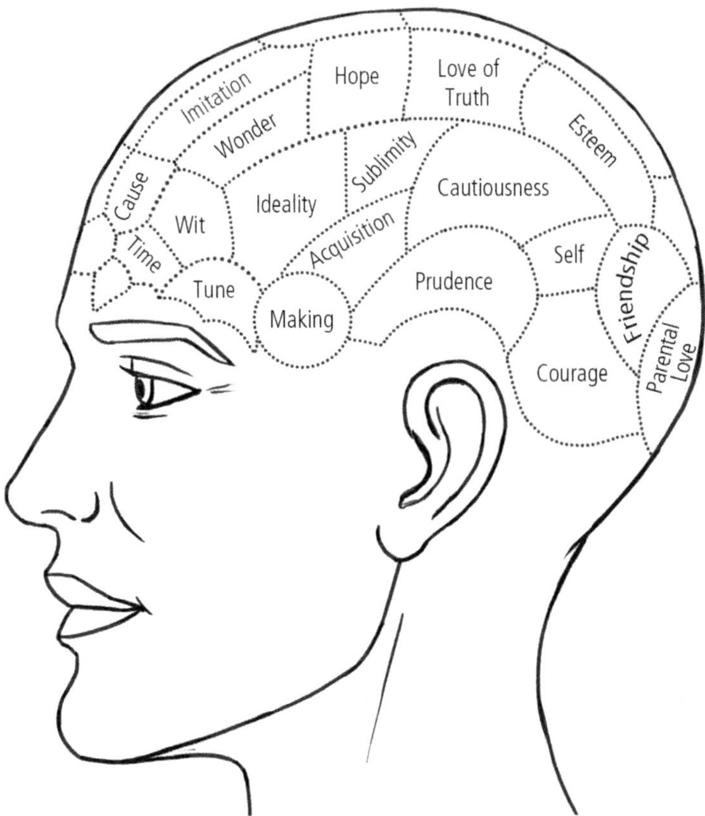


November 2008

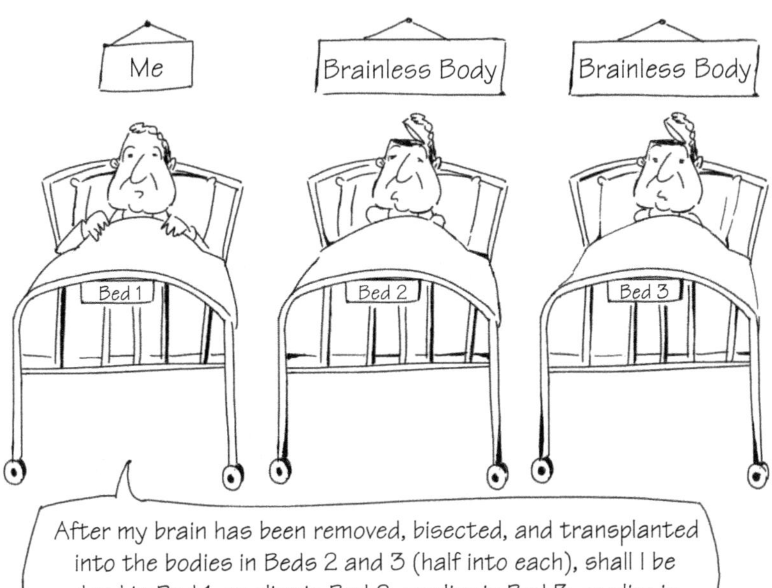


May 2012

### Activities:

1. Write down lists of word associations for the two picture stimuli above. What words, ideas, feelings, etc. do they bring to mind? (Discuss)
2. Consider how you would explain your ideas. What was your thinking process? Try to write an explanation of how the stimuli gave rise to certain thoughts. Can you show how this indicates a philosophical problem?
3. Compare what you have down for activity 2 with other people in your class. What are the differences between strong links and tenuous links to the Core Theme?

**Assessment tip**

Think quite broadly about the type of stimulus material that could lead you to discuss the mind and body; it doesn't have to be a picture of a brain or something explicitly labelled as the 'mind'. For example, stimuli which indicate the physical nature of human existence, its bodily shape, the concept of a soul, spirit, or afterlife could provide many different 'ways in' to discussions of mind and body. Or, a stimulus might remind you of a particular theory, perhaps with a computer representing functionalism or some cyclical process representing *Samsara*. Examiners will be open minded, as long as you have a strong explanation for the link from the stimulus to the issue.

## References Cited


Arberry, A. J., trans. *Mystical Poems of Rumi*. Edited by Ehsan Yarshater, with a new foreword by Franklin D. Lewis. Chicago: University of Chicago Press, 2009.

Aristotle. *On the Soul* (*De Anima*), Book II, Chapter 1 (c. 350 BC). English translation by J. A. Smith available at http://classics.mit.edu/Aristotle/soul.html (accessed 22 October 2014).

Asimov, Isaac. "Foreword". In Judith Hooper and Dicki Teresi, *The 3-Pound Universe*. New York: Macmillan, 1986.

Chalmers, David J. *The Conscious Mind: In Search of a Fundamental Theory*. Oxford: Oxford University Press, 1996.

Dennett, Daniel C. *Consciousness Explained*. Boston, MA: Little, Brown & Company, 1991.

Descartes, René. *Meditations on First Philosophy: In Which the Existence of God and the Distinction of the Soul from the Body Are Demonstrated*, 3rd edition. Translated from the Latin by Donald A. Cress. Indianapolis, IN: Hackett Publishing Company, 1993.

Ficino, Marsilio. *Platonic Theology: On the Immortality of the Soul*, 6 vols. Edited and translated by Michael J. B. Allen and James Hankins. Cambridge, MA: Harvard University Press, 2001–2006.

Plato. *Phaedo*. Translated with an introduction and notes by David Gallop. Oxford: Oxford University Press, 1999.

Ryle, Gilbert. *The Concept of Mind*, new edition with an introduction by Daniel C. Dennett. Chicago: University of Chicago Press, 2002.

Smith, Jane Idleman, and Yvonne Yazbeck Haddad. *The Islamic Understanding of Death and Resurrection*. Oxford: Oxford University Press, 2002.

Thiry, Paul-Henri. *The System of Nature, Or the Laws of the Moral and Physical World*, vol. 1. Edited by Robert R. Richardson. Mirbaud, 1770. Now available at http://www.gutenberg.org/files/8909/8909-h/8909-h.htm#link2H_4_0022 (accessed 22 October 2014).

Tucker, Robert C. *Philosophy and Myth in Karl Marx*, 3rd edition, with a new introduction by the author. New Brunswick, NJ: Transaction Publishers.

Veitch, John, and Frank Sewall. *The Method, Meditations and Philosophy of Descartes*. Washington and London: M. Walter Dunne, 1901.

# BEING HUMAN

# 5 The Self and the Other

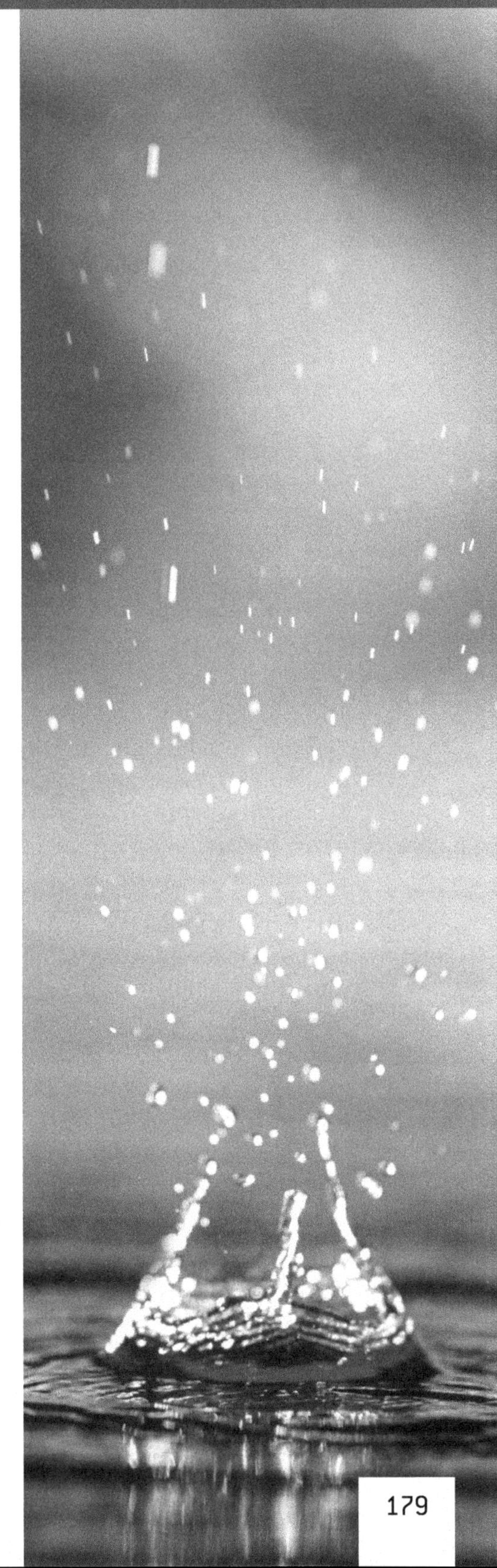

- Self/non-self
- Solipsism and inter-subjectivity
- Authenticity

## Some essential questions:

- Is there such a thing as the self?
- Is it possible to know oneself?
- In what way is how we define "the other" part of how we define "the self"?

### Stimulus 1

I thought how lovely and how strange a river is. A river is a river, always there, and yet the water flowing through it is never the same water and is never still. It's always changing and is always on the move. And over time the river itself changes too. It widens and deepens as it rubs and scours, gnaws and kneads, eats and bores its way through the land. Even the greatest rivers – the Nile and the Ganges, the Yangtze and he Mississippi, the Amazon and the great grey-green greasy Limpopo all set about with fever trees – must have been no more than trickles and flickering streams before they grew into mighty rivers.

Are people like that? I wondered. Am I like that? Always me, like the river itself, always flowing but always different, like the water flowing in the river, . . ..

Do I change like a river, widening and deepening, eddying back on myself sometimes, bursting my banks sometimes when there's too much water, too much life in me, and sometimes dried up from lack of rain? Will the I that is me grow and widen and deepen? Or will I stagnate and become an arid riverbed? Will I allow people to dam me up and confine me to wall so that I flow only where they want? Will I allow them to turn me into a canal to use for their own purposes? Or will I make sure I flow freely, coursing my way through the land and ploughing a valley of my own?

—Aidan Chambers[1]

---

1 Aidan Chambers, *This Is All: The Pillow Book of Cordelia Kenn* (London: The Bodley Head, 2005), p. 371.

## Questions

In the stimulus above, the author uses the analogy of the river to talk about their self.

1. What issues regarding the self can be identified in this passage? For example, is the river always the same river regardless of how it changes? If it changes what remains the same?
2. Relate the various states of a river to an example from real life?
3. Based on your current understanding or belief, if you had to choose from the following options, which general statement is more likely to define your position on the self?

   A fixed entity found within you and determined prior to birth

   A changing entity but only within a basic framework determined prior to birth

   An entity that can be fixed by you when you determine

   A fixed entity determined by the influences on you as you grow up

   A changing entity determined by other people in your life

   There is nothing called the self

   Return to these options when you have finished the chapter. Have you changed your mind? If you have changed your position, what was the most important factor that influenced you? If not, what the most important factor in confirming your original position?

The core theme provides an opportunity to explore a simple question, "What is it to be human?" However, as is so often the case when doing philosophy, the simple questions are the hardest to answer satisfactorily. The early attempts to answer these simple questions often generate more questions as the initial assessment of the question is found to be inadequate and many unforeseen assumptions become evident.

▲ What is a selfie?

An analysis in the concept of the self also encompasses the experience of doing philosophy. The self in everyday language tends to refer to something that defines the identity of an individual. In contemporary society, the Instagram has become synonymous with the "selfie", a picture taken by an individual of themselves. Why is it called a "selfie"? Is it because it is taken by themselves or because it is supposed to be a picture of their self? Is the self the body? Or the face? Or the pose? Or the disposition or attitude being captured? Or the experience itself? Or perhaps, the image being constructed? Is it the response that other people will provide online?

All of these questions allude to different concepts of the self, many of which will be explored in this chapter. However, the last question with its reference to "the other" highlights an issue that delineates two different approaches to the question of the self. Is our philosophical understanding of the self a result of our own reflections using introspection as the primary methodology? Or, should the role of other people and their influence and perceptions be a determining factor in identifying the self and its nature? Now with the advent of social media this possibility has taken on renewed relevance.

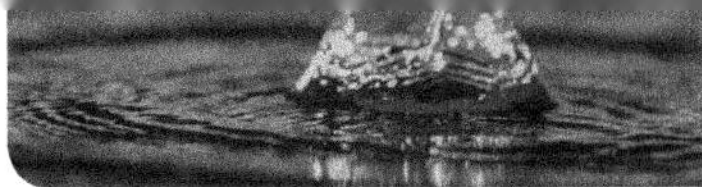

### Why is a consideration of the self important?

While the reference to a "selfie" provides an indication of the importance of the self as a philosophical concept there are other, admittedly related but even more significant, reasons for exploring the concept of the self. Contemporary philosopher Paul M. Churchland argues that a comprehensive concept of the self is essential to modern society and its ability to counter the challenges of the near future. While Churchland puts forward his own argument for the new scientifically based understanding of our selves, he makes an interesting point that understanding *what* we are will "contribute substantially toward a more peaceful and humane society".[2] In a similar way it is important to understand how we have seen ourselves at different times and in different places. These conceptions of the self have influenced thinking, and even continue to influence thinking, because of how they have framed social and political behaviour. Many of the radical changes that occurred in the 20th century, such as the progression towards racial and sexual equality, have occurred partially because the orthodox concept of the self has been challenged as part of a broader demand for change. Similarly, with arguments being offered about the imminent post-human condition, the understanding of the self is still a pertinent debate.

## What is the self?

**Questions**

1. Is the self an entity, a substance? If it is a substance, what kind of substance is it?
2. Is the self a personality trait, an attitude, or an affectation?
3. Is the self an action or a unique set of values?
4. Is the self a construction and a story that coheres an individual?
5. Is it a fabrication, a myth, or an illusion?
6. Is the self fixed or variable, in that does it evolve over time?
7. How do we know the self? Is it through introspection or through other people?

### Overview of the concept of the self

This chapter, and Chapter: Identity, look at the answers offered by accompanying philosophical inquiry over the last 3,000 years. This chapter explores the arguments for the second level of investigating the identity of an individual, better known as the question of the **self**, while Chapter 7: Identity explores the issue of how we know this identity continues over time, or the question of the **enduring self**. They are separate because not all philosophers who have directly (or indirectly) argued for a self have also argued for the continuation or persistence of this self. In fact, the issue of the enduring self is regarded as a modern issue, usually sourced from Locke's reaction to the concept of the self as put forward by Descartes.

[2] Paul M. Churchland, *Matter and Consciousness*, 3rd edition (Cambridge, MA: MIT Press, 2013), p. 77.

However, before the investigation into the self proceeds it is important to have an understanding of the conceptual frameworks that has developed over the last 2,500 years and contextualize the debates that are estential to any understanding. Idenfiying the different frameworks and analysing them is part of the process for developing your own evaluative framework that will enable you to establish your own position on the concept of the self, especially in relation to the many issues that are involved in a study of the self. These are essential to success in this subject because of the design of the assessment tasks and their assessment criteria.

**The Identity of a Human**

- Providing the ability to claim what is a human

**The Identity of an Individual**

- Providing the ability to claim the identity of *an individual human*

**An Identity of an Individual over Time**

- Providing the ability to claim they are the same individual human *over time*

## Unpacking the question of the self

When we start reflecting on the issue of the self we tend to encounter two things. We talk about "the" or "our" self all the time but have very little systematic conception of it, at least not philosophically. This is actually an important indicator for a philosophical investigation – the question might be simple but the answer is complex.

The self can be discussed in many different ways and in many different disciplines. As well as philosophy, these can be found in psychology, sociology, anthropology, religion, science, artificial intelligence, and everyday "common sense" and public discourse.

The concepts of the self in philosophy are diverse and cover many different arguments. Some of the concepts are listed below:

- a body consisting of matter
- a mind
- a body/mind
- a living organism
- an organism's behaviour and/ or functions
- a person, as defined in part by social roles and relationships
- an artefact of my culture
- an information-processing program or programs
- an immortal soul
- a kind of narrative, or a centre of narrative gravity.[3]

**Paper 3 link**

Given the different number of disciplines that investigate the concept of the self, is philosophy the most appropriate discipline to develop an understanding of the self? The Subject Guide includes a number of questions that an HL student should ask about the role of methodology in doing philosophy. These include:

- Is conceptual analysis the primary methodology of philosophy?
- How relevant are the findings of other disciplines to philosophical discussions?

As you proceed through this chapter, reflect on these questions.

[3] From Mait Edey, "Subject and Object", in Shaun Gallagher and Jonathan Shear (eds), *Models of the Self* (Thorverton, UK: Imprint Academic, 1999), p. 441.

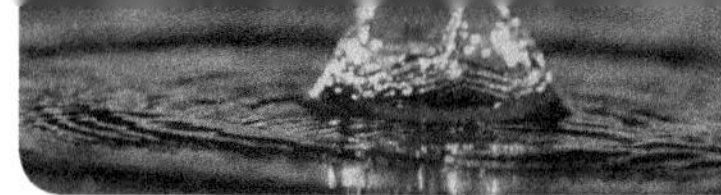



All of these are valid in that they can be argued philosophically. However, their truth is part of an ongoing debate in philosophy as well as many other disciplines. The potential positions listed above are evident in Western tradition, both the analytical and continental approaches, as well as Chinese (Confucian), Indian (Hindu and Buddhist), and Japanese (Zen). Each of these traditions will be drawn upon as part of this investigation.

Due to the longevity of the debate about the self there are a number of distinct historical phases in which the major contributions to the self have occurred within a dominant conceptual framework. In the West there have been numerous phases in history defined and discussed in philosophical writing – loosely defined as from *Ancient* to *Christian* to *Enlightenment* to *Modernity* to *Postmodern*.

A major influence on the Western concepts of the self is the religious and philosophical frameworks established in ancient Greece by **Socrates**, **Plato**, and **Aristotle**. While these philosophers drew on the ideas of the **pre-Socratics**, the approach or framework for their investigation and the focus of their interests heralded the birth of philosophy in the West. This tradition of thought was used by an emerging religious group, based on the actions and teachings of Jesus Christ, to explain its faith to the **ancient Romans**, using the philosophical works of Augustine of Hippo. This consolidated the acceptance of this particular way of thinking, and subsequent philosophical discussion has focused on the strengths and weaknesses of this approach, seeking to clarify, refine, extend, or reject its central premises.

**Challenges** to the foundation offered by Plato (and Socrates) are numerous, and include challenges from *within* the tradition, in the form of Aristotle, Hume, Heidegger, and Ludwig Wittgenstein, and numerous positions grounded in phenomenology, as well as from *without*, from philosophies and traditions of thought from Africa (Ubuntu), India (Hinduism and Buddhism), and China (Confucianism and Daoism).

As modernity emerged from the **Enlightenment** of the late 17th century, the Christian legacy of Platonic thought was initially maintained, though only to a certain degree, and then rejected. Scientific thinking, an outcome of the Enlightenment, has offered new perspectives on the self, including a rejection of the entire thesis that we actually *have* a self.

Plato's legacy was maintained to a certain extent through the work of Descartes and then rejected with the emergence of monist philosopjies, such as materialism, and the philosophical school of phenomenology. In more recent times, these traditions have become intermeshed as the intellectual ambitions of the Western tradition, established in ancient Athens and selectively reasserted in the form of the Enlightenment, led to a critique of its foundations; objectivity, the centrality of reason, realism, science, and the enlightenment project in general. This covered various schools such as post-structuralism, deconstructionism, and postmodernism. The most prominent school, postmodernism, is usually portrayed as a critique of modernism (although there were some attempts to build a replacement philosophical framework). As such, it explores the assumptions on which modernism was founded with the ambition of demonstrating how these are an outcome of power and not the search for truth.

This dynamic history of the self means that it is a rich philosophical issue with a number of perspectives worth investigating. The issue also offers you an opportunity to construct your own position of the concept of the self through an engagement with the ongoing debate lasting over 2,500 years.

## Understanding the process of philosophical analysis and evaluation

Philosophy as an activity seeks to identify issues with our understanding of the world and offer reasonable, well-thought-out solutions. An analysis of a philosophical issue involves the analysis of the relevant arguments put forward to identify the issue, the nature of the issue, and its solution. Philosophical arguments need to be justified. Generally, arguments are justified using evidence that is shown to support a point that, in turn, supports the argument. This expectation, which is a key foundation to doing philosophy, also defines the process of analysis. In broad terms, philosophical analysis and evaluation involves the systematic investigation of three elements of a philosophical position (argument). These are the **assumptions**, the **quality of the argument**, and the **implications** of the argument and resulting position.

## What is analysis and evaluation?

Analysis has always been key to the philosophical process. At a basic level it involves dismantling an argument or a position to reveal its constituent parts and assessing them. In philosophy this involves identifying and understanding the concepts, methodology and evidence used to justify the argument or position taken. The first phase of an analysis is the identification (and eventual evaluation) of the **assumptions** on which the argument is founded. A philosopher, or school of philosophy, will explicitly or implicitly use these assumptions to engage with the issue. The analysis of the assumptions involves looking at the **concepts** and resulting **conceptual framework** involved/used and the nature of the evidence used to support the argument.

The next stage of analysis is to look at the **quality of the argument** and therefore the quality of the justification of the position taken by the philosopher. This allows you to develop an understanding of the validity of the position being outlined (including the assumptions, methodologies, and evidence). A key element of any argument is the quality of the evidence used to support the point being made and how successfully it is used to support the point and therefore the overall argument.

However, you need a means to measure the quality of an argument and this is the **evaluative framework**. For example, the following questions capture the idea of an evaluative framework. What assumptions are valid assumptions? Which methodology is a valid methodology? What evidence is valid evidence and how should it be used?

The final stage of the analytical process is the **implications** of an argument and therefore position on a philosophical issue. What impact does the position have on the broader philosophical worldview? This can be extended to society, such as the recognition of difference, the accountability of the actions of individuals and so on.

Within these conceptual traditions, there are many other tensions and therefore issues that allow you numerous opportunities to explore this concept.

One of the first questions that should be asked is, how are you going to do this? How should you look for the self? In other words, what is the best methodology for conceptualizing and/or identifying the self? One of the reasons why there has been so much debate is that there are a number of different methodologies that can operate within the same conceptual tradition. For example, **rationalism** and **empiricism** both operate within the dominant tradition of Western thought – the essentialist tradition. In other words, they are different methods being used to achieve the same goal, determining the essence of the self. They share the same assumptions about what is the self but different methodologies result in different answers.

## CONCEPTUAL CLARITY

The question of the self is an **epistemological question** as well as a **metaphysical question** (and an **ethical question**).

Which one comes first? Make sure you are comfortable with the difference between these three types of question.

### The role of different methodologies

- Rationalism
- Empiricism
- Introspection
- Extrospection
- Authority
- Intuition
- Revelation

The **methodology** you use can often determine what you find. This is a common consideration in TOK. Does how you look for something influence, even determine, what you will find?

This is also a consideration in Paper 3. Does one methodology have greater validity than another? If so, how do you determine which one is best? Similarly, the **assumptions** you accept can frame the search you are undertaking. Each of the approaches mentioned above has been established by a philosopher or a school of philosophy at some stage of the various traditions of philosophy that can be included in this investigation.

### Assessment tip

The top band in the Paper 1 Section A markband has the following **Level descriptor**:

"The response contains well-developed critical analysis. There is discussion and assessment of alternative interpretations or points of view. All or nearly all of the main points are justified. The response argues from a consistently held position about the issue."

There is a clear requirement to undertake argument (justification) and analysis as part of your response in the exams, not simply describe philosophical positions. It is worth developing the skills of analysis consciously throughout the course to ensure you are prepared for this aspect of the assessment in the exam.

### Establishing the conceptual framework

There are two dominant traditions of inquiry that have considered the question of the self.

- One tradition assumes there is an **essential** self that is found through introspection and self-consciousness.
- The other tradition assumes there is an **existential** self that is found through action and other people.

There are also traditions of inquiry that reject the self, or at least the concept of the self as a unifying concept. This will also be considered in this chapter. There is also a possible division between the ancient and the modern approaches to the self:

- The ancient tradition focuses on the self as self-knowledge.
- The modern tradition focuses on the self as self-consciousness.

Each of these provide a possible framework for your analysis. However, as will be introduced soon there are a number of other possible themes that will enable you to investigate the concept of the self in a systematic manner. First, however, it is useful to reflect on the possible arguments that are available on the question of the self.

### Possible analytical frameworks

To make things easier there are a number of oppositions or binaries (both real and contrived) that can be established to frame a systematic analysis of positions taken on the issue of the self.

These can be:

- Western approaches versus Eastern approaches
- Rationalism versus Empiricism
- Materialism versus Naturalism
- Dualism versus Monism
- Soplisism versus Intersubjectivity
- Metaphysical versus Physical
- Fact versus Construct
- Individuality versus Community
- Atomistic versus Social
- Substantial versus Non-Substantial
- Private versus Public
- Introspection versus Extrospection
- Unitary versus Fragmented
- Structure versus Process
- Immanence versus Transcendence
- Subject versus Object

Each of these approaches is part of the numerous traditions of philosophical inquiry. Many of them overlap. Understanding these apparent oppositions further allows you to establish a comparative analysis as part of the exploration of the self and provides you with ideas for your own philosophy of the self. This is one of a number of **analytical strategies** available to an investigation of the self.

### Exploring the self

The following sections explore the potential analytical and evaluative frameworks further. The complex history of the philosophical concept of the self can be reduced to three approaches or *conceptual traditions*: **essentialist**, **existentialist**, and a **rejection** of the idea of the self. These will be explored in detail in this chapter. For now, the self can be conceived as an **essence** (a substance), an outcome of **existence** (an attribute or action), or a label for an **illusion** (a false concept). Each of these has a number of variations, but these broad categories provide a sense of the big picture, and, as such, you will be able to investigate them further using the suggestions in the text.

# Understanding the essentialist concept of the self

## Debates within the essentialist tradition

In philosophy essentialism defines the understanding that the necessary characteristics or properties of an entity are prior to the entity's existence. As philosopher-professor Richard L. Cartwright (1925–2010) explains, "[e]ssentialism, as I shall understand it, is the doctrine that among the attributes of a thing some are essential, others merely accidental. Its essential attributes are those it has necessarily, those it could not have lacked."[4] Consequently, the search for the self is framed by looking for

[4] Richard L. Cartwright, "Some Remarks on Essentialism", *The Journal of Philosophy* 65, no. 20 (24 October 1968): 615.

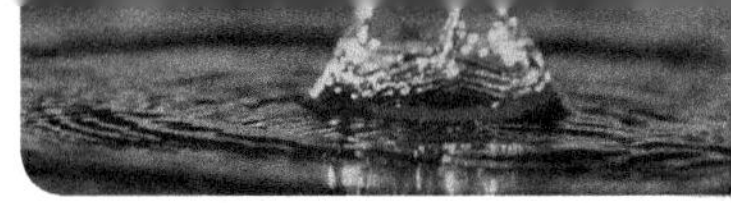

something reductive (a specific element), something identifiable, and something immutable.

### Philosophical terms

- Consciousness

  Awareness or experience of the world See also the discussion of Consciousness in Human Nature (Chapter 2)
- Essence

  An essence is the intrinsic or indispensable property or properties that characterize or identify an entity.
- Material

  The substance or substances out of which a thing is or can be made
- Substance

  That which has mass and occupies or is extended space
- Temporality

  The condition of being temporal or bounded in time as in past, present and future.
- Spatiality

  The conditions of being involved in, or having the nature of space.

## The ancient positions: Plato, Aristotle, and Augustine

The foundational concept of the self has been an enduring one. Essentialism has been the dominant framework for Western philosophy for over 2,500 years. Plato is regarded as the first significant essentialist as a result of his argument for the Form of the Good as an outcome of his famous Theory of the Forms in various dialogues throughout his life.[5] These include *Timaeus, Phaedo, The Republic, Hippias Major, The Symposium,* and *Parmenides*. It was not a perfect concept, often remaining vague with limited analysis and justification. In *Parmenides,* a later dialogue, Plato even offers six of his own objections to his Theory of the Forms. Nonetheless, the idea of a metaphysical essence was very attractive and, partly because of the overall influence of Plato's works, became the defining conceptual framework for later philosophical debate and integrated in a Christian worldview from around 400 CE onwards. Consequently, it has been the dominant concept in the Western tradition until the mid to late 19th century. The original concept is quite simple – the self is a soul that is immortal and only exists within a body for a limited amount of time.

### The self as "psyche" or soul

The "**psyche**" or **soul** is an immaterial, thinking substance, which exists so long as some form of thought is going on in this substance. It usually involves a rejection of the body (*soma*). **Plato** and **Descartes** are the key

### ESSENTIALISM VERSUS EXISTENTIALISM

Essentialism is often contrasted with existentialism. These approaches can be explained by highlighting that the existentialist understanding does not focus on conceiving identity in the same way we understand an entity. Rather, existentialism is a concept of the self that focuses on relationships, thus rejecting the notion of a predefined entity as the definitive aspect of identity. A valid question to ask is "What is an essence?" It has characteristics or properties but does it exist in time and space? Is it immutable? Essentialists frequently believe that the essence is metaphysical and accessible through introspection. This approach was established in the western tradition by Plato.

[5] Plato's *Republic* is one of the prescribed titles for Paper 2. The best-known discussion of his Theory of the Forms is found in this text, and in particular through his famous Allegory of the Cave.

philosophers who have held this view. If we start with Plato we can see how he establishes the notion of the self as a *metaphysical* issue.

Plato agrees with pre-Socratic philosophers such as Pythagoras and Heraclitus that psyche or soul is the source for our rational and moral self, as well as our biological self. This concept of the self already had a long history. It was present in ancient Greek thought through the influence of Orphism, a set of religious beliefs and practices of the Thracians and frequently associated with literature ascribed to the mythical poet Orpheus. Plato's own philosophical understanding also reflects this view, and the influence of Plato meant that this concept of the self became a common reference point in debates about the self.

### Understanding the context

The philosophical ambition throughout Plato's philosophical writings was to find certainty. This desire, arguably determined by the turbulent political times he was experiencing, drove him to create a philosophical system aimed at establishing this certainty. As a consequence, Plato was unwilling to include anything that could not provide this foundation.

In the following extract from *Phaedo*, Socrates, the Athenian philosopher and teacher featured in Plato's dialogues, is arguing for the existence of the soul. In the process, he displays a distinct attitude towards other concepts such as purity, eternity, immortality, and unchangeableness, indicating clearly an evaluative framework for determining the source of truth.

*Socrates*: And were we not saying long ago that the soul when using the body as an instrument of perception, that is to say, when using the sense of sight or hearing or some other sense (for the meaning of perceiving through the body is perceiving through the senses)—were we not saying that the soul too is then dragged by the body into the region of the changeable, and wanders and is confused; the world spins round her, and she is like a drunkard, when she touches change?

*Cebes*: Very true.

*Socrates*: But when returning into herself she reflects, then she passes into the other world, the region of purity, and eternity, and immortality, and unchangeableness, which are her kindred, and with them she ever lives, when she is by herself and is not let or hindered; then she ceases from her erring ways, and being in communion with the unchanging is unchanging. And this state of the soul is called wisdom?

*Cebes*: That is well and truly said, Socrates.

*Socrates*: And to which class is the soul more nearly alike and akin, as far as may be inferred from this argument, as well as from the preceding one?

*Cebes*: I think, Socrates, that, in the opinion of everyone who follows the argument, the soul will be infinitely more like the unchangeable—even the most stupid person will not deny that.

*Socrates*: And the body is more like the changing?

*Cebes*: Yes.

—Plato[6]

**Questions**

According to Socrates, what is the relationship between the body and the soul?

Based on this passage, how does he argue/justify this position?

[6] Plato, Phaedo, p. 65; see also Plato, The Trial and Death of Socrates: Four Dialogues, edited by Shane Weller (New York: Dover Publications, 1992), pp. 78–79.

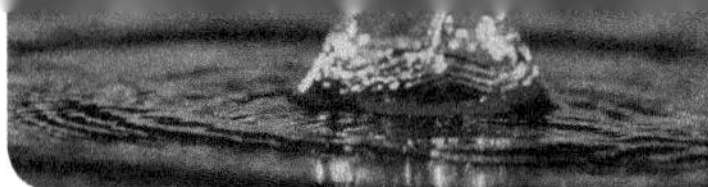

Plato argued that the self was an entity that existed in the metaphysical world. This concept is an abstract concept of the self and also a rejection of the body. As Plato states in *Phaedo*, "the body fills us with all kinds of lusts, desires, fears, phantoms and a great deal of nonsense, with the result that we really and truly never ever get a chance to think about anything at all."[7] This cannot, Plato suggests, be the foundation of the true self and the search for knowledge: "it has been well and truly proved to us that if we are ever going to gain pure knowledge of anything, we must get rid of the body. And we must look at things themselves with the soul itself."[8] This claim existed within Plato's broader philosophical system and further analysis is required to fully understand the claim Plato is making about the self.

Plato argues that reality is **dualistic**, or consists of two different realms of being. One is a realm of **change** and the other is a realm of **permanence**. The first realm, the realm of change, is transient, where things come and go. This makes it imperfect and unreliable. Socrates suggests that when the soul touches this "region" it becomes "like a drunkard". This is the realm of particulars, the realm we perceive with our senses.

The second realm is the opposite; it is the realm of "purity, and eternity, and immortality, and unchangeableness". If we were to look for our "self", as Plato did, we would surely prefer it to be present in the permanent (even perfect) realm. This was Plato's assumption. Consequently the self must exist in the permanent realm, or as he labelled it, the **metaphysical** realm, or the realm "beyond the physical".

This view of reality initially seems speculative, even mystical. This is especially the case when viewed by the modern scientific mind, an approach that looks for observable evidence to determine whether something exists. However, it underpins the Western view of reality. Plato explained, but did not argue, his theory of metaphysics in his famous Allegory of the Cave found in *The Republic*. In terms of the self, Plato identifies the physical realm with the body, and the metaphysical realm with the true self or the psyche. In doing so Plato rejects the body, even argues that it hinders the self:

> Those who rightly love wisdom are practicing dying, and death to them is the least terrible thing in the world. Look at it in this way: If they are everywhere at enmity with the body, and desire the soul to be alone by itself, and if, when this very thing happens, they shall fear and object – would not that be wholly unreasonable? Should they not willingly go to a place where there is good hope of finding what they were in love with all through life (and they loved wisdom) and of ridding themselves of the companion which they hated?
>
> —Plato[9]

[7] In Plato, *Great Dialogues of Plato*, translated by W. H. D. Rouse (New York: Signet Classic, 1999), p. 145.

[8] Ibid., p. 146.

[9] Ibid., pp. 182–183.

Plato clearly discriminates between the physical body and the metaphysical self based on a distrust of the body as a changing form. This attitude pervades Plato's concept of the body.

| The Mind/Soul | The Body |
|---|---|
| 1. must be the ruler | 1. must be ruled |
| 2. is rational | 2. is irrational |
| 3. is the crown of virtue/ knowledge and existence | 3. is shameful/degraded |
| 4. is the path to all that is good | 4. is an obstacle to all that is good |
| 5. is temporarily imprisoned | 5. is a tomb, a prison |
| 6. is important | 6. is insignificant |

When looking for a definitive expression of Plato's concept of the self, it is not always clear what he means by the psyche. The influence of Christian scholarship has usually interpreted the ancient Greek notion of psyche as soul. Neither is Plato's psyche a "mind" in the modern sense of the word. However, there is greater conceptual clarity if it is translated as "inner self" as it avoids the religious overtones that are incorporated into the notion of the soul.

Further investigation indicates that there are essentially two aspects to the Platonic inner self. The *first* is that it is the **seat of knowledge**, performing the functions that we attribute to minds. The *second* is that it is the **bringer of life**; having an inner self distinguishes a living thing from a non-living thing. (This is where calling the psyche a soul becomes attractive for Christian interpretations.) Plato has defined his self as the essence of an individual life.

Plato details the particular features of this self by using reason to draw an interesting conclusion. In the following dialogue he explains why the self is not a unitary self. Instead the self is divided and these divisions are in conflict. Again, Plato has Socrates explain his justification of this claim:

*Socrates*: Isn't it sometimes true that the thirsty person also, for some reason, may want not to drink?

*Glaucon*: Yes, often.

*Socrates*: What can we say, then, if not that in his soul there is a part that desires drink and another part that restrains him? This latter part is distinct from desire and usually can control desire.

*Glaucon*: I agree.

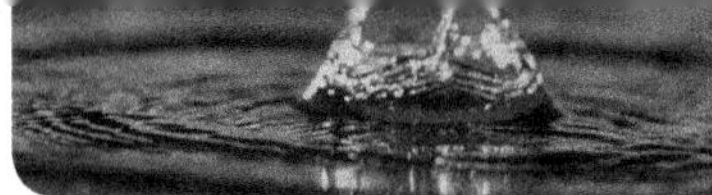



*Socrates*: And isn't it true in such cases such control originates in reason, while the urge to drink originates in something else?

*Glaucon*: So it seems.

*Socrates*: Then we can conclude that there are in us two distinct parts. One is what we call "reason", and the other we call the nonrational "appetites". The latter hungers, thirsts, desires sex, and is subject to other desires.

*Glaucon*: Yes, that is the logical conclusion.

*Socrates*: But what about our emotional or spirited element: the part in us that feels anger and indignation? ... Anger sometimes opposes our appetites as if it is something distinct from them ... Yet this emotional part of ourselves is [also] distinct from reason.

—Plato[10]

In other writings, Plato indicates that the inner self is divided into three parts: a rational part, an appetitive part, and a spirited part. This is called his **tripartite soul**. This is where Plato further develops the concept of the self as an inner self. The self is now dynamic, sometimes in conflict that can only be resolved by the dominance of one part (though, notably, not the exclusion of the others). This is a seminal concept of the self in the Western tradition.

### The tripartite soul

Plato communicates this concept of the self with a very vivid metaphor: the chariot.

## READING ACTIVITY

Read the following passage. Draw and label the images being described.

Let me speak briefly about the nature of the soul by using an image. Let the image have three parts: two winged horses and a charioteer ... One of the horses is of noble breed, the other ignoble. The charioteer controls them with great difficulty ... The vicious steed—when it has not been thoroughly trained—goes heavily, weighing down the charioteer to the earth...

Above them, in the heaven above the heaven ... there abides the true reality with which real knowledge is concerned: the Forms which are visible only to the mind and have no color, shape, or hardness. The souls that are most like gods are carried up there by their charioteer, although troubled by their steeds and only with great difficulty beholding true being ... Other souls rise only to fall again, barely glimpsing it and then altogether failing to see because their steeds are too unruly.

—Plato[11]

[10] From Plato's *Republic*, Book IV; quote taken from Manuel Velasquez, *Philosophy: A Text with Readings*, 12th edition (Wadsworth: Cengage Learning, 2014), p. 56.

[11] From Plato's *Phaedrus*, selections from 246a–247e; quoted in Velasquez, *Philosophy*, p. 56–57.

It should look something like this:

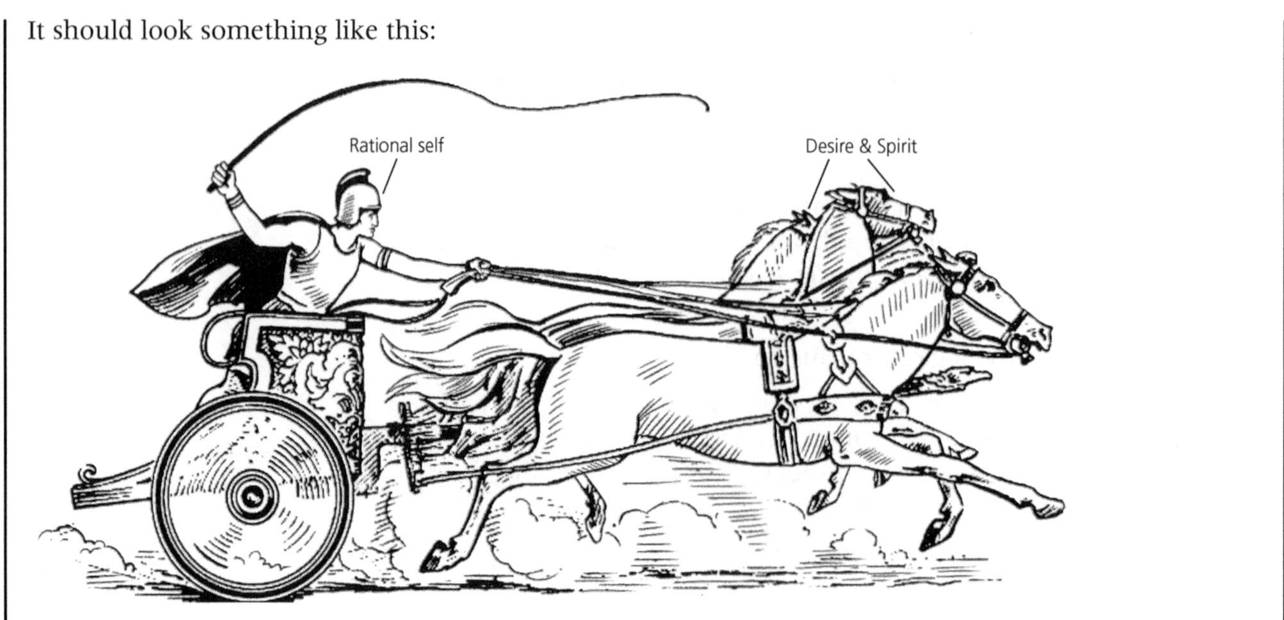


## An ancient critique: Diotima of Mantinea

Plato's views were not immediately accepted. In his dialogue *The Symposium*, Plato refers to the views of a female philosopher Diotima who, it has been suggested, was Socrates' teacher. She argued for a different perspective on the nature of the self:

> Although we speak of an individual as being the same so long as he continues to exist in the same form, and therefore assume that a man is the same person in his old age as in his infancy, yet although we call him the same, every bit of him is different, and every day he is becoming a new man, while the old man is ceasing to exist, as you can see from his hair, his flesh, his bones, his blood, and all the rest of his body. And not only his body, for the same thing happens to his soul.
>
> And neither his manners, nor his dispositions, nor his thoughts, nor his desires, nor his pleasures, nor his sufferings, nor his fears are the same throughout his life, for some of them grow, while others disappear ... Thus, unlike the gods, a mortal creature cannot remain the same throughout eternity; it can only leave behind new life to fill the vacancy that is left as it passes away .... And so it is no wonder that every creature prizes its own offspring, since everything is inspired by this love, this passion for immortality.
>
> —Plato[12]

Diotima, a character in a dialogue and possibly a real philosopher, rejects the idea of the self as a constant and therefore the foundation of identity. It was not until Locke explored the issue of personal identity (see Chapter 7: Identity) in the 17th century that philosophy systematically explored the issue of the enduring self.

[12] Plato, *The Symposium*; quote taken from Edith Hamilton and Huntington Cairns (eds), *The Collected Dialogues of Plato, including the Letters*, translated by Michael Joyce (Princeton, NJ: Princeton University Press, 1961), pp. 559–560.

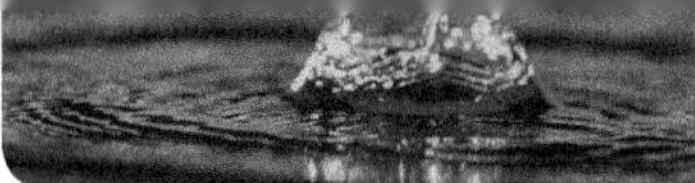

## A modern critique: a feminist critique of Plato's view of the self

There are three dominant feminist perspectives when considering the body:

1. Body as nature – biological entity.
2. Body as socially constructed – this focuses on the sex/gender distinction and theories of socialization.
3. Embodiment – this refers to the lived body and the position that "we are our bodies".

All of these are relevant to the discussion of "What is human?" and the concept of the self. However, the last is most relevant for an evaluation of Plato's concept of the self. Elizabeth V. Spelman highlights in her article "Woman as Body" a concern about Plato's emphasis on the metaphysical at the expense of the physical. Spelman argues that Plato raised the worth of the soul above that of the body:

> Plato's dialogues are filled with lessons about knowledge, reality, and goodness, and most of the lessons carry with them strong praise for the soul and strong indictments against the body. According to Plato, the body, with its deceptive senses, keeps us from real knowledge; it rivets us in a world of material things which is far removed from the world of reality; and it tempts us away from the virtuous life. It is in and through the soul, if at all, that we shall have knowledge, be in touch with reality, and lead a life of virtue. Only the soul can truly know, for only the soul can ascend to the real world, the world of the Forms or Ideas.[13]

To illustrate the superiority of the soul Plato used examples of perceived female behaviours:

> For example, how are we to know when the body has the upper hand over the soul, or when the lower part of the soul has managed to smother the higher part? We presumably can't see such conflict, so what do such conflicts translate into, in terms of actual human lives? Well, says Plato, look at the lives of women. It is women who get hysterical at the thought of death; obviously, their emotions have overpowered their reason, and they can't control themselves.[14]

While this demonstrates clearly that Plato's position on the role of women as Philosopher Queens in *The Republic* requires further investigation, it also demonstrates that he was constructing his position from a specific perspective. How viable is this perspective that involves wholesale the rejection of the body? Perhaps the body is the source of our self due to the importance of the lived experience? As Adrienne Rich suggests, "[i]n order to live a fully human life we require not only control of our bodies (though control is a prerequisite); we must touch the

[13] Elizabeth V. Spelman, "Woman as Body: Ancient and Contemporary Views", *Feminist Studies* 8, No. 1 (Spring 1982): 111.

[14] Ibid., p. 115.

unity and resonance of our physicality, our bond with the natural order, the corporeal grounds of our intelligence."[15] The physical (corporeal) dimension of our existence is being ignored in Plato's argument due to its changeability yet isn't this central to your self, especially if you are a women? For example, the power of birth means that change begins about life. Spelman questions whether or not Plato could understand this possibility. This provides a strong indication as to why essentialism in this form was rejected and a position on the embodied self (the self embedded in the body) was welcomed as an alternative. (This is a position that will be explored in more detail in the section on existentialism.)

## Aristotle and the body

Aristotle, the most famous student of Plato, continued the momentum initiated by Plato (and Socrates) but also reacted to his mentor's philosophy in a number of ways and especially its reliance on rationalism as a methodology and the influence of Pythagoras. He has a more empirical approach to philosophical issues, resulting in a different emphasis in the analysis and therefore some different conclusions. Whereas Plato had been dismissive of the body, Aristotle saw it as essential. He rejected the premise that there were two distinct and separable types of entity: soul and body. He still retained the basic outline of the mind/body but he changed the relationship. As Aristotle states in *On the Soul* (known also as *De Anima*), "The soul must be a substance in the sense of the form of a material body having life potentiality within it. But substance is actuality, and thus soul is the actuality of a body."[16]

When this short explanation is analysed the following connections are evident:

***Soul*** *= Substance* similar to *Form (of a Body) with life potentiality*
*Substance is* ***Actuality***

Therefore

*Soul = Actuality (of the Body)*

As part of Aristotle's overall philosophical framework, he regarded a "thing" as a combination of substance,[17] matter, and form. A "thing" exists (with an ontological or metaphysical reality) and is therefore *not* "nothing" because it has a substance. A substance equals matter in a form. The concept of substance is at the foundation of Aristotle's philosophical understanding and therefore essential to his conceptual framework. Aristotle argues that substance is the fundamental building block of the universe. A modern belief is that it is elementary particles. These seem similar. However, Aristotle's notion of substance is somewhat different from our modern one. For Aristotle, substance is the "whatness" of a thing. It is primary. All other features of our reality such as quantity, quality, relation, place, time, position, state, action, and affection are dependent on the category of substance.

[15] Adrienne Rich, *Of Woman Born: Motherhood as Experience and Institution* (New York: W. W. Norton, 1976), p. 62.

[16] Aristotle, *On the Soul*, Book II, Part 1, available at http://classics.mit.edu/Aristotle/soul.2.ii.html (accessed 23 October 2014).

[17] This is the first ever recorded philosophical account of substance.

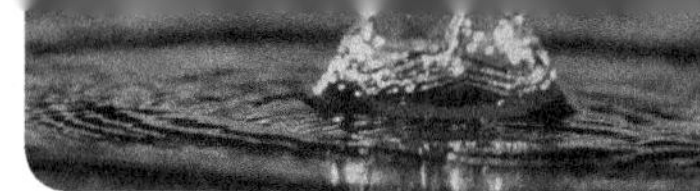



## CONCEPTUAL CLARIFICATION

### What is a substance?

First, it is worth distinguishing between a substance and a property. Properties are "things" that are attached to substances. For example, a property can be a shape, hardness, or a colour. Thus a candle will have a number of properties: it will be cylindrical, hard, and red.

The actual properties can change but the substance will continue to have a property. Another way of thinking about it is that a property cannot exist without a substance. A substance is permanent even though its properties can change. A substance is essential to the existence of a "thing". Whatever exists without properties is what Aristotle called a substance.

Aristotle thought of the soul simply as a "form" and this form is conceived in terms of behaving and thinking. Just as walking is the function of the legs, the soul is the function of the body. The soul is now the "essential whatness" of a body. It is no longer prior to the body and continues to exist even when the body is destroyed. Instead, it is a manifestation of the body or form of the body. In the same way that you cannot *see* without eyes, the soul cannot *be* without the body: "And just as there cannot be a dance without people dancing, so there cannot be ways of behaving without embodied humans to behave in those ways. Hence, for Aristotle, the soul does not exist without the body."[18]

Plato's concept of the immortal soul is clearly rejected with this understanding. Aristotle says:

> We have now given a general answer to the question, What is soul? It is substance in the sense which corresponds to the account of a thing. That means that it is what it is to be for a body of the character just assigned. Suppose that a tool, e.g. an axe, were a *natural* body, then being an axe would have been its essence, and so its soul; if this disappeared from it, it would have ceased to be an axe, except in name.[19]

The Aristotelian self is public manifestation of the body/soul, or the animate body. Therefore the self is the animal or the biological self, later defined by Aristotle as the rational animal.

This is the first level or phase of the self. This self is a singular substance and can never be otherwise. This is the ontological or biological self. The second level of a self is the unitary self of mind and action, one that is developed over time through habitation or practice and is assisted by self-knowledge. Importantly, the discussion of this aspect of the self appears amidst Artistotle's discussion of friendship and the role of friendship in a good self.

Aristotle's idea of this self can be seen in the comparison between the "good man" and the "bad man":

**TOK link** 

What does Oscar Wilde mean when he says, "Man is a rational animal who always loses his temper when he is called upon to act in accordance with the dictates of reason"?

---

[18] Richard Swinburne, "Nature and Immortality of the Soul", in Edward Craig (ed.), *Routledge Encyclopedia of Philosophy* (London: Routledge, 1998), p. 982.

[19] Aristotle, *On the Soul*, Book II, Part 1; quote taken from Peter A. Morton, "Aristotle: Selections from *On the Soul* and *Sense and Sensibilia*", in Peter A. Morton (ed.), *A Historical Introduction to the Philosophy of Mind: Readings with Commentary* (Toronto, Ontario: Braodview Press, 2010), p. 39.

### Good man

"The decent man is of one mind with himself, and he desires with his entire soul the same things. He wills for himself what is and appears to be good, and does it ... He shares the same griefs and pleasures as himself, for at all times the same thing is painful or pleasant to him and not one thing at one time and another at another."[20]

### Bad man

"That which is good is simple but what is bad is multiform. And while the good man is always alike and does not change in character, the base and the senseless man is one thing in the morning and another at night."[21]

These different descriptions make the Aristotle's position on a good and bad self very clear – a unified self is the true self. This leads to Aristotle's moral theory based on the virtuous self.

## The Christian self of Augustine

"People travel to wonder at the height of mountains, at the huge waves of the sea, at the long courses of rivers, at the vast compass of the ocean, at the circular motion of the stars, and they pass by themselves without wondering."

Augustine, *Confessions*, Book 10

▲ Augustine of Hippo

Plato had introduced a radical way of conceiving reality and how we know. The understanding that there was an existence of an immaterial reality which was separate from the physical world had provided the foundation for a radical distinction between an immaterial soul and physical body. This new conceptual framework allowed the emergence of a belief that the soul's ultimate destiny is to achieve a union with the transcendent realm. This possibility was developed by a Roman philosopher called Plotinus (205–270 CE) and in the process established an intellectual movement called Neo-Platonism. An illustration of his advocacy for Plato's conceptual framework can be seen in his consideration of the "soul, since it is a spiritual substance in it own right and can exist independently of the body, possesses a categorical superiority over the body." This even more fundamental re-assertion of Plato's metaphysical framework influenced the work of Augustine of Hippo (354–430 CE), also known at Saint Augustine. Augustine is considered the last of the great ancient philosophers. He is closely associated with the intellectual foundations of Christianity as he connected the basic

[20] Aristotle, *Nicomachean Ethics* 9.4.1166a. pp. 13–29.

[21] Aristotle, *Eudemian Ethics* 7.5.1239b. pp. 11–14.

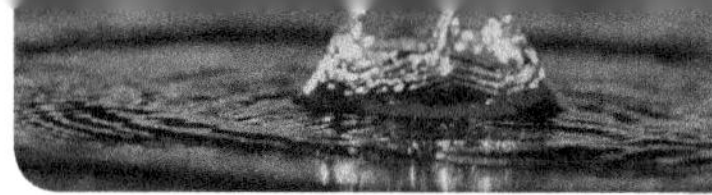

tenets of the practice of Christianity with the legitimacy of the Platonic framework – as he said, "[i]f (the Platonists) could have had this life over again with us . . . they would have become Christians, with the change of a few words and statements." In hindsight the connections were simple – the metaphysical world was the transcendental world, with the Form of the Good becoming God. (This connection also had a significant political benefit – the ideology of Christianity now became comprehendible to the Roman Empire. It was expressed in a Platonic language which was the dominant intellectual tradition of the day.)

Augustine is influential in many debates due to his original writing in the area of philosophy of language, philosophy of mind, and the philosophy of religion. However, for the present purpose his view of the self needs further explanation. Augustine conceived of the self as part of the metaphysical framework. The physical body was an inferior element of human existence and one that ensnared the soul, or the superior element. He similarly retained Plato's tripartite soul although he introduced the idea of the will into this conception, redefining the spirit to accommodate this conceptual change. The dominance of Plato remained until the re-emergence of his student, Aristotle, in the works of Thomas Aquinas. In Aquinas' writings the framework of Aristotle was integrated into Plato's. Accordingly, a person is composed of a material body informed by an immaterial soul. In the initial stage of the afterlife, the individual is merely a soul; and at the resurrection, when the individual is again reunited with the body, there is once again a complete person. This conception of the self remained dominant for over 1,500 years and was influential of the work of the next great philosopher of the self, Descartes, who wrote 1,220 years later.

### WHO WAS THOMAS AQUINAS?

Thomas Aquinas lived from 1225 to 1274. He was an immensely important philosopher and theologian. who sought to integrate the newly discovered work of Aristotle into the beliefs of Christianity. His best known work is the *Summa Theologica*, a book that seeks to explain the tenets of the Christian faith to moderates. It has become one of the most influential works on Christianity and the western philosophy.

## The essential self in modernity

### The modern debate

As the source of authority changed at the end of the Middle Ages, from the Church to the scientist, so did the questions being asked and the way in which people tried to answer them. For example, humans started to consider life not in terms of conforming to a larger order (an ordered, meaningful cosmos created by God), but rather they saw themselves in isolation, almost as biological mechanisms.

In his *Discourse on the Method*, **Descartes** provides us with the pivotal moment in modern thought when the foundation and subsequent framework for modern thinking is established – rational subjectivity. While Western thinking is still profoundly influenced by Plato's legacy, Descartes offers an opportunity to update Plato's conceptual framework. They are both rationalists: Descartes believed in "the natural light of reason", alluding to Plato's Simile of the Sun and his Allegory of the Cave and his concept of the tripartite self of reason, spirit, and passion. This self is now reason, passion, and will (the change in the latter from spirit indicates the power of Augustine's influential interpretation of Plato in the early 5th century CE). Descartes retains the priority of reason in determining the self, wary of passions and the will.

In a time of change, Descartes was one of many thinkers who decided to focus on how to understand the universe separate from the authority of the Church. Consequently, they thought that genuine knowledge needed to be based on independent, rational inquiry and experimentation. As part of the investigation, Descartes decided to assess the certainty of all his knowledge. The outcome of this sceptical methodology was the certainty of "I think, therefore I am" – the catchphrase of modernity. There was now a focus on the individual and his or her relationship to the world rather than the world and the individual's relationship to it. The self now exists in solipsistic isolation. This shift in emphasis had, and continues to have, a profound impact on the issues that are identified in modern society and the solutions that are offered in response.

### The modern self and the shift from self-knowledge to self-consciousness

This aspect of the self can be framed by treating Descartes as the "modern father of philosophy" and exploring the reactions to him through the works of Locke, Hume, and Kant. They can be categorized as **essentialists**. They believed that there was something essential that allowed a human to claim to be a human. This had traditionally been the soul and it had been debated whether or not animals also had a soul. If it was believed they did, it was argued as to whether they had the same type of soul, and so on. This provided the framework for searching for the modern self – the equivalence on the soul. In broad terms, the new soul was consciousness. For more on the concept of consciousness see the section 'Consciousness and self-consciousness' in Chapter 3: Personhood.

However, Descartes, and Locke and Kant to varying degrees, influenced the **existentialist** movement in the 20th century, through its attempt to overcome his metaphysics and to redefine the self. This should help you to understand the debate in the 20th and 21st centuries.

The way to approach this question of the self and our attempts to understand it is **dialectically** (in the Socratic sense, or with a focus on concepts). What we are looking for are the specific points at which Locke, Hume, and Kant disagree with the Cartesian view of the soul or self because of a different understanding of the key concepts, based on different methodological approaches and arguments. This leads to different issues and solutions, and these have different implications for humanity's understanding of its place in the universe and the nature of society.

## From Plato to Descartes

Plato still dominated the intellectual climate of Europe. Aristotle had re-emerged as a major thinker in the tradition after having been forgotten for almost 1,000 years until Arab scholars reintroduced him to Europe in the Middle Ages. However, Europe had changed considerably since the time of Plato. Descartes is writing after the rise of Christianity, in a period of colonial expansion, witnessing the rise of science and rapidly increasing industrialization. The Enlightenment, or secular humanism, had emerged as a new intellectual system alongside the once dominant worldview of Christianity. In fact, the Enlightenment emerged from schools of thought within the Church dating back to the 12th century. Consequently, the Enlightenment was not a revolutionary reaction to the Church, but rather the outcome of a period of personal, social, political, and therefore philosophical experimentation where

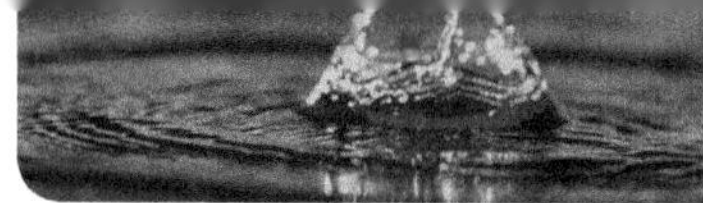



the focus had become the role of humans in a human world. This world was defined and shaped by the decisions of these humans and where change appeared to be the only constant. Most Enlightenment philosophers, such as Michel de Montaigne, John Locke, David Hume, Paul-Henri Thiry d'Holbach, Denis Diderot, Voltaire, Gottfried Leibniz, and Jean-Jacques Rousseau, felt that these decisions must be rational and universal. Reasoning had returned as the primary methodology of knowing, the inherent faculty of all humans, not revelation and authority, and the result was an underlying concept of the self as being autonomous. This led to an assumption that all issues, whether theoretical or practical, could be resolved by the application of reason and would be valid for all humans. Subsequently, this led to a sense of optimism and a focus on emancipation and therefore a sense of progress.

Descartes was one such philosopher and he was also trained in mathematics. This methodological approach was the model for his philosophical thinking, again similar to Plato. He was convinced that knowledge and absolute truths were waiting to be discovered by reasoned, disciplined reflection. With Plato still defining the intellectual framework of Europe it is no surprise that contemporary philosophers were still trained in Platonic thought. Consequently, Descartes was also a dualist (someone who believes there are two worlds, not just one). However, it is worth understanding the nature of this dualism to determine whether or not it is the same kind of dualism as Plato's. As dualists, both argue that there are two worlds; broadly defined as the physical world and the metaphysical world. In terms of a human they argue that they have something **incorporeal**, such as the soul or the mind, which is related to a body that exists in the **corporeal** world. They identify the incorporeal aspect of an individual with the "I" and therefore the self. They also both believe that the individual or self will survive the death of the body and this enables both of them to make claims about immortality. This is a transcendental theory of the self. Plato believes that the best mind is a mind in harmony and that reason should lead the mind to achieve this harmony. Descartes equally believes in the power of reason, although Descartes as a scientist was a little more appreciative of the role the senses could play in knowing the world, but in the end Descartes shares Plato's belief that mathematics and therefore ***a priori*** knowledge is superior. The cultural and therefore intellectual context in which Descartes was working – such as reason as a universal trait of all humans – meant that transcendence was still a mostly unchallenged assumption in philosophical thought at that time.

## Descartes and rational self

Descartes, firmly positioned within a dominant tradition, says that the self, and therefore identity, depends on consciousness. This is a variation, even extension, of an emphasis on self-knowledge. Self-knowledge suggests being conscious of the self. In other words, consciousness is simple self-awareness and is focused on one's own mental world. It requires introspection and reason to investigate this self. It is a personal experience, a private and therefore unique aspect of an individual and as such it cannot be experienced. Because of this dependence on rationalism, the result is an updating of Plato's tripartite self and its own emphasis on reason.

### TOK link

Do you think if you were born in a dark room, with no windows and nothing else in the room, so you couldn't see anything, and you never met anyone else, that you could understand everything in the world? This is an example of extreme rationalism.

Plato explains his understanding of knowledge as recollection in *Meno*. In this dialogue, Socrates draws a square in the dirt. He then asks a slave boy to calculate how long a side of a square would be if it had twice the area of the one he had just drawn. While the initial responses from the slave boy are incorrect Socrates uses a clever sequence of questions to enable the boy to determine the correct calculation. Plato believes that this proves his point (in the context of the dialogue). He believes it illustrates that learning does not involve discovering something new. Rather it is recollecting something the inner self already knew before a person was born but has forgotten.

As a result, the self is a thinking thing, an immaterial substantial self, and one distinct from the body. The consciousness that allows us to know that we exist composes our soul and is regarded by Descartes as a substance, albeit an immaterial substance; a substance being a thing that does not depend on anything else for its existence.

The self, while still being attached to the soul and the theistic beliefs associated with that, is the source of being human, though not necessarily an individual person's identity.

## WHAT IS THE DIFFERENCE BETWEEN DESCARTES AND PLATO?

One of the major differences between Plato and Descartes was the manner in which they established their philosophical positions. While Plato designed his epistemology to suit his metaphysics, Descartes designed his metaphysics to suit his epistemology.

### What was Descartes' project?

In his most famous work, *Meditations on First Philosophy*, Descartes says that he has two principal aims. Firstly, he seeks to demonstrate "the distinctness of the human soul from the body", and secondly, to demonstrate that "God may be more easily and certainly known than the things of the world".[22] For Descartes these two are connected. Being a self that is disconnected from the material world, Descartes argues, I can only know the world through my senses. Only the existence of God can enable me to believe there is a material world.

Similar to Plato, Descartes sought certainty but he utilized the sceptical method to determine what he could be certain of in this world. In other words, he doubted everything as a philosophical methodology, not everything as a principle of living.

However, he could not doubt the fact that he doubted his own existence as a conscious, thinking entity. Even if he was dreaming, he must be dreaming. Accordingly, his foundation of certainty was *cogito, ergo sum* (or "I think, therefore I am") and this became the first principle of Descartes' theory of knowledge. Yet, it also inadvertently became the first principle of his philosophy of identity, an identity grounded in self-consciousness.

As he also puts it in *Meditations*:

**6.** Thinking is another attribute of the soul; and here I discover what properly belongs to myself. This alone is inseparable from me. I am – I exist: this is certain; but how often?

As often as I think; for perhaps it would even happen, if I should wholly cease to think, that I should at the same time altogether cease to be. I now admit nothing that is not necessarily true. I am therefore, precisely speaking, only a thinking thing, that is, a mind, understanding, or reason, terms whose signification was before unknown to me. I am, however, a real thing, and really existent; but what thing? The answer was, a thinking thing ...

**8.** But what, then, am I? A thinking thing, it has been said. But what is a thinking thing?

It is a thing that doubts, understands, [conceives], affirms, denies, wills, refuses; that imagines also, and perceives.[23]

[22] René Descartes, *Meditations*, translated by John Veitch (New York: Cosimo, 2008), p. 62.

[23] Ibid., pp. 80–81; also see René Descartes, "Meditation II: Of the Nature of the Human Mind; And That It Is More Easily Known than the Body", available at http://oregonstate.edu/instruct/phl302/texts/descartes/meditations/Meditation2.html (accessed 23 October 2014).

The body has disappeared from Descartes' description of the self mainly because in his understanding we can conceive of ourselves existing without a body:

> **7.** The question now arises, am I anything else besides? I will stimulate my imagination with a view to discover whether I am not still something more than a thinking being. Now it is plain I am not the assemblage of members called the human body; I am not a thin and penetrating air diffused through all these members, or wind, or flame, or vapor, or breath, or any of all the things I can imagine; for I supposed that all these were not, and, without changing the supposition, I find that I still feel assured of my existence. But it is true, perhaps, that those very things which I suppose to be non-existent, because they are unknown to me, are not in truth different from myself whom I know. This is a point I cannot determine, and do not now enter into any dispute regarding it. I can only judge of things that are known to me: I am conscious that I exist, and I who know that I exist inquire into what I am. It is, however, perfectly certain that the knowledge of my existence, thus precisely taken, is not dependent on things, the existence of which is as yet unknown to me: and consequently it is not dependent on any of the things I can feign in imagination.[24]

With this, Descartes is simply continuing on the tradition of thought he has inherited from some of the great philosophical thinkers he had read in his own education. The self is an essential self and a thinking entity that is very different from the body bound by the physical world. This self is a non-material self, as well as a conscious self that is independent of the physical laws that determine the behaviour of the universe:

> To commence this examination accordingly, I here remark, in the first place, that there is a vast difference between mind and body, in respect that body, from its nature, is always divisible, and that mind is entirely indivisible. For in truth, when I consider the mind, that is, when I consider myself in so far only as I am a thinking thing, I can distinguish in myself no parts, but I very clearly discern that I am somewhat absolutely one and entire; and although the whole mind seems to be united to the whole body, yet, when a foot, an arm, or any other part is cut off, I am conscious that nothing has been taken from my mind; nor can the faculties of willing, perceiving, conceiving, etc., properly be called its parts, for it is the same mind that is exercised [all entire] in willing, in perceiving, and in conceiving, etc. But quite the opposite holds in corporeal or extended things; for I cannot imagine any one of them [how small soever it may be], which I cannot easily sunder in thought, and which, therefore, I do not know to be divisible.[25]

The result of Descartes' investigations is a human being made of two different substances – mind and body. The mind is an **immaterial substance**, which is also the soul and the self – the source of the individual – that exists in the metaphysical world. These mental states are related to the physical states of the body but they are not dependent on them, as the soul will exist after the destruction of the body. The body is a physical substance that exists in the physical world and,

[24] Descartes, *Meditations*, p. 80.

[25] Ibid., p. 120; see also René Descartes, "Meditation VI: Of the Existence of Material Things, And Of the Real Distinction Between the Mind and Body of Man", available at http://oregonstate.edu/instruct/phl302/texts/descartes/meditations/Meditation6.html (accessed 24 October 2014).

importantly, is not an essential element of who I am and therefore the self. The key to Descartes' argument is the role of consciousness.

### What did Descartes argue?

Descartes believed that:

- *First*, the mind is an immaterial thing or a substance, and its entire purpose is to think.
- *Second*, the mind is an absolutely perfect unity and indivisible; nothing can rend it apart or diminish it.
- *Third*, the mind never stops thinking, even when the body is asleep or unconscious or in a coma or suffering from a terrible trauma.
- *Fourth*, the mind enjoys a crystal clear transparency with respect to itself; the mind knows, with the utmost certainty, what it is and what it is up to – it is self-knowing.
- *Fifth*, the mind is immortal; when the brain and body die, the mind continues to be and continues to think forever.
- *Sixth*, the mind comes hard-wired with innate ideas about God, being, its own nature as a substance, and deep mathematical and logical principles; all of which are imprinted on it at the moment of its creation by God (long before it becomes embodied).

In terms of the consideration of the self, Descartes' self is an independent, solitary mind and the world is mind-dependent. Self-consciousness is the approach he uses to draw these conclusions.

What are other implications of Descartes' concept of the self? One issue that is covered in more depth in Chapter 4: Mind and Body but is worth mentioning here is the question of how two utterly different entities as mind and body can interact. This is the issue of interactionalism. Another issue is covered in Chapter 7: Identity, namely that "we can never be sure that someone is the same person we saw yesterday – we can never observe they have the same mind". This is the issue of the **enduring self**.

## Summary: What we take from Descartes

Descartes is our reference point for the modern debate about the self. Coupled with an understanding of the role of Plato in establishing and defining the conceptual framework that Descartes, to a significant extent, worked within, you are now prepared to explore the modern concepts of the self. Even if a philosophical school was rejecting this conceptual framework it was still being utilized in relation to these philosophers. As a consequence it is worth ensuring that the following concepts are understood. The following concepts are now the building blocks of the modern self:

- Rationality
- Consciousness
- Immateriality
- Unity
- Thinking
- Self-knowing
- Immortality
- Innate ideas

## Alternatives to Descartes

Before we consider a significant response to Descartes in the form of Locke's criticism of his concept of the self as soul, it is worth highlighting a number of other alternatives. These two positions do not share the same conceptual framework as Descartes (unlike Locke).

**Assessment tip**

To obtain a high mark in Paper 1 it is important to discuss your chosen philosophical issue from at least two perspectives.

## Hobbes and the materialist self

Hobbes, the radical **materialist** philosopher (see biography on p. 31 in Chapter 2: Human Nature), wrote around the same time as Descartes. Although Hobbes was English he lived in Paris where he wrote his most famous work, *The Leviathan*. During this time Hobbes and Descartes exchanged a series of letters. As a materialist Hobbes rejected Descartes' concept of the soul and his whole conceptual framework which was founded on a belief. While Hobbes did not develop an explicit concept of the self, his radical materialism meant that he conceived the individual and therefore self as simply the body, as can be seen in the following quotes: "[t]hus mind will be nothing but the motions in certain parts of an organic body" and an "essence without existence is a fiction of our mind".[26]

### Rousseau and the moral self

Before we continue with the development of Descartes' concept of the self it is worth noting a radical alternative to this tradition. Rousseau is often neglected as part of a discussion regarding the self. (See biography on p. 295 in Chapter 6: Freedom.) He never developed his own systematic epistemology or metaphysics, the foundation of a claim to be a modern philosopher. He is usually included in a political philosophy course because of his argument for a particular version of a social contract. However, his writing does contain an argument for the self but it is different in many ways from the traditional conception of the self. Rousseau rejected the rational, essentialist self of Plato and then the non-substantial and subjective self of Descartes, instead arguing for a moral self guided by feeling and a personalized sense of goodness and self-worth. The self-conscious, rational self of Descartes (and as we will find out, Locke) is a private self. This is replaced by Rousseau by a self that is expressive, unfolding within the world through action.

It is still an introspective self in many ways and is of primary importance in Rousseau's philosophical considerations, like many other philosophers in the Western tradition. However, this is not because of the epistemological and metaphysical first principles it reflects, but rather because it is important to the individual and his or her moral goodness. He retains the sense of the individual as an atomistic entity, independent of others, even if living within the community and under the general will. In fact, his distrust of society led him to believe that this society was corrupting and devoid of meaningful relationships, stripping an individual of his or her compassion and, more generally, virtues.

In many ways, Rousseau did not argue for a conception of the self, but rather a description of **self-hood** or the nature of the self.

Rousseau's philosophy and concept of the self was very influential on Friedrich Schiller, Johann Wilhelm von Goethe, Georg Wilhelm Friedrich Hegel, and Karl Marx, and, more surprisingly, on Immanuel Kant. Consequently, it has been very influential on modern life in general, though often without acknowledgement.

[26] Quotes taken from René Descartes, "Third Set of Objections with Author's Replies", in *The Philosophical Works of Descartes*, vol. 2, translated by Elizabeth S. Haldane and G. R. T. Ross (Cambridge: Cambridge University Press, 1934), pp. 65, 77.

### Hegel and the social self

Hegel (see biography on p. 161 in Chapter 4: Mind and Body) was a brilliant philosopher who responded to Kant, in turn provoking numerous responses. For example, in response Kierkegaard wrote his early Christian existential philosophy and Hegel provided Marx with the intellectual framework that became his devastating critique of Western industrialized society. If we restrict our treatment of Hegel to our current consideration of the self we find him reacting to the assumptions built into Descartes' philosophy. Aristotle and his critical rejection of some of the major arguments in Plato's philosophy inspired Hegel. In a similar way Hegel would reject Descartes' reformulation of Plato's philosophy. The key aspect that he rejects is the assumption that one's self is determined in pure isolation. Instead Hegel argues that the self can only become manifest within a complex network of social interactions and its social functions. Other selves become essential to the self and as such each person "does not see the other as an essential being, but in the other sees its own self".[27] This mutual recognition is social and therefore cannot occur if an individual is simply self-consciousness. Consciousness occurs when a self interacts with others, establishing relationships. I am because of how I fit within the world of human relationships. This approach can be taken further. As Derrick Bell argues in *Ethical Ambition: Living a Life of Meaning and Worth,* we are not even defined by our relationships, we *are* our relationships:

> However self-sufficient we may fancy ourselves, we exist only in relation – to our friend, family, and life partners; to those we teach and mentor; to our co-workers, neighbors, strangers; and even to forces we cannot fully conceive of, let alone define. In many ways, we are our relationships.[28]

**Paper 3 link** 

**The role of conflict**

Locke wrote *An Essay Concerning Human Understanding* (1690) because he was concerned that not knowing the limits of understanding would put society in moral danger. In his day Locke observed controversies, scepticism, complaints, violent expressions of dogma, even revolution.

Like Plato and Descartes, he lived through a period of political unrest but instead of seeking to resolve this conflict through the primacy of a specific authority or institution, he sought to prioritize the individual and his or her freedom.

## Locke and the psychological theory of the self as an immaterial, non-substance

Locke presents us with the first of a number of changes to the approach to the concept of the self. While Descartes followed Plato to a large degree, especially in continuing the emphasis on reason, Locke was an empiricist and a naturalist (see biography on p. 344 in Chapter 7: Identity). Like Descartes, he was also a scientist. However, he did not start out as a mathematician, but instead trained as a physician at Oxford University. Accordingly, he was taught to identify and record symptoms and then draw a conclusion about the nature of the disease and its possible cure. This process of identifying patterns and making inferences was formally a rational process, but it also involved experience as an important element in decision-making. Knowledge was accumulated, based on sense

[27] G. W. F. Hegel, "B.IV.A. Independence and Dependence of Self-Consciousness: Lordship and Bondage", Section 179, in *Phenomenology of Spirit*, translated by A. V. Miller, with analysis of the text and foreword by J. N. Findlay (Oxford: Oxford University Press, 1977), p. 111.

[28] Derrick Bell, *Ethical Ambition: Living a Life of Meaning and Worth* (London: Bloomsbury, 2002), p. 95.

perception and memory. He believed one could give an account of human understanding and our world only by appealing to natural causes. Rationalists, such as Descartes, Spinoza, and Leibniz, all appealed to God to account for the reasons why something happened. Nonetheless, Locke still believed in God, but he was a methodological naturalist, not an ontological naturalist. The difference being that methodological naturalism believes that science can explain the world while ontological naturalism refers to God for an explanation.

So, as an empiricist, Locke believed that our theories of the world must be built on experience. However, we cannot have experiences of "substances", only of their properties. Consequently, a concept of personal identity must be derived from inner experience to be valid. As a result, introspection remains key to the question of the self.

**TOK Links** 

**Experience and sense perception**

How can we know if our senses are reliable?

Can we directly perceive the world as it is or is the act of perception an active process dependent on our interpretation?

What is the role of reason in sense perception?

## What did Locke argue?

Locke's theory of personal identity and therefore the self is one of the most original and interesting parts of *An Essay Concerning Human Understanding*. Read the following passage and complete a detailed analysis of the argument presented here:

> *Personal identity*. This being premised, to find wherein personal identity consists, we must consider what person stands for; — which, I think, is a thinking intelligent being, that has reason and reflection, and can consider itself as itself, the same thinking thing, in different times and places; which it does only by that consciousness which is inseparable from thinking, and, as it seems to me, essential to it: it being impossible for any one to perceive without perceiving that he does perceive. When we see, hear, smell, taste, feel, meditate, or will anything, we know that we do so. Thus it is always as to our present sensations and perceptions: and by this every one is to himself that which he calls self: — it not being considered, in this case, whether the same self be continued in the same or divers substances. For, since consciousness always accompanies thinking, and it is that which makes every one to be what he calls self, and thereby distinguishes himself from all other thinking things, in this alone consists personal identity, i.e. the sameness of a rational being: and as far as this consciousness can be extended backwards to any past action or thought, so far reaches the identity of that person; it is the same self now it was then; and it is by the same self with this present one that now reflects on it, that that action was done.[29]
>
> [...]
>
> Consciousness is the perception of what passes in a Man's own mind.[30]

[29] John Locke, "Book II: Of Ideas", in *An Essay Concerning Human Understanding* (New York: Prometheus Books, 1995), Chapter XXVII, Section 9; see also http://oregonstate.edu/instruct/phl302/texts/locke/locke1/Book2c.html#Chapter XXVII (accessed 24 October 2014).

[30] Locke, "Book II . . .", *An Essay*, Chapter I, Section 19; see also http://oregonstate.edu/instruct/phl302/texts/locke/locke1/Book2a.html#Chapter I (accessed 24 October 2014).

## ANALYSIS ACTIVITY

Break the argument put forward by Locke in this passage into stages by answering the following guiding questions:

1. What do you have to do to discover the nature of *personal identity*?
2. According to Locke, what does a person stand for?
3. What always accompanies thinking?
4. What is Locke's definition of consciousness?
5. What is Locke's definition of personal identity and therefore the self?
6. What is not considered in this passage?
7. What is the relationship of consciousness and reason?
8. What is the relationship of consciousness and self?
9. What role do these play in personal identity?
10. What is the role of "past actions or thought" in determining the same or enduring self?

Now finally map the relationship requested by Locke:

Person = Thinking = Consciousness

### The self and a change of substance

Plato and Descartes both argued that the self was located in the form of an immortal, non-material soul (that continues to exist following the death of the body). Locke rejects this belief. He goes further, rejecting not only that the self and the soul are intimately linked, if not the same thing, but also that the self exists in any substance. He explains this using a rather gruesome example:

> That this is so, we have some kind of evidence in our very bodies, all whose particles, whilst vitally united to this same thinking conscious self, so that we feel when they are touched, and are affected by, and conscious of good or harm that happens to them, are a part of ourselves; i.e. of our thinking conscious self. Thus, the limbs of his body are to every one a part of himself; he sympathizes and is concerned for them. Cut off a hand, and thereby separate it from that consciousness he had of its heat, cold, and other affections, and it is then no longer a part of that which is himself, any more than the remotest part of matter. Thus, we see the *substance* whereof personal self consisted at one time may be varied at another, without the change of personal identity; there being no question about the same person, though the limbs which but now were a part of it, be cut off.[31]

[31] Locke, "Book II . . .", *An Essay*, Chapter XXVII, Section 11; see also http://oregonstate.edu/instruct/phl302/texts/locke/locke1/Book2c.html#Chapter XXVII (accessed 24 October 2014).

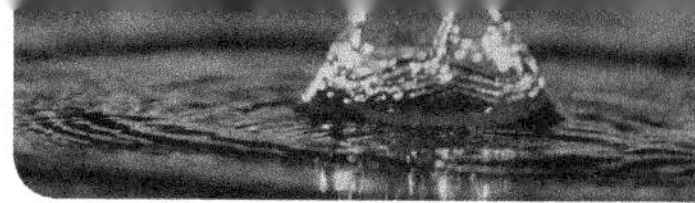



One would expect that an empiricist would be favourably disposed towards a self as a substance – something that could be experienced. Locke, however, is not a materialist as well as an empiricist. He believes that properties can also be experienced and this enables him to conclude that the essence of the self is its conscious awareness of itself as a thinking, reasoning, reflecting identity. The self does not have to be located or embedded in a single substance such as an immaterial.

The development of the self:

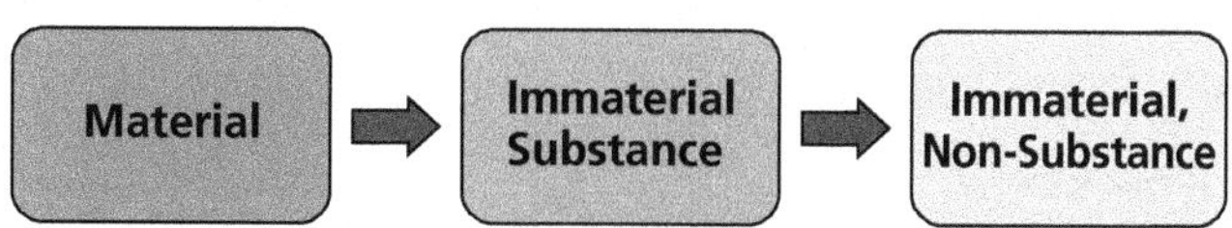


## REFLECTION QUESTIONS

Locke has been guided by the framework set up by Descartes to a certain extent. However, he is using a different methodology to Descartes.

1. How does this methodology influence the conclusions drawn by Locke?
2. What are the implications of using a different methodology to formulate an argument?

Locke comes to the conclusion that the self can reside in any number of substances or souls. This does seem viable and Locke provides an example that seems to support this:

> Self is that conscious thinking thing, whatever substance made up of ... which is sensible, or conscious of pleasure and pain ... [etc.]. Thus every one finds that, whilst comprehended under that consciousness, the little finger is as much a part of himself as what is most so. Upon separation of this little finger, should this consciousness go along with the little finger, and leave the rest of the body, it is evident the little finger would be the person, the same person...[32]

But Locke goes one step further and illustrates the full implications of his position with a famous thought experiment called the Prince and the Cobbler.

> For should the soul of a prince, carrying with it the consciousness of the prince's past life, enter and inform the body of a cobbler, as soon as deserted by his own soul, every one sees he would be the same *person* with the prince, accountable only for the prince's actions: but who would say it was the same *man*?[33]

[32] Ibid., Section 17.

[33] Ibid., Section 15.

## ANALYSIS ACTIVITY

Interpret the story of the Prince and the Cobbler according to Locke's theory of the self (personal identity).

### Questions

1. Which aspects of the argument seem valid?
   For example, how would the prince prove he was the prince even though he is in the cobbler's body? Hint – shared memories
2. Which aspects of the argument do not seem valid?
   How would the prince behave? Hint – mannerisms

### Evaluating Locke's argument

Another important aspect of Locke's argument is his claim that "consciousness always accompanies thinking". Are you currently thinking? Are you conscious of thinking? Can you be conscious of a moment when you weren't conscious of thinking? If so, what impact does this have on Locke's argument? Maybe it is fair to suggest that you are only conscious of thinking when you were asked if you were conscious of thinking. Have you ever been lost in thought? Immersed in an activity? Caught up in the moment? However, you are always potentially, if not actually, conscious of your self. Is this enough to overcome this issue?

Locke argues that we are our memories. We have self-awareness and we can remember the events that occurred when we have self-awareness. Locke assumes, however, that we have access to all our memories and that when we do remember these memories are correct or authentic. To do this we must have a self that is able to do this remembering and authenticating. Doesn't this presume a self that enables us to argue that we have a self as memories? This is called circular reasoning.

### Assumptions in Locke's argument

Locke believes that experience is either external, which is called **sensation** (= **external perception**), or internal, which is called **reflection** (= **inner perception**).

Therefore, the ideas are either ideas of sensation, which is primary, or ideas of reflection, which derived from ideas of sensation and are therefore secondary.

This is a dualistic understanding of the faculties of perception (sensation and reflection). Locke is still under the influence of Descartes and his dualism – the dichotomy of material and spiritual substance. But Locke

### TOK Links

How did Locke know?

As an empiricist, Locke is also asking his readers to inspect their own experiences to assess whether these conclusions are confirmed.

Do this yourself. What is your conclusion?

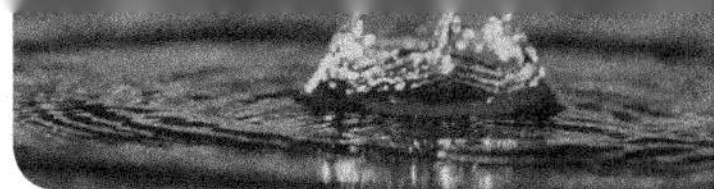

reverses the priorities defined by Descartes. His framework believed that the ideas of reflection (inner perception/knowledge) were prior to the knowledge of the world. Locke reversed this and argued that the ideas of sensation (experience) were prior to the ideas of reflection.

How does this impact on his concept of the self?

## Rejection of the essential self

### Hume and the bundle theory of the self

Like Locke, Hume was an empiricist, a philosopher who believed in an empirical appeal to the senses that provided reason with the knowledge required to understand the world (see biography on p. 31 in Chapter 2: Human Nature). While he was an Enlightenment philosopher, his use of reason eventually resulted in a set of devastating critiques of the central tenets of Enlightenment: a faith in reason and experience of the world.

Hume is renowned for his critique of inductive inference, or reasoning from the observed behaviour of a set of objects to their behaviour when they are unobserved.[34] Based on this thinking, he was able to claim that we could never justify claims of causation because we only inductively associate events and therefore only assume there is an association between them. We cannot prove there is causation.

Similarly, Hume argued that there is no relation between a descriptive statement (about what is in the world) and a prescriptive or normative statement (about what ought to be). This is a criticism of naturalism, or deriving an ethics from an understanding of nature. This is known as the "is–ought problem", but it is also referred to as "Hume's law" and "Hume's Guillotine". Unlike Descartes however this scepticism was not used to achieve certainty. Hume sought to demonstrate the lack of certainty in our understanding of the world.

Hume also challenged the arguments of Descartes and Locke on the question of the self. He argued that there was no self, only a bundle of perceptions.

**REFLECTION ACTIVITY**

Sit by yourself and close your eyes. Look for your self. Do you use your body (hands) or your thoughts (mind)?

Assuming you use your self-consciousness (thoughts), shift through your thinking, your experiences, your memories, your ideas/imagination, your sensations/moods/feelings. Can you find your self? Can you experience it?

[34] Or as Hume expresses it, how they behave when these objects are "beyond the present testimony of our senses, and the records of our memory" (Hume, "Section II . . .", *An Enquiry*, p. 22).

Hume argues that if you are diligent in your application of the empiricist methodology, you can never experience your self.

There are some philosophers who imagine we are every moment intimately conscious of what we call our SELF;[35] that we feel its existence and its continuance in existence; and are certain, beyond the evidence of a demonstration, both of its perfect identity and simplicity. The strongest sensation, the most violent passion, say they, instead of distracting us from this view, only fix it the more intensely, and make us consider their influence on *self* either by their pain or pleasure. To attempt a farther proof of this were to weaken its evidence; since no proof can be derived from any fact of which we are so intimately conscious; nor is there any thing, of which we can be certain, if we doubt of this.

Unluckily all these positive assertions are contrary to that very experience which is pleaded for them; nor have we any idea of *self*, after the manner it is here explained. For, from what impression could this idea be derived? This question it is impossible to answer without a manifest contradiction and absurdity; and yet it is a question which must necessarily be answered, if we would have the idea of self pass for clear and intelligible. It must be some one impression, that gives rise to every real idea. But self or person is not any one impression, but that to which our several impressions and ideas are supposed to have a reference. If any impression gives rise to the idea of self, that impression must continue invariably the same, through the whole course of our lives; since self is supposed to exist after that manner. But there is no impression constant and invariable. Pain and pleasure, grief and joy, passions and sensations succeed each other, and never all exist at the same time. It cannot therefore be from any of these impressions, or from any other, that the idea of self is derived; and consequently there is no such idea.

[...]

## Questions

1. How convincing does Hume believe the claims made by those who "are every moment intimately conscious of what we call our SELF"?
2. According to Hume what is the relationship between these claims and the experience used to support them?
3. Regarding the self, what does Hume conclude about the fact that an individual has numerous impressions or ideas in terms of what is missing?

But farther, what must become of all our particular perceptions upon this hypothesis? All these are different, and distinguishable, and separable from each other, and may be separately considered, and may exist separately, and have no Deed of tiny thing to support their existence. After what manner, therefore, do they belong to self; and how are they connected with it? For my part, when I enter most intimately into what I call *myself*, I always stumble on some particular perception or other, of heat or cold, light or shade, love or hatred, pain or pleasure. I never can catch myself at any time without a perception, and never can observe any thing but the perception. When my perceptions are removed for any time, as by sound sleep; so long am I insensible of *myself*, and may truly be

[35] This is commonly interpreted as a reference to Descartes and Locke as well as other contemporary philosophers influenced by their thought.

said not to exist. And were all my perceptions removed by death, and could I neither think, nor feel, nor see, nor love, nor hate after the dissolution of my body, I should be entirely annihilated, nor do I conceive what is farther requisite to make me a perfect non-entity. If any one, upon serious and unprejudiced reflection thinks he has a different notion of *himself*, I must confess I can reason no longer with him. All I can allow him is, that he may be in the right as well as I, and that we are essentially different in this particular. He may, perhaps, perceive something simple and continued, which he calls *himself*; though I am certain there is no such principle in me.

—David Hume[36]

**Questions**

1. Reread Hume's observation about his search for his essential self ("when I enter most intimately into what I call myself"). What is he looking for in relation to perceptions?
2. Can you think of an analogy to help you understand this point?
3. What does Hume say of people who differ from him?
4. According to Hume, do we really have any idea of the self?

As an empiricist, David Hume believed that our knowledge or epistemological conclusions ultimately come from experience. Consequently, if the claim were made that the self exists, the expectation should be that empirical data would be used to substantiate the claim. According to Hume, if there is to be such a thing as self it must manifest itself in the form of an impression or idea. However, "there is no such idea". As such, the idea of the self, as had been argued for in the Western tradition, cannot be tested against evidence derived from an empirical study. Hume argues that you never perceive your self, or rather the stream of consciousness never actually reveals a self. Instead, what is assumed is a unity to our transient mental experiences and this unity is actually your self. The only thing that can be ascertained in our consciousness is that it is composed of various impressions that are constantly changing. Descartes would have argued that it is logical for there to be a self that is experiencing and unifying these perceptions.

Consequently, we have no reason to believe there is a self.

## CONCEPTUAL UNDERSTANDING

### The bundle theory

1. Imagine you are sitting on a hill as a storm approaches over the horizon. Think about what will happen:
    - The air temperature will change.
    - The air pressure will change.
    - Thunder will be heard in the distance.
    - The sky will get darker.

[36] David Hume, *A Treatise of Human Nature: Being An Attempt to Introduce the Experimental Method of Reasoning into Moral Subjects, Volume I: Of the Understanding* (London: John Noon, 1739), Book I, Part IV, Section VI; available at http://davidhume.org/texts/thn.html (accessed (24 October 2014).

- The air will become more humid.
- Lightning will be seen.

These changes are all perceived. You think, "Here comes a storm." However, will you actually see the storm or just the experience of the storm?

The storm is a collection of experiences that is usually identified as a storm. Hume is rejecting the idea that there is an **essence** of the storm. To conceptualize this, imagine that as the storm passes over you you see a massive black orb with the word "STORM" written on it. This is the essence of the storm and exactly what Hume argues does not exist.

**2.** What does it mean when Hume's understanding of the self is compared to the idea of "using a flashlight to find darkness"?

## Understanding Hume's concept of the self

Does this mean that there is no self? Many commentators have argued that Hume argues for an illusionary theory of the self. However, this assumes there is a set idea of the self and Hume rejects that idea. In fact, Hume is leaving room for a new theory of the self: the self is a "bundle of perceptions": "They are the successive perceptions only, that constitute the mind".[37]

It is, however, valid to ask what ties a particular set of experiences into the bundle. In his response, Hume reveals that he is still working within the framework established by John Locke. In a similar way to Locke he argues that resemblance and causation are important elements in understanding the self. Thoughts and perceptions resemble the original experience and "mutually produce, destroy, influence, and modify each other", demonstrating a causal relationship.[38]

This leads us to believe there is a self, although on reflection, according to Hume at least, it is a fiction. The self can be conceived as a set of relations between experiences only.

In response to this lack of a self, Hume suggests, we impose a fictional self that allows us to order these experiences by referencing an "experiencer".

> For when we attribute identity, in an improper sense, to variable or interrupted objects, our mistake is not confined to the expression, but is commonly attended with a fiction, either of something invariable and uninterrupted, or of something mysterious and inexplicable, or at least with a propensity to such fictions. What will suffice to prove this hypothesis to the satisfaction of every fair enquirer, is to show from daily experience and observation, that the objects, which are variable or interrupted, and yet are supposed to continue the same, are such only as consist of a succession of parts, connected together by resemblance, contiguity, or causation.[39]

[37] Ibid.

[38] Ibid.

[39] Ibid.

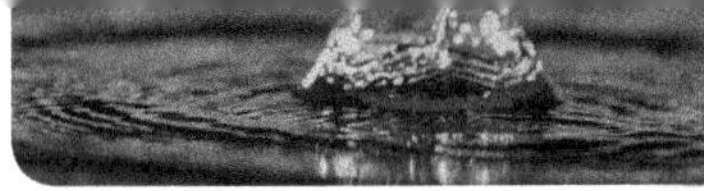

### Evaluating Hume's argument

Hume seeks to demonstrate that the self is a fiction, instead arguing for a bundle of perceptions. However, this is not enough. We have every right to challenge Hume and ask, why do we have a concept of the self if it does not exist? In order for Hume to complete his philosophical argument he must account for our established beliefs in the self and, in particular, their explanatory powers. An argument is often assessed by the quality of its reasoning and evidence. However, it should also be assessed by the philosopher's ability to provide an alternative account for our established beliefs and actions. For example, if you believe in Santa Claus, then the role of Santa Claus at Christmas explains a number of events by providing an explanation or a cause. If you are then told that there is no Santa Claus, then the person who tells you there is no Santa Claus must also provide an explanation for all the events that were previously explained by Santa Claus. Who brings the presents? Who plays Santa Claus at the local department store? And so on.

## Modern theories of the no-self

It is an opportune moment to return to the Western tradition. Contemporary psychology and neuroscience have provided some new insights into the human mind and by extension the question of the self. A number of philosophers have used these findings to re-engage with the question of the self.

### Parfit

One of these, British philosopher Derek Parfit (1942– ), offers another bundle theory, or no-self theory. Parfit has also described it as a reductionist theory of the self.

> In a sense, a Bundle Theorist denies the existence of persons ... There are persons or subjects in [a] language-dependent way. If, however, persons are believed to be more than this – to be separately existing things, distinct from our brains and bodies, and the various kinds of mental states and events – the Bundle Theorist denies that there are such things.[41]

Parfit is working within the conceptual framework set up by David Hume and is aware of the relevance to Buddhism to this position (see section on Buddhism below). In Western philosophical terms, he is arguing against any transcendental subject of consciousness. In the process he wishes to highlight the unchallenged assumptions he believes are still evident in the dominant discussions on this subject.

### Strawson

English philosopher and professor Sir Peter F. Strawson (1919–2006) rejected both the Cartesian and the no-self (or "no-ownership") theories of the self. In his book *Individuals: An Essay in Descriptive*

## A PRAGMATIC RESPONSE

William James, the 19th-century American philosopher, suggested "consciousness, then, does not appear to itself chopped up in bits. Such words as 'chain' or 'train' do not describe it fitly as it presents itself in the first instances. It is nothing jointed; it flows. A 'river' or a 'stream' is the metaphor by which it is most naturally described. In talking hereafter, let us call it the stream of thought, of consciousness, or of subjective life."[40]

How important is the right metaphor when constructing an argument in philosophy?

[40] William James, *The Principle of Psychology*, vol. 1 (New York: Henry Holt and Company, 1890), p. 239.

[41] Derek Parfit, "Divided Minds and the Nature of Persons", in Colin Blakemore and Susan Greenfield (eds), *Mindwaves: Thoughts on Intelligence, Identity and Consciousness* (Oxford: Basil Blackwell, 1987), pp. 20–21.

*Metaphysics*, he argues that they "are profoundly wrong in holding, as each must, that there are two uses of, in one of which it denotes something which it does not denote in the other".[42] Strawson rejects the position that states of consciousness do not belong to persons or, indeed, to anything at all, though it is allowed that perhaps they may be causally related to a body. When an individual says that "I am hurting" they are making a claim that the pain that is causing them to hurt is their pain. Consequently, the no-self or no-ownership doctrine argues that there is only a causal dependence upon the state of some specific body that is producing the sensation of pain. If ownership is dependent on the capability for ownership to be transferable, then experiences, such as pain, cannot be transferable.

## Kant and the transcendental ego

With the conclusion of the discussion of Plato, Descartes, Locke, and Hume, and their respective approaches of rationalism and empiricism, it becomes obvious that there is a divide in the Western intellectual tradition. The first school argued that certain *a priori* truths about the self could be deduced through the use of reason. The second school argued that the self should accept a non-substantial account of the self based on a sequence of impressions derived from the empirical data available to us. This divide became the great challenge of the Enlightenment. Which was the better way of thinking about the issues facing society in the 17th century? Kant offered the best, or at least the most influential, answer.

Kant believed that neither offered a credible answer to the most significant issues of his time. He defined them as follows:

> Two things fill the mind with ever new and increasing admiration and awe ... the starry heavens above and the moral law within.[43]

He thought that the metaphysical questions (and ontological questions) on the existence of God or whether humans were free could not be answered until the epistemological question as to whether they could know anything about these issues was answered. If not, a massive assumption was being ignored. So, similar to Descartes, Kant was seeking to establish firm foundations for thinking.

The main problem for Kant was that science understood the world as ordered by deterministic laws while man was free. Kant was impressed by science and unwilling to dismiss it out of hand as a source of knowledge. He had studied the classics, philosophy, and physics at the University of Königsberg, and been impressed by the advancements made by science, and in particular by Isaac Newton. However, he felt they could not account for the "moral law within". The answer was to seek a balance between

---

[42] Peter F. Strawson, *Individuals: An Essay in Descriptive Metaphysics* (London: Routledge, 1959), p. 98.

[43] Immanuel Kant, *Critique of Practical Reason* (translated from the German Kritik der praktischen Vernunft, 1788), Book II, Part 2, Conclusion; quote taken from Paul Gruyer (ed.), *The Cambridge Companion to Kant and Modern Philosophy* (Cambridge: Cambridge University Press, 2006), p. 1.

science and metaphysics, or between empiricism and rationalism. The result was what Kant himself described as a Copernican revolution in metaphysics and epistemology (named after Copernicus, the Renaissance mathematician and astronomer who placed the sun at the centre of the universe).

The question being asked of the self seemed to have fallen into two schools, based on two different approaches. Kant agreed with Hume (and empiricism) that knowledge starts with experience but disagreed that it was limited by it. He argued that there was also *a priori* knowledge and the question was how much: "though our knowledge begins with experience, it does not follow that it all arises out of experience".[44] This is not the place for an in-depth study of Kant's philosophy. However, this does indicate the context in which Kant was thinking. His concept of the self was immensely complex, working between these two schools, seeking to find a valid compromise between sceptical empiricism and dogmatic rationalism.

Kant was famously "awoken from his dogmatic slumber" when he was 46 during his reading of Hume's *Treatise*. He spent 11 years formulating his initial response, which resulted in his three famous *Critiques*.

Kant asked the question of Hume that we have already asked: what makes it possible for us to have a unified grasp of the world, to coordinate our bundle of perceptions? Kant argued that we perceive and experience the world around us as a world of objects, relationships, and ideas, and these all exist within a relatively stable framework of two basic organizers: space and time. He believed that this indicated a unity of the self. Without it, we would not be able to make sense of the perceptions being received, along with imagination, memory, and the capacity for synthesis. He labelled this the "transcendental unity of apperception", or the self. This is often illustrated by using the metaphor of the weaver.

Imagine opening up a box containing a jigsaw puzzle. When it is first emptied onto the table the pieces are all jumbled, many of them are not even facing upwards and recognizable. However, you slowly start to organize them and eventually place them all where they need to go to complete the picture. For us it is the construction of meaning.

> Hitherto it has been assumed that all our knowledge must conform to objects. But all attempts to extend our knowledge of objects by establishing something in regard to them by means of concepts have, on this assumption, ended in failure. We must, therefore, make trial whether we may not have more success if we suppose that objects must conform to our knowledge.
>
> —Immanuel Kant[45]

In the process Kant retains Plato's metaphysics, naming the two realities the **Phenomenal Reality** – the world as we experience it – and the **Noumenal Reality** – the purely intelligible, or non-sensual reality.

[44] Kant, "Introduction", in *Critique of Pure Reason*, translated by Norman Kemp Smith (London: Macmillan and Co., 1929), p. A1 / B1 (p. 41).

[45] Ibid., p. B 26 (p. 22).

> Sensations would be nothing to us, and would not concern us in the least, if they were not received into our (orderly) consciousness. Knowledge is impossible in any other way ... For perceptions could not be perceptions of anything for me unless they could at least be connected together into (my) one consciousness. This principle stands firm *a priori*, and may be called the "transcendental principle of unity" for all the multiplicity of our perceptions and sensations.
>
> —Immanuel Kant[46]

Kant argues that Hume got it wrong. The reason he could not find the self was because he was looking in the wrong place! Hume failed to acknowledge that while he was looking for the self he was having intelligent experiences so, Kant asked, where does this intelligence come from? The answer for Kant was the self. The self was coordinating the perceptions, making sense of them.

A suitable analogy is an eye. You never see your eye, only what you are seeing. You do not realize that your eye is seeing because you cannot see it. That is, until you look in the mirror.

Kant has also developed Descartes' "I think, therefore I am". Now, the "I" is not a simple thinking machine, rather a dynamic entity that is continually interpreting the world, synthesizing sensations and ideas into a comprehensible whole, and reliant on concepts such as substance, cause and effect, unity, plurality, possibility, necessity, and reality. This constructed, orderly world was deemed by Kant to be an objective one as the categories that constructed it were transcendental even if it was the individual's interpretation.

If you reflect upon this concept of the self you will find that it is a very abstract conception of the self. There is also nothing *personal* about it, nothing that defines the individual. It is a great intellectual answer to the challenge of Hume but it is not a satisfactory answer when reflecting upon being an individual. Kant realized this and introduced another second self or ego. This was the **empirical ego**, an ego that includes all of those elements that identify us as an individual, such as bodies, memories, personalities, ways of thinking, emotional patterns, and so on. In other words, the empirical ego determines personal identity. This appears to be a clumsy response to a challenging question and in many ways it is. It leads to more questions and more answers, increasing the complexity of the argument that Kant is seeking to put forward. These questions include:

- How do these two selves relate to one another?
- Is one self more primary or fundamental than the other?
- Which self is our "true" self, our identity, our soul?
- Are we condemned to be metaphysical schizophrenics?

---

[46] Ibid.

Kant's "self" as a "transcendental unifying principle of consciousness" does not reference the consciousness of Locke. This transcendental self or ego is not located as a separate entity *in* consciousness. Rather, it is the organizing principle that allows consciousness to occur.

Kant has now defined a "self" that is an activity and one that continues to undermine the traditional concept of the soul found in Plato and Descartes. As an activity, Kant argued that the core of the real self is the ability to choose for oneself. This conclusion of the self as activity provided later philosophers with a framework that enabled them to overhaul the traditional approach.

In conclusion it is worth reflecting on an argument made by Wittgenstein, who suggests that the subject of Western philosophy does not, in fact, exist. In his *Tractatus Logico-Philosophicus* (1921), he tells us:

> The thinking, presenting subject; there is no such thing … *in an important sense* there is no subject … The subject does not belong to the world, but is a limit of the world … There is [therefore] really a sense in which in philosophy we can talk non-psychologically of the I. The I occurs in philosophy through the fact that the "world is my world." The philosophical "I" is not the man, not the human body, or the human soul of which psychology treats, but the metaphysical subject, the limit—not a part of the world.[47]

What does Wittgenstein mean by this claim?

**TOK link** 

"The problem with introspection is that it has no end."
– Philip K. Dick

"You are who you are when nobody's watching."
– Stephen Fry

There have been a number of references to introspection so far in this chapter. It is worth reflecting on this methodology. Is it possible to know yourself? How do you know your understanding is authentic?

How valid is introspection as a way of knowing?

## REVISION ACTIVITIES

1. Flow chart

   Starting with Plato sketch out a flow chart outlining the development of the self through to Kant. What are the similarities and differences from Plato to Kant?

2. Dialogue

   Choose two philosophers and write a debate between them on the concept of the self.

   - In what ways do they end up agreeing with each other?
   - In what ways do they end up disagreeing with each other?

3. Different approach

   Phase 1

   - Select one position on the concept of the self.
   - Write up a short description of the position as if you are explaining it to a friend.
   - Break down that position into its various components. For example, what are its assumptions? How is the position justified? What are the implications of the position?
   - Decide to focus on one aspect of that position.
   - Write up a dialogue analysing that aspect with someone who agrees with the position.

   Then:

   Phase 2

   - Extend the analysis and test the understanding of that aspect and its role in the position. To do this, introduce someone into the dialogue who disagrees with the other person and asks challenging questions.

[47] Ludwig Wittgenstein, *Tractatus Logico-Philosophicus*, reproduction of 1922 edition, translated by C. K. Ogden (New York: Cosimo, 2007), Sections 5.613–5.641, p. 89.

## Understanding Eastern perspectives of the self

> One must find the source within one's own Self, one must possess it. Everything else was seeking—a detour, an error.
>
> —Hermann Hesse[48]

The Western tradition of thought is a core aspect of its cultural traditions and therefore its understanding of key issues in society, medicine, law, and even familial contexts. The essentialist concept of the self, initiated by Plato, remains dominant and is fairly entrenched in the Western philosophical understanding and its popular culture. It sees the self as a unique entity that is grounded in the ability to reason, which bestows a dignity and worth onto the individual.

Given how entrenched this view is throughout literature, theatre, the visual arts, science, and popular culture, many people in the West find it difficult to conceive of a radically different concept of the self. We have already seen how David Hume rejects the basic premise of the tradition's concept of the self. However, he solution to the issue of the self remained within the western tradition's conceptual framework. What about alternative perspective?

Two of the most significant traditions for the purpose of our inquiry into the self are found in India and China.

**TOK link** 

It is worth remembering that this experience is the same in other cultures with their own intellectual traditions when they encounter Western perspectives.

Is it possible to understand another culture's perspective? What experience and/or understanding of that culture enables a person to be able to claim they 'know' that perspective?

**Assessment tip** 

These different traditions also provide an excellent opportunity to assess aspects of the Western tradition and in the process provide compare-and-contrast opportunities. However, the traditions must be arguing about a similar concept to enable them to be successfully used in a compare-and-contrast activity.

### India

> The only one breathed breathless by Itself;
>
> Other than It there nothing since has been.
>
> From the "Hymn of Creation" in the *Rig Veda*[49]

Hinduism is not a monolithic religion. It has no single founder of the type and style of religious faiths such as Christianity and Islam. It has no single scripture or text such as the Abrahamic Old Testament or Christianity's New Testament. Similarly there is not an agreed or at least a familiar set of teachings. In fact, there is still considerable debate about

48 Herman Hesse, *Siddhartha* (New York: New Directions, 1951), p. 35.

49 Quote taken from Ramesh Chandra Majumdar, *Ancient India* (Delhi: Motilal Banarasidass, 1977), p. 63.

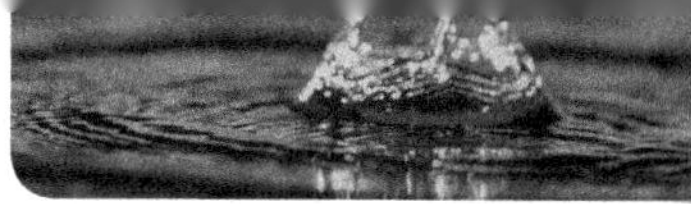



the worth of the label "Hinduism", a recent word coined by the British colonial administration and used to describe a family of religions found mainly in India in the 19th century.

There are numerous schools or traditions defined under this umbrella term. Some orthodox traditions such as Vedanta are monistic, others such as Nyaya and Vaisheshika are pluralistic, while others, such as Sankhya and Yoga, are dualistic. Heterodox systems such as the Jain and Buddhist traditions, despite their differences, both reject the authority of the texts known as the Vedas and the existence of God, while emphasizing the importance of the discipline of yoga. The Carvakans are materialists, therefore denying the existence of God, the soul, and any form of life after death.

Nonetheless, there are some similarities that enable a broad study of the philosophical arguments and systems that are part of these beliefs. For example, most Hindu traditions incorporate a profound respect for the Vedas. Similarly, most Hindu traditions believe in a common system of values known as *dharma* and in a unified subject or soul. It is this last commonality that is of interest to the investigation of the self. The role of the self is central to nearly all the philosophies of India. The self and self-knowledge are essential to the end goal of life and thought, whether it is articulated as achieving freedom, the highest good (however that is defined), and/or ultimate meaning. So despite the variations in orthodox Hindu thought a common thread is the concept of the self and the role it plays in personal enlightenment through the self-discipline of yoga and the achievement of the total integration of life in order to attain life's highest good.

A clear articulation of a concept of the self can be found in more philosophical writings called *The Upanishads*. The title refers to how they were delivered – they were taught to those who sat down beside their teachers (*upa* = near, *ni* = down, *shad* = sit).

Brahminical or orthodox schools of Indian philosophy argue that the self (or *atman*) is a substantial but non-material entity. The initial expression of this idea is found in one of the "primary" (*mukhya*) *Upanishads*, the *Chandogya Upanishad*, and it is believed by scholars to have been written in the 6th century BCE. In this text four selves are distinguished. The first three that are identified and rejected are:

- The bodily self.
- The dream self.
- The self in a dreamless sleep.

Each of these selves is rejected as the true self because the relationship between the body and the self is seen as internal. If the relationship of the soul and the body is conceived as a horse attached to a cart then, in metaphysical terms at least, the cart has been put before the horse. According to the *Chandogya Upanishad*, the correct understanding is that the relationship between the body and the self is external. The true self is one that becomes detached from the body. The true self is "deathless, bodiless, free from pleasure and pain, an inward spectator not identified with the objects of sense, the ego-identity that uses sense organs and mind as instruments of perception".[50] This initial orthodox

[50] Troy Wilson Organ, *Philosophy and the Self: East and West* (Selinsgrove, PA: Associated University Presses, 1987), p. 137.

writing defines the framework and provides the foundation for further speculation about the identity of the self and its nature in this tradition.

## READING ACTIVITY

The following extracts provide a feel for the teachings found in *The Upanishads*. Each of these extracts makes an observation about the self. As you read them, can you determine the point the extract is making about the self?

Extract one:

*Uddalaka*: Bring me a fruit from the banyan tree.

*Shvetaketu*: Here is one, Father.

*Uddalaka*: Break it open.

*Shvetaketu*: It is broken, Father.

*Uddalaka*: What do you see there?

*Shvetaketu*: These tiny seeds.

*Uddalaka*: Now break one of them open.

*Shvetaketu*: It is broken, Father.

*Uddalaka*: What do you see there?

*Shvetaketu*: Nothing, Father.

*Uddalaka*: My son, you know there is a subtle essence which you do not perceive, but through that essence the truly immense banyan tree exists. Believe it, my son. Everything that exists has its self in that subtle essence. It is Truth. It is the atman, and you, Shvetaketu, are that (*tat tvam asi*).

*Shvetaketu*: Please, Father, teach me more.

*Uddalaka*: I will, my son.

(*Chandogya Upanishad*: The Chanters' Teaching: Book VI, Part II, VI 12)

Extract two:

*Uddalaka*: Place this salt in water, and come back to me in the morning.

The son did as he was told.

*Uddalaka* (in the morning): Bring me the salt you put in the water last night.

*Shvetaketu* (after looking): Father, I cannot find it.

*Uddalaka*: Of course not; it has dissolved. Now taste the water from the surface. How does it taste?

*Shvetaketu*: It's salty.

*Uddalaka*: Taste the water from the middle of the bowl. How does it taste?

*Shvetaketu*: It's salty.

*Uddalaka*: Now taste the water from the bottom. How does it taste?

*Shvetaketu*: It's salty.

*Uddalaka*: Go, throw it away and come back to me.

He did so, and returned.

*Shvetaketu*: But, Father, although I have thrown it away, the salt remains.

*Uddalaka*: Likewise, though you cannot hear or perceive or know the subtle essence, it is here. Everything that exists has its self in that subtle essence. It is Truth. It is the atman, and you, Shvetaketu, are that (*tat tvam asi*).

*Shvetaketu*: Please, Father, teach me more.

*Uddalaka*: I will, my son.

(*Chandogya Upanishad*: The Chanters' Teaching: Book VI, Part II, VI 13)[51]

The self expressed in these extracts suggests that the self is that which a) connects all parts with the whole, and b) is the constant that remains when all else has changed.

[51] Extracts reproduced from Christopher Bartley, *An Introduction to Indian Philosophy* (London: Continuum International, 2011), p. 12.

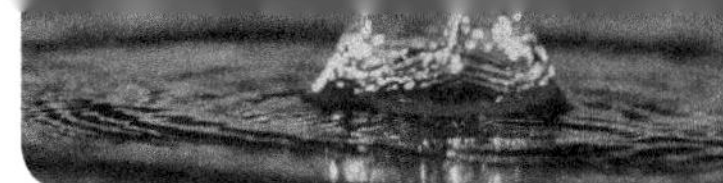



### The self in Indian thought

The concept of the self in Indian thought becomes a discussion about the nature of the self. Again the analogy of the chariot is used to illustrate the position on the self. This entry point allows a basic appreciation of some of the key features of this tradition's understanding of the self.

## THE CHARIOT

Know the self (*Atman*) as the lord of the chariot and the body as … the chariot, know the intellect (*buddhi*) as the charioteer and the mind (*manas*) as … the reins. The senses (*indriya*) are the horses; the objects of sense the paths; the self associated with the body, the senses and the mind … is the [experiencer]. He who has no understanding, whose mind is always unrestrained, his senses are out of control, as wicked horses are for a charioteer. He, however, who has understanding, whose mind is always restrained, his senses are under control, as good horses are for a charioteer.

(*Katha Upanishad* 1. 3. 3)[52]

[52] Organ, *Philosophy and the Self*, p. 137; see also http://www.ocoy.org/dharma-for-christians/upanishads-for-awakening/the-katha-upanishad/the-chariot/ (accessed 20 November 2013).

## Reading questions

1. What do the charioteer, chariot, the horses, the reins, and the paths over which the chariot travels each represent?
2. What does the sentence "Know the self (*Atman*) as the lord of the chariot" mean?
3. Plato's chariot analogy is less complicated and can be summarized in the following way: the charioteer is reason, the horses are spirit and appetite. The image describes the self. However, in the Hindu version, what does the image represent?

**Extension**

Using a diagrammatic format, compare and contrast both chariot analogies.

*The Upanishads* define the self in relation to the body, the senses, the intellect, and the mind. The body, intellect, and mind are all active in the world. However, the self is passive, being a mere observer. The key statement is "Know the self (*Atman*) as the lord of the chariot". The owner of the chariot is the self, or rather the universal self as pure consciousness. This is a characteristic feature of Hindu philosophy.

### The self as controller

Next, Yājñavalkya, in the *Brihadaranyaka Upanishad*, conceives of the self in terms of consciousness and the mind's cognitive capabilities. In a debate with his teacher, Uddaluka, Yājñavalkya argues that the self is an inner controller (*antaryamin*), evident in all sensation, thinking, and doing. Yet while this self is part of these experiences it is also distinct, understood in terms of intuition.

> The senses are said to be higher than the sense-objects. The mind is higher than the senses. The intelligent will is higher than the mind. What is higher than the intelligent will? The Atman Itself.
>
> (*Bhagavad Gita* 3:42)[53]

The self has mastery over the physical self and the mental self but the self is not made up of these selves. Consequently, it cannot be rationalized, nor can it be described in language, as this would make it an object of this world. As Jonardon Ganeri describes it in *The Concealed Art of the Soul*,

[53] See http://www.ocoy.org/dharma-for-christians/upanishads-for-awakening/the-katha-upanishad/the-chariot/ (accessed 20 November 2013).

> [h]ere is a way to reach the self—not by grasping it as an object, but catching it in its activity of sensing and thinking. Just as it is hopeless to catch a sound in the air, so it is impossible to catch the self as if it were a thing. If we cannot catch the sound once it has been released, we can catch it at the moment of its production—catch the producing of the sound. If we cannot catch the self as an object among others in the world, we can catch it in the very act of thinking.[54]

Each of these concepts of the self suggests that the self and the ultimate reality are the same.

> As a mass of salt has no distinctive core and surface; the whole thing is a single mass of flavour—so indeed, my dear, this self has no distinctive core and surface; the whole thing is a single mass of cognition. It arises out of and together with these beings and disappears after them—so I say, after death there is no awareness.
>
> (*Brhadaranyaka Upanisad* 4.6.3)[55]

Later on in the tradition of Hindu thought, the discussion of the self took a subtle but distinct turn. The concept of the self expressed by Vedanta, one of the popular orthodox systems of Indian philosophical thought, now defined the self as separate from the ultimate reality. Vedanta is the label for schools of thought that interpret the three basic texts: *The Upanishads*, the *Brahman Sutras* and the *Bhagavad Gita*.

A specific concept of the self worth reflecting upon comes from the Advaita Vedanta ("without a second") school and its most influential philosopher, Sankara.

The Advaita philosophical position on the self is monistic. It states that there is only one reality and that reality is called the Brahman. Brahman can be described in many different terms though all with an underlying principle. These are ubiquitous, absolute, formless, immaterial, immutable, without any attributes, and ineffable. According to Sankara, the true self, or the *Atman* (meaning "breath" or "spirit"), is identical to this reality or Brahman so the self is part of this reality and indistinguishable. The individual self (*Jiva*) is mere appearance (*maya*) in time and space. The reason there is a distinction is because of a failure to fully realize the nature of reality or a failure to discriminate between the true self and the non-true self. This misunderstanding can be overcome through the development of self-awareness.[56]

This conception of the self, which is representative of a significant number of Hindu traditions, is conceived in terms of the changeless and the inactive.

---

[54] Jonardon Ganeri, *The Concealed Art of the Soul: Theories of Self and Practices of Truth in Indian Ethics and Epistemology* (Oxford: Oxford University Press, 2007), p. 35.

[55] Quote reproduced from Patrick Olivelle (trans.), *Upanisads* (Oxford: Oxford University Press, 1998), p. 71.

[56] See Bina Gupta, *Perceiving in Advaita Vedanta: Epistemological Analysis and Interpretation* (London: Associated University Presses, 1991), p. 58.

This is distinct from the self defined by Yājñavalkya, who conceived of the self as active and dynamic. Yet they all tend to share an understanding of the self that is phenomenological in nature; it is understood conceptually or cognitively, rather as a feeling or a presence that is part of an experience.

This leads to the question, what does self-awareness seek to achieve? In this tradition, the self is not an entity requiring definition. Instead, it is a vehicle to a specific goal. Throughout the Hindu tradition there is a common goal for the self. The ultimate goal is the dissolution of the self and the attainment of freedom through a heightened self-awareness and therefore enlightenment. In the Advaita Verdanta, a non-dualism philosophy, for example, this is known as *moksa*. The individual is not unconscious. Rather in this state, consciousness and the other are no longer:

> Where verily, everything has become the Self, then by what and whom should one smell, then by what and whom should one see, then by what and whom should one hear, then by what and to whom should one speak, and then by what and on whom should one think, then by what and whom should one understand? By what should one know that by which all this is known. By what, my dear, should one know the knower?[57]

The result is *saccidānanda*, when defined in reference to a post-human state. This labels the three fundamental attributes of Brahman: existence, awareness, and bliss. However, even this term is inadequate for a condition that cannot be stated in any empirical sense.

## ANALYSIS ACTIVITY

1. Read the following quotations:

> Every action is really performed by the gunas [sensory energies]. Man, deluded by his egoism, thinks: "I am the doer." But he who has the true insight into the operations of the gunas and their various functions, knows that when senses attach themselves to objects, gunas are merely attaching themselves to gunas. Knowing this, he does not become attached to his actions.
>
> (*Bhagavad Gita* 3:27, 28)[58]
>
> You dream you are the doer
>
> (*Bhagavad Gita* 5:14)[59]

[57] Organ, *Philosophy and the Self*, p. 138.

[58] Reproduced from W. J. Johnson (trans.), *Bhagavad Gita* (Oxford: Oxford University Press, 2004)

[59] Ibid.

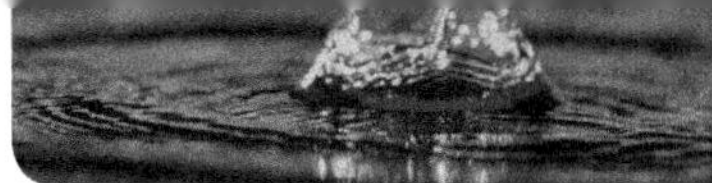

> Let the wise man know these gunas alone as the doers of every action; let him learn to know That Which is beyond them, also.
>
> (*Bhagavad Gita* 14:19)[60]

2 Write an analysis of the concept of the self that is suggested in these three quotes. As part of your analysis reflect on what the quotes are suggesting but also what they are not suggesting about the concept of the self.

## Buddhism and the anatta/anatman (or no self)

> Like vanishing dew,
> a passing apparition
> or the sudden flash
> of lightning—already gone—
> thus should one regard one's self.
>
> —Ikkyū, a Japanese Zen Buddhist monk (1394–1481)[61]
>
> To study the way is to study the self
> To study the self is to forget the self
> To forget the self is to be enlightened by all things
>
> —Zen Master Dogen[62]

### Self as dynamic interaction

Buddhism is regarded as unorthodox Hinduism. By this, it is meant that it was conceived as a response to certain aspects of the central tenets of Hinduism. So while it rejected certain aspects, it remained predominantly within the same system of thought. In many aspects, Buddhism was a political reaction to the authority that defined then contemporary society, such as the caste system. One of these aspects is the concept of the self. Instead it presented the concept of *anatta* (or *anatman* in Sanskrit), which is the negative form of *atman*. Again, in Buddhist teachings there are a number of controversies and variations. The interpretation presented here references Buddha's Second Sermon, which appears in *Anattalkkhana Sutta* and the *Mahavagga* section of the *Vinaya*. Buddha presents *anatta* as three marks: impermanence (*anicca*), suffering (*dukkha*), and non-self (*anatta*). This indicates that change, disintegration, and non-essentialism are the basic features of all things.

Buddhism retains the use of analogies to put forward its ideas and arguments.

[60] Ibid.

[61] Reproduced from Sam Hamill (trans.), *Only Companion: Japanese Poems of Love and Longing* (Boston, MA: Shambala Publications, 2013), p. 38.

[62] Sekkei Harada, *The Essence of Zen: The Teachings of Sekkei Harada*, edited and translated by Daigaku Rummé (Somerville, MA: Wisdom Publications, 2012), p. 157.

## EXERCISE: A THOUGHT EXPERIMENT

Exploring the concepts of identity and individuality

Think of a candle. You light the candle and then your friend asks you to light her candle with yours. You do so and then your candle accidentally blows out. Does the flame still exist? Or is there another flame in its place? Is it related to the flame? Is it a new flame?

Would you say it was your flame and you wanted it back?

This is a challenging thought experiment and one that highlights the manner in which we tend to define identity.

The next step is to think through a similar thought experiment involving a drop of water.

Imagine you are standing next to a bath. Using a cup, allow a drop of water to fall into the bath. Now use the same cup to retrieve the drop of water. How would you know you have been successful? People trained in the Western scientific tradition would immediately start to think about atoms. This is how we commonly understand reality and therefore identity (the defining characteristic of an entity). Return to the flame.

Does this approach make sense?

Write an analysis of these two thought experiments. Explore the fundamental metaphysical systems in Western thought, Eastern thought, and even other indigenous traditions of thought.

The Buddhists' traditional concept of the self is defined as *anatta* or "no self". In this way, they agree with Hume that the self is an illusion. This position rejects the concept of the self as a permanent self conceived as a unified entity.

What does the self refer to? According to Buddhist philosophy, the self is the collection of five aggregates or aspects (*khandha*). These are the physical form (*rupa*), sensation (*vedana*), conceptualization or perceptions (*sanna*), dispositions to act or attitudes (*sankhara*), and consciousness (*vinnana*). Buddha, discussing the issue of the self with five ascetics, asks: "And that which is impermanent, subject to decay, and not-self, is it possible to regard that in this way: This is mine, this am I, this is my self?"[63] This question is repeated for each of the aggregates and each ascetic says "no", therefore rejecting the idea of the self. The point being made by Buddha is not that there is not a self, just that a self is not evident. There is "no exercising of mastery" in each of these aggregates that would indicate a self, unlike in Hindu thought where a "leader", a "guide" or an "inner controller" exists.[64]

However, the goal of Buddhism remains the same: the achievement of enlightenment or *Nirvana*. This deconstruction of the self in Hindu thought is part of the process. Consequently, the self is present, but must be overcome. The self implied in Buddhist thought is the continual

[63] Mark Siderits, Buddhism as Philosophy: An Introduction (Aldershot, England: Ashgate Publishing, 2007), p. 38.

[64] Steven Collins, *Selfless Persons: Imagery and Thought in* Theravada *Buddhism* (Cambridge: Cambridge University Press, 1982), p. 97.

interplay between these five elements. However, there is no substance or identity beyond this interaction.

One of the most accessible Buddhist parables on the subject is the **chariot** parable. As we saw earlier, Plato and Hinduism also used a chariot to help illustrate the concept of the self. The chariot had a very high status in societies because of its effective use by nobles in warfare. This makes it a potent symbol and well known in ancient intellectual circles. The extract below is from a Buddhist text, *Milindapañha* (*Questions of King Milinda*).

## READING ACTIVITY

The following is a debate on the concept of the self and the issue of identity. The two points of view reflected are Western (ancient Greek) and Eastern (Buddhism). It occurred in the 2nd century BCE, between King Menander, a Greek ruler of northwestern India, and a Buddhist monk called Nagasena.

### The Chariot Parable

Then King Menander went up to the Venerable Nagasena, greeted him respectfully, and sat down. Nagasena replied to the greeting, and the King was pleased at heart. Then King Menander asked:

"How is your reverence known, and what is your name?"

"I'm known as Nagasena, your Majesty, that's what my fellow monks call me. But though my parents may have given me such a name it's only a generally understood term, a practical designation. There is no question of a permanent individual implied in the use of the word."

"Listen, you five hundred Greeks and eighty thousand monks!" said King Menander. "This Nagasena has just declared that there's no permanent individuality implied in his name!"

Then, turning to Nagasena,

"If, Reverend Nagasena, there is no permanent individuality, who gives you monks your robes and food, lodging and medicines? And who makes use of them? Who lives a life of righteousness, meditates, and reaches Nirvana? Who destroys living beings, steals, fornicates, tells lies, or drinks spirits? If what you say is true there's neither merit nor demerit, and no fruit or result of good or evil deeds. If someone were to kill you there would be no question or murder. And there would be no masters or teachers in the [Buddhist] Order and no ordinations. If your fellow monks call you Nagasena, what then is Nagasena? Would you say that your hair is Nagasena?"

"No, your Majesty."

"Or your nails, teeth, skin, or other parts of your body, or the outward form, or sensation, or perception, or the psychic constructions, or consciousness? Are any of these Nagasena?"

"No, your Majesty."

"Then for all my asking I find no Nagasena. Nagasena is a mere sound! Surely what your Reverence has said is false!"

Then the Venerable Nagasena addressed the King.

"Your Majesty, how did you come here – on foot, or in a vehicle?"

"In a chariot."

"Then tell me what is the chariot? Is the pole the chariot?"

"No, your Reverence."

"Or the axle, wheels, frame, reins, yoke, spokes or whip?"

"None of these things is the chariot."

"Then all these separate parts taken together are the chariot?"

"No, your Reverence."

"Then is the chariot something other than the separate parts?"

"No, your Reverence."

"Then for all my asking, your Majesty, I can find no chariot. The chariot is a mere sound. What then is the chariot? Surely what your Majesty has said is false! There is no chariot!"

When he had spoken the five hundred Greeks cried "Well done!" and said to the King, "Now, your Majesty, get out of that dilemma if you can!"

"What I said was not false," replied the King. "It's on account of all these various components, the pole, axle, wheels, and so on, that the vehicle is called a chariot. It's just a generally understood term, a practical designation."

"Well said, your Majesty! You know what the word 'chariot' means! And it's just the same with me. It's on account of the various components of my being that I'm known by the generally understood term, the practical designation Nagasena."[65]

### Activities

1. Reread the passage. What doesn't it mention about the chariot? Compare this to Plato's and the *Katha Upanishad's* use of the chariot. What conclusions can be drawn from these absences?
2. Map out the dialogue as a flow chart, expressing each stage in your own words to reflect your own understanding.
3. Having delineated each argument, evaluate them, looking for implied assumptions, the quality of their argument (justification of the position, selection of examples), and the implications of the position.

## Rejecting the self

It is worth noting what Nagasena is not doing when referring to the chariot. There is no mention of horses, or reins, or even a charioteer. Nagasena is rejecting the metaphor of a chariot and therefore the self. He does not even want to highlight the presence of an entity, guiding, directing the chariot or charioteer. Our "common sense" understanding is teased out when he asks whether "all these separate parts taken together are the chariot". We would say "yes", though only if they were properly assembled and functioning as a chariot. Buddhism says "no". They are, to use a phrase by the German philosopher Leibniz, a "borrowed reality"; the whole has a status less real than the individual parts. As such, the Buddhist rejects the self, defining the five aggregates. The self is being indicated but not the self of the immaterial, substantial tradition of Hinduism and Descartes. In this sense Buddhism is not rejecting the self, just this form of the self.

For Buddhists, there is no soul storing Karmic formations, thereby rejecting the changeless agent. However, to fully comprehend the implications of this, think of a hand grasping for something. In the Western concept of the self, grasping is something done by the hand, while in the Buddhist concept of the self, the self is something done by grasping. The action comes first and then the self or hand momentarily comes into existence. The self is in the moment – self as an event or as a response.[66]

[65] R. K. Pruthi, *Buddhism and Indian Civilization* (New Delhi: Discovery Publishing House, 2004), p. 115.

[66] See D. K. Nauriyal, M. S. Drummond, and Y. B. Lal (eds), *Buddhist Thought and Applied Psychological Research: Transcending the Boundaries* (London: Routledge, 2006).

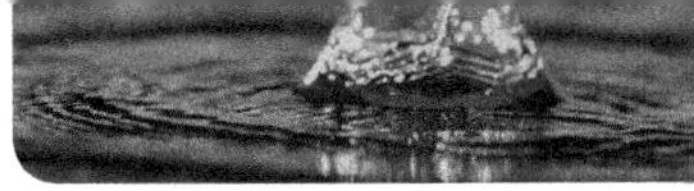

### Exploring comparative approaches

In Western commentary Buddhism is often compared with the philosophy of the self argued by Hume. This often results in superficial treatments of both positions on the self. The following activity provides an opportunity to further develop your analytical and evaluative skills.

A basic approach to compare and contrast is to initially look for shared assumptions, concepts, methodologies, and evidence and the differences. This can involve identifying something that is not acknowledged or discussed in one of the positions. If there are significant differences between two arguments of positions then looking at the nature and context of the philosophical inquiry can also be important.

A comparison between Hume and the Theravada Buddhists' concepts of the self provides an excellent opportunity to explore this skill in the context of a fascinating position on the self. It is worth starting with the understanding that while there are similarities between their positions there are also significant differences when a much more detailed analysis is undertaken.

> **FIND OUT MORE**
>
> **Compare and contrast**
>
> Compare and contrast the position of Hume and the Theravada Buddhists' concept of the self.

#### *Similarities*

Theravada Buddhists similarly believe that there is no fixed human nature. In terms of the self they also believe that there is no self with a fixed or definite existence. Instead they believe that there is just a flow of perceptions, impressions, or experiences one after another.

#### *Differences*

Theravada Buddhists believe that salvation is possible through giving up the craving for self-identity and the striving for personal success and self-fulfilment. On the other hand, Hume draws no ethical conclusions from his discovery that the self is an illusion; in fact he thinks we won't be able to really take his conclusion seriously.

Hume treats the problem of the self as chiefly an *epistemological* problem, while for Buddhism it is an *ethical* problem. What is the difference between analysing the self as an epistemological question and as an ethical question?

> **HUME AND BUDDHISM**
>
> Did Hume develop his critique of the Western self from reading Buddhist thought?
>
> It does seem remarkable that Hume developed a position that is very similar to a tradition of thinking that was very distant from him.
>
> Alison Gopnik argues that Hume did have access to materials about Buddhist thought while he was staying in France in the 1730s.[67]
>
> Does this make his contribution any less important?

## China

### Confucianism: self as a potential for selfishness

In general, owing to the influence of Descartes, the concept of the self in the West is dependent on introspection, although this is less so in contemporary thought as illustrated by existentialism (see below). When looking at different traditions of thought it is tempting to look for the familiar as a starting point. The Confucian tradition of thought offers another approach to the question of the self.

[67] See *Philosophy Bites*, "Alison Gopnik on Hume and Buddhism", 2013, available at http://philosophybites.com/2013/09/alison-gopnik-on-hume-and-buddhism.html (accessed 26 November 2013).

There is a belief by Western scholars that Confucian thought does not contain a concept of the self.

> If one had no selfish motives, but only the supreme virtues, there would be no self … If he serves selflessly, he does not know what service is [does not recognize it as service]. If he knows what service is, he has a self … [to think] only of parents but not of yourself … is what I call no self.
>
> —Zoku Kyuo dowa[68]

Service to others or at least the supreme leader requires selflessness. As Hiroshi Minami, a writer on Confucian thought, notes, "[the Confucian concept of no-self] … is identical with the spirit of service-above-self, where every spontaneous impulse is rejected as selfishness."[69]

Consequently, the concept of the self does not include discussions using the concepts of material, substance, spirit, memory, or other arguments made by Western thinkers. Rather, the focus is on personality and in particular personality developed through nurture in the context of the social or communal.

Here is a discussion on the self between a Western philosopher and an Eastern philosopher that occurred in 1957:

> *Hisamatsu*: The self is the true Formless Self only when it awakens to itself … it is always at once "one's own" and "not one's own" … the Formless Self includes, in so far as it is Self, Self-awareness. But by this formless Self (or Self-awareness) I mean the "Formless-Myself", which … expresses—or presents—Itself in its activities … The True Awakening—or Formless Self—in Itself has neither a beginning, an ending, a special place, nor a special time.
>
> *Tillich*: Then it cannot happen to a human being.
>
> *Hisamatsu*: … with this Self-awakening … one is no longer an "ordinary" human being.
>
> *Tillich* (later): Even so, you can't eliminate the "my" … Is it that there is no centered self, no self-related self, which would be a hindrance?
>
> *DeMartino* (Translator for Hisamatsu): The barrier is created by the reflectively self-conscious ego—or "I"—which discriminates itself from "not-itself"—or "not-I". *Muge* "no hindrance" [is] the overcoming of this barrier…
>
> *Tillich*: By the removal of individuality?
>
> *DeMartino*: No, by the fulfillment of individuality.
>
> *Tillich*: What is the difference … ?[70]

The Confucian concept of the self is related to the notion of potential and perfection or by fulfilment. Perfection is defined by being moral, or more specifically by being virtuous. The self is always reaching towards this perfection despite it being unobtainable. It is not an essence nor is it an existence (although it is closer to the latter). The self is not something that is static, rather it is dynamic. For example, a

---

[68] Quote reproduced from Roger T. Ames, Wimal Dissanakaye, and Thomas P. Kasulis (eds), *Self as Person in Asian Theory and Practice* (Albany, NY: State University of New York Press, 1994), pp. 64–65.
[69] Ibid., p. 65.
[70] Ibid., p. 71.

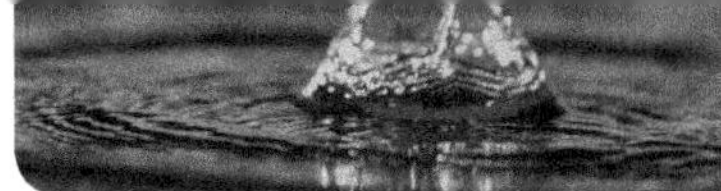

Confucian sage is not someone who has reached perfection, rather it is someone whose path towards perfection has become part of their self.

In the dialogue Paul Tillich's frustration is partly caused by the two different approaches. Tillich is being analytical while Hisamatsu is seeking to define the self in terms that could not be expressed within the conceptual framework essential to this approach.

## EXERCISE: A THOUGHT EXPERIMENT

As an editor from a philosophy publishing house you ask two philosophers to write their autobiographies. Let us say that the two examples are eminent Swiss philosopher Jean-Jacques Rousseau and the respected Japanese Confucian scholar Aria Hakuseki.

What would they understand as the proper content of an autobiography?

Regardless of whom you asked, the intention of an autobiography would appear to be the same: to tell an honest account of a person's past experiences based on his or her recollections of these events. There would also be an underlying imperative to justify the decisions made and offer the correct interpretation and evaluation of their consequences.

If we look at our first philosopher, Rousseau, we find in his *Confessions* (1782) a treatise based on what he remembered thinking at the time, the emotions he was feeling, and his perception in these terms of those around him. In other words both their presumed understanding of the event and their emotional states.

However, if we look at the second philosopher, Hakuseki, in his *Told Round a Brushwood Fire* (1716), he writes in relation to events important to His Highness Shogun Ienobu and with the intent to educate his sons and grandsons in exemplary conduct. He starts with a detailed discussion of his father and his grandfather to illustrate his own guide to loyalty and filial piety. When he turns to his own life he recounts major political and administrative events that concerned his service to Shogun Ienobu.

The first approach is a confession of the inner and hidden or introspective self. The second approach is a record of a public and honourable life. These two autobiographies illustrate the different concepts of the self in the liberal West and the Confucian influenced East.

In the Confucian influenced thought, the self is determined by the individual's place in the larger context, such as family and society.

### The Confucian self

In simple terms, every person is born with four beginnings. However, they do not constitute a self but can be seen as a potential self. These are:

- Heart of compassion – leads to Jen
- Heart of righteousness – leads to Yi
- Heart of propriety – leads to Li
- Heart of wisdom – leads to Chih

The development of these towards moral excellence provides the framework for the development of the actual self, the realization of the potential self even if this only remains an ideal.

## FIND OUT MORE

**Daoism** emerged around the same time as Confucianism and was established by Laozi (Lao Tze or Lao Tzu) or "Old Master". In Chinese society it is seen as a counterbalance to the strict social philosophy of Confucianism. Daoism is a person philosophy and emphasizes individuality and individual freedom, embracing nature, harmony, and spontaneity, by placing them at the core of the philosophy.

Research the concept of the self with a particular focus on the following:

- The role of the Dao as the way
- The role of tranquillity and activity (in contrast to the Buddhist state of Nirvana)
- The role of human attributes (in contrast to the Hindu metaphysical belief in the dissolution of the self)

# Rejection of the essential self

## Introduction to the existential self

The argument put forward by Kant is both an end and a beginning. In many ways Kant had resolved many of the outstanding issues identified in Descartes' concept of the self. The impact of Kant's work was immense and became the new reference point for modern philosophy. However, Kant was still working within the framework established by Plato and then modernized by Descartes. The concept of the self in this tradition had been concerned with *what* I am, not *who* I am as an individual. The treatment of being human remained essentially abstract and formal.

> According to Cartesian (and Platonic) metaphysics, the self is thought to be situated in a self-positing "I think" whose function is to produce representations of things in the world. And because the self is only related to its representations, which are separated from the world, it is defined as an isolated ego encapsulated in its immanent consciousness.[71]

As a result the changing nature of the context in which this self found itself had been rejected and then eventually forgotten. As Heidegger suggests, "[i]n taking over Descartes' ontological position Kant made an essential omission: he failed to provide an ontology of *Dasein*".[72] This ontology was the manner of being that is a being-in-the-world. In other words, to understand anything in the world is not simply a pure

[71] Peter Ha, "Heidegger's Concept of *solus ipse* and the Problem of Intersubjectivity", in Kwok Ying-Lau, Chan-Fai Cheung, and Tze-Wan Kwan (eds), *Identity and Alterity: Phenomenology and Cultural Traditions* (Germany: Königshausen & Neumann, 2010), p. 351.

[72] Martin Heidegger, *Being and Time*, translated by John Macquarrie and Edward Robinson, with a new foreword by Taylor Carman (New York: Harper & Row, 2008), p. 46.

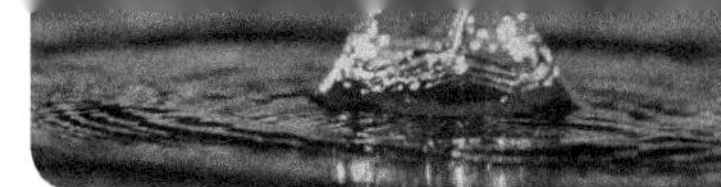



intellectual act. Similarly, the Cartesian self was merely a thinking thing, with human fellowship and empathy nowhere in consideration.

Luckily (and ironically) a neurotic, solitary genius, Rousseau, rejected this self, positing instead feeling and a sense of moral goodness as the essence of the self. The introspective self of Descartes and Locke was also rejected, being replaced by an expressive self that was extrospective. The self now had a personality. This counterbalance to the Cartesian self was not well received partly because of Rousseau's own behaviour, but his influence had a profound impact on Kant. This influence on Kant's philosophy left an avenue of inquiry that more radical philosophers sought to exploit.

## The analytical and continental tradition

The history of philosophy appears to take two divergent paths – analytical philosophy and continental philosophy. Like all generalizations these are not perfect labels or categories. Nonetheless, they provide an indication of the nature of Kant's influence. These two schools were defined by which work of Kant was seen as the most important. The two most prominent were *First Critique or Critique of Pure Reason* (1781) and *Third Critique or Critique of the Power of Judgment* (1790).

The *First Critique* is focused on epistemology and therefore the pursuit of logic and knowledge and becomes the foundational work of the analytic tradition and its association with scientific enlightenment. The *Third Critique* is focused on how to understand knowledge *through experience*. As Simon Critchley expresses it:

> Kant attempts to construct a bridge between the faculties of the **understanding** (the domain of epistemology whose concern is knowledge of nature) and **reason** (the domain of ethics whose concern is freedom), through a critique of the faculty of **judgement** ... If one takes this route, then the burning issue of Kant's philosophy becomes the plausibility of the relation of pure and practical reason, nature and freedom, or the unity of theory and practice ... Arguably, it is this route that Continental philosophy has followed ever since.[73]

## The foundation of the existential self

The relationship between existentialism and phenomenology is often debated. For our purposes they are closely related, with phenomenology laying the foundation for existentialism.

## Phenomenology as an approach to the self

This approach was exceptionally influential on philosophical schools such as **phenomenology** (which led to a number of other philosophical schools). The German philosopher **Edmund Husserl** (1859–1938)

[73] Simon Critchley, *Continental Philosophy: A Very Short Introduction* (Oxford: Oxford University Press, 2001), p. 19.

established phenomenology in the late 19th century with the ambition that "philosophy take as its primary task the description of the structures of experience as they present themselves to consciousness".[74] By this Husserl thought it possible to go "back to the things themselves"[75] without a theoretical framework, assumptions, or terminology. Later, this was defined as a return to *life-world* or a return to experience before "objectification" and "idealization" that could be explored intuitively. While some commentators saw this as irrational mysticism, Husserl was inspired by his attempt to understand the nature of mathematical and logical truths and a critique of reason. The ambition was to establish the foundation of a rigorous science. This ambition should sound familiar. Descartes and Kant sought to accomplish similar projects, lay a new foundation in response to emerging needs in society. Regardless of whether this was successful, phenomenology was regarded as a "radical, anti-traditional style of philosophising"[76] and as such provided the platform both for new approaches to old issues and the identification of new issues that could be treated philosophically.

Husserl's most famous student, and fellow German, was **Martin Heidegger** (1889–1976), who was inspired by Husserl's new approach to philosophy in the early stages of his career but also highly critical of it at the same time. As Mark Wrathall and Hubert Dreyfus explain:

> Heidegger rejected Husserl's focus on consciousness and, consequently, much of his basic phenomenological method. For Heidegger, the purpose of phenomenological description was not to discover the structures of consciousness, but to make manifest the structure of our everyday being-in-the-world. Because Heidegger's interest was worldly relations rather than mental contents, he rejected both the usefulness of the phenomenological method as practiced by Husserl and the need for mental meanings to account for many if not most forms of intentional directedness.[77]

Phenomenology focused on lived human experience in all its richness and depth, escaping the limitation of strict empiricism and reductive psychology and exploring the "affective, emotional, and imaginative" aspects of life. The "other" becomes essential to the study of an individual's existence. Experience is no longer an abstract, artificial reference point but lived, as a result of engaging with the world of others. Heidegger rejected the latent presence of Descartes' *cogito, ergo sum* that defined Husserl's project, finding his teacher's attempt to overcome the subject–object divide to be inadequate. Heidegger undertook an even more radical form of phenomenology founded on a complete rejection of the philosophy of the *cogito* and its inherent subjectivity.

**TOK link** 

Existentialists reject essentialism and tend to share an opposition to rationalism and empiricism. Many critics have argued existentialists are anti-rational, even claiming they are irrationalists.

However, this has tended to be more for rhetorical purposes than a serious claim. Regardless, all these criticisms should be seen in the context of rejecting pure rationalism defined by Platonism. Instead, embracing the validity of emotion as an epistemology.

---

[74] Mark A. Wrathall and Hubert L. Dreyfus, "A Brief Introduction to Phenomenology and Existentialism", in Hubert L. Dreyfus and Mark A. Wrathall (eds), *A Companion to Phenomenology and Existentialism* (Chichester, UK: Wiley-Blackwell, 2009), p. 2.

[75] Edmund Husserl, *Logical Investigations*, vol. 1, translated by J. N. Findlay (New York: Routledge, 2001), p. 168.

[76] Dermot Moran, *Introduction to Phenomenology* (London: Routledge, 2000), p. 4.

[77] Wrathall and Dreyfus, "A Brief Introduction . . .", p. 3.

**Jean-Paul Sartre** (1905–1980) was trained as a phenomenologist but, having attended Heidegger's lectures, he shared his focus on relationships in the world. Yet he sought to account for these relationships in a Husserlian fashion, retaining a focus on consciousness. Sartre was still a Cartesian philosopher, resisting Heidegger's attempts to overcome this aspect of Husserl's philosophy. According to Sartre, existentialism was "a doctrine which makes human life possible and, in addition, declares that every truth and every action implies a human setting and a human subjectivity".[78]

However, before these two philosophers are explored further there is a need to consider Kierkegaard and Nietzsche – two foundational thinkers in this tradition of thought.

## READING ACTIVITY

Read the following story:

The other one, the one called Borges, is the one things happen to. I walk through the streets of Buenos Aires and stop for a moment, perhaps mechanically now, to look at the arch of an entrance hall and the grillwork on the gate; I know of Borges from the mail and see his name on a list of professors or in a biographical dictionary. I like hourglasses, maps, eighteenth-century typography, the taste of coffee and the prose of Stevenson; he shares these preferences, but in a vain way that turns them into the attributes of an actor. It would be an exaggeration to say that ours is a hostile relationship; I live, let myself go on living, so that Borges may contrive his literature, and this literature justifies me. It is no effort for me to confess that he has achieved some valid pages, but those pages cannot save me, perhaps because what is good belongs to no one, not even to him, but rather to the language and to tradition. Besides, I am destined to perish, definitively, and only some instant of myself can survive in him. Little by little, I am giving over everything to him, though I am quite aware of his perverse custom of falsifying and magnifying things.

Spinoza knew that all things long to persist in their being; the stone eternally wants to be a stone and the tiger a tiger. I shall remain in Borges, not in myself (if it is true that I am someone), but I recognize myself less in his books than in many others or in the laborious strumming of a guitar. Years ago I tried to free myself from him and went from the mythologies of the suburbs to the games with time and infinity, but those games belong to Borges now and I shall have to imagine other things. Thus my life is a flight and I lose everything and everything belongs to oblivion, or to him.

I do not know which of us has written this page.[79]

What is your (philosophical) response to this passage?

[78] Jean-Paul Sartre, *Existentialism Is a Humanism* (Yale: Yale University Press, 2007), p. 12.

[79] Jorge Luis Borges, "Borges and I", in *The Aleph and Other Stories*, translated by Andrew Hurley (London: Penguin, 2000), p. 177.

## Introduction to Kierkegaard and Nietzsche

> The greatest hazard of all, losing one's self, can occur very quietly in the world, as if it were nothing at all. No other loss can occur so quietly; any other loss – an arm, a leg, five dollars, a wife, etc. – is sure to be noticed.
>
> —Søren Kierkegaard[80]

> "I am body and soul" – so speaks the child. And why should one not speak like children. But the awakened, the enlightened man says: I am body entirely, and nothing beside; and body and soul is only a word for something in the body ... You say "I" and you are proud of this word. But greater than this – although you will not believe in it – is your body and its great intelligence, which does not say "I" but performs "I" ... Behind your thoughts and feelings, my brother, stands a mighty commander, an unknown sage – he is called Self. He lives in your body, he is your body.
>
> —Friedrich Nietzsche[81]

Since Plato, the dominant tendency in Western thought was to assume that essence precedes existence. The essentialist tradition had looked for the self in a manner appropriate to this belief. However, there was an intellectual impetus to question some of the prevailing assumptions evident in the intellectual culture of the 19th century.

The father of existentialism, **Søren Kierkegaard** (1813–1855), was the first philosopher to question these assumptions, insisting that in order to have an essence an individual must first exist. Another philosopher of this period, who wrote a little later than Kierkegaard, **Nietzsche** (see biography on p. 39 in Chapter 2: Human Nature), also believed that individuals must make choices.

Both emphasized freedom in their thinking and as such expressed concern about the role of the masses and by extension the nature of society in general. They both wrote during the latter stages of the Industrial Revolution when the mood of the Enlightenment had shifted and the effects of the Industrial Revolution were becoming evident through its impact on the societies of Europe. It was a time of political revolution too and this mood filtered through to philosophy in a number of ways.

Another philosopher who was heavily influenced by these events was **Karl Marx** (1818–1883). In many ways Kierkegaard and Marx were responding to the same issues evident in European society at this time, including the ideology of religion. While each had a different response to the impacts of these issues, both highlighted the increasing alienation of the individual and were concerned about the loss of individuality with the emergence of a mass society (and culture) in the 19th century. This perceived alienation led to a concern for authenticity.

---

[80] Søren Kierkegaard, *Sickness Unto Death: A Christian Psychological Exposition for Upbuilding and Awakening, Kierkegaard's Writings Series, XIX*, edited and translated by Howard V. Hong and Edna H. Hong (Princeton, NJ: Princeton University Press, 1983), pp. 32–33.

[81] Friedrich Nietzsche, *Thus Spoke Zarathustra: A Book for None and All*, translated by Walter Kaufmann (Harmondsworth: Penguin, 1974), p. 135.

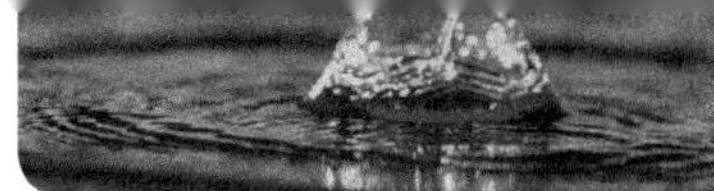



## FIND OUT MORE

- Research Marx's concept of human nature.
- Does Marx argue a concept of the self? Compare and contrast this position with the position of Hume. What are the similarities and differences?

As such Kierkegaard and Nietzsche introduced into philosophy a concern for the role of "the public" along with their concern for freedom. They urged an end to collective identity and social roles in favour of renewed respect for the individual. They demanded that an individual must act **authentically**. If they don't they will fall into the world of others, becoming simply what others expect or demand of them. Consequently, they will lose their identity and therefore their self.

This is clearly illustrated by Kierkegaard when he claims there are two different kinds of people.

> And that is what existing is like if one is to be conscious of it. Eternity is like that winged steed, infinitely quick, temporality is an old nag, and the existing person is the wagon-driver, that is, unless existing is taken to be what people usually call existing, because then the existing person is not a wagon-driver but a drunken peasant who lies in the wagon and sleeps and lets the horses take care of themselves. Of course, he also drives, he is also a carriage-driver, and likewise there perhaps are many who – also exist.[82]

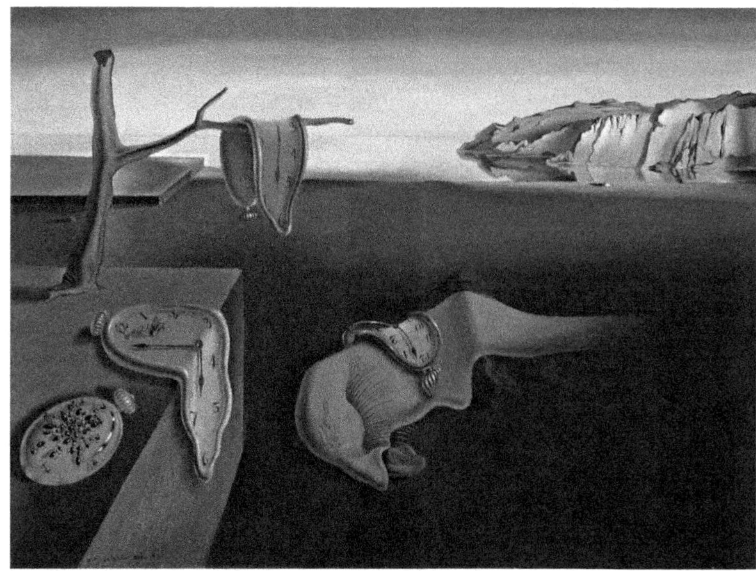

▲ *The Persistence of Memory*, by Salvador Dali

The first is the spectator and the second is the actor. He argued that the former is passive while the latter, the actor, is active and therefore authentically existing. To help explain this Kierkegaard compared two kinds of people in a wagon. The first is holding the reins while asleep. The other is holding the reins while fully awake. In the first situation, the horse pulls the wagon down a familiar road without any assistance from the sleeping person. In the second situation, the driver actually drives the wagon. Kierkegaard concedes that both individuals exist, but he makes the point that existence is a quality in the individual and consequently a person must consciously participate in an act to fully exist. Therefore, only the conscious driver exists as he is free by making active decisions about his life. In other words, both the spectator and the actor exist, but only the actor is involved in existence.

[82] Søren Kierkegaard, *Concluding Unscientific Postscript to* Philosophical Fragments, *Volume I, Kierkegaard's Writings Series, XII*, edited and translated by Howard V. Hong and Edna H. Hong (Princeton, NJ: Princeton University Press, 1992), pp. 311–312.

## Kierkegaard, authenticity and the issue of introspection

### REFLECTION

Kierkegaard encapsulated this concern with authenticity in the story of the shadow. The "shadow of the shadow" is the representative of a person who does not exist as they have lost their identity.

There was once a man who discovered his shadow. Watching its lithe motion, he assumed that it was alive. Because it followed him so faithfully, he decided that he was its master and that it was his servant. But gradually he began to believe that it was the shadow that was initiating the action and that the shadow was his irreplaceable guide and companion. He took increasing account of its comfort and welfare. He awkwardly maneuvered himself in order that it might sit in a chair or lie in bed. The importance of the shadow to the man grew to such an extent that finally the man became, in effect, "the shadow of his shadow".

What do you think Kierkegaard was trying to convey with this story?

Authenticity is a second-order question in relation to the self. As it references a position on the self, the concept of the self must be determined first. Authenticity also involves the concepts of sincerity, autonomy, and self-realization. There are a number of positions and issues on the concept of authenticity that are worth noting.

Louis P. Pojman in *Philosophy: The Pursuit of Wisdom* tells a story that captures Kierkegaard's concerns:

> There was once a man who discovered his shadow. Watching its lithe motion, he assumed that it was alive. Because it followed him so faithfully, he decided that he was its master and that it was his servant. But gradually he began to believe that it was the shadow that was initiating the action and that the shadow was his irreplaceable guide and companion. He took increasing account of its comfort and welfare. He awkwardly maneuvered himself in order that it might sit in a chair or lie in bed. The importance of the shadow to the man grew to such an extent that finally the man became, in effect, "the shadow of his shadow".[83]

Charles Taylor, in his work *Multiculturalism: Examining the Politics of Recognition*, makes the following statement:

> There is a certain way of being human that is *my* way. I am called upon to live my life in this way, and not in imitation of anyone else's life. But this notion gives a new importance to being true to myself. If I am not, I miss the point of my life; I miss what being human is for *me*.[84]

[83] Louis P. Pojman, *Philosophy: The Pursuit of Wisdom*, 2nd edition (Belmont: Wadsworth Publishing, 1998), p. 350.

[84] Charles Taylor, *Multiculturalism: Examining the Politics of Recognition* (Princeton, NJ: Princeton University Press, 1994), p. 30.

Traditionally, because of a predominantly essential concept of the self, authenticity has been defined in terms of getting in touch with an inner self. If there is no inner self the question of authenticity does not disappear, instead it is reconceptualized. In the existential tradition (French existentialism and German *existenz*) it involves an assumption that there is a unique first-person structure of existence (Heidegger terms this as "mineness" (*Jemeinigkeit*)). Kierkegaard establishes a theme that continues through Heidegger and Sartre. Often, being authentic is regarded as being true to oneself, being honest, not being involved in self-deception. This approach is strongest in Kierkegaard owing to the overtly religious intentions of his philosophy.

However, there are a number of different treatments of the issue of authenticity. Heidegger conceives of authenticity in terms of being-towards death. If an individual allows themself to be defined by their impending death, then they are living an inauthentic life. If they can escape this anxiety regarding impending death by living a life of possibility, then they can escape this inauthenticity. Heidegger does not intend his observations on authenticity to be judgmental but it is often used in his work as if it is normative, not just descriptive. For example, Heidegger argues that all human actions are informed by the norms of society or at least the masses. He conceives of these masses as anonymous social norms and practices and uses the nominalized impersonal pronoun "the one" (*das Man*) to describe the sources of these forces and their depersonalization as a result.

This indicates a number of issues. One of the major ones associated with authenticity in the existential/*existenz* traditions is the problem of authority. This perspective cannot tell you if you are being inauthentic as this itself is inauthentic. Instead an individual must determine for themselves if they are being inauthentic and then decide not to be such. But how does an individual come to realize they are being inauthentic? This problem was evident in Sartre's *Existentialism Is a Humanism* (1946). He wants to warn of the possibility of inauthenticity and how it can be identified but on the other hand he cannot do so because that would appear to provide an individual with an authority that takes away their freedom and therefore potential authenticity.

There is also the question of introspection. If it is the individual who determines when they are being authentic, how do they know? On the other hand, if it is a third person who determines the issue of authenticity then how do they know the true self of the individual in order to be able to make the judgment?

## Kierkegaard and the self

> Each age has its characteristic depravity. Ours is perhaps not pleasure or indulgence or sensuality, but rather a dissolute pantheistic contempt for individual man.
>
> —Søren Kierkegaard[85]

For Kierkegaard what is central to an individual's existence is his or her subjectivity and this condition was characterized by freedom. This is a rejection of the ideal of objectivity, an illusion that resulted in the denial of subjectivity and therefore individual freedom. Descartes had modernized this understanding offering the certainty of the "*cogito, ergo sum*" or "I think, therefore I am." However, on reflection, some philosophers feel that this statement does not answer the questions "What is thinking?" and "What is it that is doing the thinking?" This lack of clarity leads to the question "Is the 'I' that is thinking and the 'I' that exists the same self?" We are aware (or have the sensation) of thinking. In *The Science of Logic* (1816), Hegel believed he had the answer:

> By the term "I" I mean myself, a single and altogether determinate person. And yet I really utter nothing particular to myself, for every one else is an "I" or "Ego," and when I call myself "I," though I indubitably mean the single person myself, I express a thorough universal. "I" therefore, is mere being-for-self, in which everything peculiar or marked is renounced and buried out of sight; it is as it were the ultimate and unanalyzable Point of consciousness. We may say [that] "I" and thought are the same, or, more definitely, [that] "I" is thought as a thinker.[86]

Hegel defined the self as a unity of a dualism of thought and being. This, along with much of Hegel's philosophical system, becomes the departure point for Kierkegaard. Kierkegaard rejects the rational and the objective that is the driving force of Hegel's philosophy. As Kierkegaard says:

> The systematic Idea [of Hegel's] is the identity of subject and object, the unity of thought and being. Existence, on the other hand, is their separation. It does not by any means follow that existence is thoughtless but it has brought about, and brings about a separation between subject and object, thought and being.[87]

---

[85] Kierkegaard, *Concluding Unscientific . . .*, pp. 317–318.

[86] Reproduced from William Wallace (trans.), *Hegel's Logic* (Oxford: Oxford University Press, 1975), p. 38.

[87] Søren Kierkegaard, "Concluding Unscientific Postscript to the 'Philosophical Fragments'", in Robert Bretall (ed.), *A Kierkegaard Anthology*, translated by David S. Swenson, Lillian Marvin Swenson, and Walter Lowrie (Princeton, NJ: Princeton University Press, 1946), pp. 204–205.

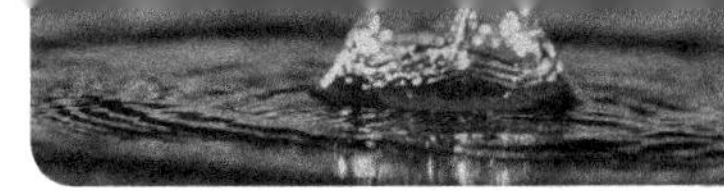



Humans exist as individuals, in the particular and not in the universal. As such they are free and defined by their free choice. It is not the capacity or potential but the choices that are made by a person that brings an individual into existence. Becoming who I am is identical with my existence and by choosing, I exist, and in the process I become a self, or a personality as Kierkegaard defines it in the following passage:

> If you will understand me aright. I should like to say that in making a choice it is not so much a question of choosing the right as of the energy, the earnestness, the pathos with which one chooses. Thereby the personality announces its inner infinity, and thereby, in turn, the personality is consolidated.[88]

Kierkegaard's subjectivity was also inspired by his observations of contemporary religious practice and in particular the Christian church service known as mass where the "masses" went through the motion of worship. Kierkegaard advocated pure subjectivity or the capacity to freely, passionately commit oneself to an authentic way of life. This commitment was not founded upon a rational decision, requiring instead an irrational, passionate "leap". As a committed Christian, Kierkegaard knew that at the heart of his belief system was faith and that there was no rational justification for faith. As William Barrett describes it in *Irrational Man: A Study in Existential Philosophy:*

> If I know that twice two is four, this knowledge is in the highest degree impersonal. Once I know it, I know it, and I need not struggle continuously to make it my own. But the truth of religion is not at all like that: it is a truth that must penetrate my own personal existence or it is nothing; and I must struggle to renew it in my life every day.[89]

**Paper 3 Link** 

Karl Jaspers commented that when reading Nietzsche there was always a contradiction evident in his work. Is it fair to ask that philosophers are consistent or argue from a single position?

This was a very different approach to philosophical problems. As a trained philosopher, Kierkegaard was familiar with the tradition of Western thought. His own beliefs became the foundation of his philosophical understanding and eventually his system of thought.

## Understanding Nietzsche

> We are unknown, we knowers, ourselves to ourselves; this has good reason. We have never searched for ourselves—how should it then come to pass, that we should ever find ourselves?
>
> —Friedrich Nietzsche[90]

[88] Søren Kierkegaard, *Either/Or: A Fragment of Life*, vol. 2, translated by David F. Swenson and Lillian Marvin Swenson (Princeton, NJ: Princeton, 1949), p. 141.

[89] William Barrett, *Irrational Man: A Study in Existential Philosophy* (New York: Anchor Books, 1990), p. 171.

[90] Friedrich Nietzsche, *The Genealogy of Morals*, republished 1913 translation by Horace B. Samuel (New York: Dover Publications, 2003), p. 1.

Nietzsche had a different view of the self. He appeared to be responding to the anonymous "despisers of the body". However, it is very clear that he had Plato in mind when he made these kinds of statements and especially Plato's emphasis on the intellect and the metaphysical.

## READING ACTIVITY

Read the following extract and complete a textual analysis.

- Break the passage and its argument down into a series of steps.
- In your own words and using your own examples, analyse what Nietzsche is arguing in this passage.

I want to speak to the despisers of the body. I would not have them learn and teach differently, but merely say farewell to their own bodies—and thus become silent.

"Body am I, and soul"—thus speaks the child. And why should one not speak like children?

But the awakened and knowing say: body am I entirely, and nothing else; and soul is only a word for something about the body.

The body is a great reason, a plurality with one sense, a war and a peace, a herd and a shepherd. An instrument of your body is also your little reason, my brother, which you call "spirit"—a little instrument and toy of your great reason.

"I," you say, and are proud of the word. But greater is that in which you do not wish to have faith—your body and its great reason: that does not say "I," but does "I."

What the sense feels, what the spirit knows, never has its end in itself. But sense and spirit would persuade you that they are the end of all things: that is how vain they are. Instruments and toys are sense and spirit: behind them still lies the self. The self also seeks with the eyes of the senses; it also listens with the ears of the spirit. Always the self listens and seeks: it compares, overpowers, conquers, destroys. It controls, and it is in control of the ego too.

Behind your thoughts and feelings, my brother, there stands a mighty ruler, an unknown sage whose name is self. In your body he dwells; he is your body.

There is more reason in your body than in your best wisdom. And who knows why your body needs precisely your best wisdom?

Your self laughs at your ego and at its bold leaps. "What are these leaps and flights of thought to me?" it says to itself. "A detour to my end. I am the leading strings of the ego and the prompter of its concepts."

The self says to the ego, "Feel pain here!" Then the ego suffers and thinks how it might suffer no more and that is why it is *made* to think.

The self says to the ego, "Feel pleasure here!" Then the ego is pleased and thinks how it might often be pleased again—and that is why it is made to think.

I want to speak to the despisers of the body. It is their respect that begets their contempt. What is it that created respect and contempt and worth and will? The creative self created respect and contempt; it created pleasure and pain. The creative body created the spirit as a hand for its will.

Even in your folly and contempt, you despisers of the body, you serve your self. I say unto you: your self itself wants to die and turns away from life. It is no longer capable of what it would do above all else: to create beyond itself. That is what it would do above all else, that is its fervent wish.

But now it is too late for it to do this: so your self wants to go under, O despisers of the body. Your self wants to go under, and that is why you have become despisers of the body! For you are no longer able to create beyond yourselves.

And that is why you are angry with life and the earth. An unconscious envy speaks out of the squint-eyed glance of your contempt.

I shall not go your way, O despisers of the body! You are no bridge to the overman.

—Friedrich Nietzsche[91]

Similar to Kierkegaard, Nietzsche also has Descartes in his sights. In particular, the Cartesian *indivisible*, immaterial soul, conceived as a substance, presented a problem for Nietzsche.

Behind thy thoughts and feelings, my brother, there is a mighty lord, an unknown sage—it is called Self; it dwells in your body, it is your body.[92]

Nietzsche rejects Descartes' (and therefore Plato's) rejection of the body. Nietzsche includes the body as well as self and ego in any discussion about what is human. He suggests that between the body and the ego is the self. He suggests that the self is in fact a pronoun for the ego (pure consciousness), its "linguistic surrogate".[93] But it is also more than that. In fact, Nietzsche believes that self is closer to the body than the ego. The self is better conceived as an expression of the body, a means of communicating itself with itself and with others. One commentator, Volker Gerhardt, argues that "[t]he self is an expression of the body understood as a unity".[94] The self allows the body to be meaningful, to have sense. The ego controls the body while the self is the body's "wisdom". Each of these descriptions indicates that Nietzsche's concept of the self is very subtle and sophisticated.

Nietzsche rejected **introspection** as a way of knowing the self, believing "our conscious life reaches only to the outer skin of our psyche". Or "consciousness is a surface".[95] In fact, Nietzsche argues that consciousness involves "a vast and thorough corruption, falsification, superficialization, and generalization".[96] Descartes – as well as others – had relied on introspection and the assumption that the mind could be perfectly known to the individual. Nietzsche rejected this assumption, instead claiming, "consciousness in general has developed only under the pressure of the need for communication" and that

[91] Nietzsche, *Thus Spoke Zarathustra*, pp. 34–35.

[92] Ibid., p. 36.

[93] Volker Gerhardt, "The Body, the Self and the Ego", in Keith Ansell-Pearson (ed.), *A Companion to Nietzsche* (Oxford: Wiley-Blackwell, 2009), p. 291.

[94] Ibid., p. 293.

[95] Friedrich Nietzsche, "Why I Am So Clever", in Friedrich Nietzsche, *Ecce Homo*, translated by Walter Kaufmann (New York: Vintage Books, 1969), p. 97.

[96] Friedrich Nietzsche, *The Gay Science*, edited by Bernard Williams, translated by Josefine Nauckhoff and Adrian del Caro (Cambridge: Cambridge University Press, 2001), pp. 213–214.

> ... human beings, like every living creature, are thinking constantly but do not know it. The thinking that becomes conscious is only the smallest part of thought, and we say it is the most superficial, the worst part – for all this conscious thought occurs in words, that is, in communicative signs, and here the origin of consciousness reveals itself... My thought is, as you see, that consciousness does not really belong to the individual existence of human beings, but rather to the social and herd nature in them ... consequently each of us, despite the best will to understand oneself as individually as possible, "to know oneself," will always just bring to one's consciousness precisely what is not individual in one, what is "average," that our very thinking constantly follows majority rule, so to speak...[97]

Similarly, he rejected the assertion that the soul is not a distinct entity from the body. What is seen as a unitary, autonomous, rational self is, in fact, the effect of a multiplicity of unconscious forces. The self is a socially induced fiction. The impetus is not our desire for order but society's desire to make human beings reliable, predictable, conformist herd animals, depriving them of independence and individuality. Nietzsche's solution to this deliberate misconception (by whom?) is to advocate the emergence of a new "man", the famous *Übermensch*.

In *The Gay Science* (1882), Nietzsche said, "We, however, want to become those we are – human beings who are new, unique, incomparable, who give themselves laws, who create themselves."[98]

These unique individuals will be able to transform themselves by organizing their drives to become an autonomous individual, able to live independently of the ideals of the majority.

> To demand of strength that it should *not* express itself as strength, that it should not be a desire to overcome [is absurd] ... A quantum of force is equivalent to a quantum of drive, will effect—more, it is nothing other than precisely this very driving, willing, effecting ... There is no such substratum; there is no "being" behind doing, effecting, becoming; "the doer" is merely a fiction added to the deed.[99]

The self is just a bundle of drives to which we create an agent and call that the self (not unlike Hume). The rejection of the traditional concept of the self, the relative unimportance of consciousness and the postulation of psychological causes of action are best accounted for in terms of the explanatory primacy of such drives. Nietzsche suggests that the self is simply an expression of the body.[100]

## FIND OUT MORE

Compare and contrast the works of Freud and Nietzsche.

Both believed that "public self is a conditioned construct of the inner psychological self."

Does this mean that their philosophies are the same? Complete an analysis of their arguments to identify their similarities and differences.

**Paper 3 Link** 

Should Freud be considered a philosopher?

If so, why? If not, why not?

---

97 Ibid.

98 Nietzsche, *The Genealogy of Morals*, Book I, Section 13.

99 Ibid.; compare with Nietzsche, *Beyond Good and Evil*, 2003.

100 Gerhardt, "The Body, . . .", pp. 292–293.

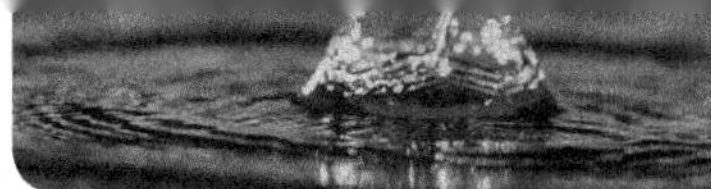

### Influence on existentialism

The self is now something that is invented as individuals can consciously choose themselves.

## VIEWING ACTIVITY: PHILOSOPHY AND FILM

In David Fincher's *Fight Club*, the film opens with a monotone narrative, as dreary as the life that Jack (the main character) lives. Watch the opening to the movie. What would an existentialist say about Jack's existence?

## Sartre and the concept of self-hood

> You are—your life, and nothing else.
>
> —Jean-Paul Sartre[101]

### Searching for a post-Cartesian self

Kierkegaard and Nietzsche both had an influence on those who took phenomenology as a new start in philosophy. But there were other philosophers who influenced existential thinking. These included Descartes, Kant, and Hegel. Sartre is the most accessible existential philosopher so his work will be used to establish the idea of the existential self.

Self-consciousness is the intersubjective dimension in the **phenomenologico-existential** philosophy of Sartre.

Sartre provided an excellent insight into his thinking on the self in one of his plays, *No Exit* (1944). The intersubjective dimension refers to how we need a second self-consciousness to reflect our self so we can see it. In this section of the play, Estelle cannot locate a mirror to help her powder her face. She asks Garcin, but is ignored. This lack of recognition produces an interesting response:

> ESTELLE: How tiresome!
>
> [ESTELLE shuts her eyes and sways, as if about to faint. INEZ runs forward and holds her up.]
>
> INEZ: What's the matter?
>
> ESTELLE: [Opens her eyes and smiles.] I feel so queer. [She pats herself.] Don't you ever feel that way too? When I can't see myself I begin to wonder if I really exist. I pat myself just to make sure, but it doesn't help.[102]

Self-consciousness is only possible when one is compelled to self-awareness with the reflective activity forced upon one by the ***look*** of the **other**.

---

101 Jean-Paul Sartre, *No Exit and Three Other Plays*, translated by Stuart Gilbert (London: Vintage, 1989), p. 43.

102 Ibid., p. 46.

### The self (but not as we know it)

The self, as the form of subjectivity and of the *cogito*, is encountered in the world that *persons* share with one another, i.e., in **an intersubjective world**. This is not the metaphysical "spirit" of **Hegel** that is transcendental in nature, yet it shares some of its features. The self and consciousness are different. The self is not *in* consciousness in the manner of Descartes, Locke, and Husserl (and therefore an essence). The self is *in* existence. In simple terms, Sartre is rejecting the traditional concept of the self, replacing it with the concept of **self-hood**.

Consequently, Sartre is both **Cartesian** and **Kantian** and yet he rejects key aspects of their respective philosophies. Fundamentally, he wishes to reject idealism, or the argument we are a *transcendental ego*. While he was a student of Husserl, who it has been argued retained this transcendental ego, and Heidegger, and was inspired by both, he rejected the former and cannibalized the latter's philosophical critique of Husserl's philosophy to construct his own philosophy.

### Framework

Sartre postulates three modes of being: being-for-itself, being-in-itself, and being-for-others. It is best to understand these using the following examples:

- *Being-for-itself* defines human consciousness
- *Being-in-itself* defines objects of the world (their essence)
- *Being-for-others* defines the role of others

Sartre rejects both **empiricism** and **idealism** that is grounded in Kant (and those before him) and therefore the **transcendental ego**, replacing it with a **transcendent ego**. (But how much he rejects Kant is an ongoing debate among his interpreters.) In other words, Sartre rejects an ego in the metaphysical world – where the mind is seen as separate from the external world and where the internal world receives information from objects and only *representations* of these objects are known by the self. Instead Sartre argues for an ego that unifies experiences. (In some ways, Sartre sits somewhere between Hume and Kant's response to Hume.)

### Kant's understanding

Kant distinguishes *appearances*

from

*reality in-itself* (the essences)

and

*the products of the senses*

from

*the concepts of understanding which synthesize these appearances.*

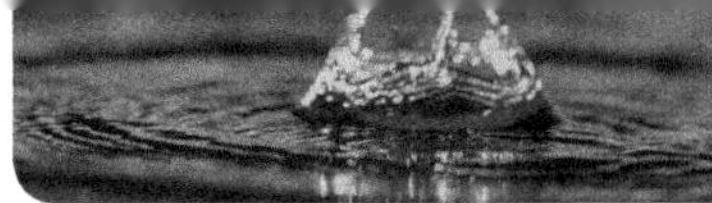

So Sartre is rejecting an understanding or an ontology that involves

- appearances (what you see),
- the unknown essences (*noumena*), and
- concepts required to understand appearances.

According to Sartre, there is no essence hidden behind the appearance and he rejects the idea that the mind is born with the ability to understand these appearances as part of a conceptual structure. However, while he rejects the existence of a Kantian **transcendental ego**, he does not necessarily reject Kant's **empirical ego**.

## Sartre's consciousness

Sartre holds firm with the idea of conscious being conscious of something (therefore being unable to exist unless it is conscious of something) thus rejecting Descartes' **pure ego**. This is the "I" of "I think, therefore I am". He rejects it because one must exist in a world to be conscious of something. He therefore rejects the dualism or metaphysics of Plato and Descartes, as well as Kant. An "I" that has nothing to think about cannot exist, therefore dualism is wrong. Descartes' "I" still exists even if it wasn't thinking (as a soul); its ongoing identity was the issue because of non-existence. Note that Sartre also rejects the position of materialism – we are our body/brain – though he believes the body/brain is important. We act in/through/with our bodies, but there is more than just our bodies.

Sartre argues for a self that is "outside, in the world. It is a being of the world, like the ego of another".[103] There is consciousness but it is not internal, rather it is external, interconnected with the world. This is a rejection of the consciousness of the introspective methodology – I look inwards for my self, which is either "in" or "behind" consciousness – the transcendental ego.

This is an **empirical ego** as the self, an ego experiencing the world by being part of it, and this includes "the other". The ego is a person's attitude towards the world, and this becomes you (such as your values). Remember, it is not in consciousness (and therefore born with it/essence/*a priori*): it emerges by being conscious of the world, and choosing how to relate to that world. It is a **psycho-physical self**.

Note that consciousness is not an object itself or an object for itself – it is not like a chair/an external essence or an essence/internal entity itself (like Descartes' immaterial, substantial self and, to a lesser extent, Locke's immaterial, non-substantial self).

Whereas idealism believes the world is constructed by consciousness, Sartre claims that consciousness has no independent existence; in fact, no existence at all apart from its world: "the ego is neither formally nor materially in consciousness: it is outside, in the world".[104]

Sartre focuses on a **pre-reflexive aspect of consciousness**, or before we use theoretical concepts to understand the world. This is the reflexive self, or the self with a structure inherent in it that allows it to understand the world. If "existence precedes essence" this cannot be the case.

[103] Jean-Paul Sartre, *Transcendence of the Ego*, translated by Forrest Williams (New York: Noonday Press, 1957), p. 31.
[104] Ibid.

Sartre stresses the practical and pre-conceptual being-in-the-world more than the various ways in which we *know* (conceptualize) the world. Sartre believes that our being-in-the-world and our encounters with the world are to be the focus when considering consciousness. This is the **empirical, psycho-physical, or practical ego**.

Imagine you lose yourself while reading a novel and drinking tea. There are three acts occurring – thinking, reading, drinking – but they are the same, there is not a separate "I" that is both reading and drinking. You can lose yourself in an activity, indicating, for Sartre, that the essential self does not exist.

There is only "consciousness of the novel", not "I am conscious of reading the novel", or the self reflecting on reading. Rather, reading is occurring and there is a relationship between self, book, and tea. You "do" something, but the "doer" occurs only after the "doing" has been done.

Sartre uses the example of running after a bus. One does not become conscious that "one's running after the bus" until one has ceased to run after the bus. This is because until this point one's consciousness is focused on the bus itself, and not on the fact that one is chasing it.

Conscious needs the book in order "to be", to exist. It cannot be conscious of nothing (being and nothingness).

### Being-with-others

The other forces you to realize your self – without the other this would not happen. Shame becomes a powerful emotion in the existence of the self. For example, imagine someone observing an event and they lose awareness of themselves. Suddenly they are observed and they become shameful and the "I" now exists. The idea of recognition can be found in Hegel's master–slave dialectic (see p. 161 in Chapter 4: Mind and Body) and the need for recognition in order to exist – you do not exist unless you are being recognized. This recognition by the other can be both a positive and a negative dimension of the self. Too much emphasis on the other's recognition takes away your freedom, by objectifying you. This subjective consciousness, which is the foundation of our choices, actions, and existential "essence", is also the ground of human freedom.

▲ Albert Camus, author of *The Stranger*

## Camus

Albert Camus' (1913–1960) novel *The Stranger* (1942) explores in a literary form the philosophical conflict between reason and experience and the concept of consciousness. The novel asks questions about the source of meaning and the worth of rationality and consciousness in human nature. Meursault, a man seemingly devoid of emotion who opens his heart to "the benign indifference of the universe", is the central character. Camus uses Meursault and the events that befall him to explore the false dichotomy between reason and emotion. More importantly, he explores the notions of consciousness and introspection, and the role of the other. The tradition of Descartes and Locke believed that introspection revealed the self. Kant's response to Hume's no-self was premised on the belief that the self must exist because something behind the experiences must be unifying them. However, consciousness can also be understood in terms of

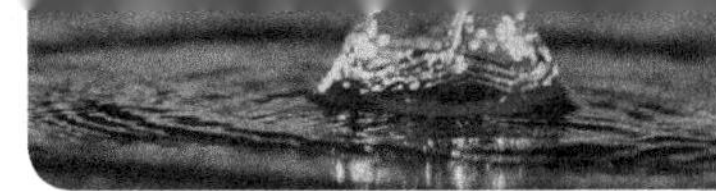

the metaphor of the mirror. The mirror is used to see oneself – it provides a reflection, enabling close examination of the self. However, it is not an introspective examination, rather seeing yourself as others see you.

The existentialists argue that the sense of reflection used by Descartes, Locke, and Kant is illusionary, or at least very dependent on the "mirror" sense of reflection and hence the role of the other. This leads to the question, "To what extent is your consciousness *your* consciousness?" The influence of Hegel can be seen here – he argued that self-comprehension depends on the recognition of others.

## de Beauvoir

> To be oneself, simply oneself, is so amazing and utterly unique an experience that it's hard to convince oneself so singular a thing happens to everybody.
>
> —Simone de Beauvoir[105]

**Question**

How is de Beauvoir's understanding of the self different from Sartre's?

Simone de Beauvoir (1908–86) was one of the leading intellectuals of the 20th century. She trained in philosophy alongside her fellow Frenchman Jean-Paul Sartre, attending lectures with him and reading many of the same texts. Consequently there are many similarities between their philosophical understanding. She too rejected the notion of solipsistic, isolated self. Instead, she used her understanding of the existentialist and phenomenological notion of the self from her reading of Hegel and Husserl and influenced by the work of Sartre and Heidegger. These influences are evident in her major philosophical work *The Ethics of Ambiguity* (1947). In this seminal work de Beauvoir defines the self as a nothingness and pure subjectivity, created through action.

### REFLECTION QUESTION

> I take pleasure in my transformations. I look quiet and consistent, but few know how many women there are in me.
>
> —Anaïs Nin[106]

With reference to an existential concept of the self, what is Anaïs Nin suggesting in her portrayal of the self?

**Question**

What did Merleau-Ponty reject in Sartre's philosophy and position on the concept of the self?

## Merleau-Ponty: the self as embodied subjectivity

Phenomenology means the study of what appears to consciousness and in doing so rejects the notion that there is a more "fundamental" level of reality. Instead phenomenologists argue that there is only the world discernible

[105] Simone de Beauvoir, *The Prime of Life: 1929–1944* [an autobiography], translated by Peter Green (New York: World Publishing, 1962), p. 27.

[106] Anaïs Nin, *The Early Diary of Anaïs Nin: 1927–1931* (New York: Harcourt Brace Jovanovich, 1985), p. 71.

by conscious human experience. As a consequence, understanding human behaviour and experience cannot reference this fictitious, more fundamental, reality. Human behaviour can only be understood from within this human experience. Maurice Merleau-Ponty (1908–1961) states it as such: "the aim of phenomenology is described as the study of experiences with a view to bringing out their 'essences', their underlying reason."[107]

This is reflected in Merleau-Ponty's *Phenomenology of Perception* (1945), with reference to our perception of the world and therefore our knowledge about it:

> Consciousness must be reckoned as a *self-contained system of Being*, as a system of *Absolute being*, into which nothing can penetrate and from which nothing can escape. On the other side, the whole spatio-temporal world, to which man and the human ego claim to belong as subordinate singular realities, is *according to its own meaning mere intentional Being*, a Being, therefore, which has the merely secondary, relative sense of a Being for a consciousness.[108]

We exist within our consciousness and are confined by it. The world surrounding the self appears to exist in time and space as an object that the consciousness recognizes. However, the consciousness recognizes the apparent object and it is an object of consciousness. Lived experience becomes fundamental to understanding existence, not a defined conceptual framework that might distort an understanding.

In Merleau-Ponty's philosophy consciousness is experiencing the world as part of understanding it – it is dynamic not static. This is in contrast to empiricists such as Hume and Locke, who saw consciousness as a repository for sensation. For Merleau-Ponty, the body is part of this experiencing as it is the context for the mind and rejects the dualist's position on the mind/body: "There is not a duality of substances but only the dialectic of living being in its biological milieu."[109]

## A Response to Solipsism: intersubjectivity

Intersubjectivity is a complex concept that emerged out of the phenomenological tradition, originating in the work of Husserl and argued in his *The Fifth Cartesian Meditation* – Empathy, Others and Intersubjectivity. Intersubjectivity can be defined in the number of different ways such as, 'a concrete self-other relation, a socially structured life-world, or a transcendental principle of justification'.[110] Each of these definitions share a common focus and that is the relation of the self to the other in the context of the shared world and another name for the problem of other minds.

---

[107] Quoted in Edo Pivcevic, *Husserl and Phenomenology* (London: Hutchinson University Library, 2014), p. 11.

[108] Quoted in John F. Bannan, *The Philosophy of Merleau-Ponty* (New York: Harcourt, Brace & World, 1967), p. 10.

[109] Ted Toadvine and Lester Embree, *Merleau-Ponty's Reading of Husserl* (Dordrecht, The Netherlands: Kluwer Academic Publishers, 2002), p. 96.

[110] Dan Zahavi, *Subjectivity and Selfhood: Investigating the First-Person Perspective* (Cambridge, MA: MIT Press, 2005), p. 178.

This is an attempt to answer the criticisms of solipsism. While to a certain extent intersubjectivity is a response to the perceived weaknesses of the argument from analogy, it offers a much more nuanced and complex answer, and one that is central to the phenomenological project. This project is seeking to overcome the mind/body and subject/object divide at the heart of Descartes' philosophy. While Descartes' self, or the ego, referenced its own world, the phenomenological self references the world it shares with others. Husserl describes this as monadological intersubjectivity. By this difficult term he means the shared world of the self and the other. The first word, 'monad' refers to a notion of the discrete self. The second word 'intersubjectivity' defines is an approach to understanding reality and knowledge that rejects the overly rational, metaphysical world of Plato and his representational theory of consciousness. The vertical hierarchy of Plato's divided line and his form of the good is rejected, replaced with a horizontal emphasis that leads to a quasi-humanist perspective and a consciousness that is not 'in' the mind, but conscious of something forming a relation with it. As Husserl argues, in this monadological intersubjectivity "the second ego [the other] is not simply there, and strictly given to himself; rather is he constituted as 'alter ego' – the ego indicated as one moment by this expression being I myself in my owness".[111] This is more simply captured by 'I cannot obtain any truth whatsoever about myself, except through the mediation of another'. This understanding is dependent on phenomenology's definition of consciousness as being conscious of, or about, something – this is known as intentionality. But this is not an ego observing the world from behind a screen, rather a self-in-a-shared-world whose existence is dependent on the same consciousness in others.

The most accessible interpretation of this idea comes from Sartre in his lecture *Existentialism Is a Humanism* when he says,

> Contrary to the philosophy of Descartes, contrary to that of Kant, when we say "I think" we are attaining to ourselves in the presence of the other, and we are just as certain of the other as we are of ourselves. Thus the man who discovers himself directly in the cogito also discovers all the others, and discovers them as the condition of his own existence. He recognises that he cannot be anything (in the sense in which one says one is spiritual, or that one is wicked or jealous) unless others recognise him as such. I cannot obtain any truth whatsoever about myself, except through the mediation of another. The other is indispensable to my existence, and equally so to any knowledge I can have of myself. Under these conditions, the intimate discovery of myself is at the same time the revelation of the other as a freedom which confronts mine, and which cannot think or will without doing so either for or against me. Thus, at once, we find ourselves in a world which is, let us say, that of "inter-subjectivity". It is in this world that man has to decide what he is and what others are.[112]

[111] Edmund Husserl, *Cartesian Meditation: An Introduction to Phenomenology*, translated by Dorion Cairns (Dordrecht, The Netherlands: Kluwer Academic Publishers, 1999), p. 94.

[112] Quoted in ibid.

With this mode of consciousness (or irreducible intentional state) as the foundation, the self overcomes solipsism by transposing itself into the other in the form of empathy which brings the other person – and their mental states – together. Sartre's development of this phenomenological position includes his radical freedom and therefore defining the individual's existential self and identity. This allows Sartre to claim that when you act you act on behalf of humankind overcoming any subjective or egocentric ethical decision-making.

## Role of culture: the other or the role of the community

In contemporary philosophy, traditional debates have included the role of culture. This leads to the question, "To what extent is our self, even our sense of self, constructed by others?"

It is worth returning to the position that this tradition of conceptualizing the self is in response to the atomistic self. Descartes argued that there is a core self that is independent of the historical-social context in which an individual finds himself or herself. This does not mean that he rejected the influence of the historical-social context, only that it existed in distinction to this context. To argue this position, Descartes tells his reader how he went about understanding himself better using the methodology of introspection. To do this he withdrew himself from others, looking within:

> After I had employed several years studying the book of the world and trying to acquire some experience, I one day formed the resolution of also making myself an object of study … Winter detained me in a place where I found no society to divert me and no cares or passions to trouble me. I remained there the whole day shut up alone in a stove-heated room, where I had complete leisure to occupy myself with my own thoughts.[113]

In this isolation, Descartes was able to search for his real self, found inside himself, determining what is true and what is false:

> I shall now close my eyes, I shall stop my ears, I shall call away all my senses, I shall efface even from my thoughts all the images of corporeal things, or at least (for that is hardly possible) I shall esteem them as vain and false; and thus holding converse only with myself and considering my own nature, I shall try little by little to reach a better knowledge of and a more familiar acquaintanceship with myself.

[113] Descartes, *Discourse on the Method*, available at http://www.gutenberg.org/ebooks/59?msg=welcome_stranger#part5 (accessed 21 October 2014).

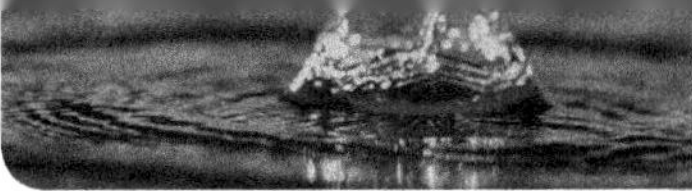

> I am a thing that thinks, that is to say, that doubts, affirms, denies, that knows a few things, that is ignorant of many, that loves, that hates, that wills, that desires, that also imagines and perceives ...
>
> In order to try to extend my knowledge further, I shall now look around more carefully and see whether I cannot still discover in myself some other things which I have not hitherto perceived. I am certain that I am a thing which thinks; but do I not then likewise know what is requisite to render me certain of a truth? Certainly in this first knowledge there is nothing that assures me of its truth, excepting the clear and distinct perception of that which I state ... And accordingly it seems to me that already I can establish as a general rule that all things which I perceive very clearly and very distinctly are true.[114]

Descartes makes several claims in this passage. He makes the claim that the real self is accessible through the use of reason. He claims that this real self, including its qualities such as its willing, desiring, imagining, and perceiving, exist independently of others – and that the best method of determining this self is by withdrawing from others. Lastly, Descartes claims that only the individual themselves can determine the truth about their self. These claims are fundamental, even foundational, to Descartes' position. The role of the other is non-existent.

However, there are those philosophers who believe that the historical-social context is primary in the construction of the self and therefore the concept of the self. Compare Descartes' famous phrase "I think, therefore I am" with an alternative from an African view of the self expressed by the philosophy of Ubuntu (human-ness): "I am because we are, and since we are, therefore I am."[115] In this conception, the role of the other, often expressed as "community", is essential to the concept of the self.

There has also been a long tradition of opposing this notion of the self in the Western tradition. Aristotle, while reacting to Plato's philosophy and therefore his concept of the self, asserted that man was a social animal. In the process, he suggested that the self was defined in relation to family and the city or state and yet remained an essential aspect of the self. As Aristotle suggests:

> The individual, when isolated, is not self-sufficing; and therefore he is like a part in relation to the whole. But he who is unable to live in society, or who has no need because he is sufficient for himself, must be either a beast or a god ... social instinct is implanted in all men by nature.[116]

Nonetheless, Platonic and Cartesian concept of the self remained dominant until the 18th century when the work of Hegel challenged

[114] René Descartes, *Discourse on Method and Meditations*, translated by Elizabeth S. Haldane and G. R. T. Ross (New York: Dover Publications, 2003), p. 79–80.

[115] John Mbiti, *African Religions and Philosophies* (New York: Doubleday, 1970), p. 141.

[116] Aristotle, *Politics*, translated by C. D. C. Reeve (London: Hackett Publishing, 1997), p. 45.

this assumption. Hegel purposefully sought to reject the atomistic self defined by Descartes. Instead Hegel, using the influence of Aristotle, argued for a **relational self**, which required recognition from another self to exist. In a fascinating passage from his *Encyclopaedia of the Philosophical Sciences* (1817), Hegel describes the relationship between a master and his slave:

> Every self wants to be united with and recognized by another self [as a free being].
>
> Yet at the same time, each self remains an independent individual and so an alien object to the other. The life of the self thus becomes a struggle for recognition ...
>
> Each self is in a struggle to convince the other that he is [a free being] worthy of the other's respect and recognition. This mutual struggle for recognition by the other is mixed with feelings of mistrust and uncertainty. The struggle carries with it all the dangers and risks that the self faces when it dares to lay itself open to the other. This life-and-death struggle can degenerate into a bloody fight in which one of the combatants is killed. But then the whole issue of recognition will be missed. Recognition requires the survival of the other as a condition and sign of one's freedom. The struggle of the self is essentially a struggle for freedom. Historically, this struggle is the basis of the rise of masters and slaves ...
>
> Preferring survival to freedom, the slave gives up his attempt to be recognized as free. The master, on the other hand, is recognized as free. The master sees in the slave the very sign of his freedom.
>
> Independent masters and dependent slaves together form a community.
>
> To preserve and protect the life of his workers becomes the concern of the master ... The slave learns to work. He acquires habits and skills. At the same time he disciplines himself. In making objects [for the master] he also makes himself. In working together with others he overcomes his isolation and is recognized for his excellence. In this process, the relation of dependence and independence is reversed. The independent master becomes dependent on the skills and virtues of the servant.[117]

This formation of the self occurs through the consciousness of others, through their recognition. This leads Hegel to claim, "an I that is a we and a we that is an I", or there can be no "I" without a "we". The need for the other is clear in this formulation. The self can only exist by being recognized by another subject. The impact of this approach can be seen clearly in the work of Sartre and other existentialists.[118]

It also has been influential on a school of philosophy called communitarianism. The major thinkers in this tradition are Alasdair MacIntyre, Charles Taylor, Michael Walzer, and Michael Sandel. While they have taken different approaches to this conception of the self they are all reacting to the atomistic concept of the self in modern philosophical liberalism in the works of John Rawls.

---

[117] Georg Hegel, *Encyclopedia of Philosophy*, translated by Gustav E. Mueller (New York: Philosophical Library, 1959), pp. 215–217.

[118] However, it is worth noting that Sartre's understanding of Hegel was defined by Alexandre Kojève's idiosyncratic but influential reading of Hegel in the 1930s. Kojève read Hegel through the lens of Marx's materialism and Heidegger's ontology. This is not an orthodox reading of Hegel.

## ASSESSMENT ACTIVITIES

1. Flow chart

   Starting with Kant sketch out a flow chart outlining the development of the self through to Sartre. What are the similarities and differences from Kant to Sartre?

2. Dialogue

   Choose two philosophers and write a debate between them on the concept of the self.

   - In what ways do they end up agreeing with each other?
   - In what ways do they end up disagreeing with each other?

## The postmodern concept of the self

While many of the positions on the self covered in this chapter have remained present in philosophical debate in the late 20th and early 21st centuries, a new movement emerged that challenged the assumptions they privileged.

### The postmodern self

> First is a shift from self-as-subject, unconsciously merged with our ground of perception, to self-as-object, directly visible to us. Second is a shift from natural self—something to be discovered—to artificial self (not "artificial" in the sense of fake but in the sense of something created, an artifact).
>
> —Walter Truett Anderson[119]

Postmodernism was a dominant philosophical movement in the late 20th century. There were other movements closely identified with postmodernism, such as deconstruction, post-structuralism, and critical theory. It emerged out of the phenomenological tradition via the critiques of the dominant essentialism, scientific-rationalism paradigm defining Western thought since Plato. The work of Heidegger and Nietzsche were seen as important to this impetus, which is regarded variously as a reaction to modernism, an extension of modernism, or even a rejection of modernism.

The major philosophers of the movement are:

- Jacques Derrida
- Jean-François Lyotard
- Michel Foucault
- Richard Rorty
- Jean Baudrillard
- Fredric Jameson

[119] Walter Truett Anderson, *The Future of the Self: Inventing the Postmodern Person* (New York: J. P. Tarcher, 1997), p. 19.

Let's look more closely at the postmodern view of the self.

Walter Truett Anderson provides a summary of four dominant concepts used by postmodernists to discuss the self. Their consistent reference throughout these concepts is change and multiple identities.

- **Multiphrenia**: Kenneth Gergen in *The Saturated Self* (1991) observed that the modern self makes the notion of the authentic self difficult and consequently "knowable characteristics" become harder to identify. The individual is exposed to multiple opinions, values, and ways of life in the course of his or her existence. Each of these impacts on an individual's sense of the self. Gergen says, "For everything that we 'know to be true' about ourselves, other voices within respond with doubt and even derision."[120] This makes an essential self a challenge as our relationships distract, undermine, and confuse, making a single and consistent self hard to identify.
- **Protean**: The protean self is able to change in response to circumstances. As Anderson summarizes, "[i]t may include changing political opinions and sexual behavior, changing ideas and ways of expressing them, changing ways of organizing one's life."[121] This does not refute the idea of an essential self as it can still be seen as a process towards discovering one's true self.
- **The decentred self**: This position rejects the possibility of the self. The self is constantly changing, being redefined through a process of existing. With a focus on the role of language, this position sees the self, and therefore the individual, as constructed by language.
- **Self-in-relation**: This self is a self that is connected to other people and even the culture in which they are contextualized. Feminist studies often articulate this concept of the self.

A theme throughout each of these concepts is that there is no inner self determining who the "I" is as a cohesive whole. According to postmodern thought, we are shaped by outside forces; in other words, we are socially constructed.

**Self and technology**

How does Facebook conceive of the self?

## Conclusion

The self is a complex issue with numerous positions available for further investigation. There is significant overlap between the self and the other topics covered in the chapters of this book. The self has had, and continues to have, a major importance in many societies around the world. From a philosophical perspective there are a number of broad conceptual frameworks that have been used to debate and explore the concept of the self over a number of years. The Western tradition's initial emphasis on an essential self was rejected by Hume's apparent no-self argument. Later on, this essential self was again rejected by the

[120] Kenneth J. Gergen, *The Saturated Self: Dilemmas of Identity in Contemporary Life* (New York: Basic Books, 1991), p. 6–7.

[121] Anderson, *Future of the Self*, p. 41.

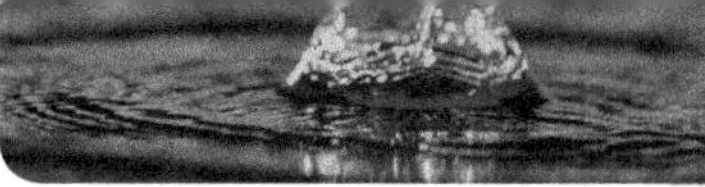

existential movement in the early 20th century. Other traditions of thinking have seen similar debates occur.

The concern throughout these debates is the attempt to find something that contains identity, whether it is the identity of being human or the identity of an individual. This overlaps with the issue of human nature and personhood and is taken further in personal identity when the question focuses on the issue of the enduring self.

## FINAL REFLECTION

Given what we know today (scientific knowledge, psychology, social philosophy, etc.) do you think the self is still an important consideration in modern society? Is there a "global identity crisis" as argued by Walter Truett Anderson?

## FIND OUT MORE

Research the Posthuman Manifesto and in particular, the "Statements on consciousness, humans and philosophy" in Part 2. This can be found in Robert Pepperell, *The Posthuman Condition: Consciousness Beyond the Brain* (Bristol, UK: Intellect, 2003), p. 178.

Read through the statements. Which ones make sense to you given our contemporary context and understanding? What impact do (will) these have on our concept of the self?

## LINK WITH THE CORE THEME

### The self and being human

The self is a complex issue with numerous positions available for further investigation. There is significant overlap between the self and the other topics covered in the chapters of this book. The self has had, and continues to have, a major importance in many societies around the world. From a philosophical perspective there are a number of broad conceptual frameworks that have been used to debate and explore the concept of the self over a number of years. The Western tradition's initial emphasis on an essential self was rejected by Hume's apparent no-self argument. Later on, this essential self was again rejected by the existential movement in the early 20th century. Other traditions of thinking have seen similar debates occur.

Indian and Chinese philosophical traditions of thought have a number of varied approaches to the self. These cover monist, dualist, and pluralist concepts. A consistent analogy in both Western and Eastern traditions has been the chariot. How this analogy has been used indicates not just the specifics of a philosophical tradition but also the nature of the conception – its sources, purpose, and conceptual framework its final manifestation in a world (if at all).

## Assessment tip: Analysing and evaluating a position on the self

The self is the key concept explored in this chapter. This key concept also includes associated concepts of introspection and the other. If you decide to respond to a non-philosophical stimulus by considering an issue associated with the concept of the self then it is advised to also determine an **analytical and an evaluative strategy**. In other words, you have to demonstrate a depth of understanding while taking a position on the issue.

Consequently, the initial decisions about the issue must be influenced by the ability to examine the issue comprehensively. This means that the issue must be framed to allow it to be detailed sufficiently as well as providing enough time to argue your own position.

Look at the markscheme accompanying each stimulus. For example, the November 2004 markscheme gives a suggestion of "the self as activity versus the self as substance". This is framed as a dichotomy but with a possibility of a relationship or an overlap. This chapter has been designed to present a number of these dichotomies but the options offered are by no means exhaustive. Consult the suggestions outlined early in the chapter.

This allows you to include a "discussion and assessment of alternative interpretations or points of view". While the number of perspectives is not prescribed, given the time allocated to complete the essay in the exam is approximately 50 minutes, it is recommended to focus on two perspectives to ensure a depth of understanding is demonstrated in your treatment of them. This should not, however, prevent you from referencing other philosophers/positions/perspectives for the purpose of illustration or example, especially if they enable you to illustrate your chosen perspectives.

Practising the phrasing of the issue will help provide guidance in the pressure of the exam. The issue should be phrased in a way which provides you with clear direction. Consequently, it should encompass both perspectives. Using the example given above you should phrase the question "To what extent is the self determined by self as activity versus the self as substance?" or "Is the self a consequence of activity or substance?"

### Activities

1. Identify a philosophical issue in response to a past paper stimuli based on an issue of the self that have been explored in this chapter.
2. Identify relevant philosophical positions in relation to the issue.
3. Write an essay plan/draft essay in response to the following instructions:

   "With explicit reference to the stimulus and your own knowledge, discuss a philosophical issue related to the question of what it means to be human *in relation to the self*."

   An essay should demonstrate a clear and concise understanding of philosophical issues and concepts. This requires a detailed knowledge of arguments and theories. Analysis should include a discussion of counter-arguments. Evaluation should provide support for a clear perspective/response.

### Assessment tip

Turn to the assessment chapter for a more detailed account of what analysis and evaluation involve, and what questions can help you make sure you are on the right track.

Use the following supports to assist you with your planning:

**Key inquiry questions**

- Is the self an entity, a substance? If it is a substance, what kind of substance is it?
- Is the self a personality trait, an attitude, or an affectation?
- Is the self an action or a unique set of values?
- Is the self a construction and a story that coheres an individual?
- Is it a fabrication, a myth, or an illusion?
- Is the self fixed or variable, in that does it evolve over time?
- How do we know the self? Is it through introspection or through other people?

## References Cited


Ames, Roger T., Wimal Dissanakaye, and Thomas P. Kasulis (eds). *Self as Person in Asian Theory and Practice*. Albany, NY: State University of New York Press, 1994.

Anaïs Nin. *The Early Diary of Anaïs Nin: 1927–1931*. New York: Harcourt Brace Jovanovich, 1985.

Anderson, Walter Truett. *The Future of the Self: Inventing the Postmodern Person*. New York: J. P. Tarcher, 1997.

Aristotle. *Politics*. Translated by C. D. C. Reeve. London: Hackett Publishing, 1997.

Bannan, John F. *The Philosophy of Merleau-Ponty*. New York: Harcourt, Brace & World, 1967.

Barrett, William. *Irrational Man: A Study in Existential Philosophy*. New York: Anchor Books, 1990.

Bartley, Christopher. *An Introduction to Indian Philosophy*. London: Continuum International, 2011.

Bell, Derrick. *Ethical Ambition: Living a Life of Meaning and Worth*. London: Bloomsbury, 2002.

Borges, Jorge Luis. "Borges and I". In Jorge Luis Borges, *The Aleph and Other Stories*. Translated by Andrew Hurley. London: Penguin, 2000, p. 177.

Cartwright, Richard L. "Some Remarks on Essentialism". *The Journal of Philosophy* 65, no. 20 (24 October 1968): 615–626.

Chambers, Aidan. *This Is All: The Pillow Book of Cordelia Kenn*. London: The Bodley Head, 2005.

Churchland, Paul M. *Matter and Consciousness*, 3rd edition. Cambridge, MA: MIT Press, 2013.

Collins, Steven. *Selfless Persons: Imagery and Thought in* Theravada *Buddhism*. Cambridge: Cambridge University Press, 1982.

Critchley, Simon. *Continental Philosophy: A Very Short Introduction*. Oxford: Oxford University Press, 2001.

de Beauvoir, Simone. *The Prime of Life: 1929–1944* [an autobiography]. Translated by Peter Green. New York: World Publishing, 1962.

Descartes, René. *Discourse on the Method of Rightly Conducting One's Reason and Seeking Truth in the Sciences*. Leiden, 1637. English translation available at http://www.gutenberg.org/ebooks/59?msg=welcome_stranger#part5 (accessed 21 October 2014).

Descartes, René. "Third Set of Objections with Author's Replies". In *The Philosophical Works of Descartes*, vol. 2. Translated by Elizabeth S. Haldane and G. R. T. Ross. Cambridge: Cambridge University Press, 1934, pp. 60–78.

Descartes, René. *Discourse on Method and Meditations*. Translated by Elizabeth S. Haldane and G. R. T. Ross. New York: Dover Publications, 2003.

Descartes, René. *Meditations*. Translated by John Veitch. New York: Cosimo, 2008.

Descartes, René. "Meditation II: Of the Nature of the Human Mind; And That It Is More Easily Known than the Body". Available at http://oregonstate.edu/instruct/phl302/texts/descartes/meditations/Meditation2.html (accessed 23 October 2014).

Descartes, René. "Meditation VI: Of the Existence of Material Things, And Of the Real Distinction Between the Mind and Body of Man". Available at http://oregonstate.edu/instruct/phl302/texts/descartes/meditations/Meditation6.html (accessed 24 October 2014).

Edey, Mait. "Subject and Object". In Shaun Gallagher and Jonathan Shear (eds), *Models of the Self*. Thorverton, UK: Imprint Academic, 1999, pp. 441–446.

Ganeri, Jonardon. *The Concealed Art of the Soul: Theories of Self and Practices of Truth in Indian Ethics and Epistemology*. Oxford: Oxford University Press, 2007.

Gerhardt, Volker. "The Body, the Self and the Ego". In Keith Ansell-Pearson (ed.), *A Companion to Nietzsche*. Oxford: Wiley-Blackwell, 2009.

Gergen, Kenneth J. *The Saturated Self: Dilemmas of Identity in Contemporary Life*. New York: Basic Books, 1991.

Gruyer, Paul (ed.). *The Cambridge Companion to Kant and Modern Philosophy*. Cambridge: Cambridge University Press, 2006.

Gupta, Bina. *Perceiving in Advaita Vedanta: Epistemological Analysis and Interpretation*. London: Associated University Presses, 1991.

Ha, Peter. "Heidegger's Concept of *solus ipse* and the Problem of Intersubjectivity'. In Kwok Ying-Lau, Chan-Fai Cheung, and Tze-Wan Kwan (eds), *Identity and Alterity: Phenomenology and Cultural Traditions*. Germany: Königshausen & Neumann, 2010, pp. 351–366.

Hamill, Sam (trans.). *Only Companion: Japanese Poems of Love and Longing*. Boston, MA: Shambala Publications, 2013.

Hamilton, Edith, and Huntington Cairns (eds). *The Collected Dialogues of Plato, including the Letters*. Translated by Michael Joyce. Princeton, NJ: Princeton University Press, 1961.

Hegel, G. W. F. "B.IV.A. Independence and Dependence of Self-Consciousness: Lordship and Bondage", section 179. In *Phenomenology of Spirit*. Translated by A. V. Miller, with analysis of the text and foreword by J. N. Findlay. Oxford: Oxford University Press, 1977, pp. 111–118.

Hegel, Georg. *Encyclopedia of Philosophy*. Translated by Gustav E. Mueller. New York: Philosophical Library, 1959.

Heidegger, Martin. *Being and Time*. Translated by John Macquarrie and Edward Robinson, with a new foreword by Taylor Carman. New York: Harper & Row, 2008.

Hesse, Herman. *Siddhartha*. New York: New Directions, 1951.

Hume, David. "Section II: Of the Origin of Ideas". In *An Enquiry Concerning Human Understanding and Concerning the Principles of Morals*. Edited by L. A. Selby-Bigge, 3rd edition revised by P. H. Nidditch. Oxford: Clarendon Press, 1975, pp. 17–22.

Husserl, Edmund. *Cartesian Meditation: An Introduction to Phenomenology*. Translated by Dorion Cairns. Dordrecht, The Netherlands: Kluwer Academic Publishers, 1999.

Husserl, Edmund. *Logical Investigations*, vol. 1. Translated by J. N. Findlay. New York: Routledge, 2001.

James, William. *The Principles of Psychology*, vol. 1. New York: Henry Holt and Company, 1890.

Johnson, W. J. (trans.). *Bhagavad Gita*. Oxford: Oxford University Press, 2004.

Kant, Immanuel. *Critique of Practical Reason*. Translated from the German *Kritik der praktischen Vernunft*, 1788, Book II, Part 2, Conclusion.

Kant, Immanuel. "Introduction". In *Critique of Pure Reason*. Translated by Norman Kemp Smith. London: Macmillan and Co., 1929.

Kierkegaard, Søren. "Concluding Unscientific Postscript to the 'Philosophical Fragments' ". In Robert Bretall (ed.), *A Kierkegaard Anthology*. Translated by David S. Swenson, Lillian Marvin Swenson, and Walter Lowrie. Princeton, NJ: Princeton University Press, 1946.

Kierkegaard, Søren. *Either/Or: A Fragment of Life*, vol. 2. Translated by David F. Swenson and Lillian Marvin Swenson. Princeton, NJ: Princeton, 1949.

Kierkegaard, Søren. *Sickness Unto Death: A Christian Psychological Exposition for Upbuilding and Awakening, Kierkegaard's Writings Series, XIX*. Edited and translated by Howard V. Hong and Edna H. Hong. Princeton, NJ: Princeton University Press, 1983.

Kierkegaard, Søren. *Concluding Unscientific Postscript to* Philosophical Fragments, *Volume I, Kierkegaard's Writings Series, XII*. Edited and translated by Howard V. Hong and Edna H.

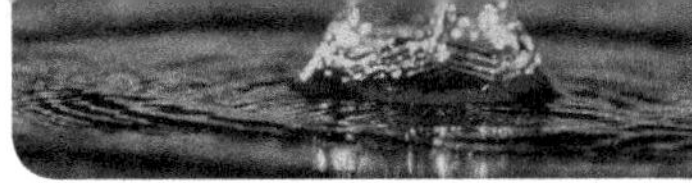



Hong. Princeton, NJ: Princeton University Press, 1992.

Locke, John. "Book II: Of Ideas". In *An Essay Concerning Human Understanding*. New York: Prometheus Books, 1995, pp. 59–320.

Majumdar, Ramesh Chandra. *Ancient India* (Delhi: Motilal Banarasidass, 1977.

Mbiti, John. *African Religions and Philosophies*. New York: Doubleday, 1970.

Moran, Dermot. *Introduction to Phenomenology*. London: Routledge, 2000.

Morton, Peter A. "Aristotle: Selections from *On the Soul* and *Sense and Sensibilia*". In Peter A. Morton (ed.), *A Historical Introduction to the Philosophy of Mind: Readings with Commentary*. Toronto, Ontario: Braodview Press, 2010, pp. 39–42.

Nauriyal, D. K., M. S. Drummond, and Y. B. Lal (eds). *Buddhist Thought and Applied Psychological Research: Transcending the Boundaries*. London: Routledge, 2006.

Nietzsche, Friedrich. "Why I Am So Clever". In Friedrich Nietzsche, *Ecce Homo*. Translated by Walter Kaufmann. New York: Vintage Books, 1969.

Nietzsche, Friedrich. *Thus Spoke Zarathustra: A Book for None and All*. Translated by Walter Kaufmann. Harmondsworth: Penguin, 1974.

Nietzsche, Friedrich. *The Gay Science*. Edited by Bernard Williams. Translated by Josefine Nauckhoff and Adrian del Caro. Cambridge: Cambridge University Press, 2001.

Nietzsche, Friedrich. *The Genealogy of Morals*. Republished 1913 English translation by Horace B. Samuel. New York: Dover Publications, 2003.

Nietzsche, Friedrich. *Beyond Good and Evil*, revised edition. Translated by R. J. Hollingdale. London: Penguin, 2003.

Olivelle, Patrick (trans.). *Upanisads*. Oxford: Oxford University Press, 1998.

Organ, Troy Wilson. *Philosophy and the Self: East and West*. Selinsgrove, PA: Associated University Presses, 1987.

Parfit, Derek. "Divided Minds and the Nature of Persons". In Colin Blakemore and Susan Greenfield (eds), *Mindwaves: Thoughts on Intelligence, Identity and Consciousness*. Oxford: Basil Blackwell, 1987, pp. 19–26.

*Philosophy Bites*. "Alison Gopnik on Hume and Buddhism", 2013. Available at http://philosophybites.com/2013/09/alison-gopnik-on-hume-and-buddhism.html (accessed 26 November 2013).

Pivcevic, Edo. *Husserl and Phenomenology*. London: Hutchinson University Library, 2014.

Plato. *The Trial and Death of Socrates: Four Dialogues* Edited by Shane Weller. New York: Dover Publications, 1992.

Plato. *Great Dialogues of Plato*. Translated by W. H. D. Rouse. New York: Signet Classic, 1999.

Pojman, Louis P. *Philosophy: The Pursuit of Wisdom*, 2nd edition. Belmont: Wadsworth Publishing, 1998.

Pruthi, R. K. *Buddhism and Indian Civilization*. New Delhi: Discovery Publishing House, 2004.

Rich, Adrienne. *Of Woman Born: Motherhood as Experience and Institution*. New York: W. W. Norton, 1976.

Sartre, Jean-Paul. *Transcendence of the Ego*. Translated by Forrest Williams. New York: Noonday Press, 1957.

Sartre, Jean-Paul. *No Exit and Three Other Plays*. Translated by Stuart Gilbert. London: Vintage, 1989.

Sartre, Jean-Paul. *Existentialism Is a Humanism*. Yale: Yale University Press, 2007.

Sekkei Harada. *The Essence of Zen: The Teachings of Sekkei Harada*. Edited and translated by Daigaku Rummé. Somerville, MA: Wisdom Publications, 2012.

Siderits, Mark. *Buddhism as Philosophy: An Introduction*. Aldershot, England: Ashgate Publishing, 2007.

Spelman, Elizabeth V. "Woman as Body: Ancient and Contemporary Views", *Feminist Studies* 8, No. 1 (Spring 1982): 109–131.

Strawson, Peter F. *Individuals: An Essay in Descriptive Metaphysics*. London: Routledge, 1959.

Swinburne, Richard. "Nature and Immortality of the Soul". In Edward Craig (ed.), *Routledge Encyclopedia of Philosophy*. London: Routledge, 1998, p. 982.

Taylor, Charles. *Multiculturalism: Examining the Politics of Recognition*. Princeton, NJ: Princeton University Press, 1994.

Toadvine, Ted, and Lester Embree. *Merleau-Ponty's Reading of Husserl*. Dordrecht, The Netherlands: Kluwer Academic Publishers, 2002.

Velasquez, Manuel. *Philosophy: A Text with Readings*, 12th edition. Wadsworth: Cengage Learning, 2014.

Wallace, William (trans.). *Hegel's Logic*. Oxford: Oxford University Press, 1975.

Wittgenstein, Ludwig. *Tractatus Logico-Philosophicus*, reproduction of 1922 edition. Translated by C. K. Ogden. New York: Cosimo, 2007.

Wrathall, Mark A., and Hubert L. Dreyfus, "A Brief Intoduction to Phenomenology and Existentialism". In Hubert L. Dreyfus and Mark A. Wrathall (eds), *A Companion to Phenomenology and Existentialism*. Chichester, UK: Wiley-Blackwell, 2009, pp. 1–6.

Zahavi, Dan. *Subjectivity and Selfhood: Investigating the First-Person Perspective*. Cambridge, MA: MIT Press, 2005.

# BEING HUMAN

# 6 Freedom

- → Freedom and determinism
- → Social conditioning
- → Existential angst

## Some essential questions:

- → Is there such a thing as free will?
- → Are freedom and determinism incompatible?
- → Why did existentialists see freedom as the source of existential angst?

## Introduction

Does being human mean being free? Is freedom an essential part of the human condition? What is left of our humanity if we remove freedom? Are the factors that influence us compatible with some human freedom?

These questions have been prominent in philosophy for centuries. Each new scientific discovery fuels the debate further as it is invariably interpreted as evidence either that human beings do indeed possess free will, or that their freedom is limited or inexistent. Recent advances in neuroscience, genetics and evolutionary psychology, as well as a better understanding of the sociocultural factors that influence us, have meant that the freedom and determinism debate is still very much at the forefront of philosophy today, and a major part of our quest to understand what it means to be human.

### Stimulus 1

▲ Dilbert cartoon by Scott Adams

## Stimulus 2

We may regard the present state of the universe as the effect of its past and the cause of its future. An intellect which at a certain moment would know all forces that set nature in motion, and all positions of all items of which nature is composed, if this intellect were also vast enough to submit these data to analysis, it would embrace in a single formula the movements of the greatest bodies of the universe and those of the tiniest atom; for such an intellect nothing would be uncertain and the future just like the past would be present before its eyes.[1]

Pierre Simon Laplace (1749–1827) was a French mathematician and scientist who lived in the late 18th and early 19th centuries. Long before computers existed, Laplace put forward a strange idea: if an "intellect" – or a "demon", as it was later referred to – was able to compute all the data of the universe as it is now, it would be able to predict the future with absolute certainty. In other words, according to Laplace, the universe is predictable because it obeys fixed laws: anyone capable of understanding those laws and knowing the current state of the universe would be able to predict the future. This assumes that the universe does indeed follow laws with no exception or surprises. The physical universe and its rules are entirely predictable because they are, according to Laplace, entirely determined.

While Laplace's idea might be acceptable when it comes to planets, the universe and perhaps most of nature, it becomes much more problematic when we include ourselves in his picture. Are human beings as predictable as the material world that surrounds them? Do we obey the same exact laws? Would a greater intellect, "demon" or supercomputer be able to predict our behaviour based on what we are today?

These are some of the questions at the heart of this chapter on Freedom. They all stem from one, central question that has preoccupied philosophers for centuries and is as far as ever from being resolved: **are human beings free?**

### Questions

1. What is your initial reaction to Stimulus 2 and to the Dilbert cartoon (Stimulus 1)? Do you think that all our actions are determined?
2. Can you think of some evidence that human beings do have free will? Conversely, what evidence is there that human beings may not be free?

### TOK link

**Ways of knowing**

Do you think your reaction is based on reason, emotion, or perhaps another way of knowing?

[1] Rephrased from Pierre-Simon Laplace, *A Philosophical Essay on Probabilities*, with an introductory note by E. T. Bell, translated from the French by Frederick William Truscott and Frederick Lincoln Emory (New York: Dover Publications, 1995), p. 4.

##  Philosophical terms and theories

**Determinism** refers to the idea that everything has a cause or a set of causes. It also means that, given that cause or set of causes, what happened had to happen and nothing else could have happened instead. This can refer to natural events and the laws of nature, but also to humans: some determinists believe that our choices do not really come from our free will, but from a series of causes that made them inevitable and, theoretically at least, predictable. Determinism comes in many forms, and not all determinists have such strong views. Determinists agree, however, that human actions and decisions are the result of a chain of causes: some determinists believe that human free will exists but is restricted by certain factors, while others believe that free will doesn't exist at all.

**Hard determinism** is the theory according to which every human action and choice is the inevitable result of a set of causes, which eliminates the possibility of human freedom. Most hard determinists are materialists who base their beliefs on the fact that human beings are material beings subjected to the laws of the material world. Since the material world follows inescapable natural laws, so must human beings. One of the consequences of hard determinism is that it may be difficult to hold people to their actions: moral responsibility, which stems from freedom, seems to disappear.

**Soft determinism** is the theory according to which there are many external factors influencing our decisions, but an element of freedom still remains. Soft determinists tend to agree that all events are the inevitable result of a set of causes. However, they also point out that some of those causes are internal causes, causes that we have some control over. We are able to determine ourselves, at least partially, out of free will. Our choices may be limited by external factors such as our environment, situation, heredity, and so on, but we still have some choice and the power to decide whether to follow one course of action over others. Soft determinists, because they believe in free will, also believe in moral responsibility.

**Libertarianism** is the theory according to which human beings are free agents. Although the material world around us is determined by the laws of nature and causation, human choices are not subjected to such laws. Of course, libertarians recognize that human beings are – at least, partly – material beings and that they are limited by certain laws of nature (for instance, gravity). Libertarians also agree that human beings are influenced by certain factors such as their sociocultural environment and their biology. They maintain, however, that free will can always be exercised: an element of choice always remains, and most human actions are the result of a choice made freely.

**Fatalism** is the idea that at least some events are set in advance and there is nothing we can do to change them. For instance, some fatalists believe that the time and manner of our death is already set. Fatalists tend to focus on an inevitable end. However much freedom we may have or think we have in the run up to that end, it is meaningless given that the final result of our actions is already predetermined.

**Compatibilism** is the idea that determinism and free will are compatible. Soft determinists are compatibilists.

**Incompatibilism** is the idea that determinism and free will are incompatible and cannot coexist. Either we are completely free, as libertarians claim, or we are not free at all, as hard determinists claim.

## EXERCISE

Match the following extracts with one or two of the philosophical terms explained above. Explain your answer.

1. Man's life is a line that nature commands him to describe upon the surface of the earth, without his ever being able to swerve from it, even for an instant. He is born without his own consent; his organization does in nowise depend upon himself; his ideas come to him involuntarily; his habits are in the power of those who cause him to contract them; he is unceasingly modified by causes, whether visible or concealed, over which he has no control, which necessarily regulate his mode of existence, give the hue to his way of thinking, and determine his manner of acting. He is good or bad, happy or miserable, wise or foolish, reasonable or irrational, without his will being for any thing in these various states.

   —Paul-Henri Thiry[2]

2. For if indeed existence precedes essence, one will never be able to explain one's action by reference to a given and specific human nature; in other words, there is no determinism – man is free, man *is* freedom. Nor, on the other hand, if God does not exist, are we provided with any values or commands that could legitimise our behaviour. Thus we have neither behind us, nor before us in a luminous realm of values, any means of justification or excuse. – We are left alone, without excuse. That is what I mean when I say that man is condemned to be free. Condemned, because he did not create himself, yet is nevertheless at liberty, and from the moment that he is thrown into this world he is responsible for everything he does. The existentialist does not believe in the power of passion. He will never regard a grand passion as a destructive torrent upon which a man is swept into certain actions as by fate, and which, therefore, is an excuse for them. He thinks that man is responsible for his passion. Neither will an existentialist think that a man can find help through some sign being vouchsafed upon earth for his orientation: for he thinks that the man himself interprets the sign as he chooses. He thinks that every man, without any support or help whatever, is condemned at every instant to invent man.

   —Jean-Paul Sartre[3]

3. Liberty and Necessity are consistent; as in the water, that has not only liberty but a necessity of descending by the channel; so likewise in the actions which men voluntarily do: which, because they proceed from their will, proceed from liberty, and yet, because every act of man's will, and every desire, and inclination proceed from some cause, and that from another cause, in a continual chain (whose first link is in the hand of God the first of all causes) they proceed from necessity. So that to him that could see the connection of those causes, the necessity of all men's voluntary actions, would appear manifest. And therefore God, that sees and disposes all things, sees also that the liberty of man in doing what he will is accompanied with the necessity of doing that which God will, & no more, nor less. For though men may do many things, which God does not command, nor is therefore Author of them; yet they can have no passion, nor appetite to any thing, of which appetite God's will is not the cause. And did not his will assure the necessity of man's will, and consequently of all that on man will dependeth, the liberty of men would be a contradiction, and an impediment to the omnipotence and liberty of God. And this shall suffice (as to the matter in hand) of that natural liberty, which only is properly called liberty.

   —Thomas Hobbes[4]

---

[2] Thiry, *The System of Nature*, p. 88; available at http://www.gutenberg.org/files/8909/8909-h/8909-h.htm#link2H_4_0022 (accessed 22 October 2014).

[3] Sartre, *Existentialism Is a Humanism*, p. 34, also available at https://www.marxists.org/reference/archive/sartre/works/exist/sartre.htm (accessed 28 October 2014).

[4] Quoted in Malcolm (trans.), *Clarendon Edition . . .: Leviathan*,

## What do we mean by a "cause"?

Since determinism is based on the idea that every event has a cause or a set of causes, it is worth spending some time examining the idea of cause. Although "cause" is a term we all use from time to time, its philosophical meaning can be rather complex.

### Question

Can you think of examples of events that have no cause?

We can start with an interesting question: is there such a thing as an uncaused event? To a large extent, the idea that some things may not have a cause is much harder to accept than the idea that everything has a cause. Even when it comes to human behaviour, finding causes is pretty easy, whereas arguing that a particular behaviour has no cause at all is a fairly difficult task. Let's imagine, for example, that your friend starts screaming at the top of his voice for no apparent reason. When you ask him why he screamed, he answers: "I have no idea. It was just random screaming." Even if you believe that he is telling the truth, you will probably start looking for a possible cause: you may think he is going mad, or is angry but doesn't realize he is. The fact is, as much as most human beings dislike being told that they are determined, they also attribute causes to everything, all the time, including to human behaviour. The idea that some events and behaviours may have no cause at all is pretty disturbing: causes and their effects help us make sense of the world and predict what may happen next. A random world where nothing can be predicted would be a very confusing place!

So, how can we reconcile our longing for freedom with the fact that we tend to look for causes everywhere?

One way is to stop thinking that causes necessarily eliminate the possibility of freedom. Free will and causation are, in theory, perfectly compatible: it all depends on the type of cause we are talking about. Causes don't necessarily need to be external to my mind, they could be *internal* to it: theoretically, *I* may well be the cause of my own actions. In fact, libertarians themselves do not claim that actions are uncaused: instead, they claim that they are often caused by internal causes.

Let's get back to your screaming friend and imagine that his explanation, instead of being "I have no idea", is the following: "I screamed because I just felt like it." That may not seem like much of an explanation, but somehow it seems better than the "random screaming" answer we first explored. This time, your friend wanted to scream, which causes his screaming. The cause of his behaviour is simply his free will, his "voluntariness", his wanting to scream. According to some philosophers, that is enough: behaviour is sometimes entirely caused by our will. Those philosophers believe that free will can be a **sufficient causal condition** of our actions: in other words, free will is enough to cause certain actions and no other explanation is needed.

### Definition of 'free will' by different schools of thought

| Definition | School |
|---|---|
| Free will is the main cause of human choices and actions. Actions are unpredictable because people are choosing from a set of options, and that choice is free. Despite some external influences, free will has the final word and can override external causes. | **Libertarianism** |
| Some actions are entirely determined by external causes and do not involve choice. Other actions are the result of internal causes such as personal desires and preferences, but those internal causes are also, ultimately, determined. | **Soft determinism** |
| Free will is never, in itself, the cause of human "choices" or actions. Actions are caused by external factors we have no control over. Free will is just a "feeling" and an illusion. | **Hard determinism** |

Of course, the question remains as to why your friend felt like screaming in the first place: the idea that the will can be so free that it can generate its own reasons to act without requiring further justification is still quite hard to accept. Instead, the will can be seen as choosing a course of action between a range of possible options. Those options may well be caused by external factors, and may be limited. In that sense, actions are not uncaused, or even caused exclusively by internal causes: they are the result of the will selecting a certain path over another. The big difference between libertarians and soft determinists is that, according to libertarians, the will is able to choose a path freely, somewhat transcending influences and causes external to itself. Soft determinists, on the other hand, believe that the will itself, although it does choose between alternative paths, is influenced and determined by a variety of factors.

This leads us to two obvious problems: soft determinism is often criticized by incompatibilists because it tries to maintain two contradictory ideas as compatible, without convincingly explaining how the will can make actual choices if it is determined. Libertarianism, on the other hand, has to defend the idea that the will can be free, in a material world that we know is ruled by causation.

This brings us back to problems explored in Chapter 4: Mind and Body: if we are entirely material beings, then our will to perform actions must be a physical process, which must have a cause, since physical processes cannot just start themselves (as far as we know). Free will coming out of nothing seems impossible in that materialist scenario. On the other hand, if we are made of both material and immaterial elements (for instance, a body and an immaterial mind or soul), free will is a possibility, but we are faced with the old mind–body problem: how can something immaterial have a causal relationship with something material? At what point does your friend's immaterial will to scream turn into an actual, physical scream? How can the connection possibly happen?

Another problem is that we know that our decisions are often influenced by many factors other than our will. Just because we do not understand the external cause of an action doesn't mean that there isn't one. Given the number of influences that can affect it, how can we know that our will is truly "free"? Isn't there always a possible cause, external to our will, that can explain every one of our decisions? To what extent is our free will undermined by the multitude of other possible causes of our behaviour? As we understand more and more about human cultures and societies, psychology, neuroscience, and the influence of genetics and evolution, free will sometimes seems to shrink.

And yet, as we will see, free will remains: it is still strangely attractive, despite all the blows it has received over the centuries. It stands on its own, like an odd possibility that refuses to disappear, perhaps supported by its strongest ally: the fact that we *feel* free.

## Other interesting points about causation

Cause and effect are related by a causal relationship: they do not happen together by chance, but because the cause precedes the effect **and** produces the effect.

▲ If I drop the ball...

**A causes B**

**For example: "I drop the ball" causes "the ball falls on the floor"**

A possible implication of this causal relationship is that the cause must trigger the effect: in other words, if the cause happens, the effect MUST follow, and there is no other alternative.

**If A happens, then B must happen**

**If I drop the ball, then it must fall on the floor**

This seems pretty obvious but this being philosophy, of course, things are not actually that simple. Some philosophers, including some empiricists, point out that causation of this type only works *given the laws of nature that are applicable in the circumstance*: my dropping the ball causes it to fall on the floor given the law of gravity. If I were to drop a ball in a space station where the law of gravity doesn't apply, then it wouldn't fall on the floor. Therefore, it isn't strictly true to say that if I drop the ball, then it must fall on the floor, as one premise is missing. The correct formulation could therefore be:

**If A happens**

**In a situation where the law "A-type events cause B-type events" applies**

**Then B will happen**

**If I drop the ball**

**In a situation where the law of gravity applies**

**Then the ball will fall to the floor**

This can be seen as weakening the causal relationship that existed between the ball being dropped and its falling on the floor: it isn't that strong if it only works in certain situations!

Another point worth making is that "A causes B" is not the same as saying that B can only happen if A happens: B could have a multitude of possible causes. It could be that C or D could also cause B. For instance, the ball falling on the floor could be caused by the wind blowing it off a table, or a cat pushing it off a shelf.

Of course, things become even more complex when we start considering the chain of causes that led to a certain event:

- What caused the wind to blow in the exact manner that made the ball roll off the table? This question could perhaps be answered by a team of expert meteorologists and physicists. They would then encounter more causes needing an explanation.
- What caused the cat to push the ball off the shelf? This becomes much more difficult than the wind example, because it involves understanding the inner workings of the mind of a cat in order to explain the sources of its behaviour. Even for a pure materialist, trying to explain the multitude of brain events that led to the cat pushing the ball would be a massive task.
- This leads us to the human example: what caused me to drop the ball? Can my action be explained using the language of neuroscience, brain chemistry, and my material body alone? Will the chain of causes eventually lead to something intangible, like a soul or a spirit? Is that even possible? What external influences make their way into the internal workings of my mind until they, too, can be counted as causes of my behaviour?

▲ What caused the cat to push the ball?

Those questions show that "A causes B" is often much too simplistic to account for human choices and actions. One of the main problems is that the laws of human behaviour are not as easily understood as the laws of nature: as discussed above in the case of the ball and the law of gravity, causation can only be established within the context of certain laws. But can we even be certain that such laws exist in the realm of human behaviour? Is behaviour subjected to mechanisms that are as reliable as the laws of nature and work every time, without exception?

There are still many questions and mysteries surrounding determinism and the concept of human free will, but one thing is certain: the influences that may cause us to behave in certain ways form an extremely complex and varied network, and very few human behaviours are the result of a single, simple cause.

In the rest of this chapter, we will explore some of the main influences that may impact on our behaviour and determine us, but first, we will examine the notion of human freedom as it is proposed by some of the philosophers who champion it.

**FIND OUT MORE**

Listen to the following podcast: Thomas Pink on free will

**http://philosophybites.com/2008/03/thomas-pink-on.html**

## Libertarianism

**Libertarianism** is the philosophical position according to which human beings possess free will, which means that they are able to choose between a range of alternatives, without their choice being determined or predictable. Most libertarians are **incompatibilists**, because they do not believe that free will is compatible with determinism. Although some libertarians are slightly closer to soft determinism and willing to acknowledge that human beings are subjected to a variety of influences, they still maintain that free will remains the ultimate cause of every human choice.

Libertarians do not deny that circumstances may prevent us from acting according to our choice: freedom of action is not the same as freedom of will. What they claim instead is that the choices we make are free ones: we are able to deliberate about them consciously and rationally.

Situations may not allow us to follow those choices but at least the will, or desire, is free. No law or necessity can rule the human will.

**Deliberation** is an important part of what it means to be free. It is the gap that exists between causes and effects, the gap in which freedom exercises itself. Our conscious self seems to be able to stop at a crossroads and consider options before choosing one. Sometimes, decisions are very quick, almost instantaneous. Other times, though, it may take months to make a decision, especially if it is a life-changing one like what university to attend or what life-partner to choose. If human beings were determined, wouldn't such decisions be much easier to make? Would it take such a long time, such effort, such calculations, and emotional turmoil, to come to a conclusion?

## FIND OUT MORE

An excellent resource on libertarianism:

http://www2.sunysuffolk.edu/pecorip/SCCCWEB/ETEXTS/INTRO_TEXT/Chapter%207%20Freedom/Freedom_Libertarianism.htm

Richard Taylor (1919–2003) is a contemporary philosopher who argues that human beings are free agents capable of causing their own behaviour. According to Taylor, there is no such thing as soft determinism: once we assume that behaviour results from causes that are besides the agent himself or herself (in other words, when we believe that the agent cannot be a sufficient cause for his or her behaviour), we are already in the same territory as hard determinists. There cannot be a halfway house between freedom and determinism. The belief in human agency is essential to Taylor and other libertarians.

Here is an extract summarizing his take on causation:

> There must, moreover, not only be this reference to myself in distinguishing my acts from all those things that are not acts, but it must be a reference to myself as an active being. Another perfectly natural way of expressing this notion of my activity is to say that, in acting, I make something happen, I cause it, or bring it about.
>
> Now it does seem odd that philosophers should construe this natural way of expressing the matter as really meaning, not that I, but rather some event, process, or state not identical with myself should be the cause of that which is represented as my act. It is plain that, whatever I am, I am never identical with any such event, process, or state as is usually proposed as the "real cause" of my act, such as some intention or state of willing.
>
> Hence, if it is really and unmetaphorically true, as I believe it to be, that I sometimes cause something to happen, this would seem to entail that it is false that any event, process, or state not identical with myself should be the real cause of it.
>
> But it is not, in fact, hard to see why philosophers should want to insist that these natural ways of expressing the matter really mean something rather different from what they seem to mean; namely, that it has been the firm conviction of most philosophers for generations that in the case of any event that occurs, another event must be at least part of its cause.
>
> If, accordingly, it is true that I am the cause of my acts, as it evidently is, then in view of this principle we must suppose that the real cause is some event intimately associated with me – and then, of course, the chase is on to find it or, failing that, at least to give it a name and create a semblance of having found it.
>
> The alternative I urge is that I am sometimes the cause of my own actions, that such an assertion is neither incomplete nor metaphorical and hence has no "real" meaning different from, much less inconsistent with, itself as it stands. In that case, however, we must conclude that the word "cause" in such contexts has not the ordinary meaning of a certain relationship between events, but has rather the older meaning of the efficacy or power of an agent to produce certain results. This idea can be otherwise expressed by saying that an agent is something that originates things, produces them, or brings them about.[5]

[5] Richard Taylor, *Action and Purpose* (Englewood Cliffs, NJ: Prentice-Hall, 1966), p. 111; extract also available at http://www.informationphilosopher.com/solutions/philosophers/taylorr/ (accessed 28 October 2014).

## Existentialism and freedom

**Existentialism** is a vast and varied philosophical school of thought. There are several different types of existentialism but focus largely on Sartre's atheist existentialism because it is the one that is the most radical when it comes to freedom.

**Main existentialist philosophers and their influences**

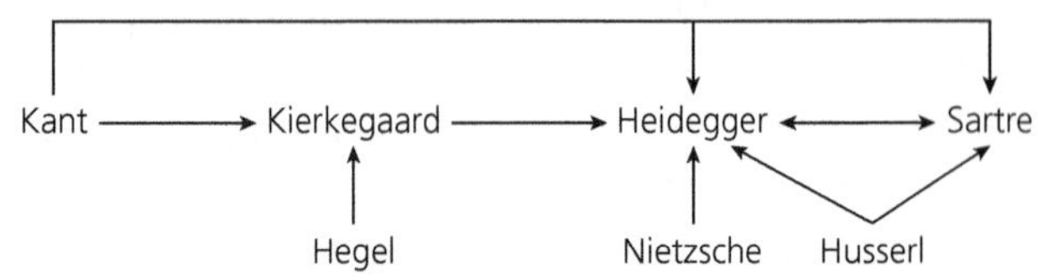


**Chronology**

**Philosophers who influenced existentialism**:

Pascal: 17th century

Kant: 18th century

Hegel: early 19th century

Nietzsche: late 19th century (arguably an existentialist philosopher himself)

Husserl: late 19th/early 20th centuries

**Main existentialist philosophers**:

Kierkegaard: 19th century

Heidegger: 20th century

Sartre: 20th century

### Questions

1. What is the main idea Taylor is trying to convey?
2. What are some of the ideas he is criticizing in this extract?
3. Why might it be difficult for determinists to accept Taylor's ideas on causation and agency?

### Main existentialist terms and ideas

Existentialism is difficult to define. However, there are some features and themes that are typical of various forms of existentialism. In short, existentialists are concerned with what **being** means for humans.

The first truly existentialist philosopher was Kierkegaard, a Christian existentialist. However, existentialism is most often associated with **atheism** (the belief that God does not exist). Some of the central themes of existentialism, like freedom and responsibility, seem even more acute if human beings are completely left to their own device, without a God.

Existentialism is a **postmodern** philosophical movement: it deconstructs, criticizes, and often rejects some of the pillars of modern philosophy such as the reliance on human reason and "objective values". As such, existentialism involves a move away from absolute claims based on religion, nature, human nature, or transcendent values like the forms in Plato's philosophy. Nothing is given from birth, nothing is innate, and nothing is given by religion (even for Christian existentialists): human beings are left to figure everything out on their own. Existentialists tend to see the loss of absolutes as a traumatic event. We have no ground to define ourselves or understand the **meaning** of our lives. Humanity is abandoned. Every single one of us is ultimately alone in our quest for values. We have to find our own meaning, alone. This generates anguish, **existential anxiety**, or what Sartre calls "**nausea**". This vocabulary is typical of existentialism and expresses the feeling of abandonment and lack of given meaning.

For existentialists, people's **identity** is not defined by a set of unchanging properties, but by the very way they change and develop through life. Therefore people *are* what they make of themselves. This involves great **responsibility**, but also great freedom. That notion of identity as what we make of ourselves is a very important point. According to existentialists, *we are what we do*, not what we could have done or wish to do. Again, it is a huge responsibility. We are self-creating beings. Each choice we make in life defines our identity.

Regarding freedom and determinism, existentialists stand on the side of freedom. Human beings are seen as free agents who must take full responsibility for their actions. Freedom is not an easy, light ability to do what we want: it is almost a burden, a responsibility we cannot escape. As Sartre wrote: "We are condemned to be free".[6]

## Biography: Jean-Paul Sartre (1905–1980)

Sartre was born in Paris in 1905 and was introduced to literature, mathematics, and philosophy at an early age by his grandfather. Sartre studied at the prestigious Ecole Normale Supérieure in Paris, where he met other future philosophers such as Raymond Aaron and Simone de Beauvoir. Beauvoir would become the love of his life, as well as an iconic and visionary feminist author.

Sartre himself quickly became an iconic figure in Parisian circles, and his fame grew all his life. Sartre was always politically active and he participated in socialist groups and publications, writing about current affairs and taking part in social movements from his student years until his death.

During the second world war, Sartre spent several months as a political prisoner. Interestingly, he planned his first major philosophical work while in captivity, and his philosophy became centred on the existence of free will. Sartre later claimed that he had never been so free as when he was a prisoner: he was put in a position of such meaningfulness that he saw it as a form of freedom. In addition, Sartre could choose how to view his situation, how to live that experience, how to describe it later and how to react to those who had imprisoned him. In other words, although he had lost his freedom of action, he kept his all-important perspective and freedom of will.

Sartre published his first major philosophical work, *Being and Nothingness*, two years after his release in 1943. Sartre's work was heavily influenced by Heidegger's *Being and Time*, an existentialist classic written 15 years earlier. In *Being and Nothingness*, Sartre lay down all the foundations of his existentialist philosophy and radical notion of freedom. *Being and Nothingness*, however, is a long and complex read, and Sartre's ideas became much more accessible when he published his lecture notes on the same topics, *Existentialism is a Humanism*, in 1946. Although Sartre refined and refuted some of his own ideas in later works such as *Critique of Dialectical Reason* (1960), *Existentialism is a Humanism* remains his most popular philosophical work thanks to its engaging simplicity.

Sartre was a prolific writer of philosophy, but also plays, short stories, novels, articles, and biographies. Works such as *No Exit* (a play) and *Nausea* (a novel) were designed as very engaging and efficient ways to explore existentialist themes without having to read complex philosophical texts.

Sartre received the Nobel Prize for Literature, which he refused, in 1964. Thanks to his controversial political activism and diverse body of work, Sartre was a real intellectual celebrity by the time he died in 1980. He remains one of the most important figures of 20th-century philosophy.

[6] For Sartre's original discussion, see Jean-Paul Sartre, *Being and Nothingness*, translated from the French by Hazel E. Barnes (New York: Philosophical Library, 1956).

## Radical freedom: Sartre

Sartre is one of the most important architects of atheist existentialism, along with Heidegger. Atheism is key in Sartre's philosophy: it alters one's whole perception of human life. The consequence of the complete absence of God and absolutes is that life is **absurd**, as it literally makes no sense (at least initially). There can be no external foundation for values and meaning: we choose those for our own lives and that choice is the only possible foundation.

Sartre's starting point is a belief that "*existence* comes before *essence* – or, if you will, that we must begin from the subjective".[7] This means that, as there is no God, there is no human nature and no given meaning of life. People exist before they are defined and determined: they are born with complete freedom and with the enormous task of creating their own essence. They do not discover the meaning of their life: they create it. Human beings must take complete responsibility for their own lives. Freedom is frightening and might not be what most people want to have to face.

According to Sartre, although there is no human nature, there is a **human condition** that he describes at length: human beings are *condemned to be free*, they cannot stop being free, and they are, therefore, infinitely responsible for their own destiny. This freedom comes from an ability to conceive of what is not the case (**nothingness**) and to desire it. We are able to envisage what is not and we are able to want it to be: we are intentional beings who project ourselves in the future and make plans (**being-for-itself**). This ability to conceive of what isn't the case is necessarily part of the human condition and human consciousness.

Human freedom is radical and double: it is a **freedom of mind** (to imagine what might be) and a **freedom of action** (to try to make it be). Psychological determinism is totally rejected with little regard for the possibility of the unconscious as a determining force. Even emotions are under our control. People can make themselves become a type of person, through some sort of training. The challenge of life is to build our personality without hiding behind excuses of what "makes us" behave in such or such a way. People have full responsibility for their actions and for who they are. Their childhood traumas, social circumstances and even genetic make-up should not be used as excuses not to take on that huge responsibility of building their identity through actions.

Our freedom is supreme and no excuse can be made not to exercise it. Even the way others perceive us is something that we can change. We are the creators of our own personality and image, and we should never use them as excuses. Statements such as "it isn't my fault if I am always late, that's just who I am" would horrify Sartre and existentialists! We are constantly making choices and we always have a choice. Even when we are just carrying on with the same routine we are choosing to do so, because we could always have chosen another path. In that sense, "[existentialism] confronts man with a possibility of choice".[8]

---

[7] Jean-Paul Sartre, *Existentialism and Humanism*, translated from the French by Philip Mairet (London: Methuen, 1948), p. 26.

[8] Ibid., p. 25.

Sartre would say that you make the choice to go to school or to work every day. You might feel like you have no choice because that is what society expects, or because your parents want you to, or because you need money, but you still have a choice. You choose to conform to what society expects, you choose to obey your parents, and you choose money over poverty and living in the street. These are choices too, choices you make every single day. We might not always be aware of the meaning of the choices we make (we might just be following the crowd) but we are still making choices. To refuse to make a choice is itself a choice constituting my identity. I am the totality of what I do, and therefore not doing something also constitutes my identity, in a negative way.

This radical freedom creates an anguish that does not come from external factors but from the fear that we might not be strong enough to make the "right" choices and to stick by them, as we are painfully aware that these choices entirely determine our identity. As we want to escape anguish, we are tempted to escape freedom but that is impossible. Hence the excuses we constantly make to try and justify our choices and behaviour. This is what Sartre calls **bad faith**. We pretend we are not free, lying to others and mainly to ourselves. The identities we assume have been chosen freely: we are like actors playing a part but we often end up believing (in bad faith) that we *are* the character we are playing. We might use the part as an excuse for our behaviour, as if the part weren't freely chosen in the first place.

Although human beings are radically free, they are thrown into a cultural, social, and historical context that constitutes their "**givenness**" (the circumstances they are born into). But humans have the ability to transcend this givenness by shaping their own identity through choice and action. To be human is to interpret our givenness, go beyond it, and achieve a certain degree of transcendence.

Although it is hard for philosophers who claim that there are no absolutes to prescribe anything, Sartre advocates that human beings turn away from bad faith and try to live more authentically, fully aware of their freedom, responsibility, and of the importance of each of their choices in the formation of their identity. The anguish generated by our freedom needs to be embraced rather than avoided, and our radical freedom needs to be affirmed and exercised consciously. Therefore, Sartre falls short of prescribing values, but he encourages certain attitudes towards our human condition: honesty, courage, responsibility, authenticity. Human beings must make a multitude of choices but also choose a general direction and project for their lives.

## Questions

1. Can you think of times when you made excuses for yourself (i.e. reasons for not doing your homework, reasons for being late, etc.) but when it was actually your fault?
2. What do you think would happen if everyone took responsibility for their actions instead of blaming them on external factors?
3. Do you agree that freedom can be a burden? Explain your answer.

Dostoevsky once wrote: "If God did not exist, everything would be permitted"; and that, for existentialism, is the starting point. Everything is indeed permitted if God does not exist, and man is in consequence forlorn, for he cannot find anything to depend upon either within or outside himself. He discovers forthwith, that he is without excuse. For if indeed existence precedes essence, one will never be able to explain one's action by reference to a given and specific human nature; in other words, there is no determinism – man is free, man *is* freedom. Nor, on the other hand, if God does not exist, are we provided with any values or commands that could legitimise our behaviour. Thus we have neither behind us, nor before us in a luminous realm of values, any means of justification or excuse. – We are left alone, without excuse. That is what I mean when I say that man is condemned to be free. Condemned, because he did not create himself, yet is nevertheless at liberty, and from the moment that he is thrown into this world he is responsible for everything he does. The existentialist does not believe in the power of passion. He will never regard a grand passion as a destructive torrent upon which a man is swept into certain actions as by fate, and which, therefore, is an excuse for them. He thinks that man is responsible for his passion. Neither will an existentialist think that a man can find help through some sign being vouchsafed upon earth for his orientation: for he thinks that the man himself interprets the sign as he chooses. He thinks that every man, without any support or help whatever, is condemned at every instant to invent man. As Ponge has written in a very fine article, "Man is the future of man." That is exactly true. Only, if one took this to mean that the future is laid up in Heaven, that God knows what it is, it would be false, for then it would no longer even be a future. If, however, it means that, whatever man may now appear to be, there is a future to be fashioned, a virgin future that awaits him – then it is a true saying. But in the present one is forsaken.

—Sartre[9]

## A few common criticisms (and counter-criticisms) of existentialism

Some authors consider that existentialism offers a wild, "anything-goes" kind of freedom. It verges on **nihilism** and its refusal to give any direction can be very unsettling.

Existentialism can seem particularly poor in terms of ethics as it seems to value individual freedom above the search for what is right or good. It is a very postmodern position: there is certain loss of values that breaks away from classical and modern philosophy. In fact, an authentic individual might well be a killer or a Nazi (it is interesting to note that Heidegger joined the Nazi party and that Sartre was a radical communist for some time: there is obviously no consistency in existentialism, given that their philosophies were so close to each other).

However, the self-formation that existentialism encourages stems from ancient philosophies (Greeks, Stoics, etc.) and is not supposed to lead to self-absorption or lack of concern for others. On the contrary, people are encouraged to teach themselves how to be better people with others in mind. Being authentic should help people be more comfortable

### FIND OUT MORE

For a good summary and interesting links:

**http://www2.sunysuffolk.edu/pecorip/SCCCWEB/ETEXTS/INTRO_TEXT/Chapter%207%20Freedom/Freedom_Existentialism.htm**

For more information about Sartre's notion of bad faith (podcast):

**http://philosophybites.com/2009/02/sebastian-gardner-on-jeanpaul-sartre-on-bad-faith.html**

9 Sartre, *Existentialism Is a Humanism*, reproduced from http://www.marxists.org/reference/archive/sartre/works/exist/sartre.htm (accessed 28 October 2014).

with themselves and therefore with others, making better and more consistent decisions.

Existentialism also calls for honesty and therefore for an individual judgment: an authentic being will be unable to blame others for her behaviour. She will have to consider the consequences of her actions and will make each choice with the conscience that her essence is being formed by her actions. Excuses like "that's just who I am" or "I had a difficult childhood" cannot be used. The authentic person will be used to living with full awareness of her responsibility.

Most existentialists insist on the importance of society and community, even if individuals also need to be independent. Refusing to blend in with the crowd and to systematically make the choices that are dictated by society is very different from refusing to take others into account at all.

Finally, the notions of independence and responsibility, which can be seen as the most important legacy of existentialism, are values in themselves and would probably encourage people to act in a more ethical way.

Another criticism is that existentialists are too worried about death and their philosophy is morbid. However, a counter-criticism is that death is a reality for all humans and needs to be addressed and confronted as an issue. It would be naive or deceitful to pretend that death is not a huge concern for most humans, especially for those who do not believe in God or in any kind of life after death.

Others accuse existentialists of being too emotional and of being "irrationalists". They try to exacerbate human emotions of anxiety and helplessness, denying the importance of reasoning for the human race. However, some of these criticisms are based on stereotypical ideas about existentialism. The origin of these criticisms is often the fact that existentialism is rather a dramatic philosophy, because it is trying to shake people out of their complacent ways in order to make them react and seek authenticity. According to most existentialists, strong emotions are required in order to give up the facticity of ordinary everyday life.

Some authors also portray existentialism as a philosophy according to which everything is absurd. This is, again, a stereotypical view: atheist existentialists believe existence is absurd in the sense that there is no given meaning. It is up to the individual to give meaning to his or her life and world. There is meaning, but it is just not pre-given or predetermined.

One of the most problematic criticisms for existentialists is the claim that existentialism is a bourgeois and elitist philosophy. The focus on existential anxiety can mask much bigger suffering. People are only able to feel and concentrate on their existential anxiety if they're not actually really suffering or fighting for survival. In other words, people who are trying to find something to eat certainly have no time to worry about the meaning of their life. According to Marxist criticisms, existential anxiety might just be typical of those who belong to the bourgeoisie and not at all a feature of the whole human race. Existentialism might just be a luxury for intellectuals and academics. The idea of authenticity is out of touch with most of the world population's worries.

Finally, it could be argued that existentialism has become an untenable position given how much we now know about the factors that determine us. Heidegger and Sartre had very little knowledge about the way the brain functions or the devastating (and very physical) effects of an abusive childhood. The following extract illustrates how it may seem difficult to reconcile existentialism with contemporary knowledge:

Because existentialism and ethic of personal responsibility appeal to some people due to their nature, those people embrace existentialism and personal responsibility and expect others to do so. Their existentialism by definition precludes them from recognising or acknowledging that non-existentialists are not of a nature such that they can embrace or practise existentialism. This leads to unrealistic expectations on the part of existentialists. Their own seeming transcendence of their nature is in fact an expression of their nature, but they nonetheless expect other people to be able to do the very same thing despite lacking natures favourable to self-transcendence. The typical existentialist response to the existence of these inherently non-existentialist individuals is one of condemnation – their unwillingness to take personal responsibility is deemed an intellectual or moral failing, when in fact it is a consequence of their nature, as immutable as the existentialist's own ability to decide to see a situation or a fact in a different light. A person inclined to self-transcendence is every bit as locked into that behaviour as a person who is disinclined is locked into disinclination.

What is the result? The widespread belief by those with the inherent natural psychological ability to overcome difficult upbringings or unfavourable genetic backgrounds that those who don't have failed to take responsibility and are themselves deficient. This leads to a lack of sympathy and a lack of compassion, and our political policies reflect the dominance of the existentialist ideology. Those who are poor are assumed to be lacking in virtue or initiative due to incompetence, immorality, or irresponsibility rather than a nature and upbringing that not only makes success difficult, but makes choosing to transcend said nature and upbringing difficult, if not biologically and psychologically impossible.

This existentialist belief that denies nature altogether either denies neuroscience and asserts that consciousness comes from something immaterial or requires that our brains act independently of their own structure. In either case, it is extremely unreasonable, and leads to equally unreasonable consequential beliefs that require the impossible from one's fellow man. It is self-delusive and a philosophical dead end. It leads to a total misunderstanding of the nature of man and of man's possibilities. It would be wise to put it aside and resume the age old discussion of what elements in man's nature are most critical in understanding what man's limits are and how man can best organise societies and projects in consequence of and in accordance with those limits. It is no more sensible to reject man's behavioural limits than it is to reject man's inability to fly or subsist underwater. Better to recognise those limits and devise tools and structures that help us to surmount them than to jump off of cliffs and hope to will ourselves to survive the splat.

—Benjamin Studebaker[10]

[10] Benjamin Studebaker, "A Critique of Existentialism", 5 September 2012; available at http://benjaminstudebaker.com/2012/09/05/a-critique-of-existentialism/ (accessed 28 October 2014).

## Questions

1. Which of the criticisms above do you think is the most damaging for existentialism, and why?
2. What are the positive things we can learn from existentialism?

## "Nature versus nurture": comparing the influence of social determinism to that of biological determinism

When studying freedom, philosophers also often spend a great deal of time thinking about what may limit it. There are many forms of determinism, and many factors that may influence our behaviour and threaten our freedom. In the rest of this chapter, we will have an in-depth look at two major factors: biology and society.

"Is it nature or nurture?" is a phrase you have most probably heard many times before, as the nature versus nurture debate has been one of the most prominent and popular debates in the history of ideas. "Nature" refers to biological influences and "nurture" to social influences and, in particular, education. The nature versus nurture debate is therefore closely related to the two types of determinism we will focus on in this chapter.

Understanding that this debate has framed many ideas for centuries is important because it can help you place certain philosophical theories in their context. When Rousseau developed his theory of the state of nature, for instance, he wanted to show that human corruption was caused by "nurture" and not "nature". Darwin, on the other hand, would have argued that human beings owe many of their traits to "nature" because they have inherited them biologically: human societies may reflect human beings, but they do not shape them to the same extent as "nature" does. As for Sartre, he believed that "nature" had very little to do with human beings: they are ultimately free beings, although they often give up their freedom to give in to society and "nurture". Those ideas are therefore useful ones and can definitely aid comprehension.

Traditionally, the two notions were presented as mutually exclusive: behaviours and personality traits were presented as either influenced by "nature" or by "nurture". However, this view has now become rather obsolete and recent research tends to suggest that nature and nurture are much more integrated than was previously thought.

## Focus topic 1: biological determinism

Biological determinism is the theory according to which our choices and actions are often strongly influenced by aspects of our biology. These can include the structure and functioning of our brain, hormones, genes, and evolutionary traits that have been passed down from our ancestors.

Recent discoveries in the fields of neuroscience and genetics make it very difficult to deny that biology influences our behaviour. The extent to which this influence encroaches on our freedom, however, remains an open question. Does our biology merely give us natural tendencies that we can choose to follow or resist, or does it compel us to act in ways we cannot truly control?

You will get a chance to explore this question in this section, as we examine biological explanations of behaviours and emotions such as attraction, impulsiveness, and aggressiveness.

## Human beings, animals, and instinct: before Darwin

For a long time, human beings seemed to believe that they were a separate species from the rest of the animal kingdom and didn't think of themselves as animals. This is exemplified in the Creation stories of many traditions, and is particularly obvious in the Judeo-Christian account of Creation.

Abrahamic faiths (Judaism, Christianity, Islam) share a common understanding of the Creation and man's place in the natural world. Although the following extract is from the Torah and therefore Judeo-Christian, the Islamic tradition is very similar when it comes to the Creation story:

> Then God said, "Let us make mankind in our image, in our likeness, so that they may rule over the fish in the sea and the birds in the sky, over the livestock and all the wild animals, and over all the creatures that move along the ground."
>
> So God created mankind in his own image, in the image of God he created them; male and female he created them.
>
> God blessed them and said to them, "Be fruitful and increase in number; fill the earth and subdue it. Rule over the fish in the sea and the birds in the sky and over every living creature that moves on the ground."
>
> Then God said, "I give you every seed-bearing plant on the face of the whole earth and every tree that has fruit with seed in it. They will be yours for food. And to all the beasts of the earth and all the birds in the sky and all the creatures that move along the ground—everything that has the breath of life in it—I give every green plant for food." And it was so.
>
> Genesis 1:26–30 (NIV)

In Genesis 2, Adam gets to name all the other animals God has created, again showing that he is different from them. In the Islamic tradition, angels bow down before Adam, emphasizing the special status God has given human beings.

One of the important implications of these Creation stories is that human beings, because they were set apart from animals, may not be subjected to the same rules. So, while it is generally accepted that animals have basic instincts and needs that determine their behaviour, human beings are often seen as having the ability to rise above their instincts and free themselves from their bodily needs.

Ancient Greek philosophers such as Plato reinforced the idea that human beings have a unique ability to control their "animal" instincts, unlike other animals. Human beings do have a body that belongs to the natural world and wants to behave in an animalistic way, but they also have a soul that belongs to a higher world and is able to control the body, or at least rein in its instincts.

Later, Descartes also made a radical distinction between animals and human beings, claiming that animals are little more than machines, whereas human beings are defined by their mind, an immaterial entity that is essentially different from the body and superior to it in every way.

The soul, spirit, or mind is where human freedom resides: in the Western, dualistic tradition, the body is often likened to a material prison, subjected to the laws of nature, whereas the mind is free from such laws and able to control itself.

In the Judeo-Christian tradition, free will is granted by God and is, essentially, what differentiates human beings from animals. In the Platonic tradition, freedom belongs to the immaterial and ideal world of forms and is present in human beings' souls. In the Cartesian tradition, freedom comes with the mind and its ability to think. In all cases, freedom forms an integral part of what distinguishes human beings from animals, and what makes them superior to the rest of nature. That is why the distinction between animals and humans is so important: closing the gap between animals and humans is compromising, and perhaps even negating, the possibility of human freedom.

## Darwin

Closing the gap between animals and humans is exactly what Darwin did, which explains why his ideas were – and still are, in some instances – met with such fierce resistance.

Darwin knew that his ideas about animal evolution would be controversial, if only because they went directly against a literal reading of the Genesis Creation story: while Genesis claims that animals were created in two days and that God was pleased with his work, evolution requires millions of years of trial and error before getting to the animals we see around us today.

The controversy regarding animals, however, was nothing in comparison to what Darwin would face when applying his theory to human beings. That is probably why he chose to avoid the subject of human evolution altogether when he first outlined his theory in *On the Origin of Species* (1859). The only sentence he included about human beings was: "Light will be thrown on the origin of man and his history."[11] That small sentence already set critics ablaze!

[11] Darwin, *On the Origin of Species*; available at http://darwin-online.org.uk/content/frameset?itemID=F373&viewtype=text&pageseq=1 (accessed 21 October 2014).

## Philosophical terms and theories

### Darwin's theory of evolution

Darwin was a 19th-century British naturalist who was made famous by his revolutionary theory of evolution. After discovering that certain animal species seemed to have adapted to their surroundings by developing traits that helped them survive in a particular environment, Darwin came up with a new hypothesis. According to Darwin, there are natural, random variations within species (i.e. imagine that some early antelopes were faster than others thanks to specific physical traits like large lungs and padded hooves). Some of these variations are an advantage, because they help individuals survive and reproduce in a particular environment (i.e. faster antelopes can escape predators more efficiently). Through a process Darwin called natural selection, the individuals with the most advantageous traits survive and reproduce, while others die or fail to reproduce: this is also known as the "survival of the fittest" (the fittest antelopes are the fastest ones, and they survive better than the slower ones that are caught by predators). More individuals are born than can possibly survive, which creates a competition for survival that will see the fittest, best-adapted individuals survive. As the individuals with the advantageous traits thrive, they reproduce with each other and pass down their traits (large lungs, padded hooves, etc.) to their offspring. Through this process, undesirable traits are gradually eliminated (smaller lungs, hard hooves, etc.), while more advantageous ones are kept. Although the traits are passed down through genes, it is important to remember that Darwin had no idea about genes, as they were not discovered until later and genetic explanations were only merged with evolutionary explanations at the beginning of the 20th century.

Though the end result may give the impression that animals – and indeed, human beings – have been *designed* to fit in their environment perfectly, evolution really needs no designer: the process is random and indiscriminate. What we observe now is the result of millions of years of evolution, which involved the death and disappearance of countless individuals and species.

It took Darwin over a decade to write about the logical extension of his theory to human beings in *The Descent of Man* (1870), a book that caused much scandal at the time. Some of Darwin's most fervent supporters suddenly deserted him, unable to accept what Darwin was saying: human beings are animals. They share a common ancestry with all other animals and are nothing more than animals themselves. They might be a very well-evolved species, but they remain animals.

One of the implications is that human beings are, to an extent, determined by nature: they are part of the larger process of evolution and a result of that process. It means that human beings have developed traits and characteristics that helped them survive and that have been passed down from generation to generation. All human beings are therefore born with certain traits that influence their behaviour and are out of their control. It is in that sense that they are determined.

Darwinism has redefined what being human means, grounding human beings more firmly in nature and amongst other animals. Being human is no longer being detached from nature and being able to transcend it: instead, nature becomes a possible explanation for much of what we are and what we do. Some of the actions that make us feel and think we are free could in fact be the result of natural tendencies that have been fine-tuned over generations.

### FIND OUT MORE

For an in-depth analysis of some of the implications of Darwinism for philosophy, watch the following video:

**http://www.open.edu/openlearn/history-in-the-arts/culture/philosophy/darwin-and-philosophy**

## Case study: evolutionary psychology and the science of attraction

Evolutionary psychology is a branch of psychology that can provide plenty of examples of human behaviour that has evolved through the process of natural selection and passed down from our ancestors. A lot of psychologists, for instance, are interested in the way we are attracted to the opposite sex and the evolutionary factors that can influence our choice of a "mate". Although we feel like we are making a conscious choice when we select a boyfriend or girlfriend, this might not be the case after all.

In a 2011 article, Anthony C. Little et al. reviewed current research on the facial traits that we tend to find attractive for evolutionary reasons. "Theoretically", they write, "preferences guide us to choose mates who will provide the best chance of our genes surviving".[12] Some facial characteristics may give us clues about the genetic quality and health of potential mates, and we may have evolved to pick those clues up in order to make the best decision. For these reasons, some facial features can seem particularly attractive. Some studies, for instance, suggest that facial symmetry is attractive because it could be an indicator of genetic strength. Other studies focus on "averageness" as an indicator of genetic diversity, which is more attractive to us than the more extreme facial features that tend to characterize less genetically varied individuals.

While there are more facial traits that we find attractive, most seem to suggest that the tastes and preferences that we think make us so unique are in fact genetically inherited to help us make the choices that will keep our offspring strong and competitive.

### FIND OUT MORE

To read the full article and explore other facial features that are supposed to be attractive for evolutionary reasons, visit

**http://www.ncbi.nlm.nih.gov/pmc/articles/PMC3130383/**

Another good example is the research that Andrew J. Elliot and Daniela Niesta conducted in 2008, concluding that men naturally tend to find women who wear red more attractive! The discussion surrounding their research was again strongly linked to evolutionary psychology and, therefore, to the idea that we are – at least partly – determined by nature (in the sense that nature and evolution have shaped our behaviour beyond what we are conscious and aware of):

> For human females, ovulation is not advertised in a conspicuous manner, but researchers are beginning to document the presence of subtle physiological, psychological, and behavioral markers of reproductive status. As with other female primates, women's estrogen–progesterone ratio is elevated near ovulation, which enhances blood flow.

[12] Anthony C. Little, Benedict C. Jones, and Lisa M. DeBruine, "Facial Attractiveness: Evolutionary Based Research", *Philosophical Transactions of the Royal Society B: Biological Sciences* 366, No. 1571 (12 June 2012): 1640; available at http://www.ncbi.nlm.nih.gov/pmc/articles/PMC3130383/ (accessed 28 October 2014).

In addition, women's general skin tone lightens mid-cycle, and women near ovulation tend to wear clothing that leaves more skin visible). Furthermore, women at mid-cycle report more sexual interest and are more easily sexually aroused, meaning the red blush of flirtation and the red flush of sexual excitation are more prevalent at this time. As such, it is likely that women, like other female primates, display red more often and more prominently when nearing ovulation. We also think it reasonable to posit that men, like their more primitive male relatives, are predisposed to interpret a display of red by a female conspecific as a sexual signal and to respond accordingly.

In sum, red is clearly linked to sex in the context of heterosexual interaction, and this link is viewed as emerging from both societal use of red and a biologically engrained predisposition to red. These two sources may contribute to the red–sex link in joint fashion. That is, we posit that the societal use of red is not random, but actually derives from the biologically based predisposition to perceive red as a sexual signal. For example, the aforementioned use of red lipstick and rouge may represent, at least in some instances, an attempt to mimic the vascularization present during ovulation and sexual excitation. Likewise, red may be used in red-light districts because it is the color that appears on the aroused female body. As these examples illustrate, the societal use of red can be seen as not only reinforcing the inherent meaning of red, but also as extending the application of this meaning beyond the tether of natural bodily processes. Thus, we posit that for men, red not only carries sexual meaning when displayed on a woman's body via vascularization, but also when displayed artificially on a woman's body with cosmetics and when exhibited on her clothing, accessories, or even in close proximity to her person.[13]

The reasons we have to choose a partner may seem free and personal to us, but research like that mentioned above suggests otherwise. The suggestion is that our biology determines our choices to a large extent, without our being aware of the influences that are at play. Philosophically, this is highly significant as it directly challenges the idea that we are entirely free to make our own choices.

**Questions**

1. Do you think the choice of a partner is as determined by "nature" as is claimed by evolutionary psychology? What role do you think "nurture" plays in such a choice?
2. Do you think evolutionary explanations of behaviour leave room for human freedom? In other words, is it possible to take a soft determinist approach and believe in both free will and evolutionary influences?

## Biological determinism in individuals

One of the features of evolutionary explanations is that they tend to focus on the human race as a species, and therefore as a whole. Evolutionary traits we have inherited are human traits that we

[13] Andrew J. Elliot and Daniela Niesta, "Romantic Red: Red Enhances Men's Attraction to Women", *Journal of Personality and Social Psychology* 95, No. 5 (2008): 1151.

share, despite some variations, and they can help us understand human nature.

This brings a new question: if human beings share evolutionary traits that unite them as a species, why are individuals still so different from one another? Even when people come from the same area, and are therefore the product of the same survival needs, they still seem to have a unique personality.

We sometimes assume that individuality is the mark of human freedom; that, despite being from the same species, we still have the freedom to behave like individuals, make our own choices, and build our own personality. It is an attractive explanation! However, biological determinists have their own, simple explanation: we are biologically and genetically unique, which gives us individuality. In the same way that our genes give us a unique physical appearance, they also give us an individual personality, and that personality may well be entirely determined by biology. In other words, individuality is not necessarily a sign of freedom.

This kind of biological determinism is philosophically significant, because it suggests that we do not build our personality out of free choice but that many of our traits are actually predetermined. This does not necessarily mean that we are entirely pre-programmed to act in a certain, fully predictable way, but that we have *tendencies* to act in a certain way. The philosophical problem here is to determine **the extent to which these tendencies affect our free will**. The greater influence they have, the less freedom we possess.

In recent years, many research studies have been conducted to look for a direct link between one biological factor and a certain type of behaviour or personality trait. Scientists have made claims about the biological roots of everything from addiction, homosexuality, and intelligence, to impulsive behaviour, attention disorders, and depression. Criminal behaviour is an area of research that has been of particular interest to scientists, and has captured the mind of the public.

## Case study: criminal behaviour

### Stimulus 3

Composite portraits showing "features common among men convicted of crimes of violence", by Francis Galton, with original photographs.[14]

[14] See DNA Learning Centre, "Criminals' Common Features, F. Galton", available at http://www.dnalc.org/view/15781-Criminals-common-features-F-Galton.html (28 October 2014).

In the late 19th century, Francis Galton (1822–1911) – who was, incidentally, Darwin's cousin – invented a new technique allowing the layering and combination of different photographs. He used his technique to combine portraits of criminals, hoping he could help identify facial features of the "typical" criminal.

Physiognomy, the discipline that establishes links between people's appearance and their personality, was popular at the time, and many researchers tried to find scientific roots for it. The belief that criminals were born with certain facial features that could help identify them was widespread, suggesting that some people were "natural born criminals". Physiognomy strongly supported biological determinism, since it was based on the idea that character and physical traits were innate as well as ultimately linked.

As no one managed to identify features that could predict criminal activity or other behaviours accurately, and as theories of human rights and equality spread in the 20th century, physiognomy was gradually abandoned.

Today, however, there is a resurgence of scientific theories linking biological factors to criminal behaviour:

- In 1989, Markku Linnoila established a link between low levels of **serotonin** (one of the chemicals responsible for passing messages between neurons in the brain) and impulsive behaviour. Linnoila studied over 1,000 arsonists in the mental institutions and prisons of New York. He found that those who had committed crimes impulsively, acting before they could think, had low levels of serotonin. On the other hand, criminals who had planned their actions and had "reasons" to turn to crime, such as the need for money, had normal levels of serotonin. Serotonin helps people control their impulses, and those with low serotonin can literally be "out of control". In 2000, Dee Higley made a very similar discovery, but this time on monkeys: those with low levels of serotonin were more likely to take risks, act impulsively, and hurt themselves through reckless behaviour and fights.
- In 1994, Adrian Raine conducted another study on prisoners, this time comparing the brain scans of 41 murderers with those of "normal" citizens. Raine discovered that the scans of murderers showed much less activity in the **prefrontal cortex** than the normal scans. The prefrontal cortex, much like serotonin, helps us control our emotions and impulses. It is responsible for decision-making, planning, problem-solving and moral reasoning. In later studies, Raine also established that some murderers not only had less activity in certain areas of the brain, but even suffered from a reduction in grey matter: in other words, their brains functioned differently, but were also physically different from normal brains.
- In 2009, finally, Rose McDermott focused on genetics and studied the ***MAOA* gene**, also commonly called the "warrior" gene. Scientists have claimed that those who have the low-activity form of the *MAOA* gene – and those missing the gene altogether – are more likely to be aggressive. McDermott conducted a study based on participants taking revenge on strangers for taking their money. Participants were led to believe that they could give unpleasant spicy sauce to the culprits as punishment

(though everything was done remotely and the "thieves" were actually imaginary). McDermott found that, when they believed a large amount of money had been taken from them, participants carrying the low-activity form of the *MAOA* gene were more than twice as likely to administer the maximum amount of "punishment" as those carrying the high-activity form of the gene. In other words, she established a direct link between a certain gene and aggressive behaviour.

**TOK and Optional Theme LInk: Ethics**

When reporting on Rose McDermott's study on the "warrior" gene, for instance, some journalists simplified findings to point out that the form of the gene that is linked with aggressive behaviour is not evenly distributed around the world: while only about half of "Westerners" carry the gene in question, as many as two-thirds of people carry it in areas that have been plagued by warfare.

What are some of the ethical implications of research into genetics and behaviour?

## EXERCISE

Before you read the following section, try to list some of the philosophical and practical implications of the kind of research listed above.

## Some philosophical and practical implications

The philosophical implications of establishing biological foundations for criminal behaviour are far-reaching. Some of these implications are very practical ones and highlight the very real impact philosophy can have on society. Lawmakers and policymakers can take completely different paths depending on their philosophical perspective.

### Freedom

First of all, there is the issue of freedom we have been focusing on. If an individual is born with key brain areas that are impaired, with low serotonin, or with the low-activity form of the *MAOA* gene, he or she will have a tendency to behave in an impulsive, perhaps even aggressive manner. This raises many philosophical questions. For instance, how difficult is it for such an individual to resist those natural tendencies? Imagine that a man possesses all three biological factors, for instance, to what extent will he be able to control his behaviour? In other words, how much freedom is left over once natural tendencies are taken into account? Some philosophers and psychologists argue that people are always, ultimately, able to exercise free will and choose one path over another. It may be more difficult for some because of their biological make-up, but an element of free choice is always present. Others, however, would point out that a strong willpower may also be the result of a combination of biological elements, making the ability to resist temptation just as determined as other behaviours. In other words, the man who resists his aggressive urges may choose to do so out of his own free will, or may have a set of genes and brain traits that counterbalance his aggressive tendencies efficiently. The ability to resist some of our own tendencies may not be the expression of free will, but another determined trait. It seems very hard to know exactly where freedom ends, and whether there is much room left for it or not.

While we can speculate blindly about what really causes behaviour, many of the gaps in our knowledge are being filled by psychological and neurobiological research, and this research sometimes seems to be squeezing freedom out of the equation. The more we know about the biological factors that influence human behaviour, the more we may be tempted to think that freedom only plays a small, or even non-existent, role in our choices.

Still, most people are reluctant to let go of the idea of human freedom. This brings up another set of important questions: why are we so unwilling to give up human freedom? What are the philosophical and practical consequences of a hard determinist view?

## Ethical and social implications: responsibility and punishment

Here, again, the example of criminal behaviour can help answer those questions. One of the main problems with hard biological determinism is that it eliminates the notion of responsibility. Indeed, if people have no real freedom to act, they cannot be held responsible for their actions. The man whose brain or genes "make him" act violently may be no more to blame than the man who is forced to be violent because someone has put a gun to his head. This possibility means that we may need to rethink the reasons why we punish criminals, and the way we do so. Should criminals who are diagnosed with brain, hormonal, or genetic abnormalities be punished as severely as if they were in control of their actions? Should they be treated like patients rather than criminals? Should punishment be retribution or simply a way for society to protect itself? Could treatments be found to help people with abnormal biological traits stay away from crime?

Raine, the British psychologist (mentioned earlier) who discovered a correlation between certain brain patterns and criminal behaviour, addressed some of these questions in a webcast filmed at the University of Pennsylvania. Here is an extract from the transcript:

One of the challenges that society is facing with new neuroscience knowledge is how we deal with prisoners who have a brain basis to their behaviour... One brief example: I defended a murderer and rapist who killed and raped a wonderful young woman in Colorado. We brain-scanned him using the same techniques we had used to brain-scan the other 41 murderers with, and we showed that he had much poorer functioning in the prefrontal cortex; that emergency brake on behaviour [was] just not there in that individual. But where do we go with that? This man was found guilty of first-degree deliberate murder, but the three-judge panel who decide punishment did not execute him, they did not give him the death penalty. They brought in the brain-imaging data and they also brought in his awful psycho-social history... Really, all the boxes were checked on this individual, he had all the social deficits, the family deficits, the brain deficits: he was a walking time-bomb waiting to explode. Is it any surprise he goes and kills and rapes somebody? So he didn't get the worst punishment, but is that really just? Where do we balance mercy with justice? Because, in a way, if you buy into the argument I gave in court, aren't you going to buy into anything? If you do something wrong, there's a reason why you do something wrong, there's always a cause. Is that going to excuse your behaviour, my behaviour, everyone else's behaviour? That's one of the issues that we're having to face with now...

Just one last point: it's not a "throw away the key" approach. Yes, there is a biological basis to crime and violence, at least in part, but that doesn't mean we throw away the key. There are beginning clues to how we might be able to, if you like, repair the brain, partly at least, of antisocial violent offenders. For example, one study gave fish oil to prisoners and, after five months, they showed much reduction in violent offending within the prison; and there are several other studies of aggressive behaviour in children showing that fish oil Omega 3 can reduce aggressive behaviour... We know Omega 3 is critical for brain structure and brain function... Could it be in the future that there are treatments for the brain bases to antisocial and violent behaviour that we are currently uncovering?

That's in the future. Right now, we've got to deal with those difficult issues about how do we deal, in court, with individuals who have all the biological, genetic and social boxes checked: are they truly responsible for their actions? Do they know, in terms of feelings, the difference between right and wrong? How moral is it of us to punish them as harshly as we do if they lack the neural circuitry underlying appropriate moral decision-making?

## Questions

1. Identify one hard-determinist argument and one soft-determinist argument outlined in Adrian Raine's speech.
2. What factor, besides biological factors, does Raine identify to help explain violent criminal behaviour?
3. Can you spot one contradiction in Raine's speech?
4. Identify one example that shows that biological determinism can actually help change people's behaviour, instead of accepting it as fixed.

## FIND OUT MORE

Watch the full webcast on

**http://www.youtube.com/watch?v=uzGfZaI6itg**

### A counter-argument: Taylor's take on psychology and determinism

I then thought I must find out more about psychology. There was certainly an abundance of books on this subject, and I thought that if any people actually know something about human nature they must surely be found among the authors of those books. I found, however, that the questions that interested me were simply ignored by these writers, that ever so many interesting things were said about brains and nerves and glands, all the names of these being duly given, and about conditioning and reflexes and the like, but nothing whatever about things so elementary as, say, a voluntary act of choice. It seemed almost as if there were a conspiracy in this branch of psychology to pretend that such things do not exist; or at least, not unless they could be twisted to resemble the model of an electrical circuit or exhibited in the perfectly comprehensible picture of a stimulus and a response. Psychological works, on the other hand, which dealt with practical problems of human motivation, with neurosis and the like, far from pretending that the questions that interested me did not exist, simply took them all for granted, speaking unabashedly of goals, freedom, the ego, and so on, with hardly the least hint of an attempt to connect these things with what was described in the aforementioned books. It seemed that these diverse approaches had almost nothing whatever in common except the name of them, that between them there yawned an abyss of human ignorance, and that, alas! it was in that vast *terra incognita* that all my philosophical torments lay.[15]

- What problems does Taylor, a contemporary philosopher, identify with a strictly psychological approach to human behaviour?

### TOK link

What does this tell you about the difference between psychology and philosophy as areas of knowledge? What questions do they respectively deal with? In what ways can knowledge be enhanced and impaired by mixing the two disciplines?

[15] Taylor, *Action and Purpose*, p. viii; also available at http://www.informationphilosopher.com/solutions/philosophers/taylorr/ (accessed 28 October 2014). http://www.informationphilosopher.com/solutions/philosophers/taylorr/

## Further ethical and philosophical considerations: are some individuals more determined than others?

As we have seen, whereas Darwinism tends to focus on the characteristics of each species, more modern discoveries have highlighted the differences that exist between people.

This leads us to an ethical and philosophical consideration raised by research into biology and criminal behaviour. This type of research tends to focus on abnormal behaviour, providing explanations for it. Although "normal" subjects are used for comparison and control purposes, their "normal" behaviour rarely seems to be explained, because it is seen as not requiring an explanation. Philosophically, this is significant because it can give the impression that "abnormal" behaviour is more biologically determined than "normal" behaviour. While criminals are viewed as individuals who cannot escape their biology and are compelled to act by factors such as low serotonin or brain abnormalities, non-criminals are not described as being compelled by anything. If this is the case and non-criminals really are freer than criminals, because they are not subjected to the same tyranny of a defective biological make-up, what could be the consequences for the human race? We live in an era where equality between human beings – a relatively recent notion – is taken for granted in many countries. People may be unequal in practice, for many reasons, but we like to think that they are equal *in theory*: they are of equal worth, because they are all human beings. Being human is the only condition and it grants everyone equality.

Once we start unpacking what a human being actually is, however, this becomes problematic. Do we grant equality and worth to all individuals simply because they are of the same biological species? Or do we grant them equality and worth because they are *persons*? If personhood is the criterion, rather than simple biological humanity, what are the elements that make someone a person? Free will and agency are usually considered important parts of personhood. Does this mean, then, that people who are less free, like biologically determined criminals, have less personhood, or even humanity, than others? Are they, therefore, not really as worthy of the equality and value we usually grant other human beings?

These questions could apply to any of the qualities that form part of personhood and humanity, and lead us to another, bigger question: should all human beings be considered equal, regardless of the extent to which they possess the qualities that define humanity? Perhaps an inclusive answer could think of all human beings and persons as *potentially* free, rational, moral, and so on. Individuals may only possess some of those qualities, and no human will possess them all to their higher degree: imperfection and incompleteness are definitely very human traits! In that sense, people who have less control over their own behaviour can be seen as possessing the same degree of personhood and humanity as the most free individuals of all.

There is another way to approach this, though perhaps not quite as attractive to most people: rather than seeing criminals as less free than non-criminals, it may make more sense to see all individuals as biologically determined in different ways. Just as some criminals are naturally destined to be impulsive and violent, non-criminals are simply biologically determined to have a calmer, more rational approach. This does not mean they are free. High serotonin or a well-functioning prefrontal cortex may give the illusion that some individuals make free choices after considering all options, but hard biological determinists would simply say that they are just as determined as those "out of control" criminals: determined to take the more sensible and peaceful route and perhaps, even, determined to feel free.

### ACTIVITY

#### Getting back to the "nature versus nurture" debate

One major problem with biologically deterministic approaches is that they tend to be reductionist: they focus on one type of explanation (biology) and ignore other possible factors.

In the case of criminal behaviour, for instance, "nurture" (sociocultural factors) is also crucially important.

Later in this chapter, we will study some of the social factors that tend to lead to criminal behaviour. In the meantime, draw up your own list of factors that are not biological but that could lead to criminal behaviour.

## Focus topic 2: social determinism

Social determinism is the theory according to which people's choices and behaviours are strongly influenced by their social and cultural environment. Social influences include family values, the education we receive at home and at school, the area we live in, the religious and cultural groups we belong to, our friendship groups, the media, and so on. In the past, social determinism was very much based on geography and social status: the main influences in people's lives were the values present in the area they lived in and the local social circles they belonged to. Today, however, the internet and the globalization of the media mean that a much wider range of social factors and values, including those we come into virtual contact with, can also influence us.

According to social determinists, the sociocultural web of influences is a particularly inescapable one, because it is everywhere around us and seems "normal" to us. We tend to adopt values and behaviours from the society that surrounds us without being aware of it, all the while convinced that we are freely choosing one set of values over another. Could it be that our most intimate beliefs and convictions are simply the product of the environment we live in? How much freedom do we exercise when we "choose" the values that form our personality and dictate our behaviour?

In this section, you will explore the philosophies of Rousseau and Marx, the "nature versus nurture" debate, as well as contemporary examples such as the social construction of gender.

## EXERCISE

1. Make a spider diagram of all the social and cultural factors that may influence you. Thinking about all the different groups you belong to may be a good start.
2. To what extent do you think these influences define you as a person?

### Stimulus 4: extract from *The Great Gatsby* (1925)

In this extract, Gatsby, a millionaire who was born poor, tells the narrator how he met Daisy, a "nice" girl – meaning a girl who was born in the upper social classes. Gatsby and Daisy's personalities are intimately linked to their social status, a status from which they never manage to free themselves.

She was the first "nice" girl he had ever known. In various unrevealed capacities he had come in contact with such people but always with indiscernible barbed wire between. He found her excitingly desirable. He went to her house, at first with other officers from Camp Taylor, then alone. It amazed him—he had never been in such a beautiful house before. But what gave it an air of breathless intensity was that Daisy lived there—it was as casual a thing to her as his tent out at camp was to him...

But he knew that he was in Daisy's house by a colossal accident. However glorious might be his future as Jay Gatsby, he was at present a penniless young man without a past, and at any moment the invisible cloak of his uniform might slip from his shoulders. So he made the most of his time. He took what he could get, ravenously and unscrupulously—eventually he took Daisy one still October night, took her because he had no real right to touch her hand.

He might have despised himself, for he had certainly taken her under false pretenses. I don't mean that he had traded on his phantom millions, but he had deliberately given Daisy a sense of security; he let her believe that he was a person from much the same stratum as herself—that he was fully able to take care of her. As a matter of fact he had no such facilities—he had no comfortable family standing behind him and he was liable at the whim of an impersonal government to be blown anywhere about the world.

But he didn't despise himself and it didn't turn out as he had imagined. He had intended, probably, to take what he could and go—but now he found that he had committed himself to the following of a grail. He knew that Daisy was extraordinary but he didn't realize just how extraordinary a "nice" girl could be. She vanished into her rich house, into her rich, full life, leaving Gatsby—nothing.
He felt married to her, that was all.

When they met again two days later it was Gatsby who was breathless, who was somehow betrayed. Her porch was bright with the bought luxury of star-shine; the wicker of the settee squeaked fashionably as she turned toward him and he kissed her curious and lovely mouth. She had caught a cold and it made her voice huskier and more charming than ever and Gatsby was overwhelmingly aware of the youth and mystery that wealth imprisons and preserves, of the freshness of many clothes and of Daisy, gleaming like silver, safe and proud above the hot struggles of the poor...[16]

---

[16] F. Scott Fitzgerald, *The Great Gatsby* (New York: Charles Scribner's, 1925), Chapter 8; reproduced here from http://texts.crossref-it.info/text/the-great-gatsby/chapter-8 (accessed 28 October 2014).

**Assessment tip**

Your internal assessment requires you to write a philosophical analysis of a non-philosophical stimulus. Similarly, the core theme examination involves a stimulus, either philosophical or non-philosophical, that needs to give rise to a philosophical reflection and discussion.

Use non-philosophical material you encounter around you, such as *The Great Gatsby* extract above, to practise thinking philosophically about non-philosophical material. Cartoons, articles, adverts, photographs, material studied in other classes, and even simple objects can all be used as triggers to great philosophical thinking!

## Society and the individual

Although *The Great Gatsby* is set in an environment where social standing was perhaps particularly important, social determinists believe that individuals are always the product of the environment they live in, whatever that environment might be. Even in a society where people are seemingly free to progress socially, express their individuality, and make unpopular choices without being in danger, social influences still shape who we are and what we believe in. Social determinists do not believe that we can simply contemplate a range of available opinions and pick the ones that suit us best: a multitude of pervasive and invisible pressures will eventually lead us towards a certain option, leaving very little room – if any – for "real" free will.

Not all social determinists are hard determinists, however. In fact, it seems that social determinism offers a certain amount of hope that is much harder to contemplate when we view the world through the lens of biological determinism: while it may seem very difficult to change biological factors such as our genetic make-up, society, at least, can be changed. If society determines who we are, the transformation of society inevitably leads to the transformation of individuals.

That is why, traditionally, many social determinists are also social reformists or even revolutionaries. A corrupt society, they argue, corrupts people, and the improvement of society would directly benefit people. For these philosophers, the first step is often consciousness-raising: if we become aware of the social influences that shape us, we can start freeing ourselves from them and moving towards a model that is more suitable. Although society shapes individuals, educated individuals can at least choose the society that shapes them, therefore exercising a certain degree of freedom.

Some thinkers, like Rousseau or Marx, criticize society as it currently exists and suggest new models that they claim would free human beings from such negative social influences. If human beings are a reflection of the society they live in, then a better society will mean better human beings, which is why social determinism often calls for political reflection and action.

## Rousseau

Rousseau was a social contract theorist. Like philosophers such as Hobbes and Locke, Rousseau used the idea of a "state of nature" to explain what human beings would be like without society, and developed the notion of a social contract that people enter into voluntarily in order to form society.

Rousseau depicted human beings in the "state of nature" as utterly free, peaceful, and dignified. Whereas Hobbes believed that the state of nature was a state of "war of man against every man", Rousseau wrote that "War, then, is a relation, not between man and man, but between State and State, and individuals are enemies only accidentally, not as men, nor even as citizens, but as soldiers [...]."[17] In other words, human beings are naturally peaceful until they enter society through the social contract.

Society, because it is not the right type of society and gives the wrong kind of education, perverts human beings and changes them for the worse. It is in that sense that Rousseau can be linked to social determinism: human beings lose part of their freedom once they become part of society, and society alienates human beings. They start adopting values that go against their nature and they become corrupt. When Rousseau says that "Man was born free, and everywhere he is in chains",[18] the chains he refers to are society itself. Man alienates himself through the social contract and the only thing that can make him free and dignified again is a new type of society and education that Rousseau seeks to construct.

Rousseau's philosophy is a good example of the relative optimism that sometimes comes with social determinism, while it often eludes biological determinism. Social determinism, as mentioned earlier, seems a little easier to free oneself from. Society is a human construct after all, something we have a little more control over than our biology.

According to Rousseau, the solution to the current situation is for individuals to rethink education and social values, to act as morally as possible, to cultivate reason, and to respect and love each other. More importantly, society needs to be transformed until it is based on a social contract: existing societies are not based on a *real* social contract, which is the cause of their corruption. In a proper social contract, the power is in the hands of the citizens rather than the government. Each citizen works for the general will and submits to it.

Rousseau's call for a deep reform of society inspired revolutionaries, who used a rather radical reading of his ideas to fuel theirs, notably during the French Revolution of 1789.

---

[17] Jean-Jacques Rousseau, *On the Social Contract, Or Principles of Political Right* (France, 1762), Book I, Chapter 4; available at http://www.constitution.org/jjr/socon_01.htm (accessed 28 October 2014).

[18] Ibid., Book I, Chapter 1.

## Biography: Jean-Jacques Rousseau (1712–1778)

Eighteenth-century philosopher, writer, and composer Rousseau was born in Geneva and spent most of his life living in France and Switzerland. Although well-educated, Rousseau was poor for most of his youth. After he moved to Paris, Rousseau befriended French philosopher Diderot and contributed many articles to his great *Encyclopaedia*. In 1750, Rousseau won an essay competition with his *Discourse on the Arts and Sciences*, where he first developed the argument he would elaborate on for the rest of his life: society and civilization have corrupted human beings. He continued with this theme in further essays such as his famous *Discourse on the Origins of Inequality* (1755) and the even more famous *Social Contract* (1762).

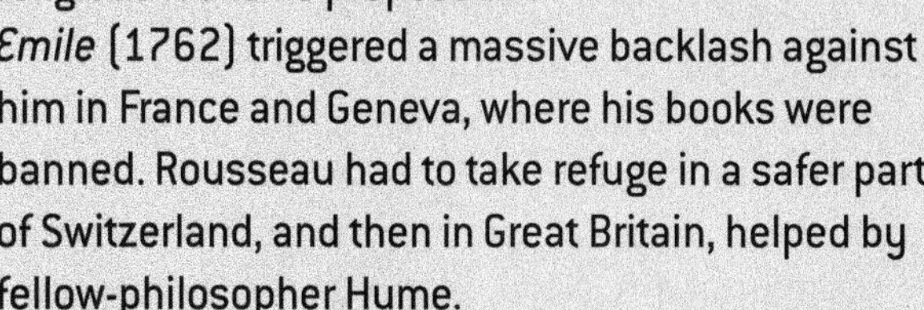

Rousseau was an opinionated man who offended a number of important people in his lifetime, including members of his own family and former friends like Diderot. The provocative religious ideas he proposed in *Emile* (1762) triggered a massive backlash against him in France and Geneva, where his books were banned. Rousseau had to take refuge in a safer part of Switzerland, and then in Great Britain, helped by fellow-philosopher Hume.

Rousseau finally made it back to Paris, in a fragile mental state, and had to live in relative secrecy, unable to publish new books. His *Confessions*, for instance, was only published after his death.

Civilised man… is always moving, sweating, toiling and racking his brains to find still more laborious occupations: he goes on in drudgery to his last moment, and even seeks death to put himself in a position to live, or renounces life to acquire immortality. He pays his court to men in power, whom he hates, and to the wealthy, whom he despises; he stops at nothing to have the honour of serving them; he is not ashamed to value himself on his own meanness and their protection; and, proud of his slavery, he speaks with disdain of those, who have not the honour of sharing it. What a sight would the perplexing and envied labours of a European minister of State present to the eyes of a Caribbean! How many cruel deaths would not this indolent savage prefer to the horrors of such a life, which is seldom even sweetened by the pleasure of doing good! But, for him to see into the motives of all this solicitude, the words *power* and *reputation*, would have to bear some meaning in his mind; he would have to know that there are men who set a value on the opinion of the rest of the world; who can be made happy and satisfied with themselves rather on the testimony of other people than on their own. In reality, the source of all these differences is, that the savage lives within himself, while social man lives constantly outside himself, and only knows how to live in the opinion of others, so that he seems to receive the consciousness of his own existence merely from the judgment of others concerning him. It is not to my present purpose to insist on the indifference to good and evil which arises from this disposition, in spite of our many fine works on morality, or to show how, everything being reduced to appearances, there is but art and mummery in even honour, friendship, virtue, and often vice itself, of which we at length learn the secret of boasting; to show, in short, how, always asking others what we are, and never daring to ask ourselves, in the midst of so much philosophy, humanity and civilisation, and of such sublime codes of morality, we have nothing to show for ourselves but a frivolous and deceitful appearance, honour without virtue, reason without wisdom, and pleasure without happiness. It is sufficient that I have proved that this is not by any means the original state of man, but that it is merely the spirit of society, and the inequality which society produces, that thus transform and alter all our natural inclinations…

—Jean-Jacques Rousseau[19]

[19] Jean-Jacques Rousseau, *Discourse on the Origin and Basis of Inequality Among Men* [Second Discourse] (France, 1755), Part 2; available at http://www.constitution.org/jjr/ineq_04.htm (accessed 28 October 2014).

That men are actually wicked, a sad and continual experience of them proves beyond doubt: but, all the same, I think I have shown that man is naturally good. What then can have depraved him to such an extent, except the changes that have happened in his constitution, the advances he has made, and the knowledge he has acquired? We may admire human society as much as we please; it will be none the less true that it necessarily leads men to hate each other in proportion as their interests clash, and to do one another apparent services, while they are really doing every imaginable mischief. What can be thought of a relation, in which the interest of every individual dictates rules directly opposite to those the public reason dictates to the community in general — in which every man finds his profit in the misfortunes of his neighbour? There is not perhaps any man in a comfortable position who has not greedy heirs, and perhaps even children, secretly wishing for his death; not a ship at sea, of which the loss would not be good news to some merchant or other; not a house, which some debtor of bad faith would not be glad to see reduced to ashes with all the papers it contains; not a nation which does not rejoice at the disasters that befall its neighbours. Thus it is that we find our advantage in the misfortunes of our fellow-creatures, and that the loss of one man almost always constitutes the prosperity of another... Let us penetrate, therefore, the superficial appearances of benevolence, and survey what passes in the inmost recesses of the heart. Let us reflect what must be the state of things, when men are forced to caress and destroy one another at the same time; when they are born enemies by duty, and knaves by interest. It will perhaps be said that society is so formed that every man gains by serving the rest. That would be all very well, if he did not gain still more by injuring them. There is no legitimate profit so great, that it cannot be greatly exceeded by what may be made illegitimately; we always gain more by hurting our neighbours than by doing them good. Nothing is required but to know how to act with impunity; and to this end the powerful employ all their strength, and the weak all their cunning...

What, then, is to be done? Must societies be totally abolished?... [Men like me] will respect the sacred bonds of their respective communities; they will love their fellow-citizens, and serve them with all their might: they will scrupulously obey the laws, and all those who make or administer them; they will particularly honour those wise and good princes, who find means of preventing, curing or even palliating all these evils and abuses, by which we are constantly threatened; they will animate the zeal of their deserving rulers, by showing them, without flattery or fear, the importance of their office and the severity of their duty. But they will not therefore have less contempt for a constitution that cannot support itself without the aid of so many splendid characters, much oftener wished for than found; and from which, notwithstanding all their pains and solicitude, there always arise more real calamities than even apparent advantages.

—Jean Jacques Rousseau[20]

## Questions

1. What are the characteristics of existing "civilized" societies Rousseau describes? How do these characteristics influence "civilized" man?
2. Do you think Rousseau's analysis of society is still valid today? Find concrete examples to support your answer.
3. In what ways can Rousseau be called a social determinist?
4. What elements of Rousseau's philosophy indicate that he is only a soft determinist?

[20] Ibid., Appendix; available at http://www.constitution.org/jjr/ineq_05.htm (accessed 28 October 2014).

## FIND OUT MORE

Listen to the following podcast: Melissa Lane on Rousseau on civilization

**http://philosophybites.com/2008/07/melissa-lane-on.html**

### Biography: Karl Marx (1818–1883)

Nineteenth-century German economist, historian, and philosopher Marx was one of the most influential thinkers of the last two centuries: he invented or transformed many of the concepts we use today (such as "class" and "alienation") and he generated enormous amounts of controversy. He was one of the founding fathers of communism and his ideas inspired many political figures – often with devastating consequences. Some say that Marx's ideas were dangerous while others argue that they were grossly misunderstood and never applied faithfully; whatever the truth may be there is no doubt that Marx is one of the most important thinkers in modern history.

Marx spent his youth in Germany where he studied law while actively educating himself in the field of philosophy, his true passion. He also became interested in radical politics and atheism from a young age. He moved to Paris when he was 25 and became more politically active, associating with various radical communist and left-wing intellectuals, including Friedrich Engels. In Paris, he continued to study intensively, adding economics and early socialism to his fields of interest.

▲ Karl Marx's grave in London's Highgate cemetery

Marx moved around, from Paris to Brussels, Cologne, and, finally, London, often trying to avoid the trouble his ideas were landing him in. He stayed in close touch with Engels, who often moved around with him, and they collaborated over several pieces of work that would result in their famous *Communist Manifesto* (1848). Marx and Engels also took an active part in the founding of the Communist League, an organization they hoped would attract the working classes and trigger a communist mass movement. The League made no secret of the fact that it was hoping to topple the capitalist system in favour of a communist society, through the means of a revolution.

Marx and Engels wrote for various newspapers around the world, and it was Marx's only source of income for a long time. In the 1860s, Marx became more successful when his political and economic work was published, culminating in his ground-breaking *Capital* (volume 1, 1867). Volumes 2 and 3 were published after his death. He died in London in 1883, where he is buried.

## Marx

According to Marx, human beings in capitalist societies are **alienated**: the economic and political system works in such a way that it enslaves people and makes them lose all their freedom. The vast majority of people are workers who are subjected to property-owners: they do not reap the fruits of their labour and they are exploited. This turns people into passive, meek prisoners who are unable to act freely and make choices.

The economic structure of society is what alienates and therefore determines people. Human nature is set by society and human beings will be different according to the type of society they live in. In that sense, Marx believed in economic and social determinism.

The capitalist society is presented as a huge, almost inescapable force that shapes people, in particular the working classes. People's actions are determined by the capitalist society they live in and are no longer a matter of personal choice: they are dictated by the roles individuals and classes play to keep capitalism going. The system is such that there is no other real alternative. According to Marx, as long as people "go with the flow" and accept the role the social system has given them, they are actively reinforcing the very system that is alienating them.

Marx's solution was to change society in order to change human beings. "Philosophers have hitherto only interpreted the world in various ways; the point is to change it," he wrote.[21] The change he proposed was a radical one: a revolution, replacing capitalist societies with a communist society in which people would be equal, and property and labour would be shared equally. According to Marx, in a communist society, people would work less and be free to pursue creative and intellectual activities, giving a new purpose to their lives. In that sense, people would be more self-determined and much less manipulated by society. In short, Marx claimed that individualistic capitalist societies enslaved people, whereas communist society would free them and give them their humanity.

This change from capitalism to communism, however, is a very difficult one, because people are determined and brainwashed to the extent that they have very little consciousness of their lack of freedom.

This is where Marx's ideas are most interesting for us: the society that determines people is described as a complete system of subjection, pervasive and pernicious, enslaving people from birth and using everything that surrounds them as propaganda. Religion itself is seen as a tool used to keep the working classes from rebelling by instilling values of meekness and promising rewards in the afterlife for those who accept their fate on earth. Every part of society is designed to keep the status quo and allow those who rule to continue exploiting those who are enslaved. The system is complete and holds people in its incredibly strong grip. Human beings become a construct, an artificial product of society, with very little freedom and independence. Typically, the working classes have no awareness of their alienation: the all-pervasive system of control means that they suffer from "false-consciousness", accepting the values thrust upon them by the dominant classes without realizing that these values are elaborate tools of mind and social control.

In addition to the socio-economic determinism described above, Marx also believed in a sort of historical determinism. Inspired by the German philosopher Hegel, Marx saw history as a series of cycles where a certain "thesis" (idea or system) first prevails, is then replaced by its "antithesis", and then progresses towards a "synthesis" of the thesis and the antithesis, combining them until they become a new "thesis", and so on. There are times where Marx suggests that the communist revolution he defends is inevitable, like the unavoidable and determined next step history is bound to take. He describes this event as the end of the cycle of history, because it puts an end to the class system and, therefore, to the endless conflicts that cause the cycle

[21] Karl Marx, *Theses on Feuerbach* (Stuttgart: J. W. H. Dietz, 1888); available at http://www.marxists.org/archive/marx/works/1845/theses/ (accessed 28 October 2014).

in the first place. This idea of historical determinism further reduces the notion of human freedom: the working classes do not decide to start a revolution. Instead, the revolution is something that will happen and that they may as well take an active part in. Paradoxically, however, it is only when the working classes do take an active part that they can free themselves. Freedom cannot be given to them by an enlightened minority working in their favour. Although they need the guidance of a philosopher to lift the veil of false-consciousness, the revolution needs to be theirs.

The enormous social, economic, and historical determining forces Marx describes seem at times inescapable. Marx, however, did believe in human freedom. His vision of a communist society clearly puts some emphasis on the importance of freely chosen occupations and work as one of the highlights of human existence. Marx also viewed freedom as something that could be achieved as a community, not the lonely pursuit described in liberal theories. Once people were free from alienation, they would be able to interact with each other, as human beings should, with freedom at the heart of their interaction. Given the situation, however, Marx had to focus on "negative freedom" – freedom *from* constraints – as a prerequisite to a more positive form of freedom – freedom *to* choose.

## Some philosophical and practical implications

### Applications of Marxism

Marx painted an idyllic picture of communist societies. In reality, however, communist societies have not been very successful: once competition is removed, workers tend to lack motivation and productivity is affected, while total equality never seems to be achieved. Indeed, some of the worst tyrants and dictators in recent history seem to have appeared in so-called communist societies. Freedom of speech always seems to suffer and dissidents are often treated brutally.

This does not mean that Marx was necessarily wrong on all accounts, and his entire theory must not be discarded simply because its applications have been less than perfect (or even totally horrific). Although Marx is often depicted as a monster by his opponents, it is very possible that his main mistake was simply to be overly optimistic about human nature and its potential for change.

What if complete equality was never possible, because human beings naturally need to compete with each other? What if human beings were bound to become corrupt by power, whatever system they live in? Can a change of system really change human nature itself?

### Can we free ourselves from social constraints?

Both Rousseau and Marx ask human beings to free themselves from social constraints, at least partially and temporarily, in order to rebuild a society whose influence on individuals is a more positive one.

However, as Marx himself points out, we are mostly unaware of the influence society has on us: so, how can we reject it? Society's influence is a powerful one, because it is constantly reinforced by our peers, our family, school, the media, and almost everything around us. Values are imposed on us until we internalize them to the extent that we become convinced that they come from us.

How can philosophers like Rousseau and Marx be sure that they are exceptions, free from the giant formatting machine that is society? If freeing oneself from society's grip is as hard as Marx describes it, how did Marx himself do it? How could he transcend all the influences he denounces, how could he see them so clearly while everyone else is blind? The claims he makes are, to an extent, paradoxical.

With hindsight, it is clear that both Marx and Rousseau themselves were deeply influenced by their era and the social circles they came into contact with. In fact, rebelling against a certain social system implies that the social system in question has influenced the rebel, even in a negative way. Marx would not have been Marx without capitalism: he was a product of the very thing he was trying to free himself from. While he did not deny it, and while it might even prove his point, this inescapable influence is a reminder that no human being can be taken away from the society he lives in. There is probably no such thing as complete freedom from society and, as some argue, attempting to understand what human beings would be like if they were not in society is perhaps feeble.

### Blaming "society"

This leads us to another related problem: both Marx and Rousseau had a tendency to blame "society" and a "system" for the corruption of human nature, as if "society" and the "system" were entities in themselves, working against human beings. But we must remember that society is made of human beings, it *is* human beings. If human beings are "good" and free, how do they ever start building societies that are alienating and corrupting? Of course, both Marx and Rousseau offer explanations and answers, but the questions seem to remain: doesn't it make more sense to say that human beings corrupt society, rather than society corrupts human beings? Since society is composed of human beings, isn't saying "society corrupts human beings" the same as saying "human beings corrupt human beings"? In which case, could it simply be the case that human nature is essentially corrupt, power-thirsty, and self-centred, therefore making Rousseau's and Marx's dreams impossible to achieve?

Finally, human beings are social animals. Society is part of what they are and is something they made, not an alien entity that has nothing to do with them. In that sense, instead of wondering what human beings would be like without society – as so many social-contract theorists have done in the past – it may make more sense to see society as a useful mirror that could help us understand human nature itself.

## Case study: gender and social conditioning

When reading about Rousseau and Marx, it is easy to think that they were talking about a society that was very different from ours and that their arguments therefore no longer apply: in many societies, human beings are now freer than ever, politically and socially, with much greater choice.

Yet, it can be argued that we are at least as determined as our ancestors, if only because society has many more ways to "condition" us than it did before. The omnipresent media, the internet, and our constant communication with others mean that it is increasingly difficult to isolate oneself from the influence of social groups. Democracy may have gained in popularity since Rousseau's time, but you have to remember that the system described by Rousseau, and even more so by Marx, is much more pervasive than a simple political system. Democracy does not prevent people from being controlled or conditioned socially. What social determinists and reformists describe is a social system that influences people through a multitude of means, such as schools, religion, public policy, moral values, advertising, language, and so on. There is no way to become aware of all the factors that influence us, as they are everywhere.

Since we are social animals belonging to a number of groups, it is normal that we should influence each other. For instance, it makes sense to try to obey certain rules and avoid conflict with others: as we attempt to be civilized, we necessarily alter our behaviour. However, social influences also worry many thinkers, because they are not always as innocent as simple attempts to "get along". Since Marx, many philosophers and political theorists have claimed that certain sections of the population actively benefit from the **social conditioning** we are all subjected to. The most powerful individuals of a society, for instance, usually try to keep things as they are, as any change could threaten their power. Since they are in power, it is easier for them to control the social system that influences people. Therefore, cultural and social influences often reflect the tastes and needs of the most powerful instead of representing the whole population.

One example that can show the extent to which social influences shape our identity and values is the example of gender. It is particularly interesting because it affects us all, and has been relevant throughout recent human history, in all cultures. It is also interesting because, for a long time, philosophers and scientists assumed that gender differences were entirely natural and had nothing to do with the influence of society.

## Philosophical terms and theories

**Feminism** is an umbrella term that is often misunderstood and caricatured. There are many branches and types of feminism, from Marxist feminism to liberal feminism, from radical feminism to essentialist feminism. Feminists often argue, debate, and disagree. However, they all have one thing in common: they all believe that women have, historically, been treated unfairly and they try to rectify the situation by seeking equality between the sexes. What they mean exactly by equality and the way to achieve it varies, though, hence the debates! A common mistake is to think that feminism claims that women are superior to men: this is not the case! Anyone (male or female) who believes that men and women should be equal can technically claim to be a feminist, especially if they think that women have suffered from discrimination.

The notion of **gender** is central to feminist theories of the 20th century. In response to widespread traditional ideas about women's nature and the natural role of women, most feminists claim that the biological differences between men and women (sex) are insignificant compared with the differences that are caused by social conditioning (gender).

This is what de Beauvoir means when she writes: "One is not born, but rather becomes, woman."[22] Most "feminine" characteristics are socially constructed and not at all derived from biology.

According to feminists, genders are socially constructed and this is what distinguishes gender from sex: whereas a person's sex is a natural and biological fact, his or her gender is artificial and a social construct. For instance, to have a beard or be able to bear children is part of one's sex, whereas to wear skirts or enjoy car racing is part of one's gender. Some characteristics, such as mood swings (for women) and aggressive behaviour (for men), are difficult to put in either category as they could belong to both. Here, we will focus on gender as a social construct in order to explore a specific type of social determinism.

Feminists believe that women are disadvantaged by the social system. They call such a system **patriarchy**. It does not refer to the power of fathers (origins of the word) but to the power of men in general. Although this concept can seem a little dated, it shaped contemporary feminist theory and is still used today, notably when feminists talk about a **"patriarchal society"** (a non-feminist society where the sexes are unequal).

According to *radical feminists*, patriarchy is an extremely complex and elaborate system of oppression. It is spread in all realms of society, from the most formal (like politics) to the most intimate (at home, in relationships, etc.). In many ways, this type of social conditioning is similar to the system denounced by Marx, and many feminists were influenced by Marxist ideas.

The subtle but constant social conditioning that constructs gender starts very early on, when a child is born and the first thing he or she hears is "It's a boy!" or "It's a girl!", making his or her sex the most important of all characteristics, defining the child's identity even before it has been named or has had a chance to meet his or her parents.

In 1969, Kate Millett, an American radical feminist, wrote one of the seminal texts of feminist theory, outlining the all-encompassing nature of the social construction of gender. Here is an extract:

> ... a disinterested examination of our system of sexual relationship must point out that the situation between the sexes now, and throughout history, is ... a relationship of dominance and subordinance. What goes largely unexamined, often even unacknowledged (yet it is institutionalized nonetheless) in our social order, is the birthright priority whereby males rule females. Through this system a most ingenious form of "internal colonization" has been achieved. It is one which tends moreover to be sturdier than any form of segregation, and more rigorous than class stratification, more uniform, and certainly more enduring. However muted its present appearance may be, sexual dominion obtains nevertheless as perhaps the most pervasive ideology of our culture and provides its most fundamental concept of power.
>
> This is so because our society, like all other historical civilizations, is a patriarchy. The fact is evident at once if one recalls that the military, industry, technology, university, science, political office and finance – in short, every avenue of power within the society, including the coercive force of the police, is entirely in male hands. As the essence of politics is power, such realization cannot fail to carry impact.
>
> —Kate Millett[23]

[22] Simone de Beauvoir, *The Second Sex*, translated by Constance Borde and Sheila Malovany-Chevallier, introduced by Judith Thurman (New York: Vintage, 2009), pp. xv, xviii.

[23] Kate Millett, *Sexual Politics* (Urbana, IL: University of Illinois Press, 2000), p. 25.

Millett carries on to say that biology cannot possibly be the origin of such disparity in power between men and women, and that society itself must be to blame:

> There is insufficient evidence for the thesis that the present social distinctions of patriarchy are physical in origin, since distinctions which we know to be culturally induced at present so outweigh them. Whatever the "real" differences between the sexes may be, we are not likely to know them until the sexes are treated differently, that is alike. And this is very far from being the case at present.[24]

Millett continues with an exploration of the social institutions that shape gender. According to her, the following institutions and factors act as conditioning agents, perpetuating and reinforcing gender roles in society to maintain the status quo:

- The family, with the father as a central power figure
- Religion, also focused on male power
- The State and laws that favour men
- The economic dependency of women
- The education system, pushing women into certain professions

Today, many women, including feminists, would say that Millett's vision is out of date. Women, partly thanks to feminism itself, have made enormous progress in the last 40 years. The education system, for instance, often favours girls and can no longer be seen as one of the instruments of a patriarchal society.

▲ Very few women appear among the most powerful political leaders in the world

[24] Ibid., p. 29.

And yet, there are still many countries where society is clearly male-dominated and where women lack the opportunities that men enjoy. Even in the most "developed" countries, institutions such as "the military, industry, technology, university, science, political office and finance" may not be "entirely in male hands", but women are certainly grossly underrepresented in their midst.

Although radical feminism is not as fashionable as it was in the 1970s, some of the questions it raised still resonate today: can biology alone really cause such a social imbalance between men and women? Is society still a powerful influence on the development of our gender identity? What social institutions and factors contribute to the construction of gender?

Thanks to feminists, such questions became much more mainstream and awareness continues to be raised on the social influences that artificially separate men and women.

In 2001, for instance, the BBC Programme *Child of Our Time* conducted an experiment, asking adults to take care of babies dressed either in a pink or in a blue outfit. The experiment revealed that the adults who thought they were taking care of a girl acted completely differently from the ones who believed they were taking care of a boy. The boys were handled more firmly and played with, while the girls were treated like fragile babies and complimented on their looks. If baby girls and boys are treated differently from birth, it becomes extremely difficult to know whether they are indeed different to start with, or they become different because of social factors. Different treatments could have a profound effect on the kind of people girls and boys grow up to be.

## ACTIVITY

Another social factor that can deeply influence the development of gender identity is the kind of games and toys that children are given.

On the internet, visit a popular toy or gift website and run a search for "girls' toys" and then "boys' toys".

- What differences do you notice?
- What social roles could these toys reinforce and encourage?
- Do you think children are *naturally* drawn towards toys that are targeted for their gender, or do you think society teaches them what toys and roles are adequate for their gender?
- What do you think happens when children refuse to conform with society's expectations? Consider different examples, for instance in different cultures and countries.

▲ Who decides which is a "girls' toy" and which is a "boys' toy"?

Far from going away, the social construction of genders has remained a relevant topic in recent years. In 2008, *Child of Our Time* explored the social construction of gender once again. Here is an extract from an article written by the programme's producer, Tessa Livingstone:

When I was very young, I thought I knew how men and women should behave: men were breadwinners and women housewives. But already the world was changing.

Now, 70 per cent of women with children have paid work, and men are taking more responsibility for housework. A survey we carried out for the Child of Our Time series showed most of our parents believe traditional gender roles are now almost irrelevant.

At the same time, we talked with their children and discovered something disturbing. The children were busy constructing new gender roles, influenced less by tradition, parents and school than by the outside world. So, are we really bridging the divide of the sexes? Or, in a culture dominated by marketing, media, and materialism, are our kids giving a different message?

The power of marketing on gender identity is illustrated by an experiment we carried out with the Child of Our Time children, now seven years old – we are tracking 25 millennium children from birth to adulthood. We filled bottles with the same lemonade. One set we packaged as "Rocket Pop" with blue labels, and the other as "Princess Pop" with pink ones.

First, we asked the children which they liked the look of and – no surprise – the girls preferred the pink and the boys, blue. We then asked them to compare the taste of the drinks. The boys told us that "Rocket Pop has more fizz", and "It's better because it's more flat". Or, as one budding scientist put it: "It's got more flavour because it's got the least amount of water." Then, the girls: "The blue one is a bit more dark and I don't like it."

We realised almost all our children believed the two identical drinks had different tastes, and they preferred the taste of the one aimed at them. The fact that the colours and design of the packaging affect their judgement attests to the power of marketing, both to deceive and drive a profitable wedge between the sexes.

This is where the media comes in. Children's television is generally benign, but children are bombarded with much more.

Advertisements, music, magazines, and many TV stations live off a diet of sex, celebrity, money, and beauty. Young children are more impressionable than their elders. They are trusting, and highly attuned to social nuances because they need to feel accepted. It is not surprising that they soak up messages crafted to seduce the population for the benefit of the market...

Other studies show boys are the more materialistic sex, a finding corroborated when we asked the Child of Our Time children about the qualities they most admired. While girls wanted to be kind and healthy, the boys chose wealth, telling us: "Money is more important than anything", and "I'd like to be rich and buy what I want".

One might think the desire to be rich would spur boys to get educated, but it doesn't appear to. Some of the able boys in our cohort told us: "Clever is so boring." They felt cleverness was not cool; influenced, perhaps, by a celebrity culture that underestimates the hard graft needed to get there.

That may go some way to help explain why boys are falling even further behind girls in school. Again, children split along gender lines, for our seven-year-old girls told us: "If you are clever, everybody likes you more", and "Clever means that you know what to do quite a lot of the time". Girls seem to expect to do well in education, and often do so.

Even so, girls' self-esteem is also under threat. The NCC [National Consumer Council] study demonstrated how the media can magnify materialism to the point where it can substantially damage children's self-esteem by making them feel inadequate. Girls respond by becoming increasingly perfectionist about their school work and their weight. Oliver James, the study's author, told me that the rates of depression and anxiety among girls from high-income families had increased from 24 to 38 per cent in just 12 years. It is a high price to pay for having it all.

—Tessa Livingstone[25]

[25] Tessa Livingstone, "The New Gender Divide", *TES Newspaper*, 9 May 2008 (updated 4 August 2008); available at http://www.tes.co.uk/article.aspx?storycode=2619363 (accessed 28 October 2014).

The construction of gender is just one example of the way society can shape our identity and influence our values and choices. Such an influence is often subtle, yet all-encompassing at the same time, raising serious philosophical questions about the amount of freedom that individuals really possess. Theoreticians such as Rousseau, Marx, and feminist scholars believe that consciousness-raising is a first step towards greater freedom, because being aware of the influences that shape us can help us detach ourselves from those influences.

For example, gender characteristics that we assumed were natural and inescapable can become more of a life choice once we perceive them as a social construct. If we know that society, and not nature, has dictated a certain way of life, we are more likely to seek alternatives and face a real choice.That is why, ultimately, freedom may depend on our awareness and understanding of the sociocultural influences that affect us.

### Questions

1. List the social factors that, according to Tessa Livingstone, influence today's children.
2. To what extent do you think such factors are determining children's values and behaviour?
3. Can you find personal examples that either reflect or contradict what Livingstone writes in this article?
4. How do you think contemporary examples relate to Rousseau's and Marx's theories?

### FIND OUT MORE

Listen to the following podcast: Janet Radcliffe Richards on men and women's natures

**http://philosophybites.com/2008/04/janet-radcliffe.html**

## Getting back to "nature versus nurture", and moving beyond it

Now that you have studied both biological and social determinism in detail, you can get a much better understanding of the nature versus nurture debate.

Let's get back to one of our case studies, criminal behaviour, in order to examine the implications of the traditional debate, and ways to get past it.

| **Nature**<br>***Some possible biological causes of criminal behaviour*** | **Nurture**<br>***Some possible social causes of criminal behaviour***[26] |
|---|---|
| • Low serotonin leading to impulsive behaviour and lack of self-control<br>• Low activity and/or damage in the prefrontal cortex, leading to poor planning abilities and lack of control over one's impulses<br>• Low activity variant of the *MAOA* "warrior" gene leading to aggressive behaviour<br>• Hormonal imbalance, for instance involving testosterones or adrenaline<br>• Biological tendency to become addicted easily | • Family: parental criminality, abuse<br>• Education: low school attendance, low-paying employment<br>• Economic factors: poverty, social inequality, unemployment<br>• Environment: criminality is common in the neighbourhood /among friends and role models<br>• Substance use: alcohol and drugs |

[26] Based on data from the Ministry of Justice, "Social Risk Factors for Involvement in Crime", in *New Zealand Criminal Justice Sector Outcomes Report: Strategic Policy Brief* (New Zealand: Ministry of Justice, 2009); available at http://www.justice.govt.nz/justice-sector/drivers-of-crime/documents/spb-social-risk-factors (accessed 28 October 2014).

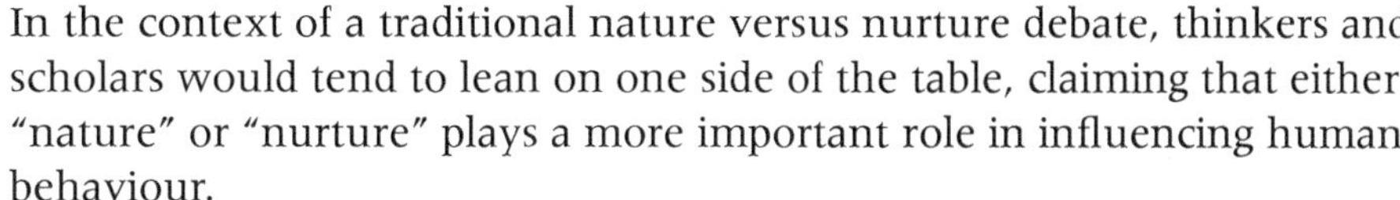

In the context of a traditional nature versus nurture debate, thinkers and scholars would tend to lean on one side of the table, claiming that either "nature" or "nurture" plays a more important role in influencing human behaviour.

## FIND OUT MORE

On social causes of criminal behaviour:

**http://www.justice.govt.nz/justice-sector/drivers-of-crime/documents/spb-social-risk-factors**

On the combination of biological and social causes of criminal behaviour:

**http://www.safe-nz.org.nz/Articles/crimecause.htm**

The position one adopts has philosophical and practical implications. As we saw in the example of biological determinism and criminal behaviour, for instance, claiming that some people are "natural" criminals means that they may need to be treated with clemency in court. Philosophically, accepting that biology can "make" people misbehave is accepting that human freedom and responsibility are limited, at least for some individuals. As we saw, those limits are problematic, because if we accept their existence for some, there is a chance that they could be extended to all human beings: non-criminal people might just be biologically determined to obey society's rules and obedience might not be a mark of their freedom after all.

Similarly, the "nurture" argument has important implications. One has to decide, for instance, whether society as a whole needs reforming or whether the particular situation of certain people has to improve without the need for radical social change. As mentioned earlier, social determinism offers some hope with the possibility of change: factors such as a bad education, poverty, or access to drugs can be tackled, even if they are complex issues. Genes and brains are difficult to modify, whereas social factors can be altered, using social policy, reforms, laws, charities, and so on. As we highlighted before, society is built by human beings and, as a human construct, it can always be deconstructed and improved to have a positive impact on individuals. This is something we see and do all the time. Social solutions do not necessarily need to be as radical as the ones proposed by Marx: simple steps like better health care or tighter rules on school attendance can have a real effect on individuals and their behaviour.

As such, in the traditional nature versus nurture debate, the "nature" position, claiming that some individuals are naturally born with strong dispositions, tends to be a little more pessimistic, as well as conservative. This is a broad generalization but it can help understand the debate better. Advocates of the "nature" argument often claim that little can be done to help or reform individuals who are born with certain negative traits. They must be dealt with accordingly and there is perhaps no point in spending too much time trying to change them. On the other hand, advocates of the "nurture" camp tend to think that such individuals are the "victims" of their environment and circumstances. Once that environment is improved or transformed, individuals are likely to change. It is therefore worth trying to reform people, but also society as a whole. Again, this doesn't need to mean that a complete transformation is needed: sometimes, social policy or simply better economic conditions are all that is needed to improve the situation and its impact on individuals.

Here, we used criminal behaviour to illustrate the nature versus nurture debate, but it has been present in many other areas. For instance, thinkers have often wondered whether differences between men and women are the result of natural factors or social ones. Likewise, researchers have been fascinated with the natural and social causes of traits such as intelligence, musical talent, or sporting abilities. In fact, it is safe to say that the nature versus nurture debate has been present in one form or another in all areas of studies related to human beings.

## Beyond "nature versus nurture": an integrated approach

However, it is important to recognize that things have moved on, and that the nature versus nurture debate is increasingly obsolete. In many areas, researchers and philosophers have been using a more integrated approach, using arguments from both sides of the debate and recognizing that behaviour is a product of a combination of natural and social elements.

We now know, for instance, that biological factors such as hormones or even genes can give us a predisposition or tendency towards certain behaviours, but that those behaviours often need to be triggered by environmental factors. For example, imagine two people: Pedro, who was born with a natural tendency to become addicted to drugs easily, and Patricia, who was born with no addictive tendencies and should be able to resist addiction for a longer time before it takes a hold of her. Now, those tendencies, in themselves, mean very little, unless they are combined with the "right" environmental factors. If Pedro was born into a loving, protective family, if he attends a school where drugs are unpopular, and lives in a neighbourhood where drugs are not available, then his natural addictive tendencies will have very little chance to become a reality. On the other hand, if Patricia's parents are abusive, all her best friends are drug addicts, and drugs are easy to obtain in her neighbourhood, her natural resistance to addiction is unlikely to be enough in the long term.

Biological determinism is not usually strong enough to be a real predictor, unless it is combined with social determinism. Even the researchers who dedicate their lives to understanding the biological factors that influence behaviour now recognize that those factors cannot be isolated from social factors. Here are a few examples taken from our biological determinism section:

- Markku Linnoila, who discovered the link between low levels of serotonin and impulsive behaviour in prisoners, also claimed that the biological factors he described needed to be combined with an environmental or social stressor, such as alcohol abuse or a violent family environment, in order to result in impulsive behaviour. Low serotonin alone is unlikely to result in impulsive criminal behaviour.

- Dee Higley, who also established a link between low serotonin and "dare-devil" behaviour in monkeys, later discovered that environmental factors such as the loss of a mother could lower the serotonin levels of young monkeys. Here, the environment triggered the biological factor that led to a certain behaviour.
- Rose McDermott, who found that people carrying the low-activity variant of the *MAOA* "warrior" gene were more likely to be aggressive, also found that they were no more aggressive than other people if the provocation was mild. In other words, carriers of the more risky gene needed to be placed in a more stressful environment before their genetic make-up really started to make a difference.

The examples above illustrate the obsolescence of the nature versus nurture debate: it is now clear that nature and nurture are so intricately linked that it is almost impossible to distinguish them from one another. Two relatively recent discoveries have further reinforced the need for an integrated approach:

- **Brain plasticity**: in the last few decades, it has become clear that the brain is not as static as previously thought. The brain is plastic, or malleable, and its structure will change depending on the environment we are in and the activities we engage in. Although children and young people's brains are particularly plastic and changeable, adult brains continue to change too. Any "natural abilities" we may be born with will disappear if unused, and any weak areas will be improved and perhaps even erased by constant practice. In other words, when it comes to the brain, nurture can reshape what nature produced.
- **Epigenetics** is a new field of studies that explores the way genes are switched on and off by environmental factors. Genes used to be seen as one of the most constant, inescapable, and determining factors of our biological make-up, but even they respond to the situation and environment!

## FIND OUT MORE

Research brain plasticity or epigenetics to find out more about the way biological, environmental, and social factors combine to make us who we are. The following pages are a good starting point:

*Brain plasticity*:

**http://www.ted.com/talks/michael_merzenich_on_the_elastic_brain.html**

**http://www.positscience.com/brain-resources/brain-plasticity/what-is-brain-plasticity**

*Epigenetics*:

**http://www.pbs.org/wgbh/nova/body/epigenetics.html**

**http://learn.genetics.utah.edu/content/epigenetics/**

**Another contemporary example of the nature and nurture combination:**

How technology wires the learning brain (brain plasticity):

**http://blogs.kqed.org/mindshift/2011/02/how-technology-wires-the-learning-brain/**

## Some philosophical implications of the nature and nurture combination

To come back to our drug addiction example, it is worth wondering what would happen to Pedro (with his genetic propensity for addiction) if he were born in Patricia's social circumstances (in an abusive family and drug-ridden environment). The blend of biological and social factors would not just mean that the risks add up, it would mean that they multiply each other and become a potent combination that would truly reduce and threaten Pedro's free will. Can anyone really escape those determining factors when they are combined?

Do you remember Raine's speech and his reference to a murderer who "checked all the boxes" and "had all the social deficits, the family deficits, the brain deficits" that made him "a walking time-bomb waiting to explode"? Raine, a fairly optimistic scientist and not a hard determinist as such, still ended up asking: "Is it any surprise he goes and kills and rapes somebody?"

Our newfound knowledge of the nature and nurture combination sometimes seems to push freedom into a corner or squeeze it out of the equation altogether.

When someone is influenced by a multitude of factors that pushes them in one direction, it is hard to deny that they are losing some freedom, up to the point where resisting all the influences may become impossible and eliminate the possibility of free will.

This brings us back to a question raised earlier in this chapter: are we all determined to the same extent? Philosophically, both hard and soft determinisms can still be maintained in the context of the nature and nurture combination. Soft determinists, on the one hand, can say that most individuals are not determined to the extreme extent of the examples cited above: most people retain an element of choice despite influences. Hard determinists, on the other hand, can claim that we are all determined to the same extent. The person who does not commit crimes was determined not to, and the one who "decides" against taking drugs was simply wired in a way that would have made her decision predictable if we knew all the parameters. It is very difficult to convince a hard determinist that freedom exists: they can claim, for instance, that some people are just determined to believe in freedom and feel free!

The nature and nurture combination, however, doesn't need to be seen in a pessimistic or hard determinist light. As we learn more about the multitude of influences that help shape our thoughts and decisions,

**Assessment tip** 

Although many of the philosophers we are studying were alive several centuries ago, it is always a good idea for you to relate their theories to contemporary examples, including ones you are personally familiar with. This will make your essays relevant to today's world and will show that you can apply philosophy to non-philosophical material. In addition, such examples will make it easier for you to give a personal response.

human freedom can resurface. Although there are rare examples of people who combine all the biological, environmental, and social elements that push them in one direction, most people are pushed in different directions all at once. They may, for instance, grow up in a drug-ridden neighbourhood but in a family that is supportive. Or they may have some genes that make them easily addicted, and others that make them strong-willed enough to resist temptation or even stop taking drugs altogether. Those contradictory influences offer a variety of possible paths. While hard determinists claim that those possibilities are just an illusion, many other thinkers believe that therein lies free will: at some point, one just has to stop at the crossroad between paths, and make a choice.

Unfortunately, there is no way to know whether this choice is illusory or real. The answer, at this point in the history of human knowledge, is more a matter of philosophical opinion than scientific calculation, since factors and their interaction are probably too complex to allow for reliable predictions. Free-will advocates would maintain that there are individuals who still do, against all odds, behave in a way that was utterly unpredictable. Hard determinists, on the other hand, would argue that such individuals must have been determined to resist their natural tendencies and the social pressures that surround them. As long as we are unable to measure and compile all the influences that affect human behaviour, there will be room for both free-will advocates and various shades of determinists.

## Other types of determinism

So far in this chapter, we have focused on two main types of determinism and their relationship with each other. Determinism, however, comes in many forms and the nature of the core theme assessment means that you should feel free to explore another form of determinism instead of the ones detailed here. Examples of topics you could study and use in an assessment include:

- **Psychological determinism**: although we may feel like we are making conscious decisions for rational, traceable reasons, many psychologists since Freud claim that we have a subconscious mind that influences our choices without our being aware of it. In that sense, we may well be determining ourselves! Psychological determinism also claims that there are laws of the human mind and that, given those laws, behaviour could be predictable. Psychological determinism can also include **behavioural determinism**, according to which people's behaviour is always a response to conditioning of some sort.
- **Environmental determinism** focuses on the impact geographical and climatic conditions have on human beings. Despite its name, it is more closely linked to biological determinism than it is to social determinism. It relies heavily on the theory of evolution, claiming that the terrain and weather conditions populations have evolved in have a great impact on their behaviour. Unfortunately, environmental determinism sometimes slips into racist and discriminatory ideology, making sweeping generalizations about certain populations and their characteristics.

- **Causal determinism** is the kind of determinism we mentioned at the beginning of this chapter. It is the belief that every event has a cause and that human behaviour does not escape or transcend that rule. Events, including human events, are the direct result of a chain of causes. This is sometimes referred to as **philosophical determinism**, although it is also closely linked to **scientific determinism**, the belief that the whole universe, including human beings and the human mind, follows laws of nature that make everything, at least in theory, predictable. Other chapters should allow you to explore this in some detail. For instance, agency, self-consciousness, materialism, and functionalism are all topics that are strongly related to determinism and that you could use in an essay on this philosophical theme. As long as you find one clear central theme and two philosophical approaches to that theme, any combination is permitted.

## THEOLOGICAL DETERMINISM

### Western religion and determinism

Most major religions deal with the topics of freedom and determinism, in one way or another. In Judaism, Christianity, and Islam, for instance, human beings possess free will, which allows them to take responsibility for their actions. God is omniscient and, as such, knows what path each human being will take, but he is not the one who makes them take the path in question: human beings make free choices and are responsible for the consequences of their actions. In certain branches of these major religions, there are more deterministic beliefs: some believe that God has a plan for each one of us and that we must follow that plan by following his signs, while others think that God already knows who is going to Heaven, regardless of their actions in this life. Despite these beliefs, however, most monotheistic believers give free will a central place, simply because morality and goodness cannot exist without it: if we are just God's puppets, we cannot ever be "good" or "bad", because our actions are not our own. A truly good person is a person who had a choice between doing the right thing and the wrong thing, and who deliberately and freely chose the right thing, for the right reasons, despite all the temptation that they might have experienced. This view can even, to an extent, explain the existence of evil and suffering in the world.

### FIND OUT MORE

**http://www.kiekeben.com/theological.html**

## AN EASTERN PERSPECTIVE

### Karma, reincarnation, and determinism

Karma is a notion that exists primarily in Eastern religions such as Hinduism and Buddhism. It is very different from the beliefs held by the main monotheistic Western religions discussed above, and yet it has certain aspects in common with them: Karma also emphasizes responsibility, free will, rewards, and punishment.

To understand Karma, you must understand reincarnation: both Hindus and Buddhists believe that, when a person dies, they can be reborn as another person. The idea is slightly different in both religions. Buddhists believe in rebirth rather than reincarnation; for Buddhists, the soul gives life to another soul, like a candle can light another, whereas Hindus believe that the same soul will pass from one body to the next. However, in both Hinduism and Buddhism, past lives do have an effect on our present life. Good and bad actions are stored up as good and bad Karma, and Karma will have a direct effect on the next life. To simplify, good actions might result in luck and good fortune, while bad actions will be punished by ill fate and difficulties in the next life.

Karma can seem like a deterministic, even fatalistic notion: our current situation is a direct consequence of our past life and we must accept it. We are receiving rewards and punishments for actions we no longer remember, and both Hinduism and Buddhism ask us to consider those as fair and justly deserved. Rebellion is futile: fate is sealed by our past actions. The family we are born into, the wealth we are born into, the social status we inherit, are all a direct consequence of Karma. Our actions, too, are influenced by Karma: we might make the same mistakes again and again, or react against a past situation.

However, it would be a mistake to think that Hinduism and Buddhism leave us as passive and powerless beings, unable to change our fate. Although it is true that certain aspects of our lives, like health or social status (notably in Hinduism), cannot be changed and must be accepted, free will is still at the centre of the notion of Karma. We are free to choose how we live our life and how we react to the life we are given. To use the metaphor of a card game, Karma means that we are dealt certain cards, but the way we play them is still up to us.

More importantly, our present choices will have a great impact on our future life: we are determining ourselves and, in that sense, we have an important responsibility towards ourselves. We are free and responsible in a way that is perhaps more profound than in any other tradition: we know that every action will be punished or rewarded, and will have direct consequences on our future, even if it is in another life. Isn't this level of control, even if we have to wait for the next life, the essence of freedom itself?

### FIND OUT MORE

**http://www.religionfacts.com/hinduism/beliefs/karma.htm**

**http://www.buddhanet.net/3-gqga.htm**

**http://buddhism.about.com/od/karmaandrebirth/a/karma.htm**

## An integrated approach

Although these types of determinism are sometimes presented as conflicting with one another, as in the nature versus nurture debate, there is really no reason to think that they are not compatible. The likely truth is that they interact with each other, sometimes reinforcing each other, sometimes counteracting each other. It makes a lot of sense to take an integrated approach combining all those factors rather than one that artificially sets them as incompatible: that is what modern psychologists, for instance, do when they try to understand people's behaviour. For the purpose of your exam, however, you might want to present two types of determinism as "two different approaches", as requested in the core theme exam instructions.

## What about freedom?

The more discoveries we make about genetics, psychology, and the role of society, the more reasons we have to think that we are determined: there are so many influences in our lives, many of which we are unaware of, that freedom seems to be increasingly unlikely. With each new discovery, determinism seems to score an extra point and freedom is squeezed out a little further, and it is hard to maintain that we can be free from any influence. However, it does not mean that we do not have any free will at all. In many ways, the idea that we are totally determined can seem just as absurd as the idea that we are totally free.

Let's start with a few problems raised by hard determinism:

- **We feel free!** It might be an obvious statement, and perhaps not one based on scientific proof or even perfect logic, but instincts can also matter in philosophy. When a theory is completely counter-intuitive, it is very difficult to give it full credit. And the idea that our whole life – every single one of our actions and decisions – is determined, is extremely counter-intuitive. Why would people feel free if freedom did not exist at all? Why would people agonize over difficult decisions if they were not really making those decisions?

  Many determinists try to offer explanations, arguing that freedom is an illusion, but none of those seems completely convincing. Whatever their argument is, however rational and logical it may seem, it just does not feel true.

  Now, of course, there are counter-criticisms: a feeling or an instinct cannot really be proof of anything, even if it is shared by most human beings. This can generate a very interesting conversation about the value of intuition in philosophy!

- Another way to look at it is to say: **if we feel free, who cares if we really are not?** There might be influences shaping our decisions, but those influences are so complex and there are so many of them that we cannot possibly predict what the decisions will be. And what is determinism without prediction? Determinism should mean that actions are predictable, and if it is unable to predict them, it falls flat. In fact, it seems that, most of the time, behaviour is explained *after it has occurred* rather than predicted accurately. This leads to another fascinating question: if determinism relies on the predictability of behaviour, could it be that free will is simply the inability to predict behaviour? In other words, since we *feel* free, and we are unable to make the calculations that can prove us wrong, could freedom just be our default hypothesis until we can show that it is indeed a complete illusion?

- Of course, as we have seen, there are predispositions and tendencies that can be identified, but those are no guarantee that certain behaviours will follow. Until we are able to predict behaviour with certainty, we will not be able to rule out freedom. It is entirely possible to think that human beings are subjected to a multitude of influences that shaped their decisions and actions, but that they still have the ability to contemplate a variety of options and exercise a certain amount of free will. Even if this amount is small, it is still there and invalidates hard determinism.

- Finally, there is also a pragmatic consideration that must enter into the equation: since we don't know whether free will really exists, it is almost reduced to a belief. However, practically speaking, aren't we all better off carrying on with this belief? What would happen without free will?

  One of the most dramatic changes would be the absence of responsibility and the death of morality. If people are not free to act as they wish, they cannot possibly take responsibility for their actions and they cannot be good or bad. They cannot be punished or rewarded. This means giving up on a major aspect of what it means to be human.

Of course, determinism has taught us to be more lenient and to look at what influences people before we condemn them: are they mentally ill? Do they have learning difficulties? Do they suffer from a chemical imbalance or perhaps an addiction? Were they brought up in terrible circumstances? Are they surrounded by criminals? Were they ever taught anything about morality? Did they act out of character?

Those influences mean that we do not see all human beings as equally responsible. However, taking people's situation into account is very different from denying the fact that they made a decision at all: only severely ill people are seen as unable to make decisions. Do we really want all human beings to be seen like puppets, unable to control themselves and help themselves?

That is a danger of extreme forms of determinism. Since we do not know whether free will truly exists, the wisest thing to do for now is probably to pretend that it does until we have proof to the contrary.

**TOK link** 

Think about the conclusion above: reason and sense experience are unable to tell us with certainty whether we are free or not. Yet most people's intuition tells them that they *are* free, because they feel like they are making decisions all the time, and not following a predictable path.

Can intuition be enough to be the foundation of our knowledge of human freedom?

## ACTIVITY: A THOUGHT EXPERIMENT

Imagine that scientists manage to prove that freedom does not exist and that all human behaviour is predictable.

1. What would be the philosophical and practical implications?
2. What would human beings think of themselves?
3. What would become easier? What would become harder?

At the end of your thought experiment, decide if humanity is better off believing in freedom (whether it is actually an illusion or not).

### FIND OUT MORE

A great way into this activity is to listen to the following podcast (Daniel Dennett talks about whether free will is worth wanting):

**http://philosophybites.com/2012/08/daniel-dennett-on-free-will-worth-wanting.html?cid=6a00d834516cc769e2017c3160 8a3b970b#comment-6a00d834516cc769e2017c31608a3b970b**

## FINAL REFLECTION

Given what we know today (scientific knowledge, psychology, social philosophy, etc.) do you think it is still possible to believe that human beings "are condemned to be free"? Can absolute freedom exist?

### Link with the core theme: *freedom* and *being human*

Our understanding of freedom and whether we believe in it at all deeply affects what it means to be human. The existentialist viewpoint, for instance, offers a view of human beings as entirely free to define themselves and ultimately responsible for whom they become. Being human *is* being free, and human beings embody freedom in a way that no other creature can match. Biological determinism, on the other hand, places human beings firmly in nature and amongst other animals. Human beings do not transcend their own biology and their freedom can only exist within the confines of genetic, chemical and evolutionary influences. Social determinism, finally, focuses on human beings as social animals that can only be understood in the context of the groups they belong to. These views do not need to be mutually exclusive, and being human may well mean a complex mixture of freedom, natural behaviours, social influences and other factors. What is important is to understand that every time we redefine freedom or focus on ways in which it is limited, we also redefine what it means to be human: the full philosophical and ethical implications of each theory must be considered.

## Assessment

Below are two stimuli taken from past papers, that can be related to the key concept of freedom:

### Stimulus 5

Source: Calvin and Hobbes © (1998) Watterson. Reprinted with permission of Universal Press Syndicate. 

### Stimulus 6

Human freedom consists in this: that we do not yet know what we shall be, not because the knowledge is too difficult to acquire, not because there are no certainties but only very great improbabilities, but because we are not yet finished. We are begun; what we have already become and are now becoming plays a part in what we shall become.

—L. Susan Stebbing[27]

## Activities

1. Write the first few sentences of an introduction for each of the three stimuli, in which you refer to the stimulus directly and identify the specific philosophical issue that your essay will be focusing on. Make sure the philosophical issue is **directly relevant** to **both** the stimulus and the core theme: *being human*.
2. There are different traditions in the academic world when it comes to introductions and whether they should include a thesis (similar to what you may call a knowledge claim in TOK) or not. A thesis is a statement that usually comes at the end of the introduction and expresses the view the writer intends to defend, or the perspective the writer will argue from.

### Assessment tip: Picking a philosophical issue related to freedom

Freedom is a key concept that we have explored in depth in this chapter. In addition, you may have read some material on your own, and your teacher no doubt gave you extra material and ideas too. This means that you probably know way too much about freedom to fit it all into an essay written in under an hour!

This is why you need to choose a specific philosophical issue. Although it is a good idea to write clearly that your issue is related to the broader key concept of freedom, "freedom" itself is not a good philosophical issue, because it is too broad. Equally, "freedom and determinism" is also too broad, and too vague, to be a good philosophical issue.

When you talk about freedom and/or determinism, it is always a good idea to specify what you intend to focus on exactly. For instance, instead of writing an essay on "whether human beings are free", you are better off narrowing it down to "whether biological determinism eliminates the possibility of human freedom". This is a precise philosophical issue that relates to both the Core theme and the key concept of freedom in a clear manner. It would also, of course, need to relate to the stimulus itself.

Since a good response would need to include a "discussion and assessment of alternative interpretations or points of view", you need to make sure you are familiar with at least two perspectives on the philosophical issue you are choosing. In fact, the issue itself could include a tension between points of view, so that you make it very clear that your essay will be a discussion. For example, you could simply ask: "To what extent are human beings determined by their biology?"; or you could include a second perspective in your question: "Are biological and social determinism equally compelling?", or something even more contrasted, like "Is a belief in radical freedom still possible today, despite scientific discoveries about the biological factors that influence human behaviour?"

Finally, another good idea is to spell things out as clearly as possible in those first few sentences. Remember that your teacher, and even more so your examiner, will have many papers to mark and will not want to hunt for clues! Instead, write in a direct and efficient manner. It is perfectly acceptable to say: "The stimulus depicts [...], which relates to the key concept of freedom in general, and to the following philosophical issue in particular: [...]" Of course, you will also need to justify the link you are making between the stimulus, the Core theme idea of being human, and the specific philosophical issue you have chosen to tackle.

---

[27] L. Susan Stebbing, *Philosophy and the Physicists* (London: Methuen, 1937), p. 249.

| Thesis in the introduction | No thesis in the introduction |
|---|---|
| The introduction ends with a thesis: a statement that clearly tells the reader what position you are going to defend or argue from in the essay. Although you will consider alternative points of view, you already know what position you will end up with. The essay intends to show why this position is the most convincing one, according to you. | The introduction explains the focus of the essay and presents the alternative points of view that will be explored, but does not yet come to any conclusion on which position is most convincing. Typically, this type of introduction may end with a question that will be answered later in the essay. |
| **Example:** "This essay will attempt to demonstrate that, although social conditioning influences our actions, human beings are still, ultimately, free to choose what path to follow". | **Example:** "Does social conditioning influence human beings' actions to the extent that the very existence of their freedom is threatened?" |
| **Advantages:** very clear beginning, that can help the reader but also the writer keep the focus of the essay in mind. The thesis can convey confidence and competence: the writer has thought about this before and knows his/her own position on the matter. This is a style that is favoured by a growing number of teachers and examiners. | **Advantages:** the essay is a genuine exploration of several points of view that mimics what a philosopher should do when presented with an issue. The point is to analyse and evaluate various perspectives before coming to a conclusion. There is more suspense and the question can really hook the reader. |
| **Disadvantages:** it can be a shame to give the game away so early on. The suspense is lost. The essay can become the defence of one point on view rather than a genuine exploration of several points of view. | **Disadvantages:** it may be harder to remain focused, and easier to digress away from the philosophical issue at hand. It can seem that the writer is actually thinking about this for the first time, which should not be the case after two years of philosophy! |

**Activity**: Pick one of the stimuli above and practise writing both styles of introduction. Is there one you prefer? It may be a good idea to discuss this with your teacher too.

3. Once you have a thesis (whether you write it down or keep it in your head!), make a list of the evidence you could use to support it. This should include historical or contemporary examples, philosophers' theories and arguments, as well as arguments from other areas of knowledge, such as sciences. Bear in mind that, in an essay, all of these will need to be **justified** and not just stated. Their relevance to your chosen philosophical issue will need to be evident or explained. Some relevance to the stimulus can make the evidence used even stronger.
4. Pick one piece of evidence listed above (perhaps the one you know in most depth), and use it to practise your analysis and evaluation skills, making a clear difference between them:

| Analysis – some guiding questions | Evaluation – some guiding questions |
|---|---|
| What perspective is this piece of evidence supporting, and why?<br>What assumptions can be found in this piece of evidence? What is the perspective of the person putting this piece of evidence forward? In what context is the piece of evidence put forward?<br>What are the implications of this piece of evidence (i.e. implications for what it means to be human, ethical implications, etc.)?<br>What are common criticisms of this piece of evidence? | How convincing is this piece of evidence? How does it compare to its criticisms, and why?<br>Are the assumptions identified problematic? Is this still a reliable piece of evidence, despite assumptions, context and perspective?<br>How useful is this piece of evidence in the development of your own argument? What do you think about it and why? What does it tell you about your main thesis? |

**Assessment tip** 

Turn to Chapter 8: IB Philosophy Assessment for a more detailed account of what analysis and evaluation involve, and what questions can help you make sure you are on the right track.

## References Cited


Andrew J. Elliot and Daniela Niesta. "Romantic Red: Red Enhances Men's Attraction to Women". *Journal of Personality and Social Psychology* 95, No. 5 (2008): 1150–1164.

Darwin, Charles. *On the Origin of Species*. John Murray, 1859. Now available at http://darwin-online.org.uk/content/frameset?itemID=F373&viewtype=text&pageseq=1 (accessed 21 October 2014).

de Beauvoir, Simone. *The Second Sex*. Translated by Constance Borde and Sheila Malovany-Chevallier. Introduced by Judith Thurman. New York: Vintage, 2009.

DNA Learning Centre. "Criminals' Common Features, F. Galton". Available at http://www.dnalc.org/view/15781-Criminals-common-features-F-Galton.html (accessed 28 October 2014).

Fitzgerald, F. Scott. *The Great Gatsby*. New York: Charles Scribner's, 1925. Reproduced here from http://crossref-it.info/text/the-great-gatsby/chapter-8 (accessed 28 October 2014).

Laplace, Pierre-Simon. *A Philosophical Essay on Probabilities*, with an introductory note by E. T. Bell. Translated from the French by Frederick William Truscott and Frederick Lincoln Emory. New York: Dover Publications, 1995.

Little, Anthony C., Benedict C. Jones, and Lisa M. DeBruine. "Facial Attractiveness: Evolutionary Based Research". *Philosophical Transactions of the Royal Society B: Biological Sciences* 366, No. 1571 (12 June 2012): 1638–1659. Available at http://www.ncbi.nlm.nih.gov/pmc/articles/PMC3130383/ (accessed 28 October 2014).

Livingstone, Tessa. "The New Gender Divide". *TES Newspaper*, 9 May 2008 (updated 4 August 2008). Available at http://www.tes.co.uk/article.aspx?storycode=2619363 (accessed 28 October 2014).

Marx, Karl. *Theses on Feuerbach* (Stuttgart: J. W. H. Dietz, 1888); available at http://www.marxists.org/archive/marx/works/1845/theses/ (accessed 28 October 2014).

Millett, Kate. *Sexual Politics*. Urbana, IL: University of Illinois Press, 2000.

Ministry of Justice. "Social Risk Factors for Involvement in Crime". In *New Zealand Criminal Justice Sector Outcomes Report: Strategic Policy Brief*. New Zealand: Ministry of Justice, 2009. Available at http://www.justice.govt.nz/justice-sector/drivers-of-crime/documents/spb-social-risk-factors (accessed 28 October 2014).

Rousseau, Jean-Jacques. *Discourse on the Origin and Basis of Inequality Among Men* [*Second Discourse*] (France, 1755. Available at http://www.constitution.org/jjr/ineq.htm (accessed 28 October 2014).

Rousseau, Jean-Jacques. *On the Social Contract, Or Principles of Political Right*. France, 1762. Available at http://www.constitution.org/jjr/socon.htm (accessed 28 October 2014).

Sartre, Jean-Paul. *Existentialism and Humanism*. Translated from the French by Philip Mairet. London: Methuen, 1948.

Sartre, Jean-Paul. *Being and Nothingness*. Translated from the French by Hazel E. Barnes. New York: Philosophical Library, 1956.

Sartre, Jean-Paul. *Existentialism Is a Humanism*. Yale: Yale University Press, 2007.

Stebbing, L. Susan. *Philosophy and the Physicists*. London: Methuen, 1937.

Studebaker, Benjamin. "A Critique of Existentialism", 5 September 2012. Available at http://benjaminstudebaker.com/2012/09/05/a-critique-of-existentialism/ (accessed 28 October 2014).

Taylor, Richard. *Action and Purpose*. Englewood Cliffs, NJ: Prentice-Hall, 1966. Extract also available at http://www.informationphilosopher.com/solutions/philosophers/taylorr/ (accessed 28 October 2014).

Thiry, Paul-Henri. *The System of Nature, Or the Laws of the Moral and Physical World*, vol. 1. Edited by Robert D. Richardson. Translated by H. D. Robinson. Mirbaud, 1770. Available at http://www.gutenberg.org/files/8909/8909-h/8909-h.htm#link2H_4_0022 (accessed 22 October 2014).

# BEING HUMAN

## 7 Identity

- → Personal identity
- → Identity over time
- → Social and cultural identity

### Some essential questions:

- → Who am I?
- → What makes me me?
- → What makes me the same person I was 10 years ago?
- → What sort of changes could I survive?
- → What would bring my existence to an end?
- → What makes it the case that some past or future being, rather than another, is you or I?
- → To what extent does culture influence or define my identity?

### Stimulus 1

Life is a valuable and unique opportunity
to discover who you are.
But it seems as soon as you near
answering that age-old question,
something unexpected always happens
to alter your course.
And who it is you thought you were
suddenly changes.

Then comes the frustrating realization
that no matter how long life endures,
no matter how many experiences
are muddled through in this existence,
you may never really be able
to answer the question....

Who am I?

Because the answer, like the seasons,
constantly, subtly, inevitably changes.
And who it is you are today,
is not the same person you will be tomorrow.

—Sha Eena, 87th Queen of Harrowbeth[1]

---

[1] see http://www.harrowbeth.com/

## Questions

1. Thinking about the stimulus above identify the issues it suggests which are associated with person identity? Write a list.
2. Which issue do you think is the most important one?
3. Can you think of any features of personal identity that are not suggested in the stimulus?

The issue of personal identity is a modern problem, although there are references to it as far back as ancient Greece. The reason why it became an issue was that it has traditionally been solved by the presumed existence of the soul (in a number of traditions including Western, Confucian, and Hindu). With the legitimacy of the soul being questioned, especially in the modern era of scientific knowledge, the question of how to define the uniqueness of an individual became a significant philosophical question. This question has been prompted by the increasingly important role that identity plays in cultural, legal, moral, religious, even scientific contexts. This concern is a relatively new one in Western thought – a concern of the modern era defined as post-17th-century. It is usually stated that the English philosopher Locke introduced this as an explicit philosophical problem in his *Essay Concerning Human Understanding* (1689). He responded to a perceived deficiency in Descartes' concept of the self. Descartes argued that "I think, therefore I am" establishing the certainty of existence. But Locke pointed out that Descartes had not secured the certainty of existence over time. According to Locke, the concept of the self now had to encompass a justification of how the self endured. While our everyday language assumes a permanent personal identity, an enduring self, it is a different question when considering the philosophical debate. Nearly all philosophical systems from around the world have attempted to answer the question of the enduring self, even occasionally rejecting the possibility of an enduring self. In contemporary philosophical debates especially, there are many positions offered with many of them highly complex in their assumptions and reasoning. There are many examples of how the enduring self has been argued and equally how it has been challenged. Consequently, this subject is an intriguing topic for analysis and evaluation. There are sound reasons why this issue needs to be explored further, even resolved, given the complexities of our modern existence.

**Create a list of elements that make up you.**

Which ones do you believe you could lose and still remain you? For example, if you get a haircut, even a radical one, are you still you? Obviously, you have lost some hair, changed your "look", even removed some hair colouring, but you are still "you".

### The question of identity: the Ship of Theseus

An interesting story that has become synonymous with the issue of personal identity is the Ship of Theseus, which is frequently referred to in philosophical discussion, so it is worth reflecting upon here. Theseus was a hero in ancient Athens who defeated the Minotaur on the island of Crete while rescuing some Athenian captives. Victorious, he then sailed them back to Athens to be hailed as a hero of the city. To honour him, the Athenian leaders secured the ship and once a year paraded it in the harbour. The ship was, of course, made of wood, so gradually it started to deteriorate. Each time it needed a repair the shipbuilders fixed the problem, replacing the various damaged parts of the ship.

▲ A 3rd-century BCE Roman mosaic floor showing Theseus returning to Athens, excavated in Tunisia

According to Greek legend, as reported by Plutarch,

> The ship wherein Theseus and the youth of Athens returned [from Crete] had thirty oars, and was preserved by the Athenians down even to the time of Demetrius Phalereus, for they took away the old planks as they decayed, putting in new and stronger timber in their place, insomuch that this ship became a standing example among the philosophers, for the logical question of things that grow; one side holding that the ship remained the same, and the other contending that it was not the same.[2]

**Guiding question**

- How do we identify something?

The ship is repaired gradually but nonetheless eventually every part of the old ship is replaced. Is it therefore the same ship as the one on which Theseus returned to Athens? Do any of the replacement parts cause the original ship to cease to exist?

Hobbes introduced a further dimension to this puzzle. He wondered what would happen if all the original parts of Theseus' ship were collected by someone from the scrap heap in the shipyard, who used them to build a second ship. He puts them all together again and claims that this is the real Ship of Theseus.

Which one is the "real" Ship of Theseus? Is it the one that is paraded each year, witnessed by the crowds attending the occasion? Or is it the one reconstructed from the original pieces discarded over time? Regardless of your answer, understanding the question requires an understanding of the various conceptual frameworks used to determine an understanding of the issue and the formulation of a position. This requires an analytical strategy to undertake developing this understanding and an evaluative framework in order to assess the various components of this philosophical issue.

In the modern debate, the issue of identity is often discussed in terms of transporter machines as seen in *Star Trek*. Discussions also include scenarios such as transplanting brains. Presently these are in the realm of science fiction, although there are claims by futurists that these possibilities are coming closer and closer. Probably one of the most famous instances of the issue of personal identity is *Doctor Who*. The Doctor, as he is known, is a Time Lord who has the ability to travel back and forth through space and time using a device called the TARDIS (which stands for Time And Relative Dimension In Space). An interesting aspect of being a Time Lord is the ability (and need) to regenerate when they die. The Doctor has regenerated in a new body and the character continues. The show actually changes this assumption of the continuity of identity in an episode called "Journey's End" (2008). In this episode an accident creates a replica of the Doctor. The replica is made of different atoms and displays a different personality (as all regenerations have). However, his memories are the memories of the "real" still existing Doctor. Rosa, his companion, asserts that this replica is not the same doctor. Is she right?

## ANOTHER VERSION

A more modern version of this story is about a collector of famous Formula One racing cars. The collector agrees to buy the championship-winning car just before its final race. In this race the driver loses control and crashes the car, damaging over 90% of the car. Engineers rebuild it, but in the process have to replace over 90% of the car. The collector refuses to buy the car, arguing it is a new car and he had wanted to buy the crashed car instead (for a lot less money!). Is it still the same car?

**Links**

Other questions are also evident in this issue. For example, this is also a question of authenticity, discussed in Chapter 5: The Self and the Other.

[2] Plutarch, *Vita Thesei*, 22–23; reproduced from https://faculty.washington.edu/smcohen/320/theseus.html (accessed 29 October 2014).

This is not only illustrated by science fiction. Raymond Martin, in *The Rise and Fall of the Soul and Self: An Intellectual History of Personal Identity*, suggests that Epicharmus, an ancient Greek comic playwright, broached the subject of personal identity in one of his plays in the 5th century BCE. Martin retells this scene in the play as follows:

> In this scene, a lender asks a debtor to pay up. The debtor replies by asking the lender whether he agrees that anything that undergoes change, such as a pile of pebbles to which one pebble has been added or removed, thereby becomes a different thing. The lender says that he agrees with that. "Well, then," says the debtor, "aren't people constantly undergoing changes?" "Yes," replies the lender. "So," says the debtor, "it follows that I am not the same person as the one who was indebted to you and, so, I owe you nothing." The lender then hits the debtor, who protests loudly at being abused. The lender replies that the debtor's complaint is misdirected since he – the lender – is not the same person as the one who hit him a moment before.[3]

To listen to an interview with Raymond Martin on the issue of personal identity – go to http://www.philosophytalk.org/shows/personal-identity-0#sthash.ul18orYN.dpuf

This captures the key elements of the issue about personal identity even in contemporary debates. How can something that is always changing have an individual identity that is the same over time? Other potential investigations are how is the concept of personal identity conceived and what are the implications for the particular type or definition of personal identity. The issue of personal identity covers the issue of attributing responsibility to the correct agent and our understanding of ourselves as individuals with free will and a future. Similarly, within philosophy a position on personal identity influences – and is influenced by – the debates on the self, human nature, mind and body, personhood, and free will.

### TOK link

Identity is not just a consideration in philosophy. Other disciplines also consider the question of identity. For example, companion issues such as individuality, social identity, and cultural identity are discussed in psychology, sociology, anthropology, law, and even the experimental sciences.

#### Questions

What methodology does each of these disciplines use to explore the issue of identity?

How is the methodology determined?

What influence does the methodology have on the outcome?

## Understanding the issue of personal identity

In Hesse's novel *Siddhartha* (1922), a friend asks the protagonist the simple question, "Who is he?" and he responds by saying, "I do not know; I know as little as you. I am on the way. I was a rich man but I am no longer, and what I will be tomorrow I do not know ... Where is Siddhartha the Brahmin, where is Siddhartha the Samana [ascetic], where is Siddhartha the rich man?"[4] The question that emerges out of this reflection is, has his identity changed? In order to understand this question the conceptual frameworks that are essential to defining the issue need to be established.

As should already be evident, the question of personal identity is an extension of the question of the self and of personhood. The question of the self explores the initial question "What is unique about being a human?" and 'What is it to be a person?' This opens up a third question: "What is unique about individual humans?"

[3] Raymond Martin, *The Rise and Fall of the Soul and Self: An Intellectual History of Personal Identity* (New York: Columbia University Press, 2006), p. 3.

[4] Hesse, *Siddhartha*; reproduced from Hilda Rosner's translation in *Siddhartha, Demian, and Other Writings*, edited by Egon Schwarz, in collaboration with Ingrid Fry (New York: Continuum Publishing, 2001), p. 70.

The question of personal identity builds upon question and explores two questions in response. The first is "What differentiates you from another person?" The second is "What makes you 'you' over time?" The first is the question of **individuality**. What makes you a different person from your friend sitting next to you? The second is called the issue of the **enduring self**. Are you the same person who broke your mother's sunglasses when you were two years old? Your father's favourite coffee mug when you were seven? When you broke your first bone when you were 12 years old and so on? There are different approaches to these questions. Both questions ask what the conditions of identity are, or the criterion or criteria of determining identity.

This topic therefore asks what conditions need to be satisfied in order for a person to be able to claim they are 1) different from the person next to them and 2) the same person as they were yesterday, in previous years, when they were five years old, and so on. Obviously, a position on the self is often assumed otherwise this question would be difficult to ask. The self provides the foundation for these questions. Consequently, the question of the self is a topic that establishes the context for this discussion and is very influential when determining an answer to an enduring self. Interestingly, as philosophers have considered the question of the enduring self they have also returned to the question of the self, revising assumptions and arguments. In this way, the enduring self can be seen as a test of the founding concept of the self.

An illustration of this shift in focus from "being human" to personal identity is provided by the following example. If it was agreed that a human (or a person) was identified by the use of reason – for example, Aristotle's claim that we are rational animals – then what differentiates, if at all, one rational being from another. In this instance it might be the ability of each human to use reason. This distinguishing factor provides individuality.

## Philosophical terms and theories

The relationship between the self and personal identity is not necessarily straight forward. There is a concern about the inclusion of the concept of the self in the issue of personal identity. Can you change your self and retain your identity? For this reason, some philosophers call it the issue of the **persistence of identity**.

### Exploring the possibilities

First, there is a need to understand initial reactions to the issue of personal identity.

Consider the following scenario: Sandra was in a car accident which resulted in her suffering severe brain damage. Her body is being kept alive by machines. The doctors state that her brain is no longer functioning cognitively and she is in a vegetative state. She has no personality. She does not respond to her surroundings, nor can she move of her own volition. The relevant question is, is Sandra still Sandra? Sandra has been stripped by the car accident of the ability to think, reason, without her memories or her aspirations. She has no emotional response to the world and no personality. She is unable to initiate actions and interact with, even create, her world. This just leaves her body. Is this enough to claim that the body is still Sandra? Or is one the factors mentioned above essential to her identity? Or is it a particular combination of these factors? This issue is close to the issue of the self but it asks, what is it that gives a person an identity?

This can be taken further, by asking how do you know a person's identity is the same over time? Peter Unger calls for an inquiry into our persistence conditions that must "appreciate what is involved in a philosophically adequate conception of ourselves. [...] such an adequate concept must be well suited for engagement with our central prudential thoughts and concerns [...]. And it must be well suited for our engagement with morality."[5] Central to his concern is the question of responsibility for an action. A classic example is the court case in 1993 of Ivan Polyukovich, a man who was accused of war crimes for the 1942 murder of 850 Jews in Ukraine, 51 years earlier. One simple question was asked, was he the same person who had committed these atrocities? He was a frail, gentle man, still happily married, adored by his grandchildren and respected for his many contributions to his local community. Was he the same man who had murdered 850 people when he was younger? Answering this question is one reason for exploring the issue of personal identity. Another is our understanding of ourselves as individuals with free will and a future. If we do not know if we will be the same person in the future, why do we plan for this future by investing in quality education, putting money aside, and seeking out opportunities. How do we know there is a continuum of identity from our context of the present moment?

## EXPLORATION ACTIVITY

### Can I borrow some money?

This activity can be used to explore the opinions of people outside your classroom. Present this scenario to your friends and family.

"A friend borrows money off you one day and agrees to pay it back in a couple of days. When it is time to pay it back your friend tells you he or she is not the same person and therefore does not have to repay the debt of someone else."

Ask: How would you prove to your friend that he or she is the same person?

Record their responses for further discussion.

The responses to the scenario in the exploration activity above often include some of the following:

- Same soul
- Same memories
- Same body
- The promise made by the individual
- The opinion of other people.

It should not be surprising that these are also reflected in the philosophical debate. For now it is worth thinking about the issue of change and its role on an understanding of the issue of personal identity.

So what changes would have to happen for you to say that you no longer exist? In other words, what can change about you yet you still survive, or are regarded as the same person? Would it be having your fingernails cut? Your hair cut? In a similar manner you can ask the question of whether

### Thought experiment

Think of a snowman. The sun comes out and the snowman starts to melt. When do you consider it to no longer be a snow man? At what point does it stop being a snowman and start being a lump of ice? What criteria do you use to judge when this point occurs?

[5] Peter Unger, "The Survival of the Sentient", *Noûs* 34, No. s14 (2000): 326; originally published in *Philosophical Perspectives* 14 (2000) 34pp.

having an organ transplant would mean that your identity would transfer with it? Is it *your* heart if it is transplanted? Your face? Your brain? Your soul? Another way of conceiving of this is to ask what the tolerance is for change before too much change means something new exists.

## In summary

This is a philosophical issue that finds its initial investigation in the concept of the self. However, if properly delineated, this is an issue of identity of a category – such as a human or a person – or an issue of individuality and an issue of the self (the personal). The enduring self asks 'what is it that must be retained in your self, whatever that is, for you to exist over time?'

### Stimulus 2

For this stimulus, identify an issue and corresponding point of discussion in relation to personal identity.

### ASSESSMENT PRACTICE

The stimulus above could suggest the following:

- the experience of disappearance or receding of an individual
- the disconnect of the other
- the issue of identity in a decontextualizing experience

How would you justify these interpretations and their connection to the philosophical issue of personal identity?

### Questions

- To what extent is the body a defining feature of the person?
- What is the importance of the other in the formation of identity?
- How important is meaning to individuality?
- How does an individual come into existence?
- Can an identity be taken from an individual?

### Understanding key philosophical distinctions

Before we explore the various positions on personal identity it is worthwhile clarify some of the key philosophical distinctions that are present in the debate regarding personal identity. These will feature in many of the secondary readings you will cover and it is therefore important to be at least familiar with them as they are part of the debate. The first distinction concerns the meaning of identical and is discussed in terms of **qualitative versus numerical**. This relates to the debate on individuality or individuation, or "What is it that differentiates one person from another?". The second distinction is **necessary and sufficient**. This distinction is important as it provides an insight into the criterion or criteria of personal identity or the enduring self, or 'What makes me 'me' over time?'. These include qualitative versus numerical, and necessary versus sufficient.

## Qualitative versus numerical

The first distinction is qualitative versus numerical. Qualitative identity refers to exact similarity and is usually illustrated by reference to identical twins or the nursery rhyme characters Tweedledum and Tweedledee from Lewis Carroll's *Through the Looking-Glass* (1872). They are the same in terms of qualities yet they are different people or characters. This is not the identity issue that is the concern of this chapter. A similar case is often illustrated by reference to Jekyll and Hyde. Robert Louis Stevenson's story *The Strange Case of Dr Jekyll and Mr Hyde* (1886) focuses on one man who has two distinct moral personalities. In modern psychiatry this condition is known as dissociative identity disorder. When Dr Jekyll transforms into Mr Hyde they are qualitatively different but they are the same person. Again this is not the identity issue being discussed in this chapter. Instead, it is the issue of numerical identity. In simple terms this is indicated by the equals sign in a mathematical statement such as 2 + 2 = 4. "2+2" and "4" are the same, standing for the same number, even if expressed differently.

This is understood by the example of a young child who does something naughty, such as breaking a vase. Twenty years later, is that child still the same person who broke that vase? Well, qualitatively she is different in that she has grown and changed form (to a certain extent). But she is not numerically different.

**Assessment tip** 

Given the assessment of the core theme, an in-depth understanding is not essential for a quality analysis of the issue of personal identity in an exam context. However, if you choose this topic for your internal assessment you might need to include this issue or aspects of this issue in your analysis.

### EXTENSION

Numerical identity is often called Leibniz's Law. This is the claim that A is the same as B only if everything true about A is also true about B. This is not strictly applicable to the issue of personal identity unless the conditional, *x* and *y* are identical if any property possessed by *x* at time *t* is also possessed by *y* at time *t*, is added. This introduces a fourth dimension (temporality) to the issue. This is a controversial addition, with some philosophers believing it compromises the principle. However, other philosophers, including John Perry, have disagreed with this objection. This position is called four-dimensionalism. This position can be used to answer the Ship of Theseus conundrum.

### Necessary versus sufficient

The second distinction is necessary versus sufficient. When we ask the question "What is a Z?", we are asking about the nature of Z, not what is the meaning of Z or what is the concept of Z. As such it is an **ontological** question, which is a **metaphysical** question. It is asking for the conditions of Z to be outlined to enable someone to identify Z. This is the **question of sufficiency**. It can, however, also

**Further reading**

For a more detailed introduction to necessary versus sufficient conditions see the discussion in Chapter 3: Personhood.

be asking what Z is made up of, what it is composed of, as well. This is the **question of necessity**. Both of these questions are answered in terms of "If ... then" or conditional statements. Conditional statements relate the truths of two propositions and connect them by stating that if the first statement (**antecedent**) is true, then the second statement (**consequent**) is true.

In terms of personal identity these conditionals can be framed in the following way:

- If I am the same person at times *t1* and *t2*, then [condition(s)].
- If [condition(s)], then I am the same person at times *t1* and *t2*.

The emphasis changes in each of these two statements between the **antecedent** and the **consequent**.

The first refers to necessity. A **necessary condition** is one that must be satisfied before whatever is being referred to can belong to a class. The focus is on the **antecedent**.

The second refers to sufficiency. A **sufficient condition** is one that is enough to conclude immediately whatever is being referred to is a member of a class. The focus is on the **consequent**.

In a basic form the difference between these two conditions is "must" and "enough".

This defines the measure of identity and in the context of personal identity indicates the conditions required in order for identity to be asserted. It is important to remember that these conditions are not causes. The presence of this aspect of a person does not cause personal identity, just provides the conditions for identity.

**LINK TO OPTIONAL THEME**

The self and therefore personal identity are key concepts in political philosophy. They are especially relevant when considering political ideologies.

## Understanding Personal Identity

We have looked at a number of different scenarios and thought experiments that highlight the issue of personal identity. The most famous example is the Ship of Theseus. Regardless of your response to this question, understanding the issue requires an understanding of the various conceptual frameworks that can be used to determine both an understanding of the issue and the formulation of a position. Understanding the conceptual framework(s) allows you to develop an analytical strategy that can be used to investigate the issue and then by assessing the various components argue a position on the issue using your own evaluative framework. Personal identity can be approached using a number of conceptual frameworks. Each of these frameworks emerges out of a particular approach to doing philosophy that has been influenced by a number of factors such as accepted or unchallenged assumptions, methodology, and purpose. In broad terms there have been three phases in the Western tradition's consideration of the issue of personal identity. the first was initiated by Plato and his arguments dominated the debate, albeit an indirect one until the publication of the works of Locke. His approach maintained its preeminence until the middle of the 1960s when a number of developments occurred including a shift from an understanding that the issue of personal identity was one about intrinsic relations to one where it was believed to be about extrinsic ones.

**Philosophical terms and theories**

The approaches to personal identity can also be divided into two categories: intrinsic and extrinsic relations. The first, intrinsic relations, refers to a physical and/or psychological relationship between two selves that is justified by a material or mental connection. The second, extrinsic relations, refers to a relationship between two selves whose connection is justified by other people.

These different approaches can be defined equally as effectively as individualism versus communitarianism.

**Individualism**

Material substance – bodily criterion of identity

Immaterial substance – soul theory of identity

Immaterial Non-substance – psychological continuity theory

**Communitarianism**

Identity in context – sociocultural identity

Individualism focuses on an essence that defines an individual's unique identity. The first argument is the bodily criterion of identity. This position argues that it is our body that defines who we are and determines how we can exist over time. The next step responds to questions about the validity of the claim that our body remains the same therefore maintaining our identity. Instead, this position argues for a substance that does not change. This is called the soul theory of identity. The final position rejects the existence of the soul and instead looks to something that is unique to an individual but does not rely on something that 1) changes and 2) is difficult to prove exists. This is called the theory of psychological continuity. All these essential positions can be rejected. Communitarians argue that out identity comes from our context: out family, our culture, our society, even our education. This position often assumes that we do not have an essential self, an innate human nature; rather, our identity is a product of our social environment.

## FIND OUT MORE

Christopher Shields presents a discussion on the issue of personal identity

http://philosophybites.com/2008/11/christopher-shi.html

## Exploring the position of individualism

### Material substance

The first position from the individualist on personal identity is the physical criterion and its focus on the body. This is the strict materialist position. One of the first issues that need to be considered with this position is what is material? This is a metaphysical question. A secondary question is the epistemological one, how do you know? These two questions are interrelated and influence each other. However, the issue of personal identity is primarily a metaphysical issue. In other words, a philosopher has a position on what is real and then determines what something can be to exist.

## Philosophical terms

**Materialism**, the theory that everything is formed of matter and nothing else exists, is closely associated with physicalism, although sometimes they are argued to be the same position expressed from slightly different approaches. In the modern era science has been involved in this discussion as scientific discoveries about matter have contributed to this position. These philosophers have included Daniel Dennett, W. V. Quine, Donald Davidson, John Searle, and Jerry Fodor.

## EXPLORATION ACTIVITY

This is illustrated by a simple activity. Ask someone to think of a unicorn. Then ask them, do they exist? If they say no, then they have indicated that something can only exist if it is made out of material and can be perceived by the senses. If they say yes, then it is likely that they believe that thoughts in their head are real and therefore the unicorn they have just thought of exists. (Or they may believe that they exist in terms of the first position but are exceptionally good at avoiding being photographed. This option is

not covered by this discussion.) An obvious response is the question, "if thoughts are real what are they made up of?". This question asks for a position on the issue of substance to be resolved. In basic terms, a position can be taken that for something to be real it must be extended in time and space. For example, it is made out of atoms. Atoms are the building block of all things that are material. However, if it is believed that thoughts are real, this rejects the assumption that things that exist are made only out of atoms.

This issue can be clearly located in the mind–body problem. If you reject the idea of the mind (not the brain) and only accept the existence of the body then this provides the context for personal identity. Consequently, a materialist accepts the assumption that material is the primary component of reality. Consequently, if anything else exists, it must be derived from material. This is the starting point for the exploration of personal identity from the individualism approach.

## The body and personal identity

The obvious way in which we identify people is through the way they look, or more **specifically** the same body. This is called the **bodily criterion of identity** (or occasionally, the **biological approach to personal identity**). This position argues that there must be spatio-temporal continuity in order for identity to persist. Therefore the role of the body is key to discussions involving an individual's identity, regardless of whether or not those involved agree with it as a primary focus. As Eric T. Olson observes:

> One of the main problems of personal identity is supposed to be how we relate to our bodies. A few philosophers endorse what is called a "bodily criterion of personal identity": they say that we *are* our bodies, or at any rate that our identity over time consists in the identity of our bodies. Many more deny this – typically on the grounds that we can imagine ourselves coming apart from our bodies. But both sides agree that the bodily criterion is an important view which anyone thinking about personal identity must consider.[6]

If the person you saw today looked the same as they did yesterday you would confidently say that they were the same person. By look we are referring to the body and most significantly the face. They might be wearing different clothes and have a different hairstyle but they would still be the same person. They might have dyed their hair, badly hurt themselves, or had some cosmetic surgery but they would still be the same person. But what if they could not remember you? Or if they referred to past events that you knew nothing of, for example they referred to a different spouse and different children?

[6] Eric T. Olson, "Is There a Bodily Criterion of Personal Identity?", in Fraser MacBride (ed.), *Identity and Modality* (Oxford: Oxford University Press, 2006), p. 242.

## REFLECTION

The reverse is also an interesting scenario. What if someone came up to you whom you had never seen before and announced he or she was your best friend, recalling an event that only you and your best friend had experienced?

Would you rely on what you saw (the person's body) or what you heard (the person's memories)?

### Understanding the issue of continuum

The question of the enduring self is a question of **continuum**. This is often defined as a pearl necklace – individual pearls do not make a necklace but when they are strung together they become a necklace. The "string" is often conceived in the idea of consciousness. However, the nature of this consciousness is debated.

Unsurprisingly, this is just one of a number of options for conceiving the issue of personal identity. Another way is to think of a flame that is continually passed from candle to candle. In the process there is a continuity but no real *personal* identity. This is a very different concept from the one based on the Western notion of consciousness.

**Reflection Questions**

What must occur for a continuum to be in place? What is being connected and how is it connected? In other words, what is the basis of this continuum?

The **physical criterion** requires that a person hold some relation of physical continuity between persons at different times. The same person is therefore the same biological object over time. A common response is to declare that the human body regenerates every seven years, suggesting that this progressive replacement means that you are a new person every seven years. There is medical research using a technique involving carbon-14 dating, which has led to some interesting facts about regeneration. It turns out that each aspect of our body has a different regeneration time. This ranges from our gut lining, which is replaced every five days, to the muscles between the ribs, which are replaced approximately every 15 years.

Some philosophers argue that the physical criterion of personal identity is solved by the existence of DNA. Michael Allen Fox, in *Philosophy Now*, discusses the composition of our bodies as part of the physical continuity approach;

> We all know that our DNA structure is unique to each of us. Philosophers who favour the physical criterion of personal identity could therefore fasten onto DNA as the source of individual continuity. They might trumpet that a scientific physicalistic solution to the identity problem is finally at hand. Curiously, they have not thus far seized the opportunity to do so. DNA certainly seems like a tempting physical carrier for personal identity, because it's as identifying of oneself as anything can be. . . . But even here, hopes are dashed for identity. The human body contains between one and ten trillion cells. Red blood cells have no DNA, but all the others do. It also turns out that only ten percent of the DNA present within our bodies belongs to our own cells: the rest reside within the ten to one hundred trillion bacteria and other organisms of several hundred species which inhabit our bodies. Hence it now looks as if what counts as 'my' body, although macroscopically quite specifiable, is, from the standpoint of genetic coding only ten percent mine. This leaves us with the awkward conclusion (which we shall have to accept) that to be me is to cohabit my body with trillions upon trillions of other organisms, whose genetic coding radically deviates from my own DNA blueprint. My body is no longer simply my body.[7]

[7] Michael Allen Fox, "A New Look at Personal Identity", *Philosophy Now*, No. 62 (July/August 2007): 11.

The actual biological criterion can be the human being (animal), the body, the brain, even the central nervous system. However, while the bodily criterion is our commonsense understanding of identity, there are situations where this understanding conflicts with other aspects of our commonsense understanding of this issue.

The first discussion of the popular thought experiment "Brain Transplant" was undertaken by Sydney Shoemaker. He described the following scenario:

> It is now possible to transplant certain organs ... [i]t is at least conceivable ... that a human body could continue to function normally if its brain were replaced by one taken from another human body ... Two men, a Mr Brown and a Mr Robinson, had been operated on for brain tumors, and brain extractions had been performed on both of them. At the end of the operations, however, the assistant inadvertently put Brown's brain in Robinson's head, and Robinson's brain in Brown's head. One of these men immediately dies, but the other, the one with Robinson's head and Brown's brain, eventually regains consciousness. Let us call the latter "Brownson"... When asked his name he automatically replies "Brown". He recognizes Brown's wife and family ... and is able to describe in detail events in Brown's life ... of Robinson's life he evidences no knowledge at all.[8]

## REFLECTION QUESTION

Which statement do you think is correct?

"Brown is the same person as Brownson."

*Or*

"Robinson acquires a new brain."

The majority of people believe that the first one is correct. The brain and the memories contained within that brain are the most important element of a human. Yet, if this is our intuitive response then the bodily criterion is false.

### Assessing the bodily criterion

With this position it is argued that our identity is determined by the identity of our bodies. The conclusion drawn by Shoemaker in the thought experiment outlined above suggests that it is not a common sense understanding of personal identity. It is worth recounting what is being argued. Brian Garrett expressed the bodily criterion argument in the following manner: "Person A at time t1 is identical to person B at time t2 if and only if A and B have the same body."[9]

This states that if we have the same body then we are the same person.

However, as we saw earlier, our bodies regenerate over time, and also as we grow we change. We look very different at the age of 50 compared to how we looked when we were five years old. Can we therefore make the claim that we are the same person?

[8] Sydney Shoemaker, *Self-Knowledge and Self-Identity* (Ithaca, NY: Cornell University Press, 1963), pp. 23–24.

[9] Brian Garrett, *What Is This Thing Called Metaphysics?* (London: Routledge, 2006), p. 45.

The immediate response is to say that change is fine as long as it is not sudden or comprehensive. Imagine a five-year-old who goes to sleep and wakes up a 50-year-old. It would be hard to believe he or she is the same person. But if the child changes over a span of 45 years? Then that is more acceptable. However, if a person is in an accident and comes out of hospital significantly different, is he or she still the same person? The suggestion is that a stable and continuous change is sufficient to determine continuity. The question for bodily criterion is what is sufficient change for it to be acceptable?

If we take the quantitative approach, what percentage is sufficient? If we return to the Ship of Theseus story, one of the questions was when does the ship stop being the ship if the change is gradual? Is it a quantity such as 51%? Or is it more to do with significant parts of the ship, such as the mast or the sails, rather than the planks of wood? With humans, is hair equivalent to the heart or the brain? This requires an answer for the position to be valid. Olson phrases it in the following way:

> ... what does it take for my body to survive? When do someone picked out at one time and someone picked out at another time have the same body? What happens to my body when you cut off my arm, for example? Does my body get a bit smaller and ten pounds lighter? Does it become a spatially scattered object? Does it make a difference if you cut off my head instead of my arm?[10]

## FIND OUT MORE

Research the argument by a defender of **animalism**, David Wiggins. The argument for animalism is relational in nature. It relies on the psychology of typical members of its kind or the psychology of other individuals.

His position is stated in the following quote:

> [P]erhaps x is a person if and only if x is an animal falling under the extension of a kind whose typical members perceive, feel, remember, imagine, desire, make projects, move themselves at will, speak, carry out projects, acquire a character as they age, are susceptible to concern for members of their own or like species ... conceive of themselves as perceiving, feeling ... etc. On this account person is a non-biological qualification of animal, and, potentially at least, a cross-classification with respect to zoological classification across the grain, so to speak, of the evolution based taxonomy.[11]

## REFLECTION ACTIVITY

Research the TV series, *The United States of Tara*. In this TV show the central character(s) has dissociative identity disorder (DID), known formerly as multiple personality disorder. These 17 different personalities exist in the same body. The fictional stories are based on a real person, known under the pseudonym of Karen Overhill, who lived their life with this disorder. Her personalities included Jensen, an 11-year-old black boy. She was diagnosed after Ms Overhill wrote a doctor a letter that said: "My name is Claire. I am seven years old. I live inside Karen."

- How does the bodily criterion of personal identity account for this possibility?

## Philosophical terms

**Animalism** argues that we are an organism of the species *Homo sapiens* and that our conditions for our personal identity or enduring self is the same as the conditions required of animals.

[10] Eric T. Olson, *The Human Animal: Personal Identity Without Psychology* (Oxford: Oxford University Press, 1997), p. 143.

[11] David Wiggins, *Sameness and Substance* (Oxford: Basil Blackwell, 1980), p. 171.

## Research Questions

- How does animalism answer the question of personal identity?
- Does animalism imply that all human animals are people? Justify your answer.
- Does animalism imply that all people are human animals? Justify your answer.
- What is the relationship between the body theory and animalism?

## REFLECTION ACTIVITY

Think about the activity earlier in the chapter where you were asked to analyse and reflect on the condition of Sandra.

What if she came out of her coma but without memories and with a propensity to get angry, even violent. Given that she was a person who prior to the accident was a kind, loving, and forgiving person, would she still be the same person even if she had the same body?

## The brain criterion

The brain is considered to be a special aspect of all animals and consequently a significant amount of importance is ascribed to this organ. This has been confirmed by neurological research in recent times. It is a part of the body and consequently is included in the arguments put forward by the body criterion position. However, because of its complex nature, some philosophers have thought that there might be a dimension to the brain that offers something significant to the theory of personal identity.

The brain is regarded as the physical seat of a person's mental life and, as such, contains something that allows personal identity to be secured. But this theory throws up an interesting aspect of identity. The brain is regarded as the secure foundation of identity but the brain is not the person in strict terms.

Garrett explores this aspect of the **brain theory** debate. He uses the example of a gold statue. Is the statue equal to the lump of gold from which it is made? If it was melted down the statue would be lost but the lump of gold would remain. Hence, they cannot be the same. As Garrett points out:

> It's true that the identity conditions of the statue are not the same as those of the lump (as the possibility of meltdown shows), but we still have a necessary connection between identity conditions, despite the numerical distinctness of the statue and the lump. Non-standard or unorthodox materialist theories of personal identity take an analogous form.[12]

This is a position argued for by Thomas Nagel (1937– ) when he says:

> I could lose everything but my functioning brain and still be me … the brain is the only part of me whose destruction I could not possibly survive … I am whatever persisting individual in the objective order underlies the subjective continuities of that mental life that I call mine … If my brain meets these conditions then the core of my self – what is essential to my existence – is my functioning brain.[13]

### Who is he?

Thomas Nagel is best known for his article "What Is it Like to Be a Bat?" (1974) in which he rejects the reductivist account of the mind. However, he is also an accomplished moral and political philosopher who published his major work *The Possibility of Altruism* in 1970. He currently teaches as University Professor of Philosophy and Law at New York University.

[12] Brian Garrett, *Personal Identity and Self-Consciousness* (London: Routledge, 1998), p. 10.

[13] Nagel, *The View from Nowhere*, p. 40.

While Nagel does not present a fully worked-out argument for this theory, leaving it more as a hypothesis, he makes the point that the brain is an important aspect of anyone's identity. As he goes on to explain:

> I am not just my brain: I weigh more than three pounds, am more than six inches high, have a skeleton, etc. But the brain is the only part of me whose destruction I could not possibly survive. The brain, but not the rest of the animal, is essential to the self.[14]

While in the end Nagel seems to commit to the *self*, and therefore identity, as a psychological concept, he raises the point that the brain needs to be fully acknowledged given the importance of its role in our existence. In fact, it is John Searle who advocates this position with his "**biological naturalism**". He makes the claim that "[c]onscious states are entirely caused by lower level neurobiological processes in the brain. Conscious states are thus *causally reducible* to neurobiological processes."[15] Nagel retains the belief that the mind is founded in the brain so the brain is the source of identity, but isn't this an argument that the self is the brain but identity comes from the mind? Obviously it depends on the relationship between the mind and the brain.[16]

## Williams: the self, the body, and the future

The thought experiment of the "Body Swap" is a common one in discussions about personal identity, whereby the memories of person A are placed in person B's body, and vice versa. The 20th-century English moral philosopher Bernard Williams (1929–2003) uses it to make a point about the role of the body in personal identity. This thought experiment first appeared in a journal article "The Self and the Future", published in *The Philosophical Review* in 1970. He asks the reader to consider what would happen if before the swap persons A and B were asked which body should receive a punishment and which one a reward. We would assume that the preference would be to ask that the reward be given to the body with person A's memories. This suggests that memories are the defining characteristic of personal identity.

But Williams gives the scenario a twist. Person A is told they are going to have their memories erased, replaced with some fictitious memories, and then they are going to be tortured. Williams asks the question, "Would you be afraid?" The suggestion is that you would still be afraid and therefore the body is important to a person's identity.

Williams continues to provide variations. These are:

1. You have your memories erased, you are given new "fake" memories, and then you are to be tortured.
2. You have your memories erased, you are given copies of another person's memories, and then you are to be tortured.

### REFLECTION ACTIVITY

Imagine someone who has been in a severe car accident. As a result of the accident they have had a personality change. Are they still the same person? Or have they changed into another person?

---

[14] Ibid.

[15] John Searle, *Mind: A Brief Introduction* (New York: Oxford University Press, 2004), p. 113.

[16] See Stephen Burwood, "Are We Our Brains?", *Philosophical Investigations* 32, No. 2 (April 2009): 113–133.

3. You have your memories erased, you are given another person's genuine memories, and then you are to be tortured.
4. You have your memories erased, you are given another person's genuine memories, that person is given your memories, and then you are to be tortured.

In each of these scenarios the assumption is that you will be afraid of being tortured. Williams uses this response to strongly suggest that personal identity and therefore the self are closely tied to the physical body. However, it is worth noting that the last scenario mentioned above is the same as the first scenario. In the first scenario the response suggested psychological continuity. However, in the final scenario the response suggested that the body was important. Williams suggests that, given this, if people were asked to choose they would prefer the latter scenario, despite their initial conclusions, making the body identity more important.

**REFLECTION ACTIVITY**

Go through Williams' thought experiment and especially the variations. Do you agree with his conclusions?

Use the philosophy Experiment's online version of Williams' thought experiment called "You're Being Tortured in the Morning" to complete this activity. It can be found at http://philosophyexperiments.com/bodyswap/Default.aspx

**Who is he?**

Bernard Williams is the former Knightbridge Professor of Philosophy at the University of Cambridge and Deutsch Professor of Philosophy at the University of California, Berkeley. He is mostly known as a moral philosopher due to his most influential book, *Ethics and the Limits of Philosophy* (1985). However, he also wrote on the topic of the self in *Problems of the Self* (1973). He refused to accept the reductionist tendencies of modern science seeking to use the insights of history, culture, politics and psychology to explore the nature of the moral individual in society through the ideals of "authenticity and self-expression".

## Immaterial substance

### The soul and personal identity

The traditional argument for the enduring identity, including enduring beyond death, is the **soul**. The belief is that if the body stops functioning, the non-physical entity, the soul, will continue to exist. The soul does not depend on the physical body as the soul is an immaterial, thinking substance that exists so long as some form of thought is going on in it. **Plato** and **Descartes** are two philosophers who have held this view. (See biographies in Chapter 4: Mind and Body and Chapter 3: Personhood, respectively.)

In ancient Greece there was a common belief that when a person died their soul escaped the body on their last breath and even as their last breath. This lead to a belief that the soul was invisible matter. While Plato never articulated a full theory of the soul in detail there is a strong suggestion in his writing, especially in *Phaedo*, that the soul was an unextended thing or an immaterial substance. In *The Republic* he suggests defining the soul in terms of empirical psychology where he rejects a unitary soul, arguing instead that the mind is in conflict. The outcome of this conflict between the three elements of the soul – reason, spirit, and desire – determines a person's behaviour and therefore directs the body. Later in *Timaeus*, the *Phaedrus* and *Laws*, he adjusts the relationship between the soul and the body, allowing the body to influence the soul as well. In terms of personal identity, Plato believed that the soul survived the death of the body and therefore the soul was the location of identity. He even suggested that only reason survived death as spirit and desire belonged to the body. Regardless of which view should be taken as his definitive view Plato makes an explicit claim that we are a thinking thing which is our soul. In the process he argues that our identity is contained in an immaterial or unextended substance. This position dominates Western thought for over 1,700 years.

What was Aristotle's position?

Aristotle, Plato's most famous student and arguably his greatest critic, responded to many of Plato's positions and arguments but strangely had little to say on the issue of the mind and body. While Aristotle rejected the emphasis Plato placed on the metaphysical dimension to reality, he still retained the idea that his 'Unmoved Mover' and possibly his concept of the rational or intellectual part of the soul (*nous*) were part of this metaphysical world. He felt that there was only one world, the physical world. Everything was therefore made up of both form and matter. This offered a form of materialism, although as noted with some exceptions. So while the conceptual framework for a theory of identity is in place for Aristotle the question did not interest him.

Over a millennia and a half of debate has passed since Plato and Aristotle and nearly all philosophical discussion in the Western tradition is dominated by their philosophies or, more accurately, various interpretations of them.

**FIND OUT MORE**

Lucretius (95?–54 BCE) was an Epicurean philosopher who wrote during the Roman era. His philosophy argued for hedonism, materialism, and atheism and denied the existence of the immaterial soul. His most influential work was a philosophical poem, *De Rerum Natura*. He influenced medieval and early modern philosophy rather than philosophers in his own time. He suggested that identity does not matter when considering the question of survival; a position that has regained popularity today.

## The Cartesian soul

While the **soul theory** was only alluded to in Plato's work, Descartes makes an explicit claim that the body and the soul are distinct. Descartes approached the issue of identity only incidentally as he sought to provide the newly emerging discipline of the natural science and its empirical methodology with a firm foundation of knowledge. Approaching philosophy from an epistemological point of view and using his famous sceptical methodology he reasoned that you could only be certain that you were thinking therefore denying the idea that material objects could hold this status of certainty and be considered real. While Descartes did not articulate a specific theory of personal identity this conclusion has specific implications regarding the role of the mind and the body in identity. By inference, you were not your body, only your mind.

Having established what can be known for certain and therefore a "first principle" of a new philosophy, Descartes sought to explore the implication of this idea. Descartes' argument is explored in Chapter 5: The Self and the Other, so the main argument need not be reiterated here. He draws the conclusion that "I had no body" and then asks the question, "So what do I have?"

Having established that "I am and I exist" Descartes reflected on the meaning of this:

> And then, examining attentively that which I was, I saw that I could conceive that I had no body, and that there was no world nor place where I might be; but yet that I could not for all that conceive that I was not ...
>
> From that I knew that I was a substance the whole essence or nature of which is to think, and that for its existence there is no need of any place, nor does it depend on any material thing; so that this "me," that is to say, the soul by which I am what I am, is entirely distinct from body.[17]

And thinking? Descartes found specific implications to its role in identity:

> What of thinking? I find here that thought is an attribute that belongs to me; it alone cannot be separate from me. I am, I exist, that is certain. But how often? Just when I think; for it might possibly be the case if I ceased entirely to think that I should likewise cease altogether to exist ...
>
> To speak accurately I am not more than a thing which thinks, that is to say a mind or a soul, or an understanding, or a reason, which are terms whose significance was formerly unknown to me. I am, however, a real thing and really exist; but what thing? I have answered: a thing which thinks.[18]

This corrected the Platonic concept of the mind/soul that had been fused with the Aristotelian one leading to thinkers such as Augustine and Avicenna to argue that the body was important to an individual and by implication personal identity. Descartes reinforced the belief that the mind was one type of substance and the body another. He still had to contend with Plato's notion that the soul's relation to the body was one of a pilot to a ship, therefore providing the body with some relevance. In other words, they were intermingled, forming a unit. Descartes argued that there was only a casual relationship and they were therefore not one singular entity. Again, the role of the body is negated.

[17] Descartes, *Discourse on Method and Meditations*, Part IV, p. 23.

[18] Ibid., p. 73.

## Assessing the non-material substance theory of personal identity

Plato's position on the soul and therefore his implied theory of personal identity is linked to his metaphysics and his theory of the forms. In his Socratic dialogue, *Phaedo*, Plato repeats an argument that he makes in *The Republic*. Here is Socrates debating with Simmias:

> Socrates: Do we say there is such a thing as justice by itself or not?
>
> Simmias: We do say so, certainly.
>
> Socrates: Such a thing as the good and beautiful?
>
> Simmias: Of course!
>
> Socrates: And did you ever see one of them with your eyes?
>
> Socrates: Never.[19]

Plato's metaphysical system allows him to claim the existence of a soul. However, this leads to difficulties. According to Plato, the soul has no gender. There is no female soul or male soul. How did he know? Consequently, major objection to this claim focuses on the question of how do you know that the soul exists, and if it does exist, how do you know that the same soul is contained within the same person? Even if the existence of the soul is accepted, it would still not provide the ability to determine if the person you are talking to is the same person whom you spoke to the day before.

So a real concern is determining that the soul exists. Yet, this is part of the broader criticism of dualism. While the concept of the soul has sound explanatory powers in certain contexts it is hard to find evidence for the existence of the mind in a metaphysical reality. If the position on the mind and the body is not tenable, then Descartes' theory of the immortal soul struggles to be valid. Surely, art of justifying the existence of the soul would be to also argue how the soul can be individuated, or how they can be differentiated from each other and over time.

These are significant criticisms and are accepted by many philosophers. However, one philosopher, Richard Swinburne argues that this criticism is problematic *because* of the expectation of empirical evidence. Swinburne argues that this is verificationalism without justification. In other words, it demands a particular standard of truth by imposing a particular process of testing. Swinburne questions the suitability of this measure of truth. In response it is argued that the theory of the soul is based on faith rather than empirical evidence. Only the activities of the soul are empirically observable and the role of the soul remain mysterious.[20]

**TOK links** 

An implication of the soul theory is a kind of scepticism. If you are unable to determine whether or not the individual in front of you has the same soul and is therefore the same person as yesterday then you might start to question whether or not the assumption that they are the same is satisfactory.

[19] Plato, *Great Dialogues*

[20] See Richard Swinburne, "Personal Identity: The Dualist Theory", in Sydney Shoemaker and Richard Swinburne, *Personal Identity* (Oxford: Basil Blackwell, 1984), pp. 1–66.

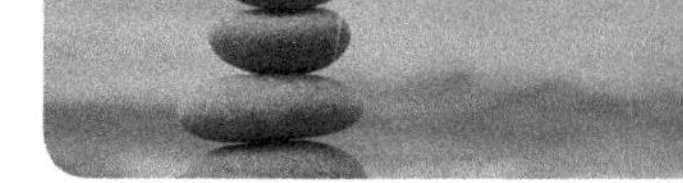

Descartes justifies his position using the argument of conceivability. We can conceive of ourselves surviving without our bodies therefore it is possible. As a consequence, we must have an immaterial source of our identity. It is often regarded as suitable because it allows us to believe that we can exist beyond the life of our physical body. The measure of conceivability needs to be further defined. Without further argument this justification remains too broad and if extended to other issues allows the justification of some farfetched ideas. It is not a sustainable justification. If you reflect on this justification you will realize that while you say 'I have a painful tooth' you believe that the 'I' being used has a direct relationship with thinking and it is not mediated through our bodies. Is this a valid assumption? Similarly if conceivability is a valid justification, why do I retain the immaterial substance of the mind/soul? Can't I exist without a mind/soul? Surely this too is conceivable? This invites the question, does conceivability as a justification lead to an acceptance of the Bundle Theory of the Self and therefore identity? (For more information see Chapter 4: Mind and Body and Chapter 5: The Self and the Other.)

Note that the position on the soul has shifted from a materialist position to a non-materialist position but not from a substantialist position. The soul is a non-material substance, an incorporeal, non-extended mental substance. There is still something substantial that composes the self and therefore personal identity, although it is not dependent upon or derived from material. Interestingly, it is unchanged by experiences in the world.

**Paper 3 links**

How do different schools of philosophy justify their claims?

Is a decision about methodology more important, than evidence?

**TOK links**

**Faith as a Way of Knowing in TOK.**

- Is it fair to ask Richard Swinburne to adhere to a specific standard of truth?
- What role does reason play in a claim based on faith?
- Is empirical evidence essential when justifying a knowledge claim?
- Is repeatability an important component in the validation of knowledge?
- Is there only one methodology for generating knowledge?

**The Nature of Evidence**

- Are there different standards for evidence in different Areas of Knowledge?
- In philosophy what is the standard for evidence?

## Immaterial non-substance and psychological continuity

### Psychological continuity and personal identity

The references to Locke so far have already established an understanding of his approach to philosophical issues. As an empiricist he believed that observation was the best method to use to discover the truth. He was reacting to the methodology of scholastic Aristotelianism, whose assumptions about knowledge were being challenged by the emergence of the new sciences. Newton's *Principia* (1687) was influential among intellectuals outside the Christian Church, including Locke. Locke rejected the neo-Platonist epistemology that was dominant and central to Descartes' philosophical argument. This led Locke to argue that we have no experiences of "substances", only of properties. To gain insight into the self, Locke similarly believed that you could use your own experiences and therefore introspection, but as a result of this different epistemological foundation he came to different conclusions to Descartes.

In the following passage from *An Essay Concerning Human Understanding* (1690) Locke lays out this method:

> To find wherein *personal identity* consists, we must consider what *person* stands for;— which, I think, is a thinking intelligent being, that has reason and reflection, and can consider itself as itself, the same thinking thing, in different times and places; which it does only by that consciousness which is inseparable from thinking, and, as it seems to me, essential to it: it being impossible for any one to perceive without perceiving that he does perceive. When we see, hear, smell, taste, feel, meditate, or will anything, we know that we do so. Thus it is always as to our present sensations and perceptions: and by this every one is to himself that which he calls *self*:—it not being considered, in this case, whether the same *self* be continued in the same or divers substances. For, since consciousness always accompanies thinking, and it is that which makes everyone to be what he calls *self*, and thereby distinguishes himself from all other thinking things; in this alone consists *personal identity*, i.e. the sameness of a rational being: and as far as this consciousness can be extended backwards to any past action or thought, so far reaches the identity of that *person*; it is the same *self* now it was then; and it is by the same *self* with this present one that now reflects on it, that that action was done.[21]

Locke identifies the issue relating to being a *person* not a man (*sic*) and as such needs to be delineated because "person" is a forensic term, involving praise and blame, and a capacity to obey laws. For Locke, a "person" is a particular type of self-reflective consciousness. The key to Locke's consideration is **consciousness**, or being aware that we are thinking. For more on the concept of consciousness see the section 'Consciousness and self-consciousness' in Chapter 3: Personhood. This, Locke believes, always accompanies thinking and consciousness is also an essential part of the thinking process. Consequently, consciousness is the aspect of our selves that makes possible our belief that we are the same identity over time and even in different locations. Locke attaches the capacity to form and retain memories to consciousness. Memories become central to the enduring self.

Augustine of Hippo (354–430) claimed a similar conclusion to Locke 12 centuries earlier when he wrote, "Great is the power of memory . . . and this thing is the mind, and this am I myself".[22]

[21] Locke, "Of Identity and Diversity", in *An Essay Concerning Human Understanding*, Book II, Chapter XXVII, p. 246. If you have difficulty with the style of writing and language refer to a version translated into modern English at http://home.sandiego.edu/~baber/metaphysics/readings/Locke.IdentityAndDiversity(JFB).pdf (accessed 30 October 2014).

[22] Saint Augustine, *The Confessions of Saint Augustine*, translated and introduced by John K. Ryan (New York: Image Books, 1960), p. 211.

According to Locke, remaining the same person has nothing to do with remaining the same substance, either physical or mental. Instead, personal identity has only to do with consciousness: it is by the consciousness of one's present thoughts and actions that the self is conceived, and it is through the continuous link of memory that the self is extended back to past consciousness thereby forming a personal identity.

## ANALYSIS ACTIVITY

### Locke's analogy of the prince and the cobbler

> For should the soul of a prince, carrying with it the consciousness of the prince's past life, enter and inform the body of a cobbler, as soon as deserted by his own soul, every one sees he would be the same person with the prince, accountable only for the prince's actions: but who would say it was the same man?
>
> —John Locke[23]

Think about what this means.

- What is Locke's purpose of presenting the analogy of the prince and the cobbler?
- What argument regarding personal identity is presented in this analogy?
- Do you think this is an effective analogy? Assess its strengths and weaknesses.

Note the change that has occurred in Locke's argument. Descartes argued for a thinking thing, which he associated with the soul. This was an immaterial substance. Locke rejects the reliance on any substance and attaches identity to an immaterial non-substance.

Locke's argument is supported by Leibniz (1646–1716), who suggested the following stimulus:

> . . . the immortality which is demanded in morals and in religion does not consist in this perpetual subsistence [of soul] alone, for without the memory of what one had been it would not be in any way desirable. Let us suppose that some individual were to become King of China at one stroke, but on condition of forgetting what he had been, as if he had been born anew, is it not as much in practice or as regards the effects which one can perceive, as if he were to be annihilated and a King of China to be created at his place at the same instant? Which this individual has no reason to desire.[24]

The suggestion is that nearly everyone would decline. The reasoning would be that being rich and all-powerful would not be worth as much as our personal (and intimate) memories. Who we are as individuals is closely connected with our memories of the past. In other words, the same body is not enough.

[23] Locke, "Of Identity and Diversity", in *An Essay . . .*, Book II, Chapter XXVII, p. 250.

[24] Gottfried Wilhelm Leibniz, *Discourse on Metaphysics*, translated by P. Lucas and L. Grint (Manchester: Manchester University Press, 1953), p. 145.

## Biography: John Locke (1632–1704)

Locke was an English philosopher who left an influential legacy, especially in political philosophy and epistemology.

Locke studied philosophy and medicine in Oxford and spent some of his life working as a physician. While in Oxford, Locke studied alongside prominent scientists of his time and even struck a friendship with Newton, which sparked his interest in epistemology.

Locke worked as a private physician and then an assistant for Lord Ashley, later Earl of Shaftesbury, who became an important political figure of his time. This marked the beginning of Locke's involvement in politics. Locke developed his political philosophy, advocating religious freedom and criticizing absolute monarchy, until his ideas were deemed too radical and he had to spend six years in exile in Holland between 1682 and 1688. During that time, Locke worked on his famous *Essay Concerning Human Understanding*, published in 1690 after his return to England.

Locke was one of the first modern empiricists and a proponent of the mind as tabula rasa, claiming that human beings are not born with innate ideas but are blank slates who learn from their experiences and their senses.

In 1690, Locke also published *Two Treatises of Civil Government*, his ground-breaking work of political philosophy, in which he established the principles of political liberalism, focusing on freedom and the natural rights of people to resist abusive power.

Under the new government and political system, Locke was able to resume his public activities and career, and carried on writing philosophical and political works until his death in 1704.

## Criticisms of Locke's theory of personal identity

The contemporary American philosopher John Perry clarifies Locke's statement that "as far as this consciousness can be extended backwards to any past action or thought, so far reaches the identity of that *person*" in the following way:

> Locke must mean something like this: "Any experience I can remember being reflectively aware of, is mine, i.e., one that happened to me." Thus the distinction between knowing of present experiences by our five external senses and knowing of them by our sixth inner sense is carried over into memory; all and only experiences I can remember having been aware of in this latter way were mine.[25]

But Locke is demanding a lot of an individual – that they remember every memory that is theirs. Nothing can be forgotten.

The 18th-century Scottish philosopher Thomas Reid (1710–1796) noticed an obvious objection to this account of personal identity. He observed:

[25] John Perry, "The Problem of Personal Identity", in John Perry (ed.), *Personal Identity* (Berkeley and Los Angeles: University of California Press, 2008), p. 14.

> [i]t is not my remembering any action of mine that makes me to be the man who did it. This remembrance makes me to know assuredly that I did it; but I might have done it, though I did not remember it.[26]

He regarded it as a mistake to treat memory as if it were just an extension of consciousness, providing it with a degree of certainty that experience suggests it does not deserve. Reid observed that memories can be clear when they are first established but as a person gets older memories can begin to fade and eventually disappear.

Reid's point is illustrated with the boy–soldier-general example. Imagine that a boy, a soldier, and a general are the same person but at different times. The general remembers the soldier's experiences. The soldier remembers the boy's experiences. However, the general is too old to remember the boy's experiences. Locke's theory cannot give an adequate explanation of this scenario.

Now, at this point it is worth abstracting the persons in this scenario to help clarify the issue:

$$\text{boy} = A$$

$$\text{soldier} = B$$

$$\text{general} = C$$

According to the scenario, C is B and B is A. Since identity is transitive, it follows that C is A (C is the same person as A).

In the scenario, however, C (the general) cannot remember A's (the boy's) experiences. Locke's theory does not allow the claim to be made that C is the same person as A. Hence, according to Locke, C both is and is not the same person as A. As with all philosophical theories there is a demand for them to be consistent. Clearly this theory is not consistent when it is considered further.

It is easy to reject the need for direct memories (as in the general remembers the boy) and to settle for indirect memories. Indirect memories are memories that the self previously had but cannot recall in the present. This allows the claim that C is B and that B is A therefore $C = A$. But Locke's **memory theory** is reliant on direct memories, not indirect memories, but as a modification it does seem to address the criticism put forward by Reid.

The question of authenticity emerges with indirect memories but also with direct memories. What about the case of false memories? How do you know which memories are authentic?

[26] Thomas Reid, "Of Identity", in John Perry (ed.), Personal Identity (Berkeley and Los Angeles: University of California Press, 2008), p. 110; originally published as "Of Memory" in Reid's *Essays on the Intellectual Powers of Man* (1785).

The following is a story of false memories:

> It was not until my 18th birthday did I realize that I had held a very significant false memory as an authentic memory. On the wall of my parent's house had been a photo of a group of boys in the backyard. In that photo was a boy jumping off a very large pile of dirt into a small, plastic paddling pool. I always thought that boy had been me (why else would my parents have had it on their wall?).
>
> I gave a speech on my 18th birthday, thanking my parents for the exciting life I had had, moving around frequently, helping my dad build or renovate house after house and in the process learning a lot about life, hard work, the rewards of persistent application, and so on. I made the observation that when little I had had the courage – and therefore belief in myself – to jump from a large pile of dirt into a small pool of water. I recalled how I had used that experience to do other challenging things in my life.
>
> Afterwards my mother came up to me and thanked me for the acknowledgement and the stories. She also quietly pointed out that the picture was not of me. I had been too scared to go up to the top of the pile of dirt so I had come inside the house crying.

A response to the issue of false memories might be to claim that the memories had to happen to me. However, as should be clear when reflecting on the story above, how do I know that these memories actually happened to me? This is called the **circularity objection**. I have to know whether or not the memories are false before I can know which memories are false.

Shoemaker has responded to this issue by introducing the concept of a "**quasi-memory**". This type of memory involved an experience that met the following criteria:

1. That we seem to remember
2. That somebody actually had
3. That is caused by an actual experience.

This is a rather technical response to the issue. However, it does raise the issue of identity without necessarily having a strong definition of the self – the location for memory. The last condition is designed to ensure that it is not a false memory. However, as Perry observed, how do you know that it was caused by an actual event? His concern is that the causal theory of memory leads to an assumption of a self, which is a conclusion that the memory theory is supposed to be designed to avoid.

### Butler and the circularity issue

Joseph Butler (1692–1752), the 18th-century English philosopher, highlighted the circularity issue in response to Locke:

> [o]ne should really think it self-evident, that consciousness of personal identity presupposes, and therefore cannot constitute personal identity, any more than knowledge … can constitute truth, which it presupposes.[27]

[27] Joseph Butler, "Of Personal Identity", in John Perry (ed.), *Personal Identity* (Berkeley and Los Angeles: University of California Press, 2008), p. 100; originally published as the first dissertation to Butler's *Analogy of Religion* (1736).

Butler's objection to Locke's theory of personal identity is very simple yet profound. He argues that in order to make sense of Locke's claim a person must genuinely remember that they did something in the past. This idea presupposes that the person was the same person who did the act that is being remembered. Genuine memory depends on having a personal identity.

Note the emphasis on "genuine" memories. I see an advertisement promoting a visit to Disneyland. This provokes a memory of my own visit to Disneyland when I was younger. This memory involves a slide where I got wet at the end. If my memory is genuine then I must have been the person who experienced it and therefore forming the memory of it. If it is genuine I am that person. Memory now depends on personal identity, not the other way round as argued by Locke.

In simple terms, the focus on memory presupposes a person who remembers. Memory implies that there is a "rememberer" or the very self or person whose nature is being defined:

> ... personal identity cannot be defined in terms of memory since one must already be in possession of the concept of personal identity, and be able to determine that it applies, in order to be in a position to operate with the concept of memory at all.[28]

Therefore memory is merely a test of personal identity over time, and does not define its essence. From Butler's perspective, a person has to be either a fixed substance or a property of a fixed substance. Anything else undermines the purpose of a personal identity.

## TOK links

In the film *Memento* (2000), Leonard makes reference, to the valid of memory in his lunch conversation with Teddy (MM 23:00): "Memory's unreliable... Memory's not perfect. It's not even that good. Ask the police. Eyewitness testimony is unreliable."

Viewing Question

Were Leonard's memories of his pre-incident self accurate? How does he know? How would you know?

What are the strengths and weaknesses of memory as a way of knowing?

## VIEWING ACTIVITY

### Philosophy and film

The film *Eternal Sunshine of the Spotless Mind* (2004) explores the relationship between our selves and our memories. Watch the film and answer the following questions:

- How do memories shape personal identity?
- Would you still be you if you had your memories erased?

### Personal identity according to Parfit

The contemporary philosopher Derek Parfit, in his seminal work *Reasons and Persons* (1984), responds to this circularity issue by proposing a moderation of the level of tolerance in personal identity. Parfit is rejecting the assumption that identity is a black and white matter. In other words, he believes that it can be dealt with through a matter of degrees in relation to **mental continuity** and **connectedness**.

[28] Harold W. Noonan, *Personal Identity*, 2nd edition (London: Routledge, 2003), p. 11.

### The criteria of continuity and connectedness

What does Parfit mean by these terms? After over a decade of developing his position he defines these terms in *Reasons and Persons*. Psychological connectedness is defined as "the holding of particular direct psychological connections" and psychological continuity is defined as "the holding of overlapping chains of *strong* connectedness".[32] These are best explained by some examples. Imagine a person who has undergone a series of experiences, or "occasions". If from a first-person perspective an individual at Occasion 2 can remember what was previously experienced at Occasion 1 then they are numerically identical.

If the connections are not strong and there is some breakage, Parfit argues that a weaker connection is still valid to ensure identity is continuous. These are overlapping memory chains. In simple terms, if on Occasion 4 I can remember what happened on Occasion 3 but not Occasion 2 but I know on Occasion 3 that I remembered what happened on Occasion 2, then I am continuous. These overlaps provide continuity if not connectedness. The question remains how much tolerance is there before the continuity is broken? Parfit makes a distinction between strong and weak connectedness and in the process maintains that strong connectedness must be evident for identity to be preserved. This strong connectedness is defined as having over half the number of connections maintained on each and every day of the person in question.

These are given the following conditions and therefore the definition of personal identity.

> (1) There is *psychological continuity* if and only if there are overlapping chains of strong connectedness. X today is one and the same person as Y at some past time if and only if (2) X is psychologically continuous with Y, (3) this continuity has the right kind of cause, and (4) it has not taken a "branching" form. (5) Personal identity over time just consists in the holding of facts like (2) to (4).[33]

While each of these are important, the fourth condition, the "branching" form, is the most demanding and worth further consideration.

## FIND OUT MORE

### A challenge to personal identity

Parfit enters the debate about personal identity by wondering whether the issue is important. In a reflection on this matter he says: "[m]y targets are two beliefs: one about the nature of personal identity, the other about its importance."[29] What are his concerns regarding the traditional concept of personal identity?

Research his concerns:

- What is his criticism of the first belief?
  To research his answer read his response from "The first is that in these cases the question about identity must have an answer…"[30]
- What is his criticism of the second belief?
  To research his answer read his response from "Against this second belief my claim will be this…"[31]

---

[29] Derek Parfit, "Personal Identity", in John Perry (ed.), *Personal Identity* (Berkeley and Los Angeles: University of California Press, 2008), p. 199; originally published in *The Philosophical Review* 80, No. 1 (January 1971): 3–27.

[30] Ibid.; also see paragraph 4 in http://mind.ucsd.edu/syllabi/03-04/phil1-spring/readings/parfit.pdf (accessed 30 October 2014).

[31] Ibid., p. 200; also see paragraph 7 in http://mind.ucsd.edu/syllabi/03-04/phil1-spring/readings/parfit.pdf (accessed 30 October 2014).

[32] Derek Parfit, *Reasons and Persons*, reprinted with corrections (Oxford: Oxford University Press, 1987), p. 206.

[33] Ibid., p. 207.

> "I enter the Teletransporter. I have been to Mars before, but only by the old method, a space-ship journey taking several weeks. The machine will send me at the speed of light. I merely have to press the green button. Like others, I am nervous. Will it work? I remind myself what I have been told to expect. When I press the button, I shall lose consciousness, and then wake up at what seems like a moment later. In fact I shall have been unconscious for about an hour. The Scanner here on earth will destroy my brain and body, while recording the exact states of all my cells. It will the transmit this information by radio. Traveling at the speed of light, the message will take three minutes to reach the Replicator on Mars. This will create, out of new matter, a brain and body exactly like mine. It will be in this new body that I shall wake up."[34]

## FIND OUT MORE

Research the teletransportation argument in Parfit's *Reasons and Persons.*

### Paper 3 link

How valid are thought experiments as evidence to support an argument in philosophy?

### Question

What is your response to this thought expeiriment? Does your response support or refute Parfit's position on personal identity?

This is called branching. This is a classic scene from many science fiction stories, especially Star Trek, and is used by Parfit to explore personal identity. However, a more potent thought experiment is appropriate at this point of the investigation.

A more fundamental argument involves the thought experiment of a brain transplant. This was used as well to illustrate an issue with psychological continuity. This is called fission. Imagine the following scenario: The brain of a person (Andree) is divided into two hemispheres and the memories of the original brain are present in each of the two hemispheres. These hemispheres are placed into two bodies. Andree is now Andree-R and Andree-L. The memories of each of the new persons are the same as the original individual and are experienced from a first-person view. However, they are not numerically identical as there are now two persons who are Andree. According to the psychological continuity theory the two people are continuous to the person from which they originated. However, they are not identical to the other Andree as they have different bodies. Nor do they have any characteristic that would allow them to claim they are continuous to the original and not the other Andree. These fission scenarios mean that psychological continuity can occur but there is no similar claim for personal identity. (They also provide examples of quasi-memories, or memory believed to be authentic and therefore support personal identity when in fact they do not.)

Say you are Andree-L and you find out that you will die in 5 minutes. Would you be worried given that Andree-R will continue to live?

## FIND OUT MORE

As a reductionist, Parfit believes that people do not exist apart from their components and that the concept of a person derives from psycholofical concepts such as memories, intetions, and desires. Consequently, he supports a bundle theory of perception familiar to us from our analysis of Hume's position, in which the continuity of experience is the basis for identity, not the self and any associated concept. In fact, Parfit compares persons to nations and clubs; saying that the identity of persons over time is analogous to the identity of nations and clubs over time. Does this make sense? Think about a club that closes down. However, a few years later it reopens and people start to attend meetings. Is it the same club? Or is it a new club? Your answer to this scenario provides an indication of whether or not you would agree with Parfit (and Hume).

[34] Ibid., p. 199.

## TOK links

**The Question of Evidence**

Parfit offers a range of evidence to support his argument. What constitutes valid evidence in philosophy? How does philosophy compare to areas of knowledge such as natural science, history, and art?

Which of these types of evidence, used in Parfit's *Reasons and Persons*, are valid?

- Cross-cultural and historical evidence (84)
- Evidence from psychology and neuropsychology (84)
- The analogy to a club (86)
- Split-brain patients thought experiment (87)

For more on valid reasoning in philosophy, research abductive reasoning.

- How does this compare to deductive reasoning and inductive reasoning?
- What does this type of reasoning say about the nature of conclusions drawn in philosophy?

### An assessment of the memory theory

The memory theory appears to be a commonsense solution to the issue of personal identity. We hold our memories dearly, capturing them in photos, through associations with people, drawing upon them frequently to tell a story that provides an insight into who we are. They also solve many of the problems evident in the body and soul theories of personal memory.

Shoemaker, a prominent critic of this memory theory, argues:

> It is, I should like to say, part of the concept of a person that persons are capable of making memory statements about their own pasts. Since it is a conceptual truth that memory statements are generally true, it is a conceptual truth that persons are capable of knowing their own pasts in a special way, a way that does not involve the use of criteria of personal identity, and it is a conceptual truth (or a logical fact) that the memory claims that a person makes can be used by others as grounds for statements about the past history of that person. This, I think, is the kernel of truth that is embodied in the view that personal identity can be defined in terms of memory.[35]

There is no denying that the debate about personal identity as presented by the tradition of essentialism is a good exercise in philosophy. However, it may be that the expectations of a satisfactory answer are too high or too demanding. Does the question require a "yes" or "no" answer? Maybe it does not require a black or white answer, rather a "to a certain extent" answer. The question is therefore about the boundaries of our tolerance. This is the position called "best-candidate theory of personal identity".

## FIND OUT MORE

Research the following arguments on best-candidate theory of personal identity:

- Robert Nozick's argument in *Philosophical Explanations* (1981).
- Sydney Shoemaker's argument in *Self-Knowledge and Self-Identity* (1963)
- David Wiggins' counter-argument in *Sameness and Substance* (1980)

[35] Sydney Shoemaker, "Personal Identity and Memory", in John Perry (ed.), *Personal Identity* (Berkeley and Los Angeles: University of California Press, 2008), pp. 133–134; originally published in *The Journal of Philosophy* 56, No. 22 (22 October 1959): 868–902.

## ARGUMENT ANALYSIS ACTIVITY

Read the following passages and identify the position of the first philosopher, Aquinas. Then read the second philosopher, Hobbes, and identify his argument in response to the first argument. Then read Locke's comment in response to Hobbes (it is assumed). Link these into a flow chart to map the progression of this dialogue, identifying the key concepts and their role in the position being established and then the criticism being made in response.

... if the soul were united to the body merely as its motor, we might say that it is not in each part of the body, but only in one part through which it would move the others. But since the soul is united to the body as its form, it must necessarily be in the whole body, and in each part thereof. For it is ... the substantial form of the body. Now the substantial form perfects not only the whole, but each part of the whole. For since a whole consists of parts, a form of the whole which does not give existence to each of the parts of the body, is a form consisting in composition and order, such as the form of a house; and such a form is accidental. But the soul is a substantial form; and therefore it must be the form and the act, not only of the whole, but also of each part. Therefore, on the withdrawal of the soul, as we do not speak of an animal or a man unless equivocally, as we speak of a painted animal or a stone animal; so is it with the hand, the eye, the flesh and bones ...

That it is entire in each part thereof, may be concluded from this ... a whole is that which is divided into parts, [and] there are three kinds of totality, corresponding to three kinds of division. There is a whole which is divided into parts of quantity, as a whole line, or a whole body. There is also a whole which is divided into logical and essential parts: as a thing defined is divided into the parts of a definition ... There is ... a third kind of whole which is potential, divided into virtual parts ...

Therefore if it be asked whether the whole whiteness is in the whole surface and in each part thereof, it is necessary to distinguish. If we mean quantitative totality ... then the whole whiteness is not in each part of the surface. The same is to be said of totality of power: since the whiteness which is in the whole surface moves the sight more than the whiteness which is in a small part ... But if we mean totality of species and essence, then the whole whiteness is in each part of a surface.

Since, however, the soul has not quantitative totality ... the whole soul is in each part of the body, by totality of perfection and of essence, but not by totality of power. For it is not in each part of the body, with regard to each of its powers; but with regard to sight, it is in the eye; and with regard to hearing, it is in the ear; and so forth.

—Thomas Aquinas[36]

For the circumscription of a thing, is nothing else but the determination, or defining of its place; and so both the terms of the distinction are the same. And in particular, of the essence of a man, which (they say) is his soul, they affirm it, to be all of it in his little finger, and all of it in every other part (how small soever) of his body; and yet no more soul in the whole body, than in any one of those parts. Can any man think that God is served with such absurdities? And yet all this is necessary to believe, to those that will believe the existence of an incorporeal soul, separated from the body.

—Thomas Hobbes[37]

Self is that conscious thinking thing, whatever substance made up of ... which is sensible, or conscious of pleasure and pain ... [etc.]. Thus every one finds that, whilst comprehended under that consciousness, the little finger is as much a part of himself as what is most so. Upon separation of this little finger, should this consciousness go along with the little finger, and leave the rest of the body, it is evident the little finger would be the person, the same person ...

—John Locke[38]

[36] Thomas Aquinas, *Summa Theologica* (1266–1268), translated by the Fathers of the English Dominican Province, 1912 (Raleigh, NC: Hayes Barton Press, 2006), Part I, Question 76, Article 8, pp. 697–698.

[37] Quoted in Malcolm (trans.), *Clarendon Edition ...: Leviathan*,

[38] Locke, "Of Identity and Diversity", in *An Essay ...*, Book II, Chapter XXVII, Section 17 also available at http://oregonstate.edu/instruct/phl302/texts/locke/locke1/Book2c.html#Chapter XXVII (accessed 30 October 2014).

## The substantial identity

### Hume: a succession of states, not a personal identity

Hume's criticism of the essentialist self extended to the issue of the enduring self. His criticism of the concept of the self as advocated by the rationalist Descartes and developed further by the empiricism of Locke was an extension of his criticism of "substance", which he argued was an assumption in Western thought.

Descartes believed a substance is that which is indivisible and therefore needs no other entity in order to exist. Locke defined substance as follows:

> The idea then we have, to which we give the general name substance, being nothing but the supposed, but unknown, support of those qualities we find existing, which we imagine cannot subsist *sine re substante*, without something to support them, we call that support *substantia*; which, according to the true import of the word, is, in plain English, standing under or upholding.[39]

This is **essentialism**, and when combined with **introspection** it leads to the essentialist concept of the self.

For Hume, substance cannot be perceived; therefore it should not be assumed that it exists, especially through introspection. This leads him to reject the substantialist theories of the self argued by many Western philosophers such as Descartes. Hume's position is illustrated by the example of a piece of wax. When I see wax I see sensory impressions and as they cohere they appear to demonstrate the existence of an object separate to myself as the perceiver. Descartes believes that this perceiver sees the underlying substance. Hume rejects this, saying instead that it is an unproven assumption and is simply a construction of the mind. Similarly, causation is an assumption and along with it a causal sequence of thoughts:

> As to causation … the true idea of the human mind, is to consider it as a system of different perceptions or different existences, which are linked together by the relation of cause and effect, and mutually produce, destroy, influence, and modify each other.[40]

The "true idea" of causation is imposed by the mind on experiences, leading Hume to claim that if the self cannot be found then an enduring self, the prerequisite of personal identity, is equally a fiction.

**Extension**

What did Hume think of his own argument?

The Appendix of his *Treatise* contains an interesting reflection by Hume. He criticized his own account of personal identity contained within the book. As Katie Javanaud summarizes in *Philosophy Now*, Hume realized that

"if there is merely a bundle of perceptions, and no enduring self that is the subject of these perceptions (i.e. a perceiver), then the entire project of the *Treatise* is invalidated, as skepticism about the self leads ultimately to an irreversible wholesale skepticism, since without the self we are not able to ground our knowledge. Hume also realised his account is guilty of raising perceptions to the status of substances ('substance' being another notion which Hume had rejected in the *Treatise*)."

So, Hume eventually writes in the Appendix: "of the section concerning personal identity, I find myself involv'd in such a labyrinth, that, I must confess, I neither know how to correct my former opinions, nor how to render them consistent."[41]

---

[39] Ibid., Book II, Chapter XXIII.

[40] Hume, *A Treatise of Human Nature*, Book I, Part IV, Section VI; available at http://davidhume.org/texts/thn.html (accessed 24 October 2014).

[41] Katie Javanaud, "David Hume's Theory of Personal Identity", *Philosophy Now*, No. 97; available at https://philosophynow.org/issues/97/A_Philosophical_Identity_Crisis (accessed 30 October 2014).

## Personal identity versus sociocultural identity

> Look, don't identify me by the size and shape of my body, my social class, my job, my gender, my ethnicity, my sexuality, my nationality, my age, my religion, my education, my friends, my lifestyle, how much money I earn, the clothes I wear, the books I read, where I go shopping, the way I decorate my house, the television programmes and movies I watch, my leisure and sports activities, the car I drive, the music I listen to, the drinks I like, the food I eat, the clubs I go to, where I go on holiday, the way I speak or my accent, the things I say, the things I do, or what I believe in. I'm just me. OK?[42]

Is this conception of identity possible? It suggests we tend to identify someone by their external features or activities, not by their internal or essential features.

All the aspects that this person has discounted are loosely defined as **sociocultural identity**. The discussion so far in this chapter has focused on the individual or an essentialist approach to the issue of personal identity. This has ignored the alternative argument that focuses on **external factors** which determine a person's identity.

### Individual versus community

The issue of personal identity focuses on the question of whether we depend on others for our identity because we need others to define who we are as individuals. In many ways it is a rejection of the tradition that has been defined as atomistic, essentialist, ego-centric, and individualist amongst others. The 20th-century Canadian philosopher Charles Taylor believes this is the case:

> There is a question about ourselves – which we roughly gesture at with the term "identity" – which cannot be sufficiently answered with any general doctrine of human nature. The search for identity can be seen as the search for what I essentially am. But this can no longer be sufficiently defined in terms of some universal description of human agency as such, as soul, reason, or will. There still remains a question about me, and that is why I think of myself as a self. This word now circumscribes an area of questioning. It designates the kind of being of which this question of identity can be asked ...[43]

**REFLECTION QUESTION**

Why is Hume's original position still studied if Hume himself did not continue to hold it?

[42] Words accompanying a cartoon in Ken Browne, *An Introduction to Sociology, 4th edition* (London: Polity, 2011), p. 398.

[43] Charles Taylor, *Sources of the Self: The Making of the Modern Identity* (Cambridge: Cambridge University Press, 1989), p. 184.

## Biography: Charles Taylor (1931– )

Taylor is one of the leading contemporary philosophers. Taylor rejects naturalism, the belief that there are inherent rules to be discovered, arguing instead from within the hermeneutic tradition. Consequently, Taylor argues that understanding is derived from meaning and therefore interpretation through context, not from verifiable facts and/or pure rationalism often seen the analytical and logical positivist approach to truth. He is associated with a communitarian critique of liberal theory's understanding of the "self" and their constructs of identity.

Taylor analyses the concept of identity, putting the issue of human nature or the characteristics of being human to one side as inadequate. He rejects a notion of identity which is based on a tradition of thought that defines identity in terms of agency, or as the initiator of action, or as the source of decision-making found inside the individual. In this next passage Taylor again reflects on the tradition related to Descartes but now starts to outline his alternative. This alternative provides the context for the individual, before they become an 'agency' with the capacity to make self-aware decisions. This context is prior to the individualization that occurs and is the source of identity.

> In the twentieth century, we may no longer believe, like Descartes, in the soul or mind as an inner space open to transparent introspection … But we retain the idea that self-understanding is getting a clear view of the desires, aversions, fears, hopes, aspirations that are within us. To know oneself is to get clear on what is within.
>
> This seems so normal and inescapable to us, that we can hardly imagine an alternative. But let us try. If I can only understand myself as part of a larger order; indeed, if man as the rational animal is just the one who is rationally aware of this order; then I only am really aware of myself, and understand myself, when I see myself against this background, fitting into this whole. I must acknowledge my belonging before I can understand myself. Engaged in an attempt to cut myself off, to consider myself quite on my own, autonomously, I should be in confusion, self-delusion, in the dark.[44]

Taylor suggests that we *are* our relationships with other people. This is a very different approach to the atomistic and introspective approach seen so far in this chapter. There is a strong philosophical foundation for this perspective – Aristotle. Aristotle took the position in his own philosophy that humans are naturally "social animals" who are not self-sufficient:

> … the individual, when isolated, is not self-sufficing; and therefore he is like a part in relation to the whole. But he who is unable to live in society, or who has no need because he is sufficient for himself, must be either a beast or a god: he is no part of a state. A social instinct is implanted in all men by nature.[45]

[44] Charles Taylor, "Legitimation Crisis?", in Charles Taylor, *Philosophy and the Human Sciences: Philosophical Papers*, vol. 2 (Cambridge: Cambridge University Press, 1985), p. 257

[45] Aristotle, *Politics*, translated by Benjamin Jowett (Stilwell, KS: Digiread.com Publishing, 2005), Book I, Part II, p. 5.

This concept of the individual was powerfully re-expressed by Hegel in the 19th century with his famous discussion of the master–slave dialectic.

> Every self wants to be united with and recognized by another self [as a free being]. Yet at the same time, each self remains an independent individual and so an alien object to the other. The life of the self thus becomes a struggle for recognition ... Each self is in a struggle to convince the other that he is [a free being] worthy of the other's respect and recognition. This mutual struggle for recognition by the other is mixed with feelings of mistrust and uncertainty. The struggle carries with it all the dangers and risks that the self faces when it dares to lay itself open to the other. This life-and-death struggle can degenerate into a bloody fight in which one of the combatants is killed. But then the whole issue of recognition will be missed. Recognition requires the survival of the other as a condition and sign of one's freedom. The struggle of the self is essentially a struggle for freedom. Historically, this struggle is the basis of the rise of masters and slaves ... Preferring survival to freedom, the slave gives up his attempt to be recognized as free. The master, on the other hand, is recognized as free. The master sees in the slave the very sign of his freedom. Independent masters and dependent slaves together form a community. To preserve and protect the life of his workers becomes the concern of the master ... The slave learns to work. He acquires habits and skills. At the same time he disciplines himself. In making objects [for the master] he also makes himself. In working together with others he overcomes his isolation and is recognized for his excellence. In this process, the relation of dependence and independence is reversed. The independent master becomes dependent on the skills and virtues of the servant.[46]

Recognition is a key concept here. Others are required to recognize our qualities before we know of them ourselves. Introspection does not suffice in the determination of our identity. More interestingly, our conception of ourselves as individual and therefore having an identity is dependent on recognition by others. This recognition is not easily given and involves a struggle to obtain it. Our identity emerges through this struggle as we force others to define us. This is, of course, a fascinating approach to the question of identity. Hegel's conception of identity through struggle is exceptionally powerful, especially in a world where power relationships are complex and society is in flux as these relationships evolve in the modern era. So it is not surprising that Hegel's thought became the central tenet of Marxism and other emancipatory ideologies.

Taylor took Hegel's (and Aristotle's) philosophy of anti-essentialism and re-assessed the issue of identity in contemporary society using the issue of recognition as central to his analysis.

> The thesis is that our identity is partly shaped by recognition or its absence, [or] by the misrecognition of others, and so a person or a group of people can suffer real damage, real distortion, if the people or society around them mirror back to them a confining or demeaning or contemptible picture of themselves ...

[46] Hegel, *Encyclopedia of Philosophy*, pp. 215–217.

Thus some feminists have argued that women in patriarchal societies have been induced to adopt a depreciatory image of themselves. They have internalized a picture of their own inferiority ... An analogous point has been made in relation to blacks: that white society has for generations projected a demeaning image of them, which some of them have been unable to resist adopting. Their own self depreciation, on this view, becomes one of the most potent instruments of their own oppression ...

Recently, a similar point has been made in relation to indigenous and colonized people in general. It is held that since 1492 Europeans have projected an image of such people as somehow inferior, "uncivilized," and through the force of conquest have often been able to impose this image on the conquered.[47]

This analysis indicates another feature that is important to identity – culture. The practices and beliefs of a group of people that encapsulate a world view expressed through art and social habits. This reflects who a person is, according to Hegel, or, in other words, recognition occurs through the culture of a community and this is the source of identity.

In order to understand the close connection between identity and recognition, we have to take into account a crucial feature of the human condition ... This crucial feature of human life is its fundamentally dialogical character. We become full human agents, capable of understanding ourselves, and hence of defining our identity, through our acquisition of rich human languages of expression. For my purposes here, I want to take language in a broad sense, covering not only the words we speak, but also other modes of expression whereby we define ourselves, including the "languages" of art, of gesture, of love, and the like. But we learn these modes of expression through exchanges with others. People do not acquire the languages needed for self-definition on their own. Rather, we are introduced to them through interaction with others who matter to us ...

Moreover, this is not just a fact about genesis, which can be ignored later on. We don't just learn the languages in dialogue and then go on to use them for our own purposes ...

We define our identity always in dialogue with, sometimes in struggle against, the things our significant others want to see in us. Even after we outgrow some of these others – our parents, for instance – and they disappear from our lives, the conversation with them continues within us as long as we live. Thus, the contribution of significant others, even when it is provided at the beginning of our lives, continues indefinitely.

—Charles Taylor[48].

[47] Charles Taylor, "The Politics of Recognition", in Amy Gutmann (ed.), *Multiculturalism [and the Politics of Recognition]*, expanded edition, with commentaries by K. Anthony Appiah, Jürgen Habermas, Steven C. Rockefeller, Michael Walzer, and Susan Wolf (Princeton, NJ: Princeton University Press, 1994), p. 25.

[48] Charles Taylor, *Philosophical Arguments* (Harvard: Harvard University Press, 1995), pp. 229–230.

## ACTIVITY

### Understanding the extract

What does Taylor mean by the following terms?

- human condition
- dialogical
- horizon
- significant others

There is a balance, however. The argument that we are socially conditioned is a reaction to a strong tradition of individualist thinking. But it can go too far. David Reisman provides an antidote:

> Social science has helped us become more aware of the extent to which individuals, great and little, are the creatures of their cultural conditioning; so we neither blame the little nor exalt the great. But the same wisdom has sometimes led us into a fallacy that, since all men have their being in culture and as a result of the culture, they owe a debt to that culture which even a lifetime of altruism could not repay. (One might argue and in fact many societies in effect do that since we are born of parents, we must feel guilt whenever we transcend their limitations!) Sometimes the point is pushed to the virtual denial of individuality: since we arise in society, it is assumed with a ferocious determinism that we can never transcend it. All such concepts are useful correctives to an earlier solipsism. But if they are extended to hold conformity with society is not only a necessity but also a duty, they destroy that margin of freedom which gives life its savor and its endless possibility for advance.[49]

According to Scott Stewart, Annette Baier offers an interesting perspective where cultural identity allows key individualist concepts of autonomy and self to remain, if reconstructed:

> Perhaps, however, we ought not to think of dependence on others, or joint identity, as problematic. Instead, we might attempt to construct a different conception of autonomy and the self, which does not perceive us as completely independent from others in the first place. Such conceptions have come from various sources, especially from communitarians and feminists, both of whom see, in their different ways, the self as inherently an embedded entity defined in large part by the communities within which they live and the relationships they have.[50]

[49] David Reisman, Individualism Reconsidered and Other Essays (Glencoe, IL: The Free Press, 1954), p. 38.

[50] Scott Stewart, "Breaking Up Is Hard to Do: A Philosophical Discussion of the End of Love", *Philosophy in the Contemporary World* 14, No. 2 (Fall 2007): 71.

In this vein, Baier has articulated a view of persons as "second persons":

> A person, perhaps, is best seen as one who was long enough dependent upon other persons to acquire the essential arts of personhood. Persons essentially are *second* persons, who grow up with other persons ... The fact that a person has a life *history*, and that a people collectively have a history depends upon the humbler fact that each person has a childhood in which a cultural heritage is transmitted, ready for adolescent rejection and adult discriminating selection and contribution. Persons come after and before other persons.[51]

If we return to the issue of the enduring self, the identity of the self and therefore personal identity is sustained by "the other", whose recognition is required or whose influence defines us as a person.

## Existentialism and the issue of personal identity

There is another aspect of this position that needs acknowledgement – the existential dimension to this type of thinking. Steven Wang, writing in *Philosophy Now* on the question of the French existential philosopher Jean-Paul Sartre and the issue of personal identity, highlights Sartre's contribution to the idea of personal identity. I am a unique being-in-the-world responsible to myself for creating my personal identity from amongst unlimited possibilities. His belief is that it is traditionally founded on a *causal* misconception. The traditional conception encompasses a pre-established personality or identity that explains the way we behave. The examples are: "She treats the patient because she is a doctor"; "He runs away because he is a coward"; "They care for their children because they are devoted parents."

Sartre believes that this kind of explanation is "back-to-front". Sartre rejects the claim that who we are determines how we behave and instead believes that, according to Wang, "it is by acting in a certain way that we establish an identity".[52] From this perspective personal identity is defined by our choices and commitments. There is no essentialism evident in this perspective. However, there is a strong influence of temporality.

Focusing on Sartre's discussion of *angoisse* ("anguish") in *Being and Nothingness* (1943), Wang illustrates how Sartre shows how this condition leads to an insecurity of identity, first using the example of a cliff-walker and then the example of a reformed gambler. The gambler's resolution is undermined when he sees a gambling table.

## VIEWING ACTIVITY

### Philosophy and film

The film *Memento* (2000) explores the relationship between our selves and our memories.

Having viewed *Memento,* do you think Leonard remained the same person throughout the movie?

**a.** According to Descartes?

**b.** According to Locke?

**c.** According to Sartre?

### Further reflection

What other factors need to be considered when discussing the self or identity?

For further discussion of the film and the issue of personal identity see Mary M. Litch's book *Philosophy Through Film* (2010).

[51] Quoted in ibid. from Annette Baier, *Postures of the Mind: Essays on Mind and Morals* (Minneapolis, MN: University of Minnesota Press, 1985), pp. 84–85.

[52] Steven Wang, "Identity and Freedom in Being and Nothingness", *Philosophy Now*, No. 64 (November/December 2007); available at https://philosophynow.org/issues/64/Identity_and_Freedom_in_Being_and_Nothingness (accessed 30 October 2014).

> What he apprehends then in anguish is precisely the total inefficacy of the past resolution. It is there, doubtless, but fixed, ineffectual, surpassed by the very fact that I am conscious *of* it. The resolution is still *me* to the extent that I realize constantly my identity with myself across the temporal flux, but it is no longer *me* – due to the fact that it has become an object *for* my consciousness. I am not subject to it, it fails in the mission which I have given it.[53]

The anguish, or anxiety, generates an understanding in an individual that any course of action is not determined, especially not by the perception of an established identity. Consequently, according to Sartre, this allows the individual to transcend and in the process create their identity. As Wang expresses it:

> A human being is neither the present static identity nor the intangible future goal. We are constituted rather by our freely chosen relationship between present identity and end. Personhood therefore necessarily involves both the facts that determine us and the movement beyond these facts to what we seek to become. It involves essence and existence, self-possession and self-dispossession, introspection and ecstasy, present and future, the real and the ideal, the indicative and the conditional. It involves what is true, and what could be. In Sartre's understanding we constitute our personal identity by accepting who we are and freely moving beyond this.[54]

Returning to Taylor, who was influenced by thinkers from the German and French hermeneutical traditions of thought similarly to Sartre, there is a context or "horizon" in which identity resides and this has an ethical dimension:

> To know who I am is a species of knowing where I stand. My identity is defined by the commitments and identifications which provide the frame or horizon within which I can try to determine from case to case what is good, or valuable, or what ought to be done, or what I endorse or oppose. In other words, it is the horizon within which I am capable of taking a stand.[55]

Taylor articulates a position on self that leads to a position on identity. The ethical consistency provides the reference for identity. This is an action or existential approach to the question of identity rather than a metaphysical or epistemological approach seen so far.

---

[53] Sartre, *Being and Nothingness*, p. 125.

[54] Wang, "Identity and Freedom . . ."; available at https://philosophynow.org/issues/64/Identity_and_Freedom_in_Being_and_Nothingness (accessed 30 October 2014).

[55] Taylor, *Sources of the Self*, p. 27.

## REVISION ACTIVITIES

Repeat the revision activities outlined on p. 217 in Chapter 5: The Self and the Other. However, use personal identity instead of the concept of the self to complete the activities. These include the Flow chart activity and the follow-up Dialogue activity.

## APPLIED METAPHYSICS

In the 20th and 21st centuries the issue of personal identity has become prominent particularly due to emerging issues in medicine, law, and ethics. Below are some scenarios that enable you to test your understanding of some of the theories of personal identity covered in this chapter by applying them to each situation. This is applied metaphysics. This activity will not only help deepen your understanding of each theory but also provide an opportunity to evaluate them. All these scenarios are based on events that have actually occurred.

**A.** A man is involved in a car accident. He is taken to hospital in a coma. Hen he wakes up he cannot remember anything about his life prior to the accident. He is also now prone to burst of anger. Prior to the accident he was a generous and good-natured person, well liked by his friends. His family and his friends declare that he is a different person.

**B.** A women trained as a doctor decides to take a sabbatical from her work and travels to Africa to undertake some humanitarian work. She leaves her husband and two children at home with the expectation they will also come to Africa to join her for an extended holiday. While taking supplies to a remote village the four-wheel drive she is driving overturns. The woman sustains a head injury and wanders off from the site of the accident. She is saved by a nomadic tribe who care for her as they travel across the desert. She recovers from the head injury but has no memory of how she became part of the tribe (who have accepted her as one of their own). She marries and has children. A camera crew filming a wildlife documentary see her and she becomes the topic of a news report on world news channels. Her first husband sees the news story and travels to Africa to return his wife to her family. When he meets her, she rejects his request, as she has no memory of any events prior to the accident and even though she feels a strong affection towards him.

**C.** Two young children abduct and brutally murder another young boy. Despite their age the two boys are sentenced to a custodial sentence. At the age of 21 they are released from jail with each claiming they are changed persons after extensive psychological (not psychiatric) rehabilitation. However, due to the outrage expressed by their local community for the murder they are given new identities and sent to another country to start a new life. They create a new life for themselves, joining a church and enter a seminary in order to seek ordination.

**D.** A man is involved in a horrific motorbike accident, which involves serious burns across his entire body. Initially he has an arm and both legs replaced with artificial limbs. An infection caught while in surgery results in the need to replace his heart and lungs with transplants. He then has his burnt face reconstructed. None of his family, friends, and former work colleagues recognize him.

Also, he has no memory of his life prior to the accident. His girlfriend volunteers to re-educate him about himself and his life by using pictures, letters and showing him places important to him throughout his life. She carefully avoids mentioning the ex-girlfriend he had fond memories of, and affection for, before dating her and the fact that she had discovered he was cheating on her with this ex-girlfriend.

Apply the following theories of personal identity and answer the question below.

**A.** If it is the same body it is the same person.

**B.** If it is the same soul it is the same person.

**C.** If someone can remember their experiences, then they are that person.

**D.** If everyone else thinks it is the same person, then it is.

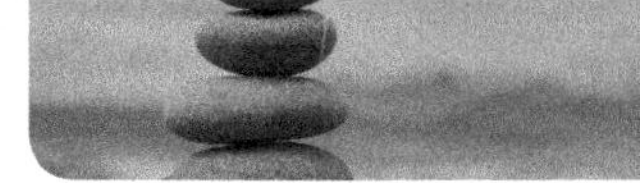



## ACTIVITY

For each scenario assess these positions on personal identity by answering the following two questions:.

1. Does the position support the claim that the person's identity has been retained?
2. Based on your application of the position to the scenario, what strengths and weaknesses are evident with this position?

## Conclusion

The issues covered in this chapter are personal identity, identity over time, and social and cultural identity. These have been considered through the questions "Who am I?", "What makes me the same person I was 10 years ago?", and "To what extent does culture shape identity?".

The positions on personal identity undertake a clear pathway of development based on a response to the previous arguments. These developments tend to occur to a changing understanding of being human, being a person and the concept of the self. Plato's initial conception of the self provided the framework for much of the Western tradition's reflection on this issue, although most of this was indirect. The rise of science and its corresponding new manner of asking questions and seeking the answers also impacted upon the issue of personal identity. The role of the soul was no longer an essential part of the analysis. Instead alternatives were explored. However, these were defined within the framework established around the soul. The result was a reliance on immaterial non-substances expressed most famously in the work of Locke who was the first philosopher to identity the issue of personal identity explicitly in his work. Locke became the seminal position of personal identity until the mid-20th century. This debate about identity became less about metaphysics and more about the sociocultural and political. However, as can be seen in Parfit's arguments a concern about the issue of personal identity led him to challenge the importance of personal identity: he felt that survival was more important than identity.

### Assessment tip

**Developing an Analytical Framework**

A good essay that demonstrates your knowledge, understanding and skills will require control over the material you have studied. One way of demonstrating a depth of understanding and the skills required to write a good philosophical essay. This can be achieved by looking for different approaches in order to formulate your own argument although still drawing upon the traditions of philosophical thought. This is the first step in creating an analytical framework that structures your treatment of the issue, responses and your own position. This allows you to undertake the experience 'doing philosophy' in the true sense of the word.

**Taking a Comparative Approach: Essentialism vs. Existentialism**

If we selected the comparison of Locke and Sartre there are still a number of different approaches or themes that can be used to explore the issue of personal identity. One example is the temporal dimension in Locke and Sartre. Locke prioritized the past in his thinking with his reliance on memory. While Sartre emphasized the the future with his belief that you choose the person you will be, and in the process choose your identity through your choices and values. This is not to suggest that they ignore the other dimension. Sartre for example included the concept of facticity in his works to counter the criticism that he did not take into account the context of the individual.

**Assessment Activity**

That I am a man, this I share with other men.

That I see and hear and that I eat and drink is what all animals do likewise.

But that I am I is only mine and belongs to me and to nobody else; to no other man, not to an angel nor to God.

**Source:** Meister Eckhart, Latin Fragments (13th century)

1. a. In response to the stimuli identify a philosophical issue in response to the stimuli based on an issue of personal identity that have been explored in this chapter.
   b. Identify relevant philosophical positions in relation to the issue.
2. Write an essay plan/draft essay in response to the following instructions:

"With explicit reference to the stimulus and your own knowledge, discuss a philosophical issue related to the question of what it means to be human in relation to the issue of personal identity."

An essay should demonstrate a clear and concise understanding of philosophical issues and concepts. This requires a detailed knowledge of arguments and theories. Analysis should include a discussion of counter-arguments. Evaluation should provide support for a clear perspective/response.

Use the following supports to assist you with your planning:

**Key Inquiry Questions**

- Is personal identity defined by a substance? If it is a substance, what kind of substance is it?
- What conditions are required for me to be the same person I was 20 years ago?
- How much can I change for my identity to survive?
- How can I continue to exist after death?
- How can I know I will exist in the future?
- To what extent does culture influence or define my identity?

Some possible key elements used to support the issue of personal identity or enduring self are listed below:

- a continuation of the body or brain
- a continuation of a soul
- a continuation of a mind
- the construction of a narrative
- a continued recognition of my existence

## References Cited

Aquinas, Thomas. *Summa Theologica (1266–1268)*. Translated by the Fathers of the English Dominican Province, 1912. Raleigh, NC: Hayes Barton Press, 2006.

Aristotle, *Politics*. Translated by Benjamin Jowett. Stilwell, KS: Digiread.com Publishing, 2005.

Baier, Annette. *Postures of the Mind: Essays on Mind and Morals*. Minneapolis, MN: University of Minnesota Press, 1985.

Browne, Ken. *An Introduction to Sociology*, 4th edition. London: Polity, 2011.

Burwood, Stephen. "Are We Our Brains?". *Philosophical Investigations* 32, No. 2 (April 2009): 113–133.

Butler, Joseph. "Of Personal Identity". In John Perry (ed.), *Personal Identity*. Berkeley and Los Angeles: University of California Press, 2008, pp. 99–105.

Descartes, René. *Discourse on Method and Meditations*. Translated by Elizabeth S. Haldane and G. R. T. Ross. New York: Dover Publications, 2003.

Fox, Michael Allen. "A New Look at Personal Identity". *Philosophy Now*, No. 62 (July/August 2007): 10–11.

Garrett, Brian. *Personal Identity and Self-Consciousness*. London: Routledge, 1998.

Garrett, Brian. *What Is This Thing Called Metaphysics?* London: Routledge, 2006.

Goodrich, Richelle E. *Eena: The Dawn and Rescue*. Pittsburgh, PA: RoseDog Books, 2012.

Hegel, Georg. *Encyclopedia of Philosophy*. Translated by Gustav E. Mueller. New York: Philosophical Library, 1959.

Hesse, Herman. "Siddhartha". Translated by Hilda Rosner. In *Siddhartha, Demian, and Other Writings*. Edited by Egon Schwarz, in collaboration with Ingrid Fry. New York: Continuum Publishing, 2001, pp. 19–104.

Hume, David. *A Treatise of Human Nature: Being An Attempt to Introduce the Experimental Method of Reasoning into Moral Subjects, Volume I: Of the Understanding* (London: John Noon, 1739), Book I, Part IV, Section VI; available at http://davidhume.org/texts/thn.html (accessed (24 October 2014).

Javanaud, Katie. "David Hume's Theory of Personal Identity". *Philosophy Now*. Available at https://philosophynow.org/issues/97/A_Philosophical_Identity_Crisis (accessed 30 October 2014).

Leibniz, Gottfried Wilhelm. *Discourse on Metaphysics*. Translated by P. Lucas and L. Grint. Manchester: Manchester University Press, 1953.

Locke, John. *An Essay Concerning Human Understanding*. New York: Prometheus Books, 1995.

Martin, Raymond. *The Rise and Fall of the Soul and Self: An Intellectual History of Personal Identity*. New York: Columbia University Press, 2006.

Nagel, Thomas. *The View from Nowhere*. New York: Oxford University Press, 1989.

Noonan, Harold W. *Personal Identity*, 2nd edition. London: Routledge, 2003.

Olson, Eric T. *The Human Animal: Personal Identity Without Psychology*. Oxford: Oxford University Press, 1997.

Olson, Eric T. "Is There a Bodily Criterion of Personal Identity?". In Fraser MacBride (ed.), *Identity and Modality*. Oxford: Oxford University Press, 2006, pp. 242–259.

Parfit, Derek. *Reasons and Persons*. Reprinted with corrections. Oxford: Oxford University Press, 1987.

Parfit, Derek. "Personal Identity". In John Perry (ed.), *Personal Identity*. Berkeley and Los Angeles: University of California Press, 2008, pp. 199–226.

Perry, John. "The Problem of Personal Identity". In John Perry (ed.), *Personal Identity*. Berkeley and Los Angeles: University of California Press, 2008, pp. 3–31.

Plato. *Great Dialogues of Plato*. Translated by W. H. D. Rouse. New York: Signet Classic, 1999.

Plutarch. *Vita Thesei*, 22–23. Available at https://faculty.washington.edu/smcohen/320/theseus.html (accessed 29 October 2014).

Reid, Thomas. "Of Identity". In John Perry (ed.), *Personal Identity*. Berkeley and Los Angeles: University of California Press, 2008, pp. 107–111.

Reisman, David. *Individualism Reconsidered and Other Essays*. Glencoe, IL: The Free Press, 1954.

Saint Augustine. *The Confessions of Saint Augustine*. Translated and introduced by John K. Ryan. New York: Image Books, 1960.

Sartre, Jean-Paul. *Being and Nothingness*. Translated from the French by Hazel E. Barnes. New York: Philosophical Library, 1956.

Searle, John. *Mind: A Brief Introduction*. New York: Oxford University Press, 2004.

Shoemaker, Sydney. *Self-Knowledge and Self-Identity*. Ithaca, NY: Cornell University Press, 1963.

Shoemaker, Sydney. "Personal Identity and Memory". In John Perry (ed.), *Personal Identity*. Berkeley and Los Angeles: University of California Press, 2008, pp. 119–134.

Stewart, Scott. "Breaking Up Is Hard to Do: A Philosophical Discussion of the End of Love". *Philosophy in the Contemporary World* 14, No. 2 (Fall 2007): 60–73.

Swinburne, Richard. "Personal Identity: The Dualist Theory". In Sydney Shoemaker and Richard Swinburne, *Personal Identity*. Oxford: Basil Blackwell, 1984, pp. 1–66.

Taylor, Charles. "Legitimation Crisis?". In Charles Taylor, *Philosophy and the Human Sciences: Philosophical Papers*, vol. 2. Cambridge: Cambridge University Press, 1985, pp. 248–288.

Taylor, Charles. *Sources of the Self: The Making of the Modern Identity*. Cambridge: Cambridge University Press, 1989.

Taylor, Charles. "The Politics of Recognition". In Amy Gutmann (ed.), *Multiculturalism [and the Politics of Recognition]*. Expanded edition, with commentaries by K. Anthony Appiah, Jürgen Habermas, Steven C. Rockefeller, Michael Walzer, and Susan Wolf. Princeton, NJ: Princeton University Press, 1994, pp. 25–74.

Taylor, Charles. *Philosophical Arguments*. Harvard: Harvard University Press, 1995.

Unger, Peter. "The Survival of the Sentient", *Noûs* 34, No. s14 (2000): 325–348. Originally published in *Philosophical Perspectives* 14 (2000) 34pp.

Wang, Steven. "Identity and Freedom in *Being and Nothingness*". *Philosophy Now*, No. 64 (November/December 2007). Available at https://philosophynow.org/issues/64/Identity_and_Freedom_in_Being_and_Nothingness (accessed 30 October 2014).

Wiggins, David. *Sameness and Substance*. Oxford: Basil Blackwell, 1980.

# BEING HUMAN

# 8 IB Philosophy Assessment

In this chapter, we will focus on the core theme component of Paper 1. However, much of the advice you will be given could be applied to other components and papers, especially when it comes to general philosophical skills and essay tips.

For **standard level (SL)** students, Paper 1 is worth 50% of the overall IB philosophy grade. The entire paper is marked out of 50, and 25 of those marks go to the core theme. This means that you should spend approximately half the time you are given for Paper 1 (1 hour 45 minutes) on your core theme essay: roughly between 45 and 55 minutes, including planning time.

For **higher level (HL)** students, Paper 1 is worth 40% of the overall IB philosophy grade. The entire paper is marked out of 75, and 25 of those marks go to the core theme. This means that you should spend approximately a third of the time you are given for Paper 1 (2 hours 30 minutes) on your core theme essay: roughly 50 minutes, including planning time.

## SL assessment outline

| Assessment component | Weighting |
|---|---|
| **External assessment (2 hours 45 minutes)** | 75% |
| **Paper 1 (1 hour 45 minutes)**<br>This paper contains two compulsory sections: section A and section B.<br>Section A consists of two stimulus-based questions on the core theme. Students are required to answer one question.<br>Section B consists of two essay questions for each of the optional themes. Students are required to answer one question. | 50% |
| **Paper 2 (1 hour)**<br>This paper consists of two questions for each of the prescribed philosophical texts. Each question is split into two parts: part A and part B. Students are required to answer one question, and to answer both part A and part B of that question. | 25% |

| | |
|---|---|
| **Internal assessment (20 hours)**<br>Students are required to complete a philosophical analysis of a non-philosophical stimulus. This component is internally assessed by the teacher and externally moderated by the IB at the end of the course. | 25% |

## HL assessment outline

| Assessment component | Weighting |
|---|---|
| **External assessment (4 hours 45 minutes)** | 80% |
| **Paper 1 (2 hours 30 minutes)**<br>This paper contains two compulsory sections: section A and section B.<br>Section A consists of two stimulus-based questions on the core theme. Students are required to answer one question.<br>Section B consists of two essay questions for each of the optional themes. Students are required to answer two questions, each from a different optional theme. | 40% |
| **Paper 2 (1 hour)**<br>This paper consists of two questions for each of the prescribed philosophical texts. Each question is split into two parts: part A and part B. Students are required to answer one question, and to answer both part A and part B of that question. | 20% |
| **Paper 3 (1 hour 15 minutes)**<br>This paper consists of one unseen text. Students are required to write a response to this text, comparing and contrasting their experience of philosophical activity with the view(s) of philosophical activity found in the text. | 20% |
| **Internal assessment (20 hours)**<br>Students are required to complete a philosophical analysis of a non-philosophical stimulus. This component is internally assessed by the teacher and externally moderated by the IB at the end of the course. | 20% |

## Introduction to important IB documents

To understand what you need to do in your assessment, it is important that you become familiar with the documents that teachers and examiners use in order to assess you. Here are some useful extracts from the *IB Philosophy Guide* and assessment material.

## Assessment objectives

The assessment objectives are based on what is expected of students once they have completed the IB Philosophy course. They are broad expectations that can help teachers and examiners, but also students, define what needs to be evident in essays and examination scripts.

The assessment objectives are similar across all Group 3 IB subjects, although they are specifically adapted to each subject, and they are broadly based on Bloom's Taxonomy:

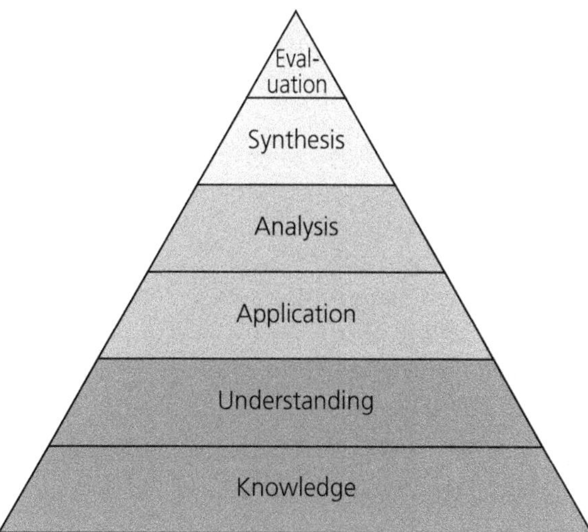


### The four assessment objectives

#### *Assessment objective 1: knowledge and understanding*

- Demonstrate knowledge and understanding of philosophical concepts, issues and arguments.
- Identify the philosophical issues present in both philosophical and non-philosophical stimuli.
- At HL only, demonstrate knowledge and understanding of the nature, function, meaning, and methodology of philosophical activity.

#### *Assessment objective 2: application and analysis*

- Analyse philosophical concepts, issues, and arguments.
- Analyse the philosophical issues present in both philosophical and non-philosophical stimuli.
- Explain and analyse different approaches to philosophical issues, making use of relevant supporting evidence/examples.
- At HL only, analysc the nature, function, meaning, and methodology of philosophical activity.

### *Assessment objective 3: synthesis and evaluation*

- Evaluate philosophical concepts, issues, and arguments.
- Construct and develop relevant, balanced, and focused arguments.
- Discuss and evaluate different interpretations or points of view.
- At HL only, evaluate the nature, function, meaning, and methodology of philosophical activity.
- At HL only, compare and contrast personal experience of philosophical activity with the issues regarding philosophical activity raised in an unseen text.

### *Assessment objective 4: selection, use, and application of appropriate skills and techniques*

- Demonstrate the ability to produce clear and well-structured written responses.
- Demonstrate appropriate and precise use of philosophical vocabulary.
- In the internal assessment task, demonstrate evidence of research skills, organization, and referencing.

As you can see, there are basic skills, like **knowledge and understanding**, which serve as a basis for all other skills. If you don't **know** any philosophy, you can't possibly write a good philosophical essay! And, of course, you also need to **understand** the theories and concepts you have learned. The way you describe and explain those theories will give your teacher or examiner a good idea of how much you know and how well you understand what you know. The point here is not only to know and understand, but also to *show* that you do.

Knowledge and understanding are like the foundations of the pyramid, and the next building blocks are **application and analysis**. This is where you get a chance to show not only that you understand philosophical ideas, but also that you can *use* them and understand their implications.

**Application** means that you are able to give examples (and if you can think of your own examples, even better) and make connections between philosophical ideas and other areas of knowledge. For instance, you might think of an example in the news or in your own experience that illustrates one of the ideas you were trying to explain; or you might find a way to connect different philosophical ideas to each other; or you could perhaps discuss whether some philosophical ideas are relevant today, etc.

**Analysis** is a very wide term and it is sometimes hard to pin it down. It involves unwrapping and unpicking ideas, looking at them in detail and trying to understand what they're made of. You could, for instance, explore what influenced the philosophers who came up with a certain theory, the assumptions that lie behind their ideas, the words they use, the implications their ideas might have, etc. This is also a good place to explore the common criticisms and counter-arguments of the idea you have chosen to explore. This will then lead you nicely into synthesis and evaluation.

At the top of the pyramid, you can find the higher-order skills of **synthesis and evaluation**. So far, you have shown that you can describe a philosophical idea clearly, explain it, give appropriate examples and make good links between the idea and other areas, explain the implications of the theory and explore its common criticisms. It already seems like a lot and it is! Sadly, many students just stop there and lose many marks as they seem to forget this last and important stage. Here, teachers and examiners will expect you to look at all the arguments you have explored so far, take one step back, weigh them carefully, and use this to build *your own* arguments.

Some questions that may help you along the way:

- Are the ideas you have explored convincing?
- Which of the criticisms and counter-criticisms are most convincing?
- Is there a flaw somewhere?
- Can you think of any criticisms of your own?
- What does your reason tell you?
- What is your gut feeling? (This will need to be justified too!)
- Do you find the ideas you have explored tempting, scary, dangerous, fascinating, life-changing?
- What impact do they have on you?
- What makes one idea stronger than the other?
- What is your perspective on the issues you have explored?
- What is your own theory on this issue, and why?

## Assessment tip: Should I say "I"?

This is a big debate in academia in general, and in philosophy in particular. The markbands state that an excellent response should "argue from a consistently held position about the issue". Some people feel that it is much easier to achieve this by saying "I" in essays, and using expressions such as *"I argue that…"*, *"These arguments lead me to believe…"* or *"My perspective on this is…"* The advantage of using such expressions is that it forces you to take a position and stick to it, and it shows a personal and deep engagement with the issues discussed. An IB examiner would not penalize you for using "I", and is likely to value this as evidence that you are *doing philosophy* and truly engaging with theories, rather than regurgitating other people's ideas.

On the other hand, many people in the academic world (and this might include your teacher!) feel that a rigorous essay should not use the first person. There are other efficient ways to show what position you hold and to be consistent. Expressions such as *"It can be argued that…"*, *"This is a more convincing argument because…"* or *"This perspective is particularly appealing because…"* can show exactly what your position is, without the use of "I". This can give your essay a more academic flavour, and it can help you choose a perspective without simply expressing an opinion that is not properly justified.

Here are some things to think about and some ways to decide whether you want to use "I" or not:

- If your teacher consistently tells you that you need to have more evaluation in your essays, that you need to engage with the issues and show a clearer, more consistent perspective in your writing, then consider using "I", at least as an exercise, in order to improve.

- If your teacher tells you that you tend to express opinions without justifying them or backing them up with proper arguments and evidence, then you may want to stop using "I" for a couple of essays, in order to practise being more objective and building your perspective in a more rational, rigorous manner.
- Ask your teacher what he or she personally thinks about this debate, and why.
- Remember that this is largely a question of academic tradition and culture: you will hear people argue passionately about using "I" or not using "I" in academic essays, but there is no right or wrong way as such. The best thing to do is probably to find your own style, but also to respect the traditions of the institutions you work within: the IB is fine with "I" and sometimes encourages it, but your future university professor may hate it!

Finally, there is one more assessment objective that doesn't quite fit into Bloom's Taxonomy: Assessment objective 4: **"Selection, use, and application of appropriate skills and techniques"**. This is an important assessment objective too and is very much present in the markbands that your teachers and examiners will use to assess your work. This involves **good essay structure, clarity of expression**, and **appropriate use of philosophical vocabulary**. *Doing philosophy* also involves these important skills: your ideas will be much more valuable if you are able to communicate them efficiently. This is also true of professional philosophers: as you read philosophical texts, don't you much prefer the ones that are clear, accessible, and engaging?

**Assessment tip: How can I use assessment objectives to improve?**

Assessment objectives are the foundation of the markbands and can really help you identify your own strengths and areas for development.

A good exercise is to analyse one of your essays using the assessment objectives and Bloom's Taxonomy. First, pick one colour for each stage of the pyramid (for example: green for knowledge and understanding, yellow for application and analysis, and red for synthesis and evaluation). Then, go through one of your essays (or, indeed, a sample essay or a friend's essay) and highlight extracts that illustrate each skill. For instance, if a paragraph is simply giving a definition or explaining a theory, you can highlight it in green.

At the end of the exercise, look at the result and ask yourself:

- Is one colour dominating the essay?
- Is one colour lacking?
- What does this tell me about the essay? Is it balanced? Is it too descriptive? For instance, is it too content-heavy, or does it now have enough content?
- What can I do to make the essay better? What skill do I need to develop (or demonstrate more clearly)?

## Specimen papers and past papers

The best way to prepare for the IB exam is to look at specimen papers (papers released by the IB to show what an exam typically looks like) and past papers (papers that become available a few months after an exam).

## Assessment tip: How can I use specimen papers and past papers to improve?

Since the assessment requires you to make "explicit reference to the stimulus", it is a great idea for you to practise writing essays and essay plans with as many stimuli as you can. Past papers offer you a chance to see the kind of material that the IB has used in the past, and to use it to get ready for the exam.

There are many ways you can practise with specimen and past papers:

- Pick a stimulus and write a quick essay plan in a few minutes, pretending you are in an exam, under timed conditions. Try to write with no material at all (textbook or notes) to see how much you remember and where the stimulus is taking your philosophical reflection.
- Write a more detailed essay plan, this time with your notes and textbook open, and be as thoughtful as you can when making the connection between the stimulus, philosophical themes and the central topic of "Being human".
- Look at a few past papers and practise choosing between the two stimuli. Make sure you pay close attention to both, and make sure you do not always choose the picture! Remember that the text may fit your tastes or what you have learned in class more closely than the picture.
- Write two or three different essay plans, on different topics, but using only one stimulus. Which topic works best with this stimulus?
- Now, do the opposite: pick a topic you would like to write about, and look at several stimuli: which stimuli best fit the topic? How would you connect each stimulus efficiently to your choice of topic? Are there cases where it isn't possible to make a credible connection between the stimulus and the topic you had chosen?
- Write a full essay based on one stimulus. Make sure you do not always choose the easiest stimulus you can find! Practising with a more challenging stimulus will help you get ready for the exam.
- When you start the course, practise writing essays with your notes and textbook open. As you get more confident, try writing essays from memory, under timed conditions, to mimic the exam.

## A WORD OF WARNING!

Although it is a great idea to browse past papers to see the range of stimuli that has been used in the past, make sure you focus on the stimuli only: the assessment format has changed quite a lot over the years and the instructions that come with the stimulus may no longer be relevant. Use the texts and images to practise, but make sure you stick to the instructions given in the latest papers, namely:

*With explicit reference to the stimulus and your own knowledge, discuss a philosophical issue related to what it means to be human.*

The same caution should be exercised when using markschemes that are based on old assessment models.

## Markbands

Here is what the *IB Philosophy Guide* says about markbands:

> Markbands are a comprehensive statement of expected performance against which responses are judged. They represent a single holistic criterion divided into level descriptors. Each level descriptor corresponds to a range of marks to differentiate student performance. A best-fit approach is used to ascertain which particular mark to use from the possible range for each level descriptor.

This is the main document your teachers and examiners will use to mark your core theme work. The "best-fit approach" means that your mark will be determined by the descriptors that best describe your work. For instance, if your work fits three out of four descriptors in the 11–15 markband, but your work would be better described by the 16–20 markband in one area only, you will still receive 11–15, because your work best fits into that markband *generally speaking*. Equally, the person marking your work will also need to decide whether it is placed at the top or the bottom of a specific markband.

Here are the markbands used for the core theme section of Paper 1:

### External assessment markbands SL and HL

#### *Paper 1: Section A – SL and HL (core theme)*

| Marks | Level descriptor |
|---|---|
| 0 | The work does not reach a standard described by the descriptors below. |
| 1–5 | • The response is poorly structured, or where there is a recognizable essay structure there is minimal focus on the task.<br>• The philosophical issues/concepts raised by the stimulus material are implied but not explicitly identified. There is minimal or no explanation of how the issues/concepts relate to the stimulus material or links to the question of what it is to be human.<br>• There is little relevant knowledge demonstrated, and the explanation is superficial. Philosophical vocabulary is not used, or is consistently used inappropriately.<br>• The essay is descriptive and lacking in analysis. |

| | |
|---|---|
| 6–10 | • There is some attempt to follow a structured approach although it is not always clear what the answer is trying to convey.<br>• The philosophical issues/concepts raised by the stimulus material are implied but not explicitly identified. There is some limited explanation of how the issues/concepts relate to the stimulus material or links to the question of what it is to be human.<br>• Knowledge is demonstrated but lacks accuracy and relevance, and there is a basic explanation of the issues/concepts. Philosophical vocabulary is used, sometimes appropriately.<br>• There is some limited analysis but the response is more descriptive than analytical. There is little discussion of alternative interpretations or points of view. Few of the main points are justified. |
| 11–15 | • There is a clear attempt to structure the response, although there may be some repetition or a lack of clarity in places.<br>• The philosophical issues/concepts raised by the stimulus material are explicitly identified. There is a basic explanation of how the issues/concepts relate to the stimulus material and to the question of what it is to be human.<br>• Knowledge is mostly accurate and relevant, and there is a satisfactory explanation of the issues/concepts. Philosophical vocabulary is used, sometimes appropriately.<br>• The response contains analysis, but this analysis lacks development. There is some discussion of alternative interpretations or points of view. Many of the main points are justified. |
| 16–20 | • The response is structured and generally organized, and can be easily followed.<br>• The philosophical issues/concepts raised by the stimulus material are explicitly identified. There is good justification of how the issues/concepts relate to the stimulus material and to the question of what it is to be human.<br>• The response contains accurate and relevant knowledge. There is a good explanation of the issues/concepts. Philosophical vocabulary is mostly used appropriately.<br>• The response contains critical analysis. There is discussion and some assessment of alternative interpretations or points of view. Most of the main points are justified. |
| 21–25 | • The response is well structured, focused and effectively organized.<br>• The philosophical issues/concepts raised by the stimulus material are explicitly identified. There is a well-developed justification of how the issues/concepts relate to the stimulus material and to the question of what it is to be human.<br>• The response contains relevant, accurate and detailed knowledge. There is a well-developed explanation of the issues/concepts. There is appropriate use of philosophical vocabulary throughout the response.<br>• The response contains well-developed critical analysis. There is discussion and assessment of alternative interpretations or points of view. All or nearly all of the main points are justified. The response argues from a consistently held position about the issue. |

## Assessment tip: How can I use the markbands to improve? 

A great way to improve your essays is to read the top markband (21–25) before you start writing, in order to remind yourself of what a great essay should look like. Then, after writing your essay, read the markbands once more and ask yourself how your work compares to each descriptor. There might be an aspect of your essay that is weaker than the rest, and using the markbands gives you a chance to edit your work until you strengthen your areas of weakness.

Once you have received your first mark from your teacher, another good exercise is to compare the markband your essay was placed into with the markband above that. So, for instance, if your essay received a 14/25, you may want to take a good look at the 16–20 markband. Ask yourself: what will take my work from this markband to the next one? For example, what is the difference between "a clear attempt to structure the response" and a response that is "structured and generally organized"? What is the difference between a "satisfactory" and a "good" explanation of the issues/concepts? What will take you from "some discussion of alternative interpretations" to a "discussion *and assessment* of alternative interpretations"?

If you have classmates whose essay was placed in the markband above yours, it may be a good idea to ask if you can read their work. Although this chapter presents you with some sample work, it will be particularly interesting to see what others can write based on the same question, the same material, and the same teaching you have experienced.

## Markschemes

What is a **markscheme**?

A markscheme is a document that examiners receive before they start marking exam papers. The note to examiners that accompanies each markscheme clearly explains that the markscheme is not a list of what *should* be found in exam scripts, but instead some suggestions and examples of what *could* be found in those answers. Read the example below:

**Note to examiners**

This markscheme outlines what members of the paper-setting team had in mind when they devised the questions. The topics listed in the bullet points indicate possible areas candidates might cover in their answers. They are not compulsory points and not necessarily the best possible points. They are only a framework to help examiners in their assessment. Examiners should be responsive to any other valid points or any other valid approaches.

## Assessment tip: How can I use markschemes to improve?

It may not always be a good idea to look at markschemes too closely before you write your essays. Instead, your essay should be based on what you know, what your teacher has decided to cover, and what you have found out through your own research. No two student answers should be the same, because they should be based on individual students' knowledge and thought processes. Modelling your answer on a markscheme may actually limit you or force you to use material that you are not confident with. Your essay may be completely different from the markscheme suggestions, and yet be a great essay. So, whatever you do, remember that markschemes are not meant to be prescriptive!

However, the markscheme could still form part of the brainstorming stage when you are preparing an "open-notes" essay plan. You may find angles and ideas you had not thought about, or perhaps suggestions you would like to explore further. Reading a markscheme in the planning stages can also help you see whether you are on the right track with your own plan, and may alert you to the fact that you had misunderstood some aspect of the stimulus (although stimuli are typically quite open-ended).

Another way to use markschemes is to read them *after* writing an essay, as a tool to help reflection. You will get new ideas about what you could do next time if a similar stimulus comes up. You will also get a better understanding of the type of material and discussion that are expected in the core theme paper.

### Sample essay analysis

#### Stimulus

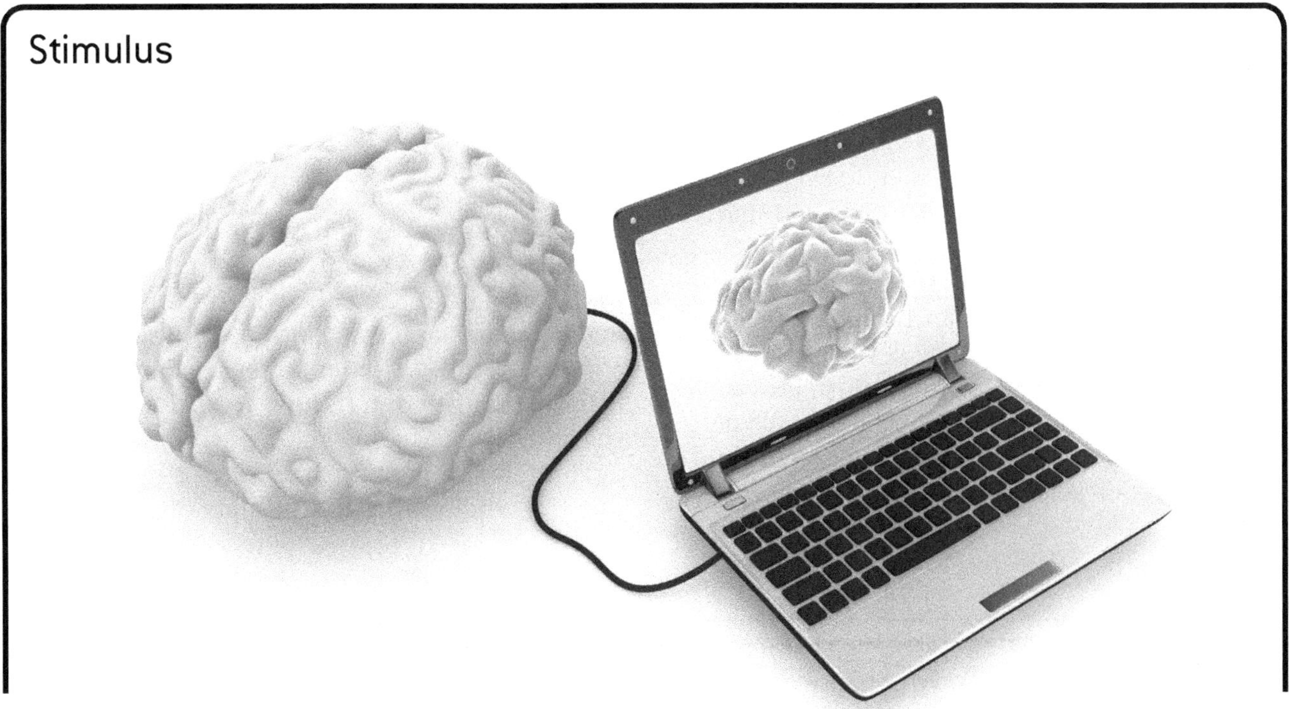

My calculator fits neatly into my bag and cost me less than £100. Nevertheless, it contains as much technology as was used, not even half a century ago, to put man on the moon. Smartphones today which sit in the palm of one's hand are hundreds of times more powerful than computers which, in my *siblings'* lifetimes took up entire rooms, and technology is briskly closing the gap on science fiction before our eyes: Artificial Intelligence that we have created, albeit in its most embryonic forms, is now a reality. As "Supercomputers" creep ever closer to our everyday life it is impossible not to ask ourselves the question, are we simply mimicking our own selves? The stimulus makes a clear connection between the brain and a computer, a connection also made by computer functionalists, who argue that our brains are like the hardware of a computer, and our minds are akin to the software. This hypothesis that we may simply be complicated computers (or, at least in some respects, indistinguishable from them) is surprisingly hard to disprove, although there are some captivating criticisms of it such as Searle's Chinese Room experiment. Computer functionalism is ruled out, to a certain extent, by property dualism, which would argue that our minds have emergent properties, which cannot be treated like physical states, but these two theories may be more compatible than they seem at first glance.

Computer functionalism is a popular, modern theory that models humans on computers, much like the stimulus image: brains are hardware, and our minds software. This solves problems of the relation between body and mind, since the analogy works and is so evident in every part of modern, western life. The theory would suggest that a modern computer possesses a mind, and there is no difference at all between the brain and a computer. Alan Turing, a computer scientist who was key in the development of computers as we know them, imagined a "Universal Turing Machine", which would be able to carry out any algorithmic program, and solve any solvable program. Is the brain simply one of these? If so, the functions become more important than the details of the working, and this can be tested using the Turing test, which simply measures whether a machine seems to, in a double blind trial, perform as well as a human being. The problem here is that the functions are determining physical difference (or lack thereof). Naturally, humans feel that there is more than that to our being human.

Searle thought up a criticism which highlights the above problem, called the Chinese Room theory. He says that, locked in a room with a rulebook (similar to a computer algorithm) for answering Chinese, he could pass the Turing test for understanding Chinese. However, he does not – he may be able to *answer* in Chinese but he does not *understand* a word, and that understanding is what the human mind brings to the world, and what being human is about. According to Searle, the computer operates by manipulating the symbols, whereas the human mind attaches meaning to the symbols.[1] In other words, Searle would disagree with the suggestion implied by the stimulus image: the human mind cannot be reduced to a computer, and comparing them like the stimulus does is misleading and simplistic. This is a far more intuitive theory, as it takes account of qualities that certainly *feel* uniquely human.

I have a couple of my own issues with computer functionalism. Firstly, how can our brains, which we know categorically have been in existence, in humans, for millions of years, be so coincidentally similar to something only decades old? This could be countered, I admit, by saying that it is not that our brains are modelled on computers, it is that computers (which, admittedly, we have created) are modelled, if subconsciously, on our brains. In fact, this is probably the way the stimulus image intends to mean, since the human brain appears on the computer screen, making its mark on the computer. However, this talk of "hardware" and "software" is so specific to modern day computers that it seems uncanny that our whole existence is simply one of these.

[1] See John R. Searle, "Is the Brain's Mind a Computer Program?", *Scientific American* 262, No. 1 (January 1990): 26–31; available at http://www.cs.princeton.edu/courses/archive/spring06/cos116/Is_The_Brains_Mind_A_Computer_Program.pdf (accessed 31 October 2014).

Computer functionalism argues that there is no difference whatsoever between the brain and a computer, but if this is so then why this one, new, modern invention? In years gone by, many philosophers have said "Our mind is like a light bulb because electricity (an input) is illuminated into something far more wonderful and different (an output, our thoughts and feelings)" simply because that was the wonder of their day? Maybe it is not that our minds are like computers, but that we see the beauty in this thing we have just created, and *want* them to be. In short, the human mind and the human brain are timeless; the computer is not. Being human cannot simply be reduced to and explained by something that human beings themselves have created.

My second criticism is that we have created computers which have intelligence far beyond our own in so many fields, so how is there still so much lacking in terms of, for example, our feelings and free will? For instance, mathematicians have spent years trying to solve the 'Four Colour Problem': four colours seem to be enough to colour any map, and can it be proved that it is. Humans had spent entire careers showing many examples of when four colours were enough, and could find no examples where four colours were not, but could not categorically prove that any map would only need four colours. The answer, in the end, was that four colours were indeed always enough, and this was proved, but only by a computer. Yes, this computer was created by a human. Yes, everything this computer had (hardware, software, algorithms) was given to it by a human, but *a computer was needed to do something that, to this day, a human has never been able to do*. This is a simple example, but increasingly common in our modern day world, and raises the issue that if computers seem to be so superior to us in so many respects, why do they lag behind us so noticeably in so many others. It seems that computers are not the same as us, after all: the stimulus image is, once again, misleading. This method of judging only by function fails to account for some of the qualities that ultimately will define our humanity, e.g. real understanding, subjectivity and free will.

In looking at property dualism, I am going to focus on one strand, emergentism, as I think it is particularly interesting. Emergentism argues that in complex systems such as the human brain (or, indeed, the human body, but that is for another day ...) the sum of all the parts is greater than the whole. There is a gap in between what a system can achieve in function and what its parts would be able to achieve individually, and the mind falls into one such gap. This is quite a nice, intuitive theory: we feel that we have real consciousness and this is not the same sort of thing as the physical world. I think of it like currencies – we can, of course, exchange currencies, but this never really is exact because "the equivalent of a pound", which you would get for a pound if you were to exchange it to go to, say, a poor African country, would buy far, far more than a pound would in London. It would not mean the same thing; it is nowhere near equivalent and is a crude misinterpretation of a pound. Emergent properties cannot be treated like other physical states because they obey different laws. I would extrapolate from this that we cannot make assumptions about such properties from, for instance, their functions, as the laws they obey are completely different.

Finally, Ned Block came up with a criticism of functionalism in which he argued that if every member of the Chinese nation performed a function representing one of the neurones of the brain, the Chinese nation would still not have a mental state as the brain does. This seems, to me, emergent: there is a gap between what a copy can achieve and what the mind can achieve. The computer may well be a copy of the human mind, as suggested by the stimulus, but it seems far from approaching its most important properties. The human mind is as mysterious as the outer reaches of the universe, and as magical as some of the phenomena that occur there. We *are*, in my opinion, more than supercomputers, because we have emergent properties that they never seem to get close to. I do not think that these emergent properties can even be explained by the "software" hypotheses, because software is not quite emergent: it is built entirely on binary algorithms in the hardware. We may never know quite what it is that makes our minds as amazing as they are, but I don't think we're about to find the answer in computers, no matter how advanced.

**Reminder:** here is the top markband, and what a great essay should achieve:

| | |
|---|---|
| 21–25 | • The response is well structured, focused and effectively organized.<br>• The philosophical issues/concepts raised by the stimulus material are explicitly identified. There is a well-developed justification of how the issues/concepts relate to the stimulus material and to the question of what it is to be human.<br>• The response contains relevant, accurate and detailed knowledge. There is a well-developed explanation of the issues/concepts. There is appropriate use of philosophical vocabulary throughout the response.<br>• The response contains well-developed critical analysis. There is discussion and assessment of alternative interpretations or points of view. All or nearly all of the main points are justified. The response argues from a consistently held position about the issue. |

## EXERCISE

Please complete *before* you read guiding comments!

- As a whole, how well do you think the essay is structured and organized? Is it a balanced essay? Is there a logical progression? Does it "flow" well?
- Read the entire essay and highlight references to the stimulus, and to the central theme of "Being human". Do you think those references are clearly present? Do you think they are clearly related to the issues and concepts discussed?
- Are the issues and concepts discussed clearly identified from the start of the essay? Does the essay remain focused on those issues and concepts?
- How relevant, accurate and detailed do you think the writer's knowledge is? Do you get the feeling that the writer truly understands what he or she is talking about? Are explanations clear and developed?
- Does the writer use philosophical language effectively and precisely?
- Are the critical analysis and discussion well developed? Are alternative points of view considered? Can you identify a consistently held perspective throughout the essay?
- Overall, what markband do you think this essay fits into?

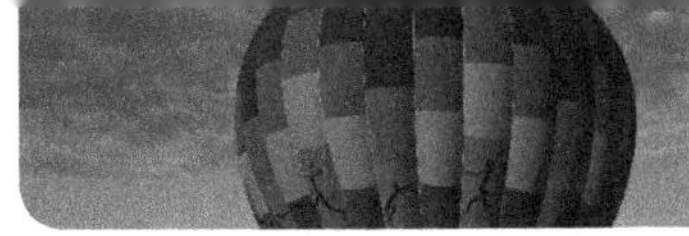

## Guiding comments

| | Strengths | Areas for development |
|---|---|---|
| **Structure** | The response is focused on a central topic and the arguments can be followed easily. The structure is fairly clear. | The essay is a little imbalanced, since the theory the writer chooses to defend only appears near the end of the essay, with little space or time left to explain it in detail. |
| **Concepts, stimulus, Being Human** | The essay is centred around specific concepts and really revolves around the stimulus, as well as "Being human". There is a genuine attempt to deal with the stimulus itself. | The key concept could be identified a little more clearly in the introduction, and the link with the stimulus could also come a little earlier, straight at the beginning of the essay. |
| **Philosophical knowledge and language** | This is a fairly strong point of this essay, as the student has a clear and detailed knowledge of the issues discussed. Examples bring this philosophical knowledge to life. Philosophical language is appropriate. | Although concepts are generally well explained, there are still a few assumptions that would need to be tackled. The relationship between property dualism and emergentism is not really explained. |
| **Analysis, alternative interpretations, position** | The analysis is another strong point. The writer is genuinely engaging with the issues and *doing philosophy*. Points are justified and the writer's position becomes pretty clear in the second part of the essay. | The writer's position could be clearer in the first part of the essay, especially in the introduction, which could benefit from a more explicit thesis. |

| | |
|---|---|
| **Overall** | The essay could be a little more balanced and the perspective could be clearer from the start. The introduction could set the scene more clearly by mentioning the stimulus straight away and identifying a key concept even more directly. The last sentence in the introduction seems like a thesis but it is never quite tackled in the essay. Finally, there is some lack of clarity when describing the relationship between emergentism and property dualism.<br><br>However, it is clear that the writer possesses a very good grasp of most of the issues discussed and engages with them in a lively and personal manner. The analysis is pretty thorough, with some depth in parts of the essay. Much of this essay demonstrates that the writer is *doing philosophy* rather than merely describing theories.<br><br>This can be placed at the bottom of the top band: 21/25 |

## Core theme: the stimulus

### What is a stimulus?

The stimulus is an image or text chosen by philosophy examiners to raise issues for discussion. It is chosen to be provocative or interesting, perhaps even ambiguous, so that different people could find different things to say about it. This should stimulate you to say something about philosophy, and the aim of this exam question is for students to discuss what they encounter in a thoughtful way, appreciating how the subject can give rise to varied reflections.

### Why is there a stimulus question in the exam?

By presenting a stimulus that goes beyond narrow philosophy (it could be literature, art, journalism, etc.), the examiners expect students to think about how philosophical issues arise in life. Philosophy is an active and reflective discipline; this type of question demands that you develop the skill of philosophical analysis and the ability to apply it in various ways.

### What skills do I need?

The interpretation of the stimulus requires the development of intellectual skills. You cannot perform well in the exam without *engaging* with the material before you. That is, *you must not ignore the stimulus* and simply write whatever essay you feel like. Take this opportunity to display your skills: describing and explaining the material; identifying and clarifying issues; supporting and justifying your choice of topic.

### How should I use the stimulus in my essay?

Use your essay introduction to unpack the material in the stimulus. This should involve discussing the stimulus, identifying an issue it raises (in the core theme), and justifying your choice of issue. You can make links to the stimulus in the body of your essay as an example, but you should *not* write the whole essay as a commentary on the stimulus. The bulk of your essay should be an analysis of the *issue* and the two approaches you are considering. Finally, use your essay conclusion to make definitive judgments about the issue you have analysed, returning to the stimulus to see how your answer applies to the material. How have you used philosophy to make sense of the material?

## Assessment markbands: dealing with the stimulus

One of the bullet points in the assessment markbands for the core theme refers to your **engagement** with the stimulus and your **identification** of the issue. The philosophy examiners have a description for attainment in this skill at different levels (see the table below).

| | |
|---|---|
| **Band 1–5 marks** | The philosophical issue raised by the stimulus material is implied but not explicitly identified. There is minimal or no explanation of how the issue relates to the stimulus material or links to the question of what it is to be human. |
| **Band 6–10 marks** | The philosophical issue raised by the stimulus material is implied but not explicitly identified. There is some limited explanation of how the issue relates to the stimulus material or links to the question of what it is to be human. |
| **Band 11–15 marks** | The philosophical issue raised by the stimulus material is explicitly identified. There is a basic explanation of how the issue relates to the stimulus material and to the question of what it is to be human. |
| **Band 16–20 marks** | The philosophical issue raised by the stimulus material is explicitly identified. There is good justification of how the issue relates to the stimulus material and to the question of what it is to be human. |
| **Band 21–25 marks** | The philosophical issue raised by the stimulus material is explicitly identified. There is a well-developed justification of how the issue relates to the stimulus material and to the question of what it is to be human. |

**Note:** You should identify a philosophical issue clearly if you want to score 11 marks or higher. The issue has to be *philosophical*. You should aim to do a good job of justifying your choice if you want to score in the top two bands.

Looking at the top markband, we can extract three key ingredients that you need to demonstrate in your response to the stimulus:

- Clear identification of a philosophical issue from the stimulus
- Developed justification of how the issue relates to the stimulus
- Developed justification of the link to the question, what is it to be human?

## EXERCISE

Write sample essay introductions to two or three stimuli of your choosing. Highlight the three ingredients above in different colours.

## Responding to a text stimulus

The text stimulus provides interesting opportunities and challenges. In past exams, many students have favoured the picture in the core theme because they see it as an easy option: pictures are open to interpretation and the details can quickly be taken in. However, working on the assumption that the picture is always best will reduce your options in the exam, and it may mean that you miss a golden opportunity to write an interesting response on a topic you know well. If you ask the right questions of the stimulus, you may find that you have a great deal to say:

### *Which core theme issues does the text raise?*

Students can go wrong by asking "what is the examiner looking for?" The texts are supposed to raise a *number* of issues and allow for a wide range of responses; *any* approach to the text is legitimate, as long as there is meaningful and justifiable explanation for how it arises. In the first of the example texts below, you will find the issues of freedom, choice, determinism, media, social forces, etc. Be open-minded, but think carefully about how you can make connections to topics you know.

### *What opinions or arguments does it present?*

Texts often supply a point of view or argument, which gives you something to sink your teeth into when doing evaluation and analysis. Although you are looking at your two chosen approaches to the issue, examiners will be pleased to see students interacting with the text also. For example, take a look at the second text below: can you agree with this pessimistic assessment of human nature, supported by the students? Could you help your discussion by arguing with/for/against the text?

### *What theories does it remind you of?*

It's helpful to see whether you can align the text with some of the theories you have studied (e.g. "isms" such as Platonism, relativism, etc.); this will start up an intelligent discussion, appropriately expressed. For example, Stimulus 3 text regards humans as intrinsically moral beings, offering a perspective that is compatible with theism or moral realism. That comparison can kick off the issue for analysis.

### *What would philosophers think?*

Imagine that you are one of the philosophers whom you have studied on the IB Philosophy course, and that you are now reading this text. What would you think about the ideas and arguments presented to you? Getting a "conversation" going between specific philosophers and the text will set you apart as a high-level candidate.

### *What terms can I use?*

The text will give you vocabulary that will improve the quality of your philosophical writing. There are many examples in the texts below: social trends, personal choice, inevitability, pessimism, character, personhood, reverence, etc. Think about how you can use these terms in your own discussion and think about the other, related terms that you know.

### *How does this link to the core theme issue?*

The text has been chosen to address the core theme question: what does it mean to be human? In exploring the connection with the core theme and the role of the "human" in the text, you give yourself interesting material for analysis and discussion. This may be particularly helpful in essay introductions and conclusions, in which you are trying to see the problem in its context.

### Text stimulus examples

#### Stimulus 1

In his recent bestseller *The Tipping Point*, the journalist Malcolm Gladwell applies [an] idea to recent social trends ... In each case the conventional wisdom attributed the trend to external social forces such as advertising, government programmes, or role models. And in each case the trend was really driven by an internal dynamic of personal choices and influences and their feedback. The naming of babies, and of things in general, is another example in which a large-scale social phenomenon – the composition of a language – emerges unpredictably out of many individual choices that influence one another.

#### Stimulus 2

I taught "War and Human Nature" again this fall. The course ponders the question, as my syllabus puts it, "Is war inevitable, or are peace and even universal disarmament possible?" During the first class, I posed that question to my undergraduate students. Thirteen said no, peace is not possible, and four said yes, it is. That pessimistic response no longer surprises me. Two years ago, I had my students ask classmates: "Will humans ever stop fighting wars, once and for all? Why or why not?" Of the 205 respondents, 185 – more than 90 percent – replied no. "From this survey," one of my students wrote, "we can conclude that most college students have little faith in mankind."

## Stimulus 3

Human beings are animals with a peculiar character and role. They are ... alert to the values of personhood, life, order, and existence as such, to his or her community, to his or her environment, to the cosmos. As a member of the community of nature, the human being may be regarded as guardian of respect for it, to exercise reverence towards it and, if it has a maker, towards its maker.

▲ Read the text before deciding on your stimulus.

**Read**
- Read the text carefully, *twice*
- Highlight terminology and concepts

**Link**
- Identify issues and arguments
- WWPT? (*what would philosophers think?*)

**Plan**
- Pick your central issue for analysis
- Quick essay plan

## Responding to a picture stimulus

The picture stimulus provides different opportunities and challenges. It is often said that "a picture tells a thousand words" and you should be open to finding a broad array of ideas and possibilities in the images presented to you. On the other hand, however, there needs to be a measure of caution; you must make a sincere attempt to *identify* and *justify* what you choose to discuss, not assuming that a picture excuses you to write about anything. Humans are capable of interpreting visual information very quickly and you may find the ideas strike you within a second or two. Yet, you should still take the time to develop techniques of analysis that will help you to *apply* the ideas effectively in the exam and show that you have depth of understanding. As with the text, you can proceed by asking the right questions (see above):

### *Which core theme issues does the picture raise?*

Be open-minded and consider a range of possibilities. Think about how all the different components of the image could relate to philosophical issues; you might want to focus on specific features of the image. If the image is combined with text (e.g. speech bubbles), consider how the text also connects with philosophical issues and works with the imagery to stimulate discussion.

### *What perspectives does it present?*

Images tend not to give specific theoretical frameworks or arguments in an unambiguous way. Images are often suggestive and open to subjective interpretation. However, images can still help you to "see" an issue in a certain way, or might be taken to imply a certain idea or perspective. Think about how you can use the perspectives of an image in dialogue or argument. You could argue for links to specific philosophies and ideologies, so long as you make intelligent links to the imagery.

### *What would philosophers think?*

Consider what the philosophers you have encountered in the course might make of the imagery. There might be connections between the visual imagery of the stimulus and the visual metaphors used by philosophers. Think about famous visual metaphors and how these compare: e.g. Plato's Cave, chariot, etc.

### *What examples can I use?*

Turn the imagery into words and phrases, short descriptions and examples. Think about how these examples can then be referred to in your writing. There might be a particular look on someone's face, an emotion or expression. There might be a symbol or visual clue. There might be an identifiable object (a computer, a car). Developing a bank of examples in the first moments of the exam will help the analysis in your writing.

### *How does this relate to the core theme issue?*

As with the text, you need to make a connection with the question of what it is to be human. There might be an implied link to one of the issues raised in this book, which are problems concerned with human self-understanding and the response to the human condition. The image might feature human beings in action or thought. You can also consider your personal response as a human encountering the issue.

## Example of picture stimulus with levels of response

| Response (essay introduction) | Grade and comment |
|---|---|
| *The stimulus shows a picture of two fat men with Alice, from* Through the Looking-Glass. *This to me represents the problem of the mind–body relationship. It is a difficult issue to solve because of the philosophical arguments for and against different theories.* | **Low score (Band 1–5 marks)**<br>• An issue is identified, but not *from* the stimulus<br>• No explanation of how the issue relates to the stimulus or the core theme |
| *The stimulus here is a picture of Tweedledum-and-Tweedledee, characters from* Through the Looking-Glass. *They are joined together and look almost identical, with Alice observing them with surprise. What do these characters mean? They are similar and appear human-like in their nature. The issue which arises from this stimulus, then, is freedom and determinism – the problem of whether humans make freely chosen decisions, or whether all actions are determined by external factors. Are these characters free?* | **Medium score (Band 11–15)**<br>• Explicit identification of the issue<br>• Basic explanation of the link to the stimulus and core theme<br>**Comment**<br>This represents a significant improvement from the previous example, because there is discussion of the material that links in a simple but logical way to a core theme issue. |
| *The stimulus presents us with an image of Tweedledum-and-Tweedledee, from* Through the Looking-Glass. *These figures are strange in their appearance; they are almost identical and seem to be joined at the hip. This further suggests some bond in mind and behaviour. Are these characters able to act as individuals? Are they free to be different from the other? They seem to be bound by a shared nature, incapable of breaking from the mould in which they are made. In that sense, they are products of the author; their lives are fixed in a rigid, fantastical way. This represents the idea of conforming to a pattern of appearance and behaviour, which leads me to think of the problem of free will. Do human agents make free and meaningful choices? Or, like the characters depicted here, are they tied to an inevitable pattern?* | **High score (Band 20–25)**<br>• Explicit identification of the issue<br>• Well-developed justification of the link to the stimulus and core theme<br>**Comment**<br>This represents a significant improvement on the previous example, because the discussion thoroughly identifies the way in which the stimulus leads to reflection about a core theme issue. Reflections develop thoughtfully to show that the issue is well chosen ("justified"). |

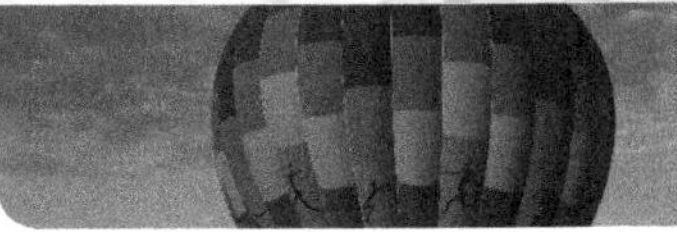

## Structuring a core theme essay

### *Why is structure important?*

Structure is a vital element of any essay and it is a key part of being successful in assessment in the core theme. Essay structure enables you to communicate your ideas, to make the reading process easier, and to make your perspective or argument more convincing. You want to show that you have a sequence of logical, developed points, and this is what well-constructed paragraphs allow.

### *What should I do?*

When preparing essays, make sure that you have a good plan before you start writing. You will be pushed for time in the exam, which makes the preparation of practice plans all the more important. Plan the rough content of each paragraph and consider how they are connected. Check that there is convincing progress in your ideas and argument. Use the tables below for an idea of how it works.

### *What about the markbands?*

The markbands demand that your response is "*well structured*". That means checking that each paragraph has a clear and coherent theme or point. Your writing must also be "*focused*", so check that your plan does not drift aimlessly between unconnected points. Where is your essay going? There must also be "*effective organization*", so your ideas should be linked together and you should make efficient use of your words (no waffle or digressions!).

## The basic threefold structure: introduction, body, conclusion

| | |
|---|---|
| **Introduction**<br>1–2 paragraphs | • Discuss stimulus<br>• Identify issue<br>• Put issue in context (why does it matter?)<br>• Identify key perspectives/approaches<br>• Identify your initial response/thesis/argument |
| **Body**<br>4–6 paragraphs | • Link or use examples from stimulus, if/where appropriate<br>• Explain and discuss issue thoroughly<br>• Analyse key perspectives/approaches, including:<br>  • Details of theories and philosophers<br>  • Counter-arguments and criticisms<br>  • Implications and effects of ideas<br>• Evaluate and make judgments, giving reasons |
| **Conclusion**<br>1 paragraph | • Apply your analysis to the stimulus<br>• Apply your analysis to the issue<br>• Make judgments, summarize your *consistent* perspective<br>• Take a wider perspective, note key implications |

**Note:** This is a suggested model, *not* the required approach.

## Mind and Body paragraph structure: worked example

| | |
|---|---|
| **1 Introduction** | Describe stimulus (e.g. brain in a jar) and the ideas it raises, focus on brain/mind connection, identify the mind–body problem as issue, contextualize, signpost dualism and monism perspectives, my approach will be to argue for dualism. |
| **2 Explain and discuss dualist perspectives** | Explain classic dualist arguments from Plato and Descartes (details, key terms, etc.), discuss distinctive ideas and strengths of dualism. |
| **3 Analyse and evaluate dualist perspectives** | Analyse implications of dualism, criticisms of Platonic and Cartesian arguments, give my comments, consider criticisms. Emphasize my approach (pro-dualism). |
| **4 Explain and discuss monist perspectives** | Explain classic monist arguments from Aristotle and Dennett (details, key terms, etc.), discuss distinctive ideas and strengths of monism. |
| **5 Analyse and evaluate monist perspectives** | Analyse implications of monism, criticisms of Aristotelian and functionalist arguments, give my comments, consider criticisms. Emphasize my approach (against monism, pro-dualism). |
| **6 Conclusion** | Wrap up by looking back on the stimulus: dualism, mind not the same as the brain, nor the body. Re-state my approach (pro-dualism) and flag up key arguments. What are the implications of my conclusion? Why does this matter? |

You could produce a very different type of structure that would enable you to address an issue arising from the stimulus, concerning mind and body. You could write an essay with a very strong argument, or something more deliberative. You could focus on a particular theory, or take a broader view of the topic. Whatever structure you decide upon, the important points of technique are:

- Each paragraph has a distinct point or purpose
- Your paragraphs advance your perspective or argument on the issue
- Your paragraphs flow with logical connections to one another
- Your paragraphs display all the necessary skills (explaining, analysing, etc.)

### EXERCISE

1. Choose a topic from this textbook and write an essay plan, implementing the advice from this chapter. Check it against the markbands. Could it lead to a good mark?
2. Get sample essays from your teacher and/or fellow students. Copy them and chop up all the paragraphs, creating a jumble of different pieces of paper. Distribute the jumbled essays and reassemble them. Is it easy? Is the structure clear enough? (Discussion)
3. Pick up a book or article on philosophy and analyse the paragraph structure. Can you pick out the plan from the text? How does the author make the writing flow between paragraphs? (Make notes)

▲ Before you write, *plan*.

**Assessment tip**

You won't have time to write a full essay plan in the exam, so write plenty of practice plans in revision; you will then have frameworks to build from. Make sure that the structures you use will hit the top level requirements for the markbands.

## Use of language in core theme answers

### *What am I aiming for?*

To get in the top markband (21–25 marks) in the core theme, your work should show that "there is appropriate use of philosophical vocabulary throughout the response". The quality of your expression, including the language and terminology you choose to use, will make a significant contribution to your grade. Your writing affects all aspects of the markband, in that you need to write well to show knowledge, analysis, and so on. Make sure that you constantly strive to improve your academic writing throughout the course.

### *How do I display "appropriate use of philosophical vocabulary"?*

This section will pick apart that skill, but there are some key observations to note initially. You should attempt to use language that is *specialist* to the subject ("philosophy"), which you will derive from reading and research, but could also develop through class discussion. It is not simply a matter of writing well, but of making the kind of linguistic distinctions made by philosophers. You should also exercise sensible *judgment* in how you use the language ("appropriate"), in terms of picking the right amount of jargon, deploying it in the right places, and using it in such a way as to improve your writing.

### *How do I develop the skills?*

The key for developing philosophical writing is to cultivate habits that improve your range and use of language throughout the course (see the suggested methods below). This should be a mix of analytical skills (finding and identifying language), application skills (writing and discussing with the language), and review skills (checking and reflecting on your language). Successful students will cycle through these skills in a constant process, striving for a better form of academic writing.

## Methods for improving philosophical language and writing

| | |
|---|---|
| **Analysis of writing** | • Read texts and keep a glossary of terms.<br>• Attempt to read technical texts and articles.<br>• Translate technical texts into plain English.<br>• Use philosophy reference works, study by word.<br>• Access word lists from textbooks, etc.<br>• Appraise essays from other students for clarity.<br>• Proofread and re-phrase your own writing. |
| **Application of writing** | • Set a checklist of terms for each essay.<br>• Include terminology in essay plans.<br>• Link theoretical terms to scholars (e.g. Kant's idealism).<br>• Less is more: apply the simplest way to say it.<br>• Choose language that helps the reader. |
| **Review of writing** | • Identify weaknesses in expression in essays.<br>• Intensively revise misunderstood/missing language.<br>• Ask a non-specialist: can anyone understand this?<br>• Reflect: did you really follow the boxes above? |

## EXERCISE

The three paragraphs below essentially have exactly the same content. Think about the following questions:

- What choices about language are these paragraphs making?
- Why write in one style or the other?
- Which fits best with "appropriate use of philosophical vocabulary"?
- How does choice of language make things clear? How does it obscure?
- Could you do a better job of writing the same paragraph?

### Example 1

*Some people say that it is not possible for people to choose anything that they are going to do because there is no way for things to be other than the way they turn out. It is nice to think that we can choose to do whatever we want, but then this might not be how things really are. It could be that everything is set out in some way and we cannot change the way things are going to be. It is out of our control. Everything is completely fixed.*

### Example 2

*It could be argued that it is impossible for us to exercise free will in making decisions – whatever we would freely choose – because events are entirely fixed by physical factors outside of the individual's control. This position is known as hard determinism. As much as we might like to believe in free will and the power of human decision-making, it may be that this conflicts with the physical reality we encounter through science and philosophy. If all events are entirely determined by their causes, then freedom of choice would be an illusion.*

### Example 3

*Hard determinists postulate the logical necessity that the physical conditions of causality operating within the universe as described by metaphysical naturalism entail the exclusion of free will as an hypothesis about the nature of human agency. The chimera of free will that is expounded in libertarianism is refuted by the formulation of empirical laws of causality through natural science that are both necessary and sufficient to expound the apparent features of decision-making.*

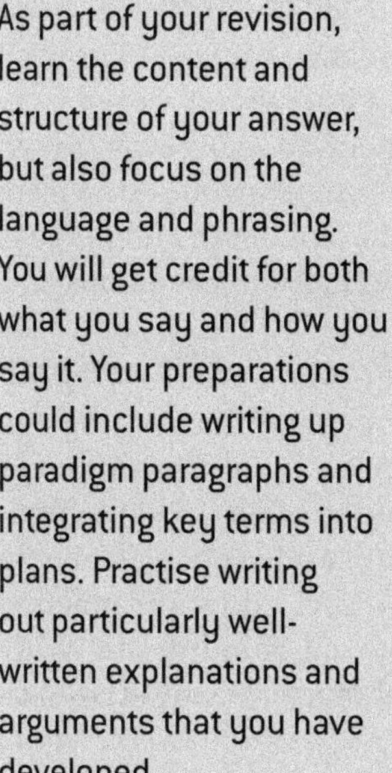

**Assessment tip**

As part of your revision, learn the content and structure of your answer, but also focus on the language and phrasing. You will get credit for both what you say and how you say it. Your preparations could include writing up paradigm paragraphs and integrating key terms into plans. Practise writing out particularly well-written explanations and arguments that you have developed.

## Revising for the core theme exam

The core theme question arises in the context of IB Diploma Philosophy Paper 1, in which HL students will be faced with three essays in total (one core, two optional themes) and SL students with two (one core, one optional theme). Writing an excellent core theme essay is particularly important for getting the exams off to a good start and making a favourable impression upon the examiner. The advice for revising here will be specific for the core theme, but the general points could also be applied to other aspects of the IB Philosophy exams.

### 1 Understand the practicalities

You need to make sure that the task of writing a core theme essay is a familiar one and that you are happy on entering the exam hall that you know what to expect. This should include the practical layout of the paper, the styles of question, and the timings of the paper. You should reckon on spending about 50 minutes on your essay (and on the optional theme essays). There is no fixed rule, but a sensible approach would be to spend 5 minutes interpreting the stimulus and planning what you will write, and 45 minutes writing up your answer. Use your revision time to familiarize yourself with specimen and past papers and practising to the time limits.

### 2 Choose and order topics

There is a lot of material in the core theme and it will not be practical to have an in-depth knowledge of every aspect of every topic. Try to strategize by mentally ordering the topics as part of your revision. A sensible policy would be to have three very strong topics that are thoroughly revised and practised, with a general appreciation of the other three as back-up topics. You should keep a rough order in your mind of which topics would be your favoured ones, but of course you should not try to make a memorized essay fit with any stimulus (the examiners will spot this!). Be prepared to be flexible on the day and write about the philosophical issues that arise from the stimulus material. As you settle upon topics for revision, gather stimulus materials from the textbook and past papers, and order them by topic, so that you have an appreciation of how you could link the words and imagery to core theme issues.

### 3 Make notes and essay plans, and learn them

There is no shortcut to exam success; you will have to gather material, condense it in note form, and learn it. The thrust of the IB Philosophy course is on doing and applying the subject, but that does not mean that you should put off learning detailed knowledge and in-depth explanations. Often, the best way to express your own ideas and comments is by reacting to the claims made by other philosophers; memorize the key points, terms, and details to make sure that you have something to engage with. Once you have sufficient knowledge, you should think about how to transform that into written answers. Look at past questions and prepare essay plans; it helps to know what to write *and* the framework within which to write it. Compare your essay plans with your notes, asking whether you have sufficient depth and range of points. A good essay should have a good mix of detailed explanations and your own personal commentary.

### 4 Practise skills and practise essays

Remember that writing an essay under timed conditions, without notes, is not a unique event; you can and should re-create it in your own time to build up your confidence and the appropriate skills. With good notes and essay plans behind you, try a mixture of practice activities. You could do short practices, e.g. by taking a stimulus and giving yourself 5 minutes to write an introduction. You should also try writing full practice essays to the clock for your favoured topics. Practice is the best way to make your writing efficient, to identify and eliminate weaknesses, and to help you feel confident and focused in the exam.

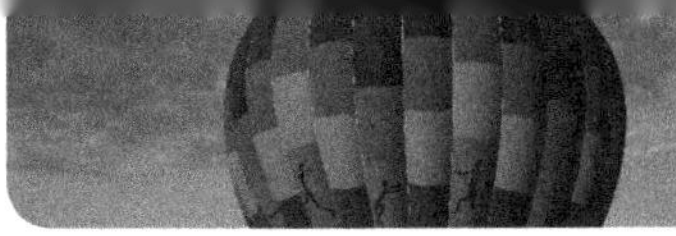

### *5 Get and use feedback*

Most importantly, do not forget your teachers. Look at the different stages of revision and think about how you could get help. Do you need advice about note taking? Are you doing enough to identify an issue in the stimulus material? Do you need to get feedback on a practice essay? The most successful students will work in a cycle of improvement, in which they get support in finding things to work on, developing notes and answers, and re-attempting work in light of feedback.

## Stimuli bank

Use the stimuli below to practise writing core theme essays based on a variety of supports.[2]

### Text stimuli

#### Stimulus 1

The controlling power of the body is the mind. The mind originates the idea, and the nature of the idea is knowledge. Wherever the idea is, we have a thing. For instance, when the idea rests on serving one's parents, then serving one's parents is a "thing"... I say there are no principles but those of the mind, and nothing exists apart from the mind.

—Wang Yangmin

#### Stimulus 2

... that gender is a choice, or that gender is a role, or that gender is a construction that one puts on, as one puts on clothes in the morning, that there is a "one" who is prior to this gender, a one who goes to the wardrobe of gender and decides with deliberation which gender it will be today.

—Judith Butler

[2] Text stimuli 1, 3 and 4 have been taken from Diané Collinson, Kathryn Plant, and Robert Wilkinson (eds), *Fifty Eastern Thinkers* (London: Routledge, 2000), pp. 286, 342, 172. Text stimulus 2 has been reproduced from Judith Butler, "Critically Queer", *GLQ: A Journal of Lesbian and Gay Studies* 1, No. 1 (1993): 21.

### Stimulus 3

To seek to know the self is invariably the wish of living beings. However, those who see the true self are rare. Only buddhas know the true self. People outside the way regard what is not the self as the self. But what buddhas call the self is the entire universe.

—Dogen Kigen

### Stimulus 4

If man were a mere object of study in physiology, if he were a mere mind described by psychology, his conduct would be governed by the laws of necessity ... [but] There is in us the Eternal different from the limited chain of causes and effects in the phenomenal world.

—Sarvepalli Radhakrishnan

## Picture stimuli

### Stimulus 5

Stimulus 6

Stimulus 7

Stimulus 8

Stimulus 9

Stimulus 10

Stimulus 11

Stimulus 12

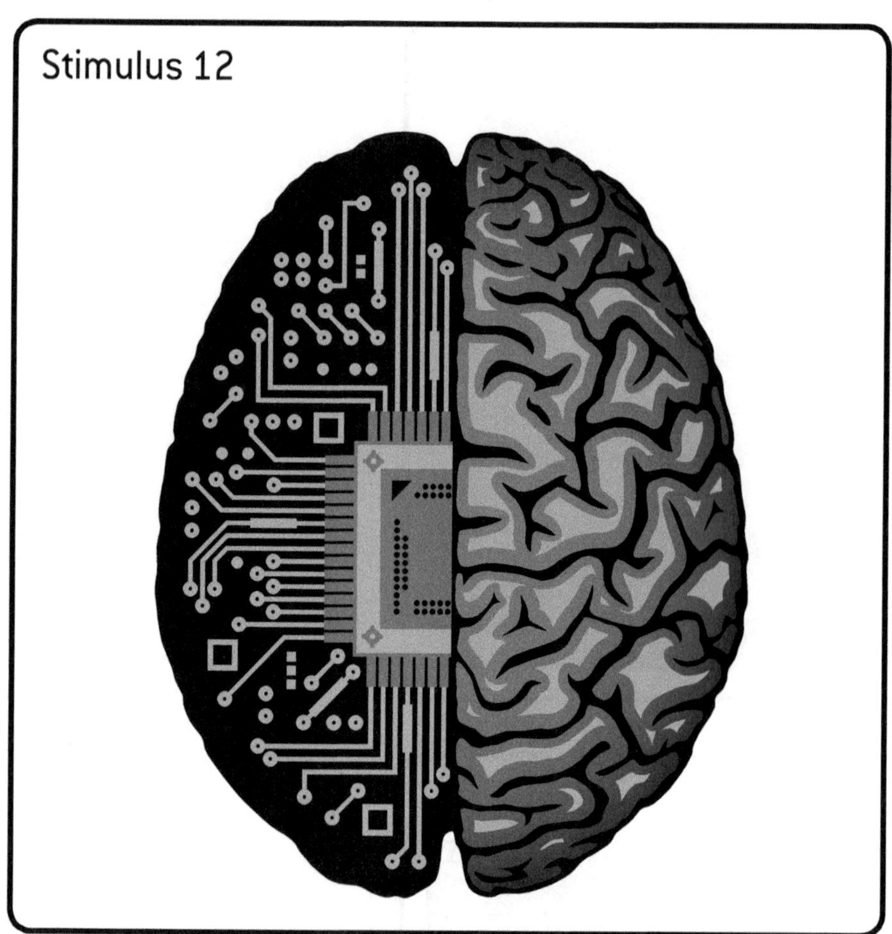

Stimulus 13

Stimulus 14

Stimulus 15

## Stimulus 16

## Stimulus 17

Stimulus 18

We hope you have found the tips in this chapter helpful. Best of luck in your assessment and beyond!

## References Cited

Judith Butler, "Critically Queer", *GLQ: A Journal of Lesbian and Gay Studies* 1, No. 1 (1993): 17–32.

Collinson, Diané, Kathryn Plant, and Robert Wilkinson (eds), *Fifty Eastern Thinkers*. London: Routledge, 2000.

Searle, John R. "Is the Brain's Mind a Computer Program?". *Scientific American* 262, No. 1 (January 1990): 26–31.

# Index

**A**
*a priori* reasoning 25–6, 199
Abrahamic religions 130, 142–50, 280
absolute 23, 161
absurdity 274
agency 86
agency as a condition of personhood 89
websites 89
what is agency? 86–7
who and what possesses agency? 87–8
alienation 297
altruism 46
kin selection 47
reciprocal altruism 47–8
analysis 10
analysing a question 12–13
analytical frameworks 186
analytical strategies 186
establishing your own position 13–14
evaluation 12, 184–5
what is analysis? 11–12
animalism 334–5
animals 71, 96, 97
agency 87–8, 89
anthropocentrism 98–109
consciousness 77–9, 81
morality 91–2
personhood 72, 74–5, 76, 97–8
self-consciousness 81, 84, 85–6
antecedent statements 329
anthropocentrism 98–100
Descartes, René 100–2
does a difference remain? 107–9
humans as animals 103–4
sentience and suffering 104–7
religious anthropocentrism 99
appetitive soul 20
Aquinas, Thomas 152, 197
argument 9–10
argument analysis activity 351
assumptions 10, 13, 184, 185
implications 10, 12, 13, 184
quality of argument 10, 11, 12, 13, 184
Aristotle 99, 152, 175, 198, 338
Aristotle and the body 194–6
biography 140
concepts of the self 183, 253, 254
On the Soul (De Anima) 141–2, 194
Plato and Aristotle 197, 204
artificial intelligence (AI) 113–16
asceticism 133, 134
assessment 365
assessment objectives 367–70
higher level (HL) 365, 366
markbands 372–4, 380–1, 387
markschemes 374–9
revising 391–3
specimen papers and past papers 370–1
standard level (SL) 365–6
stimuli 380–6, 393–401
structuring essays 387–9
use of language 389–91
associationism 59–60
atheism 272
authenticity 93–4, 237
authenticity as condition of personhood 95–6
Kierkegaard, Søren 238–9
who and what possesses authenticity? 94–5
autonomy 27, 28, 43
awareness 77, 78

**B**
babies 83–4
bad faith 93, 275
Baudrillard, Jean 255
behavioural determinism 311
behaviourism 60–1, 164
classical conditioning 61–2
trained responses 61
being 272
being human 1, 14, 119
*Being John Malkovich* 125–6, 130, 172
being-for-itself 274
Bentham, Jeremy 104–6
biography 105
biological approach to personal identity 331
biological determinism 279–80
are some individuals more determined than others? 290–1
biological determinism in individuals 284–5
criminal behaviour 285–7, 288–9
Darwin, Charles 281–2
evolutionary psychology and the science of attraction 283–4
freedom 285, 287–8
human beings, animals, and instinct 280–1
not in our genes 67–8
biological naturalism 336
blank slate 18, 58–9
associationism 59–60
behaviourism 60–2
Chomsky, Noam 64–5
conclusions 64
critique 62
Kant, Immanuel 62–4
Locke, John 59, 60
bodily criterion of identity 331
body 127, 189–90
feminist perspective 193–4
brain 127, 129
brain criterion 335–6
brain plasticity 309, 310
brain theory 335
neuroscience 125, 164, 165, 167, 175
prefrontal cortex 286
Buddhism 132, 150, 183
anatta/anatman (no self) 225
Buddha (Siddhartha Gautama) 133–4, 175
Noble Eightfold Path 134–6
rejecting the self 228
self as dynamic interaction 225–8
bundle theory of the self 209–13
Butler, Joseph 346–7
Butler, Judith 18, 68–9

**C**
Camus, Albert 248–9
*Casper the Friendly Ghost* 157–8
category mistakes 158
causal determinism 312
causation 33
cause 267
cause and effect 269–70
Chalmers, David J. 171–4
change 189
Chomsky, Noam 64–5
Christianity 133, 145–8, 175
Churchland, Paul 181
cognition 164
cognitive biases 48–54
conclusions 53
responses 53–4
communitarianism 330
compatibilism 265
concepts 11, 14, 184
conceptual engineering 4
conceptual framework 11, 14, 185
conceptual scheme 4

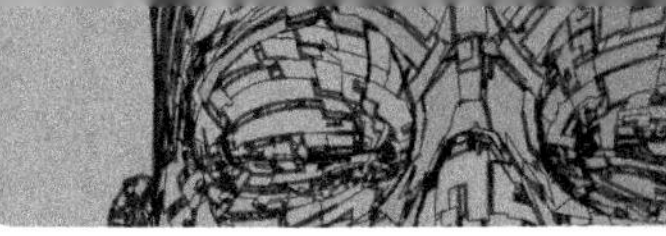

conditioning 61–2
confirmation bias 48
finance 50
juries 52
paranormal and superstitious thinking 50–2
Wason Selection Task 49–50
Confucianism 183, 229–31
Confucian self 231
connectedness 347
criteria of continuity and connectedness 348–50
consciousness 77, 127, 130, 187, 342
consciousness as a condition of personhood 79–81
ethics 80–1
hard problem of consciousness 171–4
minds, machines, and the problem of consciousness 116–18
Sartre, Jean-Paul 247–8
self-consciousness 81–6
websites 81, 86
who and what possesses consciousness? 78–9
consequent statements 329
continuum 332
corporeal 199
Cosmological Argument 25–6
Creation stories 280–1
criminal behaviour 285–7
nature versus nurture 306–8
responsibility and punishment 288–9
criteria 13
culture 252–5
sociocultural identity 353

**D**

Daoism 183, 232
Darwin, Charles 18, 42–4
evolutionary psychology 44–5
resistance to Darwin's ideas 44
theory of evolution 281–2
defence mechanisms 56–7
denial 57
rationalization 57
reaction formation 58
repression 58
sublimation 58
deliberation 271
denial 57
Dennett, Daniel 169–71, 172, 173
Consciousness Explained 157, 169
biography 169
Cartesian Theatre 170
"multiple drafts" 171
Derrida, Jacques 255
Descartes, René 18, 23–4, 181, 183
biography 100
concepts of the self 187–8, 197–8, 199–202
critiques 157–9, 160
evil demon" 155–6, 158
foundationalism 24–5, 155
I think, therefore I am (cogito ergo sum) 156
interactionism 157
machine intelligence 111
Meditations on First Philosophy 154–6, 200–2
mental distinction between human and animals 100–2
mind as immaterial substance 201–2
Plato 200, 202
"radical doubt" 155, 158
self-evidence 24–5
soul 337, 338–9
thinking thing (res cogitans) 156, 158
determinism 265
biological determinism 279–91
integrated approach 313
nature versus nurture 279, 291, 306–11
other types of determinism 311–13
social determinism 291–3
what about freedom? 313–19
dialectic 198
dialectical logic 161
master–slave dialectic 161–2
dialogue 161
Diderot, Denis 199
Diotima of Mantinea 192
discourse 66
distinctions 327–9
diversity 69
dualism 127, 128, 150, 189, 199
Cartesian dualism 157, 158

**E**

Eastern perspectives of the self 218
China 229–32
India 218–29
ego 56
empirical ego 216, 247, 248
empiricism 23, 31, 59, 185, 246
enduring self 181, 325
Enlightenment 183, 198–9
environmental determinism 311
epigenetics 309
episteme 36
epistemology 20, 150, 185
Plato 21–3
essence 186, 187, 212
essential self 185, 186–7
Aristotle and the body 194–6
from Plato to Descartes 198–202
Hegel and the social self 204
Hume and the bundle theory of the self 209–13
Immanuel Kant and the transcendental ego 214–17
Jean-Jacques Rousseau and the moral self 203
Locke and the psychological theory of the self 204–9
modern debate 197–8
modern self and the shift from self-knowledge to self-consciousness 198
modern theories of the no-self 213–14
self as "psyche" or soul 187–94
St Augustine 196–7
Thomas Hobbes and the materialist self 203
essentialism 187, 352
ethics 80–1, 85, 185
responsibility and punishment 288–9
evaluative framework 184
evidence 10
evolution 42–4
humans as animals 104–5
evolutionary psychology 44–5
altruism 46–8
evaluation 46
male aggression 45
mating preferences of humans 45–6, 283–4
morality 46
responses 53–4
existential self 185, 186, 232–3
Albert Camus 248–9
analytical and continental tradition 233
intersubjectivity 250–2
Kierkegaard and Nietzsche 236–7
Kierkegaard, authenticity and the issue of introspection 238–9
Merleau-Ponty and the self as embodied subjectivity 249–50
phenomenology as an approach to the self 233–5
postmodern self 255–6

role of culture 252–5
Sartre and the concept of self-hood 245–8
Simone de Beauvoir 249
understanding Nietzsche 241–5
existentialism 93–4, 187, 198
criticisms and counter-criticisms 276–9
existential anxiety 272
main existentialist philosophers and their influences 272
main existentialist terms and ideas 272–3
personal identity 358–61
responsibility and authenticity 94–5
responsibility and authenticity as conditions of personhood 95–6
extrinsic relations 329

**F**

facticity 93
fatalism 265
feminism 65, 68–9, 391
Ficino, Marsilio 153–4
biography 153
finance 50
Fitzgerald, F. Scott *The Great Gatsby* 292–3
forms 21–3, 139, 187
Foucault, Michel 36–7, 255
reason as a power discourse 65–7
foundationalism 24–5, 155
freedom 263–6
biological determinism 285, 287–8
causation 269–70
determinism 313–19
existentialism and freedom 272–5
free will 268–9, 285
freedom of action 274
freedom of mind 274
libertarianism 270–1
Sartre, Jean-Paul 274–6
sufficient causal condition 267
what do we mean by a "cause"? 267
Freud, Sigmund 18
biography 55
conclusions 58
defence mechanisms 56–8
tripartite theory of the unconscious 56
unconscious mind 55–6
functionalism 116–18, 164, 167–8, 171–2
Dennett, Daniel 169–71

**G**

gender and social conditioning 300–6
ghost in the machine 157, 158
givenness 275
God 32, 142–50
Goethe, Johann Wilhelm von 203

**H**

hard determinism 265, 268
Hegel, Georg Wilhelm Friedrich 161–3, 175, 203
biography 161
social self 204
Heidegger, Martin 183, 234
Heraclitus 188
heterophenomenology 169
Hinduism 132, 135, 183, 218–20
self as controller 222–5
self in Indian thought (Chariot analogy) 221–2
Hobbes, Thomas 30–1, 34
biography 31
materialist self 203
d'Holbach, Paul-Henry Thiry 160, 199
Holy Bible 99, 152
New Testament 145–6
Old Testament 142–5
Holy Koran 148–50
Horkheimer, Max 67
human condition 274
human nature 17–18
ideologies 65–8
Hume, David 30, 31–2, 199
biography 31
Buddhism 229
concepts of the self 198, 209–13, 352
conclusions 34
critique of necessary causation 33
Husserl, Edmund 233–4

**I**

*I, Robot* 126
IBM Deep Blue 110
id 56
idealism 160–3, 246
identity 273, 321–22, 327, 361–3
assessing the bodily criterion 333–5
assessing the non-material substance theory of personal identity 340–1
assessment of the memory theory 350
body and personal identity 331–3
brain criterion 335–6
Cartesian soul 338–9
criteria of continuity and connectedness 348–50
criticisms of Locke's theory of personal identity 344–7
existentialism and the issue of personal identity 358–61
exploring the position of individualism 330–1
exploring the possibilities 325–7
identity theory 168
individual versus community 353–8
individualism vs. communitarianism 330
Joseph Butler and the circularity issue 346–7
necessary and sufficient distinctions 328–9
personal identity according to Derek Parfit 347
personal identity versus sociocultural identity 353
psychological continuity and personal identity 341–3
qualitative versus numerical distinctions 327–8
Ship of Theseus 322–4
soul and personal identity 337–8
substantial identity 352
the self, the body, and the future 336–7
understanding the issue of personal identity 324–5, 329–30
ideologies 65
biological determinism 67–8
conclusions 69
feminism 68–9
neo-Marxism 67
reason as a power discourse 65–7
illusion 186
impulses 42
incommensurability 35
incompatibilism 265, 270
incorporeal 199
individualism 330
exploring the position of individualism 330–1
individualism vs. communitarianism 330
individuality 325
instincts 42
interactionism 157, 158
international-mindedness 2, 6
interpretations 39
intersubjectivity 246, 250–2

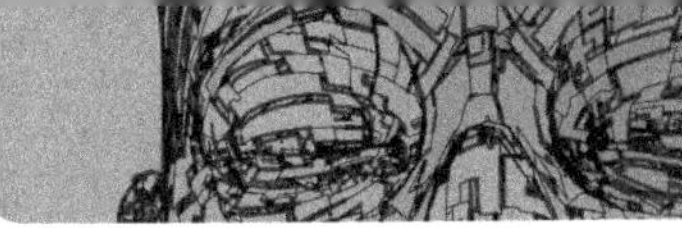

intrinsic relations 329
introspection 238–9, 243, 352
irrationalism 18, 41–2
conclusions 53
Darwin, Charles 42–4
evolutionary psychology 44–8
Freud, Sigmund 55–8
Islam 142, 143, 148–50, 175

**J**
Jainism 132
James, William 213
Jameson, Fredric 255
Jesus Christ 145, 146, 147, 183
Judaism 142–5, 175
juries 52

**K**
Kant, Immanuel 62–3, 203, 204, 233
biography 63
categories 63–4
concepts of the self 198, 214–17
Karma 312–13
Kasparov, Garry 110
key concepts 1, 15
Kierkegaard, Søren 204, 236–7
authenticity and the issue of introspection 238–9
Kierkegaard and the self 240–1
knowledge 21–3, 26–7, 28
Kuhn, Thomas 35–6

**L**
language 64–5
Leibniz, Gottfried 199, 343
libertarianism 265, 268, 270–1
Locke, John 18, 59, 181, 199
biography 344
concepts of self 192, 198, 202, 204–9
conclusions 60
criticisms of theory of personal identity 344–7
Prince and the Cobbler 207–8, 343
self and change of substance 206–8
theory of personal identity 205–6, 341–4
logic 85
logical behaviourism 166
logical principles 24–5
lucky charms 52
Lucretius 338
Lyotard, Jean-François 255

**M**
machines 71, 96, 126
agency 88, 89
artificial intelligence 113–16
consciousness 79, 81
intelligence and imitation 110–13
Kasparov versus Deep Blue 110
minds, machines, and the problem of consciousness 116–18
morality 92
personhood 76, 109–10
self-consciousness 86
male aggression 45
Mannheim, Karl 67
MAOA gene 286–7
Marx, Karl 18, 203, 204, 236, 297–301
biography 297
Marxism 65
applications of Marxism 299
neo-Marxism 67
material 187
material substance 330
materialism 160, 164, 203, 330
mating preferences, human 45–6, 283–4
*Matrix, The* 159
McGinn, Colin 176
meaning 272
mechanistic worldview 36
memory theory 345–6
assessment of the memory theory 350
circularity objection 346–7
quasi-memory 346
mental continuity 347
criteria of continuity and connectedness 348–50
Merleau-Ponty, Maurice 249–50
metaphysics 185, 189, 328
methodology 11, 185
role of different methodologies 185
mind and body 125–30, 175–8
Abrahamic religions 130, 142–50
ancient Greece 130, 136–42
ancient India 130, 131–6
ancient philosophy in perspective 150–1
cultural quotations 131
functionalism 167–71
hard problem of consciousness 171–4
idealism 160–3
mind–body problem 127, 128
naturalism and brain science 164–7
rationalism 151–9
monism 127, 128, 150
Judaism 145, 146–7
Montaigne, Michel de 199
moral responsibility 89–93
morality 32, 46
theory of the origins of morality 91
what are morality and moral responsibility? 90
who and what possesses morality and moral responsibility? 90–3

**N**
Nagel, Thomas 54–5
natural selection 42–3
naturalism 164–6
nature versus nurture 279, 291, 306–8
beyond nature versus nurture 308–9
philosophical implications 310–11
necessary and sufficient distinctions 328–9
Necessary Being 26
necessary conditions 76, 329
Neo-Platonism 196–7
neuroaesthetics 129
neuroscience 125, 164, 165, 167, 175
Nietzsche, Friedrich Wilhelm 18, 39–41, 241–4
biography 39
conclusions 40–1
"despisers of the body" 40
influence on existentialism 245
nihilism 276
nondualism 135, 150
nothingness 274
noumenal reality 215

**O**
object permanence 34
objectivity 19, 26–7, 28
ontological questions 328
optimism bias 52–3
others 3–4, 245
role of culture 252–5

**P**
paradigm shifts 35–6
paranormal thinking 50–2
Parfit, Derek 213
personal identity theory 347–50
patriarchy 68–9, 302
perception 208
perfect knowledge 21–3
permanence 189

persistence of identity 325
personhood 71–2, 119
agency 86–8
agency as a condition of personhood 89
assessment tips 120–2
authenticity as condition of personhood 95–6
consciousness 77–81
consciousness as a condition of personhood 79–81
historical perspective 73–4
legal definitions 75–6
machines 109–18
morality and moral responsibility 89–93
non-human animals 97–109
philosophical terms 76
responsibility and authenticity 93–6
responsibility as condition of personhood 95–6
self-consciousness 81–6
self-consciousness as a condition of personhood 85–6
what is a person? 73, 96–7
why is personhood important? 74–6
perspectivism 39–41
pessimistic meta-induction 38
phenomena 21, 164
phenomenal reality 215
phenomenologico-existentialism 245
phenomenology 164, 169
phenomenology as an approach to the self 233–5
philosophical behaviourism 166
philosophical determinism 312
philosophical zombies 173
philosophy 1
argument in philosophy 9–10
core theme 14
how do you start philosophizing? 9
international-mindedness 2, 6
philosophizing with attitude 6–7
philosophy and leadership 8
philosophy at work 8
relationship between TOK (theory of knowledge) and philosophy 5
understanding key philosophical distinctions 327–9
understanding the process of philosophical analysis 10
what do philosophers do? 4–5
what do we mean by concepts? 14
what is analysis? 11–14, 184–5
what is evidence? 10
what is philosophy? 1–2, 6
why do philosophy? 2–3, 7–8
why philosophize? 5–6
you as philosopher 7
physical criterion 332–3
physicalism 164, 171, 173
pineal gland 157, 158
Plato 18, 136, 152, 175
biography 137
Chariot – self-control 19–20
concepts of the self 187–94, 196–7, 198–9, 203, 204, 206, 218, 232, 236, 253
conclusions 21, 23
Descartes, René 200, 202
Diotima of Mantinea 192
epistemology – forms and perfect knowledge 21–3
feminist critique 193–4
Ficino, Marsilio 153
Kant, Imanuel 214, 215, 217
Nietzsche, Friedrich 242, 243
Phaedo 137–9, 141–2, 154
Plato's chariot 20, 191–2, 227
theory of the forms 139, 187
three parts of the soul 21, 337–8
Plotinus 196
postmodern self 255–6
decentred self 256
multiphrenia 256
protean self 256
self-in-relation 256
postmodernism 65, 69, 272
power 66–7
practical ego 248
pre-reflexive consciousness 247
pre-Socratic philosophers 183, 188
predetermined categories 69
preference utilitarianism 106–7
prerequisites of experience 63
problem of other minds 127, 159
projects 94
psyche 187–94
psycho-physical self 247, 248
psychological behaviourism 60–2
psychological determinism 311
pure ego 247
Pythagoras 188

**Q**

qualitative versus numerical distinctions 327–8
questions of necessity 329
questions of sufficiency 328

**R**

rationalism 18, 151–2, 185
conclusions 26, 27, 29
critiques of the rational view 30–4
Descartes, René 23–6, 154–9, 199–202
Ficino, Marsilio 153–4
good life 28–9
Nagel, Thomas 54–5
objectivity as rationality 26–7
perspectivism 39–41
Plato 19–23, 152–3
rationality as objectivity 19
relativism 35–8
scholasticism 152
self-awareness 54
warning against dismissing 29
why do we believe this? 28
rationalization 57
reaction formation 58
reason 20, 23, 32
reason as a power discourse 65–7
social and ecological construction 38
reductionism 164
reference points 13
reflection 208, 332
reincarnation 312
rejection of the self 186
relational self 254
relativism 35
conclusions 38
illustration 37–8
Kuhn, Thomas 35–6
repression 58
responsibility 93–4, 273
criminal behaviour 288–9
responsibility as condition of personhood 95–6
who and what possesses responsibility? 94–5
responsiveness 77, 78
resurrection 144, 145–6
Rich, Adrienne 194–5
Rome, ancient 183
Rorty, Richard 255
Rousseau, Jean-Jacques 199, 294–7, 299–301
biography 295
moral self 203
On the Origins of Inequality 295–6
Rumi, Jalal ad-Din Muhammad 149
biography 150
Ryle, Gilbert 157–8, 166

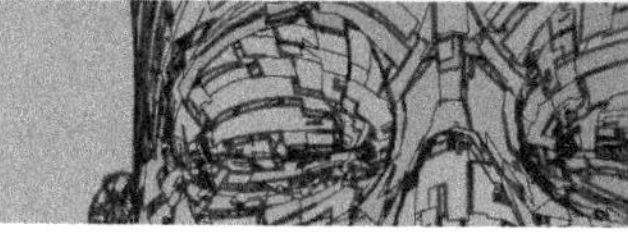


**S**

Sartre, Jean-Paul 235
being-with-others 248
biography 273
Cartesian philosophy 246
consciousness 247–8
framework of self-hood 246
Kantian philosophy 246–7
"nausea" 272
radical freedom 274–6
searching for a post-Cartesian self 245
self-hood 246
scepticism 154
Schiller, Friedrich 203
scholasticism 152
scientific determinism 312
Searle, John 114–16
self 3–4, 179–80, 256–9
bringer of life 190
seat of knowledge 190
unpacking the question of the self 182–6
what is the self? 181–2
why is a consideration of the self important? 181
self-awareness 54, 81–6
self-consciousness 81–2
personal responses 85–6
self-consciousness as a condition of personhood 85–6
websites 81, 86
who and what possesses self-consciousness? 83–4
self-control 19–20, 26–7
self-evidence 24–5
Cosmological Argument 25–6
feeling sure is not being right 38
self-hood 203
self-realization 162
sensation 208
sense experience 31
sentience 104–7
serotonin 286
Sikhism 132
Singer, Peter 106–7
Smith, Barry 167
social conditioning 300–6
social determinism 291–3
blaming "society" 300
can we free ourselves from social constraints? 299–300
gender and social conditioning 300–6
Marx, Karl 297–9
Rousseau, Jean-Jacques 294–7
society and the individual 293
sociocultural identity 353
Socrates 136–9
biography 137
concepts of the self 183, 188, 189, 190–1, 192, 194, 199
soft determinism 265, 268
solipsism 159, 250–2
soul 20–1, 127, 128–9, 136–42, 152
assessing the non-material substance theory of personal identity 340–1
Cartesian soul 338–9
mind–body theories 147–8
self as "psyche" or soul 187–94
soul and personal identity 337–8
soul theory 338
tripartite soul 191–2
space 63
spatiality 187
spirit 127
spirited soul 20
St Augustine 147–8, 152, 183, 342
biography 148
Christian self 196–7
St Paul 145–6, 150
biography 146
Strawson, Peter 213–14
subjectivity 42, 249–50
sublimation 58
substance 187
suffering 104–7
sufficient conditions 76, 329
super-ego 56
supernaturalism 165
superstitious thinking 50–2

**T**

tabula rasa 58, 59
Taylor, Charles 353–6
biography 354
Taylor, Richard 271, 289
temporality 187
theological determinism 312
time 63
TOK (theory of knowledge) 5
trained responses 61
transcendence 23
transcendent ego 246
transcendental ego 214–17, 246, 247
truth 39, 40–1
Turing, Alan 111, 113, 116
biography 112

**U**

Ubuntu 183
unconscious mind 55–6
defence mechanisms 56–8
id, super-ego and ego 56
universal grammar 65
utilitarianism 104–6

**V**

Voltaire, François-Marie Arouet 199

**W**

wakefulness 77, 78
Wason Selection Task 49–50
Watson, John B. 18
behaviourism 60–2
Williams, Bernard 336–7
Wittgenstein, Ludwig 175, 183, 217